George Washington

A COLLECTION

DAVID D'ANGERS(?). *George Washington*. Marble bust.
The Huntington Library and Art Gallery,
San Marino, California.

George Washington

A COLLECTION

COMPILED AND EDITED BY

W. B. Allen

Liberty*Classics*

INDIANAPOLIS

Editorial additions © 1988 by William B. Allen.
All rights reserved. All inquiries should be addressed to
Liberty Fund, Inc., 7440 N. Shadeland,
Indianapolis, Indiana 46250.
This book was manufactured in the United States of America.

Library of Congress Cataloging-in-Publication Data
Washington, George, 1732-1799.
George Washington: a collection.
Based almost entirely on materials reproduced from:
The writings of George Washington from the original
manuscript sources, 1745-1799 / John C. Fitzpatrick,
editor. Bibliography: p. Includes index.
1. United States—History—Revolution, 1775-1783.
2. United States—Politics and government—1783-1809.
3. Washington, George, 1732-1799—Correspondence.
I. Allen, W. B. (William Barclay), 1944-   .
II. Fitzpatrick, John Clement, 1876-1940. Writings of
George Washington from the original manuscript sources,
1745-1799. III. Title.
E312.72 1988   973.3   87-3338
ISBN 0-86597-059-9   ISBN 0-86597-060-2 (soft)

10 9 8 7 6 5 4 3 2 1

Contents

LIST OF ILLUSTRATIONS   xvii

ACKNOWLEDGMENTS   xix

EDITOR'S NOTE   xxi

CHRONOLOGY   xxiv

Prologue

2

1   TO RICHARD HENRY LEE   5

2   THE RULES OF CIVILITY AND DECENT BEHAVIOR IN COMPANY AND CONVERSATION   6

CHAPTER ONE

The Rules of Bravery and Liberty   1756–1775

15

3   ADDRESS TO HIS COMMAND, AUGUST 1756   19

4   TO GOVERNOR ROBERT HUNTER MORRIS, APRIL 9, 1756   20

5   TO FRANCIS DANDRIDGE, SEPTEMBER 20, 1765   21

6   TO GEORGE MASON, APRIL 5, 1769   23

7   TO THOMAS JOHNSON, JULY 20, 1770   26

8   TO GEORGE WILLIAM FAIRFAX, JUNE 10, 1774   29

9   TO BRYAN FAIRFAX, JULY 4, 1774   33

10   TO BRYAN FAIRFAX, JULY 20, 1774   35

11   TO BRYAN FAIRFAX, AUGUST 24, 1774   38

12   TO THE PRESIDENT OF THE SECOND CONTINENTAL CONGRESS, JUNE 16, 1775   40

Contents

13 TO MRS. MARTHA WASHINGTON, JUNE 18, 1775 40

14 GENERAL ORDERS, JULY 4, 1775 42

15 TO LIEUTENANT GENERAL THOMAS GAGE, AUGUST 11, 1775 44

16 TO THE INHABITANTS OF THE ISLAND OF BERMUDA, SEPTEMBER 6, 1775 45

17 TO THE INHABITANTS OF CANADA (undated) 46

CHAPTER TWO

Tyranny: The Scourge of Liberty   1775–1777
49

18 TO JOSEPH REED, DECEMBER 15, 1775 53

✗**19** GENERAL ORDERS, JANUARY 1, 1776 55

20 TO JOSEPH REED, JANUARY 14, 1776 57

21 TO THE PRESIDENT OF CONGRESS, FEBRUARY 9, 1776 62

22 TO JOSEPH REED, FEBRUARY 10, 1776 65

23 TO JOHN AUGUSTINE WASHINGTON, MAY 31, 1776 69

✗ **24** GENERAL ORDERS, JULY 2, 1776 70

✗**25** GENERAL ORDERS, JULY 9, 1776 72

✗**26** TO THE OFFICERS AND SOLDIERS OF THE PENNSYLVANIA ASSOCIATORS, AUGUST 8, 1776 74

27 TO THE PRESIDENT OF CONGRESS, SEPTEMBER 24, 1776 75

28 TO LUND WASHINGTON, SEPTEMBER 30, 1776 82

29 PROCLAMATION, JANUARY 25, 1777 84

30 TO AN UNIDENTIFIED CORRESPONDENT, FEBRUARY 14, 1777 85

31 TO PRESIDENT JAMES WARREN, MAY 23, 1777 86

32 TO MAJOR GENERAL PHILIP SCHUYLER, JULY 22, 1777 88

CHAPTER THREE

The Passions of Men and the Principles of Action   1778–1780
91

33 GENERAL ORDERS, MARCH 1, 1778 95

34 TO JOHN BANISTER, APRIL 21, 1778 98

35 TO JOHN AUGUSTINE WASHINGTON, JULY 4, 1778 104

36 TO COMTE D'ESTAING, SEPTEMBER 11, 1778 106

37 TO GOUVERNEUR MORRIS, OCTOBER 4, 1778 111

Contents

38 TO HENRY LAURENS, NOVEMBER 14, 1778   113

39 TO BENJAMIN HARRISON, DECEMBER 18, 1778   116

40 TO THE PRESIDENT OF CONGRESS, MARCH 15, 1779   120

41 TO THOMAS NELSON, MARCH 15, 1779   123

42 TO GEORGE MASON, MARCH 27, 1779   124

43 TO JAMES WARREN, MARCH 31, 1779   126

44 TO GOUVERNEUR MORRIS, MAY 8, 1779   129

45 SPEECH TO THE DELAWARE CHIEFS, MAY 12, 1779   131

46 CIRCULAR TO THE STATES, MAY 22, 1779   133

47 TO JOHN JAY, SEPTEMBER 7, 1779   135

48 A CONFERENCE BETWEEN CHEVALIER DE LA LUZERNE AND GENERAL WASHINGTON, SEPTEMBER 16, 1779   138

49 TO EDMUND PENDLETON, NOVEMBER 1, 1779   142

50 TO JOSEPH JONES, MAY 14, 1780   144

51 TO PRESIDENT JOSEPH REED, MAY 28, 1780   146

52 TO PRESIDENT JOSEPH REED, JULY 4, 1780   150

53 TO JOSEPH JONES, AUGUST 13, 1780   152

54 CIRCULAR TO THE STATES, AUGUST 27, 1780   154

55 TO THE PRESIDENT OF CONGRESS, OCTOBER 11, 1780   156

56 CIRCULAR TO THE STATES, OCTOBER 18, 1780   164

CHAPTER FOUR

Trials and Triumph 1780–1781

171

57 TO GEORGE MASON, OCTOBER 22, 1780   175

58 TO WILLIAM FITZHUGH, OCTOBER 22, 1780   176

59 TO JAMES DUANE, DECEMBER 26, 1780   177

60 CIRCULAR TO THE NEW ENGLAND STATES, JANUARY 5, 1781   180

61 TO LIEUTENANT COLONEL JOHN LAURENS, JANUARY 15, 1781   182

62 GENERAL ORDERS, JANUARY 30, 1781   186

63 TO JOHN SULLIVAN, FEBRUARY 4, 1781   188

64 TO JOHN PARKE CUSTIS, FEBRUARY 28, 1781   190

65 TO LUND WASHINGTON, APRIL 30, 1781   192

66 TO THE PRESIDENT OF CONGRESS, OCTOBER 19, 1781   194

67 GENERAL ORDERS, OCTOBER 20, 1781   195

Contents

CHAPTER FIVE

Washington's Knowledge of Himself and His Army 1782–1783
199

68	TO COLONEL LEWIS NICOLA, MAY 22, 1782	203
69	TO THE SECRETARY AT WAR, OCTOBER 2, 1782	204
70	TO JOSEPH JONES, DECEMBER 14, 1782	206
71	TO MAJOR GENERAL NATHANAEL GREENE, FEBRUARY 6, 1783	207
72	GENERAL ORDERS, FEBRUARY 15, 1783	209
73	TO GOVERNOR BENJAMIN HARRISON, MARCH 4, 1783	210
74	TO ALEXANDER HAMILTON, MARCH 4, 1783	211
75	TO THE PRESIDENT OF CONGRESS, MARCH 12, 1783	214
76	TO JOSEPH JONES, MARCH 12, 1783	215
77	SPEECH TO THE OFFICERS OF THE ARMY, MARCH 15, 1783	217
78	TO THE PRESIDENT OF CONGRESS, MARCH 18, 1783	221

CHAPTER SIX

Washington's Knowledge of His Countrymen 1783
225

79	TO JOSEPH JONES, MARCH 18, 1783	227
80	TO MAJOR GENERAL NATHANAEL GREENE, MARCH 31, 1783	229
81	TO ALEXANDER HAMILTON, MARCH 31, 1783	229
82	TO THEODORICK BLAND, APRIL 4, 1783	231
83	TO MARQUIS DE LAFAYETTE, APRIL 5, 1783	233
84	GENERAL ORDERS, APRIL 18, 1783	236
85	TO LIEUTENANT COLONEL TENCH TILGHMAN, APRIL 24, 1783	238
86	CIRCULAR TO THE STATES, JUNE 14, 1783	239

CHAPTER SEVEN

The General Resigns 1783
251

87	TO JOHN AUGUSTINE WASHINGTON, JUNE 15, 1783	255
88	TO REVEREND WILLIAM GORDON, JULY 8, 1783	257
89	TO JAMES DUANE, SEPTEMBER 7, 1783	260
90	FAREWELL ORDERS TO THE ARMIES OF THE UNITED STATES, NOVEMBER 2, 1783	266
91	TO THE MINISTERS, ELDERS, DEACONS, AND MEMBERS OF THE REFORMED GERMAN CONGREGATION OF NEW YORK, NOVEMBER 27, 1783	270

Contents

92 TO THE MERCHANTS OF PHILADELPHIA, DECEMBER 9, 1783   271

93 ADDRESS TO CONGRESS ON RESIGNING HIS COMMISSION,
DECEMBER 23, 1783   272

CHAPTER EIGHT

The Citizen Stirs 1784–1786

275

94 TO JONATHAN TRUMBULL, JR., JANUARY 5, 1784   277

95 TO GOVERNOR BENJAMIN HARRISON, JANUARY 18, 1784   278

96 TO MARQUIS DE LAFAYETTE, FEBRUARY 1, 1784   280

97 TO DR. JAMES CRAIK, MARCH 25, 1784   282

98 TO THOMAS JEFFERSON, MARCH 29, 1784   283

99 TO JAMES MADISON, JUNE 12, 1784   286

100 TO GOVERNOR BENJAMIN HARRISON, OCTOBER 10, 1784   287

101 TO THOMAS JOHNSON, OCTOBER 15, 1784   294

102 TO BENJAMIN HARRISON, JANUARY 22, 1785   295

103 TO THE PRESIDENT OF CONGRESS, FEBRUARY 8, 1785   297

104 TO WILLIAM GRAYSON, JUNE 22, 1785   300

105 TO DAVID HUMPHREYS, JULY 25, 1785   301

106 TO MARQUIS DE LAFAYETTE, JULY 25, 1785   304

107 TO EDMUND RANDOLPH, JULY 30, 1785   308

108 TO JAMES McHENRY, AUGUST 22, 1785   309

109 TO GEORGE MASON, OCTOBER 3, 1785   311

110 TO JAMES WARREN, OCTOBER 7, 1785   312

111 TO JAMES MADISON, NOVEMBER 30, 1785   314

112 TO HENRY LEE, APRIL 5, 1786   316

113 TO ROBERT MORRIS, APRIL 12, 1786   318

114 TO MARQUIS DE LAFAYETTE, MAY 10, 1786   319

115 TO THE SECRETARY FOR FOREIGN AFFAIRS, MAY 18, 1786   323

116 TO MARQUIS DE LAFAYETTE, AUGUST 15, 1786   324

CHAPTER NINE

Making a Constitution 1786–1788

329

117 TO JOHN JAY, AUGUST 15, 1786   333

118 TO BUSHROD WASHINGTON, SEPTEMBER 30, 1786   335

119 TO HENRY LEE, OCTOBER 31, 1786   337

Contents

120 TO JAMES MADISON, NOVEMBER 5, 1786 — 339

121 TO BUSHROD WASHINGTON, NOVEMBER 15, 1786 — 341

122 TO JAMES MADISON, NOVEMBER 18, 1786 — 343

123 TO JAMES MADISON, DECEMBER 16, 1786 — 344

124 TO GOVERNOR EDMUND RANDOLPH, DECEMBER 21, 1786 — 347

125 TO HENRY KNOX, DECEMBER 26, 1786 — 348

126 TO DAVID HUMPHREYS, DECEMBER 26, 1786 — 350

127 TO HENRY KNOX, FEBRUARY 3, 1787 — 354

128 TO HENRY KNOX, MARCH 8, 1787 — 356

129 TO THE SECRETARY FOR FOREIGN AFFAIRS, MARCH 10, 1787 — 357

130 TO GOVERNOR EDMUND RANDOLPH, MARCH 28, 1787 — 359

131 TO JAMES MADISON, MARCH 31, 1787 — 360

132 TO HENRY KNOX, APRIL 2, 1787 — 363

133 SUMMARY OF LETTERS FROM JAY, KNOX, AND MADISON, SPRING 1787 — 365

134 TO ALEXANDER HAMILTON, JULY 10, 1787 — 369

135 TO PATRICK HENRY, SEPTEMBER 24, 1787 — 370

136 TO ALEXANDER HAMILTON, NOVEMBER 10, 1787 — 370

137 TO BUSHROD WASHINGTON, NOVEMBER 10, 1787 — 371

138 TO DAVID STUART, NOVEMBER 30, 1787 — 374

139 TO JAMES MADISON, DECEMBER 7, 1787 — 376

140 TO GOVERNOR EDMUND RANDOLPH, JANUARY 8, 1788 — 378

141 TO JAMES MADISON, JANUARY 10, 1788 — 379

142 TO JAMES MADISON, FEBRUARY 5, 1788 — 380

143 TO MARQUIS DE LAFAYETTE, FEBRUARY 7, 1788 — 382

144 TO JAMES MADISON, MARCH 2, 1788 — 385

145 TO JOHN ARMSTRONG, APRIL 25, 1788 — 386

146 TO MARQUIS DE LAFAYETTE, APRIL 28, 1788 — 389

147 TO MARQUIS DE CHASTELLUX, APRIL 25 [– MAY 1], 1788 — 393

148 TO REVEREND FRANCIS ADRIAN VANDERKEMP, MAY 28, 1788 — 395

149 TO MARQUIS DE LAFAYETTE, MAY 28, 1788 — 396

150 TO HENRY KNOX, JUNE 17, 1788 — 398

151 TO MARQUIS DE LAFAYETTE, JUNE 19, 1788 — 400

152 TO BENJAMIN LINCOLN, JUNE 29, 1788 — 403

Contents

CHAPTER TEN

The Drama of Founding 1788–1789
405

153 TO THE SECRETARY FOR FOREIGN AFFAIRS, JULY 18, 1788 — 409

154 TO JONATHAN TRUMBULL, JULY 20, 1788 — 411

155 TO NOAH WEBSTER, ESQ., JULY 31, 1788 — 413

156 TO BENJAMIN LINCOLN, AUGUST 28, 1788 — 415

157 TO ALEXANDER HAMILTON, AUGUST 28, 1788 — 416

158 TO THOMAS JEFFERSON, AUGUST 31, 1788 — 418

159 TO ALEXANDER HAMILTON, OCTOBER 3, 1788 — 421

160 TO BENJAMIN LINCOLN, OCTOBER 26, 1788 — 423

161 TO MARQUIS DE LAFAYETTE, JANUARY 29, 1789 — 427

162 TO BENJAMIN LINCOLN, JANUARY 31, 1789 — 429

163 TO FRANCIS HOPKINSON, FEBRUARY 5, 1789 — 430

164 TO GEORGE STEPTOE WASHINGTON, MARCH 23, 1789 — 431

165 TO JAMES MADISON, MARCH 30, 1789 — 434

166 TO THE MAYOR, CORPORATION, AND CITIZENS OF ALEXANDRIA, APRIL 16, 1789 — 436

CHAPTER ELEVEN

Presidential Addresses 1789–1796
439

167 FRAGMENTS OF THE DISCARDED FIRST INAUGURAL ADDRESS, APRIL 1789 — 445

168 THE FIRST INAUGURAL SPEECH, APRIL 30, 1789 — 460

169 FIRST ANNUAL MESSAGE, JANUARY 8, 1790 — 467

170 SECOND ANNUAL MESSAGE, DECEMBER 8, 1790 — 470

171 THIRD ANNUAL MESSAGE, OCTOBER 25, 1791 — 474

172 FOURTH ANNUAL MESSAGE, NOVEMBER 6, 1792 — 480

173 THE SECOND INAUGURAL SPEECH, MARCH 4, 1793 — 486

174 FIFTH ANNUAL MESSAGE, DECEMBER 3, 1793 — 486

175 SIXTH ANNUAL MESSAGE, NOVEMBER 19, 1794 — 492

176 SEVENTH ANNUAL MESSAGE, DECEMBER 8, 1795 — 499

177 EIGHTH ANNUAL MESSAGE, DECEMBER 7, 1796 — 505

178 FAREWELL ADDRESS, SEPTEMBER 19, 1796 — 512

Contents

CHAPTER TWELVE

Washington the President 1789–1791
529

179 TO JAMES MADISON, MAY 5, 1789 — 531

180 TO THE UNITED BAPTIST CHURCHES IN VIRGINIA, MAY 10, 1789 — 531

181 TO THE GENERAL ASSEMBLY OF PRESBYTERIAN CHURCHES, MAY 1789 — 533

182 TO THE ANNUAL MEETING OF QUAKERS, SEPTEMBER 1789 — 533

183 THANKSGIVING PROCLAMATION, OCTOBER 3, 1789 — 534

184 SKETCH OF A PLAN OF AMERICAN FINANCE, OCTOBER 1789 — 535

185 TO CATHERINE MACAULAY GRAHAM, JANUARY 9, 1790 — 537

186 TO DAVID STUART, MARCH 28, 1790 — 539

187 TO DAVID STUART, JUNE 15, 1790 — 541

188 TO THE HEBREW CONGREGATIONS, JANUARY 1790 — 545

189 TO THE ROMAN CATHOLICS, MARCH 1790 — 546

190 TO THE HEBREW CONGREGATION IN NEWPORT, AUGUST 7, 1790 — 547

191 TO THE HEBREW CONGREGATIONS OF THE CITY OF SAVANNAH, GEORGIA (undated) — 549

192 TO THE CHIEFS AND COUNSELORS OF THE SENECA NATION, DECEMBER 29, 1790 — 550

193 TO MARQUIS DE LAFAYETTE, JULY 28, 1791 — 553

194 TO GOUVERNEUR MORRIS, JULY 28, 1791 — 555

195 TO ARTHUR YOUNG, DECEMBER 5, 1791 — 558

CHAPTER THIRTEEN

Trials of Division 1792–1796
563

196 TO JAMES MADISON, MAY 20, 1792 — 567

197 TO MARQUIS DE LAFAYETTE, JUNE 10, 1792 — 570

198 TO THE SECRETARY OF THE TREASURY, JULY 29, 1792 — 572

199 TO THE SECRETARY OF STATE, AUGUST 23, 1792 — 576

200 TO THE SECRETARY OF THE TREASURY, AUGUST 26, 1792 — 579

201 TO THE ATTORNEY GENERAL, AUGUST 26, 1792 — 581

202 PROCLAMATION, SEPTEMBER 15, 1792 — 583

203 TO THE SECRETARY OF STATE, OCTOBER 18, 1792 — 584

Contents

204 PROCLAMATION, DECEMBER 12, 1792   585

205 PROCLAMATION OF NEUTRALITY, APRIL 22, 1793   585

206 TO GOVERNOR HENRY LEE, JULY 21, 1793   586

207 PROCLAMATION, MARCH 24, 1794   588

208 PROCLAMATION, AUGUST 7, 1794   589

209 TO GOVERNOR HENRY LEE, AUGUST 26, 1794   593

210 TO BURGESS BALL, SEPTEMBER 25, 1794   596

211 PROCLAMATION, SEPTEMBER 25, 1794   598

212 TO THE SECRETARY OF STATE, OCTOBER 16, 1794   600

213 TO JOHN JAY, NOVEMBER 1794   602

214 TO THE COMMISSIONERS OF THE DISTRICT OF COLUMBIA, JANUARY 28, 1795   605

215 TO THOMAS JEFFERSON, MARCH 15, 1795   607

216 TO ALEXANDER HAMILTON, JULY 3, 1795   609

217 TO ALEXANDER HAMILTON, JULY 29, 1795   611

218 TO ALEXANDER HAMILTON, OCTOBER 29, 1795   613

219 TO GOUVERNEUR MORRIS, DECEMBER 22, 1795   617

220 TO THE HOUSE OF REPRESENTATIVES, MARCH 30, 1796   622

CHAPTER FOURTEEN

A Work Completed   1796–1799

627

221 TO ALEXANDER HAMILTON, MAY 8, 1796   629

222 TO THE EMPEROR OF GERMANY, MAY 15, 1796   632

223 TO ALEXANDER HAMILTON, MAY 15, 1796   633

224 TO THOMAS PINCKNEY, MAY 22, 1796   636

225 TO ALEXANDER HAMILTON, JUNE 26, 1796   637

226 TO THOMAS JEFFERSON, JULY 6, 1796   640

227 TO ALEXANDER HAMILTON, AUGUST 25, 1796   643

228 TALK TO THE CHEROKEE NATION, AUGUST 29, 1796   645

229 TO ALEXANDER HAMILTON, SEPTEMBER 1, 1796   649

230 TO ALEXANDER HAMILTON, NOVEMBER 2, 1796   651

231 TO JONATHAN TRUMBULL, MARCH 3, 1797   654

232 TO MARQUIS DE LAFAYETTE, DECEMBER 25, 1798   655

233 TO PATRICK HENRY, JANUARY 15, 1799   660

Contents

Epilogue
664

234 TO GOVERNOR JONATHAN TRUMBULL, AUGUST 30, 1799   665

235 LAST WILL AND TESTAMENT, JULY 9, 1799   667

INDEX OF RECIPIENTS   681

SUBJECT INDEX   683

Illustrations

GEORGE WASHINGTON by David d'Angers(?)   *Frontispiece*
Courtesy of The Henry E. Huntington Library and Art Gallery, San Marino, Calif.

WASHINGTON TAKING COMMAND OF THE ARMY AT CAMBRIDGE, 1775   *15*
Engraving by J. Rogers, from a painting by M. A. Wageman
Benson J. Lossing, Life of Washington *(Virtue and Co., 1860), Vol. I, p. 585**

WASHINGTON ENTERING TRENTON   *49*
Engraving by J. Rogers, from a painting by M. A. Wageman
Lossing, Vol. III, p. 87

WASHINGTON AT VALLEY FORGE   *91*
Engraving by J. M. Griffin
Washington Irving, The Life of George Washington *(G. P. Putnam & Sons,
1889), Vol. III, p. 282**

WASHINGTON AND HIS GENERALS AT YORKTOWN by Charles Willson Peale   *171*
Collections of the Maryland Historical Society

WASHINGTON, bust by Houdon   *199*
Courtesy of the Mt. Vernon Ladies' Association

PATRIAE PATER by Rembrandt Peale   *225*
Architect of the Capitol,
Courtesy of United States Capitol Collection, Washington, D.C.

WASHINGTON PARTING WITH HIS OFFICERS   *251*
Engraving by J. Rogers, from a painting by Chapin
Lossing, Vol. III, p. 35

WASHINGTON by R. E. Pine   *275*
Courtesy of Independence National Historical Park Collection

*Each of the Lossing and Irving facsimiles courtesy of The Huntington Library, San Marino, Calif.

Illustrations

WASHINGTON PRESIDING IN THE CONVENTION, 1787   329
Engraving by J. Rogers, from a painting by M. A. Wageman
Lossing, Vol. III, p. 62

WASHINGTON BEFORE PRINCETON by Charles Willson Peale   405
Courtesy of the Mt. Vernon Ladies' Association

THE INAUGURATION OF WASHINGTON on the balcony of   439
the old City Hall, New York
Engraving by G. R. Hall, from a painting by Darley
Irving, Vol. IV, p. 392

WASHINGTON, daguerreotype of the statue by Houdon in   529
the Capitol, Richmond, Virginia
Engraving by George Parker
Irving, Vol. III, p. 40

PRESIDENT WASHINGTON by John Trumbull   563
Copyright Yale University Art Gallery

LIFE MASK OF WASHINGTON by Houdon   627
Courtesy of Pierpont Morgan Library, New York, N.Y.

Acknowledgments

THIS WORK could not have been compiled as it has, and certainly not so well, without the able direction of Liberty Fund, Inc. Nor can I submit it to the world without acknowledging my debt to them.

Mr. Eldon Alexander, who is writing a thesis on Washington's political ideas, assisted me throughout the process of collecting, reviewing, and compiling information for this work. I am grateful for his meticulous care.

The Earhart Foundation supported my labors by affording me release-time from teaching to carry out the work. Thanks to them, the time it took to complete the project was considerably less than it might have been.

Mrs. Nathaniel Stein deserves special recognition for generously sharing with me the work of the late Dr. Stein on Washington's "discarded inaugural" and for providing information which enabled me to close the loop in tracing the derivation and circulation of those fragments in the past thirty to forty years.

Dr. W. W. Abbot and his able assistant, Dorothy Twohig, of the University of Virginia's Washington Papers Project at the Alderman Library shared generously their files and graciously received us at their facility.

The Huntington Library and Art Gallery in San Marino, California, and its reference staff were especially helpful in facilitating our research. And many other collections and repositories responded generously to our requests for information and materials. Those whose contributions deserve special note are:

Duke University Library
Lilly Library, Indiana University
Marblehead Historical Society, Marblehead, Massachusetts
Stanford University Library, Manuscript Division
Winthrop College Archives, Dacus Library, Rock Hill, South Carolina.

I also owe thanks to Harvey Mudd College and to my colleagues, without whose general support I could not have carried out this work.

W.B.A.   *Claremont, California*

William B. Allen is Professor of Government at Harvey Mudd College, Claremont, California

Editor's Note

THE MATERIALS reproduced here derive almost entirely from John C. Fitzpatrick, *The Writings of George Washington*. Where feasible, his versions have been checked against the manuscripts. Some other materials derive directly from manuscripts or other published sources.

With the exception of Chapter Eleven, where the major addresses of Washington's presidency are brought together, the materials here are presented in a straightforwardly chronological order. Critical apparatus has been held to an absolute minimum in this collection. This work is designed to be a tool of general information rather than a tool of critical study. While this work has been thoroughly checked to conform to the most recent critical judgments, readers seeking a tool of critical analysis should consult the multivolume *Papers of George Washington* in progress under the editorship of W. W. Abbot at the University of Virginia Press.

The reader will note bracketed words and phrases in the text. Except in the discarded inaugural, these are Fitzpatrick's, used to indicate that portions of the text have been crossed out, mutilated, or left out inadvertently by Washington or an aide to whom he dictated his words. Brackets sometimes enclose words that Fitzpatrick provides to fill the gap, sometimes enclose variant wordings, and sometimes indicate that the handwriting has suddenly shifted to that of another person. In the discarded inaugural, brackets have been inserted by the present editor to indicate similar textual conditions.

Modernization of spelling and grammar were applied inconsistently in Fitzpatrick. However, because it remains the most complete collection of Washington's writings published to date, we have adhered to Fitzpatrick. Changes have been introduced only in those very few cases where it is conceived that meaning would otherwise be lost. Of course, materials reprinted from other sources have not been forced to conform to the Fitzpatrick standard.

ABOUT THE FRONTISPIECE

This "best" representation of Washington remains clouded in mystery as to its provenance. Said to be the work of David d'Angers, it has also been termed a fake by some scholars. The difficulty is that this particular work, which is in marble, was uncovered earlier in this century as the "lost" David gift to the United States that, reportedly, had burned in a fire at the Library of Congress in 1851. When it surfaced, it was purchased by Henry Huntington and now forms part of the collection at The Huntington Library in San Marino, California. Because of the controversy surrounding it, it had never been publicly exhibited prior to September 1985, when it was resurrected from storage as a consequence of our researches.

Apart from the technical difficulties touching the improbability of so fine a representation in marble having survived a fire without noticeable damage, the major obstacle to considering this the work of David is the possibility that the David statue was in bronze. Indeed, a committee of French artists and statesmen in 1904 replaced the "lost" statute with a bronze copy, which now rests in the rotunda of the Capitol. Further, records of the Library of Congress contemporaneous with the fire either refer to the original as bronze or make no mention of it at all. Nor are there any other extant records uncovered to this date which make any reference to the statue. The bronze copy of 1904 was fashioned from a cast model reportedly located at David d'Angers' studio in France.

The story of the marble bust (as well as the story of the original gift), therefore, remains inconclusive. One may nevertheless attest to the extraordinarily high merit of the bronze bust attributed to David and to the virtually pinpoint precision with which its dimensions and attitudes are reproduced in the marble version now in California.

Editor's Note

The following is a list of sources for all materials that do not derive from the Fitzpatrick edition.

Letter number 4, to Robert Hunter Morris, is from the Stanford University Library and contains minor revisions by the editor.

Letter number 86, Washington's "Circular Letter," is edited from two versions: Fitzpatrick's and the South Carolina copy (thirteen manuscripts were produced—one for each state), to which I referred courtesy of the Winthrop College Archives, Dacus Library, Rock Hill, South Carolina.

Letter number 117, to John Jay, and letter number 132, to Henry Knox, are both in the collection of the University of Virginia Washington Papers Project, Alderman Library. Letter number 133, the summary Washington made of letters from Jay, Knox, and Madison, is reprinted from *North American Review* LVII, October 1827.

Letter number 155 is taken from Noah Webster, *A Collection of Papers on Political . . . Subjects*, 1843.

For letter number 167, the fragments of the discarded inaugural address, a full explanation of the sources of the fragments appears immediately after the reconstructed text. With the exception of the discarded first inaugural address and the "Farewell Address," all the material in Chapter Eleven appears as it did in the first compilation of *American State Papers*, as ordered by Congress. This editor's decision to follow those texts reflects Washington's own decision in general not to allow the publication of his official papers prior to a specific order for that purpose being given by Congress.

Letter number 188, to the Hebrew congregation, and letter number 189, to the Roman Catholics, are derived from manuscripts MH#70584 and 81529, respectively, from the Washington Papers Project.

Letter number 190, to the Hebrew congregation in Newport, and letter number 191, to the Hebrew congregation in Savannah, are as printed in *Publications of the American Jewish Historical Society* (3), 1895.

Chronology

1732

February 22 (Old Style, February 11) Birth of George Washington

1752

November 6 G. W. becomes a major in Virginia Militia

1753

October 31 G. W. undertakes mission for Governor Dinwiddie to warn French off British territory

1754

March 20 G. W., now Lt. Colonel, assumes command of expedition to Fort Duquesne

May 28 Death of Jumonville at hands of G.W.'s expeditionary force; international incident

July 4 Surrender of Fort Necessity to French

November 1 G.W. protests subordination to British regulars of lower rank; resigns commission

1755

May 10 G.W. appointed Aide-de-Camp to General Braddock, Commander-in-Chief of British forces in America

July 9 Braddock's army routed, with loss of the Commander; G.W. displays notable bravery

August 14 G.W. appointed Colonel and Commander of Virginia forces

1758

July 24 G.W. elected to Virginia House of Burgesses for Frederick County

November 23 Fort Duquesne abandoned by French; G.W. resigns commission

1759

January 6 G.W. marries Martha Dandridge Custis

1761

May 18 G.W. re-elected to House of Burgesses

1765

May 30 Patrick Henry delivers speech against the Stamp Act

July 16 G. W. elected Burgess for Fairfax County

1769

May 18 G. W. carries articles of association drawn up with G. Mason—a non-importation agreement

1770

October 5 G. W. begins exploration of Ohio Territory

1774

May 24 Virginia resolves against Boston Port Act; Assembly continues meeting after being dissolved by Governor

August 1 G. W. elected to attend First Continental Congress by Virginia Convention

September 5 First Continental Congress, Philadelphia

1775

March 25 G. W. elected to Second Continental Congress

May 10 Second Continental Congress, Philadelphia; G. W. attends in military dress

June 15 G. W. appointed Commander-in-Chief of continental forces

July 3 G. W. takes command, at Cambridge, Mass., of 16,000 armed men

1776

March 17 British evacuate Boston

July 4 Declaration of Independence

August 27 Battle of Long Island; Americans retreat, ultimately across Delaware River

December 25-26 G. W. recrosses Delaware, surprises British Hessians, takes 1,000 prisoners

1777

January 3 Battle of Trenton; British defeated

September 11 Americans defeated at Brandywine Creek

October 4 Americans defeated at Germantown

October 17 Surrender of Burgoyne at Saratoga

November 14 Articles of Confederation sent to states

1778

June 18 British evacuate Philadelphia

June 28 Battle of Monmouth; British defeated

1779

August 19 British driven from New Jersey

October 19 Battle for Savannah; Count Pulaski slain

1780

May 25 Mutiny at Morristown following winter of supply shortages and no pay for troops

1781

March 1 Articles of Confederation ratified

September 8 Battle of Eutaw Springs; British retreat to Charleston

October 19 Battle of Yorktown; Cornwallis surrenders with 7,000 men

1783

March 15 Newburgh Address

May 19 G. W. announces peace agreement, still pending ratification, to army

June 8 "Circular Address to the Governors of the Thirteen States"

September 3 Peace Treaty signed in Paris; the report reaches America in late October

November 2 G. W. bids farewell to the army

December 4 G. W. bids farewell to his officers

December 23 G. W. resigns as Commander-in-Chief before Congress at Annapolis

1785

March 28 Mount Vernon Conference on navigation of Potomac and Chesapeake

1786

September 14 Annapolis Convention; call for Constitutional Convention

October 16 G. W. appointed to Virginia delegation to Constitutional Convention

1787

January-February Shays' Rebellion in Massachusetts

February 21 Confederation Congress approves call for Convention

May 25 Constitutional Convention opens with quorum of seven states represented; G. W. unanimously elected Convention President

1788

June 21 New Hampshire becomes ninth state to ratify Constitution, making it effective

Chronology

1789

January 7 Presidential electors appointed

February 4 G. W. unanimously chosen President

April 30 G. W. inaugurated as first President

1791

December 15 Bill of Rights ratified

1792

December 5 G. W. re-elected to presidency

1793

March 4 Second Inaugural

1794

November 19 G. W. declares suppression of Whiskey Rebellion

1795

August 14 G. W. signs Jay Treaty

1796

September 19 G. W. publishes his "Farewell Address" in the *American Daily Advertiser*

1797

March 4 G. W. retires

1799

December 14 G. W. dies at Mount Vernon

George Washington

A COLLECTION

Prologue

During the final years of the war for American independence, no one was trusted more profoundly than George Washington. In its conduct of the war, the Continental Congress seemed little more than a government in name only, and so it was that Washington proved "in the absence of any real government," as Woodrow Wilson phrased it, "almost the only prop of authority and law."

This was never more poignantly evident than in the scene at Fraunces Tavern in New York City on December 4, 1783, when Washington ended his military career in a farewell meeting with his officers. After a moment of being at a loss for words, Washington raised his glass and said, "With a heart full of love and gratitude, I now take my leave of you." Washington extended his hand to shake the hands of his officers filing past. Henry Knox stood nearest, and when the moment came to shake and pass, Washington impulsively embraced and kissed his faithful general. There, in silence, he embraced each of his officers as they filed by, and then they parted.

This dramatic signature to seven years of hard travail testifies how far Washington had conquered the hearts of his countrymen, more decisively than he had conquered the armies of the enemy. The odyssey, the development of thoughts and principles, that brought Washington to this moment had begun at least thirty years earlier; and this development would not end for nearly twenty years more. The story, told in his own words, comprises nearly fifty volumes of correspondence, memoranda, and diaries. We offer here a glimpse culled from these immense resources.

How the nine-year-old whose tentative enthusiasm speaks loudly in the letter to "Dickey Lee" or the adolescent who submitted to the lengthy process of copying out and amending one hundred ten "rules of civility and decent behavior" turned into an intrepid, self-possessed, and comprehending marshall, we shall never know. The little we do know confirms Washington's birth on February 22, 1732, third son to Augustine Washington, and first to his mother Mary. Washington was only eleven years old when his father died of pneumonia. Those eleven years his family had lived first at Bridges Creek, then at Hunting Creek, and finally near Fredricksburg, all in Virginia. It was at Hunting Creek, rechristened Mount Vernon, that Washington lived from three to seven years of age.

Under the impress of the opinion that background and environment form men, commentators have exceeded themselves in trying to turn the sparse details of Washington's boyhood and the manifest poverty of his education into a set of formative influences. The strongest influence, however, seems to have been his identification with Mount Vernon. In the long career that followed, Washington always centered his labors on the expectation of returning to Mount Vernon—that is, once he had inherited the estate from his beloved brother, Lawrence. Throughout his life Mount Vernon served as a compass point.

Many have attempted to tell the story, but we lack all essential evidence to judge how far and how fast the habits of youth became the traits that were destined to blossom in Washington's adulthood. We judge it better, therefore, that Washington himself tell the story. Accordingly, the two juvenile writings here offer a glimpse of the boy that was and the man that was to be.

TO RICHARD HENRY LEE

Dear Dickey:

I thank you very much for the pretty picture book you gave me. Sam asked me to show him the pictures and I showed him all the pictures in it; and I read to him how the lame elephant took care of the master's little son. I can read three or four pages sometimes without missing a word. Ma says I may go to see you and stay all day with you next week if it be not rainy. She says I may ride my pony Hero if Uncle Sam will go with me and lead Hero. I have a little piece of poetry about the picture book you gave me, but I mustn't tell you who wrote the poetry.

> G. W.'s compliments to R.H.L.,
> And likes his book full well,
> Henceforth will count him his friend,
> And hopes many happy days he may spend.

Your good friend
George Washington

2
———

THE RULES OF CIVILITY AND DECENT BEHAVIOR IN COMPANY AND CONVERSATION

1   Every action done in company ought to be with some sign of respect to those that are present.

2   When in company, put not your hands to any part of the body not usually discovered.

3   Show nothing to your friend that may affright him.

4   In the presence of others, sing not to yourself with a humming voice, or drum with your fingers or feet.

5   If you cough, sneeze, sigh, or yawn, do it not loud but privately, and speak not in your yawning, but put your handkerchief or hand before your face and turn aside.

6   Sleep not when others speak; sit not when others stand; speak not when you should hold your peace; walk not on when others stop.

7   Put not off your clothes in the presence of others, nor go out your chamber half dressed.

8   At play and at fire, it's good manners to give place to the last comer, and affect not to speak louder than ordinary.

9   Spit not into the fire, nor stoop low before it; neither put your hands into the flames to warm them, nor set your feet upon the fire, especially if there be meat before it.

10   When you sit down, keep your feet firm and even; without putting one on the other or crossing them.

11   Shift not yourself in the sight of others, nor gnaw your nails.

12   Shake not the head, feet, or legs; roll not the eyes; lift not one eyebrow higher than the other, wry not the mouth, and bedew no man's face with your spittle by [approaching too near] him [when] you speak.

13   Kill no vermin, or fleas, lice, ticks, etc. in the sight of others; if you see any filth or thick spittle put your foot dexterously upon it; if it be upon the clothes of your companions, put it off privately, and if it be upon your own clothes, return thanks to him who puts it off.

14   Turn not your back to others, especially in speaking; jog not the table or desk on which another reads or writes; lean not upon anyone.

15   Keep your nails clean and short, also your hands and teeth clean, yet without showing any great concern for them.

16   Do not puff up the cheeks, loll not out the tongue with the hands, or beard, thrust out the lips, or bite them, or keep the lips too open or too close.

17   Be no flatterer, neither play with any that delight not to be played withal.

18   Read no letter, books, or papers in company, but when there is a necessity for the doing of it, you must ask leave; come not near the books or writings of another so as to read them unless desired, or give your opinion of them unasked; also look not nigh when another is writing a letter.

19   Let your countenance be pleasant but in serious matters somewhat grave.

20   The gestures of the body must be suited to the discourse you are upon.

21   Reproach none for the infirmities of nature, nor delight to put them that have in mind of thereof.

22   Show not yourself glad at the misfortune of another though he were your enemy.

23   When you see a crime punished, you may be inwardly pleased; but [   ] show pity to the suffering offender.

24   [damaged manuscript]

25   Superfluous compliments and all affectation of ceremonies are to be avoided, yet where due they are not to be neglected.

26   In putting off your hat to persons of distinction, as noblemen, justices, churchmen, etc., make a reverence, bowing more or less according to the custom of the better bred, and quality of the persons; among your equals expect not always that they should begin with you first; but to pull off the hat when there is no need is affectation, in the manner of saluting and resaluting in word keep to the most usual custom.

27   'Tis ill manners to bed one more eminent than yourself be covered, as well as not to do it to whom it is due. Likewise he that makes too much haste to put on his hat does not well, yet he ought to put it on at the first, or at most the second time of being asked; now what is herein spoken, of qualification in behavior or saluting, ought also to be observed in taking of place and sitting down for ceremonies without bounds are troublesome.

28   If any one come to speak to you while you are [are] sitting, stand up, though he be your inferior, and when you present seats, let it be to everyone according to his degree.

29   When you meet with one of greater quality than yourself, stop, and retire, especially if it be at a door or any straight place, to give way for him to pass.

30   In walking the highest place in most countries seems to be on the right hand; therefore place yourself on the left of him whom you desire to honor: but if three walk together the middle place is the most honorable; the wall is usually given to the most worthy if two walk together.

31   If anyone far surpasses others, either in age, estate, or merits [and] would give place to a meaner than himself, the same ought not to accept it, s[ave he offer] it above once or twice.

32   To one that is your equal, or not much inferior, you are to give the chief place in your lodging, and he to whom it is offered ought at the first to refuse it, but at the second to accept though not without acknowledging his own unworthiness.

33   They that are in dignity or in office have in all places precedency, but whilst they are young, they ought to respect those that are their equals in birth or other qualities, though they have no public charge.

34   It is good manners to prefer them to whom we speak before ourselves, especially if they be above us, with whom in no sort we ought to begin.

35   Let your discourse with men of business be short and comprehensive.

36   Artificers and persons of low degree ought not to use many ceremonies to lords or others of high degree, but respect and highly honor them, and those of high degree ought to treat them with affability and courtesy, without arrogance.

37   In speaking to men of quality do not lean nor look them full in the face, nor approach too near them at left. Keep a full pace from them.

38   In visiting the sick, do not presently play the physician if you be not knowing therein.

39   In writing or speaking, give to every person his due title according to his degree and the custom of the place.

40   Strive not with your superior in argument, but always submit your judgment to others with modesty.

41   Undertake not to teach your equal in the art himself professes; it [   ] of arrogance.

42   [damaged manuscript]; and same with a clown and a prince.

43   Do not express joy before one sick in pain, for that contrary passion will aggravate his misery.

44   When a man does all he can, though it succeed not well, blame not him that did it.

45   Being to advise or reprehend any one, consider whether it ought to be in public or in private, and presently or at some other time; in what terms to do it; and in reproving show no signs of cholor but do it with all sweetness and mildness.

46   Take all admonitions thankfully in what time or place soever given, but afterwards not being culpable take a time and place convenient to let him [him] know it that gave them.

47   Mock not nor jest at any thing of importance. Break no jests that are sharp, biting; and if you deliver any thing witty and pleasant, abstain from laughing thereat yourself.

48   Wherein [wherein] you reprove another be unblameable yourself; for example is more prevalent than precepts.

49   Use no reproachful language against any one; neither curse nor revile.

50   Be not hasty to believe flying reports to the disparagement of any.

51   Wear not your clothes foul, or ripped, or dusty, but see they be brushed once every day at least and take heed that you approach not to any uncleanness.

52   In your apparel be modest and endeavor to accommodate nature, rather than to procure admiration; keep to the fashion of your equals, such as are civil and orderly with respect to time and places.

53   Run not in the streets, neither go too slowly, nor with mouth open; go not shaking of arms, nor upon the toes, nor in a dancing [damaged manuscript].

54   Play not the peacock, looking every where about you, to see if you be well decked, if your shoes fit well, if your stockings sit neatly and clothes handsomely.

55   *Eat not in the streets, nor in your house, out of season.*

56   *Associate yourself with men of good quality if you esteem your own reputation; for 'tis better to be alone than in bad company.*

57   *In walking up and down in a house, only with one in company if he be greater than yourself, at the first give him the right hand and stop not till he does and be not the first that turns, and when you do turn let it be with your face towards him; if he be a man of great quality walk not with him cheek by jowl but somewhat behind him but yet in such a manner that he may easily speak to you.*

58   *Let your conversation be without malice or envy, for 'tis a sign of a tractable and commendable nature, and in all causes of passion permit reason to govern.*

59   *Never express anything unbecoming, nor act against the rules before your inferiors.*

60   *Be not immodest in urging your friends to discover a secret.*

61   *Utter not base and frivolous things among grave and learned men, nor very difficult questions or subjects among the ignorant, or things hard to be believed; stuff not your discourse with sentences among your betters nor equals.*

62   *Speak not of doleful things in a time of mirth or at the table; speak not of melancholy things or death and wounds, and if others mention them, change if you can the discourse; tell not your dreams, but to your intimate friend.*

63   *A man ought not to value himself of his achievements or rare qualities [damaged manuscript] virtue or kindred.*

64   *Break not a jest where none take pleasure in mirth; laugh not alone, nor at all without occasion; deride no man's misfortune though there seem to be some cause.*

65   *Speak not injurious words neither in jest nor earnest; scoff at none although they give occasion.*

66   *Be not froward but friendly and courteous, the first to salute, hear, and answer; and be not pensive when it's a time to converse.*

67   *Detract not from others, neither be excessive in commanding.*

68 Go not thither, where you know not whether you shall be welcome or not; give not advice [without] being asked, and when desired do it briefly.

69 If two contend together take not the part of either unconstrained, and be not obstinate in your own opinion; in things indifferent be of the major side.

70 Reprehend not the imperfections of others, for that belongs to parents, masters, and superiors.

71 Gaze not on the marks or blemishes of others and ask not how they came. What you may speak in secret to your friend, deliver not before others.

72 Speak not in an unknown tongue in company but in your own language and that as those of quality do and not as the vulgar; sublime matters treat seriously.

73 Think before you speak; pronounce not imperfectly, nor bring out your words too hastily, but orderly and distinctly.

74 When another speaks, be attentive yourself; and disturb not the audience. If any hesitate in his words, help him not nor prompt him without desired; interrupt him not, nor answer him till his speech has ended.

75 In the midst of discourse [damaged manuscript] but if you perceive any stop because of [damaged manuscript]; to proceed: If a person of quality comes in while you're conversing, it's handsome to repeat what was said before.

76 While you are talking, point not with your finger at him of whom you discourse, nor approach too near him to whom you talk especially to his face.

77 Treat with men at fit times about business and whisper not in the company of others.

78 Make no comparisons and if any of the company be commended for any brave act of virtue, commend not another for the same.

79 Be not apt to relate news if you know not the truth thereof. In discoursing of things you have heard, name not your author always; a secret discover not.

80 Be not tedious in discourse or in reading unless you find the company pleased therewith.

81 Be not curious to know the affairs of others, neither approach those that speak in private.

82   Undertake not what you cannot perform but be careful to keep your promise.

83   When you deliver a matter do it without passion and with discretion, however mean the person be you do it to.

84   When your superiors talk to anybody hear not neither speak nor laugh.

85   In company of those of higher quality than yourself, speak not 'til you are asked a question, then stand upright, put off your hat and answer in few words.

86   In disputes, be not so desirous to overcome as not to give liberty to each one to deliver his opinion and submit to the judgment of the major part, specially if they are judges of the dispute.

87   [damaged manuscript] as becomes a man grave, settled, and attentive [damaged manuscript] [pre]dict not at every turn what others say.

88   Be not diverse in discourse; make not many digressions; nor repeat often the same manner of discourse.

89   Speak not evil of the absent, for it is unjust.

90   Being set at meat scratch not, neither spit, cough, or blow your nose except there's a necessity for it.

91   Make no show of taking great delight in your victuals; feed not with greediness; eat your bread with a knife; lean not on the table; neither find fault with what you eat.

92   Take no salt or cut bread with your knife greasy.

93   Entertaining anyone at table it is decent to present him with meat; undertake not to help others undesired by the master.

94   If you soak bread in the sauce, let it be no more than what you put in your mouth at a time and blow not your broth at table; let it stay till cools of itself.

95   Put not your meat to your mouth with your knife in your hand; neither spit forth the stones of any fruit pie upon a dish nor cast anything under the table.

96   It's unbecoming to heap much to one's meat; keep your fingers clean; when foul wipe them on a corner of your table napkin.

97   Put not another bite into your mouth till the former be swallowed; let not your morsels be too big.

98   Drink not nor talk with your mouth full; neither gaze about you while you are a drinking.

99   Drink not too leisurely nor yet too hastily. Before and after drinking wipe your lips; breathe not then or ever with too great a noise, for it is an evil.

100   Cleanse not your teeth with the table cloth napkin, fork, or knife; but if others do it, let it be done without a peep to them.

101   Rinse not your mouth in the presence of others.

102   It is out of use to call upon the company often to eat; nor need you drink to others every time you drink.

103   In company of your betters be not [damaged manuscript] than they are; lay not your arm but [damaged manuscript].

104   It belongs to the chiefest in company to unfold his napkin and fall to meat first; but he ought then to begin in time and to dispatch with dexterity that the slowest may have time allowed him.

105   Be not angry at table whatever happens and if you have reason to be so, show it not but on a cheerful countenance especially if there be strangers, for good humor makes one dish of meat and whey.

106   Set not yourself at the upper of the table but if it be your due, or that the master of the house will have it so, contend not, lest you should trouble the company.

107   If others talk at table be attentive but talk not with meat in your mouth.

108   When you speak of God or his Attributes, let it be seriously; reverence, honor and obey your natural parents although they be poor.

109   Let your recreations be manful not sinful.

110   Labor to keep alive in your breast that little spark of celestial fire called conscience.

CHAPTER ONE

TAKING COMMAND OF THE ARMY, 1775

The Rules of Bravery
and Liberty

1756 – 1775

*W*HEN *Washington accepted the command of the Virginia militia, which was enlisted in the service of King George to prosecute the war against the French forces in 1756, the twenty-four-year-old commander could conceive no further ambition than "by rules of unerring bravery" to merit the favor of his sovereign. He seemed singularly self-possessed. Perhaps for this reason, biographers and historians have sometimes described Washington as "a born aristocrat"; at any rate, Washington believed in an adherence to eighteenth-century principles of enlightened behavior. He dedicated himself to putting a noble and virtuous code of conduct into practice in his own life. Some historians see his truly classical behavior as the real source of his greatness.*

Washington's characteristic attitude, punctilious in matters of just respect, colored his early career in a manner which cannot be more than dimly evoked in this summary presentation of those years which culminated in his being named Commander-in-Chief of the Continental Army in 1775. That attitude made a large contribution to his developing political ideas. In light of the growing revolution of the colonies, these may seem a beginning; but in fact they reflect a richer course of development.

Washington was an indefatigable letter-writer and diarist, and thus one finds the principal facts about Washington's contribution to the founding of the United States related in his own words. We find here the idea of an American union, which motivated Washington throughout the thirty years (1769–1799) of active citizenship during which he guided his country. And from the first moment of the Revolution, Washington shows a thoughtful appreciation of liberty and its political significance.

3

ADDRESS TO HIS COMMAND

August 1756

You see, gentlemen soldiers, that it hath pleased our most gracious sovereign to declare war in form against the French King, and (for divers good causes, but more particularly for their ambitious usurpations and encroachments on his American dominions) to pronounce all the said French King's subjects and vassals to be enemies to his crown and dignity; and hath willed and required all his subjects and people, and in a more especial manner commanded his captain-general of his forces, his governors, and all other his commanders and officers, to do and execute all acts of hostility in the prosecution of, this just and honorable war. And though our utmost endeavors can contribute but little to the advancement of his Majesty's honor and the interest of his governments, yet let us show our willing obedience to the best of kings, and, by a strict attachment to his royal commands, demonstrate the love and loyalty we bear to his sacred person; let us, by rules of unerring bravery, strive to merit his royal favor, and a better establishment as reward for our services.

Loyalty to the King

4

TO GOVERNOR
ROBERT HUNTER MORRIS

Winchester, April 9, 1756

Dear Sir:

French and
Indian War

I had scarce reached Williamsburg, before an express was after me with news of the French and Indians advancing within
our settlements, and doing incredible mischief to the inhabitants, which obliged me to postpone my business there, and
hurry to their assistance with all expedition.* When I came to
this place I found everything in deep confusion; and the poor
distressed inhabitants under a general consternation. I therefore collected such forces as I could immediately raise, and
sent them in such parties, and to such places as was judged
most likely to meet with the enemy, one of which, under the
command of Mr. Paris, luckily fell in with a small body of them
as they were surrounding a small fort on the No. River of
Cacapehon; whom they engaged, and after half an hour's
close firing put to flight with the loss of their commander
Monsieur Donville (killed) and three or four more mortally
wounded. The accident that has determined the fate of Monsieur, has, I believe, dispersed his party. For I don't hear of
any mischief done in this colony since, though we are not
without numbers who are making hourly discoveries.

I have sent you a copy of the Instructions that were found
about this officer; that you may see how bold and enterprising
the enemy have grown; how unconfined are the ambitious
designs of the French; and how much it will be in their power

---

*The events related here followed Washington's return from Boston,
where he had gone to confront Governor Shirley and to clear up doubts
about provincial command authority. Shirley ordered that, in joint commands, Colonel Washington would take precedence over Maryland's Captain John Dagworthy, even though Dagworthy had once held a Royal
commission and despite the general rule that provincial officers were
subordinate to officers with Royal commissions. Departing Virginia on
February 4, Washington returned to Williamsburg on March 30. The news
from the frontier hastened him westward to Winchester on April 1 or 2.
There he attempted to improve recruitment and organize colonial forces
in order to defend the frontiers. The battle related here took place between one of Washington's scouting parties and a band of Indians under
the command of Monsieur Douville (Donville in Washington's manuscript). Douville died and was scalped.

(if the colonies continue in their fatal lethargy) to give a final stab to liberty and property.

Nothing I more sincerely wish than a union of the colonies in this time of eminent danger; and that you may find your assembly in a temper of mind to act consistently with their preservation. What Maryland has, or will do I know not, but this I am certain of, that Virginia will do every thing that can be expected to promote the public good.

Union of the colonies in time of danger

I went to Williamsburg fully resolved to resign my commission, but was dissuaded from it, at least for a time. If the hurry of business in which I know your honor is generally engaged will admit of an opportunity to murder a little time in writing to me, I should receive the favor as a mark of that esteem which I could wish to merit, by showing at all times when its in my power, how much I am . . .

Dear Sir

Your honor's most Obedient
and most Humble Servant

G. Washington

PS: A letter this instant arriving from Williamsburg informs that our Assembly have voted 20,000£ more and that their forces shall be increased to 2,000 men, a laudable example this, and I hope not a singular one.

The enclosed to Col. Gage I beg the favor of you to forward.

5

TO FRANCIS DANDRIDGE

Mount Vernon, September 20, 1765

Sir:

If you will permit me after six years silence, the time I have been married to your Niece, to pay my respects to you in this Epistolary way I shall think myself happy in beginning a corrispondance which cannot but be attended with pleasure on my side.

I shoud hardly have taken the liberty Sir, of Introducing

myself to your acquaintance in this manner, and at this time, least you shoud think my motives for doing of it arose from sordid views had not a Letter which I receivd sometime this summer from Robt. Cary & Co. given me Reasons to believe that such an advance on my side woud not be altogether disagreeable on yours. Before this I rather apprehended that some disgust at the News of your Nieces Marriage with me, and why I coud not tell, might have been the cause of your silence upon that event, and discontinuing a corrispondance which before then you had kept up with her; but if I could only flatter myself, that you woud in any wise be entertaind with the few occurances that it might be in my power to relate from hence I shoud endeavour to attone for my past remissness, in this respect, by future punctuality.

At present few things are under notice of my observation that can afford you any amusement in the recital. The Stamp Act Imposed on the Colonies by the Parliament of Great Britain engrosses the conversation of the Speculative part of the Colonists, who look upon this unconstitutional method of Taxation as a direful attack upon their Liberties, and loudly exclaim against the Violation; what may be the result of this and some other (I think I may add) ill judgd Measures, I will not undertake to determine; but this I may venture to affirm, that the advantage accrueing to the Mother Country will fall greatly short of the expectations of the Ministry; for certain it is, our whole Substance does already in a manner flow to Great Britain and that whatsoever contributes to lessen our Importation's must be hurtful to their Manufacturers. And the Eyes of our People, already beginning to open, will perceive, that many Luxuries which we lavish our substance to Great Britain for, can well be dispensd with whilst the necessaries of Life are (mostly) to be had within ourselves. This consequently will introduce frugality, and be a necessary stimulation to Industry. If Great Britain therefore Loads her Manufactures with heavy Taxes, will it not facilitate these Measures? they will not compel us I think to give our Money for their exports, whether we will or no, and certain I am none of their Traders will part from them without a valuable consideration. Where then is the Utility of these Restrictions?

As to the Stamp Act, taken in a single view, one, and the first bad consequences attending it I take to be this. Our Courts of Judicature must inevitably be shut up; for it is impossible (or

Stamp Act

Frugality

next of kin to it) under our present Circumstances that the Act of Parliam't can be complyd with were we ever so willing to enforce the execution; for not to say, which alone woud be sufficient, that we have not Money to pay the Stamps, there are many other Cogent Reasons to prevent it; and if a stop be put to our judicial proceedings I fancy the Merchants of G. Britain trading to the Colonies will not be among the last to wish for a Repeal of it.

British merchants

I live upon Potomack River in Fairfax County, about ten Miles below Alexandria and many Miles distant from any of my Wifes Relations; who all reside upon York River, and who we seldom see more than once a year, not always that. My wife who is very well and Master and Miss Custis (Children of her former Marriage) all join in making a tender of their Duty and best respects to yourself and the Aunt. My Compliments to your Lady I beg may also be made acceptable and that you will do me the justice to believe that I am, etc.

6

TO GEORGE MASON

Mount Vernon, April 5, 1769

Dear Sir:

Herewith you will receive a letter and Sundry papers which were forwarded to me a day or two ago by Doctor Ross of Bladensburg. I transmit them with the greater pleasure, as my own desire of knowing your sentiments upon a matter of this importance exactly coincides with the Doctors inclinations.

At a time when our lordly Masters in Great Britain will be satisfied with nothing less than the deprication of American freedom, it seems highly necessary that some thing shou'd be done to avert the stroke and maintain the liberty which we have derived from our Ancestors; but the manner of doing it to answer the purpose effectually is the point in question.

Maintaining liberty

That no man shou'd scruple, or hesitate a moment to use arms in defence of so valuable a blessing, on which all the good and evil of life depends; is clearly my opinion; yet Arms I wou'd beg leave to add, should be the last resource; the denier resort. Addresses to the Throne, and remonstrances to parliament, we have already, it is said, proved the inefficacy of; how far then their attention to our rights and priviledges is to be awakened or alarmed by starving their Trade and manufactures, remains to be tryed.

The northern Colonies, it appears, are endeavouring to adopt this scheme. In my opinion it is a good one, and must be attended with salutary effects, provided it can be carried pretty generally into execution; but how far it is practicable to do so, I will not take upon me to determine. That there will be difficulties attending the execution of it every where, from clashing interests, and selfish designing men (ever attentive to their own gain, and watchful of every turn that can assist their lucrative views, in preference to any other consideration) cannot be denied; but in the Tobacco Colonies where the Trade is so diffused, and in a manner wholly conducted by Factors for their principals at home, these difficulties are certainly enhanced, but I think not insurmountably increased, if the Gentlemen in their several Counties wou'd be at some pains to explain matters to the people, and stimulate them to a cordial agreement to purchase none but certain innumerated Articles out of any of the Stores after such a period, not import nor purchase any themselves. This, if it did not effectually withdraw the Factors from their Importations, wou'd at least make them extremely cautious in doing it, as the prohibited Goods could be vended to none but the non-associator, or those who wou'd pay no regard to their association; both of whom ought to be stigmatized, and made the objects of publick reproach.

The more I consider a Scheme of this sort, the more ardently I wish success to it, because I think there are private, as well as public advantages to result from it; the former certain, however precarious the other may prove; for in respect to the latter I have always thought that by virtue of the same power (for here alone the authority derives) which assume's the right of Taxation, they may attempt at least to restrain our manufactories; especially those of a public nature; the same equity and justice prevailing in the one case as the other, it being no greater hardship to forbid my manufacturing, than it is to order me to buy Goods of them loaded with Duties, for the express purpose of raising a revenue. But as a measure of this sort will be an additional exertion of arbitrary power, we cannot be worsted I think in putting it to the Test. On the other hand, that the Colonies are considerably indebted to Great Britain, is a truth universally acknowledged. That many families are reduced, almost, if not quite, to penury and want, from the low ebb of their fortunes, and Estates daily selling for the discharge of Debts, the public papers furnish but too many melancholy proofs of. And that a scheme of this sort will contribute more effectually than any other I can devise to immerge the Country from the distress it at present labours under, I do most firmly believe, if it can be generally adopted. And I can see but one set of people (the Merchants excepted) who will not, or ought not, to wish well to the Scheme; and that is those who live genteely and hospitably, on clear Estates. Such as these were they, not to consider the valuable object in view, and the good of others, might think it hard to be curtail'd in their living and enjoyments; for as to the penurious Man, he saves his money, and he saves his credit, having the best plea for doing that, which before perhaps he had the most violent struggles to refrain from doing. The extravagant and expensive man has the same good plea to retrench his Expences. He is thereby furnished with a pretext to live within bounds, and embraces it, prudence dictated œconomy to him before, but his resolution was too weak to put in practice; for how can I, *says he*, who have lived in such and such a manner change my method? I am ashamed to do it; and besides such an alteration in the system of my living, will create suspicions of a decay in my fortune, and such a thought the World must not harbour; I will e'en continue my course: till at last the course discontinues the Estate, a sale of it being the consequence of his perseverance in error. This I am satisfied is the way that many who have set out in the wrong tract, have reasoned, till ruin stares them in the face. And in respect to the poor and needy man, he is only left in the same situation he was found; better I might say, because as he judges from comparison his condition is amended in proportion as it approaches nearer to those above him.

Upon the whole therefore, I think the Scheme a good one, and that it ought to be tryed here, with such alterations as the exigency of our circumstances render absolutely necessary; but how, and in what manner to begin the work, is a matter worthy of consideration, and whether it can be attempted with propriety, or efficacy (further than a communication of sentiments to one another) before May, when the Court and Assembly will meet together in Williamsburg, and a uniform plan can be concerted, and sent into the different counties to operate at the same time, and in the same manner every where, is a thing I am somewhat in doubt upon, and shou'd be glad to know your opinion of. I am Dr. Sir, etc.

7

TO THOMAS JOHNSON

Virginia, July 20, 1770

Sir:

I was honoured with your favour of the 18th. of June about the last of that Month and read it with all the attention I was capable of but having been closely engaged with my Hay and Wheat Harvests from that time till now I have not been able to enquire into the Sentiments of any of the Gentlemen of this side in respect to the Scheme of opening the Inland Navigation of Potomack by private Subscription; in the manner you have proposed, and therefore, any opinion which I may now offer on this head will be considered I hope as the result of my own private thinking, not of the Publick.

Inland navigation of Potomac

That no person more intimately concern'd in this Event wishes to see an undertaking of the sort go forward with more facility and ardour than I do, I can truely assure you; and will at all times, give any assistance in my power to promote the design; but I leave you to judge from the Tryal, which before this you undoubtedly have made; how few there are (not immediately benefited by it) that will contribute any thing worth while to the Work; and how many small sums are requisite to raise a large one.

Upon your Plan of raising money, it appears to me that there will be found but two kinds of People who will subscribe much towards it. Those who are actuated by motives of Publick spirit; and those again, who from their proximity to the Navigation will reap the salutary effects of it clearing the River. The number of the latter, you must be a competent judge of; those of the former, is more difficult to ascertain; for w'ch reason I own to you, that I am not without my doubts of your Schemes falling through, however sanguine your first hopes may be from the rapidity of Subscribers; for it is to be supposed, that your Subscription Papers (will probably) be opend among those whose Interests *must* naturally Incline them to wish well to the undertaking and consequently will aid it; but when you come to shift the Scene a little and apply to those who are unconnected with the River and the advantages of its Navigation how slowly will you advance?

This Sir, is my Sentiment, generally, upon your Plan of obtaining Subscriptions for extending the Navigation of Potomack; whereas I conceive, that if the Subscribers were vested by the two Legislatures with a kind of property in the Navigation, under certain restrictions and limitations, and to be reimbursd their first advances with a high Interest thereon by a certain easy Tolls on all Craft proportionate to their respective Burthen's, in the manner that I am told works of this sort are effected in the Inland parts of England or, upon the Plan of Turnpike Roads; you woud add thereby a third set of Men to the two I have mentioned and gain considerable strength by it: I mean the monied Gentry; who tempted by lucrative views woud advance largely on Acct. of the high Interest. This I am Inclind to think is the only method by which this desirable work will ever be accomplished in the manner it ought to be; for as to its becoming an object of Publick Expence I never expect to see it. Our Interests (in Virginia at least) are too much divided. Our Views too confind, if our Finances were better, to suffer that, which appears to rebound to the advantage of a part of the Community only, to become a Tax upon the whole, tho' in the Instance before Us there is the strongest speculative Proof in the World of the immense advantages which Virginia and Maryland might derive (and at a very small comparitive Expence) by making Potomack the Channel of Commerce between Great Britain and that immense Territory Tract of Country *which is* unfolding to our view the advantages of which are too great, and too obvious I shoud think to become the Subject of serious debate but which thro ill tim'd Parsimony and supineness may be wrested from us and conducted thro other Channels such as the Susquehanna (which I have seen recommended by some writers) the Lakes &ca.; how difficult it will be to divert it afterwards, time only can show. Thus far Sir I have taken the liberty of communicating my Sentiments on the different modes of establishing a fund but if from the efforts you have already made on the North side of Potomack it shoud be found that my fears are rather imaginary than real (as I heartily wish they may prove), I have no doubts but the same spirit may be stird up on the

South side if Gentlemen of Influence in the Counties of Hampshire, Frederick, Loudoun and Fairfax will heartily engage in it and receive occasional Sums *receivd* from those who may wish to see a work of this sort undertaken, altho they expect no benefit to themselves from it.

As to the manner in which you propose to execute the Work, in order to avoid the Inconvenience which you seem to apprehend from Locks I prefess myself to be a very incompetent judge of it. It is a general receivd opinion I know, that by reducing one Fall you too frequently create many; but how far this Inconvenience is to be avoided by the method you speak of, those who have examind the Rifts, the depth of Water above, &ca. must be infinitely the best qualified to determine. But I am inclind to think that, if you were to exhibit your Scheme to the Publick upon a more extensive Plan than the one now Printed, it woud meet with a more general approbation; for so long as it is considered as a partial Scheme so long will it be partially attended to, whereas, if it was recommended to Publick Notice upon a more enlargd Plan, and as a means of becoming the Channel of conveyance of the extensive and valuable Trade of a rising Empire, and the operations to begin at the lower landings (above the Great Falls) and to extend upwards as high as Fort Cumberland; or as far as the expenditure of the money woud carry them; from whence the Portage to the Waters of Ohio must commence; I think many woud be invited to contribute their mite, that otherwise will not. It may be said the expence of doing this will be considerably augmented; I readily grant it, but believe that the Subscribers will increase in proportion; at any rate I think that there will be at least an equal Sum raised by this means that the end of your plan will be as effectually answered by it.

Your obliging offer in respect to Miss Custis we chearfully embrace, and Mrs. Washington woud think herself much favourd in receiving those Semples and direction's for the use of them, which your Brother Adminsters for Fitts. Miss Custis's Complaint has been of two years standing, and rather Increases than abates. Mr. Boucher will do us the favour of forwarding the Medicine so soon as you can procure and commit them to his charge which it is hopd will be as soon as possible.

8

TO GEORGE WILLIAM FAIRFAX

Williamsburg, June 10, 1774

Dear Sir:

In my way to this place I met with your Letter of the 10th. of Jany. at Dumfries. In consequence of which I immediately wrote to Mr. Willis (having an opportunity so to do) desiring him to go to Belvoir, and after examining and considering every thing maturely, to give me his opinion of the Rent which ought to be set upon your Interest there (collectively or seperately) that I might, by knowing the opinion of others, be enabled, as I intended to advertise the Renting of it as soon as I came to this place, to give answers to any application's which should be made; what follows is his answer as I wrote both to Berkeley and Belvr. as he was expected at the latter place.

See his Letter from the Beginning.

Whether Mr. Willis is under, or over the Notch, time only can determine. I wish he may not have exceeded it, although I apprehend you will be disappointed at his estimate for you will please to consider, that, there are very few People who are of ability to pay a Rent equivalent to the Interest of the Money which such buildings may have cost, who are not either already provided with a Seat, or would choose to buy one, in order to Improove it; chance indeed, may throw a Person peculiarly circumstanc'd in the way, by which means a good Rent may be had, but this is to be viewed in the light of a lucky hit not as a matter of expectation; for the generalty of Renters would [   ] House than if the Land was totally divested of It; and as to your Fishery at the Racoon Branch, I think you will be disappointed there likewise as there is no Landing on this side the River that Rents for more than one half of what you expect for that, and that on the other side opposite to you (equally good they say) to be had at £15 Maryld. Curry. however Sir every notice that can, shall be given of their disposal and nothing in my power, wanting to put them of to the best advantage in the manner desir'd. I have already advertizd the Publick of this matter, also of the Sale of your Furniture, as you may see by the Inclosd Gazette, which I send, as it contains some acct. of our American transactions respecting the oppressive and arbitrary Act of Parliament for stopping up the

Port and commerce of Boston; The Advertisements are in Mr. Rinds Gazette also; and the one relative to Renting shall be put into the Papers of Maryland and Pensylvania whilst the other is already printed in hand Bills, and shall be distributed in the several Counties and Parts round about us, that notice thereof may be as general as possible; the other parts of your Letter relative to the removal of your Negro's stock &ca. shall be complied with and you may rely upon it that your Intention of not returning to Virginia shall never transpire from me though give me leave to add by way of caution to you that a belief of this sort generally prevails and hath done so for some-time whether from Peoples conjectures, or anything you may have dropt I know not. I have never heard the most distant Insinuation of Lord Dunmore's wanting Belvoir nor am I in-clined to think he does as he talks much of a Place he has purchased near the Warm Springs. In Short I do not know of any Person at present that is Inclind that way. I shall look for your Bonds when I return, and do with them as directed. Your Book of Accts. I found in your Escruitore, and never heard of a Balances drawn or Settlement thereof made by Messrs. Adam & Campbell but will now endeavour to do this myself.

[Inclosd you have a Copy of the Acct. I settled before I left home with Mr. Craven Peyton; as also of my Acct. with you in which you will perceive a charge for your Pew in the New Church at Pohick which is now conveyed to you by the Vestry and upon Record. The Balce. of this Acct. to with £   is now Exchangd for Bills and remit viz]

Dissolution of the Virginia House of Burgesses

Our Assembly met at this place the 4th. Ulto. according to Prorogation, and was dissolved the 26th. for entering into a resolve of which the Inclosd is a Copy, and which the Govr. thought reflected too much upon his Majesty, and the British Parliament to pass over unnoticed;* this Dissolution was as sudden as unexpected for there were other resolves of a much more spirited nature ready to be offerd to the House wch. would have been unanimously adopted respecting the Boston

*The Virginia House of Burgesses, the colonial legislative assembly, was dissolved by the Royal Governor, Lord Dunmore, for the next to last time when it passed a resolution naming June 1 as a day of fasting and prayer. After the dissolution the Burgesses gathered at the Raleigh Tavern and resolved to urge a congress of all the colonies and a Virginia Convention to provide for Virginia's participation in that congress. The First Conti-nental Congress convened in Philadelphia in the autumn of 1774.

Port Bill as it is calld but were withheld till the Important business of the Country could be gone through. As the case stands the assembly sat In 22 day's for nothing, not a Bill being [ ] from the rising of the Court to the day of the Dissolution and came either to advise, or [ ] the Measure. The day after this Event the Members convend themselves at the Raleigh Tavern and enterd into the Inclosd Association which being followed two days after by an Express from Boston accompanied by the Sentiments of some Meetings in our Sister Colonies to the Northwd. the proceedings mentiond in the Inclos'd Papers were had thereupon and a general meeting requested of all the late Representatives in this City on the first of August when it is hopd, and expected that some vigorous [and effectual] measures will be effectually adopted to obtain that justice which is denied to our Petitions and Remonstrances [and Prayers]; in short the Ministry may rely on it that Americans will never be tax'd without their own consent, that the cause of Boston, the despotick Measures in respect to it I mean, now is and ever will be considered as the cause of America (not that we approve their conduct in destroyg. the Tea) and that we shall not suffer ourselves to be sacrificed by piece meals though god only knows what is to become of us, threat'ned as we are with so many hoverg. evils as hang over us at present; having a cruel and blood thirsty Enemy upon our Backs, the Indians, between whom and our Frontier Inhabitants many Skirmishes have happnd, and with whom a general War is inevitable whilst those from whom we have a right to seek protection are endeavouring by every piece of Art and despotism to fix the Shackles of Slavery upon us. This Disolution which it is said and believd, will not be followed by an Election till Instructions are receivd from the Ministry has left us without the means of Defence except under the old Militia Invasion Laws which are by no means adequate to the exigency's of the Country, for from the best accts. we have been able to get, there is a confederacy of the Western, and Southern Indian's formd against us and our Settlements over the Alligany Mountains indeed in Hampshire, Augusta &ca. are in the utmost Consternation and distress; in short since the first Settlemt. of this Colony the Minds of People in it never were more disturbd, or our Situation so critical as at present; arising as I have said before from an Invasion of our Rights and Priviledges by the Mother Country; and our lives and proper-

Cause of Boston

Indian confederacy

ties by the Savages whilst Cruel Frost succeeded by as cruel a drought contributed not a little to our unhappy Situation, tho it is now thought the Injury done to wheat by the frost is not so great as was at first apprehended; the present opinion being that take the Country through half crops will be made; to these may be added and a matter of no small moment they are that a total stop is now put to our Courts of Justice (for want of a Fee Bill, which expird the 12th. of April last) and the want of Circulating Cash amongst Us; for shameful it is that the meeting of Merchants which ought to have been at this place the 25th. of April, never happend till Eight about 10 [days] ago, and I believe will break up in a manner very dissatisfactory to every one if not injurious to their Characters.

Circulating cash

I have lately been applied to by Mr. Robt. Rutherford to join (as your Attorney) in the Conveyance of the Bloomery Tract and Works; but as I never had any particular Instructions from you on this head, and know nothing of the Situation and Circumstances of the matter I have told them that I must receive directions from you on the Subject before I do anything in it and I desired him therefore to relate the case as it stands which is Inclos'd in his own Words. He is urgent to have this business executed and seems to signify that you cannot expect any part of the money till you have jond in the Conveyance. June 15th. My Patience is entirely exhausted in waiting till the business as they call it is done, or in other words till the exchange is fix'd. I have therefore left your Money with Colo. Fieldg. Lewis to dispose of for a Bill of £200 Sterg. which I suppose will be near the amt. of the Currt. Money in my hands as there are Advertisements, hand Bills, Bonds &ca. to pay for preparatory to the Sale of your Furniture and am now hurrying home, in order, if we have any wheat to Harvest that I may be present at it.

Mrs. Fairfax's Friends in this place and at Hampton are all well (I suppose she has long ago heard of the death of her Brothers Second Son) my best wishes attend her and you and I am, etc.

9

TO BRYAN FAIRFAX

Mount Vernon, July 4, 1774

Dear Sir:

John has just delivered to me your favor of yesterday, which I shall be obliged to answer in a more concise manner, than I could wish, as I am very much engaged in raising one of the additions to my house, which I think (perhaps it is fancy) goes on better whilst I am present, than in my absence from the workmen.

I own to you, Sir, I wished much to hear of your making an open declaration of taking a poll for this county, upon Colonel West's publicly declining last Sunday*; and I should have written to you on the subject, but for information then received from several gentlemen in the churchyard, of your having refused to do so, for the reasons assigned in your letter; upon which, as I think the country never stood more in need of men of abilities and liberal sentiments than now, I entreated several gentlemen at our church yesterday to press Colonel Mason to take a poll, as I really think Major Broadwater, though a good man, might do as well in the discharge of his domestic concerns, as in the capacity of a legislator. And therefore I again express my wish, that either you or Colonel Mason would offer. I can be of little assistance to either, because I early laid it down as a maxim not to propose myself, and solicit for a second.

Need of men of abilities

As to your political sentiments, I would heartily join you in them, so far as relates to a humble and dutiful petition to the throne, provided there was the most distant hope of success.

Taxation of Parliament

---

*Washington's good friend and neighbor, Bryan Fairfax, remained loyal to the Crown to the end, and his family departed for England once the revolutionary course was set. Washington always maintained a candid discourse with Fairfax and placed great confidence in his abilities. Therefore, Washington, who was himself standing for election to the Virginia House, here urges Fairfax to do so as well, their political differences notwithstanding. Fairfax chose not to do so, believing that "there are scarce any at Alexandria of my opinion; and though the few I have elsewhere conversed with on the subject are so, yet from them I could learn, that many thought otherwise; so that I believe I should at this time give general Dissatisfaction, and therefore it would be more proper to decline. . ." Fairfax's letter is in *The Papers of George Washington* (Charlottesville: University of Virginia Press).

But have we not tried this already? Have we not addressed the Lords, and remonstrated to the Commons? And to what end? Did they deign to look at our petitions? Does it not appear, as clear as the sun in its meridian brightness, that there is a regular, systematic plan formed to fix the right and practice of taxation upon us? Does not the uniform conduct of Parliament for some years past confirm this? Do not all the debates, especially those just brought to us, in the House of Commons on the side of government, expressly declare that America must be taxed in aid of the British funds, and that she has no longer resources within herself? Is there any thing to be expected from petitioning after this? Is not the attack upon the liberty and property of the people of Boston, before restitution of the loss to the India Company was demanded, a plain and self-evident proof of what they are aiming at? Do not the subsequent bills (now I dare say acts), for depriving the Massachusetts Bay of its charter, and for transporting offenders into other colonies or to Great Britain for trial, where it is impossible from the nature of the thing that justice can be obtained, convince us that the administration is determined to stick at nothing to carry its point? Ought we not, then, to put our virtue and fortitude to the severest test?

With you I think it a folly to attempt more than we can execute, as that will not only bring disgrace upon us, but weaken our cause; yet I think we may do more than is generally believed, in respect to the non-importation scheme. As to the withholding of our remittances, that is another point, in which I own I have my doubts on several accounts, but principally on that of justice; for I think, whilst we are accusing others of injustice, we should be just ourselves; and how this can be, whilst we owe a considerable debt, and refuse payment of it to Great Britian, is to me inconceivable. Nothing but the last extremity, I think, can justify it. Whether this is now come, is the question.

Debts owed Great Britain

I began with telling you, that I was to write a short letter. My paper informs me I have done otherwise. I shall hope to see you to-morrow, at the meeting of the county in Alexandria, when these points are to be considered. I am, dear Sir, your most obedient and humble servant.

10
_____

TO   BRYAN   FAIRFAX

Mount Vernon, July 20, 1774

Dear Sir:

Your letter of the 17th was not presented to me till after the resolutions, (which were adjudged advisable for this county to come to), had been revised, altered, and corrected in the committee; nor till we had gone into a general meeting in the court-house, and my attention necessarily called every moment to the business that was before it. I did, however, upon receipt of it, (in that hurry and bustle,) hastily run it over, and handed it round to the gentlemen on the bench of which there were many; but, as no person present seemed in the least disposed to adopt your sentiments, as there appeared a perfect satisfaction and acquiescence in the measures proposed (except from a Mr. Williamson, who was for adopting your advice literally, without obtaining a second voice on his side), and as the gentlemen, to whom the letter was shown, advised me not to have it read, as it was not like to make a convert, and repugnant, (some of them thought,) to the very principle we were contending for, I forbore to offer it otherwise than in the manner above mentioned; which I shall be sorry for, if it gives you any dissatisfaction in not having your sentiments read to the county at large, instead of communicating them to the first people in it, by offering them the letter in the manner I did.

That I differ very widely from you, in respect to the mode of obtaining a repeal of the acts so much and so justly complained of, I shall not hesitate to acknowledge; and that this difference in opinion may probably proceed from the different constructions we put upon the conduct and intention of the ministry may also be true; but, as I see nothing, on the one hand, to induce a belief that the Parliament would embrace a favorable opportunity of repealing acts, which they go on with great rapidity to pass, and in order to enforce their tyrannical system; and, on the other, I observe, or think I observe, that government is pursuing a regular plan at the expense of law and justice to overthrow our constitutional rights and liberties, how can I expect any redress from a measure, which has been ineffectually tried already? For, Sir, what is it we are contending against? Is it against paying the duty of three pence per

Comments on intolerable acts

35

pound on tea because burthensome? No, it is the right only, we have all along disputed, and to this end we have already petitioned his Majesty in as humble and dutiful manner as subjects could do. Nay, more, we applied to the House of Lords and House of Commons in their different legislative capacities, setting forth, that, as Englishmen, we could not be deprived of this essential and valuable part of a constitution. If, then, as the fact really is, it is against the right of taxation that we now do, and, (as I before said,) all along have contended, why should they suppose an exertion of this power would be less obnoxious now than formerly? And what reasons have we to believe, that they would make a second attempt, while the same sentiments filled the breast of every American, if they did not intend to enforce it if possible?

The conduct of the Boston people could not justify the rigor of their measures, unless there had been a requisition of payment and refusal of it; nor did that measure require an act to deprive the government of Massachusetts Bay of their charter, or to exempt offenders from trial in the place where offences were committed, as there was not, nor could not be, a single instance produced to manifest the necessity of it. Are not all these things self evident proofs of a fixed and uniform plan to tax us? If we want further proofs, do not all the debates in the House of Commons serve to confirm this? And has not General Gage's conduct since his arrival, (in stopping the address of his Council, and publishing a proclamation more becoming a Turkish bashaw, than an English governor, declaring it treason to associate in any manner by which the commerce of Great Britain is to be affected,) exhibited an unexampled testimony of the most despotic system of tyranny, that ever was practised in a free government? In short, what further proofs are wanted to satisfy one of the designs of the ministry, than their own acts, which are uniform and plainly tending to the same point, nay, if I mistake not, avowedly to fix the right of taxation? What hope then from petitioning, when they tell us, that now or never is the time to fix the matter? Shall we, after this, whine and cry for relief, when we have already tried it in vain? Or shall we supinely sit and see one province after another fall a prey to despotism? If I was in any doubt, as to the right which the Parliament of Great Britian had to tax us without our consent, I should most heartily coincide with you in opinion, that to petition, and petition only, is the proper

General Gage

*Parliamentary
taxation*

method to apply for relief; because we should then be asking a favor, and not claiming a right, which, by the law of nature and our constitution, we are, in my opinion, indubitably entitled to. I should even think it criminal to go further than this, under such an idea; but none such I have. I think the Parliament of Great Britain hath no more right to put their hands into my pocket, without my consent, than I have to put my hands into yours for money; and this being already urged to them in a firm, but decent manner, by all the colonies, what reason is there to expect any thing from their justice?

As to the resolution for addressing the throne, I own to you, Sir, I think the whole might as well have been expunged. I expect nothing from the measure, nor should my voice have accompanied it, if the non-importation scheme was intended to be retarded by it; or I am convinced, as much as I am of my existence, that there is no relief but in their distress; and I think, at least I hope, that there is public virtue enough left among us to deny ourselves every thing but the bare necessaries of life to accomplish this end. This we have a right to do, and no power upon earth can compel us to do otherwise, till they have first reduced us to the most abject state of slavery that ever was designed for mankind. The stopping our exports would, no doubt, be a shorter cut than the other to effect this purpose; but if we owe money to Great Britain, nothing but the last necessity can justify the non-payment of it; and, therefore, I have great doubts upon this head, and wish to see the other method first tried, which is legal and will facilitate these payments.

Petition to the King

I cannot conclude without expressing some concern, that I should differ so widely in sentiment from you, in a matter of such great moment and general import; and should much distrust my own judgment upon the occasion, if my nature did not recoil at the thought of submitting to measures, which I think subversive of every thing that I ought to hold dear and valuable, and did I not find, at the same time, that the voice of mankind is with me.

I must apologize for sending you so rough a sketch of my thoughts upon your letter. When I looked back, and saw the length of my own, I could not, as I am also a good deal hurried at this time, bear the thoughts of making off a fair copy. I am, &c.

11
———

TO BRYAN FAIRFAX

Mount Vernon, August 24, 1774

Dear Sir:

Your letter of the 5th instant came to this place, forwarded by Mr. Ramsay, a few days after my return from Williamsburg, and I delayed acknowledging it sooner, in the hopes that I should find time, before I began my other journey to Philadelphia, to answer it fully, if not satisfactorily; but, as much of my time has been engrossed since I came home by company, by your brother's sale and the business consequent thereupon, in writing letters to England, and now in attending to my own domestic affairs previous to my departure as above, I find it impossible to bestow so much time and attention to the subject matter of your letter as I could wish to do, and therefore, must rely upon your good nature and candor in excuse for not attempting it. In truth, persuaded as I am, that you have read all the political pieces, which compose a large share of the *Gazette* at this time, I should think it, but for your request, a piece of inexcusable arrogance in me, to make the least essay towards a change in your political opinions; for I am sure I have no new lights to throw upon the subject, or any other arguments to offer in support of my own doctrine, than what you have seen; and could only in general add, that an innate spirit of freedom first told me, that the measures, which administration hath for some time been, and now are most violently pursuing, are repugnant to every principle of natural justice; whilst much abler heads than my own hath fully convinced me, that it is not only repugnant to natural right, but subversive of the laws and constitution of Great Britain itself, in the establishment of which some of the best blood in the kingdom hath been spilt. Satisfied, then, that the acts of a British Parliament are no longer governed by the principles of justice, that it is trampling upon the valuable rights of Americans, confirmed to them by charter and the constitution they themselves boast of, and convinced beyond the smallest doubt, that these measures are the result of deliberation, and attempted to be carried into execution by the hand of power, is it a time to trifle, or risk our cause upon petitions, which with difficulty obtain access, and afterwards are thrown by with the utmost contempt? Or

Principles of natural justice

should we, because heretofore unsuspicious of design, and then unwilling to enter into disputes with the mother country, go on to bear more, and forbear to enumerate our just causes of complaint? For my own part, I shall not undertake to say where the line between Great Britain and the colonies should be drawn; but I am clearly of opinion, that one ought to be drawn, and our rights clearly ascertained. I could wish, I own, that the dispute had been left to posterity to determine, but the crisis is arrived when we must assert our rights, or submit to every imposition, that can be heaped upon us, till custom and use shall make us as tame and abject slaves, as the blacks we rule over with such arbitrary sway.

The line between Great Britain and the colonies

I intended to have wrote no more than an apology for not writing; but I find I am insensibly running into a length I did not expect, and therefore shall conclude with remarking, that, if you disavow the right of Parliament to tax us, (unrepresented as we are,) we only differ in respect to the mode of opposition, and this difference principally arises from your belief, that they—the Parliament, I mean—want a decent opportunity to repeal the acts; whilst I am as fully convinced, as I am of my own existence, that there has been a regular, systematic plan formed to enforce them, and that nothing but unanimity in the colonies (a stroke they did not expect) and firmness, can prevent it. It seems from the best advices from Boston, that General Gage is exceedingly disconcerted at the quiet and steady conduct of the people of the Massachusetts Bay, and at the measures pursuing by the other governments; as I dare say he expected to have forced those oppressed people into compliance, or irritated them to acts of violence before this, for a more colorable pretense of ruling that and the other colonies with a high hand. But I am done.

I shall set off on Wednesday next for Philadelphia, whither, if you have any commands, I shall be glad to oblige you in them; being, dear Sir, with real regard, &c.

PS: Pray what do you think of the Canada Bill?

12
_____

TO THE PRESIDENT OF THE SECOND CONTINENTAL CONGRESS

June 16, 1775

Mr. President:

Appointment to command of the army

Tho' I am truly sensible of the high Honour done me in this Appointment, yet I feel great distress from a consciousness that my abilities and Military experience may not be equal to the extensive and important Trust: However, as the congress desires I will enter upon the momentous duty, and exert every power I Possess In their Service for the Support of the glorious Cause: I beg they will accept my most cordial thanks for this distinguished testimony of their Approbation.

But lest some unlucky event should happen unfavourable to my reputation, I beg it may be remembered by every Gentn. in the room, that I this day declare with the utmost sincerity, I do not think my self equal to the Command I am honoured with.

As to pay, Sir, I beg leave to Assure the Congress that as no pecuniary consideration could have tempted me to have accepted this Arduous employment [at the expence of my domestt. ease and happiness] I do not wish to make any proffit from it: I will keep an exact Account of my expences; those I doubt not they will discharge and that is all I desire.

13
_____

TO MRS. MARTHA WASHINGTON

Philadelphia, June 18, 1775

My Dearest:

I am now set down to write to you on a subject, which fills me with inexpressible concern, and this concern is greatly aggravated and increased, when I reflect upon the uneasiness I know it will give you. It has been determined in Congress, that the whole army raised for the defence of the American cause shall be put under my care, and that it is necessary for me to proceed immediately to Boston to take upon me the command of it.

The Rules of Bravery and Liberty

You may believe me, my dear Patsy, when I assure you, in the most solemn manner that, so far from seeking this appointment, I have used every endeavor in my power to avoid it, not only from my unwillingness to part with you and the family, but from a consciousness of its being a trust too great for my capacity, and that I should enjoy more real happiness in one month with you at home, than I have the most distant prospect of finding abroad, if my stay were to be seven times seven years. But as it has been a kind of destiny, that has thrown me upon this service, I shall hope that my undertaking it is designed to answer some good purpose. You might, and I suppose did perceive, from the tenor of my letters, that I was apprehensive I could not avoid this appointment, as I did not pretend to intimate when I should return. That was the case. It was utterly out of my power to refuse this appointment, without exposing my character to such censures, as would have reflected dishonor upon myself, and given pain to my friends. This, I am sure, could not, and ought not, to be pleasing to you, and must have lessened me considerably in my own esteem. I shall rely, therefore, confidently on that Providence, which has heretofore preserved and been bountiful to me, not doubting but that I shall return safe to you in the fall. I shall feel no pain from the toil or the danger of the campaign; my unhappiness will flow from the uneasiness I know you will feel from being left alone. I therefore beg, that you will summon your whole fortitude, and pass your time as agreeably as possible. Nothing will give me so much sincere satisfaction as to hear this, and to hear it from your own pen. My earnest and ardent desire is, that you would pursue any plan that is most likely to produce content, and a tolerable degree of tranquillity; as it must add greatly to my uneasy feelings to hear, that you are dissatisfied or complaining at what I really could not avoid.

Observations on his destiny

As life is always uncertain, and common prudence dictates to every man the necessity of settling his temporal concerns, while it is in his power, and while the mind is calm and undisturbed, I have, since I came to this place (for I had not time to do it before I left home) got Colonel Pendleton to draft a will for me, by the directions I gave him, which will I now enclose. The provision made for you in case of my death will, I hope, be agreeable.

I shall add nothing more, as I have several letters to write, but to desire that you will remember me to your friends, and to assure you that I am, with the most unfeigned regard, my dear Patsy, your affectionate, &c.

14

GENERAL ORDERS

Head Quarters, Cambridge, July 4, 1775

Parole Abington. Countersign Bedford.

Exact returns to be made by the proper Officers of all the Provisions Ordnance, Ordnance Stores, Powder, Lead working Tools of all kinds, Tents, Camp Kettles, and all other Stores under their respective care, belonging to the Armies at Roxbury and Cambridge. The commanding Officer of each Regiment to make a return of the number of blankets wanted to compleat every Man with one at least.

The Hon: Artemus Ward, Charles Lee, Philip Schuyler, and Israel Putnam Esquires are appointed Major Generals of the American Army, and due obedience is to be paid them as such. The Continental Congress not having compleated the appointments of the other officers in said army nor had sufficient time to prepare and forward their Commissions; any officer is to continue to do duty in the Rank and Station he at present holds, untill further orders.

Thomas Mifflin Esqr: is appointed by the General one of his Aid-de-Camps. Joseph Reed Esqr. is in like manner appointed Secretary to the General, and they are in future to be consider'd and regarded as such.

The Continental Congress having now taken all the Troops of the several Colonies, which have been raised, or which may be hereafter raised for the support and defense of the Liberties of America; into their Pay and Service. They are now the Troops of the United Provinces of North America; and it is hoped that all Distinctions of Colonies will be laid aside; so that one and the same Spirit may animate the whole, and the only Contest be, who shall render, on this great and trying occasion, the most essential service to the Great and common cause in which we are all engaged.

It is required and expected that exact discipline be observed, and due Subordination prevail thro' the whole Army, as a Failure in these most essential points must necessarily produce extreme Hazard, Disorder and Confusion; and end in shameful disappointment and disgrace.

The General most earnestly requires, and expects, a due observance of those articles of war, established for the Government of the army, which forbid profane cursing, swearing and drunkeness; And in like manner requires and expects, of all Officers, and Soldiers, not engaged on actual duty, a punctual attendance on divine Service, to implore the blessings of heaven upon the means used for our safety and defence.

All Officers are required and expected to pay diligent Attention to keep their Men neat and clean; to visit them often at their quarters, and inculcate upon them the necessity of cleanliness, as essential to their health and service. They are particularly to see, that they have Straw to lay on, if to be had, and to make it known if they are destitute of this article. They are also to take care that Necessarys be provided in the Camps and frequently filled up to prevent their being offensive and unhealthy. Proper Notice will be taken of such Officers and Men, as distinguish themselves by their attention to these necessary duties.

The commanding Officer of each Regiment is to take particular care that not more than two Men of a Company be absent on furlough at the same time, unless in very extraordinary cases.

Col. Gardner is to be buried tomorrow at 3 O'Clock, P.M. with the military Honors due to so brave and gallant an Officer, who fought, bled and died in the Cause of his country and mankind. His own Regiment, except the company at Malden, to attend on this mournful occasion. The places of those Companies in the Lines on Prospect Hill, to be supplied by Col. Glovers regiment till the funeral is over.

No Person is to be allowed to go to Fresh-water pond a fishing or on any other occasion as there may be danger of introducing the small pox into the army.

It is strictly required and commanded that there be no firing of Cannon or small Arms from any of the Lines, or elsewhere, except in case of necessary, immediate defence, or special order given for that purpose.

All Prisoners taken, Deserters coming in, Persons coming

out of Boston, who can give any Intelligence; any Captures of any kind from the Enemy, are to be immediately reported and brought up to Head Quarters in Cambridge.

Capt. Griffin is appointed Aide-de-Camp to General Lee and to be regarded as such.

The Guard for the security of the Stores at Watertown, is to be increased to thirty men immediately.

A Serjeant and six men to be set as a Guard to the Hospital, and are to apply to Doctor Rand.

Complaint having been made against John White Quarter Master of Col. Nixon's Regmt. for misdemeanors in drawing out Provisions for more Men than the Regiment consisted of; a Court Martial consisting of one Captain and four Subalterns is ordered to be held on said White, who are to enquire, determine and report.

15

TO LIEUTENANT GENERAL THOMAS GAGE

Head Quarters, Cambridge, August 11, 1775

Sir:

Treatment of prisoners

I understand that the Officers engaged in the Cause of Liberty and their Country, who by the Fortune of War have fallen into your Hands, have been thrown, indiscriminately, into a common Gaol appropriated for Felons; That no Consideration has been had for those of the most respectable Rank, when languishing with Wounds, and Sickness; that some have been even amputated, in this unworthy Situation.

Let your Opinion, Sir, of the Principle which Actuates them, be what it may, they suppose they act from the noblest of all Principles, a Love of Freedom, and their Country: But political Opinions I conceive are foreign to this Point; the Obligations arising from the Rights of Humanity, and Claims of Rank are universally binding, and extensive (except in case of Retaliation): These I should have hoped, would have dictated a more tender Treatment of those Individuals, whom Chance or War had put in your Power. Nor can I forbear suggesting its fatal Tendency, to widen that unhappy Breach, which you, and those Ministers under whom you act, have repeatedly declared you wish'd to see forever closed.

My Duty now makes it necessary to apprize you, that for the future I shall regulate my Conduct towards those Gentlemen, who are or may be in our Possession, exactly by the Rule you shall observe towards those of ours, now in your Custody.

If Severity and Hardship mark the Line of your Conduct (painful as it may be to me) your Prisoners will feel its Effects: But if Kindness and Humanity are shewn to ours, I shall with Pleasure consider those in our Hands, only as unfortunate, and they shall receive from me that Treatment, to which the unfortunate are ever intitled.

I beg to be favoured with an Answer, as soon as possible, and am Sir, etc.

16

TO THE INHABITANTS OF THE ISLAND OF BERMUDA

Camp at Cambridge 3 Miles from Boston, September 6, 1775

Gentn:

In the great Conflict, which agitates this Continent, I cannot doubt but the Assertors of Freedom and the Rights of the Constitution, are possessed of your most favorable Regards and Wishes for Success. As Descendents of Freemen and Heirs with us of the same Glorious Inheritance, we flatter ourselves that tho' divided by our Situation, we are firmly united in Sentiment; the Cause of Virture and Liberty is Confined to no Continent or Climate, it comprehends within its capacious Limits, the Wise and good, however dispersed and seperated in Space or distance. You need not be informed, that Violence and Rapacity of a tyrannick Ministry, have forced the Citizens of America, your Brother Colonists, into Arms; We equally detest and lament the Prevalence of those Councils, which have led to the Effusion of so much human Blood and left us no Alternative but a Civil War or a base Submission. The wise disposer of all Events has hitherto smiled upon our virtuous Efforts: Those Mercenary Troops, a few of whom lately boasted of Subjugating this vast Continent, have been check'd in their earliest Ravages and are now actually encircled in a small Space; their Arms disgraced, and Suffering all the Calamities of a Siege. The Virtue, Spirit, and Union of the Provinces leave them nothing to fear, but the Want of Amunition, The applications of our Enemies to foreign States and their Vigilance upon our Coasts, are the only Efforts they have made against us with Success. Under those Circumstances, and with these Sentiments we have turned our Eyes to you Gentlemen for Relief, We are informed there is a very large Magazine in your Island under a very feeble Guard; We would not wish to involve you in an Opposition, in which from your Situation, we should be unable to support you: We knew not therefore to what extent to sollicit your Assistance in availing ourselves of this Supply; but if your Favor and Friendship to North America and its Liberties have not been misrepresented, I persuade myself you may, consistent with your own Safety, promote and further this Scheme, so as to give it the fairest prospect of Success. Be assured, that in this Case, the whole Power and Execution of my Influence will be made with the Honble. Continental Congress, that your Island may not only be Supplied with Provisions, but experience every other Mark of Affection and Friendship, which the grateful Citizens of a free Country can bestow on its Brethren and Benefactors. I am &c.

17

TO THE INHABITANTS OF CANADA

Friends and Brethren:

The unnatural Contest between the English Colonies, and Great Britian has now risen to such a height, that Arms alone must decide it.

The Colonies, confiding in the Justice of their Cause and the purity of their intentions, have reluctantly appealed to that Being, in whose hands are all Human Events: He has hitherto smiled upon their virtuous Efforts: The Hand of Tyranny has been arrested in its Ravages, and the British Arms, which have shone with so much Splendor in every part of the Globe, are now tarnished with disgrace and disappointment. Generals of approved experience, who boasted of subduing this great Continent, find themselves circumscribed within the limits of a single City and its Suburbs, suffering all the shame and distress of a Siege. While the Freeborn Sons of America, animated by the genuine principles of Liberty and Love of their Country, with increasing Union, Firmness and discipline, repel every attack and despise every Danger.

Above all we rejoice that our Enemies have been deceived with Regard to you: They have persuaded themselves, they have even dared to say, that the Canadians were not capable of distinguishing between the Blessings of Liberty and the Wretchedness of Slavery; that gratifying the Vanity of a little Circle of Nobility would blind the Eyes of the people of Canada. By such Artifices they hoped to bend you to their Views; but they have been deceived: Instead of finding in you that poverty of Soul, and baseness of Spirit, they see with a Chagrin equal to our Joy, that you are enlightened, generous, and Virtuous; that you will not renounce your own Rights, or serve as Instruments to deprive your Fellow subjects of theirs. Come then, my Brethern, Unite with us in an indissoluble Union. Let us run together to the same Goal. We have taken up Arms in Defence of our Liberty, our Property; our Wives and our Children: We are determined to preserve them or die. We look forward with pleasure to that day not far remote (we hope) when the Inhabitants of America shall have one Sentiment and the full Enjoyment of the blessings of a Free Government.

British view of Canada

Incited by these Motives and encouraged by the advice of many Friends of Liberty among you, the Great American Congress have sent an Army into your Province, under the command of General Schuyler; not to plunder but to protect you; to animate and bring forth into Action those sentiments of Freedom you have declared, and which the Tools of dispositism would extinguish through the whole Creation. To co-operate with this design and to frustrate those cruel and perfidious Schemes, which would deluge our Frontier with the Blood of Women and Children, I have detached Colonel Arnold into your Country, with a part of the Army under my Command. I have enjoined upon him, and I am certain that he will consider himself, and act as in the Country of his Patrons and best Friends. Necessaries and Accommodations of every kind which you may furnish, he will thankfully receive, and render the full Value. I invite you therefore as Friends and Brethren, to provide him with such supplies as your Country affords;

American invasion of Canada

and I pledge myself not only for your safety and security, but for ample Compensation. Let no Man desert his habitation. Let no Man flee as before an Enemy.

The cause of America and of liberty is the cause of every virtuous American Citizen Whatever may be his Religion or his descent, the United Colonies know no distinction, but such as Slavery, Corruption and Arbitrary Domination may create. Come then ye generous Citizens, range yourselves under the Standard of general Liberty, against which all the force and Artifice of Tyranny will never be able to prevail. I am, etc.

CHAPTER TWO

ENTERING TRENTON

Tyranny: The Scourge of Liberty

1775 − 1777

*G*EORGE WASHINGTON *assumed his command in the immediate aftermath of the Battle of Bunker's Hill. The first task to confront him, therefore, was to dislodge the British forces from Boston. That event set in motion a train of events which would find the main army with Washington running from battle to battle. However, the sequence of battles is only the silver frame in which is portrayed the ups and downs of efforts to recruit effective forces, to ready raw troops to confront the soldiers and mercenaries of the most powerful nation on earth, and to produce coherent political and military policies from the disarray incident to a political vacuum.*

The inspiration for so much effort was liberty—or more precisely, the determination to resist a "most tyrannical and cruel system for the destruction of our rights and liberties." But it took every bit of Washington's shrewdness to keep the resistance alive. Accordingly, this chapter shows the great breadth of the efforts required of Washington. To fix the context of these efforts firmly in mind one might read it with a regard for the sequence of battles of at least the main army during roughly the same period, remembering too that this was the season in which the Declaration of Independence was proclaimed to the world.

Siege of Boston. After the Battle of Bunker's Hill, Washington positioned his troops so as to surround Boston. Colonel Henry Knox brought more than fifty pieces of artillery from Fort George in late

February 1776. American and British troops exchanged fire for four days. Afterwards, two American redoubts crowned Dorchester Heights, a position that could control Boston and its harbor filled with British ships. The British sought to dislodge the Americans from the Heights, but their boats were dispersed by a storm. General Howe evacuated Boston on March 17, and Washington entered on the 20th. The British fleet then headed for New York.

Battle of Long Island. General Howe aimed to launch 20,000 troops against the 9,000 Americans at Brooklyn Heights and secure a land footing for operations against the city of New York. The British made their first landing on August 22, 1776, and by the 26th were ready to engage the American troops. On the 27th Howe attacked and took Brooklyn Heights. Washington retreated; his strategy was to postpone all issues which had a determining character and were beyond his army's mastery, thus wearing out the offensive by avoiding its strokes and gaining the advantage of turning upon a worn-out or over-confident and off-guard British army.

Battle of Trenton. Of the three bodies of American troops that attempted to cross the Delaware River on the night of December 25, 1776, only those commanded by Washington succeeded. The Hessians, bivouacked under Colonel Rahl in Trenton, New Jersey, were completely surprised at daybreak and forced to surrender after a brief engagement.

Battle of Princeton. On January 1, 1777, Washington received word that Lord Cornwallis was en route from Brunswick to attack him at

Trenton. Washington conceived of a plan of retreat that would allow him to attack Cornwallis's communications. Creating the deception of maintaining an encamped army, Washington moved his troops around Cornwallis and toward Brunswick. As the American troops were passing Princeton, General Hugh Mercer encountered some British patrols. Their skirmishes were decided by Washington himself, after Mercer had been mortally wounded. Then Washington's army moved on to Morristown, where they erected log huts and established winter quarters.

Battle of Brandywine. General Howe withdrew his fleet from the Delaware in August 1777. On the 22nd, Washington received word that Howe had anchored in the Chesapeake Bay. Washington promptly marched to Philadelphia. By September 7, the entire army had advanced to Newport, Pennsylvania, and on the same day Howe placed his vanguard eight miles from the Americans. With light skirmishes occurring daily, the armies finally joined battle at Brandywine on September 11. The 11,000 Americans suffered 780 casualties, while the 18,000 British took 600 casualties.

Battle of Germantown. Howe chose Germantown, six miles from Philadelphia, for his headquarters. Washington's army was near Pennebecker's Mill, about twenty miles away. Washington designed a surprise attack upon Howe, October 4, 1777. The advance was prompt, and the surprise promised success, but a dense fog arose and so confused the operations that the armies were forced to retire, Howe to Philadelphia and Washington to Valley Forge.

18

TO JOSEPH REED

Cambridge, December 15, 1775

Dear Sir:

Since my last, I have had the pleasure of receiving your *Boston rumors* favours of the 28th ultimo, and the 2d instant. I must again express my gratitude for the attention shown Mrs. Washington at Philadelphia. It cannot but be pleasing, although it did, in some measure, impede the progress of her journey on the road. I am much obliged to you for the hints contained in both of the above letters, respecting the jealousies which you say are gone abroad. I have studiously avoided in all letters intended for the public eye, I mean for that of the Congress, every expression that could give pain or uneasiness; and I shall observe the same rule with respect to private letters, further than appears absolutely necessary for the elucidation of facts. I cannot charge myself with incivility, or, what in my opinion is tantamount, ceremonious civility, to the gentlemen of this colony; but if such my conduct appears, I will endeavor at a reformation, as I can assure you, my dear Reed, that I wish to walk in such a line as will give most general satisfaction. You know, that it was my wish at first to invite a certain number of gentlemen of this colony every day to dinner, but unintentionally I believe by anybody, we somehow or other missed of it. If this has given rise to the jealousy, I can only say that I am sorry for it; at the same time I add, that it was rather owing to inattention, or, more properly, too much attention to other matters, which caused me to neglect it. The extracts of letters from this camp, which so frequently appear in the Pennsylvania papers, are not only written without my knowledge, but without my approbation, as I have always thought they must have a disagreeable tendency; but there is no restraining men's tongues, or pens, when charged with a little vanity, as in the accounts given of, or rather by, the riflemen.

With respect to what you have said of yourself, and your situation, to what I have before said on this subject I can only add, that whilst you leave the door open to my expectation of your return, I shall not think of supplying your place. If ultimately you resolve against coming, I should be glad to know it, as soon as you have determined upon it. The Congress have resolved well in respect to the pay of and advance to the men; but if they cannot get the money-signers to despatch their business, it is of very little avail; for we have not at this time money enough in camp to answer the commissary's and quartermaster's accounts, much less to pay and advance to the troops. Strange conduct this!

Army pay

The accounts which you have given of the sentiments of the people respecting my conduct, is extremely flattering. Pray God, I may continue to deserve them, in the perplexed and intricate situation I stand in. Our enlistment goes on slow. By the returns last Monday, only five thousand nine hundred and seventeen men are engaged for the ensuing campaign; and yet we are told, that we shall get the number wanted, as they are only playing off to see what advantages are to be made, and whether a bounty cannot be extorted either from the public at large, or individuals, in case of a draft. Time only can discover this. I doubt the measure exceedingly. The fortunate capture of the store-ship has supplied us with flints, and many other articles we stood in need of; but we still have our wants. We are securing our approach to Letchmore's Point, unable upon any principle whatever to account for their silence, unless it be to lull us into a fatal security to favour some attempt they may have in view about the time of the great change they expect will take place the last of this month. If this be the drift, they deceive themselves, for, if possible, it has increased my vigilance, and induced me to fortify all the avenues to our camps, to guard against any approaches upon the ice.

Enlistments

If the Virginians are wise, that arch-traitor to the rights of humanity, Lord Dunmore, should be instantly crushed, if it takes the force of the whole colony to do it; otherwise, like a snow ball, in rolling, his army will get size, some through fear some through promises, and some from inclination, joining his standard. But that which renders the measure indispensably necessary is the negroes. For if he gets formidable, numbers will be tempted to join, who will be afraid to do it without. I am exceeding happy to find that that villain Connolly is seized; I hope if there is any thing to convict him, that he will meet with the punishment due to his demerit and treachery.

We impatiently wait for accounts from Arnold. Would to God we may hear he is in Quebec, and that all Canada is in our possession. My best respects to Mrs. Reed. I am, &c.

PS: The smallpox is in every part of Boston. The soldiers there who have never had it, are, we are told, under innoculation, and considered as a security against any attempt of ours. A third shipload of people is come out to Point Shirley. If we escape the smallpox in this camp, and the country around about, it will be miraculous. Every precaution that can be is taken, to guard against this evil, both by the General Court and myself.

19

GENERAL ORDERS

Head Quarters, Cambridge, January 1, 1776

Parole The Congress. Countersign America.

This day giving commencement to the new army, which, in every point of View is entirely Continental, The General flatters himself, that a laudable Spirit of emulation, will now take place, and pervade the whole of it; without such a Spirit, few Officers have ever arrived to any degree of Reputation, nor did any Army ever become formidable: His Excellency hopes that the Importance of the great Cause we are engaged in, will be deeply impressed upon every Man's mind, and wishes it to be considered, that an Army without Order, Regularity and Discipline, is no better than a Commission'd Mob; Let us therefore, when every thing dear and valuable to Freemen is at stake; when our unnatural Parent is threat'ning of us with destruction from every quarter, endeavour by all the Skill and Discipline in our power, to acquire that knowledge, and con- *Discipline in the* duct, which is necessary in War—Our Men are brave and *continental army* good; Men who with pleasure it is observed, are addicted to fewer Vices than are commonly found in Armies; but it is Subordination and Discipline (the Life and Soul of an Army) which next under providence, is to make us formidable to our enemies, honorable in ourselves, and respected in the world; and herein is to be shewn the Goodness of the Officer.

In vain is it for a General to issue Orders, if Orders are not attended to, equally vain is it for a few Officers to exert themselves, if the same Spirit does not animate the whole; it is therefore expected, (it is not insisted upon) that each Brigadier, will be attentive to the discipline of his Brigade, to the exercise of, and the Conduct observed in it, calling the Colonels, and Field Officers of every Regiment, to severe Account for Neglect, or Disobedience of orders—The same attention is to be paid by the Field Officers to the respective Companies of their Regiments—by the Captains to their Subalterns, and so on: And that the plea of Ignorance, which is no excuse for the Neglect of Orders (but rather an Aggravation) may not be offer'd, It is order'd, and directed, that not only every regiment, but every Company, do keep an Orderly-book, to which frequent recourse is to be had, it being expected that all standing orders be rigidly obeyed, until alter'd or countermanded— It is also expected, that all Orders which are necessary to be communicated to the Men, be regularly read, and carefully explained to them.—As it is the first wish of the General to have the business of the Army conducted without punishment, to accomplish which, he assures every Officer, and Soldier, that as far as it is in his power, he will reward such as particularly distinguish themselves; at the same time, he declares that he will punish every kind of neglect, or misbehaviour, in an exemplary manner.

As the great Variety of occurrences, and the multiplicity of business, in which the General is necessarily engaged, may withdraw his attention from many objects and things which might be improved to Advantage; He takes this Opportunity of declaring, that he will thank any Officer, of whatsoever Rank, for any useful hints, or profitable Informations, but to avoid trivial matters; as his time is very much engrossed, he requires that it may be introduced through the channel of a General Officer, who is to weigh the importance before he communicates it.

All standing Orders heretofore issued for the Government

of the late Army, of which every Regiment has, or ought to have Copies; are to be strictly complied with, until changed, or countermanded.

Every Regiment now upon the new establishment, is to give in signed by the Colonel, or commanding Officer, an exact List of the Commissioned Officers, in order that they may receive Commissions—particular Care to be taken that no person is included as an Officer, but such as have been appointed by proper authority; any Attempt of that kind in the New Army, will bring severe punishment upon the author. The General will, upon any Vacancies that may happen, receive recommendations, and give them proper Consideration, but the Congress alone are competent to the appointment.

An exact Return of the strength of each Regiment, is to be given in, as soon as possible, distinguishing the Number of Militia, and such of the old Regiments, as have joined for a Month only, from the established men of the Regiment.

This being the day of the Commencement of the New-establishment, The General pardons all the Offences of the old, and commands all Prisoners (except Prisoners of war) to be immediately released.

20

TO JOSEPH REED

Cambridge, January 14, 1776

Dear Sir:

The bearer presents an opportunity to me of acknowledging the receipt of your favor of the 30th ultimo, (which never came to my hands till last night,) and, if I have not done it before, of your other of the 23rd preceding.

The hints you have communicated from time to time not only deserve, but do most sincerely and cordially meet with my thanks. You cannot render a more acceptable service, nor in my estimation give a more convincing proof of your friendship, than by a free, open, and undisguised account of every matter relative to myself or conduct. I can bear to hear of *On conduct* imputed or real errors. The man, who wishes to stand well in the opinion of others, must do this; because he is thereby enabled to correct his faults, or remove prejudices which are imbibed against him. For this reason, I shall thank you for giving me the opinions of the world, upon such points as you know me to be interested in; for, as I have but one capital object in view, I could wish to make my conduct coincide with the wishes of mankind, as far as I can consistently; I mean, without departing from that great line of duty, which, though hid under a cloud for some time, from a peculiarity of circumstances, may nevertheless bear a scrutiny. My constant attention to the great and perplexing objects, which continually rise to my view, absorbs all lesser considerations, and indeed scarcely allows me time to reflect, that there is such a body in existence as the General Court of this colony, but when I am reminded of it by a committee; nor can I, upon recollection, discover in what instances (I wish they would be more explicit) I have been inattentive to, or slighted them. They could not, surely, conceive that there was a propriety in unbosoming the secrets of an army to them; that it was necessary to ask their opinion of throwing up an intrenchment, forming a battalion, &c., &c. It must, therefore, be what I before hinted to you; and how to remedy it I hardly know, as I am acquainted with few of the members, never go out of my own lines, or see any of them in them.

I am exceeding sorry to hear, that your little fleet has been shut in by the frost. I hope it has sailed ere this, and given you some proof of the utility of it, and enabled the Congress to bestow a little more attention to the affairs of this army, which suffers exceedingly by their overmuch business, or too little attention to it. We are now without any money in our treasury, powder in our magazines, arms in our stores. We are without a brigadier (the want of which has been twenty times urged), engineers, expresses (though a committee has been appointed these two months to establish them), and by and by, when we shall be called upon to take the field, shall not have a tent to lie in. Apropos, what is doing with mine?

Enlistments at a stand

These are evils, but small in comparison of those, which disturb my present repose. Our enlistments are at a stand; the fears I ever entertained are realized; that is, the discontented officers (for I do not know how else to account for it) have thrown such difficulties or stumbling-blocks in the way of recruiting, that I no longer entertain a hope of completing the army by voluntary enlistments, and I see no move or likelihood of one, to do it by other means. In the last two weeks we have enlisted but about one thousand men; whereas I was confidently led to believe, by all the officers I conversed with, that we should by this time have had the regiments nearly completed. Our total number upon paper amounts to about ten thousand five hundred; but as a large portion of these are returned not joined, I never expect to receive them, as an ineffectual order has once issued to call them in. Another is now gone forth peremptorily requiring all officers under pain of being cashiered, and recruits as being treated as deserters, to join their respective regiments by the 1st day of next month, that I may know my real strength; but if my fears are not imaginary, I shall have a dreadful account of the advanced month's pay. In consequence of the assurances given, and my expectation of having at least men enough enlisted to defend our lines, to which may be added my unwillingness of burthening the cause with unnecessary expense, no relief of militia has been ordered in, to supply the places of those, who are released from their engagements tomorrow, and on whom, though many have promised to continue out the month, there is no security for their stay.

Thus am I situated with respect to men. With regard to arms I am yet worse off. Before the dissolution of the old army, I issued an order directing three judicious men of each brigade to attend, review, and appraise the good arms of every regiment; and finding a very great unwillingness in the men to part with their arms, at the same time not having it in my power to pay them for the months of November and December, I threatened severely, that every soldier, who carried away his firelock without leave, should never receive pay for those months; yet so many have been carried off, partly by stealth, but chiefly as condemned, that we have not at this time one hundred guns in the stores, of all that have been taken in the prize-ship and from the soldiery, notwithstanding our regiments are not half completed. At the same time I am told, and believe it, that to restrain the enlistment to men with arms, you will get but few of the former, and still fewer of the latter, which would be good for any thing.

Problems with armaments

How to get furnished I know not. I have applied to this and the neighbouring colonies, but with what success time only can tell. The reflection on my situation, and that of this army, produces many an uneasy hour when all around me are wrapped in sleep. Few people know the predicament we are in, on a thousand accounts; fewer still will believe, if any disaster happens to these lines, from what cause it flows. I have often thought how much happier I should have been, if, instead of accepting of a command under such circumstances, I had taken my musket on my shoulder and entered the ranks, or, if I could have justified the measure to posterity and my own conscience, had retired to the back country, and lived in a wigwam. If I shall be able to rise superior to these and many other difficulties, which might be enumerated, I shall most religiously believe, that the finger of Providence is in it, to blind the eyes of our enemies; for surely if we get well through this month, it must be for want of their knowing the disadvantages we labour under.

Situation around Boston

Could I have foreseen the difficulties, which have come upon us; could I have known, that such a backwardness would have been discovered in the old soldiers to the service, all the generals upon earth should not have convinced me of the propriety of delaying an attack upon Boston till this time. When it can now be attempted, I will not undertake to say; but this much I will answer for, that no opportunity can present itself earlier than my wishes. But as this letter discloses some interesting truths, I shall be somewhat uneasy until I hear it gets to your hands, although the conveyance is thought safe.

We made a successful attempt a few nights ago upon the houses near Bunker's Hill. A party under Major Knowlton crossed upon the mill-dam, the night being dark, and set fire to and burnt down eight out of fourteen which were standing, and which we found they were daily pulling down for fuel. Five soldiers, and the wife of one of them, inhabiting one of the houses, were brought off prisoners; another soldier was killed; none of ours hurt.

Securing New York City

Having undoubted information of the embarkation of troops, somewhere from three to five hundred, at Boston, and being convinced they are designed either for New York Government, (from whence we have some very disagreeable accounts of the conduct of the Tories) or Virginia, I despatched General Lee a few days ago, in order to secure the city of New York from falling into their hands, as the consequences of such a blow might prove fatal to our interests. He is also to inquire a little into the conduct of the Long-Islanders, and such others as have, by their conduct and declarations, proved themselves inimical to the common cause. To effect these purposes, he is to raise volunteers in Connecticut, and call upon the troops of New Jersey, if not contrary to any order of Congress.

By a ship just arrived at Portsmouth, New Hampshire, we have London prints to the 2d of November, containing the addresses of Parliament, which contain little more than a repetition of the speech, with assurances of standing by his Majesty with lives and fortunes. The captains (for there were three or four of them passengers) say, that we have nothing to expect but the most vigorous exertions of administration, who have a dead majority upon all questions, although the Duke of Grafton and General Conway have joined the minority, as also the Bishop of Peterborough. These captains affirm confidently, that the five regiments from Ireland cannot any of them have arrived at Halifax, inasmuch as that by a violent storm on the 19th of October, the transports were forced, in a very distressful condition, into Milford Haven (Wales) and were not in a condition to put to sea when they left London, and the weather has been such since, as to prevent heavy loaded ships from making a passage by this time. One or two transports, they add, were thought to be lost; but these arrived some considerable time ago at Boston, with three companies of the 17th regiment.

News from England

Mr. Sayre has been committed to the Tower, upon the information of a certain Lieutenant or Adjutant Richardson (formerly of your city) for treasonable practices; an intention of seizing his Majesty, and possessing himself of the Tower, it is said in the crisis, but he is admitted to bail himself in five hundred pounds, and two sureties in two hundred and fifty pounds each.

What are the conjectures of the wise ones with you, of the French armament in the West Indies? But previous to this, is there any certainty of such an armament? The captains, who are sensible men, heard nothing of this when they left England; nor does there appear any apprehensions on this score in any of the measures or speeches of administration. I should think the Congress will not, ought not, to adjourn at this important crisis.

But it is highly necessary, when I am at the end of a second sheet of paper, that I should adjourn my account of matters to another letter. I shall, therefore, in Mrs. Washington's name, thank you for your good wishes towards her, and with her compliments, added to mine, to Mrs. Reed, conclude, dear Sir, your sincere and affectionate servant.

21

TO THE PRESIDENT OF CONGRESS

Cambridge, February 9, 1776

Sir:

The purport of this Letter, will be directed to a single object; through you I mean to lay it before Congress, and at the same time that I beg their serious attention to the subject, to ask pardon for intruding an opinion, not only unasked, but in some measure repugnant to their Resolves.

The disadvantages attending the limited, Inlistment of Troops, is too apparent to those who are eye witnesses of them, to render any animadversions necessary; but to Gentlemen at a Distance, whose attention is engross'd by a thousand important objects, the case may be otherwise.

General Montgomery's defeat

That this cause precipitated the fate of the brave and much to be lamented Genl. Montgomery, and brought on the defeat which followed thereupon, I have not the most distant doubt of, for had he not been apprehensive of the Troops leaving him at so important a crisis, but continued the Blockade of Quebec, a capitulation, from the best account I have been able to collect, must inevitably have followed, and, that we were not obliged at one time to dispute these Lines under disadvantageous Circumstances (proceeding from the same cause, to wit, The Troops disbanding of themselves, before the Militia could be got in) is to me a matter of wonder and astonishment; and proves, that General Howe was either unacquainted with our Situation, or restrained by his Instructions from putting any thing to a hazard 'till his reinforcements should arrive.

The Instance of General Montgomery I mention it because it is a striking one; for a number of others might be adduced; proves, that instead of having Men to take advantage of Circumstances, you are in manner compell'd, Right or Wrong, to make Circumstances, yield to a Secondary consideration. Since the first of December I have been devising every means in my power to secure these Incampments, and though I am sensible that we never have, since that Period, been able to act upon the Offensive, and at times not in a condition to defend, yet the cost of marching home one set of Men; bringing in another, the havock and waste occasioned by the first; the repairs necessary for the Second, with a thousand incidental charges and Inconveniencies which have arisen, and which it is scarce possible either to recollect or describe, amounts to near as much as the keeping up a respectable body of Troops the whole time, ready for any emergency, would have done. To this may be added that you never can have a well Disciplined Army.

To bring Men well acquainted with the Duties of a Soldier, requires time; to bring them under proper discipline and Subordination, not only requires time, but is a Work of great difficulty; and in this Army, where there is so little distinction between the Officers and Soldiers, requires an uncommon degree of attention. To expect then the same Service from Raw, and undisciplined Recruits as from Veteran Soldiers, is to expect what never did, and perhaps never will happen. Men who are familiarized to danger, meet it without shrinking, whereas those who have never seen Service often apprehend danger where no danger is. Three things prompt Men to a regular discharge of their Duty in time of Action: natural bravery, hope of reward, and fear of punishment. The two first are common to the untutor'd, and the Disciplin'd Soldiers; but the latter, most obviously distinguishes the one from the other. A Coward, when taught to believe, that if he breaks his Ranks, and abandons his Colours, will be punished with Death by his own party, will take his chance against the Enemy; but the Man who thinks little of the one, and is fearful of the other, Acts from present feelings regardless of consequences. *Training recruits*

Again, Men of a days standing will not look forward, and from experience we find, that as the time approaches for their discharge they grow careless of their Arms, Ammunition, Camp utensils &ca. nay even the Barracks themselves have felt uncommon marks of Wanton depredation, and lays us under fresh trouble, and additional expence, in providing for every fresh sett; when we find it next to impossible to procure such Articles, as are absolutely necessary in the first Instance. To this may be added the Seasoning which new Recruits must have to a Camp, and the loss, consequent therefrom. But this *Problems with the army* is not all, Men engaged for a short, limited time only, have the Officers too much in their power; for to obtain a degree of popularity, in order to induce a second Inlistment, a kind of familiarity takes place which brings on a relaxation of Discipline, unlicensed furloughs, and other Indulgences, incompatable with order and good Government, by which means, the latter part of the time for which the Soldier was engaged, is spent in undoing what you were aiming to inculcate in the first.

To go into an enumeration of all the Evils we have experienced in this late great change of the Army, and the expence incidental to it, to say nothing of the hazard we have run, and must run, between the discharging of one Army and Inlistment of another (unless an Inormous expence of Militia is incurred) would greatly exceed the bounds of a Letter; what I have already taken the liberty of saying, will serve to convey a general Idea of the matter, and, therefore I shall with all due deference, take the freedom to give it as my opinion, that if the Congress have any reason to believe, that there will be occasion for Troops another year, and consequently of another inlistment, they would save money, and have infinitely better Troops if they were, even at the bounty of twenty, thirty or more Dollars to engage the Men already Inlisted ('till January next) and such others as may be wanted to compleat to the Establishment, for and during the War. I will not undertake to say that the Men may be had upon these terms, but I am satisfied that it will never do to let the matter alone as it was last year, till the time of service was near expiring. The hazard is too great in the first place. In the next the trouble and perplexity of disbanding one Army and raising another at the same Instant, and in such a critical situation as the last was, is scarcely in the power of Words to describe, and such as no man, who has experienced it once, will ever undergo again.

If Congress should differ from me in Sentiment upon this point, I have only to beg that they will do me the justice to believe, that I have nothing more in view than what to me appears necessary to advance the public weal, although in the first Instance it will be attended with a capital expence; and, that I have the Honor to be etc.

22

TO JOSEPH REED

Cambridge, February 10, 1776

Dear Sir:

Your obliging favors of the 28th ult. and Ist inst. are now before me, and claim my particular thanks for the polite attention you pay to my wishes in an early and regular communication of what is passing in your quarter.

If my dear sir, you conceive, that I took any thing wrong or amiss, that was conveyed in any of your former letters, you are really mistaken. I only meant to convince you, that nothing would give more real satisfaction, than to know the sentiments, which are entertained of me by the public, whether *Public reputation* they be favorable or otherwise; and I urged as a reason, that the man, who wished to steer clear of shelves and rocks, must know where they lay I know—but to declare it, unless to a friend, may be an argument of vanity—the integrity of my own heart. I know the unhappy predicament I stand in; I know that much is expected of me; I know, that without men, without arms, without ammunition, without any thing fit for the accommodation of a soldier, little is to be done; and, which is mortifying, I know, that I cannot stand justified to the world without exposing my own weakness, and injuring the cause, by declaring my wants, which I am determined not to do, further than unavoidable necessity brings every man acquainted with them.

If, under these disadvantages, I am able to keep above water, (as it were) in the esteem of mankind, I shall feel myself happy; but if, from the unknown peculiarity of my circumstances, I suffer in the opinion of the world, I shall not think you take the freedom of a friend, if you conceal the reflections that may be cast upon my conduct. My own situation feels so irksome to me at times, that, if I did not consult the public good, more than my own tranquillity, I should long ere this have put every thing to the cast of a Dye. So far from my having an army of twenty thousand men well armed &c., I have been here with less than one half of it, including sick, furloughed, and on command, and those neither armed nor clothed, as they should be. In short, my situation has been such, that I have been obliged to use art to conceal it from my own officers. The Congress, as you observe, expect, I believe, that I should do more than others—for whilst they compel me to enlist men without a bounty, they give 40 dollars to others, which will, I expect, put a stand to our enlistments; for notwithstanding all the publick virtue which is ascrib'd to these people, there is no nation under the sun, (that I ever came across) pay greater adoration to money than they do—I am pleas'd to find that your Battalions are cloathed and look well, and that they are filing off for Canada. I wish I could say that the troops here had altered much in Dress or appearance. Our regiments are little more than half compleat, and recruiting nearly at a stand—In all my letters I fail not the mention of Tents, and now perceive that notice is taken of yr. application.

General Howe

I have been convinced, by General Howe's conduct, that he has either been very ignorant of our situation (which I do not believe) or that he has received positive orders (which, I think, is natural to conclude) not to put anything to the hazard till his reinforcements arrive; otherwise there has been a time since the first of December, that we must have fought like men to have maintained these Lines, so great in their extent.

The party to Bunker's Hill had some good and some bad men engaged in it. One or two courts have been held on the conduct of part of it. To be plain, these people—among friends—are not to be depended upon if exposed; and any man will fight well if he thinks himself in no danger. I do not apply this to these people only. I suppose it to be the case with all raw and undisciplined troops. You may rely upon it, that transports left Boston six weeks ago with troops; where they are gone, unless driven to the West Indies, I know not. You may also rely upon General Clinton's sailing from Boston about three weeks ago, with about four or five hundred men; his destination I am also a stranger to. I am sorry to hear of the failures you speak of from France. But why will not Congress

Independence is necessary

forward part of the powder made in your province? They seem to look upon this as the season for action, but will not furnish the means. But I will not blame them. I dare say the demands upon them are greater than they can supply. The cause must be starved till our resources are greater, or more certain within ourselves.

With respect to myself, I have never entertained an idea of an accommodation, since I heard of the measures, which were adopted in consequence of the Bunker's Hill fight. The king's speech has confirmed the sentiments I entertained upon the news of that affair; and if every man was of my mind, the ministers of Great Britain should know, in a few words, upon what issue the cause should be put. I would not be deceived by artful declarations, nor specious pretences; nor would I be amused by unmeaning propositions; but in open, undisguised, and manly terms proclaim our wrongs, and our resolution to be redressed. I would tell them, that we had borne much, that we had long and ardently sought for reconciliation upon honorable terms, that it had been denied us, that all our attempts after peace had proved abortive, and had been grossly misrepresented, that we had done every thing which could be expected from the best of subjects, that the spirit of freedom beat too high in us to submit to slavery, and that, if nothing else could satisfy a tyrant and his diabolical ministry, we are determined to shake off all connexions with a state so unjust and unnatural. This I would tell them, not under covert, but in words as clear as the sun in its meridian brightness.

I observe what you say, in respect to the ardor of the chimney-corner heroes. I am glad their zeal is in some measure abated, because if circumstances will not permit us to make an attempt upon B[oston], or if it should be made and fail, we shall not appear altogether so culpable. I entertain the same opinion of the attempt now, which I have ever done. I believe an assault would be attended with considerable loss, and I believe it would succeed, if the men should behave well. As to an attack upon B[unker's] Hill, (unless it could be carried by surprise,) the loss, I conceive, would be greater in proportion than at Boston; and, if a defeat should follow, it would be discouraging to the men, but highly animating if crowned with success. Great good, or great evil, would consequently result from it. It is quite a different thing to what you left, being by odds the strongest fortress they possess, both in rear and front.

Assault on Boston considered

The Congress have ordered all captures to be tried in the courts of admiralty of the different governments to which they are sent, and some irreconcilable difference arising between the resolves of Congress, and the law of this colony, respecting the proceedings, or something or another which always happens to procrastinate business here, has put a total stop to the trials, to the no small injury of the public, as well as the great grievance of individuals. Whenever a condemnation shall take place, I shall not be unmindful of your advice respecting the

Treatment of captured ships

hulls, &c. Would to heaven the plan you speak of for obtaining arms may succeed. The acquisition would be great, and give fresh life and vigor to our measures, as would the arrival you speak of; our expectations are kept alive, and if we can keep ourselves so, and spirits up another summer, I have no fears of wanting the needful after that. As the number of our Inlisted men were too small to undertake any offensive operation, if the circumstances of weather, &c, should favor, I ordered in (by application to this Govt., Connecticut and New Hampshire) as many regiments of militia as would enable us to attempt something in some manner or other. They were to have been here by the first of the month, but only a few straggling companies are yet come in. The Bay towards Roxbury has been froze up once or twice pretty hard, and yesterday single persons might have crossed, I believe, from Letchmore's Point, by picking their way; a thaw, I fear, is again approaching.

We have had the most laborious piece of work at Lechmore's Point, on account of the frost, that ever you saw. We hope to get it finished on Sunday. It is within as commanding a distance of Boston as Dorchester Hill, though of a different part. Our vessels now and then pick up a prize or two. Our Commodore (Manly) was very near being catched about eight days ago but happily escaped with vessel and crew after running ashore, scuttling, and defending her.

I recollect nothing else worth giving you the trouble of, unless you can be amused by reading a letter and poem addressed to me by Mrs. or Miss Phillis Wheatley. In searching over a parcel of papers the other day, in order to destroy such as were useless, I brought it to light again. At first, with a view of doing justice to her great poetical genius, I had a great mind to publish the poem; but not knowing whether it might not be considered rather as a mark of my own vanity, than as a compliment to her, I laid it aside, till I came across it again in the manner just mentioned. I congratulate you upon your election, although I consider it as the *coup de grace* to my expectation of ever seeing you resident in this camp again. I have only to regret the want of you, if that should be the case; and I shall do it the more feelingly, as I have experienced the good effects of your aid. I am, with Mrs. Washington's compliments to Mrs. Reed, and my best respects, added, dear Sir, your most obedient and affectionate servant.

23

TO JOHN AUGUSTINE WASHINGTON

Philadelphia, May 31, 1776

Dear Brother:

Since my arrival at this place, where I came at the request of
Congress, to settle some matters relative to the ensuing Campaign I have received your Letter of the 18th. from Williamsburg, and think I stand indebted to you for another, which
came to hand some time ago, in New York.

I am very glad to find that the Virginia Convention have
passed so noble a vote, and with so much unanimity, things
have come to that pass now, as to convince us, that we have
nothing more to expect from the justice of G. Britain; also,
that she is capable of the most delusive Arts, for I am satisfied
that no Commissioners ever were design'd, except Hessians
and other Foreigners; and that the Idea was only to deceive,
and throw us off our guard; the first it has too effectually
accomplished, as many Members of Congress, in short, the
representation of whole Provences, are still feeding themselves upon the dainty food of reconciliation; and tho' they will
not allow that the expectation of it has any influence upon
their judgments (with respect to their preparations for defence) it is but too obvious that it has an operation upon every
part of their conduct and is a clog to their proceedings, it is not
in the nature of things to be otherwise, for no Man, that entertains a hope of seeing this dispute speedily, and equitably adjusted by Commissioners, will go to the same expence and run
the same hazards to prepare for the worst event as he who
believes that he must conquer, or submit to unconditional
terms, and its concomitants, such as Confiscation, hanging,
&c., &c.

To form a new Government, requires infinite care, and unbounded attention; for if the foundation is badly laid the superstructure must be bad, too much time therefore, cannot be
bestowed in weighing and digesting matters well. We have, no
doubt, some good parts in our present constitution; many bad
ones we know we have, wherefore no time can be misspent
that is employed in seperating the Wheat from the Tares. My
fear is, that you will all get tired and homesick, the consequence of which will be, that you will patch up some kind of

Virginia's vote for independence

Hessians

Forming a new government

Constitution as defective as the present; this should be avoided, every Man should consider, that he is lending his aid to frame a Constitution which is to render Million's happy, or Miserable, and that a matter of such moment cannot be the Work of a day.

I am in hopes to hear some good Accts from No. Carolina. If Clinton has only part of his force there, and not strongly Intrenched, I should think Genl. Lee will be able to give a very good acct. of those at Cape Fare. Surely Administration must intend more than 5000 Men for the Southern district, otherwise they must have a very contemptable opinion of those Colonies, or have great expectation of assistance from the Indians, Slaves, and Tories. We expect a very bloody Summer of it at New York and Canada, as it is there I expect the grand efforts of the Enemy will be aim'd; and I am sorry to say that we are not, either in Men, or Arms, prepared for it; however, it is to be hoped, that if our cause is just, as I do most religiously believe it to be, the same Providence which has in many Instances appear'd for us, will still go on to afford its aid.

Your Convention is acting very wisely in removing the disaffected, Stock, &ca., from the Counties of Princess Anne and Norfolk; and are much to be commended for their attention to the Manufacture of Salt, Salt Petre, Powder &ca. No time, nor expense should be spared to accomplish these things.

Mrs. Washington is now under Innoculation in this City; and will, I expect, have the Small pox favourably, this is the 13th day, and she has very few Pustules; she would have wrote to my Sister but thought it prudent not to do so, notwithstanding there could be but little danger in conveying the Infection in this manner. She joins me in love to you, her, and all the little ones. I am, with every Sentiment of regard, etc.

24

GENERAL ORDERS

Head Quarters, New York, July 2, 1776

Parole Armstrong. Countersign Lee.

Genl. Mifflin is to repair to the post near Kingsbridge and use his utmost endeavours to forward the works there—General Scott in the mean time to perform the duty required of

General Mifflin in the orders of the 29th of June.

No Sentries are to stop or molest the Country people coming to Market or going from it but to be very vigilant in preventing Soldiers leaving the army.

Col Cortland of the New-Jersey Brigade is to send over five-hundred of the Militia under his command to reinforce General Greene's Brigade; these troops are to be distinguished from the old Militia in future by being called New-Levies— The Quarter Master General to furnish them with Tents: The detachment from General Spencers Brigade to return when these get over. The Militia not under the immediate Command of General Heard are to be under that of Genl. Mercer until the arrival of their own General Officer.

The time is now near at hand which must probably determine, whether Americans are to be, Freemen, or Slaves; whether they are to have any property they can call their own; whether their Houses, and Farms, are to be pillaged and destroyed, and they consigned to a State of Wretchedness from which no human efforts will probably deliver them. The fate of unborn Millions will now depend, under God, on the Courage and Conduct of this army—Our cruel and unrelenting Enemy leaves us no choice but a brave resistance, or the most abject submission; this is all we can expect—We have therefore to resolve to conquer or die: Our own Country's Honor, all call upon us for a vigorous and manly exertion, and if we now shamefully fail, we shall become infamous to the whole world. Let us therefore rely upon the goodness of the Cause, and the aid of the supreme Being, in whose hands Victory is, to animate and encourage us to great and noble Actions—The Eyes of all our Countrymen are now upon us, and we shall have their blessings, and praises, if happily we are the instruments of saving them from the Tyranny meditated against them. Let us therefore animate and encourage each other, and shew the whole world, that a Freeman contending for Liberty on his own ground is superior to any slavish mercenary on earth.

Exhortations on honor, bravery, and liberty

The General recommends to the officers great coolness in time of action, and to the soldiers a strict attention and obedience with a becoming firmness and spirit.

Any officer, or soldier, or any particular Corps, distinguishing themselves by any acts of bravery, and courage, will assuredly meet with notice and rewards; and on the other hand, those who behave ill, will as certainly be exposed and punished—The General being resolved, as well for the Honor and Safety of the Country, as Army, to shew no favour to such as refuse, or neglect their duty at so important a crisis.

The General expressly orders that no officer, or soldier, on any pretence whatever, without leave in writing, from the commanding officer of the regiment, do leave the parade, so as to be out of drum-call, in case of an alarm, which may be hourly expected—The Regiments are immediately to be under Arms on their respective parades, and should any be absent they will be severely punished—The whole Army to be at their Alarm posts completely equipped tomorrow, a little before day.

Ensign Charles Miller, Capt Wrisst's Company, and Colonel Wyllys's Regiment, charged with "absenting himself from his Guard" tried by a General Court Martial and acquitted—The General approves the sentence, and orders him to be dismissed from his arrest.

As there is a probability of Rain, the General strongly recommends to the officers, to pay particular attention, to their Men's arms and ammunition, that neither may be damaged—

Lieut. Col Clark who was ordered to sit on General Court Martial in the orders of yesterday being absent on command, Lieut. Col Tyler is to sit in Court.

EVENING ORDERS

'Tis the General's desire that the men lay upon their Arms in their tents and quarters, ready to turn out at a moments warning, as their is the greatest likelihood of it.

25

GENERAL ORDERS

Head Quarters, New York, July 9, 1776

Parole Manchester. Countersign Norfolk.

John Evans of Capt. Ledyards Company Col McDougall's Regiment—Hopkins Rice of Capt. Pierce's Company Col Ritzema's Regiment having been tried by a General Court Martial whereof Col. Read was President and found guilty of "Desertion," were sentenced to receive each Thirty-nine Lashes. The General approves the Sentences and orders them to be executed at the usual time and place.

Passes to go from the City are hereafter to be granted by John Berrien, Henry Wilmot and John Ray Junr. a Committee of the City appointed for that purpose—Officers of the Guards at the Ferries and Wharves, to be careful in making this regulation known to the Sentries, who are to see that the passes are signed by one of the above persons, and to be careful no Soldier goes over the Ferry without a pass from a General officer.

The North River Guard to be removed to the Market House near the Ferry-Stairs, as soon as it is fitted up.

The Hon. Continental Congress having been pleased to allow a Chaplain to each Regiment, with the pay of Thirty-three Dollars and one third pr month—The Colonels or commanding officers of each regiment are directed to procure Chaplains accordingly; persons of good Characters and exemplary lives—To see that all inferior officers and soldiers pay them a suitable respect and attend carefully upon religious exercises. The blessing and protection of Heaven are at all times necessary but especially so in times of public distress and danger— The General hopes and trusts, that every officer and man, will endeavour so to live, and act, as becomes a Christian Soldier defending the dearest Rights and Liberties of his country.

Appointment of chaplains

The Hon. The Continental Congress, impelled by the dictates of duty, policy and necessity, having been pleased to dissolve the Connection which subsisted between this Country, and Great Britain, and to declare the United Colonies of North America, free and independent States: The several brigades are to be drawn up this evening on their respective Parades, at Six O'Clock, when the declaration of Congress, shewing the grounds and reasons of this measure, is to be read with an audible voice.

Declaration of Independence

The General hopes this important Event will serve as a fresh incentive to every officer, and soldier, to act with Fidelity and Courage, as knowing that now the peace and safety of his Country depends (under God) solely on the success of our arms: And that he is now in the service of a State, possessed of sufficient power to reward his merit, and advance him to the highest Honors of a free Country.

26

TO THE OFFICERS AND SOLDIERS OF THE PENNSYLVANIA ASSOCIATORS

Head Quarters, August 8, 1776

Gentlemen:

I had fully resolved to have paid you a Visit in New Jersey if the movements of the Enemy, and some intelligence indicating an early attack, had not induced me to suspend it.

Allow me therefore, to address you in this Mode, as fellow Citizens and fellow Soldiers engaged in the same Glorious Cause; to represent to you, that the Fate of our Country depends in all human probability, on the Exertion of a few Weeks; That it is of the utmost importance, to keep up a respectable Force for that time, and there can be no doubt that success will Crown our Efforts, if we firmly and resolutely determine, to conquer or to die.

I have placed so much confidence, in the Spirit and Zeal of the Associated Troops of Pennsylvania, that I cannot persuade myself an impatience to return Home, or a less honourable Motive will defeat my well grounded expectation, that they will do their Country essential Service, at this critical time, when the Powers of Despotism are all combined against it, and ready to strike their most decisive Stroke. If I could allow myself to doubt your Spirit and Perseverance, I should represent the ruinous Consequences of your leaving the Service, by setting before you, the discouragement it would give the Army, the confusion and shame of our Friends, and the still more· galling triumph of our Enemies. But as I have no such doubts, I shall only thank you for the Spirit and Ardor you have shewn, in so readily marching to meet the Enemy, and am most confident you will crown it by a Glorious Perseverance. The Honor and safety of our bleeding Country, and every other motive that can influence the brave and heroic Patriot, call loudly upon us, to acquit ourselves with Spirit. In short, we must now determine to be enslaved or free. If we make Freedom our choice, we must obtain it, by the Blessing of Heaven on our United and Vigorous Efforts.

I salute you Gentlemen most Affectionately, and beg leave to remind you, that Liberty, Honor, and Safety are all at stake, and I trust Providence will smile upon our Efforts, and establish us once more, the Inhabitants of a free and happy Country. I am, etc.

27

TO THE PRESIDENT OF CONGRESS

Colonel Morris's, on the Heights of Harlem,
September 24, 1776

Sir:

From the hours allotted to Sleep, I will borrow a few Moments to convey my thoughts on sundry important matters to Congress. I shall offer them, with that sincerity which ought to characterize a man of candour; and with the freedom which may be used in giving useful information, without incurring the imputation of presumption.

We are now as it were, upon the eve of another dissolution of our Army; the remembrance of the difficulties which happened upon that occasion last year, the consequences which might have followed the change, if proper advantages had been taken by the Enemy; added to a knowledge of the present temper and Situation of the Troops, reflect but a very gloomy prospect upon the appearance of things now, and satisfie me, beyond the possibility of doubt, that unless some speedy, and effectual measures are adopted by Congress, our cause will be lost.

Pay of soldiers

It is in vain to expect, that any (or more than a trifling) part of this Army will again engage in the Service on the encouragement offered by Congress. When Men find that their Townsmen and Companions are receiving 20, 30, and more Dollars, for a few Months Service, (which is truely the case) it cannot be expected; without using compulsion; and to force them into the Service would answer no valuable purpose. When Men are irritated, and the Passions inflamed, they fly hastely and chearfully to Arms; but after the first emotions are over, to expect, among such People, as compose the bulk of an Army, that they are influenced by any other principles than those of Interest, is to look for what never did, and I fear never will happen; the Congress will deceive themselves therefore if they expect it.

A Soldier reasoned with upon the goodness of the cause he is engaged in, and the inestimable rights he is contending for, hears you with patience, and acknowledges the truth of your observations, but adds, that it is of no more Importance to him than others. The Officer makes you the same reply, with this *Pay of officers* further remark, that his pay will not support him, and he cannot ruin himself and Family to serve his Country, when every Member of the community is equally Interested and benefitted by his Labours. The few therefore, who act upon Principles of disinterestedness, are, comparatively speaking, no more than a drop in the Ocean. It becomes evidently clear then, that as this Contest is not likely to be the Work of a day; as the War must be carried on systematically, and to do it, you must have good Officers, there are, in my Judgment, no other possible means to obtain them but by establishing your Army upon a permanent footing; and giving your Officers good pay; this will induce Gentlemen, and Men of Character to engage; and till the bulk of your Officers are composed of such persons as are actuated by Principles of honour, and a spirit of enterprize, you have little to expect from them. They ought to have such allowances as will enable them to live like, and support the Characters of Gentlemen; and not be driven by a scanty pittance to the low, and dirty arts which many of them practice, to filch the Public of more than the difference of pay would amount to upon an ample allowe. Besides, something is due to the Man who puts his life in his hands, hazards his health, and forsakes the Sweets of domestic enjoyments. Why a Captn. in the Continental Service should receive no more than 5/. Curry per day, for performing the same duties that an officer of the same Rank in the British Service receives 10/. Sterlg. for, I never could conceive; especially when the latter is provided with every necessary he requires, upon the best terms, and the former can scarce procure them, at any Rate. There is nothing that gives a Man consequence, and renders him fit for Command, like a support that renders him Independant of every body but the State he Serves.

Bounties in land With respect to the Men, nothing but a good bounty can obtain them upon a permanent establishment; and for no shorter time than the continuance of the War, ought they to be engaged; as Facts incontestibly prove, that the difficulty, and cost of Inlistments, increase with time. When the Army was first raised at Cambridge, I am persuaded the Men might have

been got without a bounty for the War: after this, they began
to see that the Contest was not likely to end so speedily as was
immagined, and to feel their consequence, by remarking, that
to get the Militia In, in the course of last year, many Towns
were induced to give them a bounty. Foreseeing the Evils resulting from this, and the destructive consequences which unavoidably would follow short Inlistments, I took the Liberty in
a long Letter, written by myself (date not now recollected, as
my Letter Book is not here) to recommend the Inlistments for
and during the War; assigning such Reasons for it, as experience has since convinced me were well founded. At that time
twenty Dollars would, I am persuaded, have engaged the Men
for this term. But it will not do to look back, and if the present
opportunity is slip'd, I am perswaded that twelve months more
will Increase our difficulties fourfold. I shall therefore take the
freedom of giving it as my opinion, that a good Bounty be
immediately offered, aided by the proffer of at least 100, or
150 Acres of Land and a suit of Cloaths and Blankt, to each
non-Comd. Officer and Soldier; as I have good authority for
saying, that however high the Men's pay may appear, it is
barely sufficient in the present scarcity and dearness of all
kinds of goods, to keep them in Cloaths, much less afford
support to their Families. If this encouragement then is given
to the Men, and such Pay allowed the Officers as will induce
Gentlemen of Character and liberal Sentiments to engage;
and proper care and precaution are used in the nomination
(having more regard to the Characters of Persons, than the
Number of Men they can Inlist) we should in a little time have
an Army able to cope with any that can be opposed to it, as
there are excellent Materials to form one out of: but while the
only merit an Officer possesses is his ability to raise Men; while
those Men consider, and treat him as an equal; and (in the
Character of an Officer) regard him no more than a broom-
stick, being mixed together as one common herd; no order,
nor no discipline can prevail; nor will the Officer ever meet
with that respect which is essentially necessary to due subordination.

To place any dependance upon Militia, is, assuredly, resting *The militia*
upon a broken staff. Men just dragged from the tender Scenes
of domestick life; unaccustomed to the din of Arms; totally
unacquainted with every kind of Military skill, which being
followed by a want of confidence in themselves, when opposed

to Troops regularly train'd, disciplined, and appointed, superior in knowledge, and superior in Arms, makes them timid, and ready to fly from their own shadows. Besides, the sudden change in their manner of living, (particularly in the lodging) brings on sickness in many; impatience in all, and such an unconquerable desire of returning to their respective homes that it not only produces shameful, and scandalous Desertions among themselves, but infuses the like spirit in others. Again, Men accustomed to unbounded freedom, and no controul, cannot brook the Restraint which is indispensably necessary to the good order and Government of an Army; without which, licentiousness, and every kind of disorder triumphantly reign. To bring Men to a proper degree of Subordination, is not the work of a day, a Month or even a year; and unhappily for us, and the cause we are Engaged in, the little discipline I have been labouring to establish in the Army under my immediate Command, is in a manner done away by having such a mixture of Troops as have been called together within these few Months.

Relaxed, and unfit, as our Rules and Regulations of War are, for the Government of an Army, the Militia (those properly so called, for of these we have two sorts, the Six Months Men and those sent in as a temporary aid) do not think themselves subject to 'em, and therefore take liberties, which the Soldier is punished for; this creates jealousy; jealousy begets dissatisfaction, and these by degrees ripen into Mutiny; keeping the whole Army in a confused, and disordered State; rendering the time of those who wish to see regularity and good Order prevail more unhappy than Words can describe. Besides this, such repeated changes take place, that all arrangement is set at nought, and the constant fluctuation of things, deranges every plan, as fast as adopted.

These Sir, Congress may be assured, are but a small part of the Inconveniences which might be enumerated and attributed to Militia; but there is one that merits particular attention, and that is the expence. Certain I am, that it would be cheaper to keep 50, or 100,000 Men in constant pay than to depend upon half the number, and supply the other half occasionally by Militia. The time the latter is in pay before and after they are in Camp, assembling and Marching; the waste of Ammunition; the consumption of Stores, which in spite of every Resolution, and requisition of Congress they must be furnished

with, or sent home, added to other incidental expences consequent upon their coming, and conduct in Camp, surpasses all
Idea, and destroys every kind of regularity and œconomy
which you could establish among fixed and Settled Troops;
and will, in my opinion prove (if the scheme is adhered to) the
Ruin of our Cause.

The Jealousies of a standing Army, and the Evils to be apprehended from one, are remote; and in my judgment, situated and circumstanced as we are, not at all to be dreaded; but
the consequence of wanting one, according to my Ideas,
formed from the present view of things, is certain, and inevitable Ruin; for if I was called upon to declare upon Oath,
whether the Militia have been most serviceable or hurtful upon the whole; I should subscribe to the latter. I do not mean by
this however to arraign the Conduct of Congress, in so doing I
should equally condemn my own measures, (if I did not my
judgment); but experience, which is the best criterion to work
by, so fully, clearly, and decisively reprobates the practice of
trusting to Militia, that no Man who regards order, regularity,
and oeconomy; or who has any regard for his own honour,
Character, or peace of Mind, will risk them upon this Issue.

A standing army

No less attention should be paid to the choice of Surgeons
than other Officers of the Army; they should undergo a regular examination; and if not appointed by the Director Genl.
and Surgeons of the Hospital, they ought to be subordinate
to, and governed by his directions; the Regimental Surgeons
I am speaking of, many of whom are very great Rascals,
countenancing the Men in sham Complaints to exempt them
from duty, and often receiving Bribes to Certifie Indisposi-
tions, with a view to procure discharges or Furloughs; but
independant of these practices, while they are considered as
unconnected with the Gen'l. Hospital there will be nothing
but continual Complaints of each other: The Director of the
Hospital charging them with enormity in their drafts for the
Sick; and they him, for denying such things as are necessary.
In short, there is a constant bickering among them, which
tends greatly to the Injury of the Sick; and will always subsist
till the Regimental Surgeons are made to look up to the
Director Genl. of the Hospital as a Superior. Whether this is
the case in regular Armies, or not, I cannot undertake to say;
but certain I am there is a necessity for it in this, or the Sick
will suffer; the Regimental Surgeons are aiming, I am per-

Military surgeons

suaded, to break up the Gen'l. Hospital, and have, in numberless Instances, drawn for Medicines, Stores &ca. in the most profuse and extravagant manner, for private purposes.

Military punishments

Another matter highly worthy of attention, is, that other Rules and Regulation's may be adopted for the Government of the Army than those now in existence, otherwise the Army, but for the name, might as well be disbanded. For the most attrocious offences, (one or two Instances only excepted) a Man receives no more than 39 Lashes; and these perhaps (thro' the collusion of the Officer who is to see it inflicted), are given in such a manner as to become rather a matter of sport than punishment; but when inflicted as they ought, many hardend fellows who have been the Subjects, have declared that for a bottle of Rum they would undergo a Second operation; it is evident therefore that this punishment is inadequate to many Crimes it is assigned to, as a proof of it, thirty and 40 Soldiers will desert at a time; and of late, a practice prevails, (as you will see by my Letter of the 22d) of the most alarming nature; and which will, if it cannot be checked, prove fatal both to the Country and Army; I mean the infamous practice of Plundering, for under the Idea of Tory property, or property which may fall into the hands of the Enemy, no Man is secure in his effects, and scarcely in his Person; for in order to get at them, we have several Instances of People being frightned out of their Houses under pretence of those Houses being ordered to be burnt, and this is done with a view of siezing the Goods; nay, in order that the villany may be more effectually concealed, some Houses have actually been burnt to cover the theft.

I have with some others, used my utmost endeavours to stop this horrid practice, but under the present lust after plunder, and want of Laws to punish Offenders, I might almost as well attempt to remove Mount Atlas. I have ordered instant corporal Punishment upon every Man who passes our Lines, or is seen with Plunder, that the Offenders might be punished for disobedience of Orders; and Inclose you the proceedings of a Court Martial held upon an Officer, who with a Party of Men had robbd a House a little beyond our Lines of a Number of valuable Goods; among which (to shew that nothing escapes) were four large Pier looking Glasses, Women's Cloaths, and other Articles which one would think, could be of no Earthly use to him. He was met by a Major of Brigade who ordered him to return the Goods, as taken contrary to Gen'l. Orders, which he not only peremptorily refused to do, but drew up his Party and swore he would defend them at the hazard of his Life; on which I ordered him to be arrested, and tryed for Plundering, Disobedience of Orders, and Mutiny; for the Result, I refer to the Proceedings of the Court; whose judgment appeared so exceedingly extraordinary, that I ordered a Reconsideration of the matter, upon which, and with the Assistance of fresh evidence, they made Shift to Cashier him.

I adduce this Instance to give some Idea to Congress of the Currt. Sentiments and general run of the Officers which compose the present Army; and to shew how exceedingly necessary it is to be careful in the choice of the New Sett, even if it should take double the time to compleat the levies. An Army formed of good Officers moves like Clock-work; but there is no Situation upon Earth, less enviable, nor more distressing, than that Person's who is at the head of Troops, who are regardless of Order and discipline; and who are unprovided with almost every necessary. In a word the difficulties which have forever surrounded me since I have been in the Service, and kept my Mind constantly upon the stretch; The Wounds which my Feelings as an Officer have received by a thousand things which have happened, contrary to my expectation and Wishes; the effect of my own Conduct, and present appearance of things, so little pleasing to myself, as to render it a matter of no Surprize (to me) if I should stand capitally censured by Congress; added to a consciousness of my inability to govern an Army composed of such discordant parts, and under such a variety of intricate and perplexing circumstances; induces not only a belief, but a thorough conviction in my Mind, that it will be impossible unless there is a thorough change in our Military Systems for me to conduct matters in such a manner, as to give satisfaction to the Publick which is all the recompence I aim at, or ever wished for.

On good officers

Before I conclude I must apologize for the liberties taken in this Letter and for the blots and scratchings therein, not having time to give it more correctly. With truth I can add, that with every Sentiment of respect and esteem. I am etc.

28
———

TO LUND WASHINGTON

Col. Morris's, on the Heights of Harlem,
September 30, 1776

Dear Lund:

Your letter of the 18th, which is the only one received and unanswered, now lies before me. The amazement which you seem to be in at the unaccountable measures which have been adopted by [Congress] would be a good deal increased if I had time to unfold the whole system of their management since this time twelve months. I do not know how to account for the unfortunate steps which have been taken but from that fatal idea of conciliation which prevailed so long—fatal, I call it, because from my soul I wish it may [not] prove so, though my fears lead me to think there is too much danger of it. This time last year I pointed out the evil consequences of short enlistments, the expenses of militia, and the little dependence that was to be placed in them. I assured [Congress] that the longer they delayed raising a standing army, the more difficult and chargeable would they find it to get one, and that, at the same time that the militia would answer no valuable purpose, the frequent calling them in would be attended with an expense, that they could have no conception of. Whether, as I have said before, the unfortunate hope of reconciliation was the cause, or the fear of a standing army prevailed, I will not undertake to say; but the policy was to engage men for twelve months only. The consequence of which, you have had great bodies of militia in pay that never were in camp; you have had immense quantities of provisions drawn by men that never rendered you one hour's service (at least usefully), and this in the most profuse and wasteful way. Your stores have been expended, and every kind of military [discipline?] destroyed by them; your numbers fluctuating, uncertain, and forever far short of report—at no one time, I believe, equal to twenty thousand men fit for duty. At present our numbers fit for duty (by this day's report) amount to 14,759, besides 3,427 on command, and the enemy within stone's throw of us. It is true a body of militia are again ordered out, but they come without any conveniences and soon return. I discharged a regiment the other

Raising a standing army

day that had in it fourteen rank and file fit for duty only, and several that had less than fifty. In short, such is my situation that if I were to wish the bitterest curse to an enemy on this side of the grave, I should put him in my stead with my feelings; and yet I do not know what plan of conduct to pursue. I see the impossibility of serving with reputation, or doing any essential service to the cause by continuing in command, and yet I am told that if I quit the command inevitable ruin will follow from the distraction that will ensue. In confidence I tell you that I never was in such an unhappy, divided state since I was born. To lose all comfort and happiness on the one hand, whilst I am fully persuaded that under such a system of management as has been adopted, I cannot have the least chance for reputation, nor those allowances made which the nature of the case requires; and to be told, on the other, that if I leave the service all will be lost, is, at the same time that I am bereft of every peaceful moment, distressing to a degree. But I will be done with the subject, with the precaution to you that it is not a fit one to be publicly known or discussed. If I fall, it may not be amiss that these circumstances be known, and declaration made in credit to the justice of my character. And if the men will stand by me (which by the by I despair of), I am resolved not to be forced from this ground while I have life; and a few days will determine the point, if the enemy should not change their plan of operations; for they certainly will not—I am sure they ought not—to waste the season that is now fast advancing, and must be precious to them. I thought to have given you a more explicit account of my situation, expectation, and feelings, but I have not time. I am wearied to death all day with a variety of perplexing circumstances—disturbed at the conduct of the militia, whose behavior and want of discipline has done great injury to the other troops, who never had officers, except in a few instances, worth the bread they eat. My time, in short, is so much engrossed that I have not leisure for corresponding, unless it is on mere matters of public business.

Unhappiness with situation.

I therefore in answer to your last Letter of the 18th shall say:
With respect to the chimney, I would not have you for the sake of a little work spoil the look of the fireplaces, tho' that in the parlor must, I should think, stand as it does; not so much on account of the wainscotting, which I think must be altered

Repairs to Mount Vernon

(on account of the door leading into the new building,) as on account of the chimney piece and the manner of its fronting into the room.

The chimney in the room above ought, if it could be so contrived, to be an angle chimney as the others are: but I would not have this attempted at the expence of pulling down the partition. The chimney in the new room should be exactly in the middle of it—the doors and everything else to be exactly answerable and uniform—in short I would have the whole executed in a masterly manner.

You ought surely to have a window in the gable end of the new cellar (either under the Venetian window, or one on each side of it).

Let Mr. Herbert know that I shall be very happy in getting his brother exchanged as soon as possible, but as the enemy have more of our officers than we of theirs, and some of ours have long been confined (and claim the right of being first exchanged,) I do not know how far it may be in my power at this time, to comply with his desires.

Remember me to all our neighbors and friends, particularly to Colo. Mason, to whom I would write if I had time to do it fully and satisfactorily. Without this, I think the correspondence on my part would be unavailing—I am etc.

29

PROCLAMATION

Given at Head-Quarters, Morris-Town, January 25, 1777

Whereas several persons, inhabitants of the United States of America, influenced by inimical motives, intimidated by the threats of the enemy, or deluded by a Proclamation issued the 30th of November last, by Lord and General Howe, stiled the King's Commissioners for granting pardons, &c. (now at open war, and invading these states), have been so lost to the interest and welfare of their country, as to repair to the enemy, sign a declaration of fidelity, and in some instances have been com-

Oaths of allegiance

pelled to take oaths of allegiance to and engage not to take up arms, or encourage others so to do, against the King of Great-Britain; And whereas it has become necessary to distinguish between the friends of America and those of Great-Britain, inhabitants of these States; and that every man who receives protection from, and as a subject of any State, (not being conscientiously scrupulous against bearing arms), should stand ready to defend the same against hostile invasion; I do therefore, in behalf of the United States, by virtue of the powers committed to me by Congress, hereby strictly command and require every person, having subscribed such declaration, taken such oath, and accepted such protection and certificates from Lord and General Howe or any person under their authority forthwith to repair to Head-Quarters, or to the quarters of the nearest general officer of the Continental Army, or Militia, (until further provision can be made by the Civil Authority,) and there deliver up such protections, certificates and passports, and take the oath of allegiance to the United States of America. Nevertheless hereby granting full Liberty to all such as prefer the interest and protection of Great-Britain to the freedom and happiness of their country, forthwith to withdraw themselves and families within the enemy's lines; and I do hereby declare, that all and every person, who may neglect or refuse to comply with this order, within Thirty days from the date hereof, will be deemed adherents to the King of Great-Britain, and treated as common enemies of the American States.

30

TO AN UNIDENTIFIED CORRESPONDENT

Morristown, February 14, 1777

Sir:

I have receiv'd your Letter of yesterday. In answer to it I beg leave to observe that it is not within the scan of human Wisdom to devise a perfect Plan. In all human Institutions. In the accomplishment of all great events. In the adoption of any measure for general operation, Individuals may, and will suffer; but in the case complain'd of, the matter may, I think, be answered by propounding a few questions.

Is it not a duty Incumbent upon the Members of every State to defend the rights and liberties of that State? If so, is an [oath ex]orted from them, to observe [a con]trary conduct, obligatory [   ] If such Oath was not [extorted] but the effect of a volunta[ry act] can the person taking of[fence be] considered in any other light than as an Enemy to his Country?* In either case then, where is the Injustice of calling upon them to a declaration of their Sentiments? Is a Neutral character in one of the United States, which has by her Representatives, solemnly engaged to support the Cause, a justifiable one? If it is, may it not be extended to corporate bodies; to the State at large, and to the inevitable destruction of the opposition; which under Providence, depends upon a firm union of the whole, and the spirited exertions of all its Constituent parts?

Defense of oath of allegiance

Upon the whole, it appears to me that but two kinds of People will complain much of the Proclamation, namely, those that are really disaffected, and such as want to lay by, and wait the Issue of the dispute. The first class cannot be pleased; the next are endeavouring to play a dble. game, in which their present protections may, eventually, become a sure Card.

31

TO PRESIDENT JAMES WARREN

Head Quarters, Morris Town, May 23, 1777

Dear Sir:

Your favor of the 4th. instant was duly handed me. I am fully sensible of the zeal, your State has demonstrated, in the instances you recite, and in many more. With you, I consider them as great exertions, and as a decisive evidence of your inclination to do every thing in your power to advance the Common Cause. At the same time, whatever efforts have been, or can be made, are not more than adequate to the exigency of our Situation. Tho' over sanguine and uninformed people may think differently, this is a most interesting

---

*The manuscript of this letter (in The Huntington Library, San Marino, California) is badly mutilated. The bracketed interpolations in the text, supplying missing words, were offered by Fitzpatrick, in his *The Writings of George Washington*, p. 144.

and critical period, and will not countenance the least want of Activity or attention in any quarter. I have the highest confidence, that your State will not let the great object, we are contending for, be lost, or endangered, more than is unavoidable, by any such deficiency on their part.

Your repealing the offensive part of the Act you mention, is a proof of your justice and regard to the Sense of your Sister States. It certainly bore the features of a monopoly, and was liable to the interpretation put upon it; and, though I am ready to believe, it proceeded from impolitick, rather than Selfish, motives, I am happy the Cause of complaint is removed, and the matter placed upon a more liberal footing.

I observe, your State is not a little alarmed at the prospect of an immediate invasion. Notwithstanding the intelligence from Europe, in some measure, warrants the Supposition of such an event and makes it ɾ roper not intirely to disregard it; yet I am clearly of opinion, it is not much to be apprehended. It is by no means an eligible way to the conquest of this country; your State, from its union, numbers and Situation, being capable of a much better defence than perhaps any other; and it is presumable, the Enemy will make their attacks where Circumstances promise the greatest likelihood of Success. But, be this as it may, I cannot help disapproving the project of raising Colonial regiments for your defence, at least till the Continental are filled. It is easy to perceive, as you have yourself hinted, that it will have a direct tendency to defeat your endeavours, for compleating your quota of the United Army; and it would be the most wretched policy to weaken the hands of the Continent, under the mistaken Idea of Strengthening your own. It would also be well to consider, how far it might be consistent with propriety, in the pursuit of partial schemes, to put it out of your own power to fulfill what is required of you by the Continent.

Need for a continental army

If the Several States, by levying Troops on the particular establishment of each, leave but a Small Continental Army in the Field, it will be impossible effectually to watch the Motions of the Enemy, and oppose them where they may in reality direct their operations; the consequences of which must be inevitably fatal. But if we have a sufficient Continental force on foot, we shall be able to watch them narrowly and counteract them wherever they may attempt to move. Every State will find its Security in such an Army, whose sole business it will be

Dangers of state levies

to oppose the Enemy, wherever it is most requisite. It cannot be imagined, that if your State were seriously attacked, a proportionate part of the Continental force would not be detached to Succour and protect it. My duty, inclination, and a regard to the safety of the whole would equally compel me to it. What valuable end can then be answered to you, in the Step you propose to take, which can compensate for the irretrivable injury the common cause might sustain, from our not having a Sufficient Army in the field for the purposes of general opposition? The measure, injurious in every view, can only serve to burthen the State, with an unnecessary expence, which will be intirely its own; as the Troops intended to be raised will be for local and Colonial uses, and in diminution of the common force.

I see no advantage you can derive from such an impolitic Step, which would not be fully produced, by what I assured the Assembly, on a former occasion, should be done; which is, That the Supernumerary Regiments adopted by you, should remain in your State, 'till the designs of the Enemy became so evident, as to convince us, their continuance would be no longer expedient, or useful. This assurance I repeat; and I beg you will communicate it in my name to them; earnestly recommending it to them, to relinquish the Scheme. Indeed Sir, on a Cool, dispassionate Survey of all Circumstances, it will be found replete with impolicy and danger; and I am persuaded that, either they have already, on mature deliberation laid it aside, or on a reconsideration of the matter will coincide with me in opinion, and correct the mistake. With great regard and respect, I am &c.

32

TO MAJOR GENERAL PHILIP SCHUYLER

11 Miles in the Clove, July 22, 1777

Dear Sir:

I yesterday Evening received the favour of your Letters of the 17th and 18th. instt. with their Inclosures.

I am heartily glad you have found two such advantageous spots to take post at, and I hope the progress of the Enemy will not be so rapid, as to prevent your throwing up such lines, as you may esteem necessary for their defence.

Tho' our affairs, for some days past, have worn a dark and gloomy aspect, I yet look forward to a fortunate and happy change. I trust Genl. Burgoyne's Army will meet, sooner or later an effectual check, and as I suggested before, that the success, he has had, will precipitate his ruin. From your accounts, he appears to be pursuing that line of conduct, which of all others, is most favourable to us; I mean acting in Detachment. This conduct will certainly give room for enterprise on our part, and expose his parties to great hazard. Could we be so happy, as to cut one of them off, supposing it should not exceed four, five or six hundred Men, It would inspirit the people and do away much of their present anxiety. In such an event, they would loose sight of past misfortunes, and urged at the same time by a regard for their own security, they would fly to Arms and afford every aid in their power.

Your exertions to bring the People to view things in their proper light, to impress them with a just sense of the fatal consequences that will result to themselves, their Wives, their Children and their Country, from their taking a wrong part and for preventing Toryism, cannot be too great. Genl. Burgoyne, I have no doubt, will practise every art, his Invention shall point out, to turn their minds and seduce them from their allegiance, he should be counteracted as much as possible, as it is of the last importance to keep them firm and steady in their attachments. You have already given your attention to this matter, and I am persuaded, you will omit nothing in your power to effect these great and essential points. Stopping the roads and ordering the Cattle to be removed, were certainly right and judicious. If they are well accomplished, the Enemy must be greatly retarded and distressed.

I hope, before this you have received the Supplies of Ammunition mentioned in my late Letters. I fully expected too, that the Camp Kettles, which I ordered from hence on your first application had reached you, till yesterday, when I found on inquiry, that the Quarter Master, by some accident, did not send them before three or four days ago.

There will be no occasion to transmit to Congress a Copy of your observations, suggesting the necessity of evacuating Fort George. The Gentlemen, who mentioned the holding that post, had taken up an idea, that it was defensible with the assistance of the Vessels on the Lake, which were supposed to be better equipped, and what gave countenance to the idea, was, that the Bastion was erected under the direction and superintendence of British Engineers, and was intended as part of a very large, Strong and Extensive work. I thought it expedient to submit the matter to your further consideration, wishing you at the same time to pursue such measures respecting it, as your own judgment should advise and direct.

I could heartily wish, Harmony and a good understanding to prevail thro' the whole Army, and between the Army and the people. The times are critical, big with important events, they demand our most vigorous efforts, and unless a happy agreement subsists, they will be feeble and weak. The Enemies of America, have cultivated nothing with greater or with so much industry, as to sow division and jealousy amongst us.

I cannot give you any certain account of Genl. Howe's intended Operations. His conduct is puzzling and embarrassing, beyond measure; so are the informations, which I get. At one time the Ships are standing up towards the North River. In a little while they are going up the Sound, and in an Hour after they are going out of the Hook. I think in a day or two we must know something of his intentions. I am etc.

Conduct of
General Howe

PS: I think it will not be advisable to repose too much confidence in the Works you are about to erect and from thence to collect a large Quantity of Stores. I begin to consider Lines as a Kind of Trap and not to answer the valuable purposes expected from them. Unless they are on passes that cannot be avoided by an Enemy.

CHAPTER THREE

AT VALLEY FORGE

The Passions of Men

and the

Principles of Action

1778 – 1780

WASHINGTON *and his men nearly starved at Valley Forge in the winter of 1777 – 78, yet they emerged from that trial strengthened. They became more of an army than ever, laboring under policies that were at least improved if not made perfect by Congress under constant pressure from Washington. No longer rag-tag resistance fighters, they gained international stature. An alliance with France, bringing with it the arrival of much-needed men and materiel, was pending. During this period Washington's correspondence became intense as he sought to resolve problems of recruitment, supply, and hierarchy. Through much of this time he became de facto the sole and complete ruling authority in the country.*

Setbacks were yet to come. Illusory peace overtures would paralyze American efforts, while the failure of the first French expedition would imperil the alliance. In proportion as Washington's forces gained strength the war spread, north and south, even coming to

Mount Vernon itself. The one great battle in this period bore enough import to carry the fledgling country and its troops through nearly two years of wavering.

*Battle of Monmouth. **Replacing Howe and being denied reinforcements, General Henry Clinton considered it vital to relocate his army from Philadelphia to New York with the least delay and the fewest possible engagements on the march. Washington wished to attack while the British army was strung out along its route. He placed half his army under the command of General Charles Lee, who initiated skirmishes near Monmouth Courthouse the morning of June 29, 1778. The plan seemed provident, yet Lee ordered a premature retreat, which became confused through conflicting orders and rumors and turned into a general withdrawal. Washington halted the disappointed and overheated troops and established them athwart the line of the British approach. Clinton retired, apparently for the night, but rose before midnight and retreated to New York.***

33

GENERAL ORDERS

Head-Quarters, V. Forge, Sunday, March 1, 1778
Parole Arnold. Countersigns Ashford, Almbury.

The Commander in Chief again takes occasion to return his warmest thanks to the virtuous officers and soldiery of this Army for that persevering fidelity and Zeal which they have uniformly manifested in all their conduct. Their fortitude not only under the common hardships incident to a military life, but also under the additional sufferings to which the peculiar situation of these States have exposed them, clearly proves them worthy the enviable privelege of contending for the rights of human nature, the *Freedom and Independence* of their Country. The recent Instance of uncomplaining Patience during the scarcity of provisions in Camp is a fresh proof that they possess in an eminent degree the spirit of soldiers and the magninimity of Patriots. The few refractory individuals who disgrace themselves by murmurs it is to be hoped have repented such unmanly behaviour, and resolved to emulate the noble example of their associates upon every trial which the customary casualties of war may hereafter throw in their way. Occasional distress for want of provisions and other necessaries is a spectacle that frequently occurs in every army and perhaps there never was one which has been in general so plentifully supplied in respect to the former as ours. Surely we who are free Citizens in arms engaged in a struggle for every thing valuable in society and partaking in the glorious task of laying the foundation of an *Empire*, should scorn effeminately to shrink under those accidents and rigours of War which mercenary hirelings fighting in the cause of lawless ambition, rapine and devastation, encounter with cheerfulness and alacrity, we should not be merely equal, we should be superior to them in every qualification that dignifies the man or the soldier in proportion as the motive from which we act and the final hopes of our Toils, are superior to theirs. Thank Heaven! our Country abounds with provision and with prudent management we need not apprehend want for any length of time. Defects in the Commissaries department, Contingencies of weather and other temporary impediments have subjected and may again subject us to a deficiency for a few days, but soldiers! American soldiers! will despise the meanness of repining at such trifling strokes of Adversity, trifling indeed when compared to the transcendent *Prize* which will undoubtedly crown their Patience and Perseverence, Glory and Freedom, Peace and Plenty to themselves and the Community; The Admiration of the World, the Love of their Country and the Gratitude of Posterity!

Your General unceasingly employs his thoughts on the means of relieving your distresses, supplying your wants and bringing your labours to a speedy and prosperous issue. Our Parent Country he hopes will second his endeavors by the most vigorous exertions and he is convinced the faithful officers and soldiers associated with him in the great work of rescuing our Country from Bondage and Misery will continue in the display of that patriotic zeal which is capable of smoothing every difficulty and vanquishing every Obstacle.

At a Brigade Court Martial Feby. 27th. whereof Lt. Colo. Burr was President Lieutt. Blackall William Ball of 12th. Pennsylvania Regiment tried for disobedience of orders, Insolence and ungentlemanlike behavior. The Court after mature deliberation on the evidence produced are clearly and unanimously of opinion that Lieutt. Ball is not guilty and do therefore unanimously acquit him with the highest honor of all and every of the Articles exhibited against him. The Court do further agree and determine that the charges each and all of them are groundless, frivilous and malicious, that Lt. Ball's behaviour was truly gentlemanlike, his attention and obedience to orders exemplary and his Conduct rather deserving applause than Censure.

The Commander in Chief confirms the opinion of the

Court and orders Lieutt. Ball to be immediately released from his arrest.

At a General Court Martial whereof Colonel Cortland was President, Feby. 25th. Philip Bocker an Inhabitant of this State tried for attempting to carry Provision in to the Enemy at Philadelphia and unanimously acquitted of the charge.

At the same Court Joseph De Haven, an Inhabitant of this State tried for repeatedly going into Philadelphia since the Enemy have been in possession of it and acquitted.

Also Michael Milanberger an Inhabitant of this State tried for Supporting the Enemy with Provision and acquitted.

The Commander in Chief confirms the aforegoing opinions of the Court and orders the three last mentioned Prisoners to be immediately released from confinement.

At the same Court Jacob Cross an Inhabitant of this State tried for stealing Calves and carrying them into Philadelphia, found guilty of stealing two Calves one of which he carried into Philadelphia, the other he was carrying in when taken, being a breach of a resolution of Congress dated October 8th, '77 extended by another dated December 29th. and do Sentence him to receive two hundred lashes on his bare back well laid on.

The Commander in Chief approves the sentence and orders it to be put in Execution on the Grand-Parade tomorrow morning at guard mounting.

At a General Court Martial whereof Colo. Cortland was President Feby. 24th, '78, Joseph Worrell an Inhabitant of the State of Pennsylvania tried for giving intelligence to the Enemy and for acting as guide and pilot to the Enemy; The Court are of opinion the Prisoner is guilty of acting as a guide to the Enemy (and do acquit him of the other charge against him) being a breach of a resolution of Congress dated Octr. 8th, '77, extended by another resolution of Congress dated december 29th, 1777, and they do (upwards of two thirds agreeing) sentence him to suffer death.

His Excellency the Commander in Chief approves the sentence and orders Joseph Worrell to be executed next tuesday at 10 o'Clock in the forenoon.

34

TO JOHN BANISTER

Valley Forge, April 21, 1778

Dear Sir:

On Saturday Evening, I had the pleasure to receive your favour of the 16th. Instant.

I thank you very much, for your obliging tender of a friendly intercourse between us; and you may rest assured, that I embrace it with chearfulness, and shall write you freely, as often as leisure will permit, of such points as appear to me material and interesting.*

I am pleased to find, that you expect the proposed establishment of the Army will succeed; though it is a painful consideration, that matters of such pressing importance and obvious necessity meet with so much difficulty and delay. Be assured the success of the measure is a matter of the most serious moment, and that it ought to be brought to a conclusion, as speedily as possible. The spirit of resigning Commissions has been long at an alarming height, and increases daily. [Applications from Officers on furlough are hourly arriving, and Genls. Heath, of Boston, McDougal on the No. River, and Mason of Virginia are asking what they are to do with the appliants to them.]

The Virginia Line has sustained a violent shock in this instance; [not less than Ninety havg. resigned already, to me], the same conduct has prevailed among the Officers from the other States, though not yet to so considerable a degree; and there are but too just Grounds to fear, that it will shake the very existence of the Army, unless a remedy is soon, very soon, applied. There is none, in my opinion, so effectual, as the one pointed out. This, I trust, will satisfy the Officers, and, at the same time, it will produce no present additional emission of Money. They will not be persuaded to sacrifice all views of present interest, and encounter the numerous vicissitudes of War, in the defence of their Country, unless she will be generous enough, on her part, to make a decent provision for their future support, I do not pronounce absolutely, that we shall have no Army, if the establishment fails: But the Army, we

---

*Banister was a Virginia delegate to the Continental Congress.

may have, will be without discipline, without energy, incapable of acting with vigor, and destitute of those cements necessary to promise success, on the one hand, or to withstand the shocks of adversity, on the other. It is indeed hard to say how extensive the evil may be, if the measure should be rejected, or much longer delayed. I find it a very arduous task to keep the Officers in tolerable humour, and to protract such a combination in quitting the service, as might possibly undo us forever. The difference between our service and that of the Enemy, is very striking. With us, from the peculiar, unhappy situation of things, the Officer, a few instances excepted, must break in upon his private fortune for present support, without a prospect of future relief. With them, even Companies are esteemed so honourable and so valuable, that they have sold of late from 15 to 2,200 £ Sterling, and I am credibly informed, that 4,000 Guineas have been given for a Troop of Dragoons: You will readily determine how this difference will operate; what effects it must produce. Men may speculate as they will; they may talk of patriotism; they may draw a few examples *On patriotism* from ancient story, of great atchievements performed by its influence; but whoever builds upon it, as a sufficient Basis for conducting a long and [bloody] War, will find themselves deceived in the end. We must take the passions of Men as Nature has given them, and those principles as a guide which are generally the rule of Action. I do not mean to exclude altogether the Idea of Patriotism. I know it exists, and I know it has done much in the present Contest. But I will venture to assert, that a great and lasting War can never be supported on this principle alone. It must be aided by a prospect of Interest or some reward. For a time, it may, of itself push Men to Action; to bear much, to encounter difficulties; but it will not endure unassisted by Interest.

The necessity of putting the Army upon a respectable footing, both as to numbers and constitution, is now become more essential than ever. The Enemy are beginning to play a Game more dangerous than their efforts by Arms, tho' these will not be remitted in the smallest degree, and which threatens a fatal blow to American Independence, and to her liberties of course: They are endeavouring to ensnare the people by spe- *Specious* cious allurements of Peace. It is not improbable they have had *allurements of* such abundant cause to be tired of the War, that they may be *peace* sincere, in the terms they offer, which, though far short of our pretensions, will be extremely flattering to Minds that do not penetrate far into political consequences: But, whether they are sincere or not, they may be equally destructive; for, to discerning Men, nothing can be more evident, than that a Peace on the principles of dependance, however limited, after what has happened, would be to the last degree dishonourable and ruinous. It is, however, much to be apprehended, that the Idea of such an event will have a very powerful effect upon the Country, and, if not combatted with the greatest address, will serve, at least, to produce supineness and dis-union. Men are naturally fond of Peace, and there are Symptoms which may authorize an Opinion, that the people of America are pretty generally weary of the present War. It is doubtful, whether many of our friends might not incline to an accommodation on the Grounds held out, or which may be, rather than persevere in a contest for Independence. If this is the case, it must surely be the truest policy to strengthen the Army, and place it upon a substantial footing. This will conduce to inspire the Country with confidence; enable those at the head of affairs to consult the public honour and interest, notwithstanding the defection of some and temporary inconsistency and irresolution of others, who may desire to compromise the dispute; and if a Treaty should be deemed expedient, will put it in their power to insist upon better terms, than they could otherwise expect.

Besides, the most vigorous exertions at Home, to increase and establish our Military force upon a good Basis; it appears to me advisable, that we should immediately try the full extent of our interest abroad and bring our European Negotiations to an Issue. I think France must have ratified our Independence, and will declare War immediately, on finding that serious proposals of accommodation are made; but lest, from a mistaken policy, or too exalted an Opinion of our powers, from the representations she has had, she should still remain indecisive, it were to be wished proper persons were instantly dispatched, or our envoys, already there, instructed, to insist pointedly on her coming to a final determination. It cannot be fairly supposed, that she will hesitate a moment to declare War, if she is given to understand, in a proper manner, that a reunion of the two Countries may be the consequence of procrastination. An European War, and an European Alliance would effectually answer our purposes. If the step I now men-

European negotiations

tion, should be eligible, despatches ought to be sent at once, by different conveyances, for fear of accidents. I confess it appears to me, a measure of this kind could not but be productive of the most salutary consequences. If possible, I should also suppose it absolutely necessary, to obtain good intelligence from England, pointing out the true springs of this manœuvre of Ministry; the preparations of force they are making; the prospects there are of raising it; the amount, and when it may be expected.

It really seems to me, from a comprehensive view of things, that a period is fast approaching, big with events of the most interesting importance. When the councils we pursue and the part we act, may lead decisively to liberty, or to Slavery. Under this Idea, I cannot but regret, that inactivity, that inattention, that want of something, which [unhappily, I have but too often] experienced in our public Affairs. I wish that our representation in Congress was compleat and full from every State, and that it was formed of the first Abilities among us. Whether we continue to War, or proceed to Negotiate, the Wisdom of America in Council cannot be too great. Our situation will be truly delicate. To enter into a Negotiation too hastily, or to reject it altogether, may be attended with consequences equally fatal. The wishes of the people, seldom founded in deep disquisitions, or resulting from other reasonings than their present feeling, may not intirely accord with our true policy and interest. If they do not, to observe a proper line of conduct, for promoting the one, and avoiding offence to the other, will be a Work of great difficulty. Nothing short of Independence, it appears to me, can possibly do. A Peace, on other terms, would, if I may be allowed the expression, be a Peace of War. The injuries we have received from the British Nation were so unprovoked; have been so great and so many, that they can never be forgotten. Besides the feuds, the jealousies; the animosities that would ever attend a Union with them. Besides the importance, the advantages we should derive from an unrestricted commerce; Our fidelity as a people; Our gratitude; Our Character as Men, are opposed to a coalition with them as subjects, but in case of the last extremity. Were we easily to accede to terms of dependence, no nation, upon future occasions, let the oppressions of Britain be never so flagrant and unjust, would interpose for our relief, or at least they would do it with a cautious reluctance and upon

Nothing short of independence

conditions, most probably, that would be hard, if not dishonourable to us. France, by her supplies, has saved us from the Yoke thus far, and a wise and virtuous perseverence, would and I trust will, free us entirely.

I have sent Congress, Lord North's Speech and two Bills offered by him to Parliament. They are spreading fast through the Country, and will soon become a subject of general notoriety. I therefore think, they had best be published in our papers, and persons of leisure and ability set to Work, to counteract the impressions, they may make on the Minds of the people.

Before I conclude, there are one or two points more upon which I will add an Observation or two. The first is, the indecision of Congress and the delay used in coming to determinations in matters referred to them. This is productive of a variety of inconveniences; and an early decision, in many cases, though it should be against the measure submitted, would be attended with less pernicious effects. Some new plan might then be tried; but while the matter is held in suspence, nothing can be attempted. The other point is, the *jealousy* which Congress unhappily entertain of the Army, and which, if reports are right, some Members labour to establish. You may be assured, there is nothing more injurious, or more unjustly founded. This jealousy stands upon the common, received Opinion, which under proper limitations is certainly true, that standing Armies are dangerous to a State, and from forming the same conclusion of the component parts of all, though they are totally dissimilar in their Nature. The prejudices in other Countries has only gone to them in time of *Peace*, and these from their not having, in general cases, any of the ties, the concerns or interests of Citizens or any other dependence, than what flowed from their Military employ; in short, from their being Mercenaries; hirelings. It is our policy to be prejudiced against them in time of *War;* and though they are Citizens having all the Ties, and interests of Citizens, and in most cases property totally unconnected with the Military Line. If we would pursue a right System of policy, in my Opinion, there should be none of these distinctions. We should all be considered, Congress, Army, &c. as one people, embarked in one Cause, in one interest; acting on the same principle and to the same End. The distinction, the Jealousies set up, or perhaps only incautiously let out, can answer not a single good

Indecision of Congress

Congressional jealousy

purpose. They are impolitic in the extreme. Among Individuals, the most certain way to make a Man your Enemy, is to tell him, you esteem him such; so with public bodies; and the very jealousy, which the narrow politics of some may affect to entertain of the Army, in order to a due subordination to the supreme Civil Authority, is a likely mean to produce a contrary effect; to incline it to the pursuit of those measures which that may wish it to avoid. It is unjust, because no Order of Men in the thirteen States have paid a more sanctimonious regard to their proceedings than the Army; and, indeed, it may be questioned, whether there has been that scrupulus adherence had to them by any other, [for without arrogance, or the smallest deviation from truth it may be said, that no history, now extant, can furnish an instance of an Army's suffering such uncommon hardships as ours have done, and bearing them with the same patience and Fortitude. To see Men without Cloathes to cover their nakedness, without Blankets to lay on, without Shoes, by which their Marches might be traced by the Blood from their feet, and almost as often without Provisions as with; Marching through frost and Snow, and at Christmas taking up their Winter Quarters within a day's March of the enemy, without a House or Hutt to cover them till they could be built and submitting to it without a murmur, is a mark of patience and obedience which in my opinion can scarce be parallel'd.]

There may have been some remonstrances or applications [to Congress], in the stile of complaint from the Army [and slaves indeed should we be, if this privilidge was denied], on Account of their proceedings in particular instances; but these will not Authorize nor even excuse a jealousy, that they are therefore aiming at unreasonable powers; or making strides, dangerous, or subversive of Civil Authority. Things should not be viewed in that light, more especially, as Congress, in some cases, have relieved the injuries complained of, and which had flowed from their own Acts.

I refer you to my Letter to yourself and Colonel Lee which accompanies this, upon the subject of Money for such of the Old Virginia Troops, as have or may reinlist.

In respect to the Volunteer Plan I [scarce know what opinion to give at this time.] The propriety of a requisition on this head, will depend altogether, on our operations. Such kind of Troops should not be called for, but upon the spur of the occasion and at the moment of executing an Enterprise. They will not endure a long service; and, of all Men in the Military Line, they are the most impatient of restraint and necessary Government.

[As the propositions, and the Speech of Lord North must be founded in the despair of the Nation of succeeding against us, or, from a rupture in Europe that has actually happend, or that certainly will; or from some deep political Manoeuvre; or from what I think, still more likely, a composition of the whole, would it not be good policy, in this day of uncertainty and distress to the Tories to avail ourselves of the occn. and for the sevl. States to hold out Pardon &ca. to all delinquents returng by a certain day? They are frightned, and that is the time to operate upon them. Upon a short consideration of the matter it appears to me that such a measure wd detach the Tories from the Enemy, and bring things to a much speedier conclusion and of course be a mean of saving much public treasure.]

Pardon of Tories

I will now be done, and I trust that you excuse not only the length of my Letter, but the freedom with which I have delivered my sentiments in the course of it upon several occasions. The subjects struck me as important and interesting, and I have only to wish, that they may appear to you in the same light. I am etc.

35

TO JOHN AUGUSTINE WASHINGTON

Brunswick in New Jersey, July 4, 1778

Dear Brother:

Your Letter of the 20th. Ulto. came to my hands last Night; before this will have reached you, the Acct. of the Battle of Monmouth probably will get to Virginia; which, from an unfortunate, and bad beginning, turned out a glorious and happy day.

Battle of Monmouth

The Enemy evacuated Philadelphia on the 18th. Instt. at ten o'clock that day I got intelligence of it, and by two o'clock, or soon after, had Six Brigades on their March for the Jerseys, and followed with the whole Army next Morning. On the 21st.

we completed our passage over the Delaware at Coryells ferry (abt. 33 Miles above Philadelphia) distant from Valley forge near 40 Miles. From this Ferry we moved down towards the Enemy, and on the 27th. got within Six Miles of them.

General Lee having the command of the Van of the Army, consisting of fully 5000 chosen Men, was ordered to begin the Attack next Morning so soon as the enemy began their March, to be supported by me. But, strange to tell! when he came up with the enemy, a retreat commenced; whether by his order, or from other causes, is now the subject of inquiry, and consequently improper to be descanted on, as he is in arrest, and a Court Martial sitting for tryal of him. A Retreat however was the fact, be the causes as they may; and the disorder arising from it would have proved fatal to the Army had not that bountiful Providence which has never failed us in the hour of distress, enabled me to form a Regiment or two (of those that were retreating) in the face of the Enemy, and under their fire, by which means a stand was made long enough (the place through which the enemy were pursuing being narrow) to form the Troops that were advancing, upon an advantageous piece of Ground in the rear; hence our affairs took a favourable turn, and from being pursued, we drove the Enemy back, over the ground they had followed us, recovered the field of Battle, and possessed ourselves of their dead. but, as they retreated behind a Morass very difficult to pass, and had both Flanks secured with thick Woods, it was found impracticable with our Men fainting with fatigue, heat, and want of Water, to do any thing more that Night. In the Morning we expected to renew the Action, when behold the enemy had stole off as Silent as the Grave in the Night after having sent away their wounded. Getting a Nights March of us, and having but ten Miles to a strong post, it was judged inexpedient to follow them any further, but move towards the North River least they should have any design upon our posts there.

We buried 245 of their dead on the field of Action; they buried several themselves, and many have been since found in the Woods, where, during the action they had drawn them to, and hid them. We have taken five Officers and upwards of One hundred Prisoners, but the amount of their wounded we have not learnt with any certainty; according to the common proportion of four or five to one, there should be at least a thousand or 1200. Without exagerating, their trip through the

Jerseys in killed, Wounded, Prisoners, and deserters, has cost them at least 2000 Men and of their best Troops. We had 60 Men killed, 132 Wounded, and abt. 130 Missing, some of whom I suppose may yet come in. Among our Slain Officers is Majr. Dickenson, and Captn. Fauntleroy, two very valuable ones.

I observe what you say concerning voluntary enlistments, or rather your Scheme for raising 2000 Volunteers; and candidly own to you I have no opinion of it; these measures only tend to burthen the public with a number of Officers without adding one jot to your strength, but greatly to confusion, and disorder. If the several States would but fall upon some vigorous measures to fill up their respective Regiments nothing more need be asked of them, but while these are neglected, or in other words ineffectually and feebly attended to, and these succedaniums tried, you never can have an Army to be depended upon.

The Enemy's whole force Marched through the Jerseys (that were able) except the Regiment of Anspach, which, it is said, they were affraid to trust, and therefore sent them round to New York by Water, along with the Commissioners; I do not learn that they have received much of a reinforcement as yet; nor do I think they have much prospect of any, worth Speaking of, as I believe they Stand very critically with respect to France.

As the Post waits I shall only add my love to my Sister and the family, and Strong assurances of being with the Sincerest regard and Love, Yr. most Affect. Brother.

Mr. Ballendines Letter shall be sent to New York by the first Flag. I am now moving on towards the No. River.

36

TO COMTE D'ESTAING

Head Quarters, September 11, 1778

Sir:

Regrets to Comte d'Estaing

I have had the honor of receiving your Letter of the 5th. inst: accompanied by a Copy of two Letters to Congress and Genl. Sullivan. The confidence which you have been pleased to shew in communicating these papers engage my sincere thanks. If

the deepest regret that the best concerted enterprise and brav-
est exertions should have been rendered fruitless by a disaster
which human prudence is incapable of foreseeing or preventing can alleviate disappointment, you may be assured that the
whole Continent sympathizes with you;* it will be a consolation to you to reflect that the thinking part of Mankind do not
form their judgment from events; and that their equity will
ever attach equal glory to those actions which deserve success,
as to those which have been crowned with it. It is in the trying
circumstances to which your Excellency has been exposed,
that the virtues of a great Mind are displayed in their brightest
lustre; and that the General's Character is better known than
in the moment of Victory; it was yours, by every title which can
give it, and the adverse element which robbed you of your
prize, can never deprive you of the Glory due to you. Tho
your success has not been equal to your expectations yet you
have the satisfaction of reflecting that you have rendered essential Services to the common cause.

I exceedingly lament that in addition to our misfortunes,
there has been the least suspension of harmony and good understanding between the Generals of allied Nations, whose
views, must like their interests be the same. On the first intimation of it I employed my influence in restoring what I regard
as essential to the permanence of an Union founded on mutual inclination and the strongest ties of reciprocal advantage.
Your Excellencys offer to the Council of Boston had a powerful tendency to promote the same end, and was distinguished
proof of your zeal and magnanimity.

---

*A naval fleet under the command of d'Estaing, the fruit of the alliance
with France's Louis XVI, arrived off Philadelphia in July 1778. It fulfilled
great expectations, but the great hopes to which it gave rise were blasted
by the events which followed. Unable to attack Clinton's weakened forces
at New York in the aftermath of the Battle of Monmouth, d'Estaing
turned on the British at Newport. There, however, he encountered a
greater-than-expected British force: reinforcements under Lord Howe
just then arriving. The fleets joined but were as quickly separated by a
storm. They withdrew to ports for repairs, and the French sailed to Boston. Having expected more from their allies, the disappointed Continental
troops and militia angrily withdrew. Americans suspected French intentions, an attitude fanned as much as possible by British agents. In Boston,
demonstrations and riots occurred and, eventually, left one French officer
dead for his efforts to rescue a compatriot. Washington, as evidenced in
this letter, exerted himself to minimize the damage and to save the alliance, while La Fayette returned from America to France to reinforce the
idea of a need for efficacious French support.

The present superiority of the enemy in Naval force, must, for a time, suspend all plans of offensive cooperation between us; it is not easy to foresee what change may take place by the arrival of Succours to you from Europe or what opening the enemy may give you to resume your activity; in this moment therefore, every consultation on this subject would be premature. But it is of infinite importance that we should take all the means that our circumstances will allow for the defence of a Squadron, which is so precious to the common cause of france and America, and which may have become a capital object with the enemy. Whether this really is the case can be only matter of Conjecture; the original intention of the reinforcement sent to Rhode island, was obviously the Relief of the Garrison at that post. I have to lament that, tho seasonably advised of the movement, it was utterly out of my power to counteract it. A naval force alone could have defeated the attempt; how far their views may since have been enlarged by the arrival of Byron's fleet, Your Excellency will be best able to judge. Previous to this event, I believe Genl. Clinton was waiting orders from his court, for the conduct he was to pursue; in the mean time embarking his Stores and heavy baggage in order to be the better prepared for a promt evacuation, if his instructions should require it.

But as the present posture of affairs may induce a change of operations, and tempt them to carry the war eastward for the ruin of your Squadron, it will be necessary for us to be prepared to oppose such an enterprise. I am unhappy that our situation will not admit of our contributing more effectually to this important end; but assure you at the same time, that what ever can be attempted without losing sight of objects equally essential to the interests of the two Nations, shall be put in execution.

A Candid view of our affairs which I am going to exhibit, will make you a judge of the difficulties, under which we labour. Almost all our supplies of flour and no inconsiderable part of our meat, are drawn from the States westward of Hudson's River; this renders a secure communication across that River indispensably necessary both to the support of your Squadron and the Army. The enemy being masters of that navigation, would interrupt this essential intercourse between the States. They have been sensible of these advantages, and by the attempts which they have made, to bring about a sepa-

Navigation of the Hudson; defense of New York and New England

ration of the Eastern from the Southern States, and the facility which their superiority by Sea had hitherto given him, have always obliged us besides garrisoning the Forts that immediately defend the passage, to keep a force at least, equal to that which they have had posted in New York and its dependencies.

It is incumbent upon us at this time to have a greater force in this quarter than usual, from the concentred State of the enemy's strength and the uncertainty of their designs; in addition to this it is to be observed that they derive an inestimable advantage from the facility of transporting their troops from one point to another; these rapid movements enable them to give us uneasiness for remote unguarded parts, in attempting to succour which we should be exposed to ruinous marches, and after all perhaps be the dupes of a feint. If they could by any demonstration in another part draw our attention and strength from this important point, and by anticipating our return, possess themselves of it, the consequences would be fatal. Our dispositions must therefore have equal regard to cooperating with you in a defensive plan, and securing the North River; which, the remoteness of the two objects from each other, renders peculiarly difficult. Immediately upon the change which happened in your naval affairs, my attention was directed to conciliating these two great ends.

The necessity of transporting magazines, collected relatively to our present position, and making new arrangements for ulterior operations, has hitherto been productive of delay. These points are now nearly accomplished and I hope in a day or two to begin a general movement of the Army eastward, as a commencement of this, one division marched this morning under Major General Gates towards Danbury, and the rest of the army will follow as speedily as possible.

The following is a general Idea of my disposition: The Army will be thrown into several divisions, one of which consisting of a force equal to the Enemy's in New York, will be posted about thirty miles in the rear of my present camp, and in the vicinity of the North River with a view to its defence; the other will be pushed on at different stages, as far towards Connecticut River, as can be done consistently with preserving a communication, and having them within supporting distance of each other; so as that when occasion may require, they may form a junction, either for their own immediate defence, or to oppose any attempts that may be made on the North River. The facility which the enemy have of collecting their whole force and turning it against any point they choose, will restrain us from extending ourselves so far as will either expose us to be beaten by detachment or endanger the Security of the North River.

This disposition will place the American forces as much in measure for assisting in the defence of your Squadron and the Town of Boston, as is compatible with the other great objects of our care.

It does not appear to me probable that the Enemy would hazard the penetrating to Boston by land, with the force which they at present have to the eastward. I am rather inclined to believe that they will draw together their whole Land and Naval strength, to give the greater probability of Success. in order to this, New York must be evacuated, an event which cannot take place without being announced by circumstances impossible to conceal and I have reason to hope that the time which must necessarily be exhausted in embarking and transporting their troops and Stores, would be sufficient for me to advance a considerable part of my army in measure for opposing them.

The observations which Your Excellency makes relative to the necessity of having intelligent Spies, are perfectly just; every measure that circumstances would admit has been to answer this valuable end, and our intelligence has in general been as good as could be expected from the situation of the Enemy.

The distance at which we are from our posts of observation in the first instance, and the long Journey which is afterwards to be performed before a letter can reach your Excellency hinder my communicating intelligence with such celerity as I could wish.

The letter which I sent giving an account of Lord Howes movement, was dispatched as soon as the fact was ascertained; but it did not arrive 'till you had gone to Sea, in pursuit of the British Squadron.

As your Excellency does not mention the letters which I last had the honor of writing to you, I am apprehensive of some delay, or miscarriage; their dates were the 3rd. and 4th. inst.

The sincere esteem and regard which I feel for Your Excellency, make me set the highest value upon every expression of friendship with which you are pleased to honor me; I entreat you to accept the most cordial returns on my part.

I shall count it a singular felicity if in the course of possible operations above alluded to, personal intercourse shd afford me the means of cultivating a closer intimacy with you, and of proving more particularly the respect and attachment with which I have the honor etc.

PS: My dispatches were going to be closed when your Excellency's Letter of the 8th. was delivered to me.

The State of Byron's Fleet from the best intelligence I have been able to obtain, is as follows:

Six Ships, the names of which are mentioned in the paper I had the honor of transmitting the 3rd. have arrived at New York with their Crews in very bad health.

Two vizt. The Cornwall of *74* and Monmouth of *64*, had joined Lord Howe; *two* One of which the Admirals Ship, were missing. One had put back to Portsmouth.

37

TO GOUVERNEUR MORRIS

Fish-kill, October 4, 1778

Dear Sir:

My public Letters to the President of Congress will inform you of the Wind that wafted me to this place; nothing more therefore need be said on that head.

Your Letter of the 8th. Ulto. contains three questions and answers, to wit: Can the Enemy prosecute the War? Do they mean to stay on the Continent? And is it our interest to put impediments in the way of their departure? To the first you answer in the Negative; to the second you are decided in opinion that they do not; And to the third, say, clearly No.

Much, my good Sir, may be said in favor of these answers; and *some* things against the two first of them. By way therefore of dissertation on the first, I will also beg leave to put a question, and give it an answer. Can *we* carry on the War much longer? certainly *NO*, unless some measures can be devised, and speedily executed, to restore the credit of our Currency, restrain extortion, and punish forestallers.

Financing the war effort

Without these can be effected, what funds can stand the present expences of the Army? And what Officer can bear the weight of prices, that every necessary Article is now got to? A Rat, in the shape of a Horse, is not to be bought at this time for less than £200; a Saddle under thirty or Forty; Boots twenty, and Shoes and other articles in like proportion. How is it possible therefore for Officers to stand this, without an increase of pay? And how is it possible to advance their Pay when Flour is selling (at different places) from five to fifteen pounds pr. Ct., Hay from ten to thirty pounds pr. Tunn, and Beef and other essentials, in this proportion.

The true point of light then to place, and consider this matter in, is not simply whether G. Britain can carry on the War, but whose Finances (theirs or ours) is most likely to fail: which leads me to doubt *very much* the infalibility of the answer given to your Second question, respecting the Enemy's leaving the Continent; for I believe, that they will not do it, while ever *hope* and the chapter of *accidents* can give them a *chance* of bringing us to terms short of *Independance*. But this *you* perhaps will say, they are now bereft of. *I* shall acknowledge that many things favor the idea; but add, that upon a comparative view of circumstances there is abundant matter to puzzle and confound the judgment. To your third answer, I subscribe with hand and heart. the opening is now fair, and God grant they may embrace the oppertunity of bidding an eternal adieu to our, once quit of them, happy Land. If the Spaniards would but join their Fleets to those of France, and commence hostilities, my doubts would all subside. Without it, I fear the British Navy has it too much in its power to counteract the Schemes of France.

The high prices of every necessary. The little, indeed no benefit, which Officers have derived from the intended bounty of Congress in the article of Cloathing, The change in the establishment, by which so many of them are discontinued. The unfortunate delay of this business, which kept them too long in suspence, and set a number of evil spirits to work. The unsettled Rank, and contradictory modes of adjusting it, with other causes which might be enumerated, have conspired to sour the temper of the Army exceedingly; and has, I am told, been productive of a Memorial, or representation of some kind, to Congress, which neither directly, nor indirectly did I know, or ever hear was in agitation, till some days after it was dispatched; owing, as I apprehend, to the secrecy with which it was conducted to keep it from my knowledge, as I had in a similar instance last Spring, discountenanced and stifled a child of the same illigitimacy in its birth. If you have any News worth communicating, do not put it under a bushel, but transmit it to Dr. Sir, Yrs. sincerely.

38

TO HENRY LAURENS

Fredericksburgh, November 14, 1778

Dear Sir:

This will be accompanied by an official letter on the subject of the proposed expedition against Canada. You will perceive I have only considered it in a military light; indeed I was not authorised to consider it in any other; and I am not without apprehensions, that I may be thought, in what I have done, to have exceeded the limits intended by Congress. But my solicitude for the public welfare which I think deeply interested in this affair, will I hope justify me in the eyes of all those who view things through that just medium.

I do not know, Sir, what may be your sentiments in the present case; but whatever they are I am sure I can confide in your honor and friendship, and shall not hesitate to unbosom myself to you on a point of the most delicate and important Nature.

The question of the Canadian expedition in the form it now stands appears to me one of the most interesting that has hitherto agitated our National deliberations. I have one objection to it, untouched in my public letter, which is in my estimation, insurmountable, and alarms all my feelings for the true and permanent interests of my country. This is the introduction of a large body of French troops into Canada, and putting them in possession of the capital of that Province, attached to them by all the ties of blood, habits, manners, religion and former connexion of government. I fear this would be too great a temptation, to be resisted by any power actuated by the common maxims of national policy. Let us realize for a moment the striking advantages France would derive from the posses-

Danger of French troops in Canada

sion of Canada; the acquisition of an extensive territory abounding in supplies for the use of her Islands; the opening a vast source of the most beneficial commerce with the Indian nations, which she might then monopolize; the having ports of her own on this continent independent on the precarious good will of an ally; the engrossing the whole trade of New-foundland whenever she pleased, the finest nursery of seamen in the world; the security afforded to her Islands; and finally, the facility of awing and controuling these states, the natural and most formidable rival of every maritime power in Europe. Canada would be a solid acquisition to France on all these accounts and because of the numerous inhabitants, subjects to her by inclination, who would aid in preserving it under her power against the attempt of every other.

France acknowledged for some time past the most powerful monachy in Europe by land, able now to dispute the empire of the sea with Great Britain, and if joined with Spain, I may say certainly superior, possessed of New Orleans, on our Right, Canada on our left and seconded by the numerous tribes of Indians on our Rear from one extremity to the other, a peo-ple, so generally friendly to her and whom she knows so well how to conciliate; would, it is much to be apprehended have it in her power to give law to these states.

Let us suppose, that when the five thousand French troops (and under the idea of that number twice as many might be introduced,) were entered the city of Quebec; they should de-clare an intention to hold Canada, as a pledge and surety for the debts due to France from the United States, [or, under other specious pretences hold the place till they can find a bone for contention], and [in the meanwhile] should excite the Canadians to engage in supporting [their pretences and claims]; what should we be able to say with only four or five thousand men to carry on the dispute? It may be supposed that France would not choose to renounce our friendship by a step of this kind as the consequence would probably be a reun-ion with England on some terms or other; and the loss of what she had acquired, in so violent and unjustifiable a manner, with all the advantages of an Alliance with us. This in my opinion is too slender a security against the measure to be relied on. The truth of the position will intirely depend on naval events. If France and Spain should unite and obtain a decided superiority by Sea, a reunion with England would avail very little and might be set at defiance. France, with a numerous army at command might throw in what number of land forces she thought proper to support her pretensions; and England without men, without money, and inferior on her favourite element could give no effectual aid to oppose them. Resentment, reproaches, and submission seem to be all that would be left us. Men are very apt to run into extremes; hatred to England may carry some into an excess of Confidence in France; especially when motives of gratitude are thrown into the scale. Men of this description would be unwilling to suppose France capable of acting so ungenerous a part. I am heartily disposed to entertain the most favourable sentiments of our new ally and to cherish them in others to a reasonable degree; but it is a maxim founded on the universal experience of mankind, that no nation is to be trusted farther than it is bound by its interest; and no prudent statesman or politician will venture to depart from it. In our circumstances we ought to be particularly cautious; for we have not yet attained sufficient vigor and maturity to recover from the shock of any false step into which we may unwarily fall.

If France should even engage in the scheme, in the first instance with the purest intentions, there is the greatest danger that, in the progress of the business, invited to it by circumstances and, perhaps, urged on by the solicitations and wishes of the Canadians, she would alter her views.

As the Marquis clothed his proposition when he spoke of it to me, it would seem to originate wholly with himself; but it is far from impossible that it had its birth in the Cabinet of France and was put into this artful dress, to give it the readier currency. I fancy that I read in the countenances of some people on this occasion, more than the disinterested zeal of allies. I hope I am mistaken and that my fears of mischief make me refine too much, and awaken jealousies that have no sufficient foundation.

But upon the whole, Sir, to wave every other consideration; I do not like to add to the number of our national obligations. I would wish as much as possible to avoid giving a foreign power new claims of merit for services performed, to the United States, and would ask no assistance that is not indispensible. I am, etc.

39

TO BENJAMIN HARRISON

Head Qrs., Middle Brook, December 18, 1778

My dear Sir:

You will be so obliging as to present the inclosed to the House when oppertunity, and a suitable occasion offers. I feel very sensibly the late honorable testimony of their remembrance; to stand well in the good opinion of my Countrymen constitutes my chiefest happiness; and will be my best support under the perplexities and difficulties of my present Station.

The mention of my lands in the back Country was more owing to accident than design; the Virga. Officers having solicited leave for Colo. Wood to attend the Assembly of that commonwealth with some representation of theirs respecting their claims, or wishes, brought my own matters (of a similar nature) to view; but I am too little acquainted with the minutiæ of them to ground an application on or give any trouble to the Assembly concerning them. Under the proclamation of 1763, I am entitled to 5000 Acres of Land in my own right; and by purchase from Captn. Roots, Posey, and some other Officers, I obtained rights to several thousands more, a small part of wch. I patented during the Admn. of Lord Dunmore; another part was (I believe) Surveyed, whilst the major part remains in locations; but where (without having recourse to my Memms.) and under what circumstances, I know not at this time any more than you do, nor do I wish to give trouble abt. them.

Persistence of the enemy

I can assign but two causes for the enemys continuance among us, and these balance so equally in my Mind, that I scarce know which of the two preponderates. The one is, that they are waiting the ultimate determination of Parliament; the other, that of our distresses; by which I know the Commissioners went home not a little buoyed up; and sorry I am to add, not without cause. What may be the effect of such large and frequent emissions, of the dissentions, Parties, extravagance, and a general lax of public virtue Heaven alone can tell! I am affraid even to think of It; but it appears as clear to me as ever the Sun did in its meredian brightness, that America never stood in more eminent need of the wise, patriotic, and Spirited exertions of her Sons than at this period and if it is not a sufficient cause for genl. lamentation, my misconception of

Lack of public virtue

the matter impresses it too strongly upon me, that the States seperately are too much engaged in their local concerns, and have too many of their ablest men withdrawn from the general Council for the good of the common weal; in a word, I think our political system may, be compared to the mechanism of a Clock; and that our conduct should derive a lesson from it for it answers no good purpose to keep the smaller Wheels in order if the greater one which is the support and prime mover of the whole is neglected. How far the latter is the case does not become me to pronounce but as there can be no harm in a pious wish for the good of ones Country I shall offer it as mine that each State wd. not only choose, but absolutely compel their ablest Men to attend Congress; that they would instruct them to go into a thorough investigation of the causes that have produced so many disagreeable effects in the Army and Country; in a word that public abuses should be corrected, and an entire reformation worked; without these it does not, in my judgment, require the spirit of divination to foretell the consequences of the present Administration, nor to how little purpose the States, individually, are framing constitutions, providing laws, and filling Offices with the abilities of their ablest Men. These, if the great whole is mismanaged must sink in the general wreck and will carry with it the remorse of thinking that we are lost by our own folly and negligence, or the desire perhaps of living in ease and tranquility during the expected accomplishment of so great a revolution in the effecting of which the greatest abilities and the honestest Men our (i.e. the American) world affords ought to be employed. It is much to be feared my dear Sir that the States in their seperate capacities have very inadequate ideas of the present danger. Removed (some of them) far distant from the scene of action and seeing, and hearing such publications only as flatter their wishes they conceive that the contest is at an end, and that to regulate the government and police of their own State is all that remains to be done; but it is devoutly to be wished that a sad reverse of this may not fall upon them like a thunder clap that is little expected. I do not mean to designate particular States. I wish to cast no reflections upon any one. The Public believes (and if they do believe it, the fact might almost as well be so) that the States at this time are badly represented, and that the great, and important concerns of the nation are horribly conducted, for want either of abilities or application in the

*Need for able
men in Congress*

Members, or through discord and party views of some individuals; that they should be so, is to be lamented more at this time, than formerly, as we are far advanced in the dispute and in the opinn. of many drawg. to a happy period; have the eyes of Europe upon us, and I am perswaded many political Spies to watch, discover our situation and give information of our weaknesses and wants.

The story you have related of a proposal to redeem the paper money at its present depreciated value has also come to my ears, but I cannot vouch for the authenticity of it. I am very happy to hear that the Assembly of Virginia have put the completion of their Regiment upon a footing so apparently certain, but as one great defect of your past laws for this purpose, has lain in the mode of getting the men to the Army, I shall hope that effectual measures are pointed out in the present, to remedy the evil and bring forward all that shall be raised. The Embargo upon Provisions is a most salutary measure as I am affraid a sufficiency of flour will not easily be obtained even with money of higher estimation than ours. adieu my dear Sir.

PS: Phila. 30th. This Letter was to have gone by Post from Middle brook but missed that conveyance, since which I have come to this place at the request of Congress whence I shall soon return.

I have seen nothing since I came here (on the 22d. Instt.) to change my opinion of Men or Measrs. but abundant reason to be convinced, that our Affairs are in a more distressed, ruinous, and deplorable condition than they have been in Since the commencement of the War. By a faithful labourer then in the cause. By a Man who is daily injuring his private Estate without even the smallest earthly advantage not common to all in case of a favourable Issue to the dispute. By one who wishes the prosperity of America most devoutly and sees or thinks he sees it, on the brink of ruin, you are beseeched most earnestly my dear Colo. Harrison, to exert yourself in endeavouring to rescue your Country, by, (let me add) sending your ablest and best Men to Congress; these characters must not slumber, nor sleep at home, in such times of pressing danger; they must not content themselves in the enjoyment of places of honor or *Common interests* profit in their own Country, while the common interests of *of America in* America are mouldering and sinking into irretrievable (if a *ruin* remedy is not soon applied) ruin, in which theirs also must ultimately be involved. If I was to be called upon to draw A picture of the times, and of Men; from what I have seen, heard, and in part know I should in one word say that idleness, dissipation and extravagance seem to have laid fast hold of most of them. That Speculation, peculation, and an insatiable thirst for riches seems to have got the better of every other consideration and almost of every order of Men. That party disputes and personal quarrels are the great business of the day whilst the momentous concerns of an empire, a great and accumulated debt; ruined finances, depreciated money, and want of credit (which in their consequences is the want of every thing) are but secondary considerations and postponed from day to day, from week to week as if our affairs wore the most promising aspect; after drawing this picture, which from my Soul I believe to be a true one I need not repeat to you that I am alarmed and wish to see my Countrymen roused. I have no resentments, nor do I mean to point at any particular characters; this I can declare upon my honor for I have every attention paid me by Congress than I can possibly expect and have reason to think that I stand well in their estimation but in the present situation of things I cannot help asking: Where is Mason, Wythe, Jefferson, Nicholas, Pendleton, Nelson, and another I could name; and why, if you are sufficiently impressed with your danger, do you not (as New Yk. has done in the case of Mr. Jay) send an extra Member or two for at least a certain limited time till the great business of the Nation is put upon a more respectable and happy establishmt. Your Money is now sinking 5 pr. Ct. a day in this City; and I shall not be surprized if in the course of a few months a total stop is put to the currency of it. And yet an assembly, a concert, a Dinner, or Supper (that will cost three or four hundred pounds) will not only take Men off from acting in but even from thinking of this business while a great part of the Officers of your Army from absolute necessity are quitting the Service and the more virtuous few rather than do this are sinking by sure degrees into beggery and want. I again repeat to you that this is not an exaggerated acct.; that it is an alarming one I do not deny, and confess to you that I feel more real distress on acct. of the prest. appearances of things than I have done at any one time since the commencement of the dispute; but it is time to bid you once more adieu. Providence has heretofore taken us up when all other means and hope seemed to be departing from us, in this I will confide. Yr. &ca.

Depreciation of currency

TO THE PRESIDENT OF CONGRESS

Middlebrook, March 15, 1779

Sir:

I have waited with anxious expectations, for some plan to be adopted by Congress which would have a general operation throughout the States for compleating their respective Battalions. No plan for this purpose has yet come to my knowledge, nor do I find that the several Governments are pursuing any measures to accomplish the end by particular arrangements of their own legislatures. I therefore hope Congress will excuse any appearance of importunity, in my troubling them again on the subject, as I earnestly wish to be enabled to realize some ideas on what may be expected towards the completion of our *Completion of* Battalions by the opening of the next campaign. They are *battalions* already greatly reduced, and will be much more so by that time; owing to the expiration of the term of Service of the last years drafts.

[At the Posts in the highlands, Nixons, Pattersons and Learneds Brigades alone, will suffer (by the first of April) a diminution of 847 Men, which must be replaced, illy as they can, and reluctantly as they will be spared from other Posts.]

The Committee, with whom I had the honor to confer, were of opinion, that the regimts. now in Service should be continued and completed; this was confirmed by the resolve of Congress of the 23d of Jany. last, which also directed some additional encouragements for recruiting the Army during the War. Aware that this expedient, though a very useful one, could not be altogether relied on, especially if the interference of State bounties, were still permitted; I furnished the Committee with my ideas of the mode which afforded the most certain prospect of success. I shall not trouble Congress with a repetition of these, as I doubt not they have been fully reported by the Committee.

Among the Troops of some States, recruiting in Camp on the new bounties has succeeded tolerably well; among others, where the expectations of State bounties have had more influence, very ill; Upon the whole, the success has been far short of our wishes and will probably be so of our necessities.

The measure of inlisting in the Country, in my opinion depends so much on the abolishing of State bounties, that without it, I am doubtful whether it will be worth the experiment. State bounties, have been a source of immense expence and many misfortunes. The sooner the practice can be abolished, and system introduced in our manner of recruiting and keeping up our battalions, as well as in the administration of the several departments of the Army, the sooner will our Security be established and placed out of the reach of contingencies. Temporary expedients to serve the purposes of the moment, occasion more difficulties and expence than can easily be conceived.

Abolition of state bounties

The superior information, which Congress may have, of the political State of affairs in Europe [and of combining circumstances] may induce them to believe that, there will soon be a termination of the War; and therefore, that the expence of vigorous measures to re-inforce the Army may be avoided. If this should be the case, I dare say the reasons will be well considered before a plan is adopted; which, whatever advantages of oeconomy it may promise, [in] an eventual dissappointment, may be productive of ruinous consequences. For my own part, I confess I should be cautious of admitting the supposition that the War will terminate without another desperate effort on the part of the enemy. The Speech of the Prince, and the debates of his Ministers have very little the aspect of peace; and if we reflect, that they are subsequent (as I apprehend they must have been) to the events, on which our hopes appear to be founded, they must seem no bad argumts. of a determination in the British Cabinet to continue the War. Tis true, whether this be the determination or not, tis a very natural policy that every exertion should be made by them to be in the best condition to oppose their enemies, and that there should be every appearance of vigor and preparation. But if the Ministry had serious thoughts of making peace, they would hardly insist so much as they do, on the particular point of prosecuting the American War. They would not like to raise and inflame the expectations of the People on this subject, while it was secretly their intention to disappoint them. In America, every thing has the complexion of a continuance of the War. The operations of the enemy in the Southern States do not resemble a transient incursion, but a serious conquest. At their posts in this quarter, every thing is in a state of tranquillity, and indicates a design, at least, to hold possession.

Prospects for peace

The enemy in the Southern states

These considerations joined to the preceeding. The infinite pains that are taken to keep up the Spirits of the disaffected and to assure them of support and protection; and several other circumstances, trifling in themselves but powerful when combined, amount to no contemptible evidence that the contest is not so near an end, as we could wish. I am fully sensible of many weighty reasons on the opposite side; but I do not think them sufficiently conclusive to destroy the force of what has been suggested, or to justify the sanguine inferences many seem inclined to draw.

Should the Court of Britain be able to send any reinforcements to America the next campaign, and carry on offensive operations; and should we not take some effectual means to recruit our batalions; when we shall have detached the force necessary to act decisively against the Indians, and the remaining drafts shall have returned home; the force which remains for our defence will be very inconsiderable indeed. We must *Disadvantages in* then on every exigency have recourse to the Militia, the conse-*using the militia* quence of which, besides weakness and defeat in the field, will be double or treble the necessary expence to the public. To say nothing of the injury to agriculture which attends calling out the Militia on paticular emergencies and at some critical Seasons, they are commonly twice as long coming to where they are wanted and returning home, as they are in the field; and must of course for every days real service receive two or three days pay, and consume the same proportion of provisions.

When an important matter is suspended for deliberation in Congress, I should be sorry that my sollicitude to have it determined, should contribute to a premature decision. But when I have such striking proofs of public loss and private discontent from the present management of the clothing department. When accts., inadmissible if any system existed, frequently remind me of the absolute necessity of introducing one. When I hear as I often do, of large importations of cloathing which we never see, of quantities wasting and rotting in different parts of the Country, the knowledge of which reaches me by chance. *Clothing the* When I have reason to believe that the money which has been *army* expended for cloathing the Army, if judiciously laid out [and the Cloaths regularly issued] would have effectually answered the purpose. And when I have never till now seen it otherwise than half naked. When I feel the perplexity and additional load of business thrown upon me by the irregularity in this department, and by applications from all parts of the Army for relief; I cannot forbear discovering my anxiety to have some plan decided for conducting the business hereafter, in a more provident and consistent manner. If the one proposed to the Committee does not coincide with the Sentiments of Congress, I should be happy some other could be substituted. [With the greatest respect I have the honr. etc.]

41

TO THOMAS NELSON

Middle brook, March 15, 1779

My dear Sir:

I have to thank you for your friendly letter of the 9th., and for your obliging, tho unsuccessful endeavours to procure the Horses I am indebted to my Country for. At present I have no immediate call for them, as we find it rather difficult to support the few we keep at Camp, in forage.

It gives me very singular pleasure to find that you have again taken a Seat in Congress; I think there never was a time when cool and dispassionate reasoning; strict attention and application, great integrity, and (if it was in the nature of things, unerring) wisdom were more to be wished for than the present. Our Affairs, according to my judgment, are now come to a crisis, and require no small degree of political skill, to steer clear of those shelves and Rocks which though deeply buried, may wreck our hopes, and throw us upon some inhospitable shore. Unanimity in our Councils, disinterestedness in our pursuits, and steady perseverence in our national duty, are the only means to avoid misfortunes; if they come upon us after these we shall have the consolation of knowing that we have done our best, the rest is with the Gods.

Shall I hope to have the pleasure of seeing you at Camp, when the weather gets a little settled? I can assure you that it will be a gratification of my wishes. Mrs. Washington salutes you most cordially, and offers her thanks for the letter you was kind enough to send her. I am, etc.

42

TO GEORGE MASON

Camp at Middlebrook, March 27, 1779

Dear Sir:

By some interruption of the last Weeks Mail your favor of the 8th. did not reach my hands till last Night. Under cover of this Mr. Mason (if he should not have Sailed, and) to whom I heartily wish a perfect restoration of health, will receive two letters; one of them to the Marqs. de la Fayette and the other to Doctr. Franklin; in furnishing which I am happy, as I wish for instances in which I can testify the sincerity of my regard for you.

Our Commissary of Prisoners has been invariably, and pointedly instructed to exchange those Officers first who were first captivated, as far as rank will apply; and I have every reason to believe he has obeyed the order; as I have refused a great many applications for irregular exchanges in consequence, and I did it because I would not depart from my principle, and thereby incur the charge of partiality. It sometimes happens, that officers later in captivity than others, have been exchanged before them; but it is in cases where the rank of the Enemys officers in our possession, do not apply to the latter. There is a prospect now I think of a general exchange taking place, which will be very pleasing to the parties and their connexions; and will be a mean of relieving much distress to individuals, though it may not, circumstanced as we are at this time, be advantageous to us, considered in a national and political point of view. partial exchanges have, for some time past, been discontinued by the Enemy.

Though it is not in my power to devote much time to private corrispondences, owing to the multiplicity of public letters (and other business) I have to read, write, and transact; yet I can with great truth assure you, that it would afford me very singular pleasure to be favoured at all times with your sentiments in a leizure hour, upon public matters of general concernment as well as those which more immediately respect your own State (if proper conveyances would render prudent a free communication). I am particularly desirous of it at this time, because I view things very differently, I fear, from what people in general do who seem to think the contest is at an end; and to make money, and get places, the only things now remaining to do. I have seen without dispondency (even for a moment) the hours which America have stiled her gloomy ones, but I have beheld no day since the commencement of hostilities that I have thought her liberties in such eminent danger as at present. Friends and foes seem now to combine to pull down the goodly fabric we have hitherto been raising at the expence of so much time, blood, and treasure; and unless the bodies politick will exert themselves to bring things back to first principles, correct abuses, and punish our internal foes, inevitable ruin must follow. Indeed we seem to be verging so fast to destruction, that I am filled with sensations to which I have been a stranger till within these three Months. Our Enemy behold with exultation and joy how effectually we labour for their benefit; and from being in a state of absolute despair, and on the point of evacuating America, are now on tiptoe; nothing therefore in my judgment can save us but a total reformation in our own conduct, or some decisive turn to affairs in Europe. The former alas! to our shame be it spoken! is less likely to happen than the latter, as it is now consistent with the views of the Speculators, various tribes of money makers, and stock jobbers of all denominations to continue the War for their own private emolument, without considering that their avarice, and thirst for gain must plunge every thing (including themselves) in one common Ruin.

Eminent dangers

Speculation and avarice

Were I to indulge my present feelings, and give a loose to that freedom of expression which my unreserved friendship for you would prompt me to, I should say a great deal on this subject, but letters are liable to so many accidents, and the sentiments of Men in office sought after by the enemy with so much avidity, and besides conveying useful knowledge (if they get into their hands) for the superstructure of their plans, is often perverted to the worst of purposes, that I shall be somewhat reserved, notwithstanding this Letter goes by a private hand to Mount Vernon. I cannot refrain lamenting however in the most poignant terms, the fatal policy too prevalent in most of the States, of employing their ablest Men at home in posts of honor or profit, till the great national Interests are fixed upon a solid basis. To me it appears no unjust Simile to compare the affairs of this great continent to the Mechanism of a Clock, each State representing some one or other of the smaller parts of it, which they are endeavouring to put in fine order without considering how useless and unavailing their labour, unless the great wheel, or spring which is to set the whole in motion, is also well attended to and kept in good order. I allude to no particular state, nor do I mean to cast reflections upon any one of them. Nor ought I, it may be said, to do so upon their representatives, but as it is a fact too notorious to be concealed, that C— is rent by party, that much business of a trifling nature and personal concernment withdraws their attention from matters of great national moment at this critical period. When it is also known that idleness and dissipation takes place of close attention and application, no man who wishes well to the liberties of his Country and desires to see its rights established, can avoid crying out where are our Men of abilities? Why do they not come forth to save their Country? let this voice my dear Sir call upon you, Jefferson and others; do not from a mistaken opinion that we are about to set down under our own vine and our own fig tree let our hitherto noble struggle end in ignominy; believe me when I tell you there is danger of it. I have pretty good reasons for thinking, that Administration a little while ago had resolved to give the matter up, and negotiate a peace with us upon almost any terms, but I shall be much mistaken if they do not now from the present state of our currency, dissentions, and other circumstances, push matters to the utmost extremity; nothing I am sure will prevent it but the interruption of Spain and their disappointed hope from Russia.

Congress rent by party — marginal note

I thank you most cordially for your kind offer of rendering me Services. I shall without reserve as heretofore, call upon you whenever instances occur that may require it; being with the sincerest, regard, etc.

43

TO JAMES WARREN

Middlebrook, March 31, 1779

Dear Sir:

I beseech you not to ascribe my delay in answering your obliging favor of the the 16th. of Decr. to disrespect, or want of inclination to continue a corrispondence in which I have always taken pleasure, and thought myself honord.

Your Letter of the above date came to my hands in Philadelphia where I attended at the request of Congress to settle some important matters respecting the army and its future operations; and where I was detained till some time in Feby., during that period my time was so much occupied by the immediate and pressing business which carried me down, that I could attend to little else; and upon my return to Camp I found the ordinary business of the Army had run so much behind hand, that, together with the arrangements I had to carry into execution, no leizure was left me to endulge myself sooner in making the acknowledgment I am now about to do, of the pleasure I felt at finding that I still enjoyed a share of your confidence and esteem, and now and then am to be informed of it by Letter. believe me Sir when I add, that this proof of your holding me in remembrance is most acceptable and pleasing.

Our conflict is not likely to cease so soon as every good Man would wish. The measure of iniquity is not yet filled; and unless we can return a little more to first principles, and act a little more upon patriotic ground, I do not know when it will, or, what may be the Issue of the contest. Speculation, Peculation, Engrossing, forestalling with all their concomitants, afford too many melancholy proofs of the decay of public virtue; and too glaring instances of its being the interest and desire of too many who would wish to be thought friends, to continue the War.

Nothing I am convinced but the depreciation of our Currency proceeding in a great measure from the foregoing Causes, aided by Stock jobbing, and party dissensions has fed the hopes of the Enemy and kept the B. Arms in America to this day. They do not scruple to declare this themselves, and add, that we shall be our own conquerers. Cannot our common Country Am. possess virtue enough to disappoint them? Is the paltry consideration of a little dirty pelf to individuals to be placed in competition with the essential rights and liberties of the present generation, and of Millions yet unborn? Shall a few designing men for their own aggrandizement, and to gratify their own avarice, overset the goodly fabric we have been rearing at the expence of so much time, blood, and treasure? and shall we at last become the victims of our own abominable lust of gain? Forbid it heaven! forbid it all and every State in the Union! by enacting and enforcing efficacious laws for checking the growth of these monstrous evils, and restoring

Depreciation of currency

matters, in some degree to the pristine state they were in at the commencement of the War. Our cause is noble, it is the cause of Mankind! and the danger to it, is to be apprehended from ourselves. Shall we slumber and sleep then while we should be punishing those miscreants who have brot. these troubles upon us and who are aimg. to continue us in them, while we should be striving to fill our Battalions, and devising ways and means to appreciate the currency; on the credit of wch. every thing depends? I hope not. Let vigorous measures be adopted; not to limit the prices of Articles, for this I believe is inconsistent with the very nature of things, and impracticable in itself, but to punish Speculaters, forestallers, and extortioners, and above all to sink the money by heavy taxes. To promote public and private œconomy; Encourage Manufactures &ca. Measures of this sort gone heartily into by the several States would strike at once at the root of all our evils and give the coup de grace to British hope of subjugating this Continent, either by their Arms or their Arts. The first, as I have before observed, they acknowledge is unequal to the task; the latter I am sure will be so if we are not lost to every thing that is good and virtuous.

Vigorous measures against speculators

A little time now, must unfold in some degree, the Enemys designs. Whether the state of affairs in Europe will permit them to augment their Army with more than recruits for the Regiments now on the Continent and therewith make an active and vigorous compaign, or whether with their Florida and Canadian force they will aid and abet the Indians in ravaging our Western Frontier while their Shipg. with detachments harrass (and if they mean to prosecute the predatory War threatened by Administration through their Commissioners) burn and destroy our Sea Coast; or whether, contrary to expectation, they should be more disposed to negotiate than to either is more than I can determine; the latter will depend very much upon their apprehensions from the Court of Spain, and expectations of foreign aid and powerful alliances; at present we seem to be in a Chaos but this cannot last long as I suppose the ultimate determination of the British Court will be developed at the meeting of Parliament after the Hollidays.

The enemy's designs

Mrs. Washington joins me in cordial wishes, and best respects to Mrs. Warren; she would have done herself the pleasure of writing but the present convayance was sudden. I am, etc.

44

TO GOUVERNEUR MORRIS

Hd. Qrs. Middle Brook, May 8, 1779

Monsieur Gerard did me the honor to deliver me your favour of the 26th. I shall always be obliged to you, my dear Sir, for a free communication of your sentiments on whatsoever subject may occur.

The objects of your letter were important. Mr. Gerard I dare say has made it unnecessary for me to recapitulate what passed between him and myself and has informed you of the alternative I proposed for improving the important event announced by him. From what he told me it appears that sufficient assurances cannot be given of points which are essential to justify the great undertaking you had in view at the expense of other operations very interesting. And indeed though I was desirous to convince the Minister that we are willing to make every effort in our power for striking a decisive blow; yet my judgment rather inclined to the second plan as promising more certain success, without putting so much to the hazard. The relief of the S[outhern] S[tates] appears to me an object of the greatest magnitude and what may lead to still more important advantages. I feel infinite anxiety on their account; their internal weakness, disaffection, the want of energy, the general languor that has seized the people at large makes me apprehend the most serious consequences; it would seem too, as if the enemy meant to transfer the principal weight of the war that way. If it be true that a large detachment has lately sailed from New York and that Sir Henry Clinton is gone with it, in which several accounts I have received agree (though I do not credit the latter) and these should be destined for the Southward as is most probable, there can be little doubt that this is the present plan. Charlestown it is likely will feel the next stroke. This if it succeeds will leave the enemy full possession of Georgia by obliging us to collect our forces for the defence of South Carolina and, will consequently open new sources for Men and supplies and prepare the way for a further career. The climate, I am aware is an obstacle but perhaps not so great as is imagined and, when we consider the difference in our respective means of preserving health it may possibly be found more adverse to our troops than to theirs. In this critical situa-

*Relief of the
Southern states*

tion, I hardly know any resource we have unless it be in the *event expected*; and the supposed reinforcement now on its way, for want of a competent land force on our part, may make even this dependence precarious. If it should fail, our affairs which have a very sickly aspect in many respects will receive a stroke they are little able to bear.

As a variety of accidents may disappoint our hopes here it is indispensable we should make every exertion on our part to check the enemy's progress. This cannot be done to effect, if our reliance is solely or principally on militia, for a force continually fluctuating is incapable of any material effort. The states concerned ought by all means to endeavour to draw out men for a length of time; a smaller number, on this plan would answer their purpose better; a great deal of expence would be avoided and agriculture would be much less impeded. It is to be lamented that the remoteness and weakness of this army, would make it folly to attempt to send any succour from this quarter. Perhaps for want of knowing the true state of our Foreign expectations and prospects of finance, I may be led to contemplate the gloomy side of things. But I confess they appear to me to be in a very disagreeable train. The rapid decay of our currency, the extinction of public spirit, the increasing rapacity of the times, the want of harmony in our councils, the declining zeal of the people, the discontents and distresses of the officers of the army; and I may add, the prevailing security and insensibility to danger, are symptoms, in my eye of a most alarming nature. If the enemy have it in their power to press us hard this campaign I know not what may be the consequence. Our army as it now stands is but little more than the skeleton of an army and I hear of no steps that are taking to give it strength and substance. I hope there may not be great mistakes on this head, and that our abilities in general are not overrated. The applications for succour, are numerous; but no pains are taken to put it in my power to afford them. When I endeavour to draw together the Continental troops for the most essential purposes I am embarrassed with complaints of the exhausted defenceless situation of particular states and find myself obliged either to resist solicitations, made in such a manner and with such a degree of emphasis, as scarcely to leave me a choice; or to sacrifice the most obvious principles of military propriety and risk the general safety.

I shall conclude by observing, that it is well worthy the ambi-

The gloomy side of things

tion of a patriot Statesman at this juncture, to endeavour to pacify party differences, to give fresh vigor to the springs of government, to inspire the people with confidence, and above all to restore the credit of our currency. With very great regard I am, etc.

45

SPEECH TO THE DELAWARE CHIEFS

Head Quarters, Middle Brook, May 12, 1779

Brothers: I am happy to see you here. I am glad the long Journey you have made, has done you no harm; and that you are in good health: I am glad also you left All our friends of the Delaware Nation well.

Brothers: I have read your paper. The things you have said are weighty things, and I have considered them well. The Delaware Nation have shown their good will to the United States. They have done wisely and I hope they will never repent. I rejoice in the new assurances you give of their friendship. The things you now offer to do to brighten the chain, prove your sincerity. I am sure Congress will run to meet you, and will do every thing in their power to make the friendship between the people of these States, and their Brethren of the Delaware nation, last forever.

Friendship with Indians

Brothers: I am a Warrior. My words are few and plain; but I will make good what I say. 'Tis my business to destroy all the Enemies of these States and to protect their friends. You have seen how we have withstood the English for four years; and how their great Armies have dwindled away and come to very little; and how what remains of them in this part of our great Country, are glad to stay upon Two or three little Islands, where the Waters and their Ships hinder us from going to destroy them. The English, Brothers, are a boasting people. They talk of doing a great deal; but they do very little. They fly away on their Ships from one part of our Country to an other; but as soon as our Warriors get together they leave it and go to some other part. They took Boston and Philadelphia, two of our greatest Towns; but when they saw our Warriors in a great body ready to fall upon them, they were forced to leave them.

Brothers: We have till lately fought the English all alone. Now the Great King of France is become our Good Brother and Ally. He has taken up the Hatchet with us, and we have sworn never to bury it, till we have punished the English and made them sorry for All the wicked things they had in their Hearts to do against these States. And there are other Great Kings and Nations on the other side of the big Waters, who love us and wish us well, and will not suffer the English to hurt us.

Warning to Indians

Brothers: Listen well to what I tell you and let it sink deep into your Hearts. We love our friends, and will be faithful to them, as long as they will be faithful to us. We are sure our Good brothers the Delawares will always be so. But we have sworn to take vengeance on our Enemies, and on false friends. The other day, a handful of our young men destroyed the settlement of the Onondagas. They burnt down all their Houses, destroyed their grain and Horses and Cattle, took their Arms away, killed several of their Warriors and brought off many prisoners and obliged the rest to fly into the woods. This is but the beginning of the troubles which those Nations, who have taken up the Hatchet against us, will feel.

Congress and the Indians

Brothers: I am sorry to hear that you have suffered for want of necessaries, or that any of our people have not dealt justly by you. But as you are going to Congress, which is the great Council of the Nation and hold all things in their hands, I shall say nothing about the supplies you ask. I hope you will receive satisfaction from them. I assure you, I will do every thing in my power to prevent your receiving any further injuries, and will give the strictest orders for this purpose. I will severely punish any that shall break them.

Brothers: I am glad you have brought three of the Children of your principal Chiefs to be educated with us. I am sure Congress will open the Arms of love to them, and will look upon them as their own Children, and will have them educated accordingly. This is a great mark of your confidence and of your desire to preserve the friendship between the Two Nations to the end of time, and to become One people with your Brethren of the United States. My ears hear with pleasure the other matters you mention. Congress will be glad to hear them too. You do well to wish to learn our arts and ways of life, and above all, the religion of Jesus Christ. These will make you a greater and happier people than you are. Congress will do every thing they can to assist you in this wise intention; and to tie the knot of friendship and union so fast, that nothing shall ever be able to loose it.

Brothers: There are some matters about which [I do not open my Lips, because they belong to Congress, and not to us warriors; you are going to them, they will tell you all you wish to know.

Brothers: When you have seen all you want to see, I will then wish you a good Journey to Philadelphia. I hope you may find there every thing your hearts can wish, that when you return home you may be able to tell your Nation good things of us. And I pray God he may make your Nation wise and Strong, that they may always see their own] true interest and have courage to walk in the right path; and that they never may be deceived by lies to do any thing against the people of these States, who are their Brothers and ought always to be one people with them.

46

CIRCULAR TO THE STATES

Head Quarters, Middle Brook, May 22, 1779

Sir:

The situation of our affairs at this period appears to me peculiarly critical, and this I flatter myself will apologise for that anxiety which impels me to take the liberty of addressing you on the present occasion. The state of the army in particular is *State of the army* alarming on several accounts, that of its numbers is not among the least. Our battalions are exceedingly reduced, not only from the natural decay incident to the best composed armies; but from the expiration of the term of service for which a large proportion of the men were engaged. The measures hitherto taken to replace them, so far as has come to my knowledge have been attended with very partial success; and I am ignorant of any others in contemplation that afford a better prospect. A reinforcement expected from Virginia, consisting of new levies and reinlisted men is necessarily ordered to the Southward. Not far short of one third of our whole force must be detached on a service undertaken by the direction of Congress and essential in itself. I shall only say of what remains, that when it is compared with the force of the enemy now actually at New York and Rhode Island, with the addition of the succours, they will in all probablity receive from England, at the lowest computation, it will be found to justify very serious apprehensions and to demand the zealous attention of the different legislatures.

When we consider the rapid decline of our currency, the general temper of the times the disaffection of a great part of the people, the lethargy that overspreads the rest, the increasing danger to the Southern States, we cannot but dread the consequences of any misfortune in this quarter; and must feel the impolicy of trusting our security, to a want of activity and enterprise in the Enemy.

An expectation of peace and an opinion of the Enemys inability to send more troops to this country, I fear, have had too powerful an influence in our affairs. I have never heard of any thing conclusive to authorise the former, and present appearances are in my opinion against it. The accounts we receive from Europe uniformly announce vigorous preparations to continue the war, at least another campaign. The debates and proceedings in Parliament wear this complexion. The public papers speak confidently of large reinforcements destined for America. The minister in his speech asserts positively that reinforcements will be sent over to Sir Henry Clinton; though he acknowledges the future plan of the war will be less extensive than the past. Let it be supposed, that the intended succours will not exceed five thousand men. This will give the Enemy a superiority very dangerous to our safety, if their strength be properly exerted, and our situation not materially altered for the better.

Reinforcements to General Clinton

These considerations and many more that might be suggested to point to the necessity of immediate and decisive exertions to complete our battalions and to make our military force more respectable. I thought it my duty to give an idea of its true state and to urge the attention of the States to a matter in which their safety and happiness are so interested. I hope a concern for the public good will be admitted as the motive and excuse of my importunity.

Defects in clothing supplies

There is one point which I beg leave to mention also. The want of system, which has prevailed in the clothiers department has been a source of innumerable evils; defective supplies, irregular and unequal issues, great waste loss and expence to the public, general dissatisfaction in the army, much confusion and perplexity, an additional load of business to the officers commanding make but a part of them. I have for a long time past most ardently desired to see a reformation. Congress by a resolve of the 23d of March has established an ordinance for regulating this department. According to this, there is a sub or state clothier to be appointed by each state. I know not what instructions may have been given relative to these appointments; but, if the matter now rests with the particular States, I take the liberty to press their execution without loss of time. The service suffers amazingly from the disorder in this department, and the regulations for it cannot possibly be too soon carried into effect. I have the honor, etc.

47

TO JOHN JAY

West point, September 7, 1779

Dr Sir:

I have received Your obliging Favors of the 25th. and 31st of last month and thank you for them.

It really appears impossible to reconcile the conduct Britain is pursuing, to any system of prudence or policy. For the reasons you assign, appearances are against her deriving aid from other powers; and if it is truly the case, that she has rejected the mediation of Spain, without having made allies, it will exceed all past instances of her infatuation. Notwithstanding appearances, I can hardly bring myself fully to believe that it is the case; or that there is so general a combination against the interests of Britain among the European powers, as will permit them to endanger the political ballance. I think it probable *The European political balance* enough, that the conduct of France in the affairs of the Porte and Russia will make an impression on the Empress; but I doubt whether it will be sufficient to counterballance the powerful motives she has to support England; and the Porte has been perhaps too much weakened in the last war with Russia to be overfond of renewing it. The Emperor is also the natural ally of England notwithstanding the connexions of Blood between his family and that of France; and he may prefer reasons of National policy to those of private attachment. Tis true his finances may not be in the best state, though one campaign could hardly have exhausted them, but as Holland looks up to him for her chief protection, if he should be inclined to favor England, it may give her Councils a decided biass the same way. She can easily supply what is wanting in the Article of money; and by this aid, give sinews to that confederacy. Denmark is also the natural ally of England; and though there has lately been a family bickering, her political interest may outweigh private animosity. Her marine assistance would be considerable. Portugal too, though timid and cautious at present, if she was to see connexions formed by England able to give her countenance and security, would probably declare for her interests. Russia, Denmark, The Emperor, Holland, Portugal and England would form a respectable counterpoise to the opposite scale. Though all the maritime powers of Europe were interested in the independence of this Country, as it tended to diminish the overgrown power of Britain, yet they may be unwilling to see too great a preponderacy on the side of her rivals; and when the question changes itself from the separation of America to the ruin of England as a Naval power, I should not be surprised at a proportionable change in the sentiments of some of those States which have been heretofore unconcerned Spectators or inclining to our side. I suggest these things rather as possible than probable; it is even to be expected that the decisive blow will be struck, before the interposition of the Allies England may acquire can have effect. But still as possible events, they ought to have their influence and prevent our relaxing in any measures necessary for our safety, on the supposition of a speedy peace or removal of the War from the present Theatre in America.

The account which Mr. Wharton received, of the reinforcement that came with Adml. Arbuthnot, corresponds pretty well, with respect to number, with the best information I have been able to obtain upon the subject. Some recent advices make it about Three thousand, and say that these Troops are rather in a sickly condition. It is generally said, that they are Recruits; but whether there is so great a proportion of them Scotch as his intelligence mentions, is not ascertained by any accounts I have received.

With respect to the person you recommended last Winter, he was employed in consequence; and I have not the smallest doubt of his attachment and integrity. But he has not had it in his power, and indeed it is next to impossible that any one should circumstanced as he is, to render much essential service in the way it was intended to employ him. You will readily conceive the difficulties in such a case. The business was of too delicate a nature for him to transact it frequently himself, and the Characters, he has been obliged occasionally to confide it to, have not been able to gain any thing satisfactory or material. Indeed, I believe it will seldom happen, that a person acting in this way, can render any essential advantages more than once or twice at any rate; and that what he will be compelled to do to preserve the pretended confidence of the other party, will generally counterbalance any thing he may effect. The greatest benefits are to be derived from persons who live with the other side; whose local circumstances, without subjecting them to suspicions, give them an opportunity of making observations and comparing and combining things and Sentiments. It is with such I have endeavoured to establish a correspondence, and on whose reports I shall most rely. From these several considerations, I am doubtful whether it will be of any advantage for the person to continue longer in the way he has acted. The points to which he must have alluded in his Letter, were the movements up the North River and against Charles Town and the expedition to Virginia. I believe the first certain information of the first of these events came from him. He has never received any thing from me. The Gentleman who employed him first, had some Money deposited with him for confidential purposes; but I cannot tell how much he may have paid him.

With every sentiment of esteem etc.

48

A CONFERENCE BETWEEN THE CHEVALIER DE LA LUZERNE AND GENERAL WASHINGTON

Head Quarters, West Point, September 16, 1779

The Minister opened the conference by observing, that The Council of Massachusetts had represented to him the disadvantages, which their commerce was likely to suffer from the late misfortune in Penobscot and the advantages which would result if His Excellency Count D'Estaing could detach a few ships of the line and frigates to be stationed upon their coast, for protecting their commerce and countenancing the operations of their cruisers against that of the enemy. But before he should propose such a measure to Count D'Estaing, he wished to know from The General what purposes the detachment would answer to his military operations, and whether it would enable him to prosecute any offensive enterprise against the enemy. That if he could accompany the request of the Council with assurances of this kind, a motive of such importance would have the greatest influence in determining the concurrence of Count D'Estaing, and might the better justify him in deranging or contracting his plans in the West Indies by making a detachment of his force.

Coordination of the French navy and American army in West Indies.

The General answered: That if Count D'Estaing could spare a detachment superior to the enemy's naval force upon this Continent retaining such a force in the West Indies as would put it out of the enemy's power to detach an equal force to this Continent without leaving themselves inferior in the Islands, the measure would have a high probability of many important and perhaps decisive advantages. But these would depend upon several contingencies; the time in which the detachment can arrive, and the position and force of the enemy when it arrives. That the season proper for military operations was now pretty far advanced, and to make a Winter campaign would require a disposition of our magazines peculiar to it, which could not be made without a large increase of expence; a circumstance not to be desired in the present posture of our affairs, unless the arrival of a naval succour was an event of some certainty. That with respect to the position and force of the enemy, they had now about fourteen thousand men at New York, and its dependencies and between three and four thousand at Rhode Island; that to reduce the former, if it should be concentred on the Island would require extensive preparations beforehand, both as to magazines and aids of men, which could not with propriety be undertaken on a precarious expectation of assistance. But that if the garrison of Rhode Island should continue there, we should have every reason to expect its reduction in a combined operation; it might however be withdrawn. He added: That the enemy appear to be making large detachments from New York which the present situation of their affairs seems to exact. That there is a high probability of their being left so weak as to give us an opportunity, during the Winter of acting effectually against New York, in case of the arrival of a fleet to co-operate with us; even with the force we now have and could suddenly assemble on an emergency. That at all events the French Squadron would be able to strike an important stroke, in the capture and destruction of the enemys vessels of war, with a large number of transports and perhaps seamen.

The outlook in New York and Rhode Island

He concluded with observing, That though in the great uncertainty of the arrival of a Squadron, he could not undertake to make expensive preparations for cooperating, nor pledge himself for doing it effectually; yet there was the greatest prospect of utility from the arrival of such a Squadron, and he would engage to do every thing in his power for improving its aid, if it should appear upon our coast: That if the present or future circumstances should permit His Excellency Count D'Estaing to concert a combined operation with the troops of these states against the enemy's fleets and armies within these States, he would be ready to promote the measure to the utmost of our resources and should have the highest hopes of its success; it would however, be necessary to prevent delay and give efficacy to the project that he should have some previous notice.

A combined operation suggested

The Minister replied: That The Generals delicacy upon the occasion was very proper; but as he seemed unwilling to give assurances of effectual cooperation, in conveying the application to the Admiral he would only make use of the name of the Council which would no doubt have all the weight due to the application of so respectable a body.

The General assented, observing that occasional mention

The Floridas

might be made of the military advantages to be expected from the measure.

The Minister in the next place informed The General that there had been some negotiations between Congress and Monsieur Gerard, on the subject of the Floridas and the limits of the Spanish dominions in that quarter, concerning which certain resolutions had been taken by Congress, which he supposed were known to The General. He added, that the Spaniards had in contemplation an expedition against the Floridas, which was either already begun or very soon would be begun, and he wished to know the Generals opinion of a cooperation on our part. That it was probable this expedition would immediately divert the enemy's force from South Carolina and Georgia, and the question then would be whether General Lincolns army would be necessary elsewhere, or might be employed in a cooperation with the Spanish forces. That the motive with the French court for wishing such a cooperation was that it would be a meritorious act on the side of the United States towards Spain, who though she had all along been well disposed to the revolution had entered reluctantly into the war and had not yet acknowledged our independence; that a step of this kind would serve to confirm her good dispositions and to induce her not only to enter into a Treaty with us, but perhaps to assist with a loan of money. That the forces of Spain in the Islands were so considerable as would in all appearance make our aid unnecessary; on which account the utility of it only contingent and possible, was but a secondary consideration with the Court of France; the desire to engage Spain more firmly in our interests by *a mark* of our good will to her was the leading and principal one.

The General assured the Minister, That he had the deepest sense of the friendship of France but replied to the matter in question, that he was altogether a stranger to the measures adopted by Congress relative to the Floridas and could give no opinion of the propriety of the cooperation proposed in a civil or political light; but considering it merely as a military question, he saw no objection to the measure on the supposition that the enemy's force in Georgia and South Carolina be withdrawn, without which it would of course be impossible.

The Minister then asked, in case the operation by the Spaniards against the Floridas should not induce the English to abandon the Southern States, whether it would be agreeable that the forces, either French or Spanish employed there should cooperate with our troops against those of the enemy in Georgia and South Carolina.

The General replied that he imagined such a cooperation would be desirable.

The Minister inquired in the next place, whether in case The Court of France should find it convenient to send directly from France a Squadron and a few Regiments attached to it, to act in conjunction with us in this quarter, it would be agreeable to The United States.

The General thought it would be very advancive of the common Cause.

The Minister informed, That Doctor Franklin had purchased a fifty gun ship which the King of France intended to equip, for the benefit of The United States to be sent with two or three frigates to Newfoundland to act against the enemys vessels employed in the Fishery, and afterwards to proceed to Boston to cruise from that port.

Newfoundland

He concluded the conference with stating, that in Boston several Gentlemen of influence, some of them members of Congress had conversed with him on the subject of an expedition against Canada and Nova Scotia. That his Christian Majesty had a sincere and disinterested desire to see those two provinces annexed to the American Confederacy and would be disposed to promote a plan for this purpose; but that he would undertake nothing of the kind unless the plan was previously approved and digested by The General. He added that a letter from The General to Congress some time since on the subject of an expedition to Canada had appeared in France and had been submitted to the best military judges who approved, the reasoning and thought the objections to the plan which had been proposed very plausible and powerful. That whenever the General should think the circumstances of this country favourable to such an undertaking, he should be very glad to recommend the Plan he should propose, and he was assured that the French Court would give it all the aid in their power.

Canada and Nova Scotia

The General again expressed his Sense of the good dispositions of his Christian Majesty; but observed, that while the enemy remain in force in these states, the difficulties stated in his letter alluded to by the Minister would still subsist; but that whenever that force should be removed, he doubted not it would be a leading object with the government to wrest the two forementioned provinces from the power of Britain; that in this case he should esteem himself honored in being consulted on the plan; and was of opinion, that though we should have land force enough for the undertaking, without in this respect intruding upon the generosity of our allies, a naval cooperation would certainly be very useful and necessary.

The rest of the Conference consisted in mutual assurances of friendship of the two countries &c. interspersed on the General's side with occasional remarks on the importance of removing the war from these states as it would enable us to afford ample supplies to the operations in the West Indies and to act with efficacy in annoying the commerce of the enemy and dispossessing them of their dominions on this continent.

49

TO EDMUND PENDLETON

West-point, November 1, 1779

Dear Sir:

Recollecting that I am your debtor for an obliging letter written some time last Winter, I will, while my eyes are turned Southwardly (impatiently looking for, or expecting to hear something decisively of Count D'Estaing) make my acknowledgements for it, as a proof that I am not unmindful of the favor, though I have been dilatory in thanking you for it.

Count d'Estaing

I shall not at this late period recount to you the occurrances of the past Campaign. I take it for granted that the published acc'ts. which have been officially handed to the public have regularly reached you and are as ample as I could give.

A New scene, though rather long delayed, is opening to our view and of sufficient importance to interest the hopes and fears of every well wisher to his Country and will engage the attention of all America. This I say on a supposition that the delays to the Southward and advanced season does not prevent a full and perfect co-operation with the French fleet in this quarter. Be this as it may; every thing in the preparatory way that depends upon me is done, and doing. To Count D'Estaing then, and that good Providence wch. has so remarkably aided us in all our difficulties, the rest is committed.

Stony point which has been a bone of contention the whole Campaign, and the principal business of it on the part of the enemy, is totally evacuated by them. Rhode Island is also abandoned, and the enemys whole force is drawn to a point at New York; where neither pains nor labour have been spar'd to secure the City and harbour; but in their attempts to effect the latter some unexpected disappointments have occurred (in sinking their hulks). This makes them more intent on their land batteries, wch. are so disposed as to cover the Town and the shipping equally. *Rhode Island and New York*

All lesser matters, on both sides, are suspended while we are looking at the more important object. The consequences of all these movements are not easy to be foretold; but, another Campaign having been wasted; having had their Arms disgraced, and all their projects blasted, it may be conceiv'd that the enemy like an enraged Monster summoning his whole strength, will make some violent effort, if they should be relieved from their present apprehensions of the French fleet. If they do not detach largely for the West Indies (and I do not see how this is practicable while they remain inferior at Sea) they must from the disagreeableness of their situation feel themselves under a kind of necessity of attempting some bold, enterprizing stroke, to give, in some degree, eclat to their Arms, spirits to the Tories, and hope to the Ministry, but I am under no apprehension of a capital injury from any other source than that of the continual depreciation of our Money. This indeed is truly alarming, and of so serious a nature that every other effort is in vain unless something can be done to restore its credit. Congress, the States individually, and individuals of each state, should exert themselves to effect this great end. It is the only hope; the last resource of the enemy; and nothing but our want of public virtue can induce a continuance of the War. Let them once see, that as it is in our power, so it is our inclination and intention to overcome this difficulty, and the idea of conquest, or hope of bringing us back to a state of dependance, will vanish like the morning dew; they can no more encounter this kind of opposition than the hoar frost can withstand the rays of an all chearing Sun. The liberties and safety of this Country depend upon it. the way is plain, the means are in our power, but it is virtue alone that can effect it, for without this, heavy taxes, frequently collected, (the only radical cure) and loans, are not to be obtained. Where this has been *The enemy disgraced*

Lack of public credit

the policy (in Connecticut for instance) the prices of every article have fallen and the money consequently is in demand; but in the other States you can scarce get a single thing for it, and yet it is with-held from the public by speculators, while every thing that can be useful to the public is engrossed by this tribe of black gentry, who work more effectually against us than the enemys Arms; and are a hundd. times more dangerous to our liberties and the great cause we are engaged in.

My best respects attend Mrs. Pendleton, and with much truth and regard I am, etc.

50

TO JOSEPH JONES

Morris-Town, May 14, 1780

Dear Sir:

I received the acct. of your delegation with much satisfaction and was greatly pleased to hear of your arrival in Philadelphia; as I have ever placed you among the number of my friends I mean to take this early oppertunity of giving you a mark of my confidence in an interesting moment.

Arrival of Lafayette

The arrival of the Marquis de la Fayette opens a prospect wch. offers the most important advantages to these States if proper measures are adopted to improve it. He announces an intention of his Court to send a Fleet and Army to co-operate effectually with us.

In the present state of our Finances, and in the total emptiness of our magazines a plan must be concerted to bring out the resources of the Country with vigor and decision; this I think you will agree with me cannot be effected if the measures to be taken should depend on the slow deliberations of a body so large as Congress admitting the best disposition in every member to promote the object in view. It appears to me of the greatest importance, and even of absolute necessity that a *small* Committee should be immediately appointed to reside near head Quarters vested with all the powers which Congress have so far as respects the purpose of a full co-operation with the French fleet and Army on the *Continent*. There authority should be Plenipotentiary to draw out men and supplies of every kind and give their sanction to any operations which the

Expediting French-American cooperation

Commander in chief may not think himself at liberty to undertake without it as well beyond, as within the limit of these States.

This Committee can act with dispatch and energy, by being on the spot it will be able to provide for exigencies as they arise and the better to judge of their nature and urgency. The plans in contemplation may be opened to them with more freedom and confidence than to a numerous body, where secrecy is impossible, where the indiscretion of a single member by disclosing may defeat the project.

I need not enlarge on the advantages of such a measure as I flatter myself they will occur to you and that you will be ready to propose and give it your support. The conjuncture is one of the most critical and important we have seen, all our prudence and exertions are requisite to give it a favourable issue. Hesitancy and delay would in all probability ruin our Affairs; circumstanced as we are the greatest good or the greatest ill must result. We shall probably fix the independence of America if we succeed and if we fail the abilities of the State will have been so strained in the attempt that a total relaxation and debility must ensue and the worst is to be apprehended.

These considerations should determine Congress to forego all inferior objects and unite with mutual confidence in those measures which seem best calculated to insure success. There is no man who can be more useful as a member of the Committee than General Schuyler. His perfect knowledge of the resources of the Country, the activity of his temper, His fruitfulness of expedients and his sound Military sense make me wish above all things he may be appointed. A well composed Committee is of primary importance, I need not hint that the delicacy of these intimations fits them only for your private ear.

The opinion I have of your friendship induces me thus freely and confidentially to impart my sentiments on the occasion and I shall be very happy you may agree with me in judgment. I am with the greatest esteem and regard Dr. Sir etc.

51

TO PRESIDENT JOSEPH REED

Morris Town, May 28, 1780

Dear Sir:

I am much obliged to you for your favour of the 23. Nothing could be more necessary than the aid given by your state towards supplying us with provision. I assure you, every Idea you can form of our distresses, will fall short of the reality. There is such a combination of circumstances to exhaust the patience of the soldiery that it begins at length to be worn out and we see in every line of the army, the most serious features of mutiny and sedition. All our departments, all our operations are at a stand, and unless a system very different from that which has for a long time prevailed, be immediately adopted throughout the states our affairs must soon become desperate beyond the possibility of recovery. If you were on the spot my Dear Sir, if you could see what difficulties surround us on every side, how unable we are to administer to the most ordinary calls of the service, you would be convinced that these expressions are not too strong, and that we have every thing to dread. Indeed I have almost ceased to hope. The country in general is in such a state of insensibility and indifference to its interests, that I dare not flatter myself with any change for the better.

Signs of mutiny and sedition

The Committee of Congress in their late address to the several states have given a just picture of our situation. I very much doubt its making the desired impression, and if it does not I shall consider our lethargy as incurable. The present juncture is so interesting that if it does not produce correspondent exertions, it will be a proof that motives of honor public good and even self preservation have lost their influence upon our minds. This is a decisive moment; one of the most [I will go further and say *the* most] important America has seen. The Court of France has made a glorious effort for our deliverance, and if we disappoint its intentions by our supineness we must become contemptible in the eyes of all mankind; nor can we after that venture to confide that our allies will persist in an attempt to establish what it will appear we want inclination or ability to assist them in.

Public lethargy

The Passions of Men and the Principles of Action

Every view of our own circumstances ought to determine us to the most vigorous efforts; but there are considerations of another kind that should have equal weight. The combined fleets of France and Spain last year were greatly superior of those of the enemy: The enemy nevertheless sustained no material damage, and at the close of the campaign have given a very important blow to our allies. This campaign the difference between the fleets from every account I have been able to collect will be inconsiderable, indeed it is far from clear that there will not be an equality. What are we to expect will be the case if there should be another campaign? In all probability the advantage will be on the side of the English and then what would become of America? We ought not to deceive ourselves. The maritime resources of Great Britain are more substantial and real than those of France and Spain united. Her commerce is more extensive than that of both her rivals; and it is an axiom that the nation which has the most extensive commerce will always have the most powerful marine. Were this argument less convincing the fact speaks for itself; her progress in the course of the last year is an incontestible proof.

It is true that France in a manner created a Fleet in a very short space and this may mislead us in the judgment we form of her naval abilities. But if they bore any comparison with those of great Britain how comes it to pass, that with all the force of Spain added she has lost so much ground in so short a time, as now to have scarcely a superiority. We should consider what was done by France as a violent and unnatural effort of the government, which for want of sufficient foundation, cannot continue to operate proportionable effects.

In modern wars the longest purse must chiefly determine the event. I fear that of the enemy will be found to be so. Though the government is deeply in debt and of course poor, the nation is rich and their riches afford a fund which will not be easily exhausted. Besides, their system of public credit is such that it is capable of greater exertions than that of any other nation. Speculatists have been a long time foretelling its downfall, but we see no symptoms of the catastrophe being very near. I am persuaded it will at least last out the war, and then, in the opinion of many of the best politicians it will be a national advantage. If the war should terminate successfully the crown will have acquired such influence and power that it

Strength of France and Spain compared to Great Britain's

Maritime resources of Great Britain

may attempt any thing, and a bankruptcy will probably be made the ladder to climb to absolute authority. Administration may perhaps wish to drive matters to this issue; at any rate they will not be restrained by an apprehension of it from forcing the resources of the state. It will promote their present purposes on which their all is at stake and it may pave the way to triumph more effectually over the constitution. With this disposition I have no doubt that ample means will be found to prosecute the war with the greatest vigor.

French finances

France is in a very different position. The abilities of her present Financier have done wonders. By a wise administration of the revenues aided by advantageous loans he has avoided the necessity of additional taxes. But I am well informed, if the war continues another campaign he will be obliged to have recourse to the taxes usual in time of war which are very heavy, and which the people of France are not in a condition to endure for any duration. When this necessity commences France makes war on ruinous terms; and England from her individual wealth will find much greater facility in supplying her exigencies.

Spain derives great wealth from her mines, but not so great as is generally imagined. Of late years the profits to government is essentially diminished. Commerce and industry are the best mines of a nation; both which are wanting to her. I am told her treasury is far from being so well filled as we have flattered ourselves. She is also much divided on the propriety of the war. There is a strong party against it. The temper of

*Spanish
sluggishness*

the nation is too sluggish to admit of great exertions, and tho' the Courts of the two kingdoms are closely linked together, there never has been in any of their wars a perfect harmony of measures, nor has it been the case in this; which has already been no small detriment to the common cause.

I mention these things to show that the circumstances of our allies as well as our own call for peace; to obtain which we must make one great effort this campaign. The present instance of the friendship of the Court of France is attended with every circumstance that can render it important and agreeable; that can interest our gratitude or fire our emulation. If we do our duty we may even hope to make the campaign decisive on this Continent. But we must do our duty in earnest, or disgrace and ruin will attend us. I am sincere in declaring a full persuasion, that the succour will be fatal to us if our measures are not adequate to the emergency.

Now my Dear Sir, I must observe to you, that much will depend on the State of Pennsylvania. She has it in her power to contribute without comparison more to our success than any other state; in the two essential articles of flour and transportation. New York, Jersey, Pensylvania and Maryland are our flour countries: Virginia went little on this article the last crop [and her resources are call'd for to the southward]. New York by legislative coercion has already given all she could spare for the use of the army. Her inhabitants are left with scarcely a sufficiency for their own subsistence. Jersey from being so long the place of the army's residence is equally exhausted. Maryland has made great exertions; but she can still do something more. Delaware may contribute handsomely in proportion to her extent. But Pennsylvania is our chief dependence. From every information I can obtain she is at this time full of flour. I speak to you in the language of frankness and as a friend. I do not mean to make any insinuations unfavourable to the state. I am aware of the embarrassments the government labours under, from the open opposition of one party and the underhand intrigues of another. I know that with the best dispositions to promote the public service, you have been obliged to move with circumspection. But this is a time to hazard and to take a tone of energy and decision. All parties but the disaffected will acquiesce in the necessity and give their support. The hopes and fears of the people at large may be acted upon in such a manner as to make them approve and second your views.

Importance of Pennsylvania

The matter is reduced to a point. Either Pensylvania must give us all the aid we ask of her, or we can undertake nothing. We must renounce every idea of cooperation, and must confess to our allies that we look wholly to them for our safety. This will be a state of humiliation and bitterness against which the feelings of every good American ought to revolt. Your's I am convinced will; nor have I the least doubt that you will employ all your influence to animate the Legislature and the people at large. The fate of these states hangs upon it. God grant we may be properly impressed with the consequences.

I wish the Legislature could be engaged to vest the executive with plenipotentiary powers. I should then expect every thing practicable from your abilities and zeal. This is not a time for formality or ceremony. The crisis in every point of view is extraordinary and extraordinary expedients are necessary. [I am decided in this opinion.]

I am happy to hear that you have a prospect of complying with the requisitions of Congress for specific supplies; that the spirit of the city and state seems to revive and the warmth of party decline. These are good omens of our success. Perhaps this is the proper period to unite.

I am obliged to you for the renewal of your assurances of personal regard; my sentiments for you, you are so well acquainted with as to make it unnecessary to tell you with how much esteem etc.

I felicitate you on the increase of your family. Mrs. Washington does the same and begs her particular respects and congratulations to Mrs. Reed, to which permit me to add mine.

52

TO PRESIDENT JOSEPH REED

Head Quarters, Bergen County, July 4, 1780

My Dear Sir:

Motives of friendship not less than of public good induce me with freedom to give you my sentiments on a matter, which interests you personally as well as the good of the common cause. I flatter myself you will receive what I say, in the same spirit which dictates it, and that it will have all the influence circumstances will possibly permit.

Martial law encouraged

The legislature of Pennsylvania has vested you, in case of necessity with a power of declaring Martial law throughout the state, to enable you to take such measures as the exigency may demand; so far the legislature has done its part. Europe, America, the state itself will look to you for the rest. The power vested in you will admit of all the latitude that could be desired and may be made to mean anything the public safety may require. If it is not exerted proportionably, you will be responsible for the consequences.

Nothing My Dear Sir can be more delicate and critical than your situation; a full discretionary power lodged in your hands in conjunction with the Council; great expectations in our allies and in the people of the country; ample means in the state for great exertions of every kind; a powerful party on one hand to take advantage of every opening to prejudice you; on the other popular indolence and avarice averse to every measure inconsistent with present ease and present interest; In this dilemma there is a seeming danger whatever side you take; it remains to choose that which has least real danger and will best promote the public weal. This in my Opinion clearly is to exert the powers intrusted to you with a boldness and vigor suited to the emergency.

In general I esteem it a good maxim, that the best way to preserve the confidence of the people durably is to promote their true interest; there are particular exigencies when this maxim has peculiar force. When any great object is in view, the popular mind is roused into expectation and prepared to make sacrifices both of ease and property; if those to whom they confide the management of their affairs do not call them to make these sacrifices, and the object is not attained, or they are involved in the reproach of not having contributed as much as they ought to have done towards it; they will be mortified at the disappointment; they will feel the censure, and their resentment will rise against those who with sufficient authority have omitted to do what their interest and their honor required. Extensive powers not exercised as far as was necessary, have I believe scarcely ever failed to ruin the possessor. The legislature and the people in your case, would be very glad to excuse themselves by condemning you. You would be assailed with blame from every quarter, [and your enemies would triumph.]

The party opposed to you in government are making great efforts. I am told the bank established for supplying the army is principally under the auspices of that party, It will undoubtedly give them great credit with the people; and you have no effectual way to counterbalance this but by employing all your influence and authority to render services proportioned to your station. Hitherto I confess to you frankly my Dear Sir I do not think your affairs are in the train which might be wished; and if Pensylvania does not do its part fully it is of so much importance in the general scale that we must fail of success, or limit our views to mere defence.

I have conversed with some Gentlemen on the measure of

filling your batalions. They seemed to think you could not exceed what the legislature had done for this purpose. I am of very different sentiment: The establishment of martial law implies, in my judgment the right of calling any part of your citizens into military service, and in any manner which may be found expedient; and I have no doubt the draft may be executed.

Power to conscript

I write to you with the freedom of friendship and I hope you will esteem it the truest mark I could give you of it. In this view whether you think my observations well founded or not, the motive will I am persuaded render them agreeable.

In offering my respects to Mrs. Reed, I must be permitted to accompany them with a tender of my very warm acknowledgments to her and you for the civilities and attention both of you have been pleased to show Mrs. Washington; and for the honor you have done me in calling the young Christian by my name. With the greatest regard etc.

53

TO JOSEPH JONES

Head Qrs. Tappan, August 13, 1780

Dear Sir:

The subject of this letter will be confined to a single point. I shall make it as short as possible, and write it with frankness. If any sentiment therefore is delivered which may be displeasing to you *as a member of Congress*, ascribe it to the freedom which is taken with you by a friend, who has nothg. in view but the public good.

Resignation of General Greene as Quartermaster General

In your letter without date, but which came to hand yesterday, an idea is held up as if the acceptance of General Green's resignation of the Qr. Mrs. department was not all that Congress meant to do with him. If by this it is in contemplation to suspend him from his command in the line (of which he made an express reservation at the time of entering on the other duty) and it is not already enacted, let me beseech you to consider *well* what you are about before you resolve.

I shall neither condemn, or acquit Genl. Green's conduct for the act of resignation, because all the antecedents are necessary to form a right judgment of the matter, and possibly, if the affair is ever brought before the public, you may find him treading on better ground than you seem to imagine; but this by the by. My sole aim at present is to advertise you of what I think would be the consequences of suspending him from his command in the line (a matter distinct from the other), without a proper tryal. A proceedure of this kind must touch the feelings of every Officer; it will shew in a conspicuous point of view the uncertain tenure by which they hold their Commissions. In a word it will exhibit such a specimen of power that I question much if there is an Officer in the whole line that will hold a Commission beyond the end of the Campaign if they do till then. Such an Act in the most Despotic Government would be attended at least with loud complaints.

It does not require, I am sure, with you argument at this time of day to prove, that there is no set of Men in the United States (considered as a body) that have made the same sacrafices of their Interest in support of the common cause as the Officers of the American Army; that nothing but a love of their Country, of honor, and a desire of seeing their labours crowned with success could possibly induce them to continue one moment in Service. That no Officer can live upon his pay, that hundreds having spent their little all in addition to their scant public allowance have resigned, because they could no longer support themselves as Officers; that numbers are, at this moment, rendered unfit for duty for want of Cloathing, while the rest are wasteing their property and some of them verging fast to the gulph of poverty and distress. Can it be supposed that men under these circumstances who can derive at best if the Contest ends happily, only the advantages which attend in equal proportion with Others will sit patient under such a precedent? surely they will not, for the measure, not the man, will be the subject of consideration and each will ask himself the question if Congress by its mere fiat, without enquiry and without tryal, will suspend one Officer to day; an officer of such high rank, may it not be my turn tomorrow and ought I to put it in the power of any man or body of men to sport with my Commission and character and lay me under the necessity of tamely acquiescing, or by an appeal to the public expose matters which must be injurious to its interests? The suspension of Genls. Schuyler and St. Clair, tho it was preceded by the loss of Ticonderoga which contributed not a little for the moment to excite prejudices against them, was by no means viewed with a satisfactory eye by many discerning Men, and tho it was in a manner supported by the public clamor; and the one in contemplation I am almost morally certain will be generally reprobated by the Army. Suffer not my Friend, if it is within the compass of your abilities to prevent it, so disagreeable an event to take place. I do not mean to justify; to countenance or excuse in the most distant degree any expressions of disrespect which the Gentn. in question, if he has used any, may have offered to Congress, no more than I do any unreasonable matters he may have required respecting the Q.M.G. department, but as I have already observed, my Letter is to prevent his suspension, because I *fear*, because I *feel* it must lead to very disagreeable and injurious consequences. Genl. Greene has his numerous Friends out of the Army as well as in it, and from his Character and consideration in the world, he might not, when he felt himself wounded in so summary way, withhold from a discussion that could not at best promote the public cause. As a Military Officer he stands very fair and very deservedly so, in the opinion of all his acquaintance.

These sentiments are the result of my own reflections on the matter and, I hasten to inform you of them. I do not know that Genl. Greene has ever heard of the matter and I hope he never may; nor am I acquainted with the opinion of a single Officer in the whole Army upon the subject. Nor will any tone be given by me. It is my wish to prevent the proceeding; for sure I am it cannot be brought to a happy issue if it takes place. I am &c.

54

CIRCULAR TO THE STATES

Head Quarters, near the Liberty Pole, in
Bergen County, August 27, 1780

Sir:

The Honble: the Committee of Co-operation having returned to Congress, I am under the disagreeable necessity of informing you that the Army is again reduced to an extremity of distress for want of provision. The greater part of it had been without Meat from the 21st. to the 26th. To endeavour to ob-

Lack of provisions

tain some relief, I moved down to this place, with a view of stripping the lower parts of the County of the remainder of its Cattle, which after a most rigorous exaction is found to afford between two and three days supply only, and those, consisting of Milch Cows and Calves of one or two years old. When this scanty pittance is consumed, I know not what will be our next resource, as the Commissary can give me no certain information of more than 120 head of Cattle expected from Pennsylvania and about 150 from Massachusetts. I mean in time to supply our immediate wants. Military coercion is no longer of any avail, as nothing further can possibly be collected from the Country in which we are obliged to take a position, without depriving the inhabitants of the last morsel. This mode of subsisting, supposing the desired end could be answered by it, besides being in the highest degree distressing to individuals, is attended with ruin to the Morals and discipline of the Army; during the few days which we have been obliged to send out small parties to procure provision for themselves, the most enormous excesses have been committed.

It has been no inconsiderable support of our cause, to have had it in our power to contrast the conduct of our Army with that of the enemy, and to convince the inhabitants that while their rights were wantonly violated by the British Troops, by ours they were respected. This distinction must unhappily now cease, and we must assume the odious character of the plunderers instead of the protectors of the people, the direct consequence of which must be to alienate their minds from the Army and insensibly from the cause. We have not yet been absolutely without Flour, but we have *this* day but *one* days supply in Camp, and I am not certain that there is a single Barrel between this place and Trenton. I shall be obliged therefore to draw down one or two hundred Barrels from a small Magazine which I have endeavoured to establish at West point, for the security of the Garrison in case of a sudden investiture.

From the above state of facts it may be foreseen that this army cannot possibly remain much longer together, unless very vigorous and immediate measures are taken by the States to comply with the requisitions made upon them. The Commissary General has neither the means nor the power of procuring supplies; he is only to receive them from the several Agents. Without a speedy change of circumstances, this dilemma will be involved; either the Army must disband, or what is, if possible, worse, subsist upon the plunder of the people. I would fain flatter myself that a knowledge of our situation will produce the desired relief; not a relief of a few days as has generally heretofore been the case, but a supply equal to the establishment of Magazines for the Winter. If these are not formed before the Roads are broken up by the weather, we shall certainly experience the same difficulties and distresses the ensuing Winter which we did the last. Altho' the troops have upon every occasion hitherto borne their wants with un-parralled patience, it will be dangerous to trust too often to a repetition of the causes of discontent. I have the honor etc.

55

TO THE PRESIDENT OF CONGRESS

Head Quarters, Passaic Falls, October 11, 1780

Sir:

Three days since, I received your Excellency's Letter of the 4th with the inclosed Resolutions, which, as the Army was in motion to this Post, I had it not in my power to answer before. I am much obliged to Congress for the honor they do me by the fresh mark of their attention and confidence conferred upon me in the reference they have been pleased to make. My wish to concur in sentiment with them, and a conviction that there is no time to be lost in carrying the measures relative to the Army into execution, make me reluctantly offer any objections to the plan that has been adopted; but a sense of what I owe to Congress and a regard to consistency will not permit me to suppress the difference of opinion, which happens to exist upon the present occasion, on points that appear to me far from unessential. In expressing it, I can only repeat the ideas which I have more than once taken the liberty to urge.

Reduction of regiments

That there are the most conclusive reasons for reducing the number of Regiments no person acquainted with the situation of our affairs and the state of the Army will deny. A want of officers independant of other considerations were sufficient to compel us [to it]. But that the temper of the Army produced by its sufferings requires great caution, in any reforms that are attempted, is a position not less evident than the former. In

Services the best established, where the hands of Government are strengthened, by the strongest interests of the Army to submission, the reducing of its regiments and dismissing a great part of its Officers is always a measure of delicacy and difficulty. In ours, where the Officers are held by the feeblest ties and are mouldering away by dayly resignations, it is peculiarly so. The last reduction occasioned many to quit the Service besides those who were reformed, and left durable seeds of discontent among those who remained. The general topic of declamation was, that it was as hard as dishonorable for men, who had made every sacrifice to the Service to be turned out of it at the pleasure of those in power without any adequate compensation. In the maturity to which their uneasinesses have now risen from a continuance in misery, they will be still more impatient under an attempt of a similar nature; how far these dispositions may be reasonable I pretend not to decide but in the extremity to which we are arrived policy forbids us to add new irritations. Too many of the Officers wish to get rid of their Commissions; but they are unwilling to be forced into it.

It is not the intention of these remarks to discourage a reform; but to shew the necessity of guarding against the ill effects by an ample provision both for the Officers who stay and for those who are reduced. This should be the basis of the plan and without it I apprehend the most mischievous consequences. This would obviate many scruples that will otherwise be found prejudicial in the extreme. I am convinced Congress are not a little straitened in the means of a present provision so ample as to give satisfaction; but this proves the expediency of a future one; and brings me to that which I have so frequently recommended as the most œconomical, the most politic and the most effectual that could be devised. A half pay for Life. *Half pay for life* Supported by a prospect of a permanent [in]dependence, the Officers would be tied to the Service and would submit to many momentary privations and to the inconveniences which the situation of public affairs makes unavoidable; this is exemplified in the Pensylvania Officers, who being upon this establishment are so much interested in the Service, that in the course of [five] Months, there has been only one resignation in that line.

If the objection drawn from the principle of this measure being incompatible with the genious of our government is thought insurmountable, I would propose a substitute less eligible in my opinion, but which may answer the purpose; it is to make the present half pay for Seven years whole pay for the same period to be advanced in two different payments, one half in a year after the conclusion of peace the other half in two years subsequent to the first. It will be well to have it clearly understood that the reduced Officers are to have the depreciation of their pay made good, lest any doubt should arise on this head.

No objection occurs to me, to this measure, except it be thought too great an expence; but in my judgment whatever can give consistency to our military establishment will be ultimately favourable to oeconomy. It is not easy to be conceived except by those who are witnesses to it what an additional waste and consumption of every thing and consequently what an increase of expence, results from the laxness of discipline in the Army, and where [the] Officers think they are doing the public a favor by holding their Commissions and the men are continually fluctuating it is impossible to maintain discipline. Nothing can be more obvious than that a sound Military establishment and the interests of oeconomy are the same. How much more the purposes of the War will be promoted by it in other respects will not admit of an argument.

In reasoning upon the measure of a future provision I have heard Gentlemen object the want of it in some foreign Armies, without adverting to the difference of circumstances. The Military state holds the first rank in most of the Countries of Europe and is the road to honor and emolument; the establishment is permanent, and whatever be an Officer's provision it is for life, and he has a profession for life. He has future as well as present motives of Military honor and preferment, He is attached to the Service by the spirit of the Government; By education and in most cases by early habit; his present condition if not splendid is comfortable, Pensions, distinctions, and particular privileges are commonly his rewards in retirement. In the case of the American Officers the Military character has been suddenly taken up and is to end with the War.

Reform of the regiments

The number of Regiments fixed upon by Congress is that which I should have wished; but I think the agregate number of men too small. Should the Regiments be compleated, making the usual deductions for casualties and not counting upon the three Regiments of South Carolina and Georgia we should not have in the Infantry above 18000 fighting men *rank and file*; from wch when we should have taken the garrison of West point and the different garrisons for the frontier, there would remain a force not equal even to a vigorous defensive; Intirely unequal to a decisive co-operation with our Allies, should their efforts next campaign be directed this way, as we have reason to hope. I confess too that I do not expect the States will complete their Regiments at whatever point they may be placed; if they are any thing near being full they will be apt to think the difference not material, without considering that what may be small in their quota will be very considerable in the aggregate of deficiencies, in a force originally calculated too low for our exigencies.

The enemy's whole embodied force of Infantry in these States (without speaking of the occasional aids of Militia) on a moderate estimate must amount to between Eighteen and twenty thousand fighting men. We ought on no scale of reasoning to have less than an equal number in the field (exclusive of all garrisons) for a vigorous defensive. Let us then state our

Assessment of troop needs

R and file
Armies in the field at 18000
West Point for complt. secury. reqs. 2500
Fort Schuyler fort Pitt and other frontier
  Posts require 1500
                                                  22000

By this calculation two and twenty thousand fighting men appear to be necessary on a defensive plan, to have which our total number must be thirty thousand rank and file. The Waggoners, Workmen at factories, Waiters, Men for other extra Services, Sick &ca. on an average make at least a fourth of the total numbers; which Congress may see by recurring to the returns of the Army from time to time.

Much less should we hesitate to exert ourselves to have this number, if we have any thoughts of recovering what we have lost. As to the abilities of the Country to maintain them, I am of opinion, they will be found adequate; and that they will be less strained, than they have heretofore been from the necessity we have been so frequently under of recurring to the aid of Militia.

It is my duty also to inform Congress that in the late conference with the French General and Admiral, though I could not give assurances, I was obliged to give an opinion of the force we might have the next Campaign; and I stated the Army in this quarter at fifteen thousand operative Continental Troops, wch will greatly exceed that which we should have by the proposed arrangement for it would not give us above Eleven. On this idea of fifteen thousand a memorial with a plan for next campaign has been transmitted to the Court of France.

Organization of regiments

I would therefore beg leave to propose that each Regiment of Infantry should consist of One Colonel, where the present Colonels are continued, or One Lieutt. Colonel Commandant; Two Majors, a first and Second; Nine Captains; Twenty two Subalterns; 1 Surgeon; 1 Mate; 1 Serjeant Major; 1 Qr. Mr. Serjeant; 45 Serjeants; 1 Drum Major; 1 Fife Major; 10 Drums; 10 Fifers; 612 Rank and file.

Fifty Regiments at 612 rank and file will amount to 30,600 rank and file, the force I have stated to be requisite.

Number of officers

The number of Officers to a regiment by our present establishment has been found insufficient. It is not only inconvenient and productive of irregularity in our formation and Manoeuvres; but the number taken for the different Offices of the Staff leaves the regiments destitute of Field Officers and the Companies so unprovided that they are obliged to be entrusted to the care of Serjeants and Corporals which soon ruins them. To obviate this I ask three field Officers to a Regimt; and, besides a Captain and two Subalterns to do the duties of each Company, three Supernumerary Subalterns as Paymaster, Adjutant and Quarter Master and one to reside in the State as a recruiting Officer. Officers continually employed in this way to improve every oppertunity that offered would engage men; while those who were occasionally detached for a short space of time would do nothing. I ask one Drum and fife extraordinary to attend this Officer. The supernumeraries to rank and rise in the Regiment with the other Officers. Three field Officers will be thought necessary, when we consider the great porportion employed as Adjutant General, Inspectors, Brigade Majrs.; Waggon Master, Superintendents of Hospitals &ca. In addition to which I would also propose a field Officer to reside in each State where the number of its regiments exceed two, and a Captain where it does not to direct the Recruiting Service and transact all business for the line to which he belongs with the State, which I think would be a very useful institution.

Instead of Regiments of Cavalry, I would recommend Legionary Corps which should consist of four Troops of Mounted

Dragoons of 60 each 240
Two of dismounted Do at Do 120
360

with the same number of Comd. and Non Comd. officers as at present. To make the Regiments larger will be attended with an excessive expence to purchase the horses in the first instance and to subsist them afterwards. And I think the augmentation though it would be useful, not essential. I prefer Legionary Corps because the kind of Service we have for horse almost constantly requires the aid of Infantry; in quarters, as they are commonly obliged to be remote from the Army for the benefit of forage it is indispensable for their security; and to attach to them Infantry drawn from the Regiments has many inconveniences.

Besides the four Regiments I cannot forbear recommending that two partizan Corps may be kept up Commanded by Colo. Armand and Major Lee. Tho' in general I dislike independant Corps, I think a Partizan Corps with an Army useful in many respects. Its name and destination stimulate to enterprize; and the two Officers I have mentioned have the best claims to public attention. Colonel Armand is an Officer of great merit wch. added to his being a foreigner, to his rank in life, and to the sacrifices of property he has made renders it a point of delicacy as well as justice to continue to him the means of serving honorably. Major Lee has rendered such distinguished Services and possesses so many Talents for commanding a Corps of this nature, he deserves so much credit for the perfection in which he has kept his Corps, as well as for the handsome exploits he has performed, that it would be a loss to the Service and a discouragement to merit to reduce him. And I do not see how he can be introduced into one of the Regiments in a manner satisfactory to himself and which will enable him to be equally useful, without giving too much disgust to the whole line of Cavalry. The Partizan Corps may consist of three Troops of

Mounted Dragoons of fifty each 150
3 ditto of dismted. Do 50 ea. 150
300

I would only propose one alteration in the proposed ar-

Artillery

rangement of Artillery, which is to have ten companies instead of Nine. The numerous demands of the Service have made the establishment of Companies hitherto not too great; and it would be injurious to diminish them materially. Nine Companies would be an irregular formation for a battalion of Artillery; and eight would be much too few: this makes me wish they may be fixed at Ten. The formation of nine Companies in the Infantry is with a view to one light Company to act seperately.

Terms of service

I sincerely wish Congress had been pleased to make no alternative in the term of Service but had confined it to the War, by inlistment draft or assessment as might be found necessary. On the footing upon which their requisition now stands we shall be certain of getting very few men for the War; and must continue to feel all the evils of temporary engagements. In the present humour of the States, I should entertain the most flattering hopes that they would enter upon vigorous measures to raise an army for the War, if Congress appeared decided on the point; but if they hold up a different idea as admissible, it will be again concluded, that they do not consider an Army for the War as essential; and this will encourage the opposition of Men of narrow, interested and feeble tempers, and enable them to defeat the primary object of the Resolution. Indeed if the mode by inlistment is the only one made use of to procure the men, it must necessarily fail. In my letter of the 20th. of August I say "any period short of a year is inadmissible"; but all my observations tend to prove the pernicious operation of engaging Men for any term short of the War, and the alternative is only on the supposition that the other should on experiment be found impracticable. But I regard it as of the highest importance, that the experiment should first be fairly tried; the alternative, if absolutely necessary, can be substituted hereafter.

The encouragemt. to the Officer and the bounty to the recruit are both too small in the present state of things unless the latter could be in specie, which it is probable would have a powerful influence. In case of recruits made in Camp no bounty is specified; it will be necessary here as well as in the Country, with this additional reason that a recruit made in the Army will be more valuable than one made in the Country.

I must confess also it would have given me infinite pleasure that Congress had thought proper to take the reduction and incorporation of the Regiments under their own direction. The mode of leaving it to the States is contrary to my Sentiments, because it is an adherence to the State system, and because I fear it will be productive of great confusion and discontent and it is requisite the business in contemplation should be conducted with the greatest circumspection. I fear also the *professing* to *select* the Officers retained in Service will give disgust, both to those who go and to those who remain; the former will be sent away under the public stigma of inferior merit and the latter will feel no pleasure in a present preference, when they reflect that at some future period they may experience a similar fate. I barely mention this as I am perswaded Congress did not advert to the operation of the expressions made use of, and will readily alter them.

I beg leave to remark before I conclude, that if Congress should be pleased to reconsider their Resolutions, it will be of the greatest moment that the number of men and term for wch. they are to be raised should be first determined and the requisitions transmitted to the several States. In this Article time presses; the others may be examined more at leizure, though it is very necessary the whole should be put into execution as speedily as possible.

To accelerate the business I have directed, agreeable to the tenor of the resolution returns to be immediately made which shall be without delay transmitted to the States to shew them at one view the force they have and the deficiencies for which they will have to provide, the moment they know the quotas respectively required of them. With the highest respect etc.

PS: In the establishment I submit, I mention two Subalterns to each Company; as we have few Ensigns, they must in general be both Lieutenants but in future appointments, there ought to be one Lieutenant and one Ensign as heretofore.

Congress will herewith receive a list of the Officers in New Hampshire, Massachusetts, Connecticut, New York, New Jersey, Pensylvania and Maryland line (previous to its Marching to the Southward). Also in Crane's and Lamb's Artillery, Sheldons Horse, and in Hazens, Sherburne's, Spencers and Livingstons Regiments who have *actually* had their resignations entered at Head Qrs. in the course of *this* Year, and who in general urged their necessities when they applied on the subject, and insisted, notwithstanding every persuasion to induce their continuance, that their circumstances would not admit of their remaining in Service longer. Besides these resignations there are a great many of which I have no certain account as the Officers being permitted to go home on furlough in the course of the Winter, have never rejoined the Army, and have only sent messages or written to their Regimental Officers that their own distresses and those of their families would not permit their return. As to the resignations which may have taken place in the Virginia line and the other Troops at the Southward since they were acting in that quarter, I have no account of them; but I make no doubt that many have happened. All these serve to shew the necessity of some more competent establishment than the present one, and I hold it my duty to mention, from the accts. I daily receive, unless this is the case, that I have strong reasons to believe we shall not be able to retain after the end of the Campaign, as many Officers, especially in some lines, as will be even sufficient for common duties when in Quarters. If matters fortunately should not proceed to the lengths my fears forebode, yet Congress will be sensible at the first view, of the injuries and great inconveniences which must attend such a continual change of Officers and consequent promotions which are and will be inevitable.

After having exhibited this view of the present State of the Army it is almost needless to add, that excepting in the rank of Field Officers and a very few Captains we shall have new Officers to provide rather than old ones to disband at the reduction of Regiments, and where they are to be had I know not, no disposition having been discovered of late to enter the Service. Congress have little to apprehend therefore on acct. of the expence of Supernumerary Officers when this event takes place. I am &c.

56

CIRCULAR TO THE STATES

Head Quarters, near Passaic Falls, October 18, 1780

Sir:

In obedience to the orders of Congress, I have the honor to transmit you the present state of the troops of your line, by which you will perceive how few Men you will have left after the 1st of Jany. next. When I inform you also that the Regiments of the other Lines will be in general as much reduced as yours, you will be able to judge how exceedingly weak the Army will be at that period, and how essential it is the states should make the most vigorous exertions to replace the discharged Men as early as possible.

Congress are now preparing a plan for a new establishment of their Army which when finished they will transmit to the several States with requisitions for their respective quotas. I have no doubt it will be a primary object with them to have the Levies for the War, and this appears to me a point so interesting to our Independence that I cannot forbear entering into the motives which ought to determine the States without hesitation or alternative to take their measures decisively for that object.

New plan for the army

I am religiously persuaded that the duration of the War and the greatest part of the misfortunes and perplexities we have hitherto experienced, are chiefly to be attributed to the System of temporary enlistments. Had we in the commencement raised an Army for the War, such as was within the reach of the Abilities of these States to raise and maintain we should not have suffered those military Checks which have so frequently shaken our cause, nor should we have incurred such enormous expenditures as have destroyed our paper Currency and with it all public credit. A moderate compact force on a permanent establishment capable of acquiring the discipline essential to military operations would have been able to make head against the enemy without comparison better than the throngs of Militia which at certain periods have been, not in the field, but in their way to and from the Field; for from that want of perseverance which characterises all Militia, and of that coercion which cannot be exercised upon them, it has always been found impracticable to detain the greatest part of them in service even for the term, for which they have been called out, and this has been commonly so short, that we have had a great proportion of the time two sets of Men to feed and pay, one coming to the Army and the other going from it. From this circumstance and from the extraordinary waste and consumption of provisions, stores, Camp equipage, Arms, Cloaths and every other Article incident to irregular troops, it is easy to conceive what an immense increase of public expence has been produced from the source of which I am speaking. I might add the diminution of our Agriculture by calling off at critical Seasons the labourers employed in it, as has happened in instances without number.

In the enumeration of Articles wasted, I mention Cloathes. It may be objected that the terms of engagements of the Levies do not include this, but if we want service from the Men particularly in the cold Season we are obliged to supply them notwithstanding, and they leave us before the Cloaths are half worn out.

But there are evils still more striking that have befallen us. The intervals between the dismission of one Army and the collection of another have more than once threatened us with ruin, which humanly speaking nothing but the supineness or folly of the enemy could have saved us from. How did our cause totter at the close of 76, when with a little more than two thousand Men we were driven before the enemy thro' Jersey and obliged to take post on the other side of the Delaware to make a shew of covering Philadelphia while in reallity nothing was more easy to them with a little enterprise, and industry than to make their passage good to that City and dissipate the remaining force which still kept alive our expiring opposition! What hindered them from dispersing our little Army and giving a fatal Blow to our affairs during all the subsequent winter, instead of remaining in a state of torpid inactivity and permitting us to hover about their Quarters when we had scarcely troops sufficient to mount the ordinary Guard? After having lost two Battles and Philadelphia in the following Campaign for want of those numbers and that degree of discipline which we might have acquired by a permanent force in the first instance, in what a cruel and perilous situation did we again find ourselves in the Winter of 77 at Valley Forge, within a days march of the enemy, with a little more than a third of their strength, unable to defend our position, or retreat from it, for want of the means of transportation? What but the fluctuation of our Army enabled the enemy to detach so boldly to the southward in 78 and 79 to take possession of the two States Georgia and South Carolina, while we were obliged here to be idle Spectators of their weakness; set at defiance by a Garrison of six thousand regular troops, accessible every where by a Bridge which nature had formed, but of which we were unable to take advantage from still greater weakness, apprehensive even for our own safety? How did the same Garrison insult the main Army of these States the ensuing Spring and threaten the destruction of all our Baggage and Stores, saved by a good countenance more than by an ability to defend them? And what will be our situation this winter, our Army by the 1st. of January dimished to a little more than a sufficient Garrison for West point, the enemy at liberty to range the Country wherever they please, and, leaving a handful of Men at N York, to undertake Expeditions for the reduction of other States, which for want of adequate means of defense will it is much to be dreaded add to the number of their conquests and to the examples of our want of energy and wisdom?

The loss of Canada to the Union and the fate of the brave Montgomery compelled to a rash attempt by the immediate prospect of being left without Troops might be enumerated in the catalogue of evils that have sprang from this fruitful source. We not only incur these dangers and suffer these losses for want of a constant force equal to our exigencies, but while we labor under this impediment it is impossible there can be any order or oeconomy or system in our finances. If we meet with any severe blow the great exertions which the moment requires to stop the progress of the misfortune oblige us to depart from general principles to run into any expence or to adopt any expedient however injurious on a larger scale to procure the force and means which the present emergency demands. Everything is thrown into confusion and the measures taken to remedy immediate evils perpetuate others. The same is the case if particular conjunctions invite us to offensive operations; we find ourselves unprepared without troops, without Magazines, and with little time to provide them. We are obliged to force our resources by the most burthensome methods to answer the end, and after all it is but half answered: the design is announced by the occasional effort, and the enemy have it in their power to counteract and elude the blow. The prices of every thing, Men provisions &ca. are raised to a height to which the Revenues of no Government, much less ours, would suffice. It is impossible the people can endure the excessive burthen of bounties for annual drafts and substitutes increasing at every new experiment: whatever it might cost them once for all to procure Men for the War would be a cheap bargain.

I am convinced our System of temporary inlistments has prolonged the War and encouraged the enemy to persevere.

Baffled while we had an Army in the field, they have been constantly looking forward to the period of its reduction, as the period to our opposition, and the season of their successes. They have flattered themselves with more than the event has justified; for they believed when one Army expired, we should not be able to raise another: undeceived however in this expectation by experience, they still remained convinced, and to me evidently on good grounds, that we must ultimately sink under a system which increases our expense beyond calculation, enfeebles all our measures, affords the most inviting opportunities to the enemy, and wearies and disgusts the people. This has doubtless had great influence in preventing their coming to terms and will continue to operate in the same way, The debates on the ministerial side have frequently manifested the operation of this motive, and it must in the nature of things have had great weight.

The interpositions of Neutral powers may lead to a negociation this winter: Nothing will tend so much to make the court of London reasonable as the prospect of a permanent Army in this Country, and a spirit of exertion to support it.

Disadvantages of the militia

Tis time we should get rid of an error which the experience of all mankind has exploded, and which our own experience has dearly taught us to reject; the carrying on a War with Militia, or, (which is nearly the same thing) temporary levies against a regular, permanent and disciplined force. The Idea is chimerical, and that we have so long persisted in it is a reflection on the judgment of a Nation so enlightened as we are, as well as a strong proof of the empire of prejudice over reason. If we continue in the infatuation, we shall deserve to lose the object we are contending for.

America has been almost amused out of her liberties. We have frequently heard the behavior of the Militia extolled upon one and another occasion by Men who judge only from the surface, by Men who had particular views in misrepresenting, by visionary Men whose credulity easily swallowed every vague story in support of a favorite Hypothesis. I solemnly declare I never was witness to a single instance that can countenance an opinion of Militia or raw troops being fit for the real business of fighting. I have found them useful as light parties to skirmish the Woods, but incapable of making or sustaining a serious attack. This firmness is only acquired by habit of discipline and service. I mean not to detract from the merit of the Militia; their zeal and spirit upon a variety of occasions have intitled them to the highest applause; but it is of the greatest importance we should learn to estimate them rightly. We may expect everything from ours that Militia is capable of, but we must not expect from any, service for which Regulars alone are fit. The late Battle of Campden is a melancholy comment upon this doctrine. The Militia fled at the first fire, and left the Continental troops surrounded on every side and overpowered by numbers to combat for safety instead of Victory. The enemy themselves have witnessed to their Valor.

An ill effect of short enlistments which I have not yet taken notice of, is that the constant fluctuation of their Men is one of the sources of disgust to the Officers. Just when by great trouble fatigue and vexation (with which the training of Recruits is attended) they have brought their Men to some kind of order, they have the mortification to see them go home, and to know that the drudgery is to recommence the next Campaign, In Regiments so constituted, an Officer has neither satisfaction nor credit in his command.

Every motive which can arise from a consideration of our circumstances, either in a domestic or foreign point of view calls upon us to abandon temporary expedients and substitute something durable, systematic and substantial. This applies as well to our civil administration as to our military establishment. It is as necessary to give Congress, the common Head, sufficient powers to direct the common Forces as it is to raise an Army for the War; but I should go out of my province to expatiate on Civil Affairs. I cannot forbear adding a few more remarks.

Our finances are in an alarming state of derangement. Public credit is almost arrived at its last Stage. The People begin to be dissatisfied with the feeble mode of conducting the War, and with the ineffectual burthens imposed upon them, which tho' light in comparison to what other nations feel are from their novelty heavy to them. They lose their confidence in Government apace. The Army is not only dwindling into nothing, but the discontents of the Officers as well as the Men have matured to a degree that threatens but too general a renunciation of the service, at the end of the Campaign. Since January last we have had registered at Head Quarters more than one hundred and sixty resignations, besides a number of others that were never regularly reported. I speak of the Army

Dissatisfaction with conduct of war

in this Quarter. We have frequently in the course of the campaign experienced an extremity of want. Our Officers are in general indecently defective in Cloathing. Our Men are almost naked, totally unprepared for the inclemency of the approaching season. We have no magazines for the Winter; the mode of procuring our supplies is precarious, and all the reports of the Officers employed in collecting them are gloomy.

More energy to government

These circumstances conspire to show the necessity of immediately adopting a plan that will give more energy to Government, more vigor and more satisfaction to the Army. Without it we have every thing to fear. I am persuaded of the sufficiency of our resources if properly directed.

Should the requisitions of Congress by any accident not arrive before the Legislature is about to rise, I beg to recommend that a plan be devised, which is likely to be effectual, for raising the Men that will be required for the War, leaving it to the Executive to apply it to the Quota which Congress will fix, I flatter myself however the requisition will arrive in time.

The present Crisis of our Affairs appears to me so serious as to call upon me as a good Citizen to offer my sentiments freely for the safety of the Republic. I hope the motive will excuse the liberty I have taken. I have the honor etc.

CHAPTER FOUR

AT YORKTOWN

Trials and Triumph

1780 – 1781

*W*ASHINGTON *had urged the notion of an American union, in the context of the Revolution, as early as 1775. The progress of the war made his appeals ever more insistent and strident. In the final two years of the war, when enormous labors were required to maintain his position in the face of a determined enemy, his appeals attained the status of virtual demands. Even as the Articles of Confederation, drafted and sent out to the states in 1777, were finally being ratified in 1781 (Maryland acceding and producing ratification March 1), Washington was urging upon legislators and others the necessity for a stronger national union. The struggle of the war years and the ongoing problem of maintaining a cohesive policy in the face of both a factious Congress and a populace that did not possess a clear national vision caused Washington to observe that human nature must receive its due consideration: "we must take the passions of men as nature has given them, and those principles as a guide which are generally the rule of action."*

Though few could know it, the war was swiftly approaching its end. Throughout the entire effort, or nearly so, there existed no formal apparatus of government to direct the effort. When finally in early

1781 "*The United States in Congress Assembled*" *was born, there was no place for celebration; a dangerous enemy, from Washington's perspective, still loomed before them, while inadequate provision for sustaining American forces had been made. In fact, the end of the severe trials of the war was but another step toward securing the ultimate triumph—nationhood.*

Siege of Yorktown. Washington and Rochambeau pressed General Clinton so closely in late August 1781 that Clinton believed their feints toward New York were real movements; on August 25 he ordered Cornwallis to send troops from the South to resist a threatened siege of New York. The American and French armies moved toward Yorktown, where Lafayette was checking Cornwallis's movements. On September 8, Washington received long-awaited news that Count de Grasse had arrived off the coast of Virginia. The combined strength of the allied forces was then 16,400; the British forces stood at 8,500. On September 25, the army concentrated at Williamsburg took a position within two miles of the British; four days later they had environed Yorktown. The lines fought on October 6, 9, and 11. On October 19, the British army surrendered.

57

TO GEORGE MASON

Head Quarters, Passaic Falls, October 22, 1780

Dear Sir:

In consequence of a resolve of Congress directing an enquiry into the conduct of Genl. Gates, and authorising me to appoint some other Officer in his place during this enquiry, I have made choice of Majr. Genl. Greene who will, I expect, have the honor of presenting you with this Letter.

Appointment of
General Greene

I can venture to introduce this Gentn. to you as a man of abilities bravery and coolness. He has a comprehensive knowledge of our affairs, and is a man of fortitude and resources. I have not the smallest doubt therefore, of his employing all the means which may be put into his hands to the best advantage; nor of his assisting in pointing out the most likely ones to answer the purposes of his command. With this character, I take the liberty of recommending him to your civilities and support; for I have no doubt, from the embarrassed situation of Southern affairs; of his standing much in need of the latter from every Gentn. of Influence in the Assemblies of those States.

As General Greene can give you the most perfect information, in detail of our present distresses, and future prospects, I shall content myself with giving the agregate acct. of them; and with respect to the first, they are so great and complicated, that it is scarcely within the powers of description to give an adequate idea of them; with regard to the second, unless there is a material change both in our military, and civil policy, it will be in vain to contend much longer.

We are without money, and have been so for a great length of time, without provision and forage except what is taken by Impress; without Cloathing; and shortly shall be (in a manner) without Men. In a word, we have lived upon expedients till we can live no longer, and it may truly be said that, the history of this War is a history of false hopes, and temporary devices, instead of System, and oeconomy which results from it.

Call for a new plan to conduct war

If we mean to continue our struggles (and it is to be hoped we shall not relinquish our claim) we must do it upon an entire new plan. We must have a permanent force; not a force that is constantly fluctuating and sliding from under us as a pedestal of Ice would do from a Statue in a Summers day. Involving us in expence that baffles all calculation, an expence which no funds are equal to. We must at the same time contrive ways and means to aid our Taxes by Loans, and put our finance upon a more certain and stable footing than they are at prest. Our Civil government must likewise undergo a reform, ample powers must be lodged in Congress as the head of the Federal Union, adequate to all the purposes of War. Unless these things are done, our efforts will be in vain, and only serve to accumulate expence, add to our perplexities, and dissatisfy the people without a prospect of obtaining the prize in view. but these Sentimts. do not appear well in a hasty letter, without digestion or order. I have not time to give them otherwise; and shall only assure you that they are well meant, however crude they may appear. With sincere Affectn. and esteem etc.

58

TO WILLIAM FITZHUGH

Hd. Qrs. Passaic Falls, October 22, 1780

Dear Sir:

General Greene to command Southern Army

The Gentn. who will have the honor of presenting you with this letter, is Majr. Genl. Greene, a particular friend of mine, and one who I would beg leave to recommend to your civilities. He is going to take command of the Southern Army, and calls at Annapolis to make some arrangements with the State respecting its supplies which are turned into that direction.

This Gentleman is so intimately acquainted with our situation and prospects, and can relate them with such accuracy, that I shall not trouble you with them. My best respects attend Mrs. Fitzhugh and the young Officer, whose final exchange is, I hope, not far distant; if the Prisoners we have in this quarter will reach the date of his captivity in the exchange we are about to make. The Comy. is now gone in with powers to effect this purpose. I am etc.

PS: I hope the Assemblies that are now sitting, or are about to sit, will not rise till they put three things in a fair and proper train. *Appeal to state assemblies*

First, to give full and ample powers to Congress, competent to all the purposes of War.

Secondly, by Loans and Taxes to put our finances upon a more respectable footing than they are at present. and

Thirdly, that they will endeavour to establish a permanent force. These things will secure our Independency beyond dispute, but to go on in our present Systemn; Civil as well as military is a useless and vain attempt. Tis idle to suppose that raw and undisciplined Men are fit to oppose regular Troops, and if they were, our present Military System is too expensive, for any funds except that of an Eastern Nabob; and in the Civil line instead of one head and director we have, or soon shall have, thirteen, which is as much a monster in politicks as it would be in the human form. Our prest. distresses, and future prospects of distress, arising from these and similar causes, is great beyond the powers of description and without a change must end in our ruin.

59

TO JAMES DUANE

New Windsor, December 26, 1780

My dear Sir:

I received with much thankfulness your confidential letter of the 9th. Instt. and am greatly obliged by the affectionate expressions of personl. regard wch are contained in it. An unreserved communication of Sentiments, accompanying such infomation as you are at liberty to give, will ever be pleasing to me, and cannot fail of being useful, in this light I view, and value, your last letter; some parts of wch are new, agreeable and instructive, while that part of it wch. relates to the transactn. at the Ct. of V— is wonderfully astonishing.

Greater powers to Congress, permanency in executive bodies

There are two things (as I have often declared) which in my opinion, are indispensably neccessary to the well being and good Government of our public Affairs; these are, greater powers to Congress, and more responsibility and permanency in the executive bodies. If individual States conceive themselves at liberty to reject, or alter any act of Congress, which in a full representation of them, has been solemnly debated and decided on; it will be madness in us, to think of prosecuting the War. And if Congress suppose, that Boards composed of their own body, and always fluctuating, are competent to the great business of War (which requires not only close application, but a constant and uniform train of thinking and acting) they will most assuredly deceive themselves. Many, many instances might be adduced in proof of this, but to a mind as observant as yours there is no need to enumerate them. One however, as we *feelingly* experience it, I shall name. It is the want of cloathing, when I have every reason to be convinced that the expence wch. the Public is run to in this article would Cloath our Army as well as any Troops in Europe; in place of it, we have enumerable objects of distresg. want.

Necessity alone can justify the present mode of obtaining supplies; for besides the hazard and difficulty we meet with in procuring them, I am well convinced, that the public is charged with dble. what it receives, and what it receives is doubly charged so expensive and precarious is the prest. System. When the Army marched for Winter Quarters, I visited the Hospitals and back communication from Pensa. to this place. In the Neighbourhood of Pitts town, I fell in with a parcel of Cattle that were going to be slaughtered and Salted; and can assure you upon my honor, that besides being immensely poor, they were so small that I am convinced they would not average 175 lbs. the 4 nett quarters. some could not exceed One hundd. weight, and others were mere Calves. These pass by the head and the State, or States that furnish them, will have the reputation of supplying that Numbr. of Merchantable Bullocks, when the fact is, that next Summer a starving man wd. scarce eat the Beef they were about to put up after the Salt had extracted the little fat and juices that were in it; there were about 100 in the drove I saw, and my information extended to abt. 8 or 900 more of the same kind, in the neighbourhood. I directed the Commissary to select the *best* for Salting, and let the others be eaten fresh, as it would be a waste of Salt, Barrels and time to put it up. I relate this as a matter coming under my own observation, many other instances of a similar nature might be given from information, but I avoid it.

This letter will accompany one to Congress on the subject of promotion. That of a lineal, instead of Regimental, I am perswaded, as well from the opinions I have heard, as from the reason and nature of the thing; will be most consistt. with justice and most pleasing to each State line. With respect to the rise of Colonels and promotion of General Officers, I have no wish to gratify, except that which I have expressed in my public letter of fixing some principle, to avoid discontent and the consequences which flow from it. Irregular promotion, unless there is obvious cause for it, is not only injurious in any Service, but in ours is derogatory of the dignity of Congress for the Officer who is superceded and afterwards restored, is hurt by the first act and does not feel himself obliged by the latter (considering it as an act of justice only); while the two acts stands as an undeniable proof on record, that there is an establishd principle wanting, or that there is a want of information, or a want of firmness in Congress to resist importunity because the restoring act, as I have obsd. is an incontestable proof of one or the other of these three things.

At present we are in no want of Major Generals, in this part of the Army at least; but while I am on the subject of promotion, and while the thing is in my mind, I will beg leave to mention, that if at any time hereafter, there should be a Brigr., junr. to Genl. Knox, promoted before him, he will be lost to the Service; tho' he should, thereafter, be restored to his place. I mention it because under the idea of State promotion he can never rise, and because I am well perswaded that the want of him at the head of the Artillery, would be irrepairable.

I cannot conclude without mentioning the case of Lt. Colo. Smith as deserving of notice, if a remedy can be applied. This Gentn. is of the remaining Sixteen Regiments, and though one of the oldest and (without disparagement to others) one of the best *Battalion* Officers of the whole line, must quit the Service without a chance of staying altho' he is extremely anxious to do so. He has, during the last Campaign, been in the

Inspectorate department where *I think* he may still be continued in his present Rank without injury to any one, to his own satisfaction, and the public benefit, without locating his services to any particular Corps, but to be employed as circumstances may require.

Mrs. Washington, impressed with a grateful sence of your kind intention of accompanying her to Trenton, joins me in thanks for it, and complimts. to you. Mr. Tilghman (the only person of my family at this momt. with me) also prests. his compts. with every Sentimt. of estm. etc.

60

CIRCULAR TO THE NEW ENGLAND STATES

Head Quarters, New Windsor, January 5, 1781

Sir:

It is with extreme anxiety, and pain of mind, I find myself constrained to inform Your Excellency that the event I have long apprehended would be the consequence of the complicated distresses of the Army, has at length taken place. On the night of the 1st instant a mutiny was excited by the Non Commissioned Officers and Privates of the Pennsylvania Line, which soon became so universal as to defy all opposition; in attempting to quell this tumult, in the first instance, some Officers were killed, others wounded, and the lives of several common Soldiers lost. Deaf to the arguments, entreaties, and utmost efforts of *all their Officers* to stop them, the Men moved off from Morris Town, the place of their Cantonment, with their Arms, and six pieces of Artillery: and from Accounts just received by Genl. Wayne's Aid De Camp, they were still in a body, on their March to Philadelphia, to demand a redress of their grievances. At what point this defection will stop, or how extensive it may prove God only knows; at present the Troops at the important Posts in this vicinity remain quiet, not being acquainted with this unhappy and alarming affair; but how long they will continue so cannot be ascertained, as they labor under some of the pressing hardships, with the Troops who have revolted.

*Mutiny in the
Pennsylvania line*

Trials and Triumph

The aggravated calamities and distresses that have resulted, *Poor conditions* from the total want of pay for nearly twelve Months, for want *in army* of cloathing, at a severe season, and not unfrequently the want of provisions; are beyond description. The circumstances will now point out much more forcibly what ought to be done, than any thing that can possibly be said by me, on the subject.

It is not within the sphere of my duty to make requisitions, without the Authority of Congress, from individual States: but at such a crisis, and circumstanced as we are, my own heart will acquit me; and Congress, and the States (eastward of this) whom for the sake of dispatch, I address, I am persuaded will excuse me, when once for all I give it decidedly as my opinion, that it is in vain to think an Army can be kept together much longer, under such a variety of sufferings as ours has experienced: and that unless some immediate and spirited measures are adopted to furnish at least three Months pay to the Troops, in Money that will be of some value to them; And at the same time ways and means are devised to cloath and feed them better (more regularly I mean) than they have been, the worst that can befall us may be expected.

I have transmitted Congress a Copy of this Letter, and have in the most pressing manner requested them to adopt the measure which I have above recommended, or something similar to it, and as I will not doubt of their compliance, I have thought proper to give you this previous notice, that you may be prepared to answer the requisition.

As I have used every endeavour in my power to avert the evil that has come upon us, so will I continue to exert every means I am possessed of to prevent an extension of the Mischief, but I can neither fortell, or be answerable for the issue.

That you may have every information that an officer of rank and abilities can give of the true situation of our affairs, and the condition and temper of the Troops I have prevailed upon Brigadier Genl Knox to be the bearer of this Letter, to him I beg leave to refer your Excellency for many Matters which would be too tedious for a Letter. I have the honor etc.

61

TO LIEUTENANT COLONEL
JOHN LAURENS

[New Windsor, January 15, 1781]

[Dear Sir]:

State of American affairs

In compliance with your reguest I shall commit to writing the result of our conferences on the present state of American affairs; in which I have given you my ideas, with that freedom and explicitness, which the objects of your commission, my intire confidence in you, and the exigency demand. To me it appears evident:

1st. That, considering the diffused population of these states, the consequent difficulty of drawing together its resources; the composition and temper of *a part* of its inhabitants; the want of a sufficient stock of national wealth as a foundation for Revenue and the almost total extinction of commerce; the efforts we have been compelled to make for carrying on the war, have exceeded the natural abilities of this country and by degrees brought it to a crisis, which renders immediate and efficacious succours from abroad indispensable to its safety.

2dly. That, notwithstanding from the confusion, always attendant on a revolution, from our having had governments to frame, and every species of civil and military institution to create; from that inexperience in affairs, necessarily incident to a nation in its commencement, some errors may have been committed in the administration of our finances, to which a part of our embarrassments are to be attributed, yet they are principally to be ascribed to an essential defect of means, to the want of a sufficient stock of wealth, as mentioned in the first article; which, continuing to operate, will make it impossible, by any merely interior exertions, to extricate ourselves from those embarrassments, restore public credit, and furnish the funds requisite for the support of the war.

Errors in financial administration

3dly. That experience has demonstrated the impracticability, long to maintain a paper credit without funds for its redemption. The depreciation of our currency was, in the main, a necessary effect of the want of those funds; and its restoration is impossible for the same reason; to which the general diffidence, that has taken place among the people, is an addi-

Paper credit

tional, and in the present state of things, an insuperable obstacle.

4thly. That the mode, which for want of money has been substituted for supplying the army; by assessing a proportion of the productions of the earth, has hitherto been found ineffectual, has frequently exposed the army to the most calamitous distress, and from its novelty and incompatibility with ancient habits, is regarded by the people as burthensome and oppressive; has excited serious discontents, and, in some places, alarming symptoms of opposition. This mode has besides many particular inconveniences which contribute to make it inadequate to our wants, and ineligible, but as an auxiliary.

5thly. That from the best estimates of the annual expence of the war, and the annual revenues which these states are capable of affording, there is a large balance to be supplied by public credit. The resource of domestic loans is inconsiderable because there are properly speaking few monied men, and the few there are can employ their money more profitably otherwise; added to which, the instability of the currency and the deficiency of funds have impaired the public credit.

6thly. That the patience of the army from an almost uninterrupted series of complicated distress is now nearly exhausted; their discontents matured to an extremity, which has recently had very disagreeable consequences, and which demonstrates the absolute necessity of speedy relief, a relief not within the compass of our means. You are too well acquainted with all their sufferings, for want of cloathing, for want of provisions, for want of pay.

7thly. That the people being dissatisfied with the mode of supporting the war, there is cause to apprehend, evils actually felt in the prosecution, may weaken those sentiments which begun it; founded not on immediate sufferings, but in a speculative apprehension of future sufferings from the loss of their liberties. There is danger that a commercial and free people, little accustomed to heavy burthens, pressed by impositions of a new and odious kind, may not make a proper allowance for the necessity of the conjuncture, and may imagine, they have only exchanged one tyranny for another.

Dissatisfaction of the people

8thly. That from all the foregoing considerations result:

1st. The absolute necessity of an immediate, ample and efficacious succour of money; large enough to be a foundation for substantial arrangements of finance, to revive public credit and give vigor to future operations.

2dly. The vast importance of a decided effort of the allied arms on this Continent, the ensuing campaign, to effectuate once and for all the great objects of the alliance; the liberty and independence of these states.

Without the first, we may make a feeble and expiring effort the next campaign, in all probability the period to our opposition. With it, we should be in a condition to continue the war, as long as the obstinacy of the enemy might require. The first is essential to the last; both combined would bring the contest to a glorious issue, crown the obligations, which America already feels to the magnanimity and generosity of her ally, and perpetuate the union, by all the ties of gratitude and affection, as well as mutual advantage, which alone can render it solid and indissoluble.

Need for naval superiority

9thly. That next to a loan of money a constant naval superiority on these coasts is the object most interesting. This would instantly reduce the enemy to a difficult defensive, and by removing all prospect of extending their acquistions, would take away the motives for prosecuting the war. Indeed it is not to be conceived, how they could subsist a large force in this country, if we had the command of the seas, to interrupt the regular transmission of supplies from Europe. This superiority (with an aid of money) would enable us to convert the war into a vigorous offensive. I say nothing of the advantages to the trade of both nations, nor how infinitely it would facilitate our supplies. With respect to us, it seems to be one of *two* deciding points; and it appears too, to be the interest of our allies, abstracted from the immediate benefits to this country, to transfer the naval war to America. The number of ports friendly to them, hostile to the British; the materials for repairing their disabled ships; the extensive supplies towards the subsistence of their fleet, are circumstances which would give them a palpable advantage in the contest of these seas.

10thly. That an additional succour of troops would be extremely desirable. Besides a reinforcement of numbers, the excellence of the French troops, that perfect discipline and order in the corps already sent, which have so happily tended to improve the respect and confidence of the people for our allies; the conciliating disposition and the zeal for the service, which distinguish every rank, sure indications of lasting harmony, all these considerations evince the immense utility of an accession of force to the corps now here. Correspondent with these motives, the inclosed minutes of a conference between Their Excellencies The Count De Rochambeau, The Chevalier De Ternay and myself will inform you that an augmentation to fifteen thousand men was judged expedient for the next campaign; and it has been signified to me, that an application has been made to the Court of France to this effect. But if the sending so large a succour of troops, should necessarily diminish the pecuniary aid, which our allies may be disposed to grant, it were preferable to diminish the aid in men; for the same sum of money, which would transport from France and maintain here a body of troops with all the neccessary apparatus, being put into our hands to be employed by us would serve to give activity to a larger force within ourselves, and its influence would pervade the whole administration.

11thly. That no nation will have it more in its power to repay what it borrows than this. Our debts are hitherto small. The vast and valuable tracts of unlocated lands, the variety and fertility of climates and soils; the advantages of every kind, which we possess for commerce, insure to this country a rapid advancement in population and prosperity and a certainty, its independence being established, of redeeming in a short term of years, the comparitively inconsiderable debts it may have occasion to contract. *On repayment of debts*

That notwithstanding the difficulties under which we labour and the inquietudes prevailing among the people, there is still a fund of inclination and resource in the country equal to great and continued exertions, provided we have it in our power to stop the progress of disgust, by changing the present system and adopting another more consonant with the spirit of the nation, and more capable of activity and energy in public measures; of which a powerful succour of money must be the basis. The people are discontented, but it is with the feeble and oppressive mode of conducting the war, not with the war itself. They are not unwilling to contribute to its support, but they are unwilling to do it in a way that renders private property precarious, a necessary consequence of the fluctuation of the national currency, and of the inability of government to perform its engagements, oftentimes coercively made. A large majority are still firmly attached to the independence of these states, abhor a reunion with great Britain, and are affectionate to the alliance with France, but this disposition cannot supply the place of means customary and essential in war, nor can we rely on its duration amidst the perplexities, oppressions and misfortunes, that attend the want of them.

If the foregoing observations are of any use to you I shall be happy. I wish you a safe and pleasant voyage, the full accomplishment of your mission and a speedy return; being with sentiments of perfect friendship etc.

62

GENERAL ORDERS

Head Quarters, New Windsor
Tuesday, January 30, 1781

Parole ———. Countersigns ———.

The General returns his thanks to Major General Howe for the judicious measures he pursued and to the officers and men under his command for the good conduct and alacrity with which they executed his orders for suppressing the late Mutiny in a part of the New Jersey line. It gave him inexpressible pain to have been obliged to employ their arms upon such an occasion and convinced that they themselves felt all the Reluctance which former Affection to fellow Soldiers could inspire. He considers the patience with which they endured the fatigues of march through rough and mountainous roads rendered almost impassable by the depth of the Snow and the cheerfulness with which they performed every other part of their duty as the strongest proof of their Fidelity, attachment to the service, sense of subordination and abhorrence of the principles which actuated the Mutineers in so daring and atrocious a departure from what they owed to their Country, to their Officers to their Oaths and to themselves.

Mutiny of the New Jersey line

The General is deeply sensible of the sufferings of the army. He leaves no expedient unessayed to relieve them, and he is persuaded Congress and the several States are doing every thing in their power for the same purpose. But while we look to the public for the fullfilment of its engagements we should do it with proper allowance for the embarrassments of public affairs. We began a Contest for Liberty and Independence ill provided with the means for war, relying on our own Patriotism to supply the deficiency. We expected to encounter many wants and distresses and We should neither shrink from them when they happen nor fly in the face of the Law and Government to procure redress. There is no doubt the public will in the event do ample justice to men fighting and suffering in its defence. But it is our duty to bear present Evils with Fortitude looking forward to the period when our Country will have it more in its power to reward our services.

History is full of Examples of armies suffering with patience extremities of distress which exceed those we have suffered, and this in the cause of ambition and conquest not in that of the rights of humanity of their country, of their families of themselves; shall we who aspire to the distinction of a patriot army, who are contending for every thing precious in society against every thing hateful and degrading in slavery, shall We who call ourselves citizens discover less Constancy and Military virtue than the mercenary instruments of ambition? Those who in the present instance have stained the honor of the American soldiery and sullied the reputation of patient Virtue for which they have been so long eminent can only atone for their pusillanimous defection by a life devoted to a Zealous and examplary discharge of their duty. Persuaded that the greater part were influenced by the pernicious advice of a few who probably have been paid by the enemy to betray their Associates; The General is happy in the lenity shewn in the execution of only two of the most guilty after compelling the whole to an unconditional surrender, and he flatters himself no similar instance will hereafter disgrace our military History. It can only bring ruin on those who are mad enough to make the attempt; for lenity on any future occasion would be criminal and inadmissible.

The distinction of a patriot army

The General at the same time presents his thanks to Major General Parsons for the prudent and Military dispositions he made and to Lieutenant Colonel Hull and the officers and Men under his command for the good conduct address and Courage with which they executed the enterprize against a Corps of the enemy in West Chester, having destroyed their Barracks and a large quantity of Forage, burnt a bridge across Haerlem, under the protection of one of their redoubts, brought off fifty two prisoners and a number of Horses and Cattle with inconsiderable Loss except in the death of Ensign

Thompson of the 6th. Massachusett's regiment an active and enterprizing officer.

The General also thanks Colonel Hazen and his party for their Conduct and bravery in covering Lieutenant Colonel Hull's retreat and repelling the Enemy and the Colonels Scammell and Sherman and in general all the Officers and men of General Parsons's command for their good Conduct in supporting the advanced Corps.

63

TO JOHN SULLIVAN

New Windsor, February 4, 1781

Dear Sir:

Appointment of Ministers of War, Finance, and Foreign Affairs

Colo. Armand deliver'd me your favor of the 29th. Ulto. last Evening and I thank you for the sevl. communications contained in it. The measure adopted by Congress of appointing a Minister of War, Finance, and for Foreign Affairs I think a very wise one. To give efficacy to it, proper characters will, no doubt, be chosen to conduct the business of these departments. How far Colo. Hamilton, of whom you ask my opinion as a financier, has turned his thoughts to that particular study I am unable to ansr. because I never entered upon a discussion on this point with him; but this I can venture to advance from a thorough knowledge of him, that there are few men to be found, of his age, who has a more general knowledge than he possesses, and none whose Soul is more firmly engaged in the cause, or who exceeds him in probity and Sterling virtue.

I am clearly in Sentiment with you that our cause only became distressed, and apparently desperate from an imprr. management of it. and that errors once discovered are more than half amended; I have no doubt of our abilities or resources, but we must not slumber nor Sleep; they never will be drawn forth if we do; nor will violent exertions which subside with the occasion answer our purposes. It is a provident foresight; a proper arrangement of business, system and order in the execution that is to be productive of that oeconomy which is to defeat the efforts and hopes of Great Britain. And I am happy, thrice happy on private as well as public acct; to find that these are in train; for it will ease my shoulders of an immense burthen which the deranged and perplexed situation of our Affairs and the distresses of every department of the Army which concentred in the Comr. in chief had placed upon them.

I am not less pleased to hear that, Maryland has acceded to the confederation, and that Virginia has relinquished its claim to the Land West of the Ohio, which for fertility of Soil, pleasantness of clime and other Natu'l advantages is equal to any known tract of Country in the Universe of the same extent, taking the great Lakes for its Northern boundary.

I wish most devoutly a happy completion to your plan of finance (which you say is near finished); and much success to your scheme of borrowing Coined specie, and Plate. but in what manner do you propose to apply the latter? as a fund to redeem its value in Paper, to be emitted; or to coin it? If the latter it will add one more to a thousand other reasons wch. might be offered in proof of the necessity of vesting legislative or dictatorial powers in Congress to make Laws of general utility for the purposes of War &c. that they might prohibit under the pains, and penalty of death specie and Provisions going into the Enemy for Goods. The Traffic with New York is immense. Individual States will not make it felony, lest (among other reasons) it should not become general, and nothing short of it will ever check, much less stop a practice which at the same time that it serves to drain us of our Provisions and Specie removes the barrier between us and the enemy, corrupt the morals of our people by a lucrative traffic and by degrees weaken the opposition, affords a mean to obtain regular and perfect intelligence of everything among us while even in this respect we benefit nothing from a fear of discovery. Men of all descriptions are now indiscriminately engaging in it, Whig, Tory, Speculator. By its being practiced by those of the latter class, in a mannr. with impunity, Men who, two or three yrs. ago, would have shuddered at the idea of such connexions now pursue it with avidity and reconcile it to themselves (in which their profits plead powerfully) upon a principle of equality, with the Tory, who being actuated by principle, (favourable to us) and knowing that a forfeiture of the Goods to the Informer was all he had to dread and that this was to be eluded by an agreemt. to inform against each other, went into the measure witht. risk.

This is a degression, but the subject is of so serious a nature,

Business with the enemy

and so interesting to our well being as a Nation, that I never expect to see a happy termination of the War; nor great national concerns well conducted in Peace, till there is something more than a recommendatory power in Congress. It is not possible in time of War that business can be conducted well without it. The last words therefore of my letter and the first wish of my heart concur in favor of it. I am etc.

64

TO JOHN PARKE CUSTIS

New Windsor, February 28, 1781

Dear Custis:

If you will accept a hasty letter in return for yours of last month I will devote a few moments for this purpose, and confine myself to an interesting point, or two.

Suggestions to a young Senator

I do not suppose that so young a Senator, as you are, little versed in political disquisitions can yet have much influence in a populous assembly; composed of Gentn. of various talents and of different views. But it is in your power to be punctual in your attendance (and duty to the trust reposed in you exacts it of you), to hear dispassionately, and determine cooly all great questions. To be disgusted at the decision of questions because they are not consonant to your own ideas, and to withdraw ourselves from public assemblies, or to neglect our attendance at them upon suspicion that there is a party formed who are enimical to our Cause, and to the true interest of our Country is wrong because these things may originate in a difference of opinion; but supposing the fact is otherwise and that our suspicions are well founded it is the indispensable duty of every patriot to counteract them by the most steady and uniform opposition. This advice is the result of information, that you and others being dissatisfied at the proceedings of the Virginia Assembly and thinking your attendance of little avail (as their is a majority for measures which you and a minority conceive to be repugnant to the interest of your Country) are indifferent about the Assembly.

Need for a permanent military force

The next and I believe the last thing I shall have time to touch upon is our military establishment. and here if I thought the conviction of having a permanent force had not, ere this, flashed upon every mans mind I could write a volume in support of the utility of it; for no day, nor hour arrives unaccompd. with proof of some loss, some expence, or some misfortune consequent of the want of it. No operation of War offensive or defensive can be carried on, for any length of time without it. No funds are adequate to the supplies of a fluctuating army; tho' it may go under the denomination of a regular one; much less are they competent to the support of Militia. In a word, for it is, unnecessary to go into all the reasons the subject will admit of, we have brought a cause which might have been happily terminated years ago by the adoption of proper measures to the verge of ruin by temporary enlistments and a reliance on Militia. The sums expended in bounties, waste of Arms, consumption of Military Stores, Provisions, Camp Utensils &ca.; to say nothing of Cloathing which temporary Soldiers are always receiving, and always in want of, are too great for the resources of any Nation; and prove the falacy and danger of temporary expedients which are no more than Mushrooms and of as short duration, but leave a sting (that is a debt) which is continually revolving upon us behind them.

It must be a settled plan, founded on System, order and oeconomy that is to carry us triumphantly through the war. Supiness, and indifference to the distresses and cries of a sister State when danger is far of, and a general but momentary resort to arms when it comes to our doors, are equally impolitic and dangerous, and proves the necessity of a controuling *Necessity of* power in Congress to regulate and direct all matters of *general* *Congressional* concern; without it the great business of war never can be well *power* conducted, if it can be conducted at all; while the powers of congress are only recommendatory; while one State yields obedience, and another refuses it; while a third mutilates and adopts the measure in part only, and all vary in time and manner, it is scarcely possible our affairs should prosper, or that any thing but disappointmt. can follow the best concerted plans; the willing States are almost ruined by their exertions, distrust and jealousy succeeds to it; hence proceed neglect and ill-timed compliances (one state waiting to see what another will do), this thwarts all our measures after a heavy tho' ineffectual expence is incurred.

Does not these things shew then in the most striking point of view the indispensable necessity, the great and good policy of each State's sending its ablest and best men to Congress? Men who have a perfect understanding of the constitution of their Country, of its policy and Interests, and of vesting that body with competent powers. Our Independence depends upon it; our respectability and consequence in Europe depends upon it; our greatness as a Nation, hereafter, depends upon it. the fear of giving sufficient powers to Congress for the purposes I have mentioned is futile, without it, our Independence fails, and each Assembly under its present Constitution will be annihilated, and we must once more return to the Government of G: Britain, and be made to kiss the rod preparing for our correction. A nominal head, which at present is but another name for Congress, will no longer do. That honble body, after hearing the interests and views of the several States fairly discussed and explained by their respective representatives, must dictate, not merely recommend, and leave it to the States afterwards to do as they please, which, as I have observed before, is in many cases, to do nothing at all.

When I began this letter I did not expect to have filled more than one side of the sheet but I have run on insensibly. If you are at home, give my love to Nelly and the Children. if at Richmond present my complimts. to any enquiring friends. Sincerely and affectly. I am etc.

PS: The Public Gazettes will give you all the news and occurrances of this Quarter, our eyes are anxiously turned towards the South for events.

65

TO LUND WASHINGTON

New Windsor, April 30, 1781

Dear Lund:

The British at Washington's home

Your letter of the 18th. came to me by the last Post. I am very sorry to hear of your loss; I am a little sorry to hear of my own; but that which gives me most concern, is, that you should go on board the enemys Vessels, and furnish them with refreshments. It would have been a less painful circumstance to me, to have heard, that in consequence of your non-compliance with their request, they had burnt my House, and laid the

Plantation in ruins. You ought to have considered yourself as my representative, and should have reflected on the bad example of communicating with the enemy, and making a voluntary offer of refreshments to them with a view to prevent a conflagration.

It was not in your power, I acknowledge, to prevent them from sending a flag on shore, and you did right to meet it; but you should, in the same instant that the business of it was unfolded, have declared, explicitly, that it was improper for you to yield to the request; after which, if they had proceeded to help themselves, *by force*, you could but have submitted (and being unprovided for defence) this was to be prefered to a feeble opposition which only serves as a pretext to burn and destroy.

I am thoroughly perswaded that you acted from your best judgment; and believe, that your desire to preserve my property, and rescue the buildings from impending danger, were your governing motives. But to go on board their Vessels; carry them refreshments; commune with a parcel of plundering Scoundrels, and request a favor by asking the surrender of my Negroes, was exceedingly ill-judged, and 'tis to be feared, will be unhappy in its consequences, as it will be a precedent for others, and may become a subject of animadversion.

I have no doubt of the enemys intention to prosecute the plundering plan they have begun. And, unless a stop can be put to it by the arrival of a superior naval force, I have as little doubt of its ending in the loss of all my Negroes, and in the destruction of my Houses; but I am prepared for the event, under the prospect of which, if you could deposit, in safety, at some convenient distance from the Water, the most valuable and least bulky articles, it might be consistent with policy and prudence, and a mean of preserving them for use hereafter. Such, and so many things as are necessary for common, and present use must be retained and run their chance through the firy trial of this summer.

Mrs. Washington joins me in best and affectionate regard for you, Mrs. Washington and Milly Posey; and does most sincerely regret your loss. I do not know what Negros they may have left you; and as I have observed before, I do not know what number they will have left me by the time they have done; but this I am sure of, that you shall never want assistance, while it is in my power to afford it. I am etc.

66

TO THE PRESIDENT OF CONGRESS

Head Quarters near York, October 19, 1781

Sir:

Surrender at Yorktown

I have the Honor to inform Congress, that a Reduction of the British Army under the Command of Lord Cornwallis, is most happily effected. The unremitting Ardor which actuated every Officer and Soldier in the combined Army on this Occasion, has principally led to this Important Event, at an earlier period than my most sanguine Hopes had induced me to expect.

The singular Spirit of Emulation, which animated the whole Army from the first Commencement of our Operations, has filled my Mind with the highest pleasure and Satisfaction, and had given me the happiest presages of Success.

On the 17th instant, a Letter was received from Lord Cornwallis, proposing a Meeting of Commissioners, to consult on Terms for the Surrender of the Posts of York and Gloucester. This Letter (the first which had passed between us) opened a Correspondence, a Copy of which I do myself the Honor to inclose; that Correspondence was followed by the Definitive Capitulation, which was agreed to, and Signed on the 19th. Copy of which is also herewith transmitted, and which I hope, will meet the Approbation of Congress.

Gratitude for French cooperation

I should be wanting in the feelings of Gratitude, did I not mention on this Occasion, with the warmest Sense of Acknowledgements, the very chearfull and able Assistance, which I have received in the Course of our Operations, from his Excellency the Count de Rochambeau, and all his Officers of every Rank, in their respective Capacities. Nothing could equal this Zeal of our Allies, but the emulating Spirit of the American Officers, whose Ardor would not suffer their Exertions to be exceeded.

The very uncommon Degree of Duty and Fatigue which the Nature of the Service required from the Officers of Engineers and Artillery of both Armies, obliges me particularly to mention the Obligations I am under to the Commanding and other Officers of those Corps.

I wish it was in my Power to express to Congress, how much I feel myself indebted to The Count de Grasse and the Officers of the Fleet under his Command for the distinguished

Aid and Support which have been afforded by them; between whom, and the Army, the most happy Concurrence of Sentiments and Views have subsisted, and from whom, every possible Cooperation has been experienced, which the most harmonious Intercourse could afford.

Returns of the Prisoners, Military Stores, Ordnance Shipping and other Matters, I shall do myself the Honor to transmit to Congress as soon as they can be collected by the Heads of Departments, to which they belong.

Colo. Laurens and the Viscount de Noiailles, on the Part of the combined Army, were the Gentlemen who acted as Commissioners for formg and settg the Terms of Capitulation and Surrender herewith transmitted, to whom I am particularly obliged for their Readiness and Attention exhibited on the Occasion.

Colo. Tilghman, one of my Aids de Camp, will have the Honor to deliver these Dispatches to your Excellency; he will be able to inform you of every minute Circumstance which is not particularly mentioned in my Letter; his Merits, which are too well known to need my observations at this time, have gained my particular Attention, and could wish that they may be honored with the Notice of your Excellency and Congress.

Your Excellency and Congress will be pleased to accept my Congratulations on this happy Event, and believe me to be With the highest Respect etc.

PS: Tho' I am not possessed of the Particular Returns, yet I have reason to suppose that the Number of Prisoners will be between five and Six thousand, exclusive of Seamen and others.

67

GENERAL ORDERS

Head Quarters Before York,
Saturday, October 20, 1781

Parole Congress. Countersigns York, Gloucester.

Major General the Marqs. de la
Fayette

For the Day tomorrow Colonel Walter Stewart

Major Reid

Brigade Major Cox

Brigadier General Hazen's Brigade for duty tomorrow to parade at ten o'clock on their own parade.

As a great number of the axes delivered to working parties during the siege have not been returned the Commander in Chief directs that the Commandants of Corps, continental and militia, may have an immediate and strict search made in their respective commands and that all the axes found which have not been issued for their particular use may be returned to General Elbert Superintendant of the deposit of the trenches.

The Provost Guard consisting of one sub, two serjeants, Two Corporals and twenty privates to be relieved by divisions in rotation daily. The Marquis de la Fayettes will furnish it this day; Major General Lincolns division tomorrow, and the Baron's the next day.

AFTER ORDERS

Congratulations to French and American armies

The General congratulates the Army upon the glorious event of yesterday.

The generous proofs which his most Christian Majesty has given of his attachment to the Cause of America must force conviction on the minds of the most deceived among the Enemy: relatively to the decisive good consequences of the Alliance and inspire every citizen of these States with sentiments of the most unalterable Gratitude.

His Fleet the most numerous and powerful that ever appeared in these seas commanded by an Admiral whose Fortune and Talents ensure great Events.

An Army of the most admirable composition both in officers and men are the Pledges of his friendship to the United States and their cooperation has secured us the present signal success.

The General upon his occasion entreats his Excellency Count de Rochambeau to accept his most grateful acknowledgements for his Counsels and assistance at all times. He presents his warmest thanks to the Generals Baron Viomenil, Chevalier Chastellux, Marquis de St. Simond and Count Viomenil and to Brigadier General de Choissy (who had a separate command) for the illustrious manner in which they have advanced the interest of the common cause.

He requests that Count de Rochambeau will be pleased to communicate to the Army under his immediate command the high sense he entertains of the distinguished merits of the officers and soldiers of every corps and that he will present in his name to the regiments of Gattinois and Deuxponts the two Pieces of Brass Ordnance captured by them; as a testimony of their Gallantry in storming the Enemy's Redoubt on the Night of the 14th. instant, when officers and men so universally vied with each other in the exercise of every soldierly virtue.

The General's Thanks to each individual of Merit would comprehend the whole Army. But He thinks himself bound however by Affection Duty and Gratitude to express his obligations to Major Generals Lincoln, de La Fayette and Steuben for their dispositions in the Trenches.

To General Du Portail and Colonel Carney for the Vigor and Knowledge which were conspicuous in their Conduct of the Attacks, and to General Knox and Colonel D'Aberville for their great care and attention and fatigue in bringing forward the Artillery and Stores and for their judicious and spirited management of them in the Parallels.

He requests the Gentlemen above mentioned to communicate his thanks to the officers and soldiers of their respective commands.

Ingratitude which the General hopes never to be guilty of would be conspicuous in him was he to omit thanking in the warmest terms His Excellency Governor Nelson for the Aid he has derived from him and from the Militia under his Command to whose Activity Emulation and Courage much Applause is due; the Greatness of the Acquisition will be an ample Compensation for the Hardships and Hazards which they encountered with so much patriotism and firmness.

In order to diffuse the general Joy through every Breast the General orders that those men belonging to the Army who may now be in confinement shall be pardoned released and join their respective corps.

Divine Service is to be performed tomorrow in the several Brigades or Divisions.

The Commander in Chief earnestly recommends that the troops not on duty should universally attend with that seriousness of Deportment and gratitude of Heart which the recognition of such reiterated and astonishing interpositions of Providence demand of us.

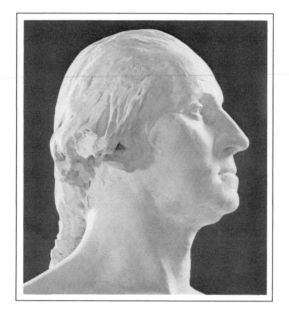

CHAPTER FIVE

WASHINGTON

Washington's Knowledge of Himself and His Army

1782 – 1783

VICTORY did not bring the end of Washington's troubles. The British remained in place on American soil for two years more. Thus, it was as difficult as it was prudent to maintain readiness in the face of general expectations of the end of conflict. Similarly, there was a very real possibility of the soldiers' countrymen simply dismissing them with thanks and forgetting the fact that they had served dutifully through great trials without compensation. Instead of elation, therefore, Washington's attitude in triumph was to preserve in his men and himself the sense of a "duty to bear present trials with fortitude." This feat proved no less valuable to his country than his skill in the field of battle.

Many charges have been made through the years that Washington's military officers plotted to make him king. A favorite villain in this set piece has always been Alexander Hamilton, but no solid evidence against him has ever surfaced. The most definite monarchical proposals that have been established were those of Colonel Lewis Nicola in a letter to Washington of May 22, 1782. Washington's immediate and stern rebuke to Nicola, often remembered since, is reprinted here. Nicola, an Irishman naturalized in America, was generally respected and had been shown a particular courtesy by Washington. He, who was himself Washington's age, was so stung by Washington's rebuke that he wrote three successive apologies in the days following.

Nicola settled into comfortable republican habits thereafter, but agitation continued to wrack an army which had been woefully mistreated by its countrymen. No one exerted himself more than Washington to obtain justice for the officers and soldiers.

In February and March of 1783, new threats arose which culminated in the famous "Newburgh Addresses" to Congress. The first of these respectfully expressed the army's dismay at the union's inefficacy. The second address, unofficial and anonymous, broached the threat of a refusal to disband without obtaining pay. This latter address led to the famous Newburgh meeting in which the officers, who were supposed to concert their plans to obtain redress, needed to be restrained by Washington. While his letters are replete with sentiments of obtaining justice for the men, the remarks he made in his Newburgh speech, reprinted here, show how well he achieved the end of restraining them. It was reported that, as Washington commenced reading his address, he fumbled in his pockets to pull out spectacles he had only recently acquired. In the delay he remarked, "I have grown not only gray, but almost blind in my country's service." Washington carried the meeting. His officers voted him unanimous thanks and rejected "with disdain, the infamous propositions" of the anonymous pamphlets.

68

TO COLONEL
LEWIS NICOLA

Newburgh, May 22, 1782

Sir:

With a mixture of great surprise and astonishment I have read with attention the Sentiments you have submitted to my perusal. Be assured Sir, no occurrence in the course of the War, has given me more painful sensations than your information of there being such ideas existing in the Army as you have expressed, and I must view with abhorrence, and reprehend with severity. For the present, the communicatn. of them will rest in my own bosom, unless some further agitation of the matter, shall make a disclosure necessary.

Astonishment at Nicola's offer to make Washington King

I am much at a loss to conceive what part of my conduct could have given encouragement to an address which to me seems big with the greatest mischiefs that can befall my Country. If I am not deceived in the knowledge of myself, you could not have found a person to whom your schemes are more disagreeable; at the same time in justice to my own feelings I must add, that no Man possesses a more sincere wish to see ample justice done to the Army than I do, and as far as my powers and influence, in a constitutional way extend, they shall be employed to the utmost of my abilities to effect it, should there be any occasion. Let me conjure you then, if you have any regard for your Country, concern for yourself or posterity, or respect for me, to banish these thoughts from your Mind, and never communicate, as from yourself, or any one else, a sentiment of the like Nature. With esteem I am.

69

TO THE SECRETARY AT WAR

Head Quarters, October 2, 1782

My dear Sir:

Painful as the task is to describe the dark side of our affairs, it some times becomes a matter of indispensable necessity. Without disguize or palliation, I will inform you candidly of the discontents which, at this moment, prevail universally throughout the Army.

Discontent in army

The Complaint of Evils which they suppose almost remediless are, the total want of Money, or the means of existing from One day to another, the heavy debts they have already incurred, the loss of Credit, the distress of their Families (i.e. such as are Maried) at home, and the prospect of Poverty and Misery before them. [It is vain Sir, to suppose that Military Men will acquiesce *contently* with bare rations, when those in the Civil walk of life (unacquainted with half the hardships they endure) are regularly paid the emoluments of Office; while the human Mind is influenced by the same passions, and have the same inclinations to endulge it cannt. be. A Military Man has the same turn to sociability as a person in Civil life; he conceives himself equally called upon to live up to his rank; and his pride is hurt when circumstans. restrain him. Only conceive then, the mortification they (even the Genl. Officers) must suffer when they cannot invite a French Officer, a visiting friend, or travelling acquaintance to a better repast than stinking Whiskey (and not always that) and a bit of Beef without Vegitables, will afford them.]

Complaints of officers

The Officers also complain of other hardships which they think might and ought to be remedied without delay, viz, the stopping Promotions where there have been vacancy's open for a long time, the withholding Commissions from those who are justly entitled to them and have Warrants or Certificates of their Appointments from the Executive of their States, and particularly the leaving the compensation for their services, in a loose equivocal state, without ascertaining their claims upon the public, or making provision for the future payment of them.

While I premise, that tho' no one that I have seen or heard of, appears opposed to the principle of reducing the Army as circumstances may require; Yet I cannot help fearing the Result of the measure in contemplation, under present circumstances when I see such a Number of Men goaded by a thousand stings of reflexion on the past, and of anticipation on the future, about to be turned into the World, soured by penury and what they call the ingratitude of the Public, involved in debts, without one farthing of Money to carry them home, after having spent the flower of their days [and many of them their patrimonies] in establishing the freedom and Independence of their Country, and suffered every thing human Nature is capable of enduring on this side of death; I repeat it, these irritable circumstances, without one thing to sooth their feelings, or frighten the gloomy prospects, I cannot avoid apprehending that a train of Evils will follow, of a very serious and distressing Nature. On the other hand could the Officers be placed in as good a situation as when they came into service, the contention, I am persuaded, would be not who should continue in the field, but who should retire to private life.

I wish not to heighten the shades of the picture, so far as the real life would justify me in doing, or I would give Anecdotes of patriotism and distress which have scarcely ever been paralleled, never surpassed in the history of Mankind; but you may rely upon it, the patience and long sufferance of this Army are almost exhausted, and that there never was so great a spirit of Discontent as at this instant: While in the field, I think it may be kept from breaking out into Acts of Outrage, but when we retire into Winter Quarters (unless the Storm is previously dissipated) I cannot be at ease, respecting the consequences. It is high time for a Peace.

Patience of army almost exhausted

To you, my dear Sir, I need not be more particular in describing my Anxiety and the grounds of it. You are too well acquainted, from your own service, with the real sufferings of the Army to require a longer detail; I will therefore only add that exclusive of the common hardships of a Military life, Our Troops have been, and still are obliged to perform more services, foreign to their proper duty, without gratuity or reward, than the Soldiers of any other Army; for example, the immense labours expended [in doing the duties of Artificers] in erecting Fortifications and Military Works; the fatigue of building themselves Barracks or Huts annually; And of cutting and transporting Wood for the use of all our Posts and Garrisons, without any expence whatever to the Public.

Of this Letter, (which from the tenor of it must be considered in some degree of a private nature) you may make such use as you shall think proper. Since the principal objects of it were, by displaying the Merits, the hardships, the disposition and critical state of the Army, to give information that might eventually be useful, and to convince you with what entire confidence and esteem. I am etc.

70

TO JOSEPH JONES

Newburgh, December 14, 1782

Dear Sir:

In the course of a few days Congress will, I expect, receive an Address from the Army on the subject of their grievances.

This Address, tho' couched in very respectful terms, is one of those things which tho' unpleasing is just now unavoidable; for I was very apprehensive once, that matters would have taken a more unfavourable turn, from the variety of discontents which prevailed at this time.

The temper of the Army is much soured, and has become more irritable than at any period since the commencement of the War. This consideration alone, prevented me (for every thing else seemed to be in a state of inactivity and almost tranquility) from requesting leave to spend this Winter in Virginia, that I might give some attention to my long neglected private concerns.

Alarming dissatisfaction of the army

The dissatisfactions of the Army had arisen to a great and alarming height, and combinations among the Officers to resign, at given periods in a body, were beginning to take place when by some address and management their resolutions have been converted into the form in which they will now appear before Congress. What that Honble. Body can, or will do in the matter, does not belong to me to determine; but policy, in my opinion, should dictate soothing measures; as it is an uncontrovertible fact, that no part of the community has undergone equal hardships, and borne them with the same patience and fortitude, that the Army has done.

Hitherto the Officers have stood between the lower order of the Soldiery and the public, and in more instances than one, at the hazard of their lives, have quelled very dangerous mutinies. But if their discontents should be suffered to rise equally high, I know not what the consequences may be.

The spirit of enthusiasm, which overcame every thing at first, is now done away; it is idle therefore to expect more from Military men, than from those discharging the Civil departments of Government. If both were to fare equally alike with respect to the emoluments of Office, I would answer for it that the Military character should not be the first to complain. But it is an invidious distinction, and one that will not stand the test of reason or policy, the one set should receive all, and the other no part (or that wch. is next to it) of their pay. In a word, the experiment is dangerous, and if it succeeded would only prove that, the one is actuated by more Zeal than the other, not that they have less occasion for their money. I am etc.

71

TO MAJOR GENERAL NATHANAEL GREENE

Newburgh, February 6, 1783

My dear Sir:

I have the pleasure to inform you that your Packet for Govr. Greene which came inclosed to me (in your private Letter of the 12th. of December) was forwarded in an hour after it came to my hands by a Gentleman returning to Rhode Island (Welcome Arnold Esquire); there can be no doubt therefore of its having got safe to the Governor.

It is with a pleasure which friendship only is susceptible of, I congratulate you on the glorious end you have put to hostilities in the Southern States; the honor and advantage of it, I hope, and trust, you will live long to enjoy. when this hemisphere will be equally free is yet in the womb of time to discover; a little while, however 'tis presumed, will disclose the determinations of the British Senate with respect to Peace or War as

Congratulations to General Greene on conclusion of hostilities

it seems to be agreed on all hands, that the present Premeir (especially if he should find the opposition powerful) intends to submit the decision of these matters to Parliament. The Speech, the Addresses, and Debates for which we are looking in every direction, will give a data from which the bright rays of the one, or the gloomy prospect of the other, may be discovered.

If Historiographers should be hardy enough to fill the page of History with the advantages that have been gained with unequal numbers (on the part of America) in the course of this contest, and attempt to relate the distressing circumstances under which they have been obtained, it is more than probable that Posterity will bestow on their labors the epithet and marks of fiction; for it will not be believed that such a force as Great Britain has employed for eight years in this Country could be baffled in their plan of Subjugating it by numbers infinitely less, composed of Men oftentimes half starved; always in Rags, without pay, and experiencing, at times, every species of distress which human nature is capable of undergoing.

I intended to have wrote you a long letter on sundry matters but Majr. Burnett popped in unexpectedly, at a time when I was preparing for the Celebration of the day; and was just going to a review of the Troops, previous to the Fue de joy. As he is impatient, from an apprehension of the Sleighing failing, and as he can give you the occurrences of this quarter more in detail than I have time to do, I will refer you to him. I cannot omit informing you however, that I let no oppertunity slip to enquire after your Son George at Princeton, and that it is with pleasure I hear he enjoys good health, and is a fine promising boy.

Mrs. Washington joins me in most Affectionate regards, and best wishes for Mrs Greene and yourself. With great truth and sincerity and every sentiment of friendship. I am etc.

72

GENERAL ORDERS

Head Quarters, Newburgh, Saturday, February 15, 1783

Parole Gottenburgh. Countersigns Hannover, Inverness.
For the day tomorrow Major Gibbs.
For duty the 2d. Jersey regiment.

The New building being so far finished as to admit the troops to attend public worship therein after tomorrow, it is directed that divine Service should be performed there every Sunday by the several Chaplains of the New Windsor Cantonment, in rotation and in order that the different brigades may have an oppertunity of attending at different hours in the same day (when ever the weather and other circumstances will permit which the Brigadiers and Commandants of brigades must determine) the General recommends that the Chaplains should in the first place consult the Commanding officers of their Brigades to know what hour will be most convenient and agreeable for attendance that they will then settle the duty among themselves and report the result to the Brigadiers and Commandants of Brigades who are desired to give notice in their orders and to afford every aid and assistance in their power for the promotion of that public Homage and adoration which are due to the supreme being, who has through his infinite goodness brought our public Calamities and dangers (in all humane probability) very near to a happy conclusion.

Completion of a chapel at headquarters

Instructions to chaplains

The General has been surprised to find in Winter Qrs. that the Chaplains have frequently been almost all absent, at the same time, under an idea their presence could not be of any utility at that season; he thinks it is proper, he should be allowed to judge of that matter himself, and therefore in future no furloughs will be granted to Chaplains except in consequence of permission from Head quarters, and any who may be now absent without such permission are to be ordered by the Commanding officers of their Brigades to join immediately, after which not more than one third of the whole number will be indulged with leave of absence at a time. They are requested to agree among themselves upon the time and length of their furloughs before any application shall be made to Head quarters on the subject.

The Commander in Chief also desires and expects the

Chaplains in addition to their public functions will in turn constantly attend the Hospitals and visit the sick, and while they are thus publickly and privately engaged in performing the sacred duties of their office they may depend upon his utmost encouragement and support on all occasions, and that they will be considered in a very respectable point of light by the whole Army.

73

TO GOVERNOR BENJAMIN HARRISON

Newburgh, March 4, 1783

Dear Sir:

Your favor of the 31st. of Jany. came to my hands the Post before last, and the Acct. from Genl. Lavalette by the last Post. Upon receipt of the latter, your Letter and Lavalettes acct. was sent to Sir Guy Carleton with a request to remit the money to Colo. Smith at Dobbs's Ferry; who is desired to forward it to the Chevr. de la Luzerne at Philadelphia.

Expectations of peace

You ask what my expectations of Peace are? I answer, I am scarcely able to form any ideas at all on the subject, since I have seen (what is called, for we have no authentic acct. of its being so) the King's Speech; and the variety of contradictory reports respecting the Negociations for it. The Enemy in New York are as impatient, and as much in the dark as we are on this occasion; not having received a Packet for more than two Months. Although I cannot give you a decided opinion, under present appearances, I will transcribe the answer I gave about the first of Jany. to a question similar to yours from a Gentleman of my acquaintance in Maryland; which as matters are yet undecided, or rather the decision, if any, unannounced, I see no occasion to depart from.

[The Fitzpatrick edition of Washington's writings omits a passage here.]

Impost Law

What, My dear Sir, could induce the State of Virginia to rescind its assent to the Impost Law? How are the numerous Creditors in Civil life and the Army to be paid if no regular and certain funds are established to discharge the Interest of Monies borrowed for these purposes? and what Tax can be more just or better calculated to this end than an Impost?

The alarm Bell, which has been rung with such tremendous sound by the State of Rhode Island, to shew the danger of entrusting Congress with the Money, is too selfish and feutile to require a serious answer. Congress are in fact, but the People; they return to them at certain short periods; are amenable at all times for their conduct, and subject to a recall at any moment. What interest therefore can a man have, under these circumstances distinct from his Constituents? Can it be supposed, that with design, he would form a junto, or pernicious Aristocracy that would operate agt. himself; in less than a month perhaps, after it was established? I cannot conceive it. But from the observations I have made in the course of this War (and my intercourse with the States in their United as well as seperate capacities has afforded ample oppertunities of judging) I am decided in my opinion, that if the powers of Congress are not enlarged, and made competent to all *general purposes*, that the Blood which has been spilt, the expence that has been incurred, and the distresses which have been felt, will avail us nothing; and that the band, already too weak, wch. holds us together, will soon be broken; when anarchy and confusion must prevail.

Discussion of Rhode Island complaints

Enlargement of powers of Congress

I shall make no apology for the freedom of these Sentiments. they proceed from an honest heart, altho' they may be the result of erroneous thinking. They will at least prove the sincerity of my friendship, as they are altogether undisguised. With the greatest esteem etc.

74

TO ALEXANDER HAMILTON

Newburgh, March 4, 1783

Dear Sir:

I have received your favor of February, and thank you for the information and observations it has conveyed to me. I shall always think myself obliged by a free communication of Sentiments, and have often thought (but suppose I thought wrong as it did not accord with the practice of Congress) that the public interest might be benefitted, if the Commander in Chief of the Army was let more into the political and pecuniary state of our Affairs than he is. Enterprises, and the adop-

Role of Commander-in-Chief

tion of Military and other arrangements that might be exceedingly proper in some circumstances would be altogether improper in others. It follows then by fair deduction, that where there is a want of information there must be chance medley; and a man may be upon the brink of a precipice before he is aware of his danger. when a little foreknowledge might enable him to avoid it. But this by the by.

Loan from Holland

The hint contained in your letter, and the knowledge I have derived from the public Gazettes respecting the non-payment of Taxes, contain all the information I have received of the danger that stares us in the face on Acct. of our funds, and so far was I from conceiving that our Finances was in so deplorable a state *at this time* that I had imbibed ideas from some source or another, that with the prospect of a loan from Holland, we should be able to rub along.

Political dissolution

To you, who have seen the danger, to which the Army has been exposed, to a political dissolution for want of subsistence, and the unhappy spirit of licentiousness which it imbibed by becoming in one or two instances its own proveditors, no observations are necessary to evince the fatal tendency of such a measure; but I shall give it as my opinion, that it would at this day be productive of Civil commotions and end in blood. Unhappy situation this! God forbid we should be involved in it.

The army, Congress, and the states

The predicament in which I stand as Citizen and Soldier, is as critical and delicate as can well be conceived. It has been the Subject of many contemplative hours. The sufferings of a complaining Army on one hand, and the inability of Congress and tardiness of the States on the other, are the forebodings of evil, and may be productive of events which are more to be deprecated than prevented; but I am not without hope, if there is such a disposition shewn as prudence and policy will dictate, to do justice, that your apprehensions, in case of Peace, are greater than there is cause for. In this however I may be mistaken, if those ideas, which you have been informed are propagated in the Army should be extensive; the source of which may be easily traced as the old leven, *it is said*, for I have no proof of it, is again, beginning to work, under a mask of the most perfect dissimulation, and apparent cordiality.

Be these things as they may, I shall pursue the same steady line of conduct which has governed me hitherto; fully convinced that the sensible, and discerning part of the Army, cannot be unacquainted (altho' I never took pains to inform them) of the Services I have rendered it on more occasions than one. This, and pursuing the suggestions of your Letter, which I am happy to find coincides with my practice for several Months past and which was the means of directing the business of the Army into the Channel it now is, leaves me under no *great* apprehension of its exceeding the bounds of reason and moderation, notwithstanding the prevailing sentiment in the Army is, that the prospect of compensation for past Services will terminate with the War.

The just claims of the Army ought, and it is to be hoped will, *Just claims of the* have their weight with every sensible Legislature in the Union, *army* if Congress point to their demands; shew (if the case is so) the reasonableness of them, and the impracticability of complying with them without their Aid. In any other point of view it would, in my opinion, be impolitic to introduce the Army on the Tapis; lest it should excite jealousy, and bring on its concomitants. The States cannot, surely, be so devoid of common sense, common honesty, and common policy as to refuse their aid on a full, clear, and candid representation of facts from Congress; more especially if these should be enforced by members of their own Body; who might demonstrate what the inevitable consequences of failure will lead to.

In my opinion it is a matter worthy of consideration how far an Adjournment of Congress for a few Months is advisable. The Delegates in that case, if they are in Unison themselves, respecting the great defects of their Constitution, may represent them fully and boldly to their Constituents. To me, who know nothing of the business which is before Congress, nor of the Arcanum, it appears that such a measure would tend to promote the public weal; for it is clearly my opinion, unless Congress have powers competent to all *general* purposes, that the distresses we have encountered, the expence we have incurred, and the blood we have spilt in the course of an Eight years war, will avail us nothing.

The contents of your letter is known only to myself, and your prudence will direct what should be done with this. With great esteem etc.

75

TO THE PRESIDENT OF CONGRESS

Head Quarters, March 12, 1783

Sir:

It is with inexpressible concern, I make the followg Report to your Excellency.

A general meeting of army officers

Two Days ago, anonymous papers were circulated in the Army, requesting a general meeting of the Officers on the next day. A Copy of one of these papers is inclosed, No. 1. About the same Time, another anonymous paper purporting to be an Address to the Officers of the Army, was handed about in a clandestine manner: a Copy of this is mark'd No 2. To prevent any precipitate and dangerous Resolutions from being taken at this perilous moment, while the passions were all inflamed; as soon as these things came to my knowledge, the next Morng. I issued the inclosed Order No. 3.* And in this situation the Matter now rests.

As all opinion must be suspended until after the meeting on Saturday, I have nothing further to add, except a Wish, that the measures I have taken to dissipate a Storm, which had gathered so suddenly and unexpectedly, may be acceptable to Congress: and to assure them, that in every vicisitude of Circumstances, still actuated with the greatest zeal in their Service, I shall continue my utmost Exertions to promote the

---

*Learning of an intended meeting by officers seeking to redress their grievances against Congress, Washington moved to avert the possibly evil consequences which could ensue. On March 11, 1783, his "General Orders" for the day (routine throughout the war) announced his awareness of the meeting (the Order No. 3 mentioned in the letter): "The Commander in Chief having heard that a general meeting of the officers of the Army was proposed . . . in an anonimous paper . . . conceives . . . his duty as well as the reputation and true interests of the Army require his disapprobation of such disorderly proceedings, at the same time he requests the General and Field officers . . . will assemble at 12 o'clock on Saturday next. . . . After mature deliberation they will devise what further measures ought to be adopted. . . ." Washington expressly disapproved of "such disorderly proceedings" and called the officers to assemble four days later to consider how best to pursue the just concerns of the army. He directed the "senior officer in Rank present" to report to him the result of the meeting, thereby implying an intention not to attend himself. When the time for the meeting arrived, however, Washington entered and delivered a dramatic appeal. The meeting was the occasion for the "Newburgh Address," reprinted below (number 77).

wellfare of my Country under the most lively Expectation, that Congress have the best Intentions of doing ample Justice to the Army, as soon as Circumstances will possibly admit. With the highest Respect etc.

PS: Since writing the foregoing another anonymous paper is put in Circulation, Copy of which is inclosed, No. 4.

76

TO JOSEPH JONES

Newburgh, March 12, 1783

Dear Sir:

I have received your letter of the 27th. Ulto., and thank you for the information and freedom of your communications.

My Official Letter to Congress of this date will inform you of what has happened in this Quarter, in addition to which, it may be necessary it should be known to you, and to such others as you may think proper, that the temper of the Army, tho very irritable on acct. of their long-protracted sufferings has been apparently extremely quiet while their business was depending before Congress untill four days past. In the mean time, it should seem reports have been propagated in Philadelphia that dangerous combinations were forming in the Army; and this at a time when there was not a syllable of the kind in agitation in Camp.

Information on the temper of the army

It also appears, that upon the arrival of a certain Gentleman from Phila. in Camp, whose name, I do not, at present, incline to mention such sentiments as these were immediately and industriously circulated. That it was universally expected the Army would not disband untill they had obtained Justice. That the public creditors looked up to them for redress of their Grievances, would afford them every aid, and even join them in the Field, if necessary. That some Members of Congress wished the Measure might take effect, in order to compel the Public, particularly the delinquent States, to do justice. With many other suggestions of a Similar Nature; from whence, and a variety of other considerations it is generally believ'd the Scheme was not only planned, but also digested and matured in Philadelphia; and that some people have been playing a double game; spreading at the Camp and in Philadelphia Reports and raising jealousies equally void of Foundation untill called into being by their vile Artifices; for as soon as the Minds of the Army were thought to be prepared for the transaction, anonymous invitations were circulated, requesting a general Meeting of the Officers next day; at the same instant many Copies of the Address to the Officers of the Army was scattered in every State line of it.

So soon as I obtained knowledge of these things, I issued the order of the 11th. (transmitted to Congress;) in order to rescue the foot, that stood wavering on the precipice of despair, from taking those steps which would have lead to the abyss of misery while the passions were inflamed, and the mind trimblingly alive with the recollection of past sufferings, and their present feelings. I did this upon the principle that it is easier to divert from a wrong to a right path, than it is to recall the hasty and fatal steps which have been already taken.

Potential dangers of officers' meeting

It is commonly supposed, if the Officers had met agreeable to the anonymous Summons, resolutions might have been formed, the consequences of which may be more easily conceived than expressed. Now, they will have leisure to view the matter more calmly and seriously. It is to be hoped they will be induced to adopt more rational measures, and wait a while longer for the settlemts. of their Accts.; the postponing of which gives more uneasiness in the Army than any other thing. there is not a man in it, who will not acknowledge that Congress have not the means of payment; but why not say they, one and all, liquidate the Accts. and certifie our dues? Are we to be disbanded and sent home without this? Are we, afterwards, to make individual applications for such settlements at Philadelphia, or any Auditing Office in our respective states; to be shifted perhaps from one board to another; dancing attendence at all, and finally perhaps be postponed till we loose the substance in pursuit of the shadow. While they are agitated by these considerations there are not wanting insiduous characters who tell them, it is neither the wish nor the intention of the public to settle your accounts; but to delay this business under one pretext or another till Peace wch. we are upon the eve of, and a seperation of the Army takes place when it is well known a generl settlement never can be effected and that individual loss, in this instance, becomes a public gain.

However derogatory these ideas are with the dignity, honor,

and justice of government yet in a matter so interesting to the Army, and at the same time so easy to be effected by the Public, as that of liquidating the Accounts, is delayed without any apparent, or obvious necessity, they will have their place in a mind that is soured and irritated. Let me entreat you therefore my good Sir to push this matter to an issue, and if there are Delegates among you, who are really opposed to doing justice to the Army, scruple not to tell them, if matters should come to extremity, that they must be answerable for all the ineffable horrors which may be occasioned thereby. I am etc.

Justice to the army

77

SPEECH TO THE OFFICERS OF THE ARMY

Head Quarters, Newburgh, March 15, 1783

Gentlemen:

By an anonymous summons, an attempt has been made to convene you together; how inconsistent with the rules of propriety! how unmilitary! and how subversive of all order and discipline, let the good sense of the Army decide.

Opposition to the call for a general meeting

In the moment of this Summons, another anonymous production was sent into circulation, addressed more to the feelings and passions, than to the reason and judgment of the Army. The author of the piece, is entitled to much credit for the goodness of his Pen and I could wish he had as much credit for the rectitude of his Heart, for, as Men see thro' different Optics, and are induced by the reflecting faculties of the Mind, to use different means, to attain the same end, the Author of the Address, should have had more charity, than to mark for Suspicion, the Man who should recommend moderation and longer forbearance, or, in other words, who should not think as he thinks, and act as he advises. But he had another plan in view, in which candor and liberality of Sentiment, regard to justice, and love of Country, have no part; and he was right, to insinuate the darkest suspicion, to effect the blackest designs.

That the Address is drawn with great Art, and is designed to answer the most insidious purposes. That it is calculated to impress the Mind, with an idea of premeditated injustice in the Sovereign power of the United States, and rouse all those resentments which must unavoidably flow from such a belief. That the secret mover of this Scheme (whoever he may be) intended to take advantage of the passions, while they were warmed by the recollection of past distresses, without giving time for cool, deliberative thinking, and that composure of Mind which is so necessary to give dignity and stability to measures is rendered too obvious, by the mode of conducting the business, to need other proof than a reference to the proceeding.

Thus much, Gentlemen, I have thought it incumbent on me to observe to you, to shew upon what principles I opposed the irregular and hasty meeting which was proposed to have been held on Tuesday last: and not because I wanted a disposition to give you every oppertunity consistent with your own honor, and the dignity of the Army, to make known your grievances. If my conduct heretofore, has not evinced to you, that I have been a faithful friend to the Army, my declaration of it at this time wd. be equally unavailing and improper. But as I was among the first who embarked in the cause of our common Country. As I have never left your side one moment, but when called from you on public duty. As I have been the constant companion and witness of your Distresses, and not among the last to feel, and acknowledge your Merits. As I have ever considered my own Military reputation as inseperably connected with that of the Army. As my Heart has ever expanded with joy, when I have heard its praises, and my indignation has arisen, when the mouth of detraction has been opened against it, it can *scarcely be supposed*, at this late stage of the War, that I am indifferent to its interests. But, how are they to be promoted? The way is plain, says the anonymous Addresser. If War continues, remove into the unsettled Country; there establish yourselves, and leave an ungrateful Country to defend itself. But who are they to defend? Our Wives, our Children, our Farms, and other property which we leave behind us. Or, in this state of hostile seperation, are we to take the two first (the latter cannot be removed), to perish in a Wilderness, with hunger, cold and nakedness? If Peace takes place, never sheath your Swords, Says he, untill you have obtained full and ample justice; this dreadful alternative, of either deserting our Country in the extremest hour of her distress, or turning our Arms against it, (which is the apparent object, unless Congress can be compelled into instant compliance) has something so shocking in it, that humanity revolts at the idea. My God! what can this writer have in view, by recommending such measures? Can he be a friend to the Army? Can he be a friend to this Country? Rather, is he not an insidious Foe? Some Emissary, perhaps, from New York, plotting the ruin of both, by sowing the seeds of discord and seperation between the Civil and Military powers of the Continent? And what a Compliment does he pay to our Understandings, when he recommends measures in either alternative, impracticable in their Nature?

But here, Gentlemen, I will drop the curtain, because it wd. be as imprudent in me to assign my reasons for this opinion, as it would be insulting to your conception, to suppose you stood in need of them. A moment's reflection will convince every dispassionate Mind of the physical impossibility of carrying either proposal into execution.

There might, Gentlemen, be an impropriety in my taking notice, in this Address to you, of an anonymous production, but the manner in which that performance has been introduced to the Army, the effect it was intended to have, together with some other circumstances, will amply justify my observations on the tendency of that Writing. With respect to the advice given by the Author, to suspect the Man, who shall recommend moderate measures and longer forbearance, I spurn it, as every Man, who regards that liberty, and reveres that justice for which we contend, undoubtedly must; for if Men are to be precluded from offering their Sentiments on a matter, which may involve the most serious and alarming consequences, that can invite the consideration of Mankind, reason is of no use to us; the freedom of Speech may be taken away, and, dumb and silent we may be led, like sheep, to the Slaughter.

I cannot, in justice to my own belief, and what I have great reason to conceive is the intention of Congress, conclude this Address, without giving it as my decided opinion, that that Honble Body, entertain exalted sentiments of the Services of the Army; and, from a full conviction of its merits and sufferings, will do it compleat justice. That their endeavors, to discover and establish funds for this purpose, have been unwearied, and will not cease, till they have succeeded, I have not a doubt. But, like all other large Bodies, where there is a variety of different interests to reconcile, their deliberations are slow.

Why then should we distrust them? and, in consequence of
that distrust, adopt measures, which may cast a shade over that
glory which, has been so justly acquired; and tarnish the reputation of an Army which is celebrated thro' all Europe, for its
fortitude and Patriotism? and for what is this done? to bring
the object we seek nearer? No! most certainly, in my opinion, it
will cast it at a greater distance.

For myself (and I take no merit in giving the assurance,
being induced to it from principles of gratitude, veracity and
justice), a grateful sence of the confidence you have ever
placed in me, a recollection of the chearful assistance, and
prompt obedience I have experienced from you, under every
vicissitude of fortune, and the sincere affection I feel for an
Army, I have so long had the honor to Command, will oblige
me to declare, in this public and solemn manner, that, in the
attainment of compleat justice for all your toils and dangers,
and in the gratification of every wish, so far as may be done
consistently with the great duty I owe my Country, and those
powers we are bound to respect, you may freely command my
Services to the utmost of my abilities.

While I give you these assurances, and pledge myself in the
most unequivocal manner, to exert whatever ability I am possessed of, in your favor, let me entreat you, Gentlemen, on
your part, not to take any measures, which, viewed in the calm
light of reason, will lessen the dignity, and sully the glory you
have hitherto maintained; let me request you to rely on the
plighted faith of your Country, and place a full confidence in
the purity of the intentions of Congress; that, previous to your
dissolution as an Army they will cause all your Accts. to be
fairly liquidated, as directed in their resolutions, which were
published to you two days ago, and that they will adopt the
most effectual measures in their power, to render ample justice to you, for your faithful and meritorious Services. And let
me conjure you, in the name of our common Country, as you
value your own sacred honor, as you respect the rights of humanity, and as you regard the Military and National character
of America, to express your utmost horror and detestation of
the Man who wishes, under any specious pretences, to overturn the liberties of our Country, and who wickedly attempts
to open the flood Gates of Civil discord, and deluge our rising
Empire in Blood. By thus determining, and thus acting, you
will pursue the plain and direct road to the attainment of your

wishes. You will defeat the insidious designs of our Enemies, who are compelled to resort from open force to secret Artifice. You will give one more distinguished proof of unexampled patriotism and patient virtue, rising superior to the pressure of the most complicated sufferings; And you will, by the dignity of your Conduct, afford occasion for Posterity to say, when speaking of the glorious example you have exhibited to Mankind, "had this day been wanting, the World had never seen the last stage of perfection to which human nature is capable of attaining."

78

TO THE PRESIDENT OF CONGRESS

Head Quarters, Newburgh, March 18, 1783

Sir:

The result of the proceedings of the grand Convention of the Officers, which I have the honor of enclosing to your Excellency for the inspection of Congress, will, I flatter myself, be considered as the last glorious proof of Patriotism which could have been given by Men who aspired to the distinction of a patriot Army; and will not only confirm their claim to the justice, but will increase their title to the gratitude of their Country.

A patriot army

Having seen the proceedings on the part of the Army terminate with perfect unanimity, and in a manner entirely consonant to my wishes; being impressed with the liveliest sentiments of affection for those who have so long, so patiently and so chearfully suffered and fought under my immediate direction; having from motives of justice, duty and gratitude, spontaneously offered myself as an advocate for their rights; and having been requested to write to your Excellency earnestly entreating the most speedy decision of Congress upon the subjects of the late Address from the Army to that Honble. Body, it now only remains for me to perform the task I have assumed, and to intercede in their behalf, as I now do, that the Sovereign Power will be pleased to verify the predictions I have pronounced of, and the confidence the Army have reposed in the justice of their Country.

Pleading the
army's cause

And here, I humbly conceive it is altogether unnecessary, (while I am pleading the cause of an Army which have done and suffered more than any other Army ever did in the defence of the rights and liberties of human nature,) to expatiate on their *Claims* to the most ample compensation for their meritorious Services, because they are perfectly known to the whole World, and because, (altho' the topics are inexhaustible) enough has already been said on the subject.

To prove these assertions, to evince that my sentiments have ever been uniform, and to shew what my ideas of the rewards in question have always been, I appeal to the Archives of Congress, and call on those sacred deposits to witness for me. And in order that my observations and Arguments in favor of a future adequate provision for the Officers of the Army may be brought to remembrance again, and considered in a single point of view without giving Congress the trouble of having recourse to their files, I will beg leave to transmit herewith an Extract from a representation made by me to a Committee of Congress so long ago as the 29th of January 1778. and also the transcript, of a Letter to the President of Congress, dated near Passaic Falls Octr. 11th. 1780 That in the critical and perilous moment when the last mentioned communication was made, there was the utmost danger of a dissolution of the Army would have taken place unless measures similar to those recommended had been adopted, will not admit a doubt. That the adoption of the Resolution granting half-pay for life has been attended with all the happy consequences I had foretold, so far as respected the good of the service; let the astonishing contrast between the State of the Army at this instant, and at the former period determine. And that the establishment of funds, and security of the payment of all the just demands of the Army will be the most certain means of preserving the National faith and future tranquillity of this extensive Continent, is my decided opinion.

By the preceeding remarks it will readily be imagined that instead of retracting and reprehending (from farther experience and reflection) the mode of compensation so strenuously urged in the Inclosures, I am more and more confirmed in the Sentiment, and if in the wrong suffer me to please myself with the grateful delusion.

For if, besides the simple payment of their Wages, a farther compensation is not due to the sufferings and sacrifices of the

Officers, then have I been mistaken indeed. If the whole Army have not merited whatever a grateful people can bestow, then have I been beguiled by prejudice, and built opinion on the basis of error. If this Country should not in the Event perform every thing which has been requested in the late Memorial to Congress, then will my belief become vain, and the hope that has been excited void of foundation. And "if, (as has been suggested for the purpose of inflaming their passions) the Officers of the Army are to be the only sufferers by this revolution; if retiring from the Field, they are to grow old in poverty wretchedness and contempt. If they are to wade thro' the vile mire of dependency and owe the miserable remnant of that life to charity, which has hitherto been spent in honor," then shall I have learned what ingratitude is, then shall I have realized a tale, which will imbitter every moment of my future life. But I am under no such apprehensions, a Country rescued by their Arms from impending ruin, will never leave unpaid the debt of gratitude.

Should any intemperate or improper warmth have mingled itself amongst the foregoing observations, I must entreat your Excellency and Congress it may be attributed to the effusion of an honest zeal in the best of Causes, and that my peculiar situation may be my apology. And I hope I need not, on this momentuous occasion make any new protestations of personal disinterestedness, having ever renounced for myself the idea of pecuniary reward. The consciousness of having attempted faithfully to discharge my duty, and the approbation of my Country will be a sufficient reccompense for my Services. I have the honor etc.

CHAPTER SIX

"PATRIAE PATER"

Washington's Knowledge of His Countrymen

1783

WASHINGTON's famous "Circular Letter" constitutes the centerpiece of his statesmanship, carrying directly to his countrymen a coherent vision of the unfinished work which lay before them in the aftermath of peace. His view of that work was that "we have a national character to establish."

TO JOSEPH JONES

Newburgh, March 18, 1783

The storm which seemed to be gathering with unfavourable prognostics, when I wrote to you last, is dispersed; and we are again in a state of tranquility. But do not, My dear Sir, suffer this appearance of tranquility to relax your endeavors to bring the requests of the Army to an issue. Believe me, the Officers are too much pressed by their present wants, and rendered too sore by the recollection of their past sufferings to be touched much longer upon the string of forbearance, in matters wherein they can see no cause for delay. Nor would I have further reliance placed on any influence of mine to dispel other Clouds if any should arise, from the causes of the last.

Requests of the army for pay

By my official Letter to Congress, and the Papers inclosed in it, you will have a full view of my assurances to, and the expectations of the Army; and I perswade myself that the well wishers to both, and of their Country, will exert themselves to the utmost to irradicate the Seeds of distrust, and give every satisfaction that justice requires, and the means which Congress possess, will enable them to do.

In a former letter I observed to you, that a liquidation of Accts, in order that the Ballances might be ascertained, is the great object of the Army; and certainly nothing can be more reasonable. To have these Ballances discharged at this, or in any short time; however desirable, they know is impracticable, and do not expect it; altho', in the meantime, they must labour under the pressure of those sufferings; which is felt more sensibly by a comparison of circumstances.

The situation of these Gentlemen merit the attention of every thinking and grateful mind. As Officers, they have been *obliged* to dress, and appear in character, to effect which, they have been *obliged* to anticipate their pay, or participate their Estates. By the first, debts have been contracted. By the latter, their patrimony is injured. To disband Men therefore under these circumstances, before their Accts. are liquidated, and the Ballances ascertained, would be, to sett open the doors of the Gaols, and then to shut them upon Seven Years faithful and painful Services. Under any circumstances which the nature of the case will admit, they must be considerable Sufferers; because necessity will compel them to part with their certificates for whatever they will fetch; to avoid the evil I have mentioned above: and how much this will place them in the hands of unfeeling, avaricious speculators a recurrence to past experience will sufficiently prove.

It may be said by those who have no disposition to compensate the Services of the Army, that the Officers have too much penetration to place dependance (in any alternative) upon the strength of their own Arm; I will readily concede to these Gentlemen that no good could result from such an attempt; but I hope they will be equally candid in acknowledging, that much mischief may flow from it, and that nothing is too extravagant to expect from men, who conceive they are ungratefully, and unjustly dealt by; especially too if they can suppose that characters are not wanting, to foment every passion which leads to discord, and that there are—but—time shall reveal the rest.

Possible response of army to unfair treatment

Let it suffice, that the very attempt, wd. imply a want of justice, and fix an indelible stain upon our national character; as the whole world, as well from the enemies publication (without any intention to serve us) as our own, must be strongly impressed with the sufferings of this army from hunger, cold and nakedness in allmost every stage of the War. Very sincerely etc.

80

TO MAJOR GENERAL NATHANAEL GREENE

Head Quarters, March 31, 1783

Dear Sir:

I have the pleasure to inclose to you a letter from the Marquis de la Fayette, which came under cover to me, by the Packet Triumph, dispatched by the Marquis and the Count de Estaing from Cadiz to Phila.

All the Accounts which this Vessel has bro't, of a Conclusion of a General Peace, you will receive before this can reach you.

You will give the highest Credit to my Sincerity, when I beg you to accept my warmest Congratulations on this glorious and happy Event, an Event which crowns all our Labors and will sweeten the Toils which we have experienced in the Course of Eight Years distressing War. The Army here, universally participate in the general Joy which this Event has diffused, and, from this Consideration, together with the late Resolutions of Congress, for the Commutation of the Half pay, and for a Liquidation of all their Accounts, their Minds are filled with the highest Satisfaction. I am sure you will join with me in this additional occasion of joy.

It remains only for the States to be Wise, and to establish their Independence on that Basis of inviolable efficacious Union, and firm Confederation, which may prevent their being made the Sport of European Policy; may Heaven give them Wisdom to adopt the Measures still necessary for this important Purpose. I have the honor etc.

81

TO ALEXANDER HAMILTON

Newburgh, March 31, 1783

Dear Sir:

I have duly received your favors of the 17th. and 24th. Ulto. I rejoice most exceedingly that there is an end to our Warfare, and that such a field is opening to our view as will, with wisdom to direct the cultivation of it, make us a great, a respectable, and happy People; but it must be improved by other means than State politics, and unreasonable jealousies and prejudices; or (it requires not the second sight to see that) we shall be instruments in the hands of our Enemies, and those European powers who may be jealous of our greatness in Union to dissolve the confederation; but to attain this, altho' the way seems extremely plain, is not so easy.

Union of the states

My wish to see the Union of these States established upon liberal and permanent principles, and inclination to contribute my mite in pointing out the defects of the present Constitution, are equally great. All my private letters have teemed with these Sentiments, and whenever this topic has been the subject of conversation, I have endeavoured to diffuse and enforce them; but how far any further essay by me might be productive of the wished for end, or appear to arrogate more than belongs to me, depends so much upon popular opinions, and the timper and dispositions of People, that it is not easy to decide. I shall be obliged to you however for the thoughts which you have promised me on this Subject, and as soon as you can make it convenient.

Need to reform the Confederation

No Man in the United States is, or can be more deeply impressed with the necessity of a reform in our present Confederation than myself. No Man perhaps has felt the bad effects of it more sensibly; for the defects thereof, and want of Powers in Congress, may justly be ascribed the prolongation of the War, and consequently the expenses occasioned by it. More than half the perplexities I have experienced in the course of my command, and almost the whole of the difficulties and distress of the Army, have their origin here; but still the prejudices of some, the designs of others, and the mere Machinery of the Majority, makes address and management necessary to give weight to opinions which are to Combat the doctrines of those different classes of Men, in the field of Politics.

I would have been more full on this subject but the bearer (in the Clothing department) is waiting. I wish you may understand what I have written. I am etc.

PS: The inclosed extract of a Letter to Mr. Livingston, I give you in confidence; I submit it to your consideration, fully perswaded that you do not want inclination to gratify the Marquis's Wishes as far as is consistent with our National honor.

82

TO THEODORICK BLAND

Newburgh, April 4, 1783

Dear Sir:

On Sunday last the Baron de Steuben handed me your obliging favor of the 22d. Ulto. permit me to offer you my unfeigned thanks for the clear and candid opinions which you
have given me of European politics. your reasonings upon the
conduct of the different Powers at War would have appeard
conclusive had not the happy event which has been since announced to us, and on which I most sincerely congratulate
you, proved how well they were founded. Peace has given rest
to speculative opinions respecting the time, and terms of it.
The first has come as soon as we could well have expected
under the disadvantages we have labd. and the latter, is abundantly satisfactory. It is now the bounden duty of every one, to
make the blessing thereof as diffusive as possible.

Nothing would so effectually bring this to pass as the removal of those local prejudices which intrude upon and embarrass
that great line of policy which alone can make us a free, happy,
and powerful people. Unless our Union can be fixed upon
such a basis as to accomplish these ends certain I am we have
toiled, bled and spent our treasure to very little purpose.

We have now a National character to establish; and it is of
the utmost importance to stamp favourable impressions upon
it; let justice then be one of its characteristics, and gratitude
another. Public Creditors of every denomination will be comprehended in the first. The Army in a particular manner will
have a claim to the latter; to say that no distinction can be
made between the claims of public Creditors, is to declare that
there is no difference in circumstances or, that the Services of
all Men are equally alike. This Army, is of near 8 years standing; 6 of which they have spent in the field, without any other
shelter from the inclemency of the Seasons than Tents, or
such Houses as they could build for themselves, without expence to the public. they have encountered hunger, cold and
Nakedness. they have fought many Battles, and bled freely.
they have lived without pay, and in consequence of it, Officers
as well as Men have been obliged to subsist upon their Rations:
they have often, very often been reduced to the necessity of

*Establishment of
a national
character*

*Payment of
national
obligations*

eating Salt Porke or Beef not for a day or a week only but months together without Vegetables of any kind or money to buy them; or a cloth to wipe on. Many of them, to do better and to dress as Officers, have contracted heavy Debts, or spent their Patrimonies; the first see the doors of Gaols opening to receive them whilst those of the latter are shut against them. Is there no discrimination then, no extra exertion to be made in favor of men under these Circumstances in the hour of their Military dissolution? Or, if no worse comes of it, are they to be turned adrift soured and discontented, complaining of the ingratitude of their Country, and under the irritation of these passions to become fit subjects for unfavourable impressions and unhappy dissentions? For permit me to add, tho' every Man in the Army feels the distress of his situatn it is not every one that reasons to the cause of it.

I would not, from the observatns. here made, be understood to mean that Congress should (because I know they cannot, nor does the Army expect it) pay the full arrearages due to them till Continental or State funds are established for the purpose; they would, from what I can learn, go home contented; nay *thankful*, to receive what I have mentioned in a more public Letter of this date, and in the manner there expressed. and surely this may be effected with proper exertions; or what possibility was there of keeping the Army together if the war had continued when the victualling, clothing and other exps were to have. . . . Another thing Sir, (as I mean to be frank and free in my communications on this subject) I will not conceal from you, it is dissimilarities in the payments of Men in Civil and Military life. the first receive every thing, the other get nothing, but bare subsistence. They ask what this is owing to? and reasons have been assigned, which say they, amount to this: that Men in Civil life have stronger passions and better pretensions to indulge them or less virtue and regd. for their Country than us; otherwise, as we are all contending for the same prize and equally interested in the attainment of it, why is not the burthen borne equally.

These, and other comparisons, which are unnecessary to enumerate, give a keener edge to their feelings, and contribute not a little to sour their tempers.

As it is the first wish of my Soul to see the war happily and speedily terminated, and those who are now in Arms return to Citizenship with good dispositions, I think it a duty which I owe to candor and to friendship to point you to such things as will have a tendency to harmony and to bring them to pass. With great esteem etc.

83

TO MARQUIS DE LAFAYETTE

Head Qrs., Newburgh, April 5, 1783

My dear Marqs.:

It is easier for you to conceive than for me to express the sensibility of my Heart at the communications in your letter of the 5th. of Feby. from Cadiz. It is to these communications we are indebted for the only acct. yet recd of a general Pacification. My mind upon the receipt of this news was instantly assailed by a thousand ideas, all of them contending for pre-eminence, but believe me my dear friend none could supplant, or ever will eradicate that gratitude, which has arisen from a lively sense of the conduct of your Nation: from my obligations to many illustrious characters of it, among whom (I do not mean to flatter, when) I place you at the head of them; And from my admiration of the Virtues of your August Sovereign; who at the same time that he stands confessed the Father of his own people, and defender of American rights has given the most exalted example of moderation in treating with his Enemies.

The report of a general peace

We now stand an Independent People, and have yet to learn political Tactics. We are placed among the Nations of the Earth, and have a character to establish; but how we shall acquit ourselves time must discover; the probability, at least I fear it is, that local, or state Politics will interfere too much with that more liberal and extensive plan of government which wisdom and foresight, freed from the mist of prejudice, would dictate; and that we shall be guilty of many blunders in treading this boundless theatre before we shall have arrived at any perfection in this Art. In a word that the experience which is purchased at the price of difficulties and distress, will alone convince us that the honor, power, and true Interest of this Country must be measured by a Continental scale; and that every departure therefrom weakens the Union, and may ultimately break the band, which holds us together. To avert

A constitution of sufficient powers

these evils, to form a Constitution that will give consistency, stability and dignity to the Union; and sufficient powers to the great Council of the Nation for general purposes is a duty which is incumbent upon every Man who wishes well to his Country, and will meet with my aid as far as it can be rendered in the private walks of life; for hence forward my Mind shall be unbent; and I will endeavor to glide down the stream of life 'till I come to that abyss, from whence no traveller is permitted to return.

The Armament wch. was preparing at Cadiz, and in which you were to have acted a distinguished part would have carried such conviction with it, that it is not to be wondered at, that Great Britain should have been impressed with the force of such reasoning. To this cause I am perswaded, the Peace is to be ascribed. Your going to Madrid from thence, instead of coming immediately to this Country, is another instance My Dear Marquis of your Zeal for the American Cause; and lays a fresh claim to the gratitude of her Sons, who will, at all times, receive you with open Arms; but as no Official dispatches are yet received, either at Phila. or New York of the completion of the treaty, nor any measures taken for the reduction of the Army, my detention therewith is quite uncertain; to say then (at this time) where I may be at the epoch for your intended visit to this Continent is too vague even for conjecture; but nothing can be more true than that the pleasure with which I shall receive you, will be equal to your wishes. I shall be better able to determine *then* than now, on the practicability of accompanying you to France. A Country to which I shall ever feel a Warm Affection; and if I do not pay it that tribute of respect which is to be derived from a visit it may be ascribed with more justice to any other cause, than a want of inclination; or the pleasure of going there under the auspices of your friendship.

Lack of congressional action on army relief

I have already observed, that the determinations of Congress, if they have come to any, respecting the Army, is yet unknown to me; but as you wish to be informed of *every thing* that concerns it, I do, for your satisfaction, transmit authentic documents of some very interesting occurrences, which have happened within the last Six Months. but I ought first to have premised, that from accumulated sufferings, and little or no prospect of relief, the discontents of the Officers last Fall put on the threatning appearance of a total resignation, till the business was diverted into the channel which produced the Address and Petition to Congress which stands first on the file herewith inclosed. I shall make no comment on these proceedings; to one as well acquainted with the sufferings of the American Army as you are, it is unnecessary, it will be sufficient to observe, that the more Virtue and forbearance of it is tried, the more resplendent it appears. My hopes, that the military exit of this valuable class of the community will exhibit such a proof of Amor patriæ as will do them honor in the page of history.

These papers with my last letter (which was intended to go by Colo. Gouvion, containing extensive details of Military Plans) will convey to you every information I can give, in the present uncertainty, worthy of attention. If you should get sleepy, and tired of reading them, recollect, for my exculpation, that it is in compliance with your request, I have run into such prolixity.

I made a proper use of the confidential part of your Letter of the 5th. of Feby.

The scheme, my dear Marqs. which you propose as a precedent, to encourage the emancipation of the black people of this Country from that state of Bondage in wch. they are held, is a striking evidence of the benevolence of your Heart. I shall be happy to join you in so laudable a work; but will defer going into a detail of the business, 'till I have the pleasure of seeing you.

Black emancipation

Lord Stirling is no more; he died at Albany in Jany. last, very much regretted. Colo. Barber was snatched from us about the same time; in a way equally unexpected, sudden and distressing; leaving many friends to bemoan his fate.

Tilghman is on the point of Matrimony with a namesake and Couzin; Sister to Mrs. Carroll of Baltimore. It only remains for me now, My dear Marqs., to make a tender of my respectful Compliments in which Mrs. Washington unites, to Madame La Fayette; and to wish you, her, and your little offspring, all the happiness this life can afford. I will extend my Compliments to the Gentlemen, with whom I have the honor of an Acquaintance, in your circle. I need not add how happy I shall be to see you in America, and more particularly at Mount Vernon; or with what truth and warmth of Affection I am etc.

84

GENERAL ORDERS

Parole Kenalal. Countersigns Litchfield, Montreal.

For the day tomorrow Brigadier Genl. Stark.
Brigd. Qr. Mr. York Brigade.

The Jersey regiment gives the Guards and the Jersey battalion the fatigues tomorrow.

Cessation of hostilities

The Commander in Chief orders the Cessation of Hostilities between the United States of America and the King of Great Britain to be publickly proclaimed tomorrow at 12 o'clock at the Newbuilding, and that the Proclamation which will be communicated herewith, be read tomorrow evening at the head of every regiment and corps of the army. After which the

Orders to chaplains

Chaplains with the several Brigades will render thanks to almighty God for all his mercies, particularly for his over ruling the wrath of man to his own glory, and causing the rage of war to cease amongst the nations.

Although the proclamation before alluded to, extends only to the prohibition of hostilities and not to the annunciation of a general peace, yet it must afford the most rational and sincere satisfaction to every benevolent mind, as it puts a period to a long and doubtful contest, stops the effusion of human blood, opens the prospect to a more splendid scene, and like another morning star, promises the approach of a brighter day than hath hitherto illuminated the Western Hemisphere; on such a happy day, a day which is the harbinger of Peace, a day which compleats the eighth year of the war, it would be ingratitude not to rejoice! it would be insensibility not to participate in the general felicity.

The Commander in Chief far from endeavouring to stifle the feelings of Joy in his own bosom, offers his most cordial Congratulations on the occasion to all the Officers of every denomination, to all the Troops of the United States in General, and in particular to those gallant and persevering men who had resolved to defend the rights of their invaded country so long as the war should continue. For these are the men who ought to be considered as the pride and boast of the American Army; And, who crowned with well earned laurels, may soon withdraw from the field of Glory, to the more tranquil walks of civil life.

While the General recollects the almost infinite variety of Scenes thro which we have passed, with a mixture of pleasure, astonishment, and gratitude; While he contemplates the prospects before us with rapture; he can not help wishing that all the brave men (of whatever condition they may be) who have shared in the toils and dangers of effecting this glorious revolution, of rescuing Millions from the hand of oppression, and of laying the foundation of a great Empire, might be impressed with a proper idea of the dignifyed part they have been called to act (under the Smiles of providence) on the stage of human affairs; for, happy, thrice happy shall they be pronounced hereafter, who have contributed any thing, who have performed the meanest office in erecting this steuendous *fabrick* of *Freedom* and *Empire* on the broad basis of Indipendency; who have assisted in protecting the rights of humane nature and establishing an Asylum for the poor and oppressed of all nations and religions. The glorius task for which we first fleu to Arms being thus accomplished, the liberties of our Country being fully acknowledged, and firmly secured by the smiles of heaven, on the purity of our cause, and the honest exertions of a feeble people (determined to be free) against a powerful Nation (disposed to oppress them) and the Character of those who have persevered, through every extremity of hardship; suffering and danger being immortalized by the illustrious appellation of the *patriot Army*: Nothing now remains but for the actors of this mighty Scene to preserve a perfect, unvarying, consistency of character through the very last act; to close the Drama with applause; and to retire from the Military Theatre with the same approbation of Angells and men which have crowned all their former vertuous Actions. For this purpose no disorder or licentiousness must be tolerated, every considerate and well disposed soldier must remember it will be absolutely necessary to wait with patience untill peace shall be declared or Congress shall be enabled to take proper measures for the security of the public stores &ca.; as soon as these Arrangements shall be made the General is confident there will be no delay in discharging with every mark of distinction and honor all the men enlisted for the war who will then have faithfully performed their engagements

The accomplishments of independence

Remaining tasks of army

with the public. The General has already interested himself in their behalf; and he thinks he need not repeat the assurances of his disposition to be useful to them on the present, and every other proper occasion. In the mean time he is determined that no Military neglects or excesses shall go unpunished while he retains the command of the Army.

The Adjutant General will have such working parties detailed to assist in making the preperations for a general rejoycing as the Chief Engineer with the Army shall call for, and the Quarter Master Genl. will also furnish such materials as he may want.

The Quarter Master General will without delay procure such a number of Discharges to be printed as will be sufficient for all the men enlisted for the War; he will please to apply to Head Quarters for the form.

An extra ration of liquor to be issued to *every* man tomorrow, to drink Perpetual Peace, Independence and Happiness to the United States of America.

85

TO LIEUTENANT COLONEL TENCH TILGHMAN

Newburgh, April 24, 1783

Dear Sir:

I received with much pleasure the kind congratulations contained in your letter of the 25th. Ulto. from Philadelphia, on the honorable termination of the War. No Man, indeed, can relish the approaching Peace with more heart felt, and grateful satisfaction than myself. A Mind always upon the stretch, and tortured with a diversity of perplexing circumstances, needed a respite; and I anticipate the pleasure of a little repose and retirement. It has been happy for me, always to have Gentlemen about me willing to share my troubles, and help me out of difficulties. To none of these can I ascribe a greater share of merit than to you.

I can scarce form an idea at this moment, when I shall be able to leave this place. The distresses of the Army for want of Money; the embarrassments of Congress, and the conseqt. de-

The approach of peace

lays, and disappointments on all sides, encompass me with difficulties; and produce, every day, some fresh source for uneasiness. But as I now see the Port opening to which I have been steering, I shall persevere till I have gained admittence. I will then leave the States to improve their present constitution, so as to make that Peace and Independencey for which we have fought and obtained, a blessing to Millions yet unborn; but to do this, liberallity must supply the place of prejudice, and *unreasonable* jealousies must yield to that confidence, which *ought* to be placed in the sovereign Power of these States. In a word the Constitution of Congress must be competent to the *general purposes of Government*; and of such a nature as to bind us together. Otherwise, we may well be compared to a rope of Sand, and shall as easily be broken and in a short time become the sport of European politics, altho' we might have no *great* inclination to jar among ourselves.

A rope of sand

From the intimation in your Letter, and what I have heard from others I presume this letter will find you in the State of Wedlock. On this happy event I pray you, and your Lady, to accept of my best wishes, and sincerest congratulations; in which Mrs. Washington joins hers most cordially. With the most Affectionate esteem, etc.

86

CIRCULAR TO THE STATES

Head Quarters, Newburgh, June 14, 1783

Sir:

The great object for which I had the honor to hold an appointment in the Service of my Country, being accomplished, I am now preparing to resign it into the hands of Congress, and to return to that domestic retirement, which, it is well known, I left with the greatest reluctance, a Retirement, for which I have never ceased to sigh through a long and painful absence, and in which (remote from the noise and trouble of the World) I meditate to pass the remainder of life in a state of undisturbed repose; But before I carry this resolution into effect, I think it a duty incumbent on me, to make this my last official communication, to congratulate you on the glorious events

Domestic retirement

Congratulations

which Heaven has been pleased to produce in our favor, to offer my sentiments respecting some important subjects, which appear to me, to be intimately connected with the tranquility of the United States, to take my leave of your Excellency as a public Character, and to give my final blessing to that Country, in whose service I have spent the prime of my life, for whose sake I have consumed so many anxious days and watchfull nights, and whose happiness being extremely dear to me, will always constitute no inconsiderable part of my own.

Impressed with the liveliest sensibility on this pleasing occasion, I will claim the indulgence of dilating the more copiously on the subjects of our mutual felicitation. When we consider the magnitude of the prize we contended for, the doubtful nature of the contest, and the favorable manner in which it has terminated, we shall find the greatest possible reason for gratitude and rejoicing; this is a theme that will afford infinite delight to every benevolent and liberal mind, whether the event in contemplation, be considered as the source of present enjoyment or the parent of future happiness; and we shall have equal occasion to felicitate ourselves on the lot which Providence has assigned us, whether we view it in a natural, a political or moral point of light.

America's future   The Citizens of America, placed in the most enviable condition, as the sole Lords and Proprietors of a vast Tract of Continent, comprehending all the various soils and climates of the World, and abounding with all the necessaries and conveniencies of life, are now by the late satisfactory pacification, acknowledged to be possessed of absolute freedom and Independency; They are, from this period, to be considered as the Actors on a most conspicuous Theatre, which seems to be peculiarly designated by Providence for the display of human greatness and felicity; Here, they are not only surrounded with every thing which can contribute to the completion of private and domestic enjoyment, but Heaven has crowned all its other blessings, by giving a fairer oppertunity for political happiness, than any other Nation has ever been favored with. Nothing can illustrate these observations more forcibly, than a recollection of the happy conjuncture of times and circumstances, under which our Republic assumed its rank among the Nations; The foundation of our empire was not laid in the gloomy age of Ignorance and Superstition, but at an Epocha when the rights of mankind were better understood and more

Foundation of American empire

clearly defined, than at any former period; the researches of the human mind, after social happiness, have been carried to a great extent; the Treasures of knowledge, acquired through a long succession of years, by the labours of Philosophers, Sages and Legislatures, are laid open for our use, and their collected wisdom may be happily applied in the Establishment of our forms of Government; the free cultivation of Letters, the unbounded extension of Commerce, the progressive refinement of Manners, the growing liberality of sentiment, and above all, the pure and benign light of Revelation, have had a meliorating influence on mankind and increased the blessings of Society. At this auspicious period, the United States came into existence as a Nation, and if their Citizens should not be completely free and happy, the fault will be intirely their own.

Such is our situation, and such are our prospects: but notwithstanding the cup of blessing is thus reached out to us, notwithstanding happiness is ours, if we have a disposition to seize the occasion and make it our own; yet, it appears to me there is an option still left to the United States of America, that it is in their choice, and depends upon their conduct, whether they will be respectable and prosperous, or contemptible and miserable as a Nation; This is the time of their political probation; this is the moment when the eyes of the whole World are turned upon them; this is the moment to establish or ruin their national Character forever; this is the favorable moment to give such a tone to our Federal Government, as will enable it to answer the ends of its institution; or this may be the ill-fated moment for relaxing the powers of the Union, annihilating the cement of the Confederation, and exposing us to become the sport of European politics, which may play one State against another to prevent their growing importance, and to serve their own interested purposes. For, according to the system of Policy the States shall adopt at this moment, they will stand or fall; and by their confirmation or lapse, it is yet to be decided, whether the Revolution must ultimately be considered as a blessing or a curse: a blessing or a curse, not to the present age alone, for with our fate will the destiny of unborn Millions be involved.

A time of political probation

With this conviction of the importance of the present Crisis, silence in me would be a crime; I will therefore speak to your Excellency, the language of freedom and of sincerity, without disguise; I am aware, however, that those who differ from me

The importance of the present crisis

in political sentiment, may perhaps remark, I am stepping out of the proper line of my duty, and they may possibly ascribe to arrogance or ostentation, what I know is alone the result of the purest intention, but the rectitude of my own heart, which disdains such unworthy motives, the part I have hitherto acted in life, the determination I have formed, of not taking any share in public business hereafter, the ardent desire I feel, and shall continue to manifest, of quietly enjoying in private life, after all the toils of War, the benefits of a wise and liberal Government, will, I flatter myself, sooner or later convince my Countrymen, that I could have no sinister views in delivering with so little reserve, the opinions contained in this Address.

Four pillars of independence

There are four things, which I humbly conceive, are essential to the well being, I may even venture to say, to the existence of the United States as an Independent Power:

1st. An indissoluble Union of the States under one Federal Head.

2dly. A Sacred regard to Public Justice.

3dly. The adoption of a proper Peace Establishment, and

4thly. The prevalence of that pacific and friendly Disposition, among the People of the United States, which will induce them to forget their local prejudices and policies, to make those mutual concessions which are requisite to the general prosperity, and in some instances, to sacrifice their individual advantages to the interest of the Community.

These are the Pillars on which the glorious Fabrick of our Independency and National Character must be supported; Liberty is the Basis, and whoever would dare to sap the foundation, or overturn the Structure, under whatever specious pretexts he may attempt it, will merit the bitterest execration, and the severest punishment which can be inflicted by his injured Country.

On the three first Articles I will make a few observations, leaving the last to the good sense and serious consideration of those immediately concerned.

Principles of union

Under the first head, altho' it may not be necessary or proper for me in this place to enter into a particular disquisition of the principles of the Union, and to take up the great question which has been frequently agitated, whether it be expedient and requisite for the States to delegate a larger proportion of Power to Congress, or not, Yet it will be a part of my duty, and that of every true Patriot, to assert without reserve, and to insist upon the following positions, That unless the States will suffer Congress to exercise those prerogatives, they are undoubtedly invested with by the Constitution, every thing must very rapidly tend to Anarchy and confusion, That it is indispensable to the happiness of the individual States, that there should be lodged somewhere, a Supreme Power to regulate and govern the general concerns of the Confederated Republic, without which the Union cannot be of long duration. That there must be a faithfull and pointed compliance on the part of every State, with the late proposals and demands of Congress, or the most fatal consequences will ensue, That whatever measures have a tendency to dissolve the Union, or contribute to violate or lessen the Sovereign Authority, ought to be considered as hostile to the Liberty and Independency of America, and the Authors of them treated accordingly, and lastly, that unless we can be enabled by the concurrence of the States, to participate of the fruits of the Revolution, and enjoy the essential benefits of Civil Society, under a form of Government so free and uncorrupted, so happily guarded against the danger of oppression, as has been devised and adopted by the Articles of Confederation, it will be a subject of regret, that so much blood and treasure have been lavished for no purpose, that so many sufferings have been encountered without a compensation, and that so many sacrifices have been made in vain. Many other considerations might here be adduced to prove, that without an entire conformity to the Spirit of the Union, we cannot exist as an Independent Power; it will be sufficient for my purpose to mention but one or two which seem to me of the greatest importance. It is only in our united Character as an Empire, that our Independence is acknowledged, that our power can be regarded, or our Credit supported among Foreign Nations. The Treaties of the European Powers with the United States of America, will have no validity on a dissolution of the Union. We shall be left nearly in a state of Nature, or we may find by our own unhappy experience, that there is a natural and necessary progression, from the extreme of anarchy to the extreme of Tyranny; and that arbitrary power is most easily established on the ruins of Liberty abused to licentiousness.

Union and liberty

As to the second Article, which respects the performance of Public Justice, Congress have, in their late Address to the United States, almost exhausted the subject, they have ex-

Justice to public creditors

plained their Ideas so fully, and have enforced the obligations the States are under, to render compleat justice to all the Public Creditors, with so much dignity and energy, that in my opinion, no real friend to the honor and Independency of America, can hesitate a single moment respecting the propriety of complying with the just and honorable measures proposed; if their Arguments do not produce conviction, I know of nothing that will have greater influence; especially when we recollect that the System referred to, being the result of the collected Wisdom of the Continent, must be esteemed, if not perfect, certainly the least objectionable of any that could be devised; and that if it shall not be carried into immediate execution, a National Bankruptcy, with all its deplorable consequences will take place, before any different Plan can possibly be proposed and adopted, So pressing are the present circumstances! and such is the alternative now offered to the States!

The ability of the Country to discharge the debts which have been incurred in its defence, is not to be doubted; an inclination, I flatter myself, will not be wanting; the path of our duty is plain before us; honesty will be found on every experiment, to be the best and only true policy; let us then as a Nation be just; let us fulfil the public Contracts, which Congress had undoubtedly a right to make for the purpose of carrying on the War, with the same good faith we suppose ourselves bound to perform our private engagements; in the mean time, let an attention to the chearfull performance of their proper business, as Individuals, and as members of Society, be earnestly inculcated on the Citizens of America, then will they strengthen the hands of Government, and be happy under its protection: every one will reap the fruit of his labours; every one will enjoy his own acquisitions without molestation and without danger.

Taxation   In this state of absolute freedom and perfect security, who will grudge to yield a very little of his property to support the common interest of Society, and insure the protection of Government? Who does not remember, the frequent declarations, at the commencement of the War, that we should be compleatly satisfied, if at the expence of one half, we could defend the remainder of our possessions? Where is the Man to be found, who wishes to remain indebted, for the defence of his own person and property, to the exertions, the bravery, and the blood of others, without making one generous effort to repay the debt of honor and of gratitude? In what part of the Continent shall we find any Man, or body of Men, who would not blush to stand up and propose measures, purposely calculated to rob the Soldier of his Stipend, and the Public Creditor of his due? and were it possible that such a flagrant instance of Injustice could ever happen, would it not excite the general indignation, and tend to bring down, upon the Authors of such measures, the aggravated vengeance of Heaven?

If after all, a spirit of disunion or a temper of obstinacy and perverseness, should manifest itself in any of the States, if such an ungracious disposition should attempt to frustrate all the happy effects that might be expected to flow from the Union, if there should be a refusal to comply with the requisitions for Funds to discharge the annual interest of the public debts, and if that refusal should revive again all those jealousies and produce all those evils, which are now happily removed, Congress, who have in all their Transaction shewn a great degree of magnanimity and justice, will stand justified in the sight of God and Man, and the State alone which puts itself in opposition to the aggregate Wisdom of the Continent, and follows such mistaken and pernicious Councils, will be responsible for all the consequences. *. . . and disunion*

For my own part, conscious of having acted while a Servant of the Public, in a manner I conceived best suited to promote the real interests of my Country; having in consequence of my fixed belief in some measure pledged myself to the Army, that their Country would finally do them compleat and ample Justice; and not wishing to conceal any instance of my official conduct from the eyes of the World, I have thought proper to transmit to your Excellency the inclosed collection of Papers, relative to the half pay and commutation granted by Congress to the Officers of the Army; From these communications, my decided sentiment will be clearly comprehended, together with the conclusive reasons which induced me, at an early period, to recommend the adoption of the measure, in the most earnest and serious manner. As the proceedings of Congress, the Army, and myself are open to all, and contain in my opinion, sufficient information to remove the prejudices and errors which may have been entertained by any; I think it unnecessary to say any thing more, than just to observe, that the Resolutions of Congress, now alluded to, are undoubtedly as absolutely binding upon the United States, as the most sol- *Military pay* emn Acts of Confederation or Legislation. As to the Idea, which I am informed has in some instances prevailed, that the half pay and commutation are to be regarded merely in the odious light of a Pension, it ought to be exploded forever; that Provision, should be viewed as it really was, a reasonable compensation offered by Congress, at a time when they had nothing else to give, to the Officers of the Army, for services then to be performed. It was the only means to prevent a total dereliction of the Service, It was a part of their hire, I may be allowed to say, it was the price of their blood and of your Independency, it is therefore more than a common debt, it is a debt of honour, it can never be considered as a Pension or gratuity, nor be cancelled until it is fairly discharged.

Compensation for soldiers

With regard to a distinction between Officers and Soldiers, it is sufficient that the uniform experience of every Nation of the World, combined with our own, proves the utility and propriety of the discrimination. Rewards in proportion to the aids the public derives from them, are unquestionably due to all its Servants; In some Lines, the Soldiers have perhaps generally had as ample a compensation for their Services, by the large Bounties which have been paid to them, as their Officers will receive in the proposed Commutation, in others, if besides the donation of Lands, the payment of Arrearages of Cloathing and Wages (in which Articles all the component parts of the Army must be put upon the same footing) we take into the estimate, the Bounties many of the Soldiers have received and the gratuity of one Year's full pay, which is promised to all, possibly their situation (every circumstance being duly considered) will not be deemed less eligible than that of the Officers. Should a farther reward, however, be judged equitable, I will venture to assert, no one will enjoy greater satisfaction than myself, on seeing an exemption from Taxes for a limited time, (which has been petitioned for in some instances) or any other adequate immunity or compensation, granted to the brave de-

Commutation of half pay

fenders of their Country's Cause; but neither the adoption or rejection of this proposition will in any manner affect, much less militate against, the Act of Congress, by which they have offered five years full pay, in lieu of the half pay for life, which had been before promised to the Officers of the Army.

Before I conclude the subject of public justice, I cannot omit to mention the obligations this Country is under, to that meritorious Class of veteran Non-commissioned Officers and Privates, who have been discharged for inability, in consequence of the Resolution of Congress of the 23d of April 1782, on an annual pension for life, their peculiar sufferings, their singular merits and claims to that provision need only be known, to interest all the feelings of humanity in their behalf: nothing but a punctual payment of their annual allowance can rescue them from the most complicated misery, and nothing could be a more melancholy and distressing sight, than to behold those who have shed their blood or lost their limbs in the service of their Country, without a shelter, without a friend, and without the means of obtaining any of the necessaries or comforts of Life; compelled to beg their daily bread from door to door! Suffer me to recommend those of this discription, belonging to your State, to the warmest patronage of your Excellency and your Legislature.

Disabled soldiers

It is necessary to say but a few words on the third topic which was proposed, and which regards particularly the defence of the Republic, As there can be little doubt but Congress will recommend a proper Peace Establishment for the United States, in which a due attention will be paid to the importance of placing the Militia of the Union upon a regular and respectable footing; If this should be the case, I would beg leave to urge the great advantage of it in the strongest terms. The Militia of this Country must be considered as the Palladium of our security, and the first effectual resort in case of hostility; It is essential therefore, that the same system should pervade the whole; that the formation and discipline of the Militia of the Continent should be absolutely uniform, and that the same species of Arms, Accoutrements and Military Apparatus, should be introduced in every part of the United States; No one, who has not learned it from experience, can conceive the difficulty, expence, and confusion which result from a contrary system, or the vague Arrangements which have hitherto prevailed.

A regular and uniform militia

If in treating of political points, a greater latitude than usual has been taken in the course of this Address, the importance of the Crisis, and the magnitude of the objects in discussion, must be my apology: It is, however, neither my wish or expectation, that the preceding observations should claim any regard, except so far as they shall appear to be dictated by a good intention, consonant to the immutable rules of Justice; calculated to produce a liberal system of policy, and founded on whatever experience may have been acquired by a long and close attention to public business. Here I might speak with the more confidence from my actual observations, and, if it would not swell this Letter (already too prolix) beyond the bounds I had prescribed myself: I could demonstrate to every mind open to conviction, that in less time and with much less expence than has been incurred, the War might have been brought to the same happy conclusion, if the resourses of the Continent could have been properly drawn forth, that the distresses and disappointments which have very often occurred, have in too many instances, resulted more from a want of energy, in the Continental Government, than a deficiency of means in the particular States. That the inefficiency of measures, arising from the want of an adequate authority in the Supreme Power, from a partial compliance with the Requisitions of Congress in some of the States, and from a failure of punctuality in others, while it tended to damp the zeal of those which were more willing to exert themselves; served also to accumulate the expences of the War, and to frustrate the best concerted Plans, and that the discouragement occasioned by the complicated difficulties and embarrassments, in which our affairs were, by this means involved, would have long ago produced the dissolution of any Army, less patient, less virtuous and less persevering, than that which I have had the honor to command. But while I mention these things, which are notorious facts, as the defects of our Federal Government, particularly in the prosecution of a War, I beg it may be understood, that as I have ever taken a pleasure in gratefully acknowledging the assistance and support I have derived from every Class of Citizens, so shall I always be happy to do justice to the unparalleled exertion of the individual States, on many interesting occasions.

Defects of federal government in time of war

I have thus freely disclosed what I wished to make known, before I surrendered up my Public trust to those who committed it to me, the task is now accomplished, I now bid adieu to your Excellency as the Chief Magistrate of your State, at the same time I bid a last farewell to the cares of Office, and all the imployments of public life.

It remains then to be my final and only request, that your Excellency will communicate these sentiments to your Legislature at their next meeting, and that they may be considered as the Legacy of One, who has ardently wished, on all occasions, to be useful to his Country, and who, even in the shade of Retirement, will not fail to implore the divine benediction upon it.

I now make it my earnest prayer, that God would have you, *An earnest prayer* and the State over which you preside, in his holy protection, that he would incline the hearts of the Citizens to cultivate a spirit of subordination and obedience to Government, to entertain a brotherly affection and love for one another, for their fellow Citizens of the United States at large, and particularly for their brethren who have served in the Field, and finally, that he would most graciously be pleased to dispose us all, to do Justice, to love mercy, and to demean ourselves with that Charity, humility and pacific temper of mind, which were the Characteristicks of the Divine Author of our blessed Religion, and without an humble imitation of whose example in these things, we can never hope to be a happy Nation.

CHAPTER SEVEN

PARTING WITH HIS OFFICERS

The General Resigns

1783

ASHINGTON'S transition from statesman-general to citizen-statesman occurred almost effortlessly. The year-and-a half delay between the decisive victory at Yorktown and the achievement of a negotiated peace, with the subsequent six-month delay before all appropriate ratifications had been secured, imposed upon Washington the difficult and sensitive task of maintaining an army prepared to fight at the same time as the new nation was yearning to reacquire the arts of peace. Washington acted on the principle that the army had to remain standing less for the sake of defending the nation's freedom than for the sake of symbolizing a free nation until the rest of the world officially concurred in its existence. From the beginning of this time, however, he inculcated lessons—which were acts of legislation in all but form—of political responsibility which entailed strengthening the federal union, honoring its debts, and regulating its orderly expansion through the continent. His wide correspondence bears universally the mark of his solicitude—above all for the just compensation of the soldiers.

Washington disbanded the army just as soon as the peace was made final. In taking leave of his troops he no less exhorted them to a republican faith than he had exhorted their fellow-republicans, the civilians, to keep faith with the troops. The war struggle had lasted eight years, and its effect on Washington and the soldiers is best symbolized, perhaps, in Washington's farewell, when he assembled his officers at a tavern and endeavored to utter some parting sentiments. In the end, he could do no more than reach out in a warm embrace of the portly General Henry Knox, who stood nearest. The other officers filed by, silence pervading, and reenacted the ritual.

The effect of the war on the country is perhaps best symbolized by Washington's resignation of his commission immediately after disbanding the army. At that point the United States stood as a free republic under no armed domination. Congress then sat at Annapolis, Maryland, to which Washington journeyed. He inquired how Congress would prefer to receive his farewell, by letter or public address. Congress summoned him to appear and speak; he did so as recorded in this chapter, resigning "with satisfaction the appointment [he] accepted with diffidence."

87

TO JOHN AUGUSTINE WASHINGTON

Newburgh, June 15, 1783

My dear Brother:

I have received your favor of the 12th. of April from Berkley, and am obliged to you for the Acct. contained in it of our deceased brothers affairs. I have since heard that his Widow survived him but a little while. I am also obliged to you for taking upon you the direction of my mothers Interest at the little Fall Quarter, which I believe has been under most wretched Management. equally burthensome to me, and teazing to her.

In answer to the question you have propounded to me, respecting our Nephew Ferdinand, I must observe to you, that the *presumption* is, for I cannot speak with certainty, that our Navy, if it can be called one, will be laid up, or otherwise disposed of; consequently there can be no birth for Ferdinand there. It follows then, that there is only the other alternative of getting him on board a Merchant Ship, and this, possibly, may be the best of the two; your knowledge, together with that of his mothers friends, of the Trade, and Trading people of Virginia (where his Connections and Interest lyes) will point him much better than I can do, to the proper channel for employment.

I wait here with much impatience, the arrival of the Definitive Treaty; this event will put a period not only to my military Service, but also to my public life; as the remainder of my natural one shall be spent in that kind of ease and repose

Desire for private life

which a man enjoys that is free from the load of public cares, and subject to no other Controul than that of his own judgment, and a proper conduct for the walk of private Life.

It is much to be wished (but I think a good deal to be doubted) that the States would adopt a liberal and proper line of Conduct for the Government of this Country. It should be founded in justice. Prejudices, unreasonable jealousies, and narrow policy should be done away. Competent powers for all *general* purposes should be bested in the Sovereignty of the United States, or Anarchy and Confusion will soon succeed.

On liberty

Liberty, when it degenerates into licenciousness, begets confusion, and frequently ends in Tyranny or some woeful catastrophe, and to suppose that the Affairs of this Continent can be conducted by thirteen distinct Sovereignties, or by one without adequate powers, are mere solecisms in politicks. It is in our United capacity we are known, and have a place among the Nations of the Earth. Depart from this, and the States separately would stand as unknown in the World and as contemptable (comparatively speaking) as an individual County in any one State is to the State itself; and in others perhaps, has never been heard of and would be as little attended to but for the sport of Politicians to answer their sinister views, or the purposes of designing Courts, if they should grow jealous of our rising greatness as an Empire, and wish to play off one State against another. We are a young Nation and have a character to establish. It behoves us therefore to set out right for first impressions will be lasting, indeed are all in all. If we do not fulfil our public engagement, if we do not religeously observe our Treaties. If we shall be faithless to, and regardless of those who have lent their money, given their personal Services, and spilt their Blood; and who are now returning home poor and pennyless; in what light shall we be considered? And that there is but too much reason to apprehend these, none who see the daily publications, and will attend to the c[onduct] of some of the States, can har[dly] have any doubt of. So far therefore as the claims of the Army are concerned, and the Half pay or commutation of it is to be effected, I have suffered Extracts of Original Papers, in my possession, to be published; to shew the justice, oeconomy, and even the necessity that Congress were under of granting this, to keep the Army in the Field at so early a period as 1778. One of these I herewith send you.

My love, in which Mrs. Washington joins me, is offered to my Sister and your family; present my Complimts. to all enquiring friends, and be assured etc.

88

TO REVEREND WILLIAM GORDON

Head Qrs., Newburgh, July 8, 1783

Dear Sir:

Your favor of the 19th. of June came to my hands on Sunday last by the Southern Mail; from this circumstance, and the date of it I conclude it has been to Philadelphia, a mistake not very unusual for the Post master at Fishkiln to commit.

I delayed not a moment to forwd. the letters which came to me under your cover of the 26th. of Feby. to New York. I did not answer the letter which accompanied them in due Season; not so much from the hurry of business, as because my Sentiments on the essential part of it had been communicated to you before; and because the Annunciation of Peace, which came close upon the heels of it, put an end to all speculative opinions with respect to the time and terms of it.

I now thank you for your kind congratulations on this event. I feel sensibly the flattering expressions, and fervent wishes with which you have accompanied them, and make a tender of mine, with much cordiality, in return. It now rests with the Confederated Powers, by the line of conduct they mean to adopt, to make this Country great, happy, and respectable; or to sink it into littleness; worse perhaps, into Anarchy and Confusion; for certain I am, that unless adequate Powers are given to Congress for the *general* purposes of the Federal Union that we shall soon moulder into dust and become contemptable in the Eyes of Europe, if we are not made the sport of their politicks; to suppose that the general concern of this Country can be directed by thirteen heads, or one head without competent powers, is a solecism, the bad effects of which every Man who has had the practical knowledge to judge from, that I have, is fully convinced of; tho' none perhaps has felt them in so forcible, and distressing a degree. The People at large, and at a distance from the theatre of Action, who only know that the Machine was kept in motion, and that they are at last ar-

Power to Congress

rived at the first object of their Wishes are satisfied with the event, without investigating the causes of the slow progress to it, or of the Expences which have accrued and which they now seem unwilling to pay; great part of which has arisen from that want of energy in the Federal Constitution which I am complaining of, and which I wish to see given to it by a Convention of the People, instead of hearing it remarked that as we have worked through an arduous Contest with the Powers Congress already have (but which, by the by, have been gradually diminishing) why should they be invested with more?

On Providence

To say nothing of the invisible workings of Providence, which has conducted us through difficulties where no human foresight could point the way; it will appear evident to a close Examiner, that there has been a concatenation of causes to produce this Event; which in all probability at no time, or under any Circumstances, will combine again. We deceive ourselves therefore by this mode of reasoning, and what would be much worse, we may bring ruin upon ourselves by attempting to carry it into practice.

Sovereignty of the State

We are known by no other character among Nations than as the United States; Massachusetts or Virginia is no better defined, nor any more thought of by Foreign Powers than the County of Worcester in Massachusetts is by Virginia, or Glouster County in Virginia is by Massachusetts (respectable as they are); and yet these Counties, with as much propriety might oppose themselves to the Laws of the State in wch. they are, as an Individual State can oppose itself to the Federal Government, by which it is, or ought to be bound. Each of these Counties has, no doubt, its local polity and Interests. these should be attended to, and brought before their respective legislatures with all the force their importance merits; but when they come in contact with the general Interest of the State; when superior considerations preponderate in favor of the whole, their Voices should be heard no more; so should it be with individual States when compared to the Union. Otherwise I think it may properly be asked for what purpose do we farcically pretend to be United? Why do Congress spend Months together in deliberating upon, debating, and digesting plans, which are made as palatable, and as wholesome to the Constitution of this Country as the nature of things will admit of, when some States will pay no attention to them, and others regard them but partially; by which means all those evils which proceed from delay, are felt by the whole; while the compliant States are not only suffering by these neglects, but in many instances are injured most capitally by their own exertions; which are wasted for want of the United effort. A hundd. thousand men coming one after another cannot move a Ton weight; but the united strength of 50 would transport it with ease. so has it been with great part of the expence which has been incurred this War. In a Word, I think the blood and treasure which has been spent in it has been lavished to little purpose, unless we can be better Cemented; and that is not to be effected while so little attention is paid to the recommendations of the Sovereign Power.

To me it would seem not more absurd, to hear a traveller, who was setting out on a long journey, declare he would take no Money in his pocket to defray the Expences of it but rather depend upon chance and charity lest he should misapply it, than are the expressions of so much fear of the powers and means of Congress. For Heavens sake who are Congress? are *Congress is not a* they not the Creatures of the People, amenable to them for *danger* their Conduct, and dependant from day to day on their breath? Where then can be the danger of giving them such Powers as are adequate to the great ends of Government, and to all the general purposes of the Confederation (I repeat the word *genl*, because I am no advocate for their having to do with the particular policy of any State, further than it concerns the Union at large). What may be the consequences if they have not these Powers I am at no loss to guess; and deprecate the worst; for sure I am, we shall, in a little time, become as contemptable in the great Scale of Politicks as we now have it in our power to be respectable; and that, when the band of Union gets once broken, every thing ruinous to our future prospects is to be apprehended; the best that can come of it, in my humble opinion is, that we shall sink into obscurity, unless our Civil broils should keep us in remembrance and fill the page of history with the direful consequences of them.

You say that, Congress loose time by pressing a mode that does not accord with the genius of the People, and will thereby, endanger the Union; and that it is the quantum they want. Permit me to ask if the quantum has not already been demanded? Whether it has been obtained? and whence proceed the accumulated evils, and poignant distresses of many of the public Creditors, particularly in the Army? For my own part I hesitate not a moment to confess, that I see nothing wherein the Union is endangered by the late requisition of that body; but a prospect of much good, justice, and propriety from the compliance with it. I know of no Tax more convenient; none so agreeable, as that which every man may pay, or let it alone as his convenience, abilities, or Inclination shall prompt. I am therefore a warm friend to the Impost.

I can only repeat to you, that whenever Congress shall think proper to open the door of their Archives to you, (which can be best known, and with more propriety discovered through the Delegates of your own State), All my Records and Papers shall be unfolded to your View, and I shall be happy in your Company at Mt. Vernon, while you are taking such Extracts from them, as you may find convenient. It is a piece of respect wch. I think is due to the Sovereign Power to let it take the lead in this business (without any interference of mine). And another reason why I choose to withhold mine, to this epoch is, that I am positive no History of the Revolution can be perfect if the Historiographer has not free access to that fund of Information.

Mrs. Washington joins me in Compliments to Mrs. Gordon and I am etc.

89

TO JAMES DUANE

Rocky Hill, September 7, 1783

Sir:

I have carefully perused the Papers which you put into my hands relative to Indian Affairs.

Conduct toward Indians and citizens in western lands

My Sentiments with respect to the proper line of Conduct to be observed towards these people coincides precisely with those delivered by Genl. Schuyler, so far as he has gone in his Letter of the 29th. July to Congress (which, with the other Papers is herewith returned), and for the reasons he has there assigned; a repetition of them therefore by me would be unnecessary. But independant of the arguments made use of by him the following considerations have no small weight in my Mind.

To suffer a wide extended Country to be over run with

Land Jobbers, Speculators, and Monopolisers or even with scatter'd settlers, is, in my opinion, inconsistent with that wisdom and policy which our true interest dictates, or that an enlightened People ought to adopt and, besides, is pregnant of disputes both with the Savages, and among ourselves, the evils of which are easier, to be conceived than described; and for what? But to aggrandize a few avaricious Men to the prejudice of many, and the embarrassment of Government. For the People engaged in these pursuits without contributing in the smallest degree to the Support of government, or considering themselves as amenable to its Laws, will involve it by their unrestrained conduct, in inextricable perplexities, and more than probable in a great deal of Bloodshed.

My ideas therefore of the line of conduct proper to be observed not only towards the Indians, but for the government of the Citizens of America, in their Settlement of the Western Country (which is intimately connected therewith) are simply these.

First and as a preliminary, that all Prisoners of whatever age or Sex, among the Indians shall be delivered up.

That the Indians should be informed, that after a Contest of eight years for the Sovereignty of this Country G: Britain has ceded all the Lands of the United States within the limits discribed by the arte. of the Provisional Treaty.

That as they (the Indians) maugre all the advice and admonition which could be given them at the commencemt; and during the prosecution of the War could not be restrained from acts of Hostility, but were determined to join their Arms to those of G Britain and to share their fortune; so, consequently, with a less generous People than Americans they would be made to share the same fate; and be compelld to retire along with them beyond the Lakes. But as we prefer Peace to a state of Warfare, as we consider them as a deluded People; as we perswade ourselves that they are convinced, from experience, of their error in taking up the Hatchet against us, and that their true Interest and safety must now depend upon *our* friendship. As the Country, is large enough to contain us all; and as we are disposed to be kind to them and to partake of their Trade, we will from these considerations and from motives of Compn., draw a veil over what is past and establish a boundary line between them and us beyond which we will *endeavor* to restrain our People from Hunting or Settling, and within which they shall not come, but for the purposes of Trading, Treating, or other business unexceptionable in its nature.

In establishing this line, in the first instance, care should be taken neither to yield nor to grasp at too much. But to endeavor to impress the Indians with an idea of the generosity of our disposition to accommodate them, and with the necessity we are under, of providing for our Warriors, our Young People who are growing up, and strangers who are coming from other Countries to live among us. And if they should make a point of it, or appear dissatisfied at the line we may find it necessary to establish, compensation should be made them for their claims within it.

It is needless for me to express more explicitly because the tendency of my observns. evinces it is my opinion that if the Legislature of the State of New York should insist upon expelling the Six Nations from all the country they Inhabited previous to the War, within their Territory (as General Schuyler seems to be apprehensive of) that it will end in another Indian War. I have every reason to believe from my enquiries, and the information I have received, that they will not suffer their Country (if it was our policy to take it before we could settle it) to be wrested from them without another struggle. That they would compromise for a part of it I have very little doubt, and that it would be the cheapest way of coming at it, I have no doubt at all. The same observations, I am perswaded, will hold good with respect to Virginia, or any other state which has powerful Tribes of Indians on their Frontiers; and the reason of my mentioning New York is because General Schuyler has expressed his opinion of the temper of its Legislature; and because I have been more in the way of learning the Sentimts. of the Six Nations, than of any other Tribes of Indians on the Subject.

The Six Nations

The limits being sufficiently extensive (in the New Ctry.) to comply with all the engagements of Government and to admit such emigrations as may be supposed to happen within a given time not only from the several States of the Union but from Foreign Countries, and moreover of such magnitude as to form a distinct and proper Government; a Proclamation in my opinion, should issue, making it Felony (if there is power for the purpose and if not imposing some very heavy restraint) for any person to Survey or Settle beyond the Line; and the Officers Commanding the Frontier Garrison should have pointed and peremptory orders to see that the Proclamation is carried into effect.

Measures of this sort would not only obtain Peace from the Indians, but would, in my opinion, be the surest means of preserving it. It would dispose of the Land to the best advantage; People the Country progressively, and check Land Jobbing and Monopolizing (which is now going forward with great avidity) while the door would be open, and the terms known for every one to obtain what is reasonable and proper for himself upon legal and constitutional ground.

Every advantage that could be expected or even wished for would result from such a mode of procedure. Our Settlements would be compact, Government well established, and our Barrier formidable, not only for ourselves but against our Neighbours, and the Indians as has been observed in Genl Schuylers Letter will ever retreat as our Settlements advance upon them and they will be as ready to sell, as we are to buy; That it is the cheapest as well as the least distressing way of dealing with them, none who are acquainted with the Nature of Indian warfare, and has ever been at the trouble of estimating the expence of one, and comparing it with the cost of purchasing their Lands, will hesitate to acknowledge.

Unless some such measures as I have here taken the liberty of suggesting are speedily adopted one of two capital evils, in my opinion, will inevitably result, and is near at hand; either that the settling, or rather overspreading the Western Country will take place, by a parcel of Banditti, who will bid defiance to all Authority while they are skimming and disposing of the Cream of the Country at the expence of many suffering officers and Soldiers who have fought and bled to obtain it, and are now waiting the decision of Congress to point them to the promised reward of their past dangers and toils, or a renewal of Hostilities with the Indians, brought about more than probably, by this very means.

How far agents for Indian Affrs. are indispensably necessary I shall not take upon me to decide; but if any should be appointed, their powers in my opinion should be circumscribed, accurately defined, and themselves rigidly punished for every infraction of them. A recurrence to the conduct of these People under the British Administration of Indian Affairs will manifest the propriety of this caution, as it will there

Indian affairs agents

be found, that self Interest was the principle by which their Agents were actuated; and to promote this by accumulating Lands and passing large quantities of Goods thro their hands, the Indians were made to speak any language they pleased by their representation; were pacific or hostile as their purposes were most likely to be promoted by the one or the other. No purchase under any pretence whatever should be made by any other authority than that of the Sovereign power, or the Legislature of the State in which such Lands may happen to be. Nor should the Agents be permitted directly or indirectly to trade; but to have a fixed, and ample Salary allowed them as a full compensation for their trouble.

Indian trade

Whether in practice the measure may answer as well as it appears in theory to me, I will not undertake to say; but I think, if the Indian Trade was carried on, on Government Acct., and with no greater advance than what would be necessary to defray the expence and risk, and bring in a small profit, that it would supply the Indians upon much better terms than they usually are; engross their Trade, and fix them strongly in our Interest; and would be a much better mode of treating them than that of giving presents; where a few only are benefitted by them. I confess there is a difficulty in getting a Man, or set of Men, in whose Abilities and integrity there can be a perfect reliance; without which, the scheme is liable to such abuse as to defeat the salutary ends which are proposed from it. At any rate, no person should be suffered to Trade with the Indians without first obtaining a license, and giving security to conform to such rules and regulations as shall be prescribed; as was the case before the War.

Settlers in western lands

In giving my Sentiments in the Month of May last (at the request of a Committee of Congress) on a Peace Establishmt. I took the liberty of suggesting the propriety, which in my opinion there appeared, of paying particular attention to the French and other Settlers at Detroit and other parts within the limits of the Western Country; the perusal of a late Pamphlet entitled "Observations on the Commerce of the American States with Europe and the West Indies" impresses the necessity of it more forcibly than ever on my Mind. The author of that Piece strongly recommends a liberal change in the Government of Canada, and tho' he is too sanguine in his expectations of the benefits arising from it, there can be no doubt of the good policy of the measure. It behooves us therefore to counteract them, by anticipation. These People have a disposition towards us susceptible of favorable impressions; but as no Arts will be left unattempted by the British to withdraw them from our Interest, the prest. moment should be employed by us to fix them in it, or we may loose them forever; and with them, the advantages, or disadvantages consequent of the choice they may make. From the best information and Maps of that Country, it would appear that from the Mouth of the Great Miami River wch. empties into the Ohio to its confluence with the Mad River, thence by a Line to the Miami Fort and Village on the other Miami River wch. empties into Lake Erie, and Thence by a Line to include the Settlement of Detroit would with Lake Erie to the No.ward, Pensa. to the Eastwd. and the Ohio to the Soward form a Governmt. sufficiently extensive to fulfill all the public engagements, and to receive moreover a large population by Emigrants, and to confine The Settlement of the New States within these bounds would, in my opinion, be infinitely better even supposing no disputes were to happen with the Indians and that it was not necessary to guard against those other evils which have been enumerated than to suffer the same number of People to roam over a Country of at least 500,000 Square Miles contributing nothing to the support, but much perhaps to the Embarrassment of the Federal Government.

Was it not for the purpose of comprehending the Settlement of Detroit within the Jurisdn. of the New Governmt a more compact and better shaped district for a State would be for the line to proceed from the Miami Fort and Village along the River of that name to Lake Erie leaving In that case the Settlement of Detroit, and all the Territory No. of the Rivers Miami and St. Josephs between the Lakes Erie, St. Clair, Huron, and Michigan to form, hereafter, another State equally large compact and water bounded.

At first view, it may seem a little extraneous, when I am called upon to give an opinion upon the terms of a Peace proper to be made with the Indians, that I should go into the formation of New States; but the Settlemt. of the Western Country and making a Peace with the Indians are so analogous that there can be no definition of the one without involving considerations of the other. For I repeat it, again, and I am clear in my opinion, that policy and economy point very strongly to the expediency of being upon good terms with the Indians, and the propriety of purchasing their Lands in preference to attempting to drive them by force of arms out of their Country; which as we have already experienced is like driving the Wild Beasts of the Forest which will return as soon as the pursuit is at an end and fall perhaps on those that are left there; when the gradual extension of our Settlements will as certainly cause the Savage as the Wolf to retire; both being beasts of prey tho' they differ in shape. In a word there is nothing to be obtained by an Indian War but the Soil they live on and this can be had by purchase at less expence, and without that bloodshed, and those distresses which helpless Women and Children are made partakers of in all kinds of disputes with them.

If there is any thing in these thoughts (which I have fully and freely communicated) worthy attention I shall be happy and am Sir Yr. etc.

PS: A formal Address, and memorial from the Oneida Indians when I was on the Mohawk River, setting forth their Grievances and distresses and praying relief, induced me to order a pound of Powder and 3 lbs. of Lead to be issued to each Man, from the Military Magazines in the care of Colo. Willet; this, I presume, was unknown to Genl. Schuyler at the time he recommended the like measure in his Letter to Congress.

90

FAREWELL ORDERS TO THE ARMIES
OF THE UNITED STATES

Rock Hill, near Princeton, November 2, 1783

The United States in Congress assembled after giving the most honorable testimony to the merits of the foederal Armies, and presenting them with the thanks of their country for their long, eminent, and faithful services, having thought proper by their proclamation bearing date the 18th. day of October last to discharge such part of the Troops as were engaged for the war, and to permit the Officers on furlough to retire from service from and after to-morrow; which proclamation having been communicated in the publick papers for the information and government of all concerned; it only remains for the

Comdr in Chief to address himself once more, and that for the last time, to the Armies of the U.States (however widely dispersed the individuals who compose them may be) and to bid them an affectionate, a long farewell.

But before the Comdr in Chief takes his final leave of those he holds most dear, he wishes to indulge himself a few moments in calling to mind a slight review of the past. He will then take the liberty of exploring, with his military friends, their future prospects, of advising the general line of conduct, which in his opinion, ought to be pursued, and he will conclude the Address by expressing the obligations he feels himself under for the spirited and able assistance he has experienced from them in the performance of an arduous Office.

Recollection of the war

A contemplation of the compleat attainment (at a period earlier than could have been expected) of the object for which we contended against so formidable a power cannot but inspire us with astonishment and gratitude. The disadvantageous circumstances on our part, under which the war was undertaken, can never be forgotten. The singular interpositions of Providence in our feeble condition were such, as could scarcely escape the attention of the most unobserving; while the unparalleled perseverence of the Armies of the U States, through almost every possible suffering and discouragement for the space of eight long years, was little short of a standing miracle.

It is not the meaning nor within the compass of this address to detail the hardships peculiarly incident to our service, or to describe the distresses, which in several instances have resulted from the extremes of hunger and nakedness, combined with the rigours of an inclement season; nor is it necessary to dwell on the dark side of our past affairs. Every American Officer and Soldier must now console himself for any unpleasant circumstances which may have occurred by a recollection of the uncommon scenes in which he has been called to Act no inglorious part, and the astonishing events of which he has been a witness, events which have seldom if ever before taken place on the stage of human action, nor can they probably ever happen again. For who has before seen a disciplined Army form'd at once from such raw materials? Who, that was not a witness, could imagine that the most violent local prejudices would cease so soon, and that Men who came from the different parts of the Continent, strongly disposed, by the habits of education, to despise and quarrel with each other, would instantly become but one patriotic band of Brothers, or who, that was not on the spot, can trace the steps by which such a wonderful revolution has been effected, and such a glorious period put to all our warlike toils?

It is universally acknowledged, that the enlarged prospects of happiness, opened by the confirmation of our independence and sovereignty, almost exceeds the power of description. And shall not the brave men, who have contributed so essentially to these inestimable acquisitions, retiring victorious from the field of War to the field of agriculture, participate in all the blessings which have been obtained; in such a republic, who will exclude them from the rights of Citizens and the fruits of their labour. In such a Country, so happily circumstanced, the pursuits of Commerce and the cultivation of the soil will unfold to industry the certain road to competence. To those hardy Soldiers, who are actuated by the spirit of adventure the Fisheries will afford ample and profitable employment, and the extensive and fertile regions of the West will yield a most happy asylum to those, who, fond of domestic enjoyments are seeking for personal independence. Nor is it possible to conceive, that any one of the U States will prefer a national bankruptcy and a dissolution of the union, to a compliance with the requisitions of Congress and the payment of its just debts; so that the Officers and Soldiers may expect considerable assistance in recommencing their civil occupations from the sums due to them from the public, which must and will most inevitably be paid.

Payment of soldiers

In order to effect this desirable purpose and to remove the prejudices which may have taken possession of the minds of any of the good people of the States, it is earnestly recommended to all the Troops that with strong attachments to the Union, they should carry with them into civil society the most conciliating dispositions; and that they should prove themselves not less virtuous and useful as Citizens, than they have been persevering and victorious as Soldiers. What tho, there should be some envious individuals who are unwilling to pay the debt the public has contracted, or to yield the tribute due to merit; yet, let such unworthy treatment produce no invective or any instance of intemperate conduct; let it be remembered that the unbiassed voice of the free Citizens of the United States has promised the just reward, and given the merited applause; let it be known and remembered, that the reputation of the foederal Armies is established beyond the reach of malevolence; and let a consciousness of their achievements and fame still incite the men, who composed them to honourable actions; under the persuasion that the private virtues of oeconomy, prudence, and industry, will not be less amiable in civil life, than the more splendid qualities of valour, perseverance, and enterprise were in the Field. Every one may rest assured that much, very much of the future happiness of the Officers and Men will depend upon the wise and manly conduct which shall be adopted by them when they are mingled with the great body of the community. And, altho the General has so frequently given it as his opinion, in the most public and explicit manner, that, unless the principles of the federal government were properly supported and the powers of the union increased, the honour, dignity, and justice of the nation would be lost forever. Yet he cannot help repeating, on this occasion, so interesting a sentiment, and leaving it as his last injunction to every Officer and every Soldier, who may view the subject in the same serious point of light, to add his best endeavours to those of his worthy fellow Citizens towards effecting these great and valuable purposes on which our very existence as a nation so materially depends.

The Commander in chief conceives little is now wanting to enable the Soldiers to change the military character into that of the Citizen, but that steady and decent tenor of behaviour which has generally distinguished, not only the Army under his immediate command, but the different detachments and seperate Armies through the course of the war. From their good sense and prudence he anticipates the happiest consequences; and while he congratulates them on the glorious occasion, which renders their services in the field no longer necessary, he wishes to express the strong obligations he feels himself under for the assistance he has received from every Class, and in every instance. He presents his thanks in the most serious and affectionate manner to the General Officers, as well for their counsel on many interesting occasions, as for their ardor in promoting the success of the plans he had adopted. To the Commandants of Regiments and Corps, and to the other Officers for their great zeal and attention, in carrying his orders promptly into execution. To the Staff, for their alacrity and exactness in performing the Duties of their

Thanks to all troops

several Departments. And to the Non Commissioned Officers and private Soldiers, for their extraordinary patience in suffering, as well as their invincible fortitude in Action. To the various branches of the Army the General takes this last and solemn opportunity of professing his inviolable attachment and friendship. He wishes more than bare professions were in his power, that he were really able to be useful to them all in future life. He flatters himself however, they will do him the justice to believe, that whatever could with propriety be attempted by him has been done, and being now to conclude these his last public Orders, to take his ultimate leave in a short time of the military character, and to bid a final adieu to the Armies he has so long had the honor to Command, he can only again offer in their behalf his recommendations to their grateful country, and his prayers to the God of Armies. May ample justice be done them here, and may the choicest of heaven's favours, both here and hereafter, attend those who, under the devine auspices, have secured innumerable blessings for others; with these wishes, and this benediction, the Commander in Chief is about to retire from Service. The Curtain of seperation will soon be drawn, and the military scene to him will be closed for ever.

91

TO THE MINISTERS, ELDERS, DEACONS, AND MEMBERS OF THE REFORMED GERMAN CONGREGATION OF NEW YORK

New York, November 27, 1783

Gentlemen:

The illustrious and happy event on which you are pleased to congratulate and wellcome me to this City, demands all our gratitude; while the favorable sentiments you have thought proper to express of my conduct, intitles you to my warmest acknowledgements.

Disposed, at every suitable opportunity to acknowledge publicly our infinite obligations to the Supreme Ruler of the Universe for rescuing our Country from the brink of destruction; I cannot fail at this time to ascribe all the honor of our late successes to the same glorious Being. And if my humble exertions have been made in any degree subservient to the execution of the divine purposes, a contemplation of the benediction of Heaven on our righteous Cause, the approbation of my virtuous Countrymen, and the testimony of my own Conscience, will be a sufficient reward and augment my felicity beyond anything which the world can bestow.

The establishment of Civil and Religious Liberty was the Motive which induced me to the Field; the object is attained, and it now remains to be my earnest wish and prayer, that the Citizens of the United States would make a wise and virtuous use of the blessings, placed before them; and that the reformed german Congregation in New York; may not only be conspicuous for their religious character, but as examplary, in support of our inestimable acquisitions, as their reverend Minister has been in the attainment of them.

92

TO THE MERCHANTS OF PHILADELPHIA

Philadelphia, December 9, 1783

Gentlemen:

The perfect establishment of American Independence is indeed an event of such infinite importance as to fill the mind with gratitude and Joy; and afford the fairest occasion for mutal congratulations.

The honorable sentiments you are pleased to express respecting the Merits of the Army; the just idea you entertain of their bravery, sufferings and magnanimity; and the honest desire you manifest of making an adequate compensation for their Services; are circumstances highly satisfactory to me, as well as extremely flattering to the gallant Men who are more immediately concerned. And I must take the liberty to add, that the punctuality of the Merchants and other Citizens of Philadelphia in raising their proportion of Taxes for the support of the War, and their chearfulness in affording every other assistance in their power, are marks of Patriotism which deserve the warmest acknowledgements.

I am happy in having one more opportunity of expressing the personal obligations I feel myself under to You Gentlemen, for your favorable opinion and for the present as well as for every former instance of your polite attention.

Having long since been convinced of the expediency and even necessity of rendering compleat justice to all the public Creditors; and having at the same time been impressed with a belief that the good sense of my Countrymen would ultimately induce them to comply with the requisitions of Congress, I could not avoid being greatly pleased with the Example set by the State of Pennsylvania; nor can I conceal my satisfaction at finding your sentiments coincide so exactly with my own. Let us flatter ourselves, that the day is not remote, when a wise and just system of policy will be adopted by every State in the Union; then will national faith be inviolably preserved, public credit durably established, the blessings of Commerce extensively diffused, and the reputation of our new-formed Empire supported with as much *Eclat* as has been acquired in laying the foundation of it.

93

ADDRESS TO CONGRESS ON RESIGNING HIS COMMISSION

[Annapolis, December 23, 1783]

Mr. President:

The great events on which my resignation depended having at length taken place; I have now the honor of offering my sincere Congratulations to Congress and of presenting myself before them to surrender into their hands the trust committed to me, and to claim the indulgence of retiring from the Service of my Country.

Happy in the confirmation of our Independence and Sovereignty, and pleased with the oppertunity afforded the United States of becoming a respectable Nation, I resign with satisfaction the Appointment I accepted with diffidence. A diffidence in my abilities to accomplish so arduous a task, which however was superseded by a confidence in the rectitude of our Cause, the support of the Supreme Power of the Union, and the patronage of Heaven.

The Successful termination of the War has verified the most sanguine expectations, and my gratitude for the interposition of Providence, and the assistance I have received from my Countrymen, encreases with every review of the momentous Contest.

While I repeat my obligations to the Army in general, I should do injustice to my own feelings not to acknowledge in this place the peculiar Services and distinguished merits of the Gentlemen who have been attached to my person during the War. It was impossible the choice of confidential Officers to compose my family should have been more fortunate. Permit me Sir, to recommend in particular those, who have continued in Service to the present moment, as worthy of the favorable notice and patronage of Congress.

I consider it an indispensable duty to close this last solemn act of my Official life, by commending the Interests of our dearest Country to the protection of Almighty God, and those who have the superintendence of them, to his holy keeping.

Having now finished the work assigned me, I retire from the great theatre of Action; and bidding an Affectionate farewell to this August body under whose orders I have so long acted, I here offer my Commission, and take my leave of all the employments of public life.

CHAPTER EIGHT

WASHINGTON

The Citizen Stirs

1784 – 1786

*W*ASHINGTON *returned to Mount Vernon, which was in considerable disrepair, to resume the domestic arts he had so long pined for. Martha Washington had visited him in the army's camp when occasion permitted and shared with him and his men their many privations. Her ministrations to the soldiers were a source of comfort to them and George Washington. He had returned home but once during the long war, taking a brief stop there during the Yorktown campaign. He could already see at that time the labors which lay before him to bring Mount Vernon back to its former glory. He also saw what could not be restored: Martha's son Jack Custis had died just after the victory at Yorktown. Both her children were now gone, and she and Washington had none of their own.*

Though Washington plunged back into the managing of his estates, he found himself under no less weight of correspondence than formerly. He assured one friendly inquirer, "I have not leisure to turn my thoughts to commentaries." Public concerns still pressed in on him; everyone, it seemed, sought his opinion, and he disappointed none. He resumed his prewar efforts to produce a waterway connecting the transappalachian region and the Potomac, as much for reasons of state—"to cement the union"—as for reasons of commerce. Continuing to press for a strengthening of the Union, between the end of 1783 and 1786 Washington drew a coterie of reform-minded men around him whose efforts at length gave hope of a general reform of the Confederation.

94

TO JONATHAN TRUMBULL, JR.

Mount Vernon, January 5, 1784

Dear Trumbull:

Your obliging Letter of the 15th. of Novembr. did not reach me until some days after we had taken possession of the city of New York. The scene that followed, of festivity, congratulation, addresses and resignation, must be my apology for not replying to it sooner.

I sincerely thank you for the copy of the address of Govr. Trumbull to the Genl. Assembly and free Men of your State; the sentiments contained in it are such as would do honor to a patriot of any age or Nation; at least, they are too coincident with my own, not to meet with my warmest approbation. Be so good as to present my most cordial respects to the Governor and let him know that it is my wish, the mutual friendship and esteem which have been planted and fostered in the tumult of public life, may not wither and die in the serenity of retirement: tell him we shou'd rather amuse our evening hours of Life in cultivating the tender plants, and bringing them to perfection, before they are transplanted to a happier clime. *Governor Trumbull's address*

Notwithstanding the jealous and contracted temper which seems to prevail in some of the States, yet I cannot but hope and believe that the good sense of the people will ultimately get the better of their prejudices; and that order and sound policy, tho' they do not come so soon as one wou'd wish, will be produced from the present unsettled and deranged state of *Local jealousies* public affairs. Indeed I am happy to observe that the political disposition is actually meliorating every day; several of the States have manifested an inclination to invest Congress with more ample powers; most of the Legislatures appear disposed to do perfect justice; and the Assembly of this Commonwealth have just complied with the requisitions of Congress, and I am informed without a dissentient voice. Every thing My Dear Trumbull will come right at last, as we have often prophesied; my only fear is that we shall lose a little reputation first.

After having passed with as much prosperity as could be expected, through the career of public Life, I have now reached the goal of domestic enjoyment; in which state, I assure you I find your good wishes most acceptable to me. The family at Mount Vernon joins in the same compliments and cordiality, with which I am, &c.

95

TO GOVERNOR BENJAMIN HARRISON

Mount Vernon, January 18, 1784

My dear Sir:

Return to private life

I have just had the pleasure to receive your letter of the 8th., for the friendly and affectionate terms in which you have welcomed my return to this Country and to private life; and for the favourable light in which you are pleased to consider, and express your sense of my past services, you have my warmest and most grateful acknowledgments.

American prospects

That the prospect before us is, as you justly observe, fair, none can deny; but what use we shall make of it, is exceedingly problematical; not but that I believe, all things will come right at last; but like a young heir, come a little prematurely to a large inheritance, we shall wanton and run riot until we have brought our reputation to the brink of ruin, and then like him shall have to labor with the current of opinion, when *compelled* perhaps, to do what prudence and common policy pointed out as plain as any problem in Euclid, in the first instance.

State jealousies of Congress and of one another

The disinclination of the individual States to yield competent powers to Congress for the Federal Government, their unreasonable jealousy of that body and of one another, and the disposition which seems to pervade each, of being all-wise and all-powerful within itself, will, if there is not a change in the system be our downfal as a nation. This is as clear to me as the A, B, C; and I think we have opposed Great Britain, and have arrived at the present state of peace and independency, to very little purpose, if we cannot conquer our own prejudices. The powers of Europe begin to see this, and our newly acquired friends the British, are already and professedly acting upon this ground; and wisely too, if we are determined to persevere in our folly. They know that individual opposition to their measures is futile, and *boast* that we are not sufficiently united as a Nation to give a general one! Is not the indignity alone, of this declaration, while we are in the very act of peacemaking and conciliation, sufficient to stimulate us to vest more extensive and adequate powers in the sovereign of these United States? For my own part, altho' I am returned to, and am now mingled with the class of private citizens, and like them must suffer all the evils of a Tyranny, or of too great an extension of federal powers; I have no fears arising from this source, in my mind, but I have many, and powerful ones indeed which predict the worst consequences from a half-starved, limping Government, that appears to be always moving upon crutches, and tottering at every step. Men, chosen as the Delegates in Congress are, cannot officially be dangerous; they depend upon the breath, nay, they are so much the creatures of the people, under the present constitution, that they can have no views (which could possibly be carried into execution,) nor any interests, distinct from those of their constituents. My political creed therefore is, to be wise in the choice of *Political creed* Delegates, support them like Gentlemen while they are our representatives, give them competent powers for all federal purposes, support them in the due exercise thereof, and lastly, to compel them to close attendance in Congress during their delegation. These things under the present mode for, and termination of elections, aided by annual instead of constant Sessions, would, or I am exceedingly mistaken, make us one of the most wealthy, happy, respectable and powerful Nations, that ever inhabited the terrestrial Globe, without them, we shall in my opinion soon be every thing which is the direct reverse of them.

I shall look for you, in the first part of next month, with such other friends as may incline to accompany you, with great pleasure, being with best respects to Mrs. Harrison, in which Mrs. Washington joins me, dear Sir, &c.

96

TO MARQUIS DE LAFAYETTE

Mount Vernon, February 1, 1784

At length my Dear Marquis I am become a private citizen on the banks of the Potomac, and under the shadow of my own Vine and my own Fig-tree, free from the bustle of a camp and the busy scenes of public life, I am solacing myself with those tranquil enjoyments, of which the Soldier who is ever in pursuit of fame, the Statesman whose watchful days and sleepless nights are spent in devising schemes to promote the welfare of his own, perhaps the ruin of other countries, as if this globe was insufficient for us all, and the Courtier who is always watching the countenance of his Prince, in hopes of catching a gracious smile, can have very little conception. I am not only retired from all public employments, but I am retiring within myself; and shall be able to view the solitary walk, and tread the paths of private life with heartfelt satisfaction. Envious of none, I am determined to be pleased with all; and this my dear friend, being the order for my march, I will move gently down the stream of life, until I sleep with my Fathers.

Except an introductory letter or two, and one countermanding my request respecting plate, I have not written to you since the middle of October by Genl. Duportail. To inform you at this late hour, that the city of New York was evacuated by the British forces on the 25th. of November; that the American Troops took possession of it the same day, and delivered it over to the civil authority of the State; that good order, contrary to the expectation and predictions of Gl. Carleton, his Officers and all the loyalists, was immediately established; and that the harbour of New York was finally cleared of the British flag about the 5th. or 6th. of Decemr., would be an insult to your intelligence. And to tell you that I remained eight days in New York after we took possession of the city; that I was very much hurried during that time, which was the reason I did not write to you from thence; that taking Phila. in my way, I was obliged to remain there a week; that at Annapolis, where Congress were then, and are now sitting, I did, on the 23d. of December present them my commission, and made them my last bow, and on the Eve of Christmas entered these doors an

Tranquil enjoyments of private life

British evacuation of New York

older man by near nine years, than when I left them, is very uninteresting to any but myself. Since that period, we have been fast locked up in frost and snow, and excluded in a manner from all kinds of intercourse, the winter having been, and still continues to be, extremely severe.

I have now to acknowledge, and thank you for your favors of the 22d of July and 8th of September, both of which, altho' the first is of old date, have come to hand since my letter to you of October. The accounts contained therein of the political and commercial state of affairs as they respect America, are interesting, and I wish I could add that they were altogether satisfactory; and the agency you have had in both, particularly with regard to the free ports in France, is a fresh evidence of your unwearied endeavours to serve this country; but there is no part of your Letters to Congress My Dear Marquis, which bespeaks the excellence of your heart more plainly than that, which contains those noble and generous sentiments on the justice which is due to the faithful friends and Servants of the public; but I must do Congress the justice to declare, that as a body, I believe there is every disposition in them, not only to acknowledge the merits, but to reward the services of the army: There is a contractedness, I am sorry to add, in some of the States, from whence all our difficulties on this head, proceed; but it is to be hoped, the good sense and perseverance of the rest, will ultimately prevail, as the spirit of *meanness* is beginning to subside.

From a letter which I have just received from the Governor of this State I expect him here in a few days, when I shall not be unmindful of what you have written about the bust, and will endeavour to have matters respecting it, placed on their proper basis. I thank you most sincerely My Dear Marqs. for your kind invitation to your house, if I should come to Paris. At present I see but little prospect of such a voyage, the deranged situation of my private concerns, occasioned by an absence of almost nine years, and an entire disregard of all private business during that period, will not only suspend, but may put it for ever out of my power to gratify this wish. This not being the case with you, come with Madame la Fayette and view me in my domestic walks. I have often told you, and repeat it again, that no man could receive you in them with more friendship and affection than I should do; in which I am sure Mrs. Washington would cordially join me. We unite in

Little prospect of trip to France

respectful compliments to your Lady, and best wishes for your little flock. With every sentiment of esteem, Admiration and Love, I am etc.

97

TO DR. JAMES CRAIK

Mount Vernon, March 25, 1784

Dear Sir:

In answer to Mr. Bowie's request to you, permit me to assure that Gentleman, that I shall at all times be glad to see him at this retreat. That whenever he is here, I will give him the

Use of public papers

perusal of any public papers antecedent to my appointment to the command of the American army, that he may be laying up materials for his work. And whenever Congress shall have opened *their* Archives to any Historian for information, that he shall have the examination of all others in my possession which are subsequent thereto; but that 'till this epoch, I do not think myself at liberty to unfold papers which contain all the occurrences and transactions of my *late* command; first, because I conceive it to be respectful to the sovereign power to let them take the lead in this business; and next, because I have, upon this principle, refused Doctr. Gordon and others who are about to write the History of the revolution, this priviledge.

Publication of biographies

I will frankly declare to you, My Dr. Doctor that any memoirs of my life, distinct and unconnected with the general history of the war, would rather hurt my feelings than tickle my pride whilst I lived. I had rather glide gently down the stream of life, leaving it to posterity to think and say what they please of me, than by any act of mine to have vanity or ostentation imputed to me. And I will further more confess that I was rather surprised into a consent, when Doctr. Witherspoon (very unexpectedly) made the application, than considered the tendency of that consent. It did not occur to me at that moment, from the manner in which the question was propounded, that no history of my life, without a very great deal of trouble indeed, could be written with the least degree of accuracy, unless recourse was had to me, or to my papers for information; that it would not derive sufficient authenticity without a promulgation of this fact; and that such a promulgation would subject me to the imputation I have just mentioned, which would hurt me the more, as I do not think vanity is a trait of my character.

It is for this reason, and candour obliges me to be explicit, that I shall stipulate against the publication of the memoirs Mr. Bowie has in contemplation to give the world, 'till I shou'd see more probability of avoiding the darts which *I think* would be pointed at me on such an occasion; and how far, under these circumstances, it wou'd be worth Mr. Bowie's while to spend time which might be more usefully employed in other matters, is with him to consider; as the practicability of doing it efficiently, without having free access to the documents of this War, which must fill the most important pages of the Memoir, and which for the reasons already assigned cannot be admitted at present, also is. If nothing happens more than I at present foresee, I shall be in Philadelphia on or before the first of May; where 'tis probable I may see Mr. Bowie and converse further with him on this subject; in the mean while I will thank you for communicating these Sentiments. I am, etc.

98

TO THOMAS JEFFERSON

Mount Vernon, March 29, 1784

Dear Sir:

It was not in my power to answer your favor of the 15th. by the last post, for the reason then assigned. I wish I may be able to do it to your satisfaction now, as I again am obliged to pay my attention to other Company, (the Govr. being gone).

My opinion coincides perfectly with yours respecting the practicability of an easy, and short communication between the Waters of the Ohio and Potomac. Of the advantages of that communication, and the preference it has over *all* others. And of the policy there would be in this State, and Maryland to adopt and render it facile; but I confess to you freely, I have no expectation that the public will adopt the measure; for besides the jealousies wch. prevail, and the difficulty of proportioning such funds as may be allotted for the purposes you have mentioned, there are two others, which, in my opinion, will be yet harder to surmount; these are (if I have not imbibed

On need for connection between Potomac and Ohio rivers

too unfavourable an opinion of my Countrymen) the impracticability of bringing the great, and truly wise policy of the measure to their view; and the difficulty of drawing money from them, for such a purpose if you could do it. for it appears to me, maugre all the sufferings of the public creditors, breach of public faith, and loss of public reputation, that payment of the taxes which are already laid, will be postponed as long as possible! how then are we to expect new ones, for purposes more remote?

I am not so disinterested in this matter as you are; but I am made very happy to find that a man of discernment and liberality (who has no particular interest in the plan) thinks as I do, who have Lands in that Country the value of which would be enhanced, by the adoption of such a Scheme.

Previous history of Potomac navigation

More than ten years ago I was struck with the importance of it, and despairing of any aid from the public, I became a principal Mover of a Bill to empower a number of Subscribers to undertake, at their own expence, (upon conditions which were expressed) the extension of the Navigation from tide Water to Wills's Creek (about 150 Miles) and I devoutly wish that this may not be the only expedient by which it can be effected now. To get this business in motion, I was obliged, even upon *that ground*, to comprehend James River, in order to remove the jealousies which arose from the attempt to extend the Navigation of the Potomack. The plan however, was in a tolerable train when I set out for Cambridge in 1775, and would have been in an excellent way had it not been for the difficulties which were met with in the Maryland Assembly; from the opposition which was given (according to report) by the Baltimore Merchants; who were alarmed, and perhaps not without cause, at the consequence of Water transportation to George Town of the produce which usually came to their Market.

Local jealousies and war defeat project

The local interest of that place (Baltimore) joined with the short sighted politics, or contracted views of another part of that Assembly, gave Mr. Thomas Johnson who was a warm promoter of the Scheme on the No. side of the River, a great deal of trouble. In this situation things were when I took command of the Army; the War afterwards called Mens attention to different objects, and all the Money they could or would raise, were applied to other purposes; but with you, I am satisfied that not a moment ought to be lost in recommencing this business; for I *know* the Yorkers will delay no time to remove

New York

every obstacle in the way of the other communication, so soon as the Posts at Oswego and Niagara are surrendered; and I shall be mistaken if they do not build Vessels for the Navigation of the Lakes, which will supercede the necessity of coasting on either side.

It appears to me that the Interest and policy of Maryland is proportionably concerned with that of Virginia to remove obstructions, and to invite the trade of the Western territory into the channel you have mentioned. You will have frequent oppertunities of learning the Sentiments of the principal characters of that State, respecting this matter, and if you should see Mr. Johnson (formerly Govr. of the State) great information may be derived from him. How far, upon more mature consideration I may depart from the resolution I had formed of living perfectly at my ease, exempt from all kinds of responsibility, is more than I can, at present, absolutely determine. The Sums granted, the manner of granting them, the powers and objects, would merit consideration. The trouble, if my situation at the time would permit me to engage in a work of this sort would be set at naught; and the immense advantages which this Country would derive from the measure, would be no small stimulus to the undertaking; if that undertaking could be made to comport with those ideas, and that line of conduct with which I meant to glide gently down the stream of life; and it did not interfere with any other plan I might have in contemplation. *(marginal note: Virginia and Maryland)*

I am not less in sentiment with you respecting the impolicy of this State's grasping at more territory than they are competent to the Government of. And for the reasons you assign, I very much approve of a Meridian from the Mouth of the Great Kanhawa as a convenient and very proper line of seperation. But I am mistaken if our chief Magistrate will coincide with us in this opinion. *(marginal note: The extension of Virginia)*

I will not enter upon the subject of Commerce, it has its advantages and disadvantages, but which of them preponderates is not the question. From Trade our Ctizens *will not* be restrained, and therefore it behoves us to place it in the most convenient channels, under proper regulation, freed *as much as possible*, from those vices which luxury, the consequence of wealth and power, naturally introduce. *(marginal note: Commerce)*

The incertitude which prevails in Congress, and the non-attendance of its Members, is discouraging to those who are *(marginal note: Congress)* willing, and ready to discharge the trust which is reposed in them; whilst it is disgraceful, in a high degree to our Country. but I believe the case will never be otherwise, so long as that body persist in their present mode of doing business; and will hold constant, instead of annual Sessions; against the former of which, my mind furnishes me with a variety of Arguments, but not one, in times of peace, in favor of the latter.

Annual Sessions would always produce a full representation, and alertness at business. The Delegates, after a recess of 8 or 10 Months would meet each other with glad Countenances; they would be complaisant; they would yield to each other as much as the duty they owed their constituents would permit; and they would have oppertunities of becoming better acquainted with the Sentiments of them and removing their prejudices, during the recess. Men who are always together get tired of each others Company; they throw off the proper restraint; they say and do things which are personally disgusting; this begets opposition; opposition begets faction; and so it goes on till business is impeded, often at a stand. I am sure (having the business prepared by proper Boards or a Committee) an Annual Session of two Months would dispatch more business than is now done in twelve; and this by a full representation of the Union.

Long as this letter is, I intended to be more full on some of the points, and to have touched upon some others; but it is not in my power, as I am obliged to snatch the moments which give you this hasty production from Co. With very great esteem &c.

Quoery, have you not made the distance from Cuyahoga to New York too great?

99

TO JAMES MADISON

Mount Vernon, June 12, 1784

Dear Sir:

Thomas Paine

Can nothing be done in our Assembly for poor Paine? Must the merits, and Services of *Common Sense* continue to glide down the stream of time, unrewarded by this Country? His writings certainly have had a powerful effect on the public mind; ought they not then to meet an adequate return? He is poor! he is chagreened! and almost, if not altogether, in despair of relief. New York it is true, not the least distressed, nor best able State in the Union, has done something for him. This kind of provision he prefers to an allowance from Congress; he has reasons for it, which to him are conclusive, and such I think as would have weight with others. His views are moderate; a decent independency is, I believe, all he aims at. Should he not obtain this? If you think so, I am sure you will not only move the matter, but give it your support. For me, it only remains to feel for his Situation, and to assure you of the sincere esteem and regard with which I have the honor &c.

100

TO GOVERNOR BENJAMIN HARRISON

Mount Vernon, October 10, 1784

Dear Sir:

Upon my return from the western Country a few days ago, I had the pleasure to receive your favor of the 17th. ulto. It has always been my intention to pay my respects to you before the chance of *another* early and hard winter should make a warm fireside too comfortable to be relinquished. And I shall feel an additional pleasure in offering this tribute of friendship and respect to you, by having the company of the Marqs. de la Fayette, when he shall have revisited this place from his Eastern tour; now every day to be expected.

I shall take the liberty now, my dear sir, to suggest a matter, which would (if I am not too shortsighted a politician) mark your administration as an important era in the Annals of this Country, if it should be recommended by you, and adopted by the Assembly.

It has been long my decided opinion that the shortest, easiest, and least expensive communication with the invaluable and extensive Country back of us, would be by one, or both of the rivers of this State which have their sources in the Apalachian mountains. Nor am I singular in this opinion. Evans, in his Map and Analysis of the middle Colonies which (considering the early period at which they were given to the public) are done with amazing exactness. And Hutchins since,

Need for an inland waterway

in his topographical description of the Western Country, (a good part of which is from actual surveys), are decidedly of the same sentiments; as indeed are all others who have had opportunities, and have been at the pains to investigate and consider the subject.

But that this may not now stand as mere matter of opinion or assertion, unsupported by facts (such at least as the best maps now extant, compared with the oral testimony, which my opportunities in the course of the war have enabled me to obtain); I shall give you the different routs and distances from Detroit, by which all the trade of the North Western parts of the United territory, must pass; unless the Spaniards, contrary to their present policy, should engage part of it; or the British should attempt to force nature by carrying the trade of the upper Lakes by the river Outawaies into Canada, which I scarcely think they will or could effect. Taking Detroit then (which is putting ourselves in as unfavourable a point of view as we can be well placed, because it is upon the line of the British territory) as a point by which, as I have already observed, all that part of the trade must come, it appears from the statement enclosed, that the tide waters of this State are nearer to it by 168 miles than that of the river St. Lawrence; or than that of the Hudson at Albany by 176 miles.

Maryland, Pennsylvania, New York prospects

Maryland stands upon similar ground with Virginia. Pennsylvania altho' the Susquehanna is an unfriendly water, much impeded it is said with rocks and rapids, and nowhere communicating with those which lead to her capital; has it in contemplation to open a communication between Toby's Creek (which empties into the Alleghany river, 95 miles above Fort Pitt) and the west branch of Susquehanna; and to cut a canal between the waters of the latter, and the Schuylkill; the expence of which is easier to be conceived than estimated or described by me. A people however, who are possessed of the spirit of commerce, who see, and who will pursue their advantages, may achieve almost anything. In the mean time, under the uncertainty of these undertakings, they are smoothing the roads and paving the ways for the trade of that western World. That New York will do the same so soon as the British Garrisons are removed, which are at present, insurmountable obstacles in *their* way, no person who knows the temper, genius, and policy of those people as well as I do, can harbour the smallest doubt.

Thus much with respect to rival States; let me now take a short view of our own; and being aware of the objections which are in the way, I will enumerate, in order to contrast them with the advantages.

The first and principal one is, the *unfortunate Jealousy*, which ever has and it is to be feared ever will prevail, lest one part of the State should obtain an advantage over the other part (as if the benefits of trade were not diffusive and beneficial to all); then follow a train of difficulties viz: that our people are already heavily taxed; that we have no money; that the advantages of this trade are remote that the most *direct* rout for it is thro' *other* States, over whom we have no controul; that the routs over which we have controul, are as distant as either of those which lead to Philadelphia, Albany or Montreal; That a sufficient spirit of commerce does not pervade the citizens of this commonwealth; that we are in fact doing for others, what they ought to do for themselves.

Without going into the investigation of a question, which has employed the pens of able politicians, namely, whether trade with Foreigners is an advantage or disadvantage to a country. This State as a part of the confederated States (all of whom have the spirit of it very strongly working within them) must adopt it, or submit to the evils arising therefrom without receiving its benefits; common policy therefore points clearly and strongly, to the propriety of our enjoying all the advantages which nature and our local situation afford us; and evinces clearly that unless this spirit could be totally eradicated in other States, as well as in this, and every man made to become either a cultivator of the Land, or a manufacturer of such articles as are prompted by necessity, such stimulas should be employed as will *force* this spirit; by shewing to our Countrymen the superior advantages we possess beyond others; and the importance of being upon a footing with our Neighbours.

If this is fair reasoning, it ought to follow as a consequence, that we should do our part towards opening the communication with the fur and peltry trade of the Lakes; and for the produce of the Country which lies within; and which will, so soon as matters are settled with the Indians, and the terms on which Congress means to dispose of the Land, and found to be favourable, are announced, settle faster than any other ever did, or any one would imagine. This then when considered in an interested point of view, is alone sufficient to excite our endeavours; but in my opinion, there is a political consideration for so doing, which is of still greater importance.

Political considerations

I need not remark to you Sir, that the flanks and rear of the United States are possessed by other powers, and formidable ones too; nor how necessary it is to apply the cement of interest, to bind all parts of the Union together by indissoluble bonds, especially that part of it, which lies immediately west of us, with the middle States. For, what ties, let me ask, shou'd we have upon those people? How entirely unconnected with them shall we be, and what troubles may we not apprehend, if the Spaniards on their right, and Gt. Britain on their left, instead of throwing stumbling blocks in their way as they now do, should hold out lures for their trade and alliance. What, when they get strength, which will be sooner than most people conceive (from the emigration of foreigners who will have no particular predilection towards us, as well as from the removal of our own citizens) will be the consequence of their having formed close connexions with both, or either of those powers in a commercial way? It needs not, in my opinion, the gift of prophecy to foretell.

Western settlers discussed

The Western settlers, (I speak now from my own observation) stand as it were upon a pivot; the touch of a feather, would turn them any way. They have look'd down the Mississippi, until the Spaniards (very impoliticly I think, for themselves) threw difficulties in their way; and they looked that way for no other reason, than because they could glide gently down the stream; without considering perhaps, the fatigues of the voyage back again, and the time necessary to perform it in; and because they have no other means of coming to us but by a long Land transportation and unimproved roads. These causes have hitherto checked the industry of the present settlers; for except the demand for provisions, occasioned by the increase of population, and a little flour which the necessities of Spaniards compel them to buy, they have no incitements to labour. But smooth the road once, and make easy the way for them, and then see what an influx of articles will be poured upon us; how amazingly our exports will be encreased by them, and how amply we shall be compensated for any trouble and expence we may encounter to effect it.

Virginia's advantages

A combination of circumstances makes the present conjuncture more favourable for Virginia, than for any other State in the Union, to fix these matters. The jealous and untoward disposition of the Spaniards on one hand, and the private views of some individuals, coinciding with the general policy of the Court of Great Britain, on the other, to retain as long as possible the Posts of Detroit, Niagara, and Oswega &c. (which, tho' done under the letter of the Treaty, is certainly an infraction of the spirit of it, and injurious to the Union) may be improved to the greatest advantage by this State; if she would open the avenues to the trade of that Country, and embrace the present moment to establish it. It only wants a beginning; the Western Inhabitants wou'd do their part towards its execution. Weak as they are, they would meet us at least half way, rather than be *driven* into the arms of, or be made dependant upon foreigners; which would, eventually, either bring on a separation of them from us, or a war between the United States and one or the other of those powers, most probably with the Spaniards.

The preliminary steps to the attainment of this great object, would be attended with very little expence, and might, at the same time that it served to attract the attention of the Western Country, and to convince the wavering Inhabitants thereof of our disposition to connect ourselves with them, and to facilitate their commerce with us, would be a mean of removing those jealousies which otherwise might take place among ourselves.

These, in my opinion are; to appoint Commissioners, who from their situation, integrity and abilities, can be under no suspicion of prejudice or predilection to one part more than to another. Let these Commissioners make an actual survey of James river and Potomack from tide-water to their respective sources. Note with great accuracy the kind of navigation, and the obstructions in it; the difficulty and expence attending the removal of these obstructions; the distances from place to place thro' the whole extent; and the nearest and best Portages between these waters and the Streams capable of improvement which run into the Ohio; traverse these in like manner to *their* junction with the Ohio, and with equal accuracy. The navigation of this river (i.e., the Ohio) being well known, they will have less to do in the examination of it; but nevertheless, let the courses and distances of it be taken to the mouth of the Muskingum, and up that river (notwithstanding it is in the ceded lands) to the carrying place with Cayahoga; down the

Appointment of commissioners

Cayahoga to Lake Erie, and thence to Detroit. Let them do the same with big Bever creek, although part of it is in the State of Pennsylvania; and with the Scioto also. In a word, let the Waters East and West of the Ohio, which invite our notice by their proximity, and the ease with which Land transportation may be had between them and the Lakes on one side, and the rivers Potomac and James on the other, be explored, accurately delineated, and a correct and connected Map of the whole be presented to the public. These things being done, I shall be mistaken if prejudice does not yield to facts; jealousy to candour, and finally, that reason and nature thus aided, will dictate what is right and proper to be done.

In the meanwhile, if it should be thought that the lapse of time which is necessary to effect this work, may be attended with injurious consequences, could not there be a sum of money granted towards opening *the best,* or if it should be deemed *more eligible,* two of the nearest communications, one to the Northward and another to the Southward, with the settlements to the westward? And an act be passed (if there should not appear a manifest disposition in the Assembly to make it a public undertaking) to incorporate, and encourage private Adventurers if any should associate and sollicit the same, for the purpose of extending the navigation of Potomac or James river? And, in the former case, to request the concurrence of Maryland in the measure. It will appear from my statement of the different routs (and as far as my means of information have extended, I have done it with the utmost candour), that all the produce of the settlements about Fort Pitt can be brought to Alexandria by the Yohoghaney in 304 Miles; whereof only 31 is land transportation: And by the Monongahela and Cheat river in 300 miles; 20 only of which are land carriage. Whereas the common road from Fort Pitt to Philadelphia is 320 miles, all Land transportation; or 476 miles, if the Ohio, Toby's Creek, Susquehanna and Schuylkill are made use of for this purpose: how much of this is by land, I know not; but from the nature of the Country it must be very considerable. How much the interests and feelings of people thus circumstanced would be engaged to promote it, requires no illustration.

For my own part, I think it highly probable, that upon the strictest scrutiny (if the Falls of the Great Kanhawa can be made navigable, or a short portage be had there), it will be

A public or private venture

Geographic consideration

found of equal importance and convenience to improve the
navigation of both the James and Potomac. The latter I am
fully persuaded, affords the nearest communication with the
Lakes; but James river may be more convenient for all the
settlers below the mouth of the Gt. Kanhawa, and for some
distance perhaps above, and west of it: for I have no expectation that any part of the trade *above* the falls of the Ohio will go
down that river and the Mississippi, much less that the returns
will ever come up them; unless our want of foresight and good
management is the occasion of it. Or upon trial, if it should be
found that these rivers, from the beforementioned Falls, will
admit the descent of Sea vessels; in which case, and the navigation of the former's becoming free, it is probable that both
vessels and the cargoes will be carried to foreign markets and
sold; but the returns for them will never in the natural course
of things, ascend the long and rapid current of that river;
which with the Ohio to the Falls, in their meanderings, is little
if any short of 2000 miles. Upon the whole, the object, in my
estimation is of vast commercial and political importance: in
these lights I think posterity will consider it, and regret (if our
conduct should give them cause) that the present favourable
moment to secure so great a blessing for them, was neglected.

One thing more remains, which I had like to have forgot, *Position of*
and that is the supposed difficulty of obtaining a passage thro'   *Pennsylvania*
the State of Pennsylvania. How an application to its Legisla-
ture would be relished, in the first instance, I will not undertake to decide; but of one thing I am almost certain, such an
application would place that body in a very delicate situation.
There is in the State of Pennsylvania at least 100,000 souls west
of the Laurel hill, who are groaning under the inconveniences
of a long land transportation; they are wishing, indeed they
are looking for the improvement and extension of inland navigation; and if this cannot be made easy for them, to Philada (at
any rate it must be lengthy), they will seek a mart elsewhere;
the consequence of which would be, that the State, tho' contrary to the policy and interests of its Sea-ports, must submit to
the loss of so much of its trade, or hazard not only the trade
but the loss of the Settlement also; for an opposition on the
part of Government to the extension of water transportation,
so consonant with the essential interests of a large body of
people, or any extraordinary impositions upon the exports or
imports to, or from another State, would ultimately bring on a

separation between its Eastern and Western Settlements; towards which, there is not wanting a disposition at this moment in that part of it, which is beyond the mountains. I consider Rumsey's discovery for working Boats against stream, by mechanical powers (principally) as not only a very fortunate invention for these States in general, but as one of those circumstances which have combined to render the present epocha favourable above all others for fixing, if we are disposed to avail ourselves of them, a large portion of the trade of the Western Country in the bosom of this State irrevocably.

Lengthy as this letter is, I intended to have written a fuller and more digested one, upon this important subject, but have met with so many interruptions since my return home, as almost to have precluded my writing at all. What I now give is crude; but if you are in sentiment with me, I have said enough; if there is not an accordance of opinion I have said too much and all I pray in the latter case is, that you will do me the justice to believe my motives are pure, however erroneous my judgment may be on this matter, and that I am with the most perfect esteem etc.

101

TO THOMAS JOHNSON

Mount Vernon, October 15, 1784

Dear Sir:

On a supposition that you are now at Annapolis, the petition of the Potomack Company is enclosed to your care. A duplicate has been forwarded to the Assembly of this state; the fate of which I have not yet heard, but entertain no doubt of its favorable reception, as there are many auspicious proofs of liberality and justice already exhibited in the proceedings of the present session. I hope the same spirit will mark the proceedings of yours. The want of energy in the Federal government, the pulling of one State and party of States against another and the commotion amongst the Eastern people have sunk our national character much below par; and has brought our politics and credit to the brink of a precipice; a step or two farther must plunge us into a Sea of Troubles, perhaps anarchy and confusion. I trust that a proper sense of justice and unanimity in those States which have not drunk so deep of the cup of folly may yet retrieve our affairs. But no time is to be lost in essaying them. I have written to no gentlemen in your Assembly respecting the Potomack business but yourself. The justice of the cause and your management of it will insure success. With great regard and respect I am etc.

102

TO BENJAMIN HARRISON

Mount Vernon, January 22, 1785

My dear Sir:

It is not easy for me to decide by which my mind was most affected upon the receipt of your letter of the 6th. inst., surprise or gratitude: both were greater than I have words to express. The attention and good wishes which the Assembly have evidenced by their act for vesting in me 150 shares in the navigation of each of the rivers Potomac and James, are more than mere compliment; there is an unequivocal and substantial meaning annexed. But believe me sir, notwithstanding these, no circumstance has happened to me since I left the walks of public life, which has so much embarrassed me. On the one hand, I consider this act, as I have already observed, as a noble and unequivocal proof of the good opinion, the affection, and disposition of my Country to serve me; and I should be hurt, if by declining the acceptance of it, my refusal should be construed into disrespect, or the smallest slight upon the generous intention of the country: or, that an ostentatious display of disinterestedness or public virtue, was the source of the refusal. On the other hand, it is really my wish to have my mind, and my actions which are the result of contemplation, as free and independent as the air, that I may be more at liberty (in things which my opportunities and experience have brought me to the knowledge of) to express my sentiments, and if necessary, to suggest what may occur to me, under the fullest conviction, that altho' my judgment may be arraigned, there will be no suspicion that sinister motives had the smallest

Gift of shares in navigation company

influence in the suggestion. Not content then with the bare consciousness of my having, in all this navigation business, acted upon the clearest conviction of the political importance of the measure; I would wish that every individual who may hear that it was a favorite plan of mine, may know also that I had no other motive for promoting it, than the advantage I conceived it would be productive of to the Union, and to this State in particular, by cementing the Eastern and Western Territory together, at the same time that it will give vigor and encrease to our commerce, and be a convenience to our Citizens.

How would this matter be viewed then by the eye of the world; and what would be the opinion of it, when it comes to be related that G W—n exerted himself to effect this work, and G. W— has received 20,000 Dollars, and £5,000 Sterling of the public money as an interest therein? Would not this in the estimation of it (if I am entitled to any merit for the part I have acted; and without it there is no foundation for the act) deprive me of the principal thing which is laudable in my conduct? Would it not, in some respects, be considered in the same light as a pension? And would not the apprehension of this make me more reluctantly offer my sentiments in future? In a word, under what ever pretence, and however customary these gratuitous gifts are made in other Countries, should I not thence forward be considered as a dependant? One moments thought of which would give me more pain, than I should receive pleasure from the product of all the tolls, was every farthing of them vested in me: altho' I consider it as one of the most certain and increasing Estates in the Country.

I have written to you with an openness becoming our friendship. I could have said more on the subject; but I have already said enough to let you into the State of my mind. I wish to know whether the ideas I entertain occurred to, and were expressed by any member in or out of the House. Upon the whole, you may be assured my Dr. Sir, that my mind is not a little agitated. I want the best information and advice to settle it. I have no inclination (as I have already observed) to avail myself of the generosity of the Country: nor do I want to appear ostentatiously disinterested (for more than probable my refusal would be ascribed to this motive) or that the Country should harbour an idea that I am disposed to set little value on her favours, the manner of granting which is as flattering, as the grant is important. My present difficulties however shall be no impediment to the progress of the undertaking. I will receive the full and frank opinions of my friends with thankfulness. I shall have time enough between the sitting of the next Assembly to consider the tendency of the act, and in this, as in all other matters, will endeavor to decide for the best.

My respectful compliments and best wishes, in which Mrs. Washington and Fanny Bassett (who is much recovered) join, are offered to Mrs. Harrison and the rest of your family. It would give us great pleasure to hear that Mrs. Harrison had her health restored to her. With every sentiment of esteem, regard and friendship. I am, etc.

103

TO THE PRESIDENT OF CONGRESS

Mount Vernon, February 8, 1785

Dear Sir:

Since my last, I have had the honor to receive your favors of the 26th. of Decr. and 16th. of January. I have now the pleasure to inform you, that the Assemblies of Virginia and Maryland have enacted Laws, of which the enclosed is a copy; they are exactly similar in both States. At the same time and at the joint and equal expence of the two Governments, the sum of 6666⅔ Dollars are voted for opening and keeping in repair a road from the highest practicable navigation of this river, to that of the river Cheat or Monongahela, as commissioners (who are appointed to survey and lay out the same) shall find most convenient and beneficial to the Western Settlers: and have concurred in an application to the State of Pennsylvania for permission to open another road from Fort Cumberland to the Yohoganey, at the three forks or Turkey foot. A similar Bill to the one enclosed, is passed by our Assembly, respecting the navigation of James river, and the communication between it and the waters of the great Kanhawa, and the Executive authorised by a resolve of the Assembly to appoint Commissioners to examine and report the most convenient course for a canal between Elizabeth river and the waters of Roanoke; with an estimate of the expence: and if the best communication shall be found to require the concurrence of the State of

Inland communications with western territory

No. Carolina thereto, to make application to the Legislature thereof accordingly.

A plan to spread Christianity among the Indians

Towards the latter part of the year 1783 I was honored with a letter from the Countess of Huntington, briefly reciting her benevolent intention of spreading Christianity among the Tribes of Indians inhabiting our Western Territory; and expressing a desire of my advice and assistance to carry this charitable design into execution. I wrote her Ladyship for answer, that it would by no means comport with the plan of retirement I had promised myself, to take an active or responsible part in this business; and that it was my belief, there was no other way to effect her pious and benevolent designs, but by first reducing these people to a state of greater civilization, but that I wou'd give every aid in my power, consistent with the ease and tranquility, to which I meant to devote the remainder of my life, to carry her plan into effect. Since that I have been favored with other letters from her, and a few days ago under cover from Sir James Jay the papers herewith enclosed.

As the plan contemplated by Lady Huntington, according to the outlines exhibited, is not only unexceptionable in its design and tendency, but has humanity and charity for its object; and may I conceive, be made subservient to valuable political purposes, I take the liberty of laying the matter before you for your free and candid sentiments thereon; the communication I make of this matter to you sir, is in a private way, but you are at full liberty to communicate the plan of Lady Huntington, to the members individually; or officially to Congress, as the importance and propriety of the measure may strike you. My reasons for it are these: 1st. I do not believe that any of the States to whom she has written (unless it may be New York) are in circumstances, since their cession of Territory, to comply with the requisition respecting emigration; for it has been privately hinted to me, and ought not to become a matter of public notoriety, that notwithstanding the indefinite expressions of the Address respecting the numbers or occupations of the emigrants, which was purposely omitted to avoid giving alarms in England, the former will be great, and the useful artisans among them, many. 2d Because such emigration, if it should effect the object in view, besides the humane and charitable purposes which would be thereby answered, will be of immense political consequence; and even if this should not succeed to her Ladyships wishes, it must nevertheless, be of considerable importance from the encrease of population by orderly and well disposed characters, who would at once form a barrier and attempt the conversion of the Indians without involving an expence to the Union. I see but one objection to a compact, unmixed and powerful settlement of this kind, if it is likely to be so, the weight of which you will judge. It is, (and her Ladyship seems to have been aware of it, and endeavours to guard against it) placing a people in a body upon our exterior, where they will be contiguous to Canada, who may bring with them strong prejudices against us, and our form of Government, and equally strong attachments to the country and Constitution they leave, without the means, being detached and unmixed with Citizens of different sentiments, of having them eradicated. Her Ladyship has spoken so feelingly and sensibly, on the religeous and benevolent purposes of the plan, that no language of which I am possessed, can add aught to enforce her observations. And no place I think bids so fair to answer her views as that spot in Hutchin's map, mark'd Miami Village and Fort, from hence there is a communication to all parts by water and at which, in my opinion we ought to have a Post.

Do not think it strange my good Sir, that I send you the original papers from Lady Huntington. Many, mistakenly, think I am retired to ease and that kind of tranquility which would grow tiresome for want of employment; but at no period of my life, not in the eight years I served the public, have I been *obliged* to write so much *myself*, as I have done since my retirement. Was this confined to friendly communications, and to my own business, it would be equally pleasing and trifling; but I have a thousand references of old matters with which I ought not to be troubled; but which, nevertheless, must receive some answer; these, with applications for certificates, copies of Orders &c. &c. &c. deprive me of my usual and necessary exercise.

I have tryed, but hitherto in vain, to get a Secretary or Clerk, to take upon him the drudging part of this business: that you might not wonder at my parting with original papers on an important subject, I thought it incumbent upon me to assign the reason, and I beg you to be assured, that I have *no* other motive for it. *Seeks secretary*

Please to accept my thanks for the pamphlet you sent me, and for the resolutions respecting the temporary and permanent seat of Government. If I might be permitted to hazard an opinion of the latter, I would say, that by the time your Federal buildings on the banks of the Delaware, along the point of triangle, are fit for the reception of Congress; it will be found that they are very improperly placed for the seat of the Empire, and will have to undergo a second edition in a more convenient one. If the union continues, and this is not the case, I will agree to be classed among the false prophets, and suffer for evil prediction. The letter for the Marqs. de la Fayette, I pray you to forward by the Packet. With great esteem and regard, I am etc.

104

TO WILLIAM GRAYSON

Mount Vernon, June 22, 1785

Dr. Sir:

Since my last to you I have been favored with your letters of the 5th, 27th, and — of May, and beg your acceptance of my thanks for their enclosures, and for the communications you were pleased to make me therein.

I am very glad to find you have pass'd an Ordinance of Congress respecting the sale of the Western Lands: I am too well acquainted with the local politics of individual States, not to have foreseen the difficulties you met with in this business; these things are to be regretted, but not to be altered until liberallity of sentiment is more universal. Fixing the Seat of Empire at any spot on the Delaware, is in my humble opinion, demonstrably wrong: to incur an expence for what may be call'd the *permanent* seat of Congress, at this time, is I conceive evidently impolitic; for without the gift of prophecy, I will venture to predict that under any circumstance of confederation, it will not remain so far to the Eastward long; and that until the public is in better circumstances, it ought not to be built at all. Time, too powerful for sophistry, will point out the place and disarm localities of their power. In the meanwhile let the widow, the Orphan and the suffering Soldier, who are crying to you for their dues, receive *that* which can very well be rendered to them.

Establishment of a site for a national capital

There is nothing new in this quarter of an interesting nature, to communicate, unless you should not have been informed that the Potomac navigation proceeds under favourable auspices: At the general meeting of the subscribers in May last, it appeared that upwards of 400 of the 500 shares had been engaged; many more have been subscribed since; a Board of Directors have been chosen, proper characters and Labourers advertized for, to commence the work in the least difficult parts of the river, 'till a skillful Engineer can be engaged to undertake those which are more so; and it is expected the work will be begun by the 10th. of next month. With great esteem, &c.

105

TO DAVID HUMPHREYS

Mount Vernon, July 25, 1785

My dr. Humphreys:

Since my last to you, I have received your letter of the 15th. of January, and I believe that of the 11th. of November, and thank you for them. It always gives me pleasure to hear from you; and I should think if *amusements* would spare you, business could not so much absorb your time as to prevent your writing more frequently, especially as there is a regular conveyance once a month by the Packet.

As the complexion of European politics seems now (from letters I have received from the Marqs. de la Fayette, Chevrs. Chartellux, De la Luzerne, &c.,) to have a tendency to Peace, I will say nothing of war, nor make any animadversions upon the contending powers; otherwise, I might possibly have said that the retreat from it seemed impossible after the explicit declaration of the parties: My first wish is to see this plague to mankind banished from off the Earth, and the sons and Daughters of this world employed in more pleasing and innocent amusements, than in preparing implements and exercising them for the destruction of mankind: rather than quarrel about territory let the poor, the needy and oppressed of the Earth, and those who want Land, resort to the fertile plains of our western country, the *second land of Promise*, and there dwell in peace, fulfilling the first and great commandment.

European politics: war, peace, emigration

Praise of
Humphreys

In a former letter, I informed you my Dr. Humphreys, that if I had *talents* for it, I have not *leisure* to turn my thoughts to commentaries: a consciousness of a defective education, and a certainty of the want of time, unfit me for such an undertaking; what with company, letters and other matters, many of them quite extraneous, I have not been able to arrange my own private concerns so as to rescue them from that disorder'd state into which they have been thrown by the war, and to do which is become absolutely necessary for my support, whilst I remain on this stage of human action. The sentiments of your last letter on this subject gave me great pleasure; I should be pleased indeed to see you undertake this business: your abilities as a writer; your discernment respecting the principles which lead to the decision by arms; your personal knowledge of many facts as they occurred in the progress of the War; your disposition to justice, candour and impartiality, and your diligence in investigating truth, combining fit you, when joined with the vigor of life, for this task; and I should with great pleasure, not only give you the perusal of all my papers, but any oral information of circumstances, which cannot be obtained from the former, that my memory will furnish: and I can with great truth add that my house would not only be at your service during the period of your preparing this work, but (and without an unmeaning compliment I say it) I should be exceedingly happy if you would make it your home. You might have an apartment to yourself, in which you could command your own time; you wou'd be considered and treated as one of the family; and meet with that cordial reception and entertainment which are characteristic of the sincerest friendship.

To reverberate European news would be idle, and we have little of domestic kind worthy of attention: We have held treaties indeed, with the Indians; but they were so unseasonably delayed, that these people by our last accounts from the westward, are in a discontented mood, supposed by many to be instigated thereto by our late enemies, now, to be sure, *fast friends*; who from any thing I can learn, under the indefinite expression of the treaty hold, and seem resolved to retain possession of our western Posts. Congress have also, after a long and tedious deliberation, passed an ordinance for laying off the Western Territory into States, and for disposing of the land; but in a manner and on terms which few people (in the

Congressional
ordinance on
western lands

Southern States) conceive can be accomplished: Both sides are sure, and the event is appealed to, let time decide it. It is however to be regretted that local politics and self-interested views obtrude themselves into every measure of public utility: but to such characters be the consequences.

My attention is more immediately engaged in a project which I think big with great political, as well as commercial consequences to these States, especially the middle ones: it is, by removing the obstructions, and extending the inland navigation of our rivers, to bring the States on the Atlantic in close connexion with those forming to the westward, by a short and easy transportation: without this, I can easily conceive they will have different views, separate interests and other connexions. I may be singular in my ideas; but they are these, that to open a door to, and make easy the way for those Settlers to the westward (which ought to progress regularly and compactly) before we make any stir about the navigation of the Mississippi, and before our settlements are far advanced towards that river, would be our true line of policy. It can, I think, be demonstrated, that the produce of the western Territory (if the navigations which are now in hand succeed, and of which I have no doubt) as low down the Ohio as the Great Kanhawa, I *believe* to the Falls, and between the parts above and the Lakes, may be brought either to the highest shipping port on this or James river, at a less expence, with more ease, (including the return) and in a much shorter time, than it can be carried to New Orleans if the Spaniards instead of restricting, were to throw open their ports and invite our trade. But if the commerce of that country should embrace this channel, and connexions be formed; experience has taught us (and there is a very recent proof with G: Britain) how next to impracticable it is to divert it; and if that should be the case, the Atlantic States (especially as those to the westward will in a great degree fill with foreigners) will be no more to the present union, except to excite perhaps very justly our fears, than the Country of California which is still more to the westward, and belonging to another power.

Mrs. Washington presents her compliments to you, and with every wish for your happiness, I am etc.

Inland navigation

106

TO MARQUIS DE LAFAYETTE

Mount Vernon, July 25, 1785

My Dear Marquis:

I have to acknowledge and thank you for your several favors of the 9th. of February, 19th. of March and 16th. of April, with their enclosures; all of which (the last only yesterday) have been received since I had the honor to address you in February.

I stand before you as a Culprit: but to *repent* and *be forgiven* are the precepts of Heaven: I do the former, do you practice the latter, and it will be participation of a divine attribute. Yet I am not barren of excuses for this seeming inattention; frequent absences from home, a round of company when at it, and the pressure of many matters, might be urged as apologies for my long silence; but I disclaim all of them, and trust to the forbearance of friendship and your wonted indulgence: indeed so few things occur, in the line on which I now move, worthy of attention, that this also might be added to the catalogue of my excuses; especially when I further add, that one of my letters, if it is to be estimated according to its length, would make three of yours.

I now congratulate you, and my heart does it more effectually than my pen, on your safe arrival at Paris, from your voyage to this Country, and on the happy meeting with Madame la Fayette and your family in good health. May the blessing of this long continue to them, and may every day add increase of happiness to yourself.

Peace and the Ohio lands

As the clouds which overspread your hemisphere are dispersing, and peace with all its concomitants is dawning upon your Land, I will banish the sound of War from my letter: I wish to see the sons and daughters of the world in Peace and busily employed in the more agreeable amusement of fulfilling the first and great commandment, *Increase and Multiply*: as an encouragement to which we have opened the fertile plains of the Ohio to the poor, the needy and the oppressed of the Earth; any one therefore who is heavy laden, or who wants land to cultivate, may repair thither and abound, as in the Land of promise, with milk and honey: the ways are preparing, and the roads will be made easy, thro' the channels of Potomac and James river.

Speaking of these navigations, I have the pleasure to inform you that the subscriptions, (especially for the first) at the surrender of the books, agreeably to the act which I enclosed you in my last, exceeded my most sanguine expectation: for the latter, that is James river, no comparison of them has yet been made.

Of the £50,000 Sterlg. required for the Potomac navigation, upwards of £40,000, was subscribed before the middle of May, and encreasing fast. A President and four Directors, consisting of your hble. Servant, Govrs. Johnson and Lee of Maryland, and Colo. Fitzgerald and Gilpin of this State, were chosen to conduct the undertaking. The first dividend of the money was paid in on the 15th. of this month; and the work is to be begun the first of next, in those parts which require least skill; leaving the more difficult 'till an Engineer of abilities and practical knowledge can be obtained; which reminds me of the question which I propounded to you in my last, on this subject, and on which I should be glad to learn your sentiments. This prospect, if it succeeds and of which I have no doubt, will bring the Atlantic States and the Western Territory into close connexion, and be productive of very extensive commercial and political consequences; the last of which gave the spur to my exertions, as I could foresee many, and great mischiefs which would naturally result from a separation, and that a separation would inevitably take place, if the obstructions between the two countries remained, and the navigation of the Mississippi should be made free.

Potomac navigation

Great Britain, in her commercial policy is acting the same unwise part, with respect to herself, which seems to have influenced all her Councils; and thereby is defeating her own ends: the restriction of our trade, and her heavy imposts on the staple commodities of this Country, will I conceive, immediately produce powers in Congress to regulate the Trade of the Union; which, more than probably would not have been obtained without in half a century. The mercantile interests of the *whole* Union are endeavouring to effect this, and will no doubt succeed; they see the necessity of a controuling power, and the futility, indeed the absurdity, of each State's enacting Laws for this purpose independent of one another. This will

Commercial policy of Great Britain

be the case also, after a while, in all matters of common concern. It is to be regretted, I confess, that Democratical States must always *feel* before they can *see*: it is this that makes their Governments slow, but the people will be right at last.

Congressional disposal of western lands

Congress after long deliberation, have at length agreed upon a mode for disposing of the Lands of the United States in the Western territory: it may be a good one, but it does not comport with my ideas. The ordinance is long, and I have none of them by me, or I would send one for your perusal. They seem in this instance, as in almost every other, to be surrendering the little power they have, to the States individually which gave it to them. Many think the price which they have fixed upon the Lands too high; and all to the Southward I believe, that disposing of them in Townships, and by square miles alternately, they will be a great let to the sale: but experience, to which there is an appeal, must decide.

A donkey from the King of Spain

Soon after I had written to you in Feby., Mr. Jefferson, and after him Mr. Carmichael informed me that in consequence of an application from Mr. Harrison for permission to export a Jack for me from Spain, his Catholic Majesty had ordered *two* of the first race in his Kingdom (lest an accident might happen to *one*) to be purchased and presented to me as a mark of his esteem. Such an instance of condescension and attention from a crowned head is very flattering, and lays me under great obligation to the King; but neither of them is yet arrived: these I presume are the two mentioned in your favor of the 16th. of April; one as having been shipped from Cadiz, the other as expected from the Isle of Malta, which you would forward. As they have been purchased since December last, I began to be apprehensive of accidents; which I wish may not be the case with respect to the one from Cadiz, if he was actually shipped at the time of your account: should the other pass thro' your hands you cannot oblige me more, than by requiring the greatest care, and most particular attention to be paid to him. I have long endeavoured to procure one of a good size and breed, but had little expectation of receiving two as a royal gift.

Hounds and seeds

I am much obliged to you my dear Marquis, for your attention to the hounds, and not less sorry that you should have met the smallest difficulty, or experienced the least trouble in obtaining them: I was no way anxious about these, consequently should have felt no regret, or sustained no loss if you had not succeeded in your application. I have commissioned three or four persons (among whom Colo. Marshall is one,) to procure for me in Kentucke, for the use of the Kings Garden's at Versailles or elsewhere, the seeds mentioned in the list you sent me from New York, and such others as are curious, and will forward them as soon as they come to my hands; which cannot be 'till after the growing Crop has given its seeds.

My best wishes will accompany you to Potsdam, and into the Austrian Dominions whenever you set out upon that tour. As an unobserved spectator, I should like to take a peep at the troops of those Monarch's at their manoeuverings, upon a grand field day; but as it is among the unattainable things, my philosophy shall supply the place of curiosity, and set my mind at ease.

In your favor of the 19th. of March you speak of letters which were sent by a Mr. Williams; but none such have come to hand. The present for the little folks did not arrive by Mr. Ridouts Ship as you expected; to what cause owing I know not. Mrs. Washington has but indifferent health; and the late loss of her mother, and only brother Mr. Barthw. Dandridge (one of the Judges of our Supreme Court) has rather added to her indisposition. My mother and friends enjoy good health. George has returned after his peregrination thro' the West Indies, to Bermuda, the Bahama Islands, and Charlestown; at the last place he spent the winter. He is in better health than when he set out, but not quite recovered: He is now on a journey to the Sweet Springs, to procure a stock sufficient to fit him for a matrimonial voyage in the Frigate F. Bassett, on board which he means to embark at his return in October: how far his case is desperate, I leave you to judge, if it is so, the remedy however pleasing at first, will certainly be violent.

The latter end of April I had the pleasure to receive in good order, by a Ship from London, the picture of yourself, Madame la Fayette and the children, which I consider as an invaluable present, and shall give it the best place in my House. Mrs. Washington joins me in respectful compliments, and in every good wish for Madame de la Fayette, yourself and family, all the others who have come under your kind notice present their compliments to you. For myself, I can only repeat the sincere attachment, and unbounded affection of My Dr. Marqs., &c.

107

TO EDMUND RANDOLPH

Mount Vernon, July 30, 1785

Dear Sir:

Altho' it is not my intention to derive any pecuniary advantage from the generous vote of the Assembly of this State, consequent of its gratuitous gift of fifty shares in each of the navigations of the rivers Potomac and James; yet, as I consider these undertakings as of vast political and commercial importance to the States on the Atlantic, especially to those nearest the centre of the Union, and adjoining the Western Territory, I can let no act of mine impede the progress of the work: I have therefore come to the determination to hold the shares which the Treasurer was directed to subscribe on my account, in trust for the use and benefit of the public; unless I shall be able to discover, before the meeting of the Assembly, that it would be agreeable to it to have the product of the Sales arising from these shares, applied as a fund on which to establish two Charity schools, one on each river, for the Education and support of the Children of the poor and indigent of this Country who cannot afford to give it; particularly the children of those men of this description, who have fallen in defence of the rights and liberties of it. If the plans succeed, of which I have no doubt, I am sure it will be a very productive and encreasing fund, and the monies thus applied will be a beneficial institun.

Shares in waterways companies for charitable purposes

I am aware that my non-acceptance of these shares will have various motives ascribed to it, among which an ostentatious display of disinterestedness, perhaps the charge of disrespect or slight of the favors of my Country, may lead the van: but under a consciousness that my conduct herein is not influenced by considerations of this nature, and that I shall act more agreeably to my own feelings and more consistent with my early declarations, by declining to accept them; I shall not only hope for indulgence, but a favorable interpretation of my conduct: my friends, I persuade myself, will acquit me, the World I hope will judge charitably.

Perceiving by the advertisement of Messrs. Cabell, Buchanan and Southa; that half the sum required by the Act, for opening and extending the navigation of James river, is subscribed; and the 20th. of next month appointed for the subscribers to meet at Richmond, I take the liberty of giving you a power to act for me on that occasion. I would (having the accomplishment of these navigations much at heart) have attended in person; but the President and Directors of the Potomac Company by their own appointment, are to commence the survey of this river in the early part of next month; for which purpose I shall leave home tomorrow. Besides which, if the Ejectments which I have been obliged to bring for my Land in Pennsylva. are to be tried at the September Term, as Mr. Smith, my Lawyer, conceived they would, and is to inform me, I shall find it necessary I fear, to attend the trial; an intermediate journey therefore, in addition, to Richmond would be impracticable for me to accomplish. I am, etc.

108

TO JAMES McHENRY

Mount Vernon, August 22, 1785

Dr. Sir:

Your letter of the first inst: came to this place whilst I was absent on a tour up the river, or an earlier acknowledgment of it shou'd have been sent to you: the inclosure shall, either by this or the next post, be sent to Dr. Gordon for his information, and that justice may be done to a character so deserving American gratitude and the pen of an historian, as the Marqs. de la Fayette.

I am very glad to hear that Congress are relieved from the embarrassment which originated with Longchamp: had the demand of him been persisted in, it might have involved very serious consequences; it is better for the Court of France to be a little vexed, than for it to have perservered in the demand of him.

As I have ever been a friend to adequate powers of Congress, without which it is evident to me we never shall establish a national character, or be considered as on a respectable footing by the powers of Europe, I am sorry I cannot agree with you in sentiment not to enlarge them for the regulating of commerce. I have neither time nor abilities to enter into a full discussion of this subject, but it should seem to me that your arguments against it; principally, that some States may be

Powers of Congress over regulation of commerce

more benefited than others by a commercial regulation, apply
to every matter of general utility; for can there be a case enumerated in which this argument has not its force in a greater
or less degree? We are either a united people under one head,
and for federal purposes; or we are thirteen independant sovereignties, eternally counteracting each other: if the former,
whatever such a majority of the States as the Constitution
points out, conceives to be for the benefit of the whole, should,
in my humble opinion, be submitted to by the minority; let the
southern States always be represented; let them act more in
union; let them declare freely and boldly what is for the interest of, and what is prejudicial to their constituents; and there
will, there *must* be an accommodating spirit; in the establishment of a navigation act, this in a particular manner ought,
and will doubtless be attended to. If the assent of nine (or as
some propose, of eleven) States is necessary to give validity to a
Commercial system; it insures this measure, or it cannot be
obtained: Wherein then lies the danger? But if your fears are
in danger of being realized, cannot certain provisos in the
ordinance guard against the evil? I see no difficulty in this, if
the southern Delegates would give their attendance in Congress, and follow the example, if it should be set them, of
hanging together to counteract combinations. I confess to you
candidly, that I can foresee no evil greater than disunion than
those *unreasonable* jealousies (I say *unreasonable*, because I
would have a *proper* jealousy always awake, and the United
States on the watch to prevent individual States from in-
fracting the constitution with impunity) which are continually
poisoning our minds and filling them with imaginary evils to
the prevention of real ones.

Imposts on trade with Great Britain

As you have asked the question, I answer, I do not know that
we can enter upon a war of Imposts with Gt: Britain, or any
other foreign power; but we are certain that this war has been
waged agst. us by the former, *professedly* upon a belief that we
never could unite in opposition to it; and I *believe* there is no
way of putting an end to, or at least of stopping the encrease of
it, but to convince them of the contrary. Our trade in all points
of view, is as essential to G: B: as hers is to us; and she will
exchange it upon reciprocal and liberal terms, if better cannot
be had. It can hardly be supposed, I think, that the carrying
business will devolve wholly on the States you have named, or
remain long with them if it should; for either G: B: will depart

from her present contracted system; or the policy of the southern States in framing the Act of navigation, or by Laws passed by themselves individually, will devise ways and means to encourage seamen for the transportation of the product of their respective Countries, or for the encouragement of _____ . But admitting the contrary; if the Union is considered as permanent, (and on this I presume all superstructures are built) had we not better encourage seamen among ourselves, with less imports, than divide it with foreigners, and by increasing the amount of them, ruin our Merchants and greatly injuring the mass of our Citizens?

To sum up the whole, I foresee, or think I do it, the many advantages which will arise from giving powers of this kind to Congress (if a sufficient number of States are required to exercise them) without any evil, save that which may proceed from inattention, or want of wisdom in the formation of the act; whilst without them we stand in a ridiculous point of view in the eyes of the nations of the world with whom we are attempting to enter into Commercial treaties, without means of carrying them into effect; who must see and feel that the Union, or the States individually are sovereigns as best suits their purposes; in a word, that we are one nation today, and thirteen tomorrow, who will treat with us on such terms? But perhaps I have gone too far, and therefore will only add that Mrs. Washington offers her compliments and best wishes for you and that with great esteem etc.

109

TO GEORGE MASON

Mount Vernon, October 3, 1785

Dr. Sir:

I have this moment received yours of yesterday's date, enclosing a memorial and remonstrance against the Assessment Bill, which I will read with attention. At *present* I am unable to do it, on account of company. The bill itself I do not recollect ever to have read; with *attention* I am certain I never did, but will compare them together.

Altho, no man's sentiments are more opposed to *any kind* of restraint upon religious principles than mine are; yet I must

On taxes for the support of teachers of Christianity in Virginia

confess, that I am not amongst the number of those who are so much alarmed at the thoughts of making people pay towards the support of that which they profess, if of the denomination of Christians; or declare themselves Jews, Mahomitans or otherwise, and thereby obtain proper relief. As the matter now stands, I wish an assessment had never been agitated, and as it has gone so far, that the Bill could die an easy death; because I think it will be productive of more quiet to the State, than by enacting it into a Law; which, in my opinion, would be impolitic, admitting there is a decided majority for it, to the disquiet of a respectable minority. In the first case the matter will soon subside; in the latter, it will rankle and perhaps convulse, the State. The Dinner Bell rings, and I must conclude with an expression of my concern for your indisposition. Sincerely and affectionately, I am &c.

110

TO JAMES WARREN

Mount Vernon, October 7, 1785

Dear Sir:

The assurances of your friendship, after a silence of more than six years, are extremely pleasing to me. Friendships, formed under the circumstances that ours commenced, are not easily eradicated; and I can assure you, that mine has undergone no diminution; every occasion, therefore, of renewing it, will give me pleasure, and I shall be happy at all times to hear of your welfare.

The war, as you have justly observed, has terminated most advantageously for America, and a fair field is presented to our view; but I confess to you freely, My Dr. Sir, that I do not think we possess wisdom or Justice enough to cultivate it properly. Illiberality, Jealousy, and local policy mix too much in all our public councils for the good government of the Union. In a word, the confederation appears to me to be little more than a shadow without the substance; and Congress a nugatory body, their ordinances being little attended to. To *me*, it is a solecism in politics: indeed it is one of the most extraordinary things in nature, that we should confederate as a Nation, and yet be afraid to give the rulers of that nation, who are the creatures of our making, appointed for a limited and short duration, and who are amenable for every action, and recallable at any moment, and are subject to all the evils which they may be instrumental in producing, sufficient powers to order and direct the affairs of the same. By such policy as this the wheels of Government are clogged, and our brightest prospects, and that high expectation which was entertained of us by the wondering world, are turned into astonishment; and from the high ground on which we stood, we are descending into the vale of confusion and darkness.

Wheels of government clogged

That we have it in our power to become one of the most respectable Nations upon Earth, admits, in my humble opinion, of no doubt; if we would but pursue a wise, just, and liberal policy towards one another, and would keep good faith with the rest of the World: that our resources are ample and encreasing, none can deny; but while they are grudgingly applyed, or not applyed at all, we give a vital stab to public faith, and shall sink, in the eyes of Europe, into contempt.

It has long been a speculative question among Philosophers and wise men, whether foreign Commerce is of real advantage to any Country; that is, whether the luxury, effeminacy, and corruptions which are introduced along with it; are counterbalanced by the convenience and wealth which it brings with it; but the decision of this question is of very little importance to us; we have abundant reason to be convinced, that the spirit for Trade which pervades these States is not to be restrained; it behooves us then to establish just principles; and this, any more than other matters of national concern, cannot be done by thirteen heads differently constructed and organized. The necessity, therefore, of a controuling power is obvious; and why it should be withheld is beyond my comprehension.

Usefulness of foreign commerce

The Agricultural Society, lately established in Philadelphia, promises extension usefulness if it is prosecuted with spirit. I wish most sincerely that every State in the Union would institute similar ones; and that these Societies would correspond fully and freely with each other, and communicate all useful discoveries founded on practice, with a due attention to climate, soil, and Seasons to the public.

Philadelphia Agricultural Society

The great works of improving and extending the inland navigations of the two large rivers Potomac and James, which interlock with the waters of the Western Territory, are already begun, and I have little doubt of their success. The conse-

Union and inland navigation

quences to the Union, in my judgment are immense: more so in a political, than in a commercial view; for unless we can connect the new States which are rising to our view in those regions, with those on the Atlantic by *interest*, (the only binding cement, and no otherwise to be effected but by opening such communications as will make it easier and cheaper for them to bring the product of their labour to our markets, instead of going to the Spaniards southerly, or the British northerly), they will be quite a distinct people; and ultimately may be very troublesome neighbours to us. In themselves considered merely as a hardy race, this *may* happen; how much more so, if linked with either of those powers in politics and commerce.

It would afford me great pleasure to go over those grounds in your State with a mind more at ease, than when I travelled them in 1775 and 1776; and to unite in congratulating on the happy change, with those characters, who participated of the anxious moments we passed in those days, and for whom I entertain a sincere regard; but I do not know whether to flatter myself with the enjoyment of it: the deranged state of my affairs, from an absence and total neglect of them for almost nine years, and a pressure of other matters, allow me little leisure for gratifications of this sort. Mrs. Washington offers her compliments and best wishes to Mrs. Warren, to which be pleased to add those of, dear Sir, &c.

111

TO JAMES MADISON

Mount Vernon, November 30, 1785

My dear Sir:

Receive my thanks for your obliging communications of the 11th. I hear with much pleasure that the Assembly are engaged, seriously, in the consideration of the revised Laws. A short and simple code, in my opinion, tho' I have the sentiments of some of the Gentlemen of the long robe against me, would be productive of happy consequences, and redound to the honor of this or any Country which shall adopt such.

A simple law code

I hope the resolutions which were published for the consideration of the House, respecting the reference to Congress for the regulation of a Commercial system will have passed. The

Resolution on regulation of commerce

proposition in my opinion is so self evident that I confess I am at a loss to discover wherein lyes the weight of the objection to the measure. We are either a United people, or we are not. If the former, let us, in all matters of general concern act as a nation, which have national objects to promote, and a national character to support. If we are not, let us no longer act a farce by pretending to it. For whilst we are playing a dble. game, or playing a game between the two we never shall be consistent or respectable; but *may* be the dupes of some powers and, most assuredly, the contempt of all. In any case it behoves us to provide good Military Laws, and look well to the execution of them, but, if we mean by our conduct that the States shall act independently of each other it becomes *indispensably* necessary, for therein will consist our strength and respectabity in the Union.

It is much to be wished that public faith may be held inviolate. Painful is it even in thought that attempts should be made to weaken the bands of it. It is a dangerous experiment, once slacken the reins and the power is lost, and it is questionable with me whether the advocates of the measure foresee all the consequences of it. It is an old adage that honesty is the best policy; this applies to public as well as private life, to States as well as individuals. I hope the Port and assize Bills no longer sleep, but are awakened to a happy establishment. The first with some alterations, would, in my judgment be productive of great good to this Country; without it, the Trade thereof I conceive will ever labor and languish; with respect to the Second if it institutes a speedier Administration of Justice it is equally desirable.

It gives me great pleasure to hear that our assembly were in a way of adopting a mode for establishing the Cut betwn. Elizabeth river and Pasquotank which was likely to meet the approbation of the State of No. Carolina. It appears to me that no Country in the Universe is better calculated to derive benefits from inland Navigation than this is, and certain I am, that the conveniences to the Citizens individually, and the sources of wealth to the Country generally, which will be opened thereby will be found to exceed the most sanguine imagination; the Mind can scarcely take in at one view all the benefits which will result therefrom. The saving in draught Cattle, preservation of Roads &ca. &ca. will be felt most interestingly. This business only wants a beginning. Rappahanock, Shan-

Rivers, roads, and canals

nondoah, Roanoke, and the branches of York River will soon perceive the advantages which water transportation (in ways hardly thought of at first) have over that of Land and will extend Navigation to almost every mans door.

From the complexion of the debates in the Pensylvania it should seem as if that Legislature intended their assent to the proposition from the States of Virginia and Maryland respecting a road to the Yohiogany should be conditional of permission given to open a Communication between the Chesapeak and Delaware by way of the rivers Elk and Christeen, which I am sure will never be obtained if the Baltimore interest can give it effectual opposition.

The Directors of the Potomack Company have sent to the Delegates of this County to be laid before the Assembly a Petition (which sets forth the reasons) for relief in the depth of the Canals which it may be found necessary to open at the great and little Falls of the River. As public oeconomy and private interest equally prompt the measure and no possible disadvantage that we can see will attend granting the prayer of it, we flatter ourselves no opposition will be given to it.

To save trouble to expidite the business, and to secure uniformity without delay, or an intercourse between the Assemblies on so trivial a matter we have taken the liberty of sending the draught of a Bill to Members of both Assemblies which if approved will be found exactly similar. With the highest esteem etc.

112

TO HENRY LEE

Mount Vernon, April 5, 1786

My Dr. Sir:

Ascribe my silence to any cause rather than a want of friendship, or to a disclination to keep up a friendly intercourse with you, by letter. Absences from home, hurry of business, Company &c., however justly they might be offered, are too stale and common place to be admitted. I therefore discard them; throwing myself upon your lenity, and depending more upon your goodness, than on any apology I can make as an excuse for not having acknowledged the receipt of your favours of the 16th. of Feby. and 2d. of March, before this time.

The first came to hand just after I had made one trip to our works at the great Falls of this River; and when I was upon the eve of another to the same place, where the Board of Directors by appointment met the first of last month. I can therefore inform you from my own observation, that this business is progressing in a manner that exceeds our most sanguine expectation, difficulties vanish as we proceed, the time and expence which it was supposed we should have to encounter at this place, will both be considerably reduced. After a thorough investigation of the ground there *we* have departed from Ballandine's rout for the Canal, and marked a fresh cut, which in our judgments will save 4/5th. of the labour, consequently proportionate time and expence, and in the opinion of Mr. Brindley who has just been to see it, 9/10ths., and be equally good when effected. Upon the whole, to be laconic, if there are any doubts remaining of the success of this work, they must be confined to three classes of men, viz: those who have not opportunities of investigations, who will not be at the trouble of doing it when it is in their power, and those whose interests being opposed, do not *wish* to be convinced. The great Fall is the only place where, under our present view of the River, we conceive it necessary to establish Locks; the ground favors them, and there can be no doubt (this being the case) of Locks succeeding as well in this as in other Countries, as the materials for erecting them are abundant. What difficulties may be found where no difficulty was apprehended, I will not take upon me to declare: where they were thought wholly to lie, we are free from apprehension.

My sentiments with respect to the foederal Government, are well known, publicly and privately have they been communicated without reserve; but my *opinion* is, that there is more wickedness than ignorance in the conduct of the States, or in other words, in the conduct of those who have too much influence in the government of them; and until the curtain is withdrawn, and the private views and selfish principles upon which these men act, are exposed to public notice, I have little hope of amendment without another convulsion. The picture of our Affairs as drawn by the Committee, approved by Congress and handed to the public, did not at all surprise me: before that report, tho' I could not go into the minutiae of

Visit to canal works

Conduct of the states

matters, I was more certain of the agregate of our [Here the available manuscript is blank.] than I am now of the remedy which will be applied; without the latter I do not see upon what ground your Agent at the Court of Morocco, and the other at Algiers, are to treat, unless, having to do with new hands, they mean to touch the old string, and make them dance awhile to the tune of promises.

I thank you for the pamphlet which contains the correspondence between Mr. Jay and Mr. Littlepage; and shall be obliged to you for a Gazette containing the publication of the latter, which appears to have given rise to them. I am, etc.

113

TO ROBERT MORRIS

Mount Vernon, April 12, 1786

Dear Sir:

Society of Quakers

I give you the trouble of this letter at the instance of Mr. Dalby of Alexandria; who is called to Philadelphia to attend what he conceives to be a vexatious lawsuit respecting a slave of his, which a Society of Quakers in the city (formed for such purposes) have attempted to liberate; The merits of this case will no doubt appear upon trial. but from Mr. Dalby's state of the matter, it should seem that this Society is not only acting repugnant to justice so far as its conduct concerns strangers, but, in my opinion extremely impolitickly with respect to the State, the City in particular; and without being able, (but by acts of tyranny and oppression) to accomplish their own ends. He says the conduct of this society is not sanctioned by Law: had the case been otherwise, whatever my opinion of the Law might have been, my respect for the policy of the State would on this occasion have appeared in my silence; because against the penalties of promulgated Laws one may guard; but there is no avoiding the snares of individuals, or of private societies. And if the practice of this Society of which Mr. Dalby speaks, is not discountenanced, none of those whose *misfortune* it is to have slaves as attendants, will visit the City if they can possibly avoid it; because by so doing they hazard their property; or they must be at the expence (and this will not always succeed) of providing servants of another description for the trip.

I hope it will not be conceived from these observations, that *Slavery* it is my wish to hold the unhappy people, who are the subject of this letter, in slavery. I can only say that there is not a man living who wishes more sincerely than I do, to see a plan adopted for the abolition of it; but there is only one proper and effectual mode by which it can be accomplished, and that is by Legislative authority; and this, as far as my suffrage will go, shall never be wanting. But when slaves who are happy and contented with their present masters, are tampered with and seduced to leave them; when masters are taken unawares by these practices; when a conduct of this sort begets discontent on one side and resentment on the other, and when it happens to fall on a man, whose purse will not measure with that of the Society, and he looses his property for want of means to defend it; it is oppression in the latter case, and not humanity in any; because it introduces more evils than it can cure.

I will make no apology for writing to you on this subject; for if Mr. Dalby has not misconceived the matter, an evil exists which requires a remedy; if he has, my intentions have been good, though I may have been too precipitate in this address. Mrs. Washington joins me in every good and kind wish for Mrs. Morris and your family, and I am, &c.

114

TO MARQUIS DE LAFAYETTE

Mount Vernon, May 10, 1786

My dear Marquis:

The Letter which you did me the favor to write to me by Mr. Barrett dated the 6th. of Feby., together with the parcel and packages which accompanied it, came safely to hand; and for which I pray you to accept my grateful acknowledgments.

The account given of your tour thro' Prussia and other *Lafayette's* States of Germany, to Vienna and back; and of the Troops *European tour* which you saw reviewed in the pay of those Monarchs, at different places, is not less pleasing than it is interesting; and must have been as instructive as entertaining to yourself. Your reception at the Courts of Berlin, Vienna, and elsewhere must have been pleasing to you: to have been received by the King of Prussia, and Prince Henry his brother, (who as soldiers and politicians can yield the palm to none) with such marks of attention and distinction, was as indicative of their discernment, as it is of your merit, and will encrease my opinion of them. It is to be lamented however that great characters are seldom without a blot. That one man should tyranise over millions, will always be a shade in that of the former; whilst it is pleasing to hear that a due regard to the rights of mankind, is characteristic of the latter: I shall revere and love him for this trait of his character. To have viewed the several fields of Battle over which you passed, could not, among other sensations, have failed to excite this thought, here have fallen thousands of gallant spirits to satisfy the ambition of, or to support their sovereigns perhaps in acts of oppression or injustice! melancholy reflection! For what wise purposes does Providence permit this? Is it as a scourge for mankind, or is it to prevent them from becoming too populous? If the latter, would not the fertile plains of the Western world receive the redundancy of the old?

For the several articles of intelligence with which you have been so good as to furnish me, and for your sentimts. on European politics, I feel myself very much obliged; on these I can depend. Newspaper accounts are too sterile, vague and contradictory, on which to form any opinion, or to claim even the smallest attention.

One evil of democratic government

The account of and observations which you have made on the policy and practice of Great Britain at the other Courts of Europe, respecting these States, I was but too well informed and convinced of before. Unhappily for us, though their accounts are greatly exaggerated, yet our conduct has laid the foundation for them. It is one of the evils of democratical governments, that the people, not always seeing and frequently misled, must often feel before they can act right; but then evils of this nature seldom fail to work their own cure. It is to be lamented, nevertheless, that the remedies are so slow, and that those, who may wish to apply them seasonably are not attended to before they suffer in person, in interest and in reputation. I am not without hopes, that matters will take a more favorable turn in the foederal Constitution. The discerning part of the community have long since seen the necessity of giving adequate powers to Congress for national purposes; and the ignorant and designing must yield to it ere long. Several late Acts of the different Legislatures have a tendency thereto; among these, the Impost which is now acceded to by every State in the Union, (tho' clogged a little by that of New York) will enable Congress to support the national credit in pecuniary matters better than it has been; whilst a measure in which this state has taken the lead at its last session, will it is to be hoped give efficient powers to that Body for all commercial purposes. This is a nomination of some of its first characters to meet other Commissioners from the several States in order to consider of and decide upon such powers as shall be necessary for the sovereign power of them to act under; which are to be reported to the respective Legislatures at their autumnal sessions for, it is to be hoped, final adoption; thereby avoiding those tedious and futile deliberations, which result from recommendations and partial concurrences; at the same time that it places it at once in the power of Congress to meet European Nations upon decisive and equal ground. All the Legislatures, which I have heard from, have come into the proposition, and have made very judicious appointments: much good is expected from this measure, and it is regretted by many, that more objects were not embraced by the meeting. A General Convention is talked of by many for the purpose of revising and correcting the defects of the foederal government; but whilst this is the wish of some, it is the dread of others from an opinion that matters are not yet sufficiently ripe for such an event.

Nomination of commissioners to revise congressional powers

The British still occupy our Posts to the Westward, and will, I am persuaded, continue to do so under one pretence or another, no matter how shallow, as long as they can: of this, from some circumstances which had occurred, I have been convinced since August, 1783 and gave it as my opinion at that time, if not officially to Congress as the sovereign, at least to a number of its members, that they might act accordingly. It is indeed evident to me, that they had it in contemplation to do this at the time of the Treaty; the expression of the Article which respects the evacuation of them, as well as the tenor of their conduct since relative to this business, is strongly marked with deception. I have not the smallest doubt but that every secret engine is continually at work to inflame the Indian mind, with a view to keep it at variance with these States, for the purpose of retarding our settlements to the Westward, and depriving us of the fur and peltry trade of that country.

British in the west

Donkeys from Spain

Your assurances my dear Marquis, respecting the male and female Asses, are highly pleasing to me, I shall look for them with much expectation and great satisfaction, as a valuable acquisition and important service.

The Jack which I have already received from Spain, in appearance is fine; but his late royal master, tho' past his grand climacteric, cannot be less moved by female allurements than he is; or when prompted, can proceed with more deliberation and majestic solemnity to the work of procreation. The other Jack perished at Sea.

Potomac Company

Mr. Littlepage in his dispute with Mr. Jay seems to have forgot his former situation. It is a pity, for he appears to be a young man of abilities. At the next meeting of the Potomac Company (which I believe will not be 'till August) I will communicate to them your sentiments respecting the terms on which a good Ingénieur des ponts and chaussées may be had and take their opinion thereon.

Emancipation of slaves

The benevolence of your heart my Dr. Marqs. is so conspicuous upon all occasions, that I never wonder at any fresh proofs of it; but your late purchase of an estate in the colony of Cayenne, with a view of emancipating the slaves on it, is a generous and noble proof of your humanity. Would to God a like spirit would diffuse itself generally into the minds of the people of this country; but I despair of seeing it. Some petitions were presented to the Assembly, at its last Session, for the abolition of slavery, but they could scarcely obtain a reading. To set them afloat at once would, I really believe, be productive of much inconvenience and mischief; but by degrees it certainly might, and assuredly ought to be effected; and that too by legislative authority.

I give you the trouble of a letter to the Marqs. de St. Simon, in which I have requested to be presented to Mr. de Menonville. The favourable terms in which you speak of Mr. Jefferson gives me great pleasure: he is a man of whom I early imbibed the highest opinion. I am as much pleased, therefore, to meet confirmations of my discernment in these matters, as I am mortified when I find myself mistaken.

I send herewith the copies of your private Letters to me, promised in my last, and which have been since copied by your old aid. As Mrs. Washington and myself have both done ourselves the honor of writing to Madame de la Fayette, I shall not give you the trouble at this time of presenting my respects to her; but pray to accept every good wish which this family can render for your health and every blessing this life can afford you. I cannot conclude without expressing to you the earnest enquiries and ardent wishes of your friends (among whom, I claim to stand first) to see you in America, and of giving you repeated assurances of the sincerity of my friendship, and of the Affectionate regard with which I am etc.

115

TO THE SECRETARY
FOR FOREIGN AFFAIRS

Mount Vernon, May 18, 1786

Dear Sir:

In due course of post, I have been honored with your favors of the 2d. and 16th. of March; since which I have been a good deal engaged and pretty much from home. For the enclosure which accompanied the first, I thank you. Mr. Littlepage seems to have forgot what had been his situation, forgot what was due to you, and indeed what was necessary to his own character: and his guardian, I think, seems to have forgotten every thing.

I coincide perfectly in sentiment with you, my Dr. Sir, that there are errors in our national Government which call for correction, loudly I would add; but I shall find myself happily mistaken if the remedies are at hand. We are certainly in a delicate situation, but my fear is that the people are not yet sufficiently *misled* to retract from error. To be plainer, I think there is more wickedness than ignorance mixed in our Councils. Under this impression, I scarcely know what opinion to entertain of a general convention. That it is necessary to revise and amend the articles of confederation, I entertain *no* doubt; but what may be the consequences of such an attempt is doubtful. Yet something must be done, or the fabrick must fall, for it certainly is tottering.

Errors in government

Ignorance and design are difficult to combat. Out of these proceed illiberal sentiments, *improper* jealousies, and a train of evils which oftentimes, in republican governments, must be sorely felt before they can be removed. The former, that is ignorance, being a fit soil for the latter to work in, tools are employed by them which a generous mind would disdain to use; and which nothing but time, and their own puerile or wicked productions can show the inefficacy and dangerous tendency of. I think often of our situation and view it with concern. From the high ground we stood upon, from the plain path which invited our footsteps, to be so fallen! so lost! it is really mortifying; but virtue, I fear has, in a great degree, taken its departure from us; and the want of disposition to do justice is the source of the national embarrassments; for whatever guise or colorings are given to them, this I apprehend is the origin of the evils we now feel, and probably shall labour under for some time yet. With respectful complimts. to Mrs. Jay, and sentiments of sincere friendship, I am &c.

116

TO MARQUIS DE LAFAYETTE

Mount Vernon, August 15, 1786

My dr. Marqs:

I will not conceal that my numerous correspondencies are daily becoming irksome to me; yet I always receive your letters with augmenting satisfaction, and therefore rejoice with you in the measures which are likely to be productive of a more frequent intercourse between our two nations. Thus, motives of a private as well as of a public nature conspire to give me pleasure, in finding that the active policy of France is preparing to take advantage of the supine stupidity of England, with respect to our commerce.

French and English commercial policy

While the latter by its impolitic duties and restrictions is driving our Ships incessantly from its harbours; the former seems by the invitations it is giving to stretch forth the friendly hand to invite them into its Ports. I am happy in a conviction, that there may be established between France and the U.S., such a mutual intercourse of good offices and reciprocal interests, as cannot fail to be attended with the happiest consequences. Nations are not influenced, as individuals may be, by disinterested friendships; but, when it is their interest to live in amity, we have little reason to apprehend any rupture. This principle of union can hardly exist in a more distinguished

French and American friendship and commerce

manner between two nations, than it does between France and the United States. There are many articles of manufacture which we stand absolutely in need of and shall continue to have occasion for so long as we remain an agricultural people, which will be while lands are so cheap and plenty, that is to say, for ages to come.

In the mean time we shall have large quantities of timber, fish, oil, wheat, Tobo., rice, Indigo, &c. to dispose of: Money we have not. Now it is obvious that we must have recourse for the Goods and manufactures we may want, to the nation which will enable us to pay for them by receiving our Produce in return. Our commerce with any of the great manufacturing Kingdoms of Europe will therefore be in proportion to the facility of making remittance, which such manufacturing nation may think proper to afford us. On the other hand, France has occasion for many of our productions and raw materials; let her judge whether it is most expedient to receive them by direct importation and to pay for them in goods; or to obtain them thro' the circuitous channel of Britain and to pay for them in money as she formerly did.

I know that Britain arrogantly expects we will sell our produce wherever we can find a market and bring the money to purchase goods from her; I know that she vainly hopes to retain what share she pleases in our trade, in consequence of our prejudices in favor of her fashions and manufactures; but these are illusions, which will vanish and disappoint her, as the dreams of conquest have already done. Experience is constantly teaching us, that these predilections were founded in error. We find the quality and price of the French goods we receive in many instances, to be better than the quality and price of the English. Time, and a more thorough acquaintance with the business may be necessary to instruct your merchants in the choice and assortment of Goods necessary for such a Country. As to an ability for giving credit, in which the English merchants boast a superiority, I am confident it would be happy for America if the practice could be entirely abolished.

British trade expectations

However unimportant America may be considered at present, and however Britain may affect to despise her trade, there will assuredly come a day, when this country will have some weight in the scale of Empires. While connected with us as Colonies only, was not Britain the first power in the World? Since the dissolution of that connexion, does not France occu-

Future growth of American commercial influence

py the same illustrious place? Your successful endeavors my Dr. Marqs., to promote the interests of your two Countries (as you justly call them) must give you the most unadulterated satisfaction: be assured the measures which have lately been taken with regard to the two Articles of *Oil* and *Tobacco*, have tended very much to endear you to your fellow Citizens on this side of the Atlantic.

Influence of commerce on humanity

Altho' I pretend to no peculiar information respecting commercial affairs, nor any foresight into the scenes of futurity; yet as the member of an infant empire, as a Philanthropist by character, and (if I may be allowed the expression) as a Citizen of the great republic of humanity at large; I cannot help turning my attention sometimes to this subject. I would be understood to mean, I cannot avoid reflecting with pleasure on the probable influence that commerce may hereafter have on human manners and society in general. On these occasions I consider how mankind may be connected like one great family in fraternal ties. I indulge a fond, perhaps an enthusiastic idea, that as the world is evidently much less barbarous than it has been, its melioration must still be progressive; that nations are becoming more humanized in their policy, that the subjects of ambition and causes for hostility are daily diminishing, and, in fine, that the period is not very remote, when the benefits of a liberal and free commerce will, pretty generally, succeed to the devastations and horrors of war.

Prussia, the Barbary states

Some of the late treaties which have been entered into, and particularly that between the King of Prussia and the Ud. States, seem to constitute a new era in negotiation, and to promise the happy consequences I have just now been mentioning. But let me ask you my Dr. Marquis, in such an enlightened, in such a liberal age, how is it possible the great maritime powers of Europe should submit to pay an annual tribute to the little piratical States of Barbary? Would to Heaven we had a navy able to reform those enemies to mankind, or crush them into non-existence.

I forbear to enter into a discussion of our domestic Politics, because there is little interesting to be said upon them, and perhaps it is best to be silent, since I could not disguise or palliate where I might think them erroneous. The British still hold the frontier Posts, and are determined to do so. The Indians commit some trifling ravages, but there is nothing like a general or even open war. You will have heard what a loss we have met with by the death of poor Genl. Greene. General McDougal and Colo. Tilghman are also dead.

It is a great satisfaction to have it in my power to pay some attention to Monsr. Du Plessis, by whom I had the happiness of receiving your last letter: he is now at Mount Vernon on his way to Georgia.

You will see by the length to which I have extended this letter, that I can never find myself weary of conversing with you. Adieu, My Dr. Marqs.

CHAPTER NINE

PRESIDING IN THE CONVENTION, 1787

Making a Constitution

1786 — 1788

*W*ASHINGTON's replies to Bushrod Washington in *1786* distill much of his political judgment in the period of constitutional turmoil immediately prior to the Constitutional Convention. Our understanding is bettered in knowing the context set forth by Bushrod's letter of September *27*, *1786*. In that letter, Bushrod announced to Washington the formation of a "Patriotic Society" whose object was "to inquire into the state of public affairs; to consider in what the true happiness of the people consists, and what are the evils which have pursued, and still continue to molest us; the means of attaining the former, and escaping the latter; to inquire into the conduct of those who represent us, and to give them our sentiments upon those laws, which ought to be or are already made." In reply to Washington's initial response, which questioned the motives of such an association, Bushrod answered: "we thought that an appearance of corruption was discoverable in the mass of the people. . . ." He held that the Patriotic Society did not aim to usurp the privileges of duly constituted representatives, but only to reinforce the most salutary aspects of republican government. Washington's second letter (November *15*) closed the correspondence.

The expectant air of Washington's correspondence during this period justifies his observation that "the present era is pregnant of great and strange events." The role he played in these events becomes central in constructing an accurate view of his political ideas. In the Constitutional Convention, Washington played a pivotal though quiet role. Elected to preside, he did not participate in the debates, with one notable exception. On the final day of the Convention, after the Constitution had been readied for signing, a motion was made to alter the rule of representation to facilitate greater participation by the people. The Convention had debated and rejected that proposition more than once in the preceding weeks. Washington stepped down from the presiding chair and declared "his wish that the alteration proposed might take place." The debate ceased there, and a unanimous vote of approval followed. The influence which was visible on that singular occasion had been exercised invisibly throughout the course of the Convention, as Washington maintained regular though informal conversation with the diverse delegates.

117

TO JOHN JAY

Mount Vernon, August 15, 1786

Dear Sir:

I have to thank you very sincerely for your interesting letter of the 27th of June, as well as for the other communications you had the goodness to make at the same time.

I'm sorry to be assured, of what indeed I had little doubt before, that we have been guilty of violating the treaty in some instances. What a misfortune it is the British should have so well grounded a pretext for their palpable infractions? And what a disgraceful part, out of the choice of difficulties before us, are we to act?

Violation of peace treaty with Great Britain

Your sentiments, that our affairs are drawing rapidly to a crisis, accord with my own. What the event will be is also beyond the reach of my foresight. We have errors to correct. We have probably had too good an opinion of human nature in forming our confederation. Experience has taught us, that men will not adopt & carry into execution, measures the best calculated for their own good without the intervention of a coercive power. I do not conceive we can exist long as a nation, without having lodged somewhere a power which will pervade the whole Union in as energetic a manner, as the authority of the different state governments extend over the several States. To be fearful of vesting Congress, constituted as that body is, with ample authorities for national purposes, appears to me the very climax of popular absurdity and madness.

Could Congress exert them for the detriment of the public without injuring themselves in as equal or greater proportion? Are not their interests inseparably connected with those of their constituents? By the rotation of appointment must they not mingle frequently with the mass of citizens? Is it not rather to be apprehended, if they were possessed of the power before described, that the individual members would be induced to use them, on many occasions, very timidly & inefficaciously for fear of losing their popularity & future election? We must take human nature as we find it. Perfection falls not to the share of mortals. Many are of opinion that Congress have too frequently made use of the suppliant humble tone of requisition, in applications to the States, when they had a right to assume their imperial dignity and command obedience. Be that as it may, requisitions are a perfect nihility, where thirteen sovereign, independent, disunited States are in the habit of discussing & refusing compliance with them at their option. Requisitions are actually little better than a jest and a bye word throughout the Land. If you tell the Legislatures they have violated the treaty of peace and invaded the prerogatives of the confederacy they will laugh in your face. What then is to be done? Things cannot go on in the same manner forever. It is much to be feared, as you observe, that the better kind of people being disgusted with the circumstances will have their minds prepared for any revolution whatever. We are apt to run from one extreme into another. To anticipate & prevent disastrous contingencies would be the part of wisdom & patriotism.

Monarchical government

What astonishing changes a few years are capable of producing! I am told that even respectable characters speak of a monarchical form of government without horror. From thinking proceeds speaking, thence to acting is often but a single step. But how irrevocable and tremendous! What a triumph for the advocates of despotism to find that we are incapable of governing ourselves, and that systems founded on the basis of equal liberty are merely ideal and fallacious! Would to God that wise measures may be taken in time to avert the consequences we have but too much reason to apprehend.

Retired as I am from the world, I frankly acknowledge I cannot feel myself an unconcerned spectator. Yet having happily assisted in bringing the ship into port & having been fairly discharged; it is not my business to embark again on the sea of troubles. Nor could it be expected that my sentiments and opinions would have much weight on the minds of my countrymen—they have been neglected, tho' given as a last legacy in the most solemn manner. I had then perhaps some claims to public attention. I consider myself as having none at present. With sentiments of sincere esteem & friendship

I am, my dear Sir,

Yr. Most Obed. & Affect.

Hble Servant

G. Washington

118

TO BUSHROD WASHINGTON

Mount Vernon, September 30, 1786

Dear Bushrod:

I was from home when your servant arrived, found him in a hurry to be gone when I returned; have company in the House, and am on the eve of a journey up the river to meet the Directors of the Potomac Company; these things combining, will not allow me time to give any explicit answer to the question you have propounded.*

Generally speaking, I have seen as much evil as good result *On societies* from such Societies as you describe the Constitution of yours to be; they are a kind of imperium in imperio, and as often clog as facilitate public measures. I am no friend to institutions† except in local matters which are wholly or in a great measure confined to the County of the Delegates. To me it appears much wiser and more politic, to choose able and honest representatives, and leave them in all national questions to determine from the evidence of reason, and the facts which shall be adduced, when internal and external information is given to them in a collective state. What certainty is there that Societies in a corner or remote part of a State can possess that knowledge which is necessary for them to decide on many

---

*The letters from Bushrod Washington are printed in footnotes to Washington's answer in the Fitzpatrick edition.

†In Washington's manuscript the word in all probability was "instructions." See the end of the following paragraph.

important questions which may come before an Assembly? What reason is there to expect, that the society itself may be accordant in opinion on such subjects? May not a few members of this society (more sagacious and designing than the rest) direct the measures of it to private views of their own? May not this embarrass an honest, able Delegate, who hears the voice of his Country from all quarters, and thwart public measures?

These are first thoughts, but I give no decided opinion. Societies nearly similar to such as you speak of, have lately been formed in Massachusetts: but what has been the consequence? Why they have declared the Senate useless; many other parts of the Constitution unnecessary; salaries of public officers burthensome &c. To point out the defects of the constitution (if any existed) in a decent way, was proper enough; but they have done more: they first vote the Court of Justice, in the present circumstances of the State, oppressive; and next, by violence stop them; which has occasioned a very solemn Proclamation and appeal from the Governor to the people. You may say no such matters are in contemplation by your Society: granted: a snow-ball gathers by rolling; possibly a line may be drawn between occasional meetings for special purposes, and a standing Society to direct with local views and partial information the affairs of the Nation, which cannot be well understood but by a large and comparative view of circumstances. Where is this so likely to enter as in the general Assembly of the people? What figure then must a Delegate make who comes there with his hands tied, and his judgment forestalled? His very instructors, perhaps (if they had nothing sinister in view) were they present at all the information and arguments, which would come forward, might be the first to change sentiments.

Hurried as this letter is, I am sensible I am writing to you upon a very important subject. I have no time to copy, correct, or even peruse it; for which reason I could wish to have it or a copy returned to me. George and his wife set off yesterday for the races at Fredericksburg; the rest of the family are well and join in love and good wishes for all at Bushfield. I am, &c.

119

TO HENRY LEE

Mount Vernon, October 31, 1786

My Dr. Sir:

I am indebted to you for your several favors of the 1st. 11th. and 17th. of this instt: and shall reply to them in the order of their dates; but first let me thank you for the interesting communications imparted by them.

The picture which you have exhibited, and the accounts which are published of the commotions, and temper of numerous bodies in the Eastern States, are equally to be lamented and deprecated. They exhibit a melancholy proof of what our trans-Atlantic foe has predicted; and of another thing perhaps, which is still more to be regretted, and is yet more unaccountable, that mankind when left to themselves are unfit for their own Government. I am mortified beyond expression when I view the clouds that have spread over the brightest morn that ever dawned upon any Country. In a word, I am lost in amazement when I behold what intrigue, the interested views of desperate characters, ignorance and jealousy of the minor part, are capable of effecting, as a scourge on the major part of our fellow Citizens of the Union; for it is hardly to be supposed that the great body of the people, tho' they will not act, can be so shortsighted, or enveloped in darkness, as not to see rays of a distant sun thro' all this mist of intoxication and folly.

On mankind and government

You talk, my good Sir, of employing influence to appease the present tumults in Massachusetts. I know not where that influence is to be found; and if attainable, that it would be a proper remedy for the disorders. Influence is no Government. Let us have one by which our lives, liberties and properties will be secured; or let us know the worst at once. Under these impressions, my humble opinion is, that there is a call for decision. Know precisely what the insurgents aim at. If they have *real* grievances, redress them if possible; or acknowledge the justice of them, and your inability to do it in the present moment. If they have not, employ the force of government against them at once. If this is inadequate, *all* will be convinced that the superstructure is bad, or wants support. To be more exposed in the eyes of the world, and more contemptible than

Insurgency in Massachusetts

we already are, is hardly possible. To delay one or the other of these, is to exasperate on the one hand, or to give confidence on the other, and will add to their numbers; for, like snow-balls, such bodies increase by every movement, unless there is something in the way to obstruct and crumble them before the weight is too great and irresistible.

These are my sentiments. Precedents are dangerous things; let the reins of government then be braced and held with a steady hand, and every violation of the Constitution be repre-hended: if defective, let it be amended, but not suffered to be trampled upon whilst it has an existence.

Navigation of the
Mississippi River
With respect to the navigation of the Mississippi, you al-ready know my sentiments thereon: they have been uniformly the same, and as I have observed to you in a former letter, are controverted by one consideration *only* of weight, and that is the operation the occlusion of it may have on the minds of the western settlers, who will not consider the subject in a relative point of view or on a comprehensive scale, and may be influ-enced by the demagogues of the country to acts of extrava-gance and desperation, under a popular declamation that their interests are sacrificed. Colo. Mason, at present, is in a fit of the gout; what [his] sentiments on the subject are, I know not, nor whether he will be able to attend the Assembly during the present Session. For some reasons, however, (which need not be mentioned) I am inclined to believe he will advocate the navigation of that river. But in all matters of great national moment, the only true line of conduct, in my opinion, is, dis-passionately to compare the advantages and disadvantages of the measure proposed, and decide from the balance. The lesser evil, where there is a choice of them, should always yield to the greater. What benefits (more than we now enjoy) are to be obtained by such a Treaty as you have delineated with Spain, I am not enough of a Commercial man to give any opinion on. The China came to hand without much damage; and I thank you for your attention in procuring and forward-ing of it to me. Mrs. Washington joins me in best wishes for Mrs. Lee and yourself and I am &c.

120

TO JAMES MADISON

Mount Vernon, November 5, 1786

My dear Sir:

I thank you for the communications in your letter of the first instt. The decision of the House on the question respecting a paper emission, is portentous I hope, of an auspicious Session. It may certainly be classed among the important questions of the present day; and merited the serious consideration of the Assembly. Fain would I hope, that the great, and most important of all objects, the foederal governmt., may be considered with that calm and deliberate attention which the magnitude of it so loudly calls for at this critical moment. Let prejudices, unreasonable jealousies, and local interest yield to reason and liberality. Let us look to our National character, and to things beyond the present period. No morn ever dawned more favourably than ours did; and no day was ever more clouded than the present! Wisdom, and good examples are necessary at this time to rescue the political machine from the impending storm. Virginia has now an opportunity to set the latter, and has enough of the former, I hope, to take the lead in promoting this great and arduous work. Without some alteration in our political creed, the superstructure we have been seven years raising at the expence of so much blood and treasure, must fall. We are fast verging to anarchy and confusion!

Concern for fate of federal government

A letter which I have just received from Genl Knox, who had just returned from Massachusetts (whither he had been sent by Congress consequent of the commotion in that State) is replete with melancholy information of the temper, and designs of a considerable part of that people. Among other things he says,

there creed is, that the property of the United States, has been protected from confiscation of Britain by the joint exertions of *all*, and therefore ought to be the *common property* of all. And he that attempts opposition to this creed is an enemy to equity and justice, and ought to be swept from off the face of the Earth.

Again:

They are determined to anihillate all debts public and private, and have Agrarian Laws, which are easily effected by the means of unfunded paper money which shall be a tender in all cases whatever.

He adds:

The numbers of these people amount in Massachusetts to about one fifth part of several populous Counties, and to them may be collected, people of similar sentiments from the States of Rhode Island, Connecticut, and New Hampshire, so as to constitute a body of twelve or fifteen thousand desperate, and unprincipled men. They are chiefly of the young and active part of the Community.

How melancholy is the reflection, that in so short a space, we should have made such large strides towards fulfilling the prediction of our transatlantic foe! "Leave them to themselves, and their government will soon dissolve." Will not the wise and good strive hard to avert this evil? Or will their supineness suffer ignorance, and the arts of self-interested designing disaffected and desperate characters, to involve this rising empire in wretchedness and contempt? What stronger evidence can be given of the want of energy in our governments than these disorders? If there exists not a power to check them, what security has a man for life, liberty, or property? To you, I am sure I need not add aught on this subject, the consequences of a lax, or inefficient government, are too obvious to be dwelt on. Thirteen Sovereignties pulling against each other, and all tugging at the foederal head will soon bring ruin on the whole; whereas a liberal, and energetic Constitution, well guarded and closely watched, to prevent incroachments, might restore us to that degree of respectability and consequence, to which we had a fair claim, and the brightest prospect of attaining. With sentiments of the sincerest esteem etc.

121

TO BUSHROD WASHINGTON

Mount Vernon, November 15, 1786

Dear Bushrod:

Your letter of the 31st. of October in reply to mine of the 30th. of Septr. came safe to hand. It was not the intention of my former letter either to condemn, or give my voice in favor of the Patriotic Society, of which you have now, but not before, declared yourself a member; nor do I mean to do it now. I offered observations under the information I had then received, the weight of which was to be considered. As first thoughts, they were undigested, and might be very erroneous.

The Patriotic Society

That representatives ought to be the mouth of their Constituents, I do not deny, nor do I mean to call in question the right of the latter to instruct them. It is to the embarrassment, into which they may be thrown by these instructions in *national matters* that my objections lie. In speaking of national matters I look to the foederal Government, which in my opinion it is the interest of every State to support; and to do this, as there are a variety of interests in the union, there must be a yielding of the parts to coalesce the whole. Now a County, a District, or even a State might decide on a measure which, tho' apparently for the benefit of it in its unconnected state, may be repugnant to the interests of the nation, and eventually to the State itself as a part of the confederation. If then, members go instructed, to the Assembly, from certain Districts, the requisitions of Congress repugnant to the sense of them, and all the lights which they may receive from the communications of that body to the Legislature, must be unavailing; altho' the nature and necessity of them, when the reasons therefor are fully expounded; which can only be given by Congress to the Assembly thro' the Executive, and which come before them in their legislative capacity, are as clear as the sun. In local matters which concern the District; or things which respect the internal police of the State, there may be nothing amiss in instructions. In national matters also, the *sense*, but not the *Law* of the District may be given, leaving the Delegates to judge from the nature of the case and the evidence before them.

The instructions of your Society as far as they have gone, meet my entire approbation, except in the article of commutables. Here, if I understand the meaning and design of the clause, I must disagree to it most heartily; for if the intention of it is to leave it optional with the person taxed to pay any staple commodity (Tobo. would be least exceptionable) in lieu of specie, the people will be burthened, a few speculators enriched, and the public derive no benefit from it. Have we not had a recent and melancholy proof of this during the war in the provision tax? Did not the people pay this in some way or other, perhaps badly; and was not the army almost starved? Can any instance be given where the public has sold Tobacco, Hemp, Flour or any other commodity upon as good terms as individuals have done it? Must not there be places of deposit for these commutables; Collectors, Storekeepers &c. &c. employed? These, rely on it, will sink one half, and a parcel of Speculators will possess themselves of the other half. It was to these things that we owe the present depravity of the minds of so many people of this Country, and filled it with so many knaves and designing characters.

Among the great objects which you took into consideration at your meeting at Richmond, how comes it to pass, that you never turned your eyes to the inefficacy of the Foederal Government, so as to instruct your Delegates to accede to the propositions of the Commrs. at Annapolis; or to devise some other mode to give it that energy, which is necessary to support a national character? Every man who considers the present constitution of it, and sees to what it is verging, trembles. The fabrick which took nine years, at the expense of much blood and treasure, to rear, now totters to the foundation, and without support must soon fall.

The determination of your Society to promote frugality and industry by example, to encourage manufactures, and to avoid dissipation, is highly praise-worthy: these, and premiums for the most useful discoveries in Agriculture within your district, the most profitable course of cropping, and the best method of fencing to save timber &c. would soon make us a rich and happy people. With every good wish for you and yours, in which your aunt joins. I am, &c.

122

TO JAMES MADISON

Mount Vernon, November 18, 1786

My Dr. Sir:

Not having sent to the Post Office with my usual regularity, your favor of the 8th. did not reach me in time for an earlier acknowledgment than of this date. It gives me the most sensible pleasure to hear that the acts of the present session* are marked with wisdom, justice and liberality. They are the palladium of good policy, and the sure paths that lead to national happiness. Would to God every State would let these be the leading features of their constituent characters: those threatening clouds, which seem ready to burst on the Confederacy, would soon dispel. The unanimity with which the Bill was received, for appointing Commissioners agreeably to the recommendation of the Convention at Annapolis; and the uninterrupted progress it has met with since, are indications of a favourable issue. It is a measure of equal necessity and magnitude; and may be the spring of reanimation.

Appointment of Delegates to the Constitutional Convention

Altho' I had bid adieu to the public walks of life in a public manner, and had resolved never more to tread that theatre; yet, if upon an occasion so interesting to the well-being of the Confederacy it should have been the wish of the Assembly that I should have been an associate in the business of revising the foederal System; I should, from a sense of the obligation I am under for repeated proofs of confidence in me, more than from any opinion I should have entertained of my usefulness, have obeyed its call; but it is now out of my power to do this with any degree of consistency, the cause I will mention.

I presume you heard Sir, that I was first appointed, and have since been rechosen, President of the Society of the Cincinnati; and you may have understood also, that the triennial Genl. Meeting of this body is to be held in Philada. the first Monday in May next. Some particular reasons combining with the peculiar situation of my private concerns; the necessity of paying attention to them; a wish for retirement and relaxation from public cares, and rheumatic pains which I begin to feel very sensibly, induced me on the 31st ulto. to address a circular

Society of the Cincinnati

---

*The Virginia Assembly.

letter to each State society informing them of my intention not to be at the next meeting, and of my desire not to be rechosen President. The Vice President is also informed of this, that the business of the Society may not be impeded by my absence. Under these circumstances it will readily be perceived that I could not appear at the same time and place on any other occasion, without giving offence to a very respectable and deserving part of the Community, the late officers of the American Army. I feel as you do for our acquaintance Colo. Lee; better never have delegated than left him out, unless some glaring impropriety of conduct had been ascribed to him. I hear with pleasure that you are in the new choice. With sentiments of the highest esteem and affectn. I am &c.

123

TO JAMES MADISON

Mount Vernon, December 16, 1786

My dear Sir:

Your favor of the 7th. came to hand the evening before last. The resolutions which you say are inserted in the Papers, I have not yet seen. The latter come irregularly, tho' I am a subscriber to Hay's Gazette.

Besides the reasons which are assigned in my circular letter to the several State Societies of the Cincinnati, for my nonattendance at the next General meeting to be holden at Philadelphia the first Monday of May, there existed one of a political nature, which operates more forceably on my mind than all the others; and which, in confidence, I will now communicate to you.

Purpose of the Society of the Cincinnati

When this Society was first formed, I am persuaded not a member of it conceived that it would give birth to those Jealousies, or be chargeable with those dangers (real or imaginary) with which the minds of many, and some of respectable characters, were filled. The motives which induced the Officers to enter into it were, I am confident, truly and frankly recited in the Institution: one of which, indeed the principal, was to establish a charitable fund for the relief of such of their compatriots, the Widows, and descendants of them, as were fit objects for their support; and for whom no public provision had been made. But the trumpet being sounded, the alarm was spreading far and wide; I readily perceived therefore that unless a modification of the plan could be effected (to anihilate the Society altogether was impracticable on acct. of the foreign officers who had been admitted), that irritations wd. arise which would soon draw a line betwn. the Society, and their fellow Citizens.

To prevent this, To conciliate the affections, And to convince the world of the purity of the plan, I exerted myself, and with much difficulty, effected the changes which appeared in the recommendation from the General Meeting to those of the States; the accomplishment of which was not easy; and I have since heard, that whilst some States acceded to the recommendation, others are not disposed thereto, alledging that, unreasonable prejudices, and ill founded jealousies ought not to influence a measure laudable in its institution, and salutary in its objects and operation.

Under these circumstances, there will be no difficulty in conceiving, that the part I should have had to have acted, would have been delicate. On the one hand, I might be charged with dereliction to the Officers, who had nobly supported me, and had treated me with uncommon marks of attention and attachment. On the other, with supporting a measure incompatible (some say) with republican principles. I thought it best therefore without assigning this (the principal reason) to decline the Presidency, and to excuse my attendance at the meeting on the ground, which is firm and just; the necessity of paying attention to my private concerns; to conformity to my determination of passing the remainder of my days in a state of retirement; and to indisposition; occasioned by Rheumatic complaints with which, at times, I am a good deal afflicted. Professing at the sametime my entire approbation of the institution as altered, and the pleasure I feel at the subsidence of those Jealousies which yielded to the change. *Presuming*, on the general adoption of them.

I have been thus particular to shew, that under circumstances like these, I should feel myself in an aukward situation to be in Philadelphia on another public occasion during the sitting of this Society. That the prest. era is pregnant of great, and *strange* events, none who will cast their eyes around them, can deny; what may be brought forth between this and the first of May to remove the difficulties which at present labour in my mind, against the acceptance of the honor which has lately been conferred on me by the Assembly, is not for me to predict; but I should think it incompatible with that candour which ought to characterize an honest mind, not to declare that under my present view of the matter, I should be too much embarrassed by the meetings of these two bodies in the same place, in the same moment (after what I have written) to be easy in the situation; and consequently, that it wd. be improper to let my appointment stand in the way of another. Of this, you who have had the whole matter fully before you, will judge; for having received no other than private intimation of my election, and unacquainted with the formalities which are, or ought to be used on these occasions, silence may be deceptious, or considered as disrespectful; The imputation of both, or either, I would wish to avoid. This is the cause of the present disclosure, immediately on the receipt of your letter, which has been locked up by Ice; for I have had no communication with Alexandria for many days, till the day before yesterday.

My Sentiments are decidedly against Commutables; for sure I am it will be found a tax without a revenue. That the people will be burthened. The public expectation deceived, and a few Speculators *only*, enriched. Thus the matter will end, after the morals of *some*, are more corrupted than they now are; and the minds of *all*, filled with more leaven, by finding themselves taxed, and the public demands in full force. Tobacco, on acct. of the public places of deposit, and from the accustomed mode of negotiating the article, is certainly better fitted for a Commutable than any other production of this Country; but if I understand the matter rightly (I have it from report only) will any man pay five pound in Specie for five taxables, when the same sum (supposing Tobo. not to exceed 20/. per Ct.) will purchase 500 lbs. of Tobo. and this, if at 28/. will discharge the tax on Seven? And will not the man who neither makes, nor can easily procure this commodity, complain of the inequality of such a mode, especially when he finds that the revenue is diminished by the difference be it what it may, between the real and nominal price? and that he is again to be taxed to make this good. These, and such like things, in my humble opinion, are extremely hurtful, and are among the principal causes that present depravity and corruption without accomplishing the object in view for it is not the shadow, but the substance with which Taxes must be paid, if we mean to be honest. With sentiments of sincere esteem etc.

124

TO GOVERNOR EDMUND RANDOLPH

Mount Vernon, December 21, 1786

Sir:

I had not the honor of receiving your Excellency's favor of the 6th, with its enclosures, till last night. Sensible as I am of the honor conferred on me by the General Assembly, in appointing me one of the Deputies to a Convention proposed to be held in the City of Philadelphia in May next, for the purpose of revising the Foederal Constitution; and desirous as I am on all occasions, of testifying a ready obedience to the calls of my Country; yet, Sir, there exists at this moment, circumstances, which I am persuaded will render my acceptance of this fresh mark of confidence incompatible with other measures which I had previously adopted; and from which, seeing little prospect of disengaging myself, it would be disengenuous not to express a wish that some other character, on whom greater reliance can be had, may be substituted in my place; the probability of my non-attendance being too great to continue my appointment.

Appointment to the Philadelphia Convention

As no mind can be more deeply impressed than mine is with the awful situation of our affairs; resulting in a great measure from the want of efficient powers in the foederal head, and due respect to its Ordinances, so, consequently, those who do engage in the important business of removing these defects, will carry with them every good wish of mine which the best dispositions towards the attainment can bestow. I have the honr. etc.

125

TO HENRY KNOX

Mount Vernon, December 26, 1786

My dear Sir:

Nothing but the pleasing hope of seeing you under this roof in the course of last month, and wch. I was disposed to extend even to the present moment, has kept me till this time from acknowledging the receipt of your obliging favor of the 23d of October. Despairing now of that pleasure, I shall thank you for the above letter, and the subsequent one of the 17th. instt., which came to hand yesterday evening.

Insurgency in Massachusetts

Lamentable as the conduct of the Insurgents of Massachusetts is, I am exceedingly obliged to you for the advices respecting them; and pray you, most ardently, to continue the acct. of their proceedings; because I can depend upon them from you without having my mind bewildered with those vague and contradictory reports which are handed to us in Newspapers, and which please one hour, only to make the moments of the next more bitter. I feel, my dear Genl. Knox, infinitely more than I can express to you, for the disorders which have arisen in these States. Good God! who besides a Tory could have foreseen, or a Briton predicted them! were these people wiser than others, or did they judge of us from the corruption, and depravity of their own hearts? The latter I am persuaded was the case, and that notwithstanding the boasted virtue of America, we are far gone in every thing ignoble and bad.

I do assure you, that even at this moment, when I reflect on the present posture of our affairs, it seems to me to be like the vision of a dream. My mind does not know how to realize it, as a thing in actual existence, so strange, so wonderful does it appear to me! In this, as in most other matter, we are too slow. When this spirit first dawned, probably it might easily have been checked; but it is scarcely within the reach of human ken, at this moment, to say when, where, or how it will end. There are combustibles in every State, which a spark might set fire to. In this State, a perfect calm prevails at present, and a prompt disposition to support, and give energy to the foederal System is discovered, if the unlucky stirring of the dispute respecting the navigation of the Mississippi does not become a leaven that will ferment, and sour the mind of it.

The resolutions of the prest. Session respecting a paper emission, military certificates, &ca., have stamped justice and liberality on the proceedings of the Assembly, and By a late act, *it* seems very desirous of a General Convention to revise and amend the foederal Constitution. Apropos, what prevented the Eastern States from attending the September meeting at Annapolis? Of all the States in the Union it should have seemed to me, that a measure of this sort (distracted as they were with internal commotions, and experiencing the want of energy in the government) would have been most pleasing to them. What are the prevailing sentiments of the one now proposed to be held in Philadelphia, in May next? and how will it be attended? You are at the fountain of intelligence, and where the wisdom of the Nation, it is to be presumed, has concentered; consequently better able (as I have had abundant experience of your intelligence, confidence, and candour to solve these questions).

Political issues in Virginia

. . . and the Eastern states

The Maryland Assembly has been violently agitated by the question for a paper emission. It has been carried in the House of Delegates, but what has, or will be done with the Bill in the Senate I have not yet heard. The partisans in favor of the measure in the lower House, threaten, it is said, a secession if it is rejected by that Branch of the Legislature. Thus are we advancing. In regretting, which I have often done with the deepest sorrow, the death of our much lamented frd. General Greene, I have accompanied it of late with a quaere, whether he would not have prefered such an exit to the scenes which it is more than probable many of his compatriots may live to bemoan.

. . . and Maryland

In both your letters you intimate, that the men of reflection, principle and property in New England, feeling the inefficacy of their present government, are contemplating a change; but you are not explicit with respect to the nature of it. It has been supposed, that, the Constitution of the State of Massachusetts was amongst the most energetic in the Union; May not these disorders then be ascribed to an endulgent exercise of the powers of Administration? If your laws authorized, and your powers were adequate to the suppression of these tumults, in the first appearances of them, delay and temporizing expedients were, in my opinion improper; these are rarely well

. . . and Massachusetts

349

applied, and the same causes would produce similar effects in any form of government, if the powers of it are not enforced. I ask this question for information, I know nothing of the facts.

Actions of Great Britain

That G. B will be an unconcerned Spectator of the present insurrections (if they continue) is not to be expected. That she is at this moment sowing the Seeds of jealousy and discontent among the various tribes of Indians on our frontier admits of no doubt, in my mind. And that she will improve every opportunity to foment the spirit of turbulence within the bowels of the United States, with a view of distracting our governments, and promoting divisions, is, with me, not less certain. Her first Manoeuvres will, no doubt, be covert, and may remain so till the period shall arrive when a decided line of conduct may avail her. Charges of violating the treaty, and other pretexts, will not then be wanting to colour overt acts, tending to effect the grt. objects of which she has long been in labour. A Man is now at the head of their American Affairs well calculated to conduct measures of this kind, and more than probably was selected for the purpose. We ought not therefore to sleep nor to slumber. Vigilance in watching, and vigour in acting, is, in my opinion, become indispensably necessary. If the powers are inadequate amend or alter them, but do not let us sink into the lowest state of humiliation and contempt, and become a byword in all the earth. I think with you that the Spring will unfold important and distressing Scenes, unless much wisdom and good management is displayed in the interim. Adieu; be assured no man has a higher esteem and regard for you than I have; none more sincerely your friend, and more Affecte. etc.

126

TO DAVID HUMPHREYS

Mount Vernon, December 26, 1786

My Dr. Humphreys:

I am much indebted to you for your several favors of the 1st. 9th. and 16th. of Novr. the last came first. Mr. Morse, having in mind the old proverb, was determined not to make more haste than good speed in prosecuting his journey to Georgia, so I got the two first lately.

For your publication respecting the treatment of Captn. Asgill, I am exceedingly obliged to you. The manner of making it is the best that cou'd be devised; whilst the matter will prove the illiberality, as well as the fallacy of the reports which have been circulated on that occasion, and which are fathered upon that officer as the author.

It is with the deepest and most heartfelt concern, I perceive by some late paragraphs extracted from the Boston papers, that the Insurgents of Massachusetts, far from being satisfied with the redress offered by their general Court, are still acting in open violation of law and government, and have obliged the chief Magistrate in a decided tone to call upon the Militia of the State to support the Constitution. What, gracious God, is man! that there should be such inconsistency and perfidiousness in his conduct? It is but the other day, that we were shedding our blood to obtain the Constitutions under which we now live; Constitutions of our own choice and making; and now we are unsheathing the sword to overturn them. The thing is so unaccountable, that I hardly know how to realize it, or to persuade myself that I am not under the illusion of a dream.

Insurgency in Massachusetts

My mind, previous to the receipt of your letter of the 1st. ulto., had often been agitated by a thought similar to the one you have expressed respecting an old friend of your's; but Heaven forbid that a crisis should come when he shall be driven to the necessity of making choice of either of the alternatives there mentioned. Let me entreat you, my dr. Sir, to keep me advised of the situation of affairs in your quarter. I can depend on your accounts. Newspaper paragraphs unsupported by other testimony, are often contradictory and bewildering. At one time these insurgents are spoken of as a mere mob; at other times as systematic in all their proceedings. If the first, I would fain hope that like other Mobs it will, however formidable, be of short duration. If the latter there are surely men of consequence and abilities behind the curtain who move the puppets; the designs of whom may be deep and dangerous. They may be instigated by British counsel; actuated by ambitious motives, or being influenced by dishonest principles, had rather see the Country in the horror of civil discord, than do what justice would dictate to an honest mind.

I had scarcely despatched my circular letters to the several State Societies of the Cincinnati, when I received letters from

Society of the Cincinnati

some of the principal members of our Assembly expressing a wish that they might be permitted to name me as one of the Deputies of this State to the Convention proposed to be held at Philadelphia the first of May next. I immediately wrote to my particular friend Mr. Madison (and gave similar reasons to the others) the answer is contained in the extract No. 1; in reply I got the extract No. 2. This obliged me to be more explicit and confidential with him on points which a recurrence to the conversations we have had on this subject will bring to your mind and save me the hazard of a recital in this letter. Since this interchange of letters I have received from the Governor the letter No. 4 and have written No. 5 in answer to it. Should this matter be further pressed, (which I hope it will not, as I have no inclination to go) what had I best do? You as an indifferent person, and one who is much better acquainted with the sentiments and views of the Cincinnati than I am; (for in this State where the recommendations of the General Meeting have been agreed to hardly any thing is said about it) as also with the temper of the people and state of politics at large, can determine upon better ground and fuller evidence than myself; especially as you have opportunities of knowing in what light the States to the Eastward consider the Convention, and the measures they are pursuing to contravene, or to give efficiency to it.

On the last occasion, only five States were represented; none East of New York. Why the Nw. England Governments did not appear, I am yet to learn; for of all others the distractions and turbulent temper of these people would, I should have thought, have afforded the strongest evidence of the *necessity* of competent powers somewhere. That the Foederal Government is nearly, if not quite at a stand, none will deny. The first question then is, shall it be annihilated or supported? If the latter, the proposed convention is an object of the first magnitude, and should be supported by all the friends of the present Constitution. In the other case, if on a full and dispassionate revision thereof, the continuance shall be adjudged impracticable or unwise, as only delaying an event which must 'ere long take place; would it not be better for such a Meeting to suggest some other, to avoid if possible civil discord or other impending evils? I must candidly confess, as we could not remain quiet more than three or four years in time of peace, under the Constitutions of our own choosing; which it was

Philadelphia Convention

believed, in many States at least, were formed with deliberation and wisdom, I see little prospect either of our agreeing upon any other, or that we should remain long satisfied under it if we could. Yet I would wish any thing, and every thing essayed to prevent the effusion of blood, and to avert the humiliating and contemptible figure we are about to make in the annals of mankind.

If this second attempt to convene the States for the purposes proposed by the report of the partial representation at Annapolis in September, should also prove abortive, it may be considered as an unequivocal evidence that the States are not likely to agree on any general measure which is to pervade the Union, and of course that there is an end of Foederal Government. The States therefore which make the last dying essay to avoid these misfortunes, would be mortified at the issue, and their deputies would return home chagrined at their ill success and disappointment. This would be a disagreeable circumstance for any one of them to be in, but more particularly so for a person in my situation. If no further application is made to me, of course I do not attend; if there is, I am under no obligation to do it, but as I have had so many proofs of your friendship, know your abilities to judge, and your opportunities of learning the politics of the day, on the points I have enumerated, you would oblige me by a full and confidential communication of your sentiments thereon.

Peace and tranquillity prevail in this State. The Assembly by a very great majority, and in very emphatical terms, have rejected an application for paper money, and spurned the idea of fixing the value of military Certificates by a scale of depreciation. In some other respects too the proceedings of the present Session have been marked with justice and a strong desire of supporting the foederal system. Altho' I lament the effect, I am pleased at the cause which has deprived us of the pleasure of your aid in the attack of Christmas pies; we had one yesterday on which all the company, tho' pretty numerous, were hardly able to make an impression. Mrs. Washington and George and his wife (Mr. Lear I had occasion to send to the Western Country) join in affectione. regards for you, and with sentiments, &c.

127

TO HENRY KNOX

Mount Vernon, February 3, 1787

My dear Sir:

I feel myself exceedingly obliged to you for the full, and friendly communications in your letters of the 14th. 21st. and 25th. ult; and shall (critically as matters are described in the latter) be extremely anxious to know the issue of the movements of the forces that were assembling, the one to support, the other to oppose the constitutional rights of Massachusetts. The moment is, indeed, important! If government shrinks, or is unable to enforce its laws; fresh manoeuvres will be displayed by the insurgents, anarchy and confusion must prevail, and every thing will be turned topsy turvy in that State; where it is not probable the mischiefs will terminate.

Attendance at the Philadelphia Convention

In your letter of the 14th. you express a wish to know my intention respecting the Convention, proposed to be held in Philada. in May next. In *confidence* I inform you, that it is not, at this time, my purpose to attend it. When this matter was first moved in the Assembly of this State, some of the principal characters of it wrote to me, requesting to be permitted to put my name in the delegation. To this I objected. They again pressed, and I again refused; assigning among other reasons my having declined meeting the Society of the Cincinnati at that place, about the same time, and that I thought it would be disrespectfull to that body (to whom I ow'd much) to be there on any other occasion. Notwithstanding these intimations, my name was inserted in the Act; and an official communication thereof made by the Executive to me, to whom, at the same-time that I expressed my sense for the confidence reposed in me, I declared, that as I saw no prospect of my attending, it was my wish that my name might not remain in the delegation, to the exclusion of another. To this I have been requested, in emphatical terms, not to decide absolutely, as no inconvenience would result from the non-appointment of another, at least for sometime.

Thus the matter stands, which is the reason of my saying to you in *confidence* that at present I retain my first intention, not to go. In the meanwhile as I have the fullest conviction of your friendship for, and attachment to me; know your abilities to judge; and your means of information, I shall receive any communications from you, respecting this business, with thankfulness. My first wish is, to do for the best, and to act with propriety; and you know me too well, to believe that reserve or concealment of any circumstance or opinion, would be at all pleasing to me. The legallity of this Convention I do not mean to discuss, nor how problematical the issue of it may be. That powers are wanting, none can deny. Through what medium they are to be derived, will, like other matters, engage public attention. That which takes the shortest course to obtain them, will, in my opinion, under present circumstances, be found best. Otherwise, like a house on fire, whilst the most regular mode of extinguishing it is contended for, the building is reduced to ashes. My opinion of the energetic wants of the foederal government are well known; publickly and privately I have declared it; and however constitutionally it may be for Congress to point out the defects of the foederal System, I am strongly inclined to believe that it would be found the most efficatious channel for the recommendation, more especially the alterations, to flow, for reasons too obvious to enumerate.

The System on which you seem disposed to build a National government is certainly more energetic, and I dare say, in every point of view more desirable than the present one; which, from experience, we find is not only slow, debilitated, and liable to be thwarted by every breath, but is defective in that secrecy, which for the accomplishment of many of the most important national purposes is indispensably necessary; and besides, having the Legislative, Executive and Judiciary departments concentered, is exceptionable. But at the same-time I give this opinion, I believe that the political machine will yet be much tumbled and tossed, and possibly be wrecked altogether, before such a system as you have defined will be adopted. The darling Sovereignties of the States individually, The Governors elected and elect. The Legislators, with a long train of et cetera whose political consequence will be lessened, if not anihilated, would give their weight of opposition to such a revolution. But I may be speaking without book, for scarcely ever going off my own farms I see few people who do not call upon me; and am very little acquainted with the Sentiments of the great world; indeed, after what I have seen, or rather after what I have heard, I shall be surprized at nothing; for if three years since any person had told me that at this day, I should see such a formidable rebellion against the laws and constitutions of our own making as now appears I should have thought him a bedlamite, a fit subject for a mad house. Adieu, you know how much, and how sincerely I am etc.

Mrs. Washington joins me in every good wish for yourself, Mrs. Knox and the family.

128

TO HENRY KNOX

Mount Vernon, March 8, 1787

My dear Sir:

Will you permit me to give you the trouble of making an indirect, but precise enquiry, into the alligations of the enclosed letters. I flatter myself that from the vicinity of Elizabeth Town to New York, and the constant intercourse between the two, you will be able to do it without much trouble. It is but little in my power to afford the pecuniary aids required by the writer; but if the facts as set forth be true, I should feel very happy in offering my mite, and rendering any services in my power on the occasion. Be so good, when you write to me on this subject, to return the letters and translations.

The observations contained in your letter of the 22d. Ulto. (which came duly to hand) respecting the disfranchisement of a number of the Citizens of Massachusetts for their rebellious conduct may be just; and yet, without exemplary punishment, similar disorders may be excited by other ambitious and discontented characters. Punishments however ought to light on the principals.

The Philadelphia Convention

I am glad to hear that Congress are about to remove some of the stumbling blocks which lay in the way of the proposed Convention; a Convention is an expedient I wish to see tried; after which, if the present government is not efficient, conviction of the propriety of a change of it, will dissiminate through every rank, and class of people and may be brought about in place; till which however necessary it may appear in the eyes of the more descerning, my opinion is, that it cannot be effected without great contention, and much confusion. It is among the evils, and perhaps is not the smallest, of democratical governments, that the people must *feel*, before they will *see*. When this happens, they are roused to action; hence it is that this form of governments is so slow. I am indirectly and delicately pressed to attend this convention. Several reasons are opposed to it in my mind, and not the least my having declined attending the General Meeting of the Cincinnati, which is to be holden in Philadelphia, at the same time on account of the disrespect it might *seem* to offer to that Society, to be there on another occasion. A thought however has lately run through my mind, which is attended with embarrassment. It is, wheather my non-attendance in this Convention will not be considered as deriliction to republicanism, nay more, whether other motives may not (however injuriously) be ascribed to me for not exerting myself on this occasion in support of it. Under these circumstances let me pray you, my dear Sir, to inform me confidentially what the public expectation is on this head, that is, whether I will, or ought to be there? You are much in the way of obtaining this knowledge, and I can depend upon your friendship, candour, and judgment in the communication of it, as far as it shall appear to you. My final determination (if what I have already given to the Executive of this State is not considered in that light) cannot be delayed beyond the time necessary for your reply. With great truth etc.

129

TO THE SECRETARY FOR FOREIGN AFFAIRS

Mount Vernon, March 10, 1787

Dear Sir:

I stand indebted to you for two letters. The first, introductory of Mr. Anstey, needed no apology, nor will any be necessary on future similar occasions. The other of the 7th of January is on a very interesting subject deserving very particular attention.

How far the revision of the federal system, and giving more adequate powers to Congress may be productive of an efficient government, I will not under my present view of the matter, presume to decide. That many inconveniences result from the present form, none can deny. Those enumerated in your letter are so obvious and sensibly felt that no logic can

Revision of federal system

controvert, nor is it likely that any change of conduct will remove them, and that attempts to alter or amend it will be like the proppings of a house which is ready to fall, and which no shoars can support (as many seem to think) may also be true. But, is the public mind matured for such an important change as the one you have suggested? What would be the consequences of a premature attempt? My opinion is, that this Country must yet feel and see more, before it can be accomplished.

State opposition to revisions

A thirst for power, and *the bantling, I had liked to have said monster*, for sovereignty, which have taken such fast hold of the States individually, will when joined by the many whose personal consequence in the control of State politics will in a manner be annihilated, form a strong phalanx against it; and when to these the few who can hold posts of honor or profit in the National Government are compared with the many who will see but little prospect of being noticed, and the discontent of others who may look for appointments, the opposition will be altogether irresistable till the mass, as well as the more discerning part of the Community shall see the necessity. Among men of reflection, few will be found I believe, who are not *beginning* to think that our system is more perfect in theory than in practice; and that notwithstanding the boasted virtue of America it is more than probable we shall exhibit the last melancholy proof, that mankind are not competent to their own Government without the means of coercion in the Sovereign.

Legality of the Philadelphia Convention

Yet, I would fain try what the wisdom of the proposed Convention will suggest: and what can be effected by their Councils. It may be the last peaceable mode of essaying the practicability of the present form, without a greater lapse of time than the exigency of our affairs will allow. In strict propriety a Convention so holden may not be legal. Congress, however, may give it a colouring by recommendation, which would fit it more to the taste without proceeding to a definition of the powers. This however constitutionally it might be done would not, in my opinion, be expedient; for delicacy on the one hand, and Jealousy on the other, would produce a mere nihil.

My name is in the delegation to this Convention; but it was put there contrary to my desire, and remains contrary to my request. Several reasons at the time of this appointment and which yet exist, conspired to make an attendance inconvenient, perhaps improper, tho' a good deal urged to it. with sentiments of great regard &c.

PS: Since writing this letter, I have seen the resolution of Congress recommendatory of the Convention to be holden in Philadelphia the 2d Monday in May.

130

TO GOVERNOR EDMUND RANDOLPH

Mount Vernon, March 28, 1787

Dear Sir:

Your favor of the 11th. did not come to my hand till the 24th; and since then, till now, I have been too much indisposed to acknowledge the receipt of it.

To what cause to ascribe the detention of the [letter] I know not, as I never omit sending once, and oftener twice a week to the Post Office in Alexandria. It was the decided intention of the letter I had the honor of writing to your Excellency the 21st. of December last, to inform you, that it would not be convenient for me to attend the Convention proposed to be holden in Philadelphia in May next; and I had entertained hopes that another had been, or soon would be, appointed in my place; inasmuch as it is not only inconvenient for me to leave home, but because there will be, I apprehend, too much cause to charge my conduct with inconsistency, in again appearing on a public theatre after a public declaration to the contrary; and because it will, I fear, have a tendency to sweep me back into the tide of public affairs, when retirement and ease is so essentially necessary for, and is so much desired by me.

Attendance at the Philadelphia Convention

However, as my friends, with a degree of sollicitude which is unusual, seem to wish for my attendance on this occasion, I have come to a resolution to go, if my health will permit, provided, from the lapse of time between the date of your Excellency's letter and this reply, the Executive may not, the reverse of which wd. be highly pleasing to me, have turned its thoughts to some other character; for independantly of all other considerations, I have, of late, been so much afflicted with a rheumatic complaint in my shoulder that at times I am hardly able to raise my hand to my head, or turn myself in bed. This, consequently, might prevent my attendance, and eventually a representation of the State; which wd. afflict me more sensibly than the disorder that occasioned it.

If after the expression of these sentiments, the Executive should consider me as one of the Delegates, I would thank your Excellency for the earliest advice of it; because, if I am able, and should go to Philadelpa., I shall have some previous arrangements to make, and would set off for that place the first, or second day of May, that I may be there in time to account, personally, for my conduct to the General Meeting of the Cincinnati which is to convene on the first Monday of that month. My feelings would be much hurt if that body should otherwise, ascribe my attendance on the one, and not on the other occasion, to a disrespectful inattention to the Society; when the fact is, that I shall ever retain the most lively and affectionate regard for the members of which it is composed, on acct. of their attachment to, and uniform support of me, upon many trying occasions; as well as on acct. of their public virtues, patriotism, and sufferings.

I hope your Excellency will be found among the *attending* delegates. I should be glad to be informed who the others are; and cannot conclude without once more, and in emphatical terms, praying that if there is not a *decided* representation in *prospect,* without me, that another, for the reason I have assigned, may be chosen in my room without ceremony and without delay; for it would be unfortunate indeed if the State which was the mover of this Convention, should be unrepresented in it. With great respect I have the honor etc.

131

TO JAMES MADISON

Mount Vernon, March 31, 1787

My Dear Sir:

At the sametime that I acknowledge the receipt of your obliging favor of the 21st. ult. from New York I promise to avail myself of your indulgence of writing only when it is convenient to me. If this should not occasion a relaxation on your part, I shall become very much your debtor, and possibly like others in similar circumstances (when the debt is burthensome) may feel a disposition to apply the spunge, or, what is nearly a-kin to it, pay you off in depreciated paper, which being a legal tender, or what is tantamount, being *that* or *nothing*, you cannot refuse. You will receive the nominal value, and that you know quiets the conscience, and makes all things easy, with the debtor.

I am glad to find that Congress have recommended to the States to appear in the Convention proposed to be holden in Philadelphia in May. I think the reasons in favor, have the preponderancy of those against the measure. It is idle in my opinion to suppose that the Sovereign can be insensible of the inadequacy of the powers under which it acts, and that seeing, it should not recommend a revision of the Foederal system when it is considered by many as the *only* Constitutional mode by which the defects can be remedied. Had Congress proceeded to a delineation of the Powers, it might have sounded an Alarm; but as the case is, I do not conceive that it will have that effect.

Congress and the Philadelphia Convention

From the acknowledged abilities of the Secretary for Foreign Affairs, I could have had no doubt on his having ably investigated the infractions of the Treaty on both sides. Much is it be regretted however, that there should have been any on ours. We seem to have forgotten, or never to have learnt, the policy of placing ones enemy in the wrong. Had we observed good faith on our part, we might have told our tale to the world with a good grace; but complts. illy become those who are found to be the first agressors.

I am fully of opinion that those who lean to a Monarchial governmt. have either not consulted the public mind, or that they live in a region where the levelling principles in which they were bred, being entirely irradicated, is much more productive of Monarchical ideas than are to be found in the Southern States, where, from the habitual distinctions which have always existed among the people, one would have expected the first generation, and the most rapid growth of them. I also am clear, that even admitting the utility; nay necessity of the form, yet that the period is not arrived for adopting the change without shaking the Peace of this Country to its foundation. That a thorough reform of the present system is indispensable, none who have capacities to judge will deny; and with hand (and heart) I hope the business will be essayed

Monarchical ideas

Need for revisions of government

in a full Convention. After which, if more powers, and more decision is not found in the existing form. If it still wants energy and that secrecy and dispatch (either from the nonattendance, or the local views of its members) which is characteristick of good Government. And if it shall be found (the contrary of which however I have always been more afrd. of, than of the abuse of them) that Congress will upon all proper occasions exercise the powers with a firm and steady hand, instead of frittering them back to the Individual States where the members in place of viewing themselves in their National character, are too apt to be looking. I say after this essay is made if the system proves inefficient, conviction of the necessity of a change will be dissiminated among all classes of the People. Then, and not till then, in my opinion can it be attempted without involving all the evils of civil discord.

I confess however that my opinion of public virtue is so far changed that I have my doubts whether any system without the means of coercion in the Sovereign, will enforce Obedience to the Ordinances of a Genl. Government; without which, every thing else fails. Laws or Ordinances unobserved, or partially attended to, had better never have been made; because the first is a mere nihil, and the 2d. is productive of much jealousy and discontent. But the kind of coercion you may ask? This indeed will require thought; though the noncompliance of the States with the late requisition, is an evidence of the necessity. It is somewhat singular that a State (New York) which used to be foremost in all foederal measures, should now turn her face against them in almost every instance.

I fear the State of Massachusetts have exceeded the bounds of good policy in its disfranchisements; punishment is certainly due to the disturbers of a government, but the operations of this Act is too extensive. It embraces too much, and probably will give birth to new instead of destroying the old leven. Some Acts passed at the last Session of our Assembly respecting the trade of this Country, has given great, and general discontent to the Merchants of it. An application from the whole body of those at Norfolk has been made, I am told, to convene the assembly.

I had written thus far, and was on the point of telling you how much I am your obliged Servant, when your favor of the 18th. calls upon me for additional acknowledgments. I thank you for the Indian Vocabulary which I dare say will be very acceptable in a general comparison. Having taken a copy, I return you the original with thanks.

It gives me great pleasure to hear that there is a probability of a full representation of the States in Convention; but if the delegates come to it under fetters, the salutary ends proposed will in my opinion be greatly embarrassed and retarded, if not altogether defeated. I am anxious to know how this matter really is, as my wish is, that the Convention may adopt no temporizing expedient, but probe the defects of the Constitution to the bottom, and provide radical cures; whether they are agreed to or not; a conduct like this, will stamp wisdom and dignity on the proceedings, and be looked to as a luminary, which sooner or later will shed its influence.

Expectations for the Philadelphia Convention

I should feel pleasure, I confess, in hearing that Vermont is received into the Union upon terms agreeable to all parties. I took the liberty years ago to tell some of the first characters in the State of New York, that sooner or later it would come to that. That the longer it was delayed the terms on their part, would, probably be more difficult; and that the general interest was suffering by the suspence in which the business was held; as the asylem wch. it afforded, was a constant drain from the Army in place of an aid which it offered to afford. And lastly, considering the proximity of it to Canada if they were not with us, they might become a sore thorn in our sides, wch. I verily believe would have been the case if the war had continued. The Western Settlements without good and wise management of them, may be equally troublesome.

With sentimts. of the sincerest friendship &c. Be so good as to forward the enclosed. Mrs. Washington intended to have sent it by Colo. Carrington, but he did not call here.

132

TO HENRY KNOX

April 2, 1787

My dear Sir,

The early attention which you were so obliging as to pay to my letter of the 8th Ulto. is highly pleasing and flattering. Were you to continue to give me information on the same point you would add to the favor, as I see, or think I see reasons for and against my attendance in the Convention so near an equilibrium as will cause me to determine upon either with diffidence—one of the reasons against it is a fear that all the States will not be represented. As some of them appear to have been unwillingly drawn into the measure, their Delegates will come with such fetters as will embarrass and perhaps render nugatory the whole proceeding. In either of these circumstances—that is a partial representation—or cramped powers, I should not like to be a sharer in the business. If the Delegates assemble with such powers as will enable the Convention to probe the defects of the Constitution to the bottom, and point out radical cures—it would be an honourable employment; but not otherwise. These are matters you may possibly come at by means of your acquaintance with the Delegates in Congress who undoubtedly know what powers are given by their respective States. You also can inform me what is the prevailing opinion with respect to my attendance or non attendance; and I would sincerely thank you for the confidential communication of it.

The delegates to the Philadelphia Convention

If I should attend the Convention, I will be in Philadelphia previous to the meeting of the Cincinnati where I shall hope and expect to meet you and some others of my particular friends the day before, in order that I may have a free and unreserved conference with you on the subject of it, for I assure you this is, in my estimation, a business of a delicate nature. That the design of the Institution was pure I have not a particle of doubt—that it may be so still is perhaps equally unquestionable. But, is not the subsiding of the Jealousies respecting it to be ascribed to the modifications which took place at the last General Meeting? Are not these rejected in toto by some of the State Societies, and partially acceded to by others? Has any State so far overcome its prejudices as to grant a Charter?

Society of the Cincinnati

Will the modifications and alterations be insisted on in the next meeting, or given up? If the first, will it not occasion warmth, and divisions? If the latter, and I should remain at the head of this order, in what light would my signature appear in recommendations, having different tendencies? In what light will this versatility appear to the foreign members who perhaps are acting agreeably to the recommendations? These & other matters which may be agitated will, I fear, place me in a disagreeable situation if I should attend the meeting; and were among the causes which induced me to decline previously the honor of the presidency. Indeed my health is become very precarious. A rheumatic complaint which has followed me more than 6 months is frequently so bad that it is sometimes with difficulty I can raise my hand to my head, or turn myself in bed. This, however smooth and agreeable other matters might be, might, almost in the moment of my departure, prevent my attendance on either occasion. I will not at present touch upon any other points of your letter but will wish you to ponder on all these matters, and write to me as soon as you can. With sentiments of the sincerest friendship. I am your Most affect. G. Washington

133

SUMMARY OF LETTERS FROM JAY, KNOX, AND MADISON*

Mr. Jay

Does not think the giving any further powers to Congress will answer our purposes,

Because some of the members will have partial and personal purposes in view, which, and ignorance, prejudice, and interested views of others, will always embarrass those who are well disposed.

Because secrecy and dispatch will be too uncommon, and foreign as well as local interests will frequently oppose, and sometimes frustrate, the wisest measures.

---

*Washington's summary of the Jay, Knox, and Madison letters, when published, was prefaced by the following note by the editors of *North American Review* (October 1827):

We are now about to insert a document, which we possess, in General Washington's handwriting, and which is a summary of three letters received by him from Jay, Knox, and Madison, not long before the convention at Philadelphia. It will show at the same time the opinions of these eminent persons, as to the plan of a constitution, and the earnest attention, which Washington bestowed on the subject. After obtaining the views of others in detail, it was his custom to draw out, arrange, and note on paper the prominent points, that he might bring them into a compass, which his mind could more easily grasp. The following quotation is an exact transcript of such a summary.

Because large assemblies often misunderstand, or neglect the obligations of character, honor, and dignity, and will collectively do, or omit, things which an individual gentleman in his private capacity would not approve.

The executive business of sovereignty, depending on so many wills, and those wills moved by such a variety of contradictory motives and inducements, will, in general, be but feebly done; and

Such a sovereign, however theoretically responsible, cannot be effectually so in its department and officers, without adequate judicatories. He, therefore,

Does not promise himself anything very desirable from any change, which does not divide the sovereignty into its proper departments. Let Congress legislate; let others execute; let others judge. Proposes

A Governor General, limited in his prerogatives and duration; that Congress should be divided into an upper and lower house, the former appointed for life, the latter annually; that the Governor General (to preserve the balance) with the advice of a council, formed, for that *only* purpose, of the great judicial officers, have a negative on their acts.

What powers should be granted to the government so constituted, is a question which deserves much thought; the more [powers], however, he thinks, the better; the *states* retaining only so much as may be necessary for domestic purposes, and all their principal officers, civil and military, being commissioned and removed by the national government.

Questions the policy of the Convention, because it ought to have originated with, and the proceedings be confirmed by, the people, the only source of just authority.

General Knox

It is out of all question, that the foundation of the government must be of republican principles, but so modified and wrought together, that whatever shall be erected thereon should be durable and efficient. He speaks entirely of the Federal Government, or, what would be better, one government, instead of an association of governments.

Were it possible to effect a government of this kind, it might be constituted of an assembly, or lower house, chosen for one, two, or three years; a Senate chosen for five, six, or seven years; and the executive under the title of Governor General, chosen by the Assembly and Senate for the term of seven years, but liable to an impeachment of the lower house, and triable by the Senate.

A judiciary to be appointed by the Governor General during good behavior, but impeachable by the lower house and triable by the Senate.

The laws passed by the General Government, to be obeyed by the local governments, and if necessary, to be enforced by a body of armed men.

All national objects to be designed and executed by the General Government, without any reference to the local governments.

This is considered as a government of the least possible powers, to preserve the confederated government. To attempt to establish less, will be to hazard the existence of republicanism, and to subject us either to a division of the European powers, or to a despotism arising from high handed commotions.

Mr. Madison

Thinks an individual independence of the states utterly irreconcilable with their aggregate sovereignty, and that a consolidation of the whole into one simple republic, would be as inexpedient as it is unattainable. He, therefore, proposes a middle ground, which may at once support a due supremacy of the national authority, and not exclude the local authorities whenever they can be subordinately useful. As the ground work, he proposes that a change be made in the principle of representation, and thinks there would be no great difficulty in effecting it.

Next, that in addition to the present federal powers, the national government should be armed with positive and complete authority in all cases which require uniformity; such as the regulation of trade, including the right of taxing both exports and imports, the fixing the terms and forms of naturalization, &c.

Next, that in addition to the present federal powers, a negative *in all cases* whatever on the legislative acts of the states, as heretofore exercised by the kingly prerogative, appears to him absolutely necessary, and to be the least possible encroachment on the state jurisdictions. Without this defensive power he conceives that every positive [law?], which can be given on paper, will be evaded.

This control over the laws would prevent the internal vicissitudes of state policy, and the aggressions of interested majorities.

The national supremacy ought also to be extended, he thinks, to the judiciary departments; the oaths of the judges should at least include a fidelity to the general as well as the local constitution; and that an appeal should be to some national tribunals in all cases, to which foreigners or inhabitants of other states may be parties. The admiralty jurisdictions to fall entirely within the purview of the national government.

The national supremacy in the executive departments is liable to some difficulty, unless the officers administering them could be made appointable by the supreme government. The militia ought entirely to be placed in some form or other under the authority, which is interested with the general protection and defence.

A government composed of such extensive powers should be well organized and balanced.

The legislative department might be divided into two branches, one of them chosen every _____ years by the people at large, or by the legislatures: the other to consist of fewer members, to hold their places for a longer term, and to go out in such a rotation as always to leave in office a large majority of old members.

Perhaps the negative on the laws might be most conveniently exercised by this branch.

As a further check, a council of revision, including the great ministerial officers, might be superadded.

A national executive must also be provided. He has scarcely ventured as yet to form his own opinion, either of the manner in which it ought to be constituted, or of the authorities with which it ought to be clothed.

An article should be inserted expressly guarantying the tranquillity of the states against internal, as well as external dangers.

In like manner, the right of coercion should be expressly declared. With the resources of commerce in hand, the national administration might always find means of exerting it either by sea or land; but the difficulty and awkwardness of operating by force on the collective will of a state, render it particularly desirable that the necessity of it might be precluded. Perhaps the negative on the laws might create such a mutual dependence between the general and particular authorities as to answer; or perhaps some defined objects of taxation might be submitted along with commerce to the general authority.

To give a new system its proper validity and energy, a ratification must be obtained from the people, and not merely from the ordinary authority of the legislatures. This will be the more essential, as inroads on the *existing constitutions* of the states will be unavoidable.

---

¹34

TO ALEXANDER HAMILTON

Philadelphia, July 10, 1787

Dear Sir:

I thank you for your Communication of the 3d. When I refer you to the state of the Councils which prevailed at the period you left this City, and add, that they are now, if possible, in a worse train than ever; you will find but little ground on which the hope of a good establishment can be formed. In a word, I *almost* despair of seeing a favourable issue to the proceedings of our Convention, and do therefore repent having had any agency in the business.

Reaction to the events of the Philadelphia Convention

The Men who oppose a strong and energetic government are, in my opinion, narrow minded politicians, or are under the influence of local views. The apprehension expressed by them that the *people* will not accede to the form proposed is the *ostensible*, not the *real* cause of the opposition; but admitting that the *present* sentiment is as they prognosticate, the question ought nevertheless to be, is it, or is it not, the best form? If the former, recommend it, and it will assuredly obtain mauger opposition. I am sorry you went away. I wish you were back. The crisis is equally important and alarming, and no opposition under such circumstances should discourage exertions till the signature is fixed. I will not, at this time trouble you with more than my best wishes and sincere regards. I am &c.

135

TO PATRICK HENRY

Mount Vernon, September 24, 1787

Dear Sir:

The Constitution

In the first moment after my return I take the liberty of sending you a copy of the Constitution which the Foederal Convention has submitted to the People of these States. I accompany it with no observations; your own Judgment will at once discover the good, and the exceptionable parts of it. and your experience of the difficulties, which have ever arisen when attempts have been made to reconcile such variety of interests and local prejudices as pervade the several States will render explanation unnecessary. I wish the Constitution which is offered had been made more perfect, but I sincerely believe it is the best that could be obtained at this time; and, as a constitutional door is opened for amendment hereafter, the adoption of it under the present circumstances of the Union, is in my opinion desirable.

From a variety of concurring accounts it appears to me that the political concerns of this Country are, in a manner, suspended by a thread. That the Convention has been looked up to by the reflecting part of the community with a solicitude which is hardly to be conceived, and that if nothing had been agreed on by that body, anarchy would soon have ensued, the seeds being richly sown in every soil. I am &c.

136

TO ALEXANDER HAMILTON

Mount Vernon, November 10, 1787

Dear Sir:

I thank you for the Pamphlet and for the Gazette contained in your letter of the 30th Ult. For the remaining numbers of Publius, I shall acknowledge myself obliged, as I am persuaded the subject will be well handled by the Author.

Opposition to the Constitution

The new Constitution has, as the public prints will have informed you, been handed to the people of this state by a unanimous vote of the Assembly; but it is not to be inferred from hence that its opponants are silenced; on the contrary, there are many, and some powerful ones. Some of whom, it is said by overshooting the mark, have lessened their weight: be this as it may, their assiduity stands unrivalled, whilst the friends to the Constitution content themselves with barely avowing their approbation of it. Thus stands the matter with us, at present; yet, my opinion is, that the Major voice is favourable.

Application has been made to me by Mr. Secretary Thompson (by order of Congress) for a copy of the report, of a Committee, which was appointed to confer with the Baron de Steuben on his first arrival in this Country; forwarded to me by Mr. President Laurens. This I have accordingly sent. It throws no other light on the subject than such as are to be derived from the disinterested conduct of the Baron. No terms are made by him "nor will he accept of any thing but with general approbation." I have however, in my letter enclosing this report to the Secretary, taken occasion to express an unequivocal wish, that Congress would reward the Baron for his Services, sacrafices and merits, to his entire satisfaction. It is the only way in which I could bring my Sentiments before that honble. body, as it has been an established principle with me, to ask nothing from it. With very great esteem and regard etc.

137

TO BUSHROD WASHINGTON

Mount Vernon, November 10, 1787

Dear Bushrod:

In due course of Post, your letters of the 19th. and 26th. Ult. came to hand and I thank you for the communications therein; for a continuation in matters of importance, I shall be obliged to you. That the Assembly would afford the People an opportunity of deciding on the proposed Constitution I had scarcely a doubt, the only question with me was, whether it would go forth under favourable auspices, or receive the stamp of disapprobation. The opponents I expected, (for it ever has been that the adversaries to a measure are more active than its Friends) would endeavor to stamp it with unfavourable impressions, in order to bias the Judgment that is ulti-

Opponents of the Constitution

mately to decide on it, this is evidently the case with the writers in opposition, whose objections are better calculated to alarm the fears, than to convince the Judgment, of their readers. They build their objections upon principles that do not exist, which the Constitution does not support them in, and the existence of which has been, by an appeal to the Constitution itself flatly denied; and then, as if they were unanswerable, draw all the dreadful consequences that are necessary to alarm the apprehensions of the ignorant or unthinking. It is not the interest of the major part of those characters to be convinced; nor will their local views yield to arguments, which do not accord with their present, or future prospects.

Thoughts on adoption of the Constitution by the states

A Candid solution of a single question to which the plainest understanding is competent does, in my opinion, decide the dispute: namely is it best for the States to unite, or not to unite? If there are men who prefer the latter, then unquestionably the Constitution which is offered must, in their estimation, be wrong from the words, we the People to the signature inclusively; but those who think differently and yet object to parts of it, would do well to consider that it does not lye with any *one* State, or the *minority* of the States to superstruct a Constitution for the whole. The separate interests, as far as it is practicable, must be consolidated; and local views must be attended to, as far as the nature of the case will admit. Hence it is that every State has some objection to the present form and these objections are directed to different points. that which is most pleasing to one is obnoxious to another, and so vice versa. If then the Union of the whole is a desirable object, the componant parts must yield a little in order to accomplish it. Without the latter, the former is unattainable, for again I repeat it, that not a single State nor the minority of the States can force a Constitution on the Majority; but admitting the power it will surely be granted that it cannot be done without involving scenes of civil commotion of a very serious nature let the opponents of the proposed Constitution in this State be asked, and it is a question they certainly ought to have asked themselves, what line of conduct they would advise it to adopt, if nine other States, of which I think there is little doubt, should accede to the Constitution? would they recommend that it should stand single? Will they connect it with Rhode Island? or even with two others checkerwise and remain with them as outcasts from the Society, to shift for themselves? or will they return to their dependence on Great Britain? or lastly, have the mortification to come in when they will be allowed no credit for doing so?

The warmest friends and the best supporters the Constitution has, do not contend that it is free from imperfections; but they found them unavoidable and are sensible, if evil is likely to arise there from, the remedy must come hereafter; for in the present moment, it is not to be obtained; and, as there is a Constitutional door open for it, I think the People (for it is with them to Judge) can as they will have the advantage of experience on their Side, decide with as much propriety on the alterations and amendments which are necessary [as] ourselves. I do not think we are more inspired, have more wisdom, or possess more virtue, than those who will come after us.

Imperfections in the Constitution

The power under the Constitution will always be in the People. It is entrusted for certain defined purposes, and for a certain limited period, to representatives of their own chusing; and whenever it is executed contrary to their Interest, or not agreeable to their wishes, their Servants can, and undoubtedly will be, recalled. It is agreed on all hands that no government can be well administered without powers; yet the instant these are delegated, altho' those who are entrusted with the administration are no more than the creatures of the people, act as it were but for a day, and are amenable for every false step they take, they are, from the moment they receive it, set down as tyrants; their natures, one would conceive from this, immediately changed, and that they could have no other disposition but to oppress. Of these things, in a government constituted and guarded as *ours* is, I have no idea; and do firmly believe that whilst many *ostensible* reasons are assigned to prevent the adoption of it, the real ones are concealed behind the Curtain, because they are not of a nature to appear in open day. I believe further, supposing them pure, that as great evils result from too great Jealousy as from the want of it. We need look I think no further for proof of this, than to the Constitution, of some if not all of these States. No man is a warmer advocate for proper restraints and wholesome checks in every department of government than I am; but I have never yet been able to discover the propriety of placing it absolutely out of the power of men to render essential Services, because a possibility remains of their doing ill.

If Mr. Ronald can place the Finances of this Country upon so respectable a footing as he has intimated, he will deserve much of its thanks. In the attempt, my best wishes, I have nothing more to offer, will accompany him. I hope there remains virtue enough in the Assembly of this State to preserve inviolate public treaties and private Contracts; if these are infringed, farewell to respectability and safety in the Government.

I have possessed a doubt, but if any had existed in my breast, reiterated proofs would have convinced me of the impolicy of *all* commutable Taxes. If we cannot learn wisdom from experience, it is hard to say where it is to be found. But why talk of learning it; these things are *mere* Jobs by which few are enriched at the public expense; for whether premeditation, or ignorance, is the cause of this destructive scheme, it ends in oppression.

You have I find broke the Ice; the only advice I will offer to you on the occasion (if you have a mind to command the attention of the House) is to speak seldom, but to important Subjects, except such as particularly relate to your Constituents, and, in the former case make yourself *perfectly* master of the Subject. Never exceed a *decent* warmth, and submit your sentiments with diffidence. A dictatorial Stile, though it may carry conviction, is always accompanied with disgust. I am, &c.

138

TO DAVID STUART

Mount Vernon, November 30, 1787

Dear Sir:

Opposition to the Constitution

Your favor of the 14th. came duly to hand. I am sorry to find by it that the opposition is gaining strength. At this however I do not wonder. The adversaries to a measure are generally, if not always, more active and violent than the advocates; and frequently employ means which the others do not, to accomplish their ends.

I have seen no publication yet, that ought, in my judgment, to shake the proposed Government in the mind of an impartial public. In a word, I have hardly seen any that is not addressed to the passions of the people; and obviously calculated to rouse their fears. Every attempt to amend the Constitution at this time, is, in my opinion, idly vain. If there are characters who prefer disunion, or seperate Confederacies to the general Government which is offered to them, their opposition may, for ought I know, proceed from principle; but as nothing in my conception is more to be depricated than a disunion, or these seperate Confederacies, my voice, as far as it will extend, shall be offered in favor of the latter. That there are some writers (and others perhaps who may not have written) who wish to see these States divided into several confederacies is pretty evident. As an antidote to these opinions, and in order to investigate the ground of objections to the Constitution which is submitted to the People, the Foederalist, under the signature of Publius, is written. The numbers which have been published I send you. If there is a Printer in Richmond who is really well disposed to support the New Constitution he would do well to give them a place in his Paper. They are (I think I may venture to say) written by able men; and before they are finished, will, if I am mistaken not, place matters in a true point of light. Altho' I am acquainted with some of the writers who are concerned in this work, I am not at liberty to disclose their names, nor would I have it known that they are sent by *me* to *you* for promulgation.

The Federalist

You will recollect that the business of the Potomack Company is withheld from the Assembly of Maryland until it is acted upon in this State. That the sitting of that Assembly is expected to be short. And that our operations may be suspended if no other recourse is to be had than to common law processes to obtain the dividends, which are called for by the Directors, and not paid by the Subscribers.

Certificate, and Commutation taxes I hope will be done away by this Assembly. And that it will not interfere either with public treaties, or private contracts. Bad indeed must the situation of that Country be, when this is the case. With great pleasure I received the information respecting the commencement of my Nephews political course. I hope he will not be so buoyed up by the favourable impression it has made as to become a babbler. If the Convention *was* such a tumultuous, and disorderly body as a certain Gentleman has represented it to be, it may be ascribed, in a great degree to some dissatisfied characters who would not submit to the decisions of a majority thereof. I shall depend upon the Corn from Mr. Henley. All here are well and join me in good wishes for you. I am etc.

139

TO JAMES MADISON

Mount Vernon, December 7, 1787

My dear Sir:

Since my last to you, I have been favored with your letters of the 28th. of October and 18th. of November. With the last came 7 numbers of the Foederalist, under the signature of Publius, for which I thank you. They are forwarded to a Gentleman in Richmond for republication; the doing of which in this State will I am persuaded, have a good effect as there are certainly characters in it who are no friends to a general government; perhaps I should not go too far was I to add, who have no great objection to the introduction of anarchy and confusion.

State legislatures and the Constitution

The Sollicitude to discover what the several State Legislatures would do with the Constitution is now transferred to the several Conventions. The decisions of which being more interesting and conclusive is, consequently, more anxiously expected than the other. What Pennsylvania and Delaware have done, or will do must soon be known. Other Conventions to the Northward and Eastward of them are treading closely on their heels; but what the three Southern States have done, or in what light the new Constitution is viewed by them, I have not been able to learn. North Carolina it has been said (by some accts. from Richmond) will be governed in a great measure by the conduct of Virginia. The pride of South Carolina will not I conceive suffer this influence to work in her councils; and the disturbances in Georgia will or I am mistaken show the people of it the propriety of being United, and the necessity there is for a general Government. If these with the States Eastward and Northward of us, should accede to the Foederal Government, I think the citizens of this State will have no cause to bless the opposers of it here if they should carry their point. A paragraph in the Baltimore Paper has announced a change in the Sentiments of Mr. Jay on this subject; and adds that, from being an admirer of the new form, he has become a bitter enemy to it. This relation (without knowing Mr. Jay's opinion) I disbelieve, from a Conviction that he would consider the matter well before he would pass any Judgment. It is very unlikely therefore that a man of his knowledge and fore-

John Jay

sight should turn on both sides of a question in so short a space. I am anxious however to know the foundation (if any) for this.

PS: Since writing the foregoing, I have received a letter from a member (of the Assembly) in Richmond dated the 4th. Inst. giving the following information.

I am sorry to inform you, that the Constitution has lost ground so considerably that it is doubted whether it has any longer a majority in its favor. From a vote which took place the other day, this would appear certain, tho' I cannot think it so decisive as the enemies to it consider it. It marks however the inconsistency of some of its opponents. At the time the resolutions calling a Convention were entered into Colo M——— sided with the friends to the Constitution, and opposed any hint being given, expressive of the Sentiments of the House as to amendments. But as it was unfortunately omitted at that time to make provision for the subsistence of the Convention, it became necessary to pass some resolution providing for any expence whh. may attend an attempt to make amendments. As M——— had on the former occasion declared, that it would be improper to make any discovery of the Sentiments of the House on the subject, and that we had no right to suggest any thing to a body paramt. to us, his advocating such a resolution was a matter of astonishment. It is true, he declared it was not declaratory of our opinion; but the contrary must be very obvious. As I have heard many declare themselves friends to the Constitution since the vote, I do not consider it as altogether decisive of the opinion of the House with respect to it.

I am informed, both by Genl. Wilkinson (who is just arrived here from New Orleans by way of No. Carolina) and Mr. Ross, that North Carolina is almost unanimous for adopting it. The latter received a letter from a member of that Assembly now sitting.

In a debating Society here, which meets once a week, this subject has been canvassed at two successive meetings, and is to be finally decided on tomorrow evening; as the whole Assembly, almost has attended on these occasions, their opinion will then be pretty well ascertained; and as the opinion on this occasion will have much influence, some of Colo. Innis's friends have obtained a promise from him to enter the list.

The bill respecting British debts has passed our house but with such a clause as I think makes it worse than a rejection.

The letter, of which I enclose you a printed copy, from Colo. R H Lee to the Govr. has been circulated with great industry in manuscript, four weeks before it went to press, and said to have had a bad influence. The enemies to the Constitution leave no stone unturned to encrease the opposition to it. I am, &c.

140

TO GOVERNOR EDMUND RANDOLPH

Mount Vernon, January 8, 1788

Dear Sir:

The letter, which you did me the honor of writing to me on the 27th Ulto. with the enclosure, came duly to hand. I receive them as a fresh instance of your friendship and attention. For both I thank you.

Opposition to the Constitution

The diversity of Sentiments upon the important matter which has.been submitted to the People, was as much expected as it is regretted, by me. The various passions and motives, by which men are influenced are concomitants of fallibility, engrafted into our nature for the purposes of unerring wisdom; but had I entertained a latent hope (at the time you moved to have the Constitution submitted to a second Convention) that a more perfect form would be agreed to, in a word that any Constitution would be adopted under the impressions and instructions of the members, the publications, which have taken place since would have eradicated every form of it. How do the sentiments of the influential characters in *this* State who are opposed to the Constitution, and have favoured the public with their opinions, quadrate with each other? Are they not at variance on some of the most important points? If the opponents in the *same* State cannot agree in *their* principles what prospect is there of a coalescence with the advocates of the measure when the different views, and jarring interests of so wide and extended an Empire are to be brought forward and combated?

Constitutional amendments

To my Judgment, it is more clear than ever, that an attempt to amend the Constitution which is submitted, would be productive of more heat and greater confusion than can well be conceived. There are some things in the new form, I will readily acknowledge, wch. never did, and I am persuaded never will, obtain my *cordial* approbation; but I then did conceive, and do now most firmly believe, that, in the aggregate, it is the best Constitution that can be obtained at this Epocha, and that this, or a dissolution of the Union awaits our choice, and are the only alternatives before us. Thus believing, I had not, nor have I now any hesitation in deciding on which to lean.

I pray your forgiveness for the expression of these sentiments. In acknowledging the receipt of your Letter on this subject, it was hardly to be avoided, although I am well disposed to let the matter rest entirely on its own merits, and mens minds to their own workings. With very great esteem &c.

141

TO JAMES MADISON

Mount Vernon, January 10, 1788

My dear Sir:

I stand indebted to you for your favors of the 20th. and 26th. Ulto. and I believe for that of the 14th. also, and their enclosures. It does not appear to me, that there is any *certain* criterion in this State, by which a decided judgment can be formed, as to the opinion which is entertained by the mass of its citizens with respect to the new Constitution. My belief on this occasion is, that whenever the matter is brought to a final decision, that not only a majority, but a large one, will be found in its favor. That the opposition should have gained strength, among the members of the Assembly at Richmond, admitting the fact, is not to be wondered at when it is considered that the powerful adversaries to the Constitution are all assembled at that place, acting conjunctly, with the promulgated sentiments of Col. R— H— L— as auxiliary. It is said however, and I believe it may be depended upon, that the latter, (tho' he may retain his sentiments) has withdrawn, or means to withdraw his opposition; because as he has expressed himself, or as others have done it for him, he finds himself in bad company; such as with M— Sm—th &c, &c. His brother, Francis L. Lee on whose judgment the family place much reliance, is decidedly in favor of the new form, under a conviction that it is the best that can be obtained, and because it promises energy, stability, and that security which is, or ought to be, the wish of every good Citizen of the Union.

Virginia and the Constitution

How far the determination of the question before the debating club (of which I made mention in a former letter) may be considered as auspicious of the final decision of the Convention, I shall not prognosticate; but in this club, the question it seems, was determined by a very large majority in favor of the Constitution; but of all arguments which may be used at this time, none will be so forcible, I expect, as that nine States have acceded to it. And if the unanimity, or majorities in those which are to follow, are as great as in those which have acted, the power of those arguments will be irrisistable. The Governor has given his reasons to the Publick for with holding his Signature to the Constitution. A copy of them I send you.

Our Assembly has been long in Session, employed chiefly (according to my information) in rectifying the mistakes of the last, and committing others for emendations at the next. Yet "who so wise as we are" We are held in painful suspence with respect to European Intelligence. Peace or War, by the last accts. are equally balanced a grain added to either scale will give it the preponderancy. I have no regular corrispondt. in Massachusetts; otherwise, as the occasional subject of a letter I should have had no objection to the communication of my sentiments on the proposed Government as they are unequivocal and decided. With the greatest esteem etc.

PS: I have this momt. been informed, that the Assembly of No Carolina have postponed the meeting of the Convention of that State until July; this seems evidently calculated to take the Tone from Virginia.

142

TO JAMES MADISON

Mount Vernon, February 5, 1788

My dear Sir:

I am indebted to you for several of your favors, and thank you for their enclosures. The rumours of War between France and England have subsided; and the poor Patriots of Holland, it seems, are left to fight their own Battles or negotiate, in neither case with any great prospect of advantage. They must have been deceived, or their conduct has been divided, precipitate, and weak. The former, with some blunders, have, I conceive, been the causes of their misfortunes.

I am sorry to find by yours, and other accts. from Massachusetts, that the decision of its Convention (at the time of their dates) remains problematical. A rejection of the New form by that State will invigorate the opposition, not only in New York, but in all those which are to follow; at the same time that it will afford materials for the Minority in such as have adopted it, to blow the Trumpet of discord more loudly. The acceptance by a *bare* majority, tho' preferable to a rejection, is also to be deprecated. It is scarcely possible to form any decided opinion of the general sentiment of the people of this State, on this important subject. Many have asked me with anxious solicitude, if you did not mean to get into the Convention; conceiving it of indispensable necessity. Colo Mason, who returned only yesterday, has offered himself, I am told for the County of Stafford; and his friends add, he can be elected not only there, but for Prince William and Fauquier also. The truth of this I know not. I rarely go from home, and my visitors, who, for the most part are travellers and strangers, have not the best information.

At the time you suggested for my consideration, the expediency of a communication of my sentiments on the proposed Constitution, to any correspondent I might have in Massachusetts, it did not occur to me that Genl Lincoln and myself frequently interchanged letters; much less did I expect, that a hasty, and indigested extract of one which I had written, intermixed with a variety of other matter to Colo Chas Carter, in answer to a letter I had received from him respecting Wolf dogs, Wolves, Sheep, experiments in Farming &c &c &c. was then in the press, and would bring these sentiments to public view by means of the extensive circulation I find that extract has had. Altho' I never have concealed, and am perfectly regardless who becomes acquainted with my sentiments on the proposed Constitution, yet nevertheless, as no care had been taken to dress the ideas, or any reasons assigned in support of my opinion, I feel myself hurt by the publication; and informed my friend the Colonel of it. In answer, he has fully exculpated himself of the *intention*, but his zeal in the cause prompted him to distribute copies, under a prohibition (which was disregarded) that they should not go to the press. As you

Massachusetts and the Constitution

have seen the rude, or crude extract (as you may please to term it) I will add no more on the subject.

Perceiving that the Foederalist, under the signature of Publius, is about to be republished, I would thank you for forwarding to me three or four Copies, one of which to be neatly bound, and inform me of the cost. Altho' we have not had many, or deep Snows yet we have since the commencement of them, had a very severe Winter; and if the cold of this day is proportionately keen with you a warm room, and a good fire will be found no bad, or uncomfortable antidote to it. With sentiments of perfect esteem etc.

143

TO MARQUIS DE LAFAYETTE

Mount Vernon, February 7, 1788

My dear Marqs:

You know it always gives me the sincerest pleasure to hear from you, and therefore I need only say that your two kind letters of the 9th and 15th of Octr. so replete with personal affection and confidential intelligence, afforded me inexpressible satisfaction. I shall myself be happy in forming an acquaintance and cultivating a friendship with the new Minister Plenipotentiary of France, whom you have commended as a "sensible and honest man;" these are qualities too rare and too precious not to merit one's particular esteem. You may be persuaded, that he will be well received by the Congress of the United States, because they will not only be influenced in their conduct by his individual merits, but also by their affection for the nation of whose Sovereign he is the Representative. For it is an undoubted fact, that the People of America entertain a grateful remembrance of past services as well as a favourable disposition for commercial and friendly connections with your Nation.

New French Minister

You appear to be, as might be expected from a real friend to this Country, anxiously concerned about its present political situation. So far as I am able I shall be happy in gratifying that friendly solicitude. As to my sentiments with respect to the merits of the new Constitution, I will disclose them without reserve, (although by passing through the Post offices they

Views on the Constitution

should become known to all the world) for, in truth, I have nothing to conceal on that subject. It appears to me, then, little short of a miracle, that the Delegates from so many different States (which States you know are also different from each other in their manners, circumstances and prejudices) should unite in forming a system of national Government, so little liable to well founded objections. Nor am I yet such an enthusiastic, partial or undiscriminating admirer of it, as not to perceive it is tinctured with some real (though not radical) defects. The limits of a letter would not suffer me to go fully into an examination of them; nor would the discussion be entertaining or profitable, I therefore forbear to touch upon it. With regard to the two great points (the pivots upon which the whole machine must move,) my Creed is simply,

1st. That the general Government is not invested with more Powers than are indispensably necessary to perform the functions of a good Government; and, consequently, that no objection ought to be made against the quantity of Power delegated to it.

2ly. That these Powers (as the appointment of all Rulers will for ever arise from, and, at short stated intervals, recur to the free suffrage of the People) are so distributed among the Legislative, Executive, and Judicial Branches, into which the general Government is arranged, that it can never be in danger of degenerating into a monarchy, an Oligarchy, an Aristocracy, or any other despotic or oppressive form, so long as there shall remain any virtue in the body of the People.

Distribution of powers

I would not be understood my dear Marquis to speak of consequences which may be produced, in the revolution of ages, by corruption of morals, profligacy of manners, and listlessness for the preservation of the natural and unalienable rights of mankind; nor of the successful usurpations that may be established at such an unpropitious juncture, upon the ruins of liberty, however providently guarded and secured, as these are contingencies against which no human prudence can effectually provide. It will at least be a recommendation to the proposed Constitution that it is provided with more checks and barriers against the introduction of Tyranny, and those of a nature less liable to be surmounted, than any Government hitherto instituted among mortals, hath possessed. We are not to expect perfection in this world; but mankind, in modern times, have apparently made some progress in the science of

. . . and checks and barriers

government. Should that which is now offered to the People of America, be found on experiment less perfect than it can be made, a Constitutional door is left open for its amelioration.

Some respectable characters have wished, that the States, after having pointed out whatever alterations and amendments may be judged necessary, would appoint another federal Convention to modify it upon those documents. For myself I have wondered that sensible men should not see the impracticability of the scheme. The members would go fortified with such Instructions that nothing but discordant ideas could prevail. Had I but slightly suspected (at the time when the late Convention was in session) that another convention would not be likely to agree upon a better form of Government, I should now be confirmed in the fixed belief that they would not be able to agree upon any System whatever. So many, I may add, such contradictory, and, in my opinion unfounded objections have been urged against the System in contemplation; many of which would operate equally against every efficient Government that might be proposed. I will only add, as a further opinion founded on the maturest deliberation, that there is no alternative, no hope of alteration, no intermediate resting place, between the adoption of this, and a recurrence to an unqualified state of Anarchy, with all its deplorable consequences.

Since I had the pleasure of writing to you last, no material alteration in the political state of affairs has taken place to change the prospect of the Constitution's being adopted by nine States or more, Pennsylvania, Delaware, New Jersey and Connecticut have already done it. It is also said Georgia has acceded. Massachusetts, which is perhaps thought to be rather more doubtful than when I last addressed you, is now in convention.

Emigration to the western lands

A spirit of emigration to the western Country is very predominant. Congress have sold, in the year past, a pretty large quantity of lands on the Ohio, for public Securities, and thereby diminished the domestic debt considerably. Many of your military acquaintances such as the Generals Parsons, Varnum, and Putnam, the Colos. Tupper, Sprout and Sherman, with many more, propose settling there. From such beginnings much may be expected.

The storm of war between England and your Nation, it seems, is dissipated. I hope and trust the political affairs in

France are taking a favorable turn. If the Ottomans wd. suffer themselves to be precipitated into a war, they must abide the consequences. Some Politicians speculate on a triple Alliance between the two Imperial Courts and Versailles. I think it was rather fortunate, than otherwise, that the incaution of Ambassador and the rascality of a Rhinegrave prevented you from attempting to prop a falling fabric.

It gives me great pleasure to learn that the present ministry of France are friendly to America; and that Mr. Jefferson and yourself have a prospect of accomplishing measures which will mutually benefit and improve the commercial intercourse between the two Nations. Every good wish attend you and yrs. I am, &c.

144

TO JAMES MADISON

Mount Vernon, March 2, 1788

Sir:

The decision of Massachusetts, notwithstanding its concomitants, is a severe stroke to the opponents of the proposed Constitution in this State; and with the favorable determination of the States which have gone before, and such as are likely to follow after, will have a powerful operation on the Minds of Men who are not actuated more by disappointment, passion and resentment, than they are by moderation, prudence and candor. Of the first description however, it is to be lamented that there are so many; and among them, *some* who would hazard *every* thing rather than their opposition should fail, or have the sagacity of their prognostications impeached by an issue contrary to their predictions.

Massachusetts and the Constitution

The determination you have come to, will give pleasure to your friends. From those in your County you will learn with more certainty than from me, the expediency of your attending the election in it. With *some*, to have differed in sentiment, is to have passed the Rubicon of their friendship, altho' you should go no further. With others (for the honor of humanity) I hope there is more liberality; but the consciousness of having discharged that duty which we owe to our Country, is superior to all other considerations, will place small matters in a secondary point of view.

His Most Ch—n M—y speaks, and acts in a style not very pleasing to republican ears or to republican forms; nor do I think this language is altogether so to the temper of his own subjects at *this* day. Liberty, when it begins to take root, is a plant of rapid growth. The checks he endeavors to give it, however warrantable by ancient usage, will, more than probably, kindle a flame, which may not be easily extinguished; tho' for a while it may be smothered by the Armies at his command, and the Nobility in his interest. When the people are oppressed with Taxes, and have cause to suspect that there has been a misapplication of their money, the language of despotism is but illy brooked. This, and the mortification which the pride of the Nation has sustained in the affairs of Holland (if one may judge from appearances) may be productive of events which prudence will not mention.

To-morrow, the Elections for delegates to the Convention of this State commences; and as they will tread close upon the heels of each other this month becomes interesting and important. With the most friendly sentiments and affectionate regard &c.

145

TO JOHN ARMSTRONG

Mount Vernon, April 25, 1788

Dear Sir:

From some cause or other which I do not know your favor of the 20th of February did not reach me till very lately. This must apologize for its not being sooner acknowledged. Altho' Colo Blaine forgot to call upon me for a letter before he left Philadelphia, yet I wrote a few lines to you previous to my departure from that place; whether they ever got to your hands or not you best know.

I well remember the observation you made in your letter to me of last year, "that my domestic retirement must suffer an interruption." This took place, notwithstanding it was utterly repugnant to my feelings, my interests and my wishes; I sacrificed every private consideration and personal enjoyment to the earnest and pressing solicitations of those who saw and knew the alarming situation of our public concerns, and had no other end in view but to promote the interests of their Country; and conceiving, that under those circumstances, and at so critical a moment, an absolute refusal to act, might, on my part, be construed as a total dereliction of my Country, if imputed to no worse motives. Altho' you say the same motives induce you to think that another tour of duty of this kind will fall to my lot, I cannot but hope that you will be disappointed, for I am so wedded to a state of retirement and find the occupations of a rural life so congenial; with my feelings, that to be drawn into public at my advanced age, could be a sacrifice that would admit of no compensation.

Your remarks on the impressions which will be made on the manners and sentiments of the people by the example of those who are first called to act under the proposed Government are very just; and I have no doubt but (if the proposed Constitution obtains) those persons who are chosen to administer it will have wisdom enough to discern the influence which their example as rulers and legislators may have on the body of the people, and will have virtue enough to pursue that line of conduct which will most conduce to the happiness of their Country; as the first transactions of a nation, like those of an individual upon his first entrance into life, make the deepest impression, and are to form the leading traits in its character, they will undoubtedly pursue those measures which will best tend to the restoration of public and private faith and of consequence promote our national respectability and individual welfare.

Conduct of individuals called to act under the proposed government

That the proposed Constitution will admit of amendments is acknowledged by its warmest advocates; but to make such amendments as may be proposed by the several States the condition of its adoption would, in my opinion amount to a complete rejection of it; for upon examination of the objections, which are made by the opponents in different States and the amendments which have been proposed, it will be found that what would be a favorite object with one State, is the very thing which is strenuously opposed by another; the truth is, men are too apt to be swayed by local prejudices and those who are so fond of amendments which have the particular interest of their own States in view cannot extend their ideas to the general welfare of the Union; they do not consider that for

State amendments to the Constitution

every sacrifice which they make they receive an ample compensation by the sacrifices which are made by other States for their benefit; and that those very things, which they give up operate to their advantage through the medium of the general interest.

In addition to these considerations it should be remembered that a constitutional door is open for such amendments as shall be thought necessary by nine States. When I reflect upon these circumstances I am surprised to find that any person who is acquainted with the critical state of our public affairs, and knows the variety of views, interests, feelings and prejudices which must be consulted in framing a general Government for these States, and how little propositions in themselves so opposite to each other, will tend to promote that desirable end, can wish to make amendments the ultimatum for adopting the offered system.

I am very glad to find, that the opposition in your State, however formidable it has been represented, is, generally speaking, composed of such characters, as cannot have an extensive influence; their fort, as well as that of those in the same class in other States seems to lie in misrepresentation, and a desire to inflame the passions and to alarm the fears by noisy declamation rather than to convince the understanding by sound arguments or fair and impartial statements. Baffled in their attacks upon the constitution they have attempted to vilify and debase the Characters, who formed it, but even here I trust they will not succeed. Upon the whole I doubt whether the opposition to the Constitution will not ultimately be productive of more good than evil; it has called forth, in its defence, abilities which would not perhaps have been otherwise exerted that have thrown new light upon the science of Government, they have given the rights of man a full and fair discussion, and explained them in so clear and forcible a manner, as cannot fail to make a lasting impression upon those who read the best publications on the subject, and particularly the pieces under the signature of Publius. There will be a greater weight of abilities opposed to the system in the convention of this State than there has been in any other, but notwithstanding the unwearied pains which have been taken, and the vigorous efforts which will be made in the Convention to prevent its adoption, I have not the smallest doubt but it will obtain here.

Benefits of opposition to the Constitution

I am sorry to hear, that the College in your neighbourhood is in so declining a state as you represent it, and that it is likely to suffer a further injury by the loss of Dr. Nisbet whom you are afraid you shall not be able to support in a proper manner on account of the scarcity of Cash which prevents parents from sending their Children thither. This is one of the numerous evils which arise from the want of a general regulating power, for in a Country like this where equal liberty is enjoyed, where every man may reap his own harvest, which by proper attention will afford him much more than is necessary for his own consumption, and where there is so ample a field for every mercantile and mechanical exertion, if there cannot be money found to answer the common purposes of education, not to mention the necessary commercial circulation, it is evident that there is something amiss in the ruling political power which requires a steady, regulating and energetic hand to correct and control. That money is not to be had, every mans experience tells him, and the great fall in the price of property is an unequivocal and melancholy proof of it; when, if that property was well secured, faith and justice well preserved, a stable government well administered, and confidence restored, the tide of population and wealth would flow to us, from every part of the Globe, and, with a due sense of the blessings, make us the happiest people upon earth. With sentiments of very great esteem &c.

Stable government and the circulation of cash

146

TO MARQUIS DE LAFAYETTE

Mount Vernon, April 28, 1788

I have now before me, my dear Marqs. your favor of the 3d of August in the last year; together with those of the 1st. of January, the 2d. of January and the 4th. of February in the present. Though the first is of so antient a date, they all come to hand lately, and nearly at the same moment. The frequency of your kind remembrance of me, and the endearing expressions of attachment, are by so much the more satisfactory, as I recognise them to be a counterpart of my own feelings for you. In truth, you know I speak the language of sincerity and not of flattery, when I tell you, that your letters are ever most welcome and dear to me.

War in Europe

This I lay out to be a letter of Politics. We are looking anxiously across the Atlantic for news and you are looking anxiously back again for the same purpose. It is an interesting subject to contemplate how far the war, kindled in the north of Europe, may extend its conflagrations, and what may be the result before its extinction. The Turk appears to have lost his old and acquired a new connection. Whether England has not, in the hour of her pride, overacted her part and pushed matters too far for her own interest, time will discover: but, in my opinion (though from my distance and want of minute information I should form it with diffidence) the affairs of that nation cannot long go on in the same prosperous train: in spite of expedients and in spite of resources, the Paper bubble will one day burst. And it will whelm many in the ruins. I hope the affairs of France are gradually sliding into a better state. Good effects may, and I trust will ensue, without any public convulsion. France, were her resources properly managed and her administrations wisely conducted, is (as you justly observe) much more potent in the scale of empire, than her rivals at present seem inclined to believe.

French and American trade

I notice with pleasure the additional immunities and facilities in trade, which France has granted by the late Royal arret to the United States. I flatter myself it will have the desired effect, in some measure, of augmenting the commercial intercourse. From the productions and wants of the two countries, their trade with each other is certainly capable of great amelioration, to be actuated by a spirit of unwise policy. For so surely as ever we shall have an efficient government established, so surely will that government impose retaliating restrictions, to a certain degree, upon the trade of Britain. at present, or under our existing form of Confederations, it would be idle to think of making commercial regulations on our part. One State passes a prohibitory law respecting some article, another State opens wide the avenue for its admission. One Assembly makes a system, another Assembly unmakes it. Virginia, in the very last session of her Legislature, was about to have passed some of the most extravagant and preposterous Edicts on the subject of trade, that ever stained the leaves of a Legislative Code. It is in vain to hope for a remedy of these and innumerable other evils, untill a general Government shall be adopted.

Making a Constitution

The Conventions of Six States only have as yet accepted the new Constitution. No one has rejected it. It is believed that the Convention of Maryland, which is now in session; and that of South Carolina, which is to assemble on the 12th of May, will certainly adopt it. It is, also, since the elections of Members for the Convention have taken place in this State, more generally believed that it will be adopted here than it was before those elections were made. There will, however, be powerful and eloquent speeches on both sides of the question in the Virginia Convention; but as Pendleton, Wythe, Blair, Madison, Jones, Nicholas, Innis and many other of our first characters will be advocates for its adoption, you may suppose the weight of abilities will rest on that side. Henry and Mason are its great adversaries. The Governor, if he opposes it at all will do it feebly.

On the general merits of this proposed Constitution, I wrote to you, some time ago, my sentiments pretty freely. That letter had not been received by you, when you addressed to me the last of yours which has come to my hands. I had never supposed that perfection could be the result of accommodation and mutual concession. The opinion of Mr. Jefferson and yourself is certainly a wise one, that the Constitution ought by all means to be accepted by nine States before any attempt should be made to procure amendments. For, if that acceptance shall not previously take place, men's minds will be so much agitated and soured, that the danger will be greater than ever of our becoming a disunited People. Whereas, on the other hand, with prudence in temper and a spirit of moderation, every essential alteration, may in the process of time, be expected.

You will doubtless, have seen, that it was owing to this conciliatory and patriotic principle that the Convention of Massachusetts adopted the Constitution in toto; but recommended a number of specific alterations and quieting explanations, as an early, serious and unremitting subject of attention. Now, although it is not to be expected that every individual, in Society, will or can ever be brought to agree upon what is, exactly, the best form of government; yet, there are many things in the Constitution which only need to be explained, in order to prove equally satisfactory to all parties. For example: there was not a member of the convention, I believe, who had the least objection to what is contended for by the Advocates for a

Bill of Rights

Bill of Rights and *Tryal by Jury*. The first, where the people evidently retained every thing which they did not in express terms give up, was considered nugatory as you will find to have been more fully explained by Mr. Wilson and others: And as to the second, it was only the difficulty of establishing a mode which should not interfere with the fixed modes of any of the States, that induced the Convention to leave it, as a matter of future adjustment.

The Constitution and the Presidency

There are other points on which opinions would be more likely to vary. As for instance, on the ineligibility of the same person for President, after he should have served a certain course of years. Guarded so effectually as the proposed Constitution is, in respect to the prevention of bribery and undue influence in the choice of President: I confess, I differ widely myself from Mr. Jefferson and you, as to the necessity or expediency of rotation in that appointment. The matter was fairly discussed in the Convention, and to my full convictions; though I cannot have time or room to sum up the argument in this letter. There cannot, in my judgment, be the least danger that the President will by any practicable intrigue ever be able to continue himself one moment in office, much less perpetuate himself in it; but in the last stage of corrupted morals and political depravity: and even then there is as much danger that any other species of domination would prevail. Though, when a people shall have become incapable of governing themselves and fit for a master, it is of little consequence from what quarter he comes. Under an extended view of this part of the subject, I can see no propriety in precluding ourselves from the services of any man, who on some great emergency shall be deemed universally, most capable of serving the Public.

In answer to the observations you make on the probability of my election to the Presidency (knowing me as you do) I need only say, that it has no enticing charms, and no fascinating allurements for me. However, it might not be decent for me to say I would refuse to accept or even to speak much about an appointment, which may never take place: for in so doing, one might possibly incur the application of the moral resulting from that Fable, in which the Fox is represented as inveighing against the sourness of the grapes, because he could not reach them. All that it will be necessary to add, my dear Marquis, in order to show my decided predilection, is, that, (at my time of life and under my circumstances) the encreasing infirmities of nature and the growing love of retirement do not permit me to entertain a wish beyond that of living and dying an honest man on my own farm. Let those follow the pursuits of ambition and fame, who have a keener relish for them, or who may have more years, in store, for the enjoyment.

Mrs. Washington, while she requests that her best compliments may be presented to you, joins with me in soliciting that the same friendly and affectionate memorial of our constant remembrance and good wishes may be made acceptable to Madame de la Fayette and the little ones. I am &c.

PS: May 1st. Since writing the foregoing letter, I have received Authentic Accounts that the Convention of Maryland have ratified the new Constitution by a Majority of 63 to 11.

147

TO MARQUIS DE CHASTELLUX

Mount Vernon, April 25[– May 1], 1788

My dear Marquis:

In reading your very friendly and acceptable letter of 21st. December 1787, which came to hand by the last mail, I was, as you may well suppose, not less delighted than surprised to come across that plain American word "my wife." A wife! well *Domestic felicity* my dear Marquis, I can hardly refrain from smiling to find you are caught at last. I saw, by the eulogium you often made on the happiness of domestic life in America, that you had swallowed the bait and that you would as surely be taken (one day or another) as you was a Philosopher and a Soldier. So your day has, at length, come. I am glad of it with all my heart and soul. It is quite good enough for you. Now you are well served for coming to fight in favor of the American Rebels, all the way across the Atlantic Ocean, by catching that terrible Contagion, domestic felicity, which time like the small pox or the plague, a man can have only once in his life: because it commonly lasts him (at least with us in America, I dont know how you manage these matters in France) for his whole life time. And yet after all the maledictions you so richly merit on the subject, the worst wish which I can find in my heart to make against Madame de Chastellux and yourself is, that you may neither of you ever get the better of this same domestic felicity during the entire course of your mortal existence.

If so wonderful an event should have occasioned me, my dear Marquis, to have written in a strange style, you will understand me as clearly as if I had said (what in plain English, is the simple truth) do me the justice to believe that I take a heartfelt interest in whatever concerns your happiness. And in this view, I sincerely congratulate you on your auspicious Matrimonial connection. I am happy to find that Madame de Chastellux is so intimately connected with the Dutchess of Orleans, as I have always understood that this noble lady was an illustrious pattern of connubial love, as well as an excellent model of virtue in general.

While you have been making love, under the banner of Hymen, the great Personages in the North have been making war, under the inspiration, or rather under the infatuation of Mars. Now, for my part, I humbly conceive, you have had much the best and wisest of the bargain. For certainly it is more consonant to all the principles of reason and religion (natural and revealed) to replenish the earth with inhabitants, rather than to depopulate it by killing those already in existence, besides it is time for the age of Knight-Errantry and mad-heroism to be at an end. Your young military men, who

Waste of war

want to reap the harvest of laurels, don't care (I suppose) how many seeds of war are sown; but for the sake of humanity it is devoutly to be wished, that the manly employment of agriculture and the humanizing benefits of commerce, would supersede the waste of war and the rage of conquest; that the swords might be turned into plough-shares, the spears into pruning hooks, and, as the Scripture expresses it, "the nations learn war no more."

Now I will give you a little news from this side of the water, and then finish. As for us, we are plodding on in the dull road of peace and politics. We, who live in these ends of the earth, only hear of the rumors of war like the roar of distant thunder. It is to be hoped, that our remote local situation will prevent us from being swept into its vortex.

Adoption of the Constitution by the states

The Constitution, which was proposed by the foederal Convention, has been adopted by the States of Massachusetts, Connecticut, Jersey, Pennsylvania, Delaware, and Georgia. No State has rejected it. The Convention of Maryland is now sitting and will probably adopt it; as that of South Carolina is expected to do in May. The other Conventions will assemble early in the summer. Hitherto there has been much greater unanimity in favour of the proposed government than could have reasonably been expected. Should it be adopted (and I think it will be) America will lift up her head again and in a few years become respectable among the nations. It is a flattering and consolatory reflection, that our rising Republics have the good wishes of all the Philosophers, Patriots, and virtuous men in all nations: and that they look upon them as a kind of Asylum for mankind. God grant that we may not disappoint their honest expectations, by our folly or perverseness.

With sentiments of the purest attachment &c.

148

TO REVEREND FRANCIS ADRIAN VANDERKEMP

Mount Vernon, May 28, 1788

Sir:

The letter which you did me the favor to address to me the 15th. of this instt. from New York has been duly received, and I take the speediest occasion to well-come your arrival on the American shore.

I had always hoped that this land might become a safe and *Holland* agreeable Asylum to the virtuous and persecuted part of mankind, to whatever nation they might belong; but I shall be the more particularly happy, if this Country can be, by any means, useful to the Patriots of Holland, with whose situation I am peculiarly touched, and of whose public virtue I entertain a great opinion.

You may rest assured, Sir, of my best and most friendly sentiments of your suffering compatriots, and that, while I deplore the calamities to which many of the most worthy members of your Community have been reduced by the late foreign interposition in the interior affairs of the United Netherlands; I shall flatter myself that many of them will be able with the wrecks of their fortunes which may have escaped the extensive devastation, to settle themselves in comfort, freedom and ease in some corner of the vast regions of America.

The spirit of the Religions and the genius of the political Institutions of this Country must be an inducement. Under a good government (which I have no doubt we shall establish) this Country certainly promises greater advantages, than almost any other, to persons of moderate property, who are determined to be sober, industrious and virtuous members of Society. And it must not be concealed, that a knowledge that these are the general characteristics of your compatriots would be a principal reason to consider their advent as a valuable acquisition to our infant settlements. If you should meet with as favorable circumstances, as I hope will attend your first operations; I think it probable that your coming will be the harbinger for many more to adventure across the Atlantic.

In the meantime give me leave to request that I may have the pleasure to see you at my house whensoever it can be convenient to you, and to offer whatsoever services it may ever be in my power to afford yourself, as well as to the other Patriots and friends to the rights of Mankind of the Dutch Nation. I am etc.

149

TO MARQUIS DE LAFAYETTE

Mount Vernon, May 28, 1788

My dear Marquis:

I have lately had the pleasure to receive the two letters by which you introduced to my acquaintance M. Du Pont and M. Vanderkemp and altho' those gentlemen have not as yet been to visit me, you may be persuaded that whensoever I shall have the satisfaction of receiving them, it will be with all that attention to which their merits and your recommendations entitle them.

Joel Barlow

Notwithstanding you are acquainted with Mr. Barlow in person, and with his works by reputation, I thought I would just write you a line by him, in order to recommend him the more particularly to your civilities. Mr. Barlow is considered by those who are good Judges to be a genius of the first magnitude; and to be one of those Bards who hold the keys of the gate by which Patriots, Sages and Heroes are admitted to immortality. Such are your Antient Bards who are both the priest and door-keepers to the temple of fame. And these, my dear Marquis, are no vulgar functions. Men of real talents in Arms have commonly approved themselves patrons of the liberal arts and friends to the poets of their own as well as former times. In some instances by acting reciprocally, heroes have made poets, and poets heroes. Alexander the Great is said to have been enraptured with the Poems of Homer and to have lamented that he had not a rival muse to celebrate his actions. Julius Caesar is well known to have been a man of a highly cultivated understanding and taste. Augustus was the professed and magnificent rewarder of poetical merit, nor did he lose the return of having his atcheivments immortalized in song. The Augustan age is proverbial for intellectual refinement and elegance in composition; in it the harvest of laurels and bays was wonderfully mingled together. The age of your Louis the fourteenth, which produced a multitude of great Poets and great Captains, will never be forgotten: nor will that of Queen Ann in England, for the same cause, ever cease to reflect a lustre upon the Kingdom. Although we are yet in our cradle, as a nation, I think the efforts of the human mind with us are sufficient to refute (by incontestable facts) the doctrines of those who have asserted that every thing degenerates in America. Perhaps we shall be found, at this moment, not inferior to the rest of the world in the performances of our poets and painters; notwithstanding many of the incitements are wanting which operate powerfully among older nations. For it is generally understood, that excellence in those sister Arts has been the result of easy circumstances, public encouragements and an advanced stage of society. I observe that the Critics in England, who speak highly of the American poetical geniuses (and their praises may be the more relied upon as they seem to be reluctantly extorted,) are not pleased with the tribute of applause which is paid to your nation. It is a reason why they should be the more caressed by your nation. I hardly know how it is that I am drawn thus far in observations on a subject so foreign from those in which we are mostly engaged, farming and politics, unless because I had little news to tell you.

On the liberal arts and poetry

Since I had the pleasure of writing to you by the last Packet, the Convention of Maryland has ratified the federal Constitution by a majority of 63 to 11 voices. That makes the seventh State which has adopted it, next Monday the Convention in

Political fate of America

Virginia will assemble; we have still good hopes of its adoption here: though by no great plurality of votes. South Carolina has probably decided favourably before this time. The plot thickens fast. A few short weeks will determine the political fate of America for the present generation and probably produce no small influence on the happiness of society through a long succession of ages to come. Should every thing proceed with harmony and consent according to our actual wishes and expectations; I will confess to you sincerely, my dear Marquis; it will be so much beyond any thing we had a right to imagine or expect eighteen months ago, that it will demonstrate as visibly the finger of Providence, as any possible event in the course of human affairs can ever designate it. It is impracticable for you or any one who has not been on the spot, to realise the change in men's minds and the progress towards rectitude in thinking and acting which will then have been made.

Adieu, my dear Marquis, I hope your affairs in France will subside into a prosperous train without coming to any violent crisis. Continue to cherish your affectionate feelings for this country and the same portion of friendship for me, which you are ever sure of holding in the heart of your most sincere, &c.

150

TO HENRY KNOX

Mount Vernon, June 17, 1788

My dear Sir:

I received your letter of the 25th. of May, just when I was on the eve of a departure for Fredericksburgh to pay a visit to my mother from whence I returned only last evening. The information of the accession of South Carolina to the New Government, since your letter, gives us a new subject for mutual felicitations. It was to be hoped that this auspicious event would have considerable influence upon the proceedings of the Convention of Virginia; but I do not find that to have been the case. Affairs in the Convention, for some time past, have not worn so good an aspect as we could have wished: and, indeed, the acceptance of the Constitution has become more doubtful than it was thought to be at their first meeting.

Making a Constitution

The purport of the intelligence, I received from my private letters by the last nights mail, is, that every species of address and artifice has been put in practice by the Antifederalists to create jealousies and excite alarms. Much appears to depend upon the final part which the Kentucke members will take; into many of whose minds apprehensions of unreal dangers, respecting the navigation of the Mississipi and their organization into a separate State, have been industriously infused. Each side seems to think, at present, that it has a small majority, from whence it may be augered that the majority, however it shall turn, will be very inconsiderable. Though, for my own part, I cannot but imagine, if any decision is had, it will be in favor of the adoption. My apprehension is rather that a strenuous, possibly, successful effort may be made for an adjournment; under an idea of opening a corrispondence with those who are opposed to the Constitution in other States. Colo. Oswald has been at Richmond, it is said with letters from Antifoederalists in New York and Pensylvania to their Coadjutors in this State.

The Antifederalists

The Resolution, which came from the Antifederalists (much to the astonishment of the other party) that no question should be taken until the whole Plan should have been discussed paragraph by paragraph; and the remarkable tardiness in their proceedings (for the Convention have been able as yet only to get through the 2d. or 3d. Section), are thought by some to have been designed to protract the business until the time when the Assembly is to convene, that is the 23d. instant, in order to have a more colorable pretext for an adjournment. But notwithstanding the resolution, there has been much desultory debating and the opposers of the Constitution are reported to have gone generally into the merits of the question. I know not how the matter may be, but a few days will now determine.

I am sorry to find not only from your intimations, but also from many of the returns in the late Papers, that there should be so great a majority against the Constitution in the Convention of New York. And yet I can hardly conceive, from motives of policy and prudence, they will reject it absolutely, if either this State or New-Hampshire should make the 9th. in adopting it; as that measure which gives efficacy to the system, must place any State that shall actually have refused its assent to the New-Union in a very awkward and disagreeable predicament.

New York opposition to the Constitution

By a letter which I have just recd. from a young Gentleman who lives with me, but who is now at home in New-Hampshire, I am advised that there is every prospect that the Convention of that State will adopt the Constitution almost immediately upon the meeting of it. I cannot but hope then, that the States which may be disposed to make a secession will think often and seriously on the consequences. Colo. Humphreys who is still here, occupied with literary pursuits, desires to be remembered in terms of the sincerest friendship to you and yours.

Mrs. Washington and the family offer, with me, their best Compliments to Mrs. Knox and the little ones. You will ever believe me to be, with great esteem etc.

151

TO MARQUIS DE LAFAYETTE

Mount Vernon, June 19, 1788

I cannot account for your not having received some of my letters, my dear Marquis, before you wrote yours of the 18th of March, as I have been writing to you, at short intervals, constantly since last autumn. To demonstrate the satisfaction I enjoy on the receipt of your favours; I always answer them almost as soon as they arrive. Although, on account of my retirement from the busy scenes of life and the want of diversity in the tenour of our affairs, I can promise to give you little novelty or entertainment in proportion to what I expect in return. Were you to acknowledge the receipt of my letters, and give the dates of them when you write to me, I should be able to ascertain which of them had reached you, and which of them had miscarried. I am left in doubt whether the Indian Vocabularies &c. &c. have got to you or not.

War in Europe There seems to be a great deal of bloody work cut out for this summer in the North of Europe. If war, want and plague are to desolate those huge armies that are assembled, who that has the feelings of a man can refrain from shedding a tear over the miserable victims of Regal Ambition? It is really a strange thing that there should not be room enough in the world for men to live, without cutting one anothers throats. As France, Spain and England have hardly recovered from the wounds of the late war, I would fain hope they will hardly be dragged into this. However, if the war should be protracted (and not end in a campaign as you intimate it possibly may) there seems to be a probability of other powers being engaged on one side or the other. by the British papers (which are our principal source of intelligence, though not always to be relied upon, as you know) it appears that the Spaniards are fitting out a considerable fleet and that the English Ministry have prohibited the subjects of their Kingdom from furnishing transports for the Empress of Russia. France must be too intent on its own domestic affairs to wish to interfere, and we have not heard that the King of Prussia, since his exploits in Holland, has taken it into his head [not to] meddle with other people's business. I cannot say that I am sorry to hear that the Algerines and other piratical powers are about to assist the Porte, because I think Russia will not forget and that she will take some leisure moment, just to keep her fleets in exercise, for exterminating those nests of Miscreants.

I like not much the situation of affairs in France. The bold demands of the parliaments, and the decisive tone of the King, shew that but little more irritation would be necessary to blow up the spark of discontent into a flame, that might not easily be quenched. If I were to advise, I would say that great moderation should be used on both sides. Let it not, my dear Marquis, be considered as a derogation from the good opinion, that I entertain of your prudence, when I caution you, as an individual desirous of signalizing yourself in the cause of your country and freedom, against running into extremes and prejudicing your cause. The King, though, I think from every thing I have been able to learn, he is really a good-hearted tho' a warm-spirited man, if thwarted injudiciously in the execution of prerogatives that belonged to the Crown, and in plans which he conceives calculated to promote the national good, may disclose qualities he has been little thought to possess. On the other hand, such a spirit seems to be awakened in the Kingdom, as, if managed with extreme prudence, may produce a gradual and tacit Revolution much in favor of the subjects, by abolishing Lettres de Cachet and defining more accurately the powers of government. It is a wonder to me, there should be found a single monarch, who does not realize that his own glory and felicity must depend on the prosperity and happiness of his People. How easy is it for a sovereign to do

Affairs in France

The King of France

that which shall not only immortalize his name, but attract the blessings of millions.

Adoption of the Constitution by the states

In a letter I wrote you a few days ago by Mr. Barlow (but which might not possibly have reached New York until after his departure) I mentioned the accession of Maryland to the proposed government, and gave you the state of politics to that period. Since which the Convention of South Carolina has ratified the Constitution by a great majority: that of this State has been setting almost three weeks; and so nicely does it appear to be ballanced, that each side asserts that it has a preponderancy of votes in its favour. It is probable, therefore, the majority will be small, let it fall on whichever part it may; I am inclined to believe it will be in favour of the adoption. The Conventions of New York and New Hampshire assemble both this week; a large proportion of members, with the Governor at their head, in the former, are said to be opposed to the government in contemplation: New Hampshire it is thought will adopt it without much hesitation or delay. It is a little strange that the men of large property in the South, should be more afraid that the Constitution will produce an Aristocracy or a Monarchy, than the genuine democratical people of the East. Such are our actual prospects. The accession of one State more will complete the number, which by the Constitutional provision, will be sufficient in the first instance to carry the Government into effect.

Blessings of the new government

And then, I expect, that many blessings will be attributed to our new government, which are now taking their rise from that industry and frugality into the practice of which the people have been forced from necessity. I really believe, that there never was so much labour and economy to be found before in the country as at the present moment. If they persist in the habits they are acquiring, the good effects will soon be distinguishable. When the people shall find themselves secure under an energetic government, when foreign nations shall be disposed to give us equal advantages in commerce from dread of retaliation, when the burdens of war shall be in a manner done away by the sale of western lands, when the seeds of happiness which are sown here shall begin to expand themselves, and when every one (under his own vine and fig-tree) shall begin to taste the fruits of freedom, then all these blessings (for all these blessings will come) will be referred to the fostering influence of the new government. Whereas many causes will have conspired to produce them. You see I am not less enthusiastic than ever I have been, if a belief that peculiar scenes of felicity are reserved for this country, is to be denominated enthusiasm. Indeed, I do not believe, that Providence has done so much for nothing. It has always been my creed that we should not be left as an awful monument to prove, "that Mankind, under the most favourable circumstances for civil liberty and happiness, are unequal to the task of Governing themselves, and therefore made for a Master."

We have had a backward spring and summer, with more rainy and cloudy weather than almost ever has been known: still the appearance of crops in some parts of the country is favorable, as we may generally expect will be the case, from the difference of soil and variety of climate in so extensive a region; insomuch that, I hope, some day or another, we shall become a storehouse and granary for the world. In addition to our former channels of trade, salted provisions, butter, cheese &c. are exported with profit from the eastern States to the East Indies. In consequence of a Contract, large quantities of flour are lately sent from Baltimore for supplying the garrison of Gibraltar. With sentiments of tenderest affection etc.

152

TO BENJAMIN LINCOLN

Mount Vernon, June 29, 1788

Mr dear Sir:

I beg you will accept my thanks for the communications handed to me in your letter of the 3d. instant, and my congratulations of the encreasing good dispositions of the Citizens of your State of which the late elections are strongly indicative. No one *can* rejoice more than I do at every step the people of this great Country take to preserve the Union, establish good order and government, and to render the Nation happy at home and respectable abroad. No Country upon Earth ever had it more in its power to attain these blessings than United America. Wondrously strange then, and much to be regretted indeed would it be, were we to neglect the means, and to depart from the road which Providence has pointed us to, so plainly; I cannot believe it will ever come to pass. The great

Governor of the Universe has led us too long and too far on the road to happiness and glory, to forsake us in the midst of it. By folly and improper conduct, proceeding from a variety of causes, we may now and then get bewildered; but I hope and trust that there is good sense and virtue enough left to recover the right path before we shall be entirely lost.

Virginia ratification

You will, before this letter can have reached you, have heard of the Ratification of the new Government by this State. The final question without previous amendments was taken the 25th. Ayes, 89. Noes, 79; but something recommendatory, or declaratory of the rights, [accompanied] the ultimate decision. This account and the news of the adoption by New Hampshire arrived in Alexandria nearly about the same time on Friday evening; and, as you will suppose, was cause for great rejoicing among the Inhabitants who have not I believe an Antifederalist among them. Our Accounts from Richmond are, that the debates, through all the different Stages of the business, though [brisk] and animated, have been conducted with great dignity and temper; that the final decision exhibited an awful and solemn scene, and that there is every reason to expect a perfect acquiescence therein by the minority; not only from

Patrick Henry

the declaration of Mr. Henry, the great leader of it, who has signified that though he can never be reconciled to the Constitution in its present form, and shall give it every *constitutional* opposition in his power yet that he will submit to it peaceably, as he thinks every good Citizen ought to do when it is in exercise and that he will both by precept and example inculcate this doctrine to all around him.

There is little doubt entertained here *now* of the ratification of the proposed Constitution by North Carolina; and however great the opposition to it may be in New York the leaders thereof will, I should conceive, consider well the conseqences before they reject it. With respect to Rhode Island, the power that governs there has so far baffled all calculation on this question that no man would chuse to hazard an opinion lest he might be suspected of participating in its phrensy. You have every good wish of this family and the sincere regard of your affectionate, &c.

BEFORE PRINCETON

The Drama of Founding

1788 – 1789

*I*n Washington's writings in this chapter he comments on the prospects for the new government in the aftermath of the ratification of the Constitution. He also reflects on the past; in particular, he responds to an inquiry from Noah Webster in *1788* touching the dispute about whose strategy it was that produced the battle of Yorktown. Today, still, commentators assert that it was nevertheless not the idea of an assault against Clinton at New York which had seized Rochambeau. For Rochambeau the decisive combat would take place not in New York but in Virginia. In order to do so, he had to convince General Washington himself. This rendition finds a Washington stuck on the idea of relying on French naval forces to assault Clinton, as opposed to Cornwallis, over whom victory, and with it the war, was finally gained. In Washington's own time this version of events had emerged, prompting Webster to inquire just what did occur. Washington's lengthy response, read in the light of letters stretching back to *1777*, places the matter in a truer light.

Washington looked forward even as he looked back. He approached the installation of the new government with that characteristic diffidence noted throughout his military career. It was universally believed that the Constitutional Convention settled on the design it did, above all on the strong executive, because of the expectation that Washington would be the first President. Nevertheless, just as at length he had been persuaded to attend the Constitutional Convention he had done so much to bring about, at length he had to be persuaded to accept the presidency. Washington seemed genuinely uncertain whether events were unfolding around him or whether he in fact was producing them, giving credibility to his opinion that "a greater drama is now acting on this theatre than has heretofore been brought on the American stage, or any other in the world." Whether he was merely acting or directing, the last act in this drama was his inauguration on April 30, 1789.

153

TO THE SECRETARY
FOR FOREIGN AFFAIRS

Mount Vernon, July 18, 1788

Dear Sir:

A few days ago, I had the pleasure to receive your letter from Poughkeepsie; since which I have not obtained any authentic advices of the proceedings of your Convention. The clue you gave me, to penetrate into the principles and wishes of the four classes of men among you who are opposed to the Constitution, has opened a large field for reflection and conjecture. The accession of Ten States must operate forcibly with all the opposition, except the class which is comprehended in your last description. Before this time you will probably have come to some decision. While we are waiting the result with the greatest anxiety, our Printers are not so fortunate as to obtain any papers from the Eastward. Mine which have generally been more regular, have, however, frequently been interrupted for some time past.

It is extremely to be lamented, that a new arrangement in the Post Office, unfavorable to the circulation of intelligence, should have taken place at the instant when the momentous question of a general Government was to come before the People. I have seen no good apology, not even in Mr. Hazard's publication, for deviating from the old custom, of permitting Printers to exchange their Papers by the Mail. That practice was a great public convenience and gratification. If the privi-

Newspapers in the mail

lege was not from convention an original right, it had from prescription strong pretensions for continuance, especially at so interesting a period. The interruption in that mode of conveyance, has not only given great concern to the friends of the Constitution, who wished the Public to be possessed of every thing, that might be printed on both sides of the question; but it has afforded its enemies very plausible pretexts for dealing out their scandals, and exciting jealousies by inducing a belief that the suppression of intelligence, at that critical juncture, was a wicked trick of policy, contrived by an Aristocratic Junto. Now, if the Post Master General (with whose character I am unacquainted and therefore would not be understood to form an unfavorable opinion of his motives) has any candid Advisers who conceive that he merits the public employment they ought to counsel him to wipe away the aspersion he has incautiously brought upon a good cause; if he is unworthy of the office he holds, it would be well that the ground of a complaint, apparently so general, should be inquired into, and, if [well] founded, redressed through the medium of a better appointment.

It is a matter in my judgment of primary importance that the public mind should be relieved from inquietude on this subject. I know it is said that the irregularity or defect has happened accidentally, in consequence of the contract for transporting the Mail on horseback, instead of having it carried in the *Stages*; but I must confess, I could never account, upon any satisfactory principles, for the inveterate enmity with which the Post Master General is asserted to be actuated against that valuable institution. It has often been understood by wise politicians and enlightened patriots that giving a facility to the means of travelling for Strangers and of intercourse for citizens, was an object of Legislative concern and a circumstance highly beneficial to any country. In England, I am told, they consider the Mail Coaches as a great modern improvement in their Post Office Regulations. I trust we are not too old, or too proud to profit by the experience of others. In this article the materials are amply within our reach. I am taught to imagine that the horses, the vehicles, and the accommodations in America (with very little encouragement,) might in a short period become as good as the same articles are to be found in any Country of Europe. and at the same time, I am sorry to learn that the line of Stages is at present interrupted in some

Mail coaches

parts of New England and totally discontinued at the South-ward.

I mention these suggestions only as my particular thoughts on an Establishment, which I had conceived to be of great importance. Your proximity to the Person in question and connection with the characters in Power, will enable you to decide better than I can on the validity of the allegations; and, in that case, to weigh the expediency of dropping such hints as may serve to give satisfaction to the Public. With sentiments of the highest consideration &c.

PS: Since writing the foregoing, I have been favored with your letter which was begun on the 4th and continued till the 8th. and thank you for the information therein contained. Your next will, I hope, announce the ratification by your State without previous amendments.

154

TO JONATHAN TRUMBULL

Mount Vernon, July 20, 1788

My dear Trumbull:

I have received your favor of the 20th of June and thank you heartily for the confidential information contained in it. The character given of a certain great Personage, who is remarkable for neither forgetting nor forgiving, I believe to be just. What effect the addition of such an extraordinary weight of power and influence as the new Arrangement of the East India affairs gives to one branch of the British Government cannot be certainly foretold; but one thing is certain, that is to say, it will always be wise for America to be prepared for events. Nor can I refrain from indulging the expectation that the time is not very distant, when it shall be more in the power of the United States than it hath hitherto been, to be forearmed as well as forewarned against the evil contingencies of European politics.

You will have perceived from the public Papers, that I was not erroneous in my calculation, that the Constitution would be accepted by the Convention of this State. The Majority, it is true, was small, and the minority respectable in many points of view. But the great part of the minority here, as in most other

Ratification proceedings

States, have conducted themselves with great prudence and political moderation; insomuch that we may anticipate a pretty general and harmonious acquiescence. We shall impatiently wait the result from New York and North Carolina. The other State which has not yet acted is nearly out of the question.

As the infamy of the conduct of Rhode Island outgoes all precedent, so the influence of her counsels can be of no prejudice. There is no State or description of men but would blush to be involved in a connection with the Paper-Money Junto of that Anarchy. God grant that the honest men may acquire an ascendency before irrevocable ruin shall confound the innocent with the guilty.

I am happy to hear from Genl. Lincoln and others that affairs are taking a good turn in Massachusetts; but the Triumph of salutary and liberal measures over those of an opposite tendency seems to be as complete in Connecticut as in any other State and affords a particular subject of congratulation. Your friend Colo. Humphreys informs me, from the wonderful revolution of sentiment in favour of federal measures, and the marvellous change for the better in the elections of your State, that he shall begin to suspect that miracles have not ceased; indeed, for myself, since so much liberality has been displayed in the construction and adoption of the proposed General Government, I am almost disposed to be of the same opinion. Or at least we may, with a kind of grateful and pious exultation, trace the finger of Providence through those dark and mysterious events, which first induced the States to appoint a general Convention and then led them one after another (by such steps as were best calculated to effect the object) into an adoption of the system recommended by that general Convention; thereby, in all human probability, laying a lasting foundation for tranquillity and happiness; when we had but too much reason to fear that confusion and misery were coming rapidly upon us. That the same good Providence may still continue to protect us and prevent us from dashing the cup of national felicity just as it has been lifted to our lips, is the earnest prayer of, My Dear Sir, your faithful friend, &c.

155

TO NOAH WEBSTER, ESQ.

Mount Vernon, July 31, 1788

Sir:

I duly received your letter of the 14th inst., and can only answer you briefly and generally from memory; that a combined operation of the land and naval forces of France in America, for the year 1781, was preconcerted the year before; that the point of attack was not absolutely agreed upon,* because it could not be foreknown where the enemy would be most susceptible of impression; and because we (having the command of the water with sufficient means of conveyance) could transport ourselves to any spot with the greatest celerity; that it was determined by me, nearly twelve months beforehand, at all hazards, to give out and cause it to be believed by the highest military as well as civil officers, that New York was the destined place of attack, for the important purpose of inducing the eastern and middle states to make greater exertions in furnishing specific supplies, than they otherwise would have done, as well as for the interesting purpose of rendering the enemy less prepared elsewhere; that by these means, and these alone, artillery, boats, stores, and provisions, were in seasonable preparation to move with the utmost rapidity to any part of the continent; for the difficulty consisted more in providing, than knowing how to apply the military apparatus; that before the arrival of the Count de Grasse, it was the fixed determination *to strike the enemy in the most vulnerable quarter*, so as to ensure success with moral certainty, as our affairs were then in the most ruinous train imaginable; that New York was thought to be beyond our effort, and consequently that the only hesitation that remained, was between an attack upon the British army in Virginia and that in Charleston: and finally, that by the intervention of several communications, and some incidents which can not be detailed in a letter, the hostile post in Virginia, from being a *provisional and strongly expected*, became the *definitive and certain object* of the campaign.

French-American military cooperation in 1781

---

*Because it would be easy for the Count de Grasse, in good time before his departure from the West Indies, to give notice, by express, at what place he could most conveniently first touch to receive advice. [G.W.]

I only add, that it never was in contemplation to attack New York, unless the garrison should first have been so far degarnished to carry on the southern operations, as to render our success in the siege of that place, as infallible as any future military event can ever be made. For I repeat it, and dwell upon it again, some splendid advantage (whether upon a larger or smaller scale was almost immaterial) was so essentially necessary, to revive the expiring hopes and languid exertions of the country, at the crisis in question, that I never would have consented to embark in any enterprise, wherein, from the most rational plan and accurate calculations, the favorable issue should not have appeared as clear to my view as a ray of light. The failure of an attempt against the posts of the enemy, could, in no other possible situation during the war, have been so fatal to our cause.

That much trouble was taken and finess used to misguide and bewilder Sir Henry Clinton, in regard to the real object, by fictitious communications, as well as by making a deceptive provision of ovens, forage, and boats, in his neighborhood, is certain. Nor were less pains taken to deceive our own army; for I had always conceived, where the imposition did not completely take place at home, it could never sufficiently succeed abroad.

Your desire of obtaining truth, is very laudable; I wish I had more leisure to gratify it, as I am equally solicitous the undisguised verity should be known. Many circumstances will unavoidably be misconceived and misrepresented. Notwithstanding most of the papers, which may properly be deemed official, are preserved; yet the knowledge of innumerable things, of a more delicate and secret nature, is confined to the perishable remembrance of some few of the present generation. With esteem, I am sir, Your most obedient humble servant, G. WASHINGTON

156

TO BENJAMIN LINCOLN

Mount Vernon, August 28, 1788

My dear Sir:

I received with your letter of the 9th. instant, one from Mr. Minot, and also his History of the Insurrections in Massachusetts. The work seems to be executed with ingenuity, as well as to be calculated to place facts in a true point of light, obviate the prejudices of those who are unacquainted with the circumstances and answer good purposes in respect to our government in general. I have returned him my thanks for his present, by this conveyance.

The public appears to be anxiously waiting for the decision of Congress, respecting the *place* for convening the National Assembly under the new government, and the Ordinance for its organization. Methinks it is a great misfortune, that local interests should involve themselves with federal concerns at this moment.

So far as I am able to learn, foederal principles are gaining ground considerably. The declaration of some of the most respectable characters in this state (I mean of those who were opposed to the government) is now explicit, that they will give the Constitution a fair chance, by affording it all the support in their power. Even in Pennsylvania, the Minority, who were more violent than in any other place, say they will only seek for amendments in the mode pointed out by the Constitution itself. *Support for the new Constitution*

I will however just mention by way of caveat, there are suggestions, that attempts will be made to procure the election of a number of antifoederal characters to the first Congress, in order to embarrass the wheels of government and produce premature alterations in its Constitution. How these hints, which have come through different channels, may be well or ill founded, I know not: but, it will be advisable, I should think, for the foederalists to be on their guard so far as not to suffer any secret machinations to prevail, without taking measures to frustrate them. That many amendments and explanations might and should take place, I have [no] difficulty in conceding; but, I will confess, my apprehension is, that the New York Circular letter is intended to bring on a general Convention at *Federalist-Antifederalist election intrigue*

Amendments to the Constitution

too early a period, and in short, by referring the subject to the Legislatures, to set every thing afloat again. I wish I may be mistaken in imagining, that there are persons, who, upon finding they could not carry their point by an open attack against the Constitution, have some sinister designs to be silently effected, if possible. But I trust in that Providence, which has saved us in six troubles yea in seven, to rescue us again from any imminent, though unseen, dangers. Nothing, however, on our part ought to be left undone. I conceive it to be of unspeakable importance, that whatever there be of wisdom, and prudence, and patriotism on the Continent, should be concentred in the public Councils, at the first outset. Our habits of intimacy will render an apology unnecessary. Heaven is my witness, that an inextinguishable desire [that] the felicity of my country may be promoted is my only motive in making these observations. With sentiments of sincere attachment etc.

157

TO ALEXANDER HAMILTON

Mount Vernon, August 28, 1788

Dear Sir:

I have had the pleasure to receive your letter dated the 13th. accompanied by one addressed to Genl. Morgan. I will forward the letter to General Morgan by the first conveyance, and add my particular wishes, that he would comply with the request contained in it. Although I can scarcely imagine how the watch of a British officer, killed within their lines, should have fallen into his hands who was many miles distant from the scene of action, yet, if it so happened, I flatter myself there will be no reluctance or delay in restoring it to the family.

Comments on "Publius"

As the perusal of the political papers under the signature of Publius has afforded me great satisfaction, I shall certainly consider them as claiming a most distinguished place in my Library. I have read every performance which has been printed on one side and the other of the great question lately agitated (so far as I have been able to obtain them) and, without an unmeaning compliment, I will say, that I have seen no other so well calculated (in my judgment) to produce conviction on an unbiased Mind, as the *Production* of your *triumvirate*.

When the transient circumstances and fugitive performances which attended this Crisis shall have disappeared, That Work will merit the Notice of Posterity; because in it are candidly and ably discussed the principles of freedom and the topics of government, which will be always interesting to mankind so long as they shall be connected in Civil Society.

The circular letter from your Convention, I presume, was the equivalent by which you obtained an acquiescence in the proposed Constitution. Notwithstanding I am not very well satisfied with the tendency of it, yet the foederal affairs had proceeded, with few exceptions, in so good a train, that I hope the political Machine may be put in motion, without much effort or hazard of miscarrying.

On the delicate subject with which you conclude your letter, I can say nothing; because the event alluded to may never happen; and because, in case it should occur, it would be a point of prudence to defer forming one's ultimate and irrevocable decision, so long as new data might be afforded for one to act with the greater wisdom and propriety. I would not wish to conceal my prevailing sentiment from you. For you know me well enough, my good Sir, to be persuaded, that I am not guilty of affectation, when I tell you, that it is my great and sole desire to live and die, in peace and retirement on my own farm. Were it even indispensable a different line of conduct should be adopted; while you and some others who are acquainted with my heart would *acquit*, the world and Posterity might probably accuse me [of] *inconsistency* and *ambition*. Still I hope I shall always possess firmness and virtue enough to maintain (what I consider the most enviable of all titles) the character of *an honest man*, as well as prove (what I desire to be considered in reality) that I am, with great sincerity and esteem, etc.

On the possibility of becoming President

TO THOMAS JEFFERSON

Mount Vernon, August 31, 1788

Dear Sir:

I was very much gratified by the receipt of your letter, dated the 3d. of May. You have my best thanks for the political information contained in it, as well as for the satisfactory account of the Canal of Languedoc. It gives me pleasure to be made acquainted with the particulars of that stupendous Work, tho' I do not expect to derive any but speculative advantages from it.

Canals at Languedoc

... and in America

When America will be able to embark in projects of such pecuniary extent, I know not; probably not for very many years to come; but it will be a good example and not without its use, if we can carry our present undertakings happily into effect. Of this we have now the fairest prospect. Notwithstanding the real scarcity of money, and the difficulty of collecting it, the labourers employed by the Potomack Company have made very great progress in removing the obstructions at the Shenandoah, Seneca and Great Falls. Insomuch that, if this Summer had not proved unusually rainy and if we could have had a favourable autumn, the Navigation might have been sufficiently opened (though not completed) for Boats to have passed from Fort Cumberland to within nine miles of a Shipping port by the first of January next. There remains now no doubt of the practicability of the Plan, or that, upon the ulterior operations being performed, this will become the great avenue into the Western Country; a country which is now settg. in an extraordinarily rapid manner, under uncommonly favorable circumstances, and which promises to afford a capacious asylum for the poor and persecuted of the Earth.

I do not pretend to judge how far the flames of war, which are kindled in the North of Europe, may be scattered; or how soon they will be extinguished. The European politics have taken so strange a turn, and the Nations formerly allied have become so curiously severed, that there are fewer sure premises for calculation, than are usually afforded, even on that precarious and doubtful subject. But it appears probable to me, that peace will either take place this year, or hostility be greatly extended in the course of the next. The want of a hearty co-operation between the two Imperial Powers against the Porte; or the failure of success from any other cause, may accelerate the first contingency; the irritable state into wch. several of the other Potentates seem to have been drawn, may open the way to the secd. Hitherto the event of the contest has proved different from the general expectation. If, in our speculations, we might count upon discipline, system and resource, and certainly these are the articles which generally give decisive advantages in War, I had thought full-surely the Turks must, at least, have been driven out of Europe.

Is it not unaccountable that the Russians and Germans combined, are not able to effect so much, as the former did alone in the late War? But perhaps these things are all for the best and may afford room for pacification. I am glad our Commodore Paul Jones has got employment, and heartily wish him success. His new situation may possibly render his talents and services more useful to us at some future day. I was unapprised of the circumstances which you mention, that Congress had once in contemplation to give him promotion. They will judge now how far it may be expedient.

By what we can learn from the late foreign Gazettes, affairs seem to have come to a crisis in France; and I hope they are beginning to meliorate. Should the contest between the King and the Parliaments result in a well constituted National Assembly, it might ultimately be a happy event for the kingdom. But I fear that Kingdom will not recover its reputation and influence with the Dutch for a long time to come. Combinations appear also to be forming in other quarters. It is reported by the last European accounts that England has actually entered into a Treaty with Prussia; and that the French Ambassador at the Court of London has asked to be informed of its tenor. In whatever manner the Nations of Europe shall endeavor to keep up their prowess in war and their ballance of power in peace, it will be obviously our policy to cultivate tranquility at home and abroad; and extend our agriculture and commerce as far as possible.

I am much obliged by the information you give respecting the credit of different Nations among the Dutch Money-holders; and fully accord with you with regard to the manner in which our own ought to be used. I am strongly impressed with the expediency of establishing our National faith beyond imputation, and of having recourse to loans only on critical occasions. Your proposal for transferring the whole foreign debt to

Holland is highly worthy of consideration. I feel mortified that there should have been any just grd. for the clamour of the foreign Officers who served with us; but, after having received a quarter of their whole debt in specie and their interest in the same for sometime, they have infinitely less reason for complaint than our native Officers, of whom the suffering and neglect have only been equalled by their patience and patriotism. A great proportion of the Officers and Soldiers of the American Army have been compelled by indigence to part with their securities for one eighth of the nominal value. Yet their conduct is very different from what you represented that of the French Officers to have been.

The new Constitution and proposed amendments

The merits and defects of the proposed Constitution have been largely and ably discussed. For myself, I was ready to have embraced any tolerable compromise that was competent to save us from impending ruin; and I can say, there are scarcely any of the amendments which have been suggested, to which I have *much* objection, except that which goes to the prevention of direct taxation; and that, I presume, will be more strenuously advocated and insisted upon hereafter, than any other. I had indulged the expectation, that the New Government would enable those entrusted with its Administration to do justice to the public creditors and retrieve the National character. But if no means are to be employed but requisitions, that expectation was vain and we may as well recur to the old Confoederation. If the system can be put in operation without touching much the Pockets of the People, perhaps, it may be done; but, in my judgment, infinite circumspection and prudence are yet necessary in the experiment. It is nearly impossible for anybody who has not been on the spot to conceive (from any description) what the delicacy and danger of our situation have been. Though the peril is not past entirely; thank God! the prospect is somewhat brightening.

You will probably have heard before the receipt of this letter, that the general government has been adopted by eleven States; and that the actual Congress have been prevented from issuing their ordinance for carrying it into execution, in consequence of a dispute about the place at which the future Congress shall meet. It is probable that Philadelphia or New York will soon be agreed upon.

I will just touch on the bright side of our national State, before I conclude: and we may perhaps rejoice that the People have been ripened by misfortune for the reception of a good government. They are emerging from the gulf of dissipation and debt into which they had precipitated themselves at the close of the war. Oeconomy and industry are evidently gaining ground. Not only Agriculture; but even Manufactures are much more attended to than formerly. Notwithstanding the shackles under which our trade in general labours; commerce to the East Indies is prosecuted with considerable success: Salted provisions and other produce (particularly from Massachusetts) have found an advantageous market there. The Voyages are so much shorter and the vessels are navigated at so much less expence, that we hope to rival and supply (at least through the West Indies) some part of Europe, with commodities from thence. This year the exports from Massachusetts have amounted to a great deal more than their exports [*sic*]. I wish this was the case everywhere.

Agriculture, manufacturing, and commerce

On the subject of our commerce with France, I have received several quaeries from the Count de Moustiers; besides the information he desired relative to articles of importation from and exportation to France, he wished to know my opinion of the advantage or detriment of the Contract between Mr. Morris and the Farm; as also what emoluments we had to give in return for the favors we solicited in our intercourse with the Islands. As I knew that these topics were also in agitation in France, I gave him the most faithful and satisfactory advice I could: but in such a cautious manner as might not be likely to contradict your assertions or impede your negotiations in Europe. With sentiments of the highest regard etc.

Commerce with France

159

TO ALEXANDER HAMILTON

Mount Vernon, October 3, 1788

Dear Sir:

In acknowledging the receipt of your candid and kind letter by the last Post; little more is incumbent upon me, than to thank you sincerely for the frankness with which you communicated your sentiments, and to assure you that the same manly tone of intercourse will always be more than barely welcome, indeed it will be highly acceptable to me. I am particularly glad in the present instance, that you have dealt thus freely and like a friend.

Speculations on vote of the Electoral College

Although I could not help observing, from several publications and letters that my name had been sometimes spoken of, and that it was possible the *Contingency* which is the subject of your letter might happen; yet I thought it best to maintain a guarded silence and to seek the counsel of my best friends (which I certainly hold in the highest estimation) rather than to hazard an imputation unfriendly to the delicacy of my feelings. For, situated as I am, I could hardly bring the question into the slightest discussion, or ask an opinion even in the most confidential manner, without betraying, in my judgment, some impropriety of conduct, or without feeling an apprehension, that a premature display of anxiety might be construed into a vain-glorious desire of pushing myself into notice as a candidate. Now, if I am not grossly deceived in myself, I should unfeignedly rejoice, in case the Electors, by giving their votes in favor of some other person, would save me from the dreaded Dilemma of being forced to accept or refuse.

If that may not be, I am, in the next place, earnestly desirous of searching out the truth, and of knowing whether there does not exist a probability that the government would be just as happily and effectually carried into execution without my aid, as with it. I am *truly* solicitous to obtain all the previous information which the circumstances will afford, and to determine (when the determination can with propriety be no longer postponed) according to the principles of right reason, and the dictates of a clear conscience; without too great a reference to the unforeseen consequences, which may affect my person or reputation. Untill that period, I may fairly hold myself open to conviction; though I allow your sentiments to have weight in them; and I shall not pass by your arguments without giving them as dispassionate a consideration, as I can possibly bestow upon them.

In taking a survey of the subject, in whatever point of light I have been able to place it, I will not suppress the acknowledgment, my Dr. Sir that I have always felt a kind of gloom upon my mind, as often as I have been taught to expect, I might, and perhaps must ere long, be called to make a decision. You will, I am well assured, believe the assertion (though I have little expectation it would gain credit from those who are less acquainted with me) that if I should receive the appointment and if I should be prevailed upon to accept it, the acceptance would be attended with more diffidence and reluctance than I ever experienced before in my life. It would be, however, with a fixed and sole determination of lending whatever assistance might be in my power to promote the public weal, in hopes that at a convenient and early period my services might be dispensed with, and that I might be permitted once more to retire, to pass an unclouded evening after the stormy day of life, in the bosom of domestic tranquility.

But why these anticipations? if the friends to the Constitution conceive that my administering the government will be a means of its acceleration and strength, is it not probable that the adversaries of it may entertain the same ideas, and of course make it an object of opposition? That many of this description will become Electors, I can have no doubt of, any more than that their opposition will extend to any character who (from whatever cause) would be likely to thwart their measures. It might be impolitic in them to make this declaration *previous* to the Election; but I shall be out in my conjectures if they do not act conformably thereto, and that the seeming moderation by which they appear to be actuated at present is neither more or less than a finesse to lull and deceive. Their plan of opposition is systematized, and a regular intercourse, I have much reason to believe between the Leaders of it in the several States is formed to render it more effectual. With sentiments of sincere regard &c.

160

TO BENJAMIN LINCOLN

Mount Vernon, October 26, 1788

My dear Sir:

I have been lately favored with the receipt of your letters of the 24th and 30th of September, with their enclosures, and thank you sincerely for your free and friendly communications. As the period is now rapidly approaching which must decide the fate of the new Constitution, as to the manner of its being carried into execution, and probably as to its usefulness, it is not wonderful that we should all feel an unusual degree of anxiety on the occasion. I must acknowledge my fears have

A critical period for the new Constitution in various states

been greatly alarmed, but still I am not without hopes. From the good beginning that has been made in Pennsylvania, a State from which much was to be feared, I cannot help foreboding well of the others. That is to say, I flatter myself a majority of them will appoint foederal members to the several branches of the new government. I hardly should think that Massachusetts, Connecticut, New Jersey, Delaware, Maryland, South Carolina, and Georgia, would be for attempting premature amendments. Some of the rest may, also, in all probability be apprehensive of throwing our affairs into confusion, by such ill-timed expedients.

There will however, be no room for the advocates of the Constitution to relax in their exertions; for if they should be lulled into security, appointments of Antifoederal men may probably take place, and the consequences, which you so justly dread, be realized. Our Assembly is now in session; it is represented to be rather antifoederal, but we have heard nothing of its doings. Mr. Patrick Henry, R.H. Lee and Madison are talked of for the Senate. Perhaps as much opposition, or, in other words, as great an effort for early amendments, is to be apprehended from this State, as from any but New York. The constant report is, that North Carolina will soon accede to the new Union. A new Assembly is just elected in Maryland, in which it is asserted the number of Foederalists greatly predominates; and that being the case, we may look for favorable appointments, in spite of the rancour and activity of a few discontented, and I may say *apparently* unprincipled men.

Possibility of becoming President

I would willingly pass over in silence that part of your letter, in which you mention the persons who are Candidates for the two first Offices in the Executive, if I did not fear the omission might seem to betray a want of confidence. Motives of delicacy have prevented me hitherto from conversing or writing on this subject, whenever I could avoid it with decency. I may, however, with great sincerity and I believe without offending against modesty or propriety say to *you*, that I most heartily wish the choice to which you allude may not fall upon me: and that, if it should, I must reserve to myself the right of making up my final decision, at the last moment when it can be brought into one view, and when the expediency or inexpediency of a *refusal* can be more judiciously determined than at present. But be assured, my dear Sir, if from any inducement I shall be persuaded ultimately to accept, it will not be (so far as

I know my own heart) from any of a private or personal nature. Every personal consideration conspires to rivet me (if I may use the expression) to retirement. At my time of life, and under my circumstances, nothing in this world can ever draw me from it, unless it be a *conviction* that the partiality of my Countrymen had made my services absolutely necessary, joined to a *fear* that my refusal might induce a belief that I preferred the conservation of my own reputation and private ease, to the good of my Country. After all, if I should conceive myself in a manner constrained to accept, I call Heaven to witness, that this very act would be the greatest sacrifice of my personal feelings and wishes that ever I have been called upon to make. It would be to forego repose and domestic enjoyment, for trouble, perhaps for public obloquy: for I should consider myself as entering upon an unexplored field, enveloped on every side with clouds and darkness.

From this embarrassing situation I had naturally supposed that my declarations at the close of the war would have saved me; and that my sincere intentions, then publicly made known, would have effectually precluded me for ever afterwards from being looked upon as a Candidate for any office. This hope, as a last anchor of worldly happiness in old age, I had still carefully preserved; until the public papers and private letters from my Correspondents in almost every quarter, taught me to apprehend that I might soon be obliged to answer the question, whether I would go again into public life or not.

You will see, my dear Sir, from this train of reflections, that I have lately had enough of my own perplexities to think of, without adverting much to the affairs of others. So much have I been otherwise occupied, and so little agency did I wish to have in electioneering, that I have never entered into a single discussion with any person nor to the best of my recollection expressed a single sentiment orally or in writing respecting the appointment of a Vice President. From the extent and respectability of Massachusetts it might reasonably be expected, that he would be chosen from that State. But having taken it for granted, that the person selected for that important place would be a true Foederalist; in that case, I was altogether disposed to acquiesce in the prevailing sentiments of the Electors, without giving any unbecoming preference or incurring any unnecessary ill-will. Since it here seems proper to touch a little

Vice-Presidential considerations

more fully upon that point, I will frankly give you my manner of thinking, and what, under certain circumstances, would be my manner of acting.

For this purpose I must speak again hypothetically for argument's sake, and say, supposing I should be appointed to the Administration and supposing I should accept it, I most solemnly declare, that whosoever shall be found to enjoy the confidence of the States so far as to be elected Vice President, cannot be disagreeable to me in that office. And even if I had any predilection, I flatter myself, I possess patriotism enough to sacrifice it at the shrine of my Country; where, it will be unavoidably necessary for me to have made infinitely greater sacrifices, before I can find myself in the supposed predicament: that is to say, before I can be connected with others, in any possible political relation. In truth, I believe that I have no prejudices on the subject, and that it would not be in the power of any evil-minded persons, who wished to disturb the harmony of those concerned in the government, to infuse them into my mind. For, to continue the same hypothesis one step farther, supposing myself to be connected in office with any gentleman of character, I would most certainly treat him with perfect sincerity and the greatest candour in every respect. I would give him my full confidence, and use my utmost endeavours to co-operate with him, in promoting and rendering permanent the national prosperity; this should be my great, my only aim, under the fixed and irrevocable resolution of leaving to other hands the helm of the State, as soon as my service could possibly with propriety be dispensed with.

I have thus, my dear Sir, insensibly been led into a longer detail than I intended; and have used more egotism than I could have wished; for which I urge no other apology, than but my opinion of your friendship, discretion and candour. With sentiments of real esteem etc.

161

TO MARQUIS DE LAFAYETTE

Mount Vernon, January 29, 1789

My dear Marquis:

By the last post I was favored with the receipt of your letter, dated the 5th of September last. Notwithstanding the distance of its date, it was peculiarly welcome to me: for I had not in the mean time received any satisfactory advices respecting yourself or your country. By that letter, my mind was placed much more at its ease, on both those subjects, than it had been for many months.

The last letter, which I had the pleasure of writing to you, was forwarded by Mr. Gouverneur Morris. Since his departure from America, nothing very material has occurred. The minds of men, however, have not been in a stagnant State. But patriotism, instead of faction, has generally agitated them. It is not a matter of wonder, that, in proportion as we approach to the time fixed for the organization and operation of the new government, their anxiety should have been encreased, rather than diminished.

The choice of Senators, Representatives, and Electors, *Federal elections* which (excepting in that of the last description) took place at different times, in the different States, has afforded abundant topics for domestic News, since the beginning of Autumn. I need not enumerate the several particulars, as I imagine you see most of them detailed, in the American Gazettes. I will content myself with only saying, that the elections have been hitherto vastly more favorable than we could have expected, that federal sentiments seem to be growing with uncommon rapidity, and that this encreasing unanimity is not less indicative of the good disposition than the good sense of the Americans. Did it not savour so much of partiality for my Countrymen I might add, that I cannot help flattering myself the new Congress on account of the self-created respectability and various talents of its Members, will not be inferior to any Assembly in the world. From these and some other circumstances, I really entertain greater hopes, that America will not finally disappoint the expectations of her Friends, than I have at almost any former period. Still however, in such a fickle state of existence I would not be too sanguine in indulging myself with the contemplation of scenes of uninterrupted prosperity; lest some unforeseen mischance or perverseness should occasion the greater mortification, by blasting the enjoyment in the very bud.

Reluctance to become President

I can say little or nothing new, in consequence of the repetition of your opinion, on the expediency there will be, for my accepting the office to which you refer. Your sentiments, indeed, coincide much more nearly with those of my other friends, than with my own feelings. In truth my difficulties encrease and magnify as I draw towards the period, when, according to the common belief, it will be necessary for me to give a definitive answer, in one way or another. Should the circumstances render it, in a manner inevitably necessary, to be in the affirmative: be assured, my dear Sir, I shall assume the task with the most unfeigned reluctance, and with a real diffidence for which I shall probably receive no credit from the world. If I know my own heart, nothing short of a conviction of duty will induce me again to take an active part in public affairs; and, in that case, if I can form a plan for my own conduct, my endeavours shall be unremittingly exerted (even at the hazard of former fame or present popularity) to extricate my country from the embarrassments in which it is entangled, through want of credit; and to establish a general system of policy, which if pursued will ensure permanent felicity to the Commonwealth. I think I see a *path*, as clear and as direct as a ray of light, which leads to the attainment of that object. Nothing but harmony, honesty, industry and frugality are necessary to make us a great and happy people. Happily the present posture of affairs and the prevailing disposition of my countrymen promise to co-operate in establishing those four great and essential pillars of public felicity.

Useful arts and domestic manufacturing

What has been considered at the moment as a disadvantage, will probably turn out for our good. While our commerce has been considerably curtailed, for want of that extensive credit formerly given in Europe, and for default of remittance; the useful arts have been almost imperceptibly pushed to a considerable degree of perfection.

Though I would not force the introduction of manufactures, by extravagant encouragements, and to the prejudice of agriculture; yet, I conceive much might be done in that way by women, children and others; without taking one really necessary hand from tilling the earth. Certain it is, great savings are already made in many articles of apparel, furniture and consumption. Equally certain it is, that no diminution in agriculture has taken place, at the time when greater and more substantial improvements in manufactures were making, than were ever before known in America. In Pennsylvania they have attended particularly to the fabrication of cotton cloths, hats, and all articles in leather. In Massachusetts they are establishing factories of Duck, Cordage, Glass, and several other extensive and useful branches. The number of shoes made in one town and nails in another is incredible. In that State and Connecticut are also factories of superfine and other broad cloths. I have been writing to our friend Genl. Knox this day, to procure me homespun broad cloth, of the Hartford fabric, to make a suit of cloaths for myself. I hope it will not be a great while, before it will be unfashionable for a gentleman to appear in any other dress. Indeed we have already been too long subject to British prejudices. I use no porter or cheese in my family, but such as is made in America: both those articles may now be purchased of an excellent quality.

While you are quarrelling among yourselves in Europe; *American* while one King is running mad, and others acting as if they *tranquillity* were already so, by cutting the throats of the subjects of their neighbours, I think you need not doubt, my dear Marquis, we shall continue in tranquility here. And that population will be progressive so long as there shall continue to be so many easy means for obtaining a subsistence, and so ample a field for the exertion of talents and industry. All my family join in Compliments to Madame la Fayette and yours. Adieu.

162

TO BENJAMIN LINCOLN

Mount Vernon, January 31, 1789

My dear Sir:

Your two letters of December 20th and January 4th are before *Antifederalist* me. I am much obliged to you for the intelligence contained in *intrigues* them: because it enabled me to contradict a report in circulation among the Antifederalists, that your State had made choice of only one Representative to Congress, that no more would probably be appointed and that every thing was in very great confusion. Though facts will ultimately become known; yet much mischief to the federal cause may be done, by suffering misrepresentation to pass unnoticed or unrefuted. Last winter the Antifederalists in Philadelphia published, that Connecticut had been surprised into an adoption of the Constitution, while a great majority of the freemen were opposed to it. Now it is certain, nothing can fix the stigma of falsehood upon that assertion better than the late respectable appointments in that State. Much the same thing has happened in Maryland. The Federal Ticket has been carried by a Majority of thousands. In the County which bears my name, there was not a dissenting vote.

By the best information I can obtain, federal sentiments are spreading perhaps, faster than ever in this Commonwealth. It is generally supposed that six, if not seven, of the Representatives from it to Congress, will be decided friends to the Constitution. I will only add, that, in Maryland and this State, it is probable Mr. John Adams will have a considerable number of the votes of the Electors. Some of those gentlemen will have been advised that this measure would be entirely agreeable to me, and that I considered it to be the only certain way to prevent the election of an Antifederalist. With sentiments of the greatest esteem &c.

163

TO FRANCIS HOPKINSON

Mount Vernon, February 5, 1789

Dear Sir:

Hopkinson's music

We are told of the amazing powers of musick in ancient times; but the stories of its effects are so surprizing that we are not obliged to believe them unless they had been founded upon better authority than Poetic assertion; for the Poets of old (whatever they may do in these days) were strangely addicted to the Marvellous; and If I before *doubted* the truth of their relations with respect to the power of musick, I am now fully convinced of their falsity, because I would not, for the honor of my Country, allow that we are left by Ancients at an immeasurable distance in everything; and if they could sooth the ferocity of wild beasts, could draw the trees and Stones after them, and could even charm the powers of Hell by their music, I am sure that your productions would have had at least virtue enough in them (without the aid of voice or instrument) to melt the Ice of the Delaware and Potomack, and in that case you should have had an earlier acknowledgment of your favor of the 1st. of December which came to hand but last Saturday.

I readily admit the force of your distinction between "a thing *done* and a thing *to be done*," and as I do not believe that you would do "a very bad thing indeed" I must even make a virtue of necessity, and defend your performance, if necessary, to the last effort of my musical Abilities.

But, my dear Sir, if you had any doubts about the reception which your work would meet with, or had the smallest reason to think that you should need any assistance to defend it, you have not acted with your usual good Judgement in the choice which you have made of a Coadjutor; for should the tide of prejudice not flow in favor of it (and so various are the tastes, opinions and whims of men that even the sanction of divinity does not ensure universal concurrence) what, alas! can I do to support it? I can neither sing one of the songs, nor raise a single note on any instrument to convince the unbelieving, but I have, however one argument which will prevail with persons of true taste (at least in America), I can tell them that it is the production of Mr. Hopkinson.

With the compliments of Mrs. Washington added to mine for you and yours, I am, etc.

164

TO GEORGE STEPTOE WASHINGTON

Mount Vernon, March 23, 1789

Dear George:

As it is probable I shall soon be under the necessity of quitting this place, and entering once more into the bustle of public life, in conformity to the voice of my Country, and the earnest entreaties of my friends, however contrary it is to my own desires or inclinations, I think it incumbent on me as your uncle and friend, to give you some advisory hints, which, if properly attended to, will, I conceive, be found very useful to you in regulating your conduct and giving you respectability,

Advice for youth on conduct and character

not only at present, but thro' every period of life. You have now arrived to that age when you must quit the trifling amusements of a boy, and assume the more dignified manners of a man.

At this crisis your conduct will attract the notice of those who are about you, and as the first impressions are generally the most lasting, your doings now may mark the leading traits of your character through life. It is therefore absolutely necessary if you mean to make any figure upon the stage, that you should take the first steps right. What these steps are, and what general line is to be pursued to lay the foundation of an honorable and happy progress, is the part of age and experience to point out. This I shall do, as far as in my power with the utmost chearfulness; and, I trust, that your own good sense will shew you the necessity of following it. The first and great object with you at present is to acquire, by industry, and application, such knowledge as your situation enables you to obtain, as will be useful to you in life. In doing this two other important advantages will be gained besides the acquisition of knowledge: namely, a habit of industry, and a disrelish of that profusion of money and dissipation of time which are ever attendant upon idleness. I do not mean by a close application to your studies that you should never enter into those amusements which are suited to your age and station: they can be made to go hand in hand with each other, and, used in their proper seasons, will ever be found to be a mutual assistance to one another. But what amusements, and when they are to be taken, is the great matter to be attended to. Your own judgement, with the advice of your *real* friends who may have an opportunity of a personal intercourse with you, can point out the particular manner in which you may best spend your moments of relaxation, better than I can at a distance. One thing, however, I would strongly impress upon you, vizt. that when you have leisure to go into company that it should always be of the best kind that the place you are in will afford; by this means you will be constantly improving your manners and cultivating your mind while you are relaxing from your books; and good company will always be found much less expensive than bad. You cannot offer, as an excuse for not using it, that you cannot gain admission there; or that you have not a proper attention paid you in it: this is an apology made only by those whose manners are disgusting, or whose character is exceptionable; neither of which I hope will ever be said of you. I cannot enjoin too strongly upon you a due observance of oeconomy and frugality, as you well know yourself, the present state of your property and finances will not admit of any unnecessary expense. The article of clothing is now one of the chief expences, you will incur, and in this, I fear, you are not so oeconomical as you should be. Decency and cleanliness will always be the first object in the dress of a judicious and sensible man; a conformity to the prevailing fashion in a certain degree is necessary; but it does not from thence follow that a man should always get a new Coat, or other clothes, upon every trifling change in the mode, when perhaps he has two or three very good ones by him. A person who is anxious to be a leader of the fashion, or one of the first to follow it will certainly appear in the eyes of judicious men, to have nothing better than a frequent change of dress to recommend him to notice. I would always wish you to appear sufficiently decent to entitle you to admission into any company where you may be; but I cannot too strongly enjoin it upon you, and your own knowledge must convince you of the truth of it, that you should be as little expensive in this respect as you properly can. You should always keep some clothes to wear to Church, or on particular occasions, which should not be worn everyday; this can be done without any additional expence; for whenever it is necessary to get new clothes, those which have been kept for particular occasions will then come in as every-day ones, unless they should be of a superior quality to the new. What I have said with respect to clothes will apply perhaps more pointedly to Lawrence than to you; and as you are much older than he is, and more capable of judging of the propriety of what I have here observed, you must pay attention to him in this respect, and see that he does not wear his clothes improperly or extravagantly. Much more might be said to you, as a young man, upon the necessity of paying due attention to the moral virtues; but this may, perhaps, more properly be the subject of a future letter when you may be about to enter into the world. If you comply with the advice herein given to pay a diligent attention to your studies, and employ your time of relaxation in proper company, you will find but few opportunities and little inclination, while you continue at an Acadimy, to enter into those scenes of vice and dissipation which too often present themselves to youth in every place, and particularly in towns.

If you are determined to neglect your books, and plunge into extravagance and dissipation, nothing I could say now would prevent it; for you must be employed, and if it is not in pursuit of those things which are profitable, it must be in pursuit of those which are destructive. As your time of continuing with Mr. Hanson will expire the last of this month and I understand Dr. Craik has expressed an inclination to take you and Lawrence to board with him, I shall know his determination respecting the matter; and if it is agreeable to him and Mrs. Craik to take you, I shall be pleased with it, for I am certain that nothing will be wanting on their parts to make your situation agreeable and useful to you. Should you live with the Doctor I shall request him to take you both under his peculiar care; provide such clothes for you, from time to time, as he shall judge necessary, and do by you in the same manner as he would if you were his own children. Which if he will undertake, I am sensible, from knowledge which I have of him, and the very amiable character and disposition of Mrs. Craik, that they will spare no proper exertions to make your situation pleasing and profitable to you. Should you or Lawrence therefore behave in such a manner as to occasion any complaint being made to me, you may depend upon losing that place which you now have in my affections, and any future hopes you may have from me. But if, on the contrary, your conduct is such as to merit my regard, you may always depend upon the warmest attachment, and sincere affection of Your friend and Uncle.

165

TO JAMES MADISON

Mount Vernon, March 30, 1789

My dear Sir:

I have been favored with you Letter of the 19th; by which it appears that a quoram of Congress was hardly to be expected until the beginning of the *past* week. As this delay must be very irksome to the attending Members, and every days continuance of it (before the Government is in operation) will be more sensibly felt; I am resolved, no interruption shall proceed from me that can well be avoided (after notice of the Election is announced); and therefore take the liberty of requesting the favor of you to engage Lodgings for me previous to my arrival. Colo. Humphreys, I presume, will be of my party; and Mr. Lear who has already lived three years with me as a private Secretary, will accompany, or preceed me in the stage.

On the subject of lodgings I will frankly declare, I mean to go into none but hired ones. If these cannot be had tolerably convenient (I am not very nice) I would take rooms in the most decent Tavern, till a house can be provided for the more permanent reception of the President. I have already declined a very polite and pressing offer from the Governor, to lodge at his house till a place could be prepared for me; after which should any other of a similar nature be made, there would be no propriety in the acceptance. But as you are fully acquainted with sentiments on this subject, I shall only add, that as I mean to avoid private families on the one hand, so on another, I am not desirous of being placed *early* in a situation for entertaining. Therefore, hired (private) lodgings would not only be more agreeable to my own wishes, but, possibly, more consistent with the dictates of sound policy. For, as it is my wish and intention to conform to the public desire and expectation, with respect to the style proper for the Chief Magistrate to live in, it might be well to know (as far as the nature of the case will admit) what these are before he enters upon it.

After all, something may perhaps have been decided upon with respect to the accommodations of the President, before this letter wd. have reached you that may render this application nugatory. If otherwise, I will sum up all my wishes in one word, and that is to be placed in an independent situation, with the prospect I have alluded to, before me. With strong, and Affectionate friendship I am etc.

Plans for New York lodgings

˙66

TO THE MAYOR, CORPORATION, AND
CITIZENS OF ALEXANDRIA

[Alexandria, April 16, 1789]

Gentlemen:

*Election to
Presidency*

Although I ought not to conceal, yet I cannot describe, the painful emotions which I felt in being called upon to determine whether I would accept or refuse the Presidency of the United States.

The unanimity of the choice, the opinion of my friends, communicated from different parts of Europe, as well as of America, the apparent wish of those, who were not altogether satisfied with the Constitution in its present form, and an ardent desire on my own part, to be instrumental in conciliating the good will of my countrymen towards each other have induced an acceptance.

Those, who have known me best (and you, my fellow citizens, are from your situation, in that number) know better than any others that my love of retirement is so great, that no earthly consideration, short of a conviction of duty, could have prevailed upon me to depart from my resolution, *"never more to take any share in transactions of a public nature."* For, at my age, and in my circumstances, what possible advantages could I propose to myself, from embarking again on the tempestuous and uncertain ocean of public-life?

*Farewell to
Alexandria
neighbors*

I do not feel myself under the necessity of making public declarations, in order to convince you, Gentlemen, of my attachment to yourselves, and regard for your interests. The whole tenor of my life has been open to your inspection; and my past actions, rather than my present declarations, must be the pledge of my future conduct.

In the mean time I thank you most sincerely for the expressions of kindness contained in your valedictory address. It is true, just after having bade adieu to my domestic connexions, this tender proof of your friendship is but too well calculated still farther to awaken my sensibility, and encrease my regret at parting from the enjoyments of private life.

All that now remains for me is to commit myself and you to the protection of that beneficent Being, who, on a former occasion has happily brought us together, after a long and distressing separation. Perhaps the same gracious Providence will again indulge us with the same heartfelt felicity. But words, my fellow-citizens, fail me: *Unutterable sensations must then be left to more expressive silence: while, from an aching heart, I bid you all, my affectionate friends and kind neighbours, farewell!*

CHAPTER ELEVEN

THE INAUGURATION OF WASHINGTON

Presidential Addresses

1789 – 1796

*T*OO LONG and too radical, Washington's first draft of his first inaugural address was never delivered. Its pages scattered by a thoughtless scholar, it is here partially recreated." Those are the words with which Dr. Nathaniel Stein opened his publication of the most extensive collection of fragments from the "discarded inaugural" heretofore published. The "thoughtless scholar" to whom he referred was Jared Sparks, the nineteenth-century compiler of Washington's papers. Sparks took James Madison's judgment that the address would be an embarrassment to Washington not only as reason to exclude it from Washington's published works, but also to scissor it into samples of Washington's autograph for Sparks's numerous friends and acquaintances throughout the country.

Long presumed to be the work of David Humphreys, Washington's friend and secretary—in spite of existing in Washington's own handwriting—this work has been largely ignored. Even the casual reader of this collection, however, will find echos of its ideas throughout Washington's correspondence reaching back as far as six years. We can only speculate about the meaning of Washington's having apparently written to James Madison that this was Humphreys' work, but we cannot rule out the possibility that he did so from a desire to encourage the most candid response from Madison.

It is clear from the fragments we do have (and we now publish here the most extensive compilation yet and in the most coherent order) that if we had the whole of the "discarded inaugural" it would rank alongside and perhaps above Washington's *1783* "Circular Address" as a comprehensive statement of his political understanding. *Standing even in its defective form, it is a manifest contribution to our knowledge of how far Washington's* understanding *as opposed to his* image *contributed to the founding of the United States. We have corrected previous versions against the manuscripts, often resulting in material changes. To give one example: in the manuscript, the line that in previous versions has read,* "I presume not *to assert that better may not still be devised" should read* "presume now" *instead of* "presume not." *The difference in the sense is great; this is Washington's retrospective judgment on the work of the Constitutional Convention, many of whose members he had warned beforehand to aim not for the most that is acceptable, but for the best possible.*

In this version, I signal alternative readings in the text with brackets. Empty brackets signal missing text. The order in which the fragments appear here is based solely on a reading of the manuscripts and comparison of sense. I believe that the present order is the natural order. This runs counter to the hand pagination of the extant manuscript sheets. I maintain, however, that that pagination is manifestly not in Washington's hand: it could have been applied subsequently, even by Sparks, who had no particular regard for the order of the leaves. Immediately following the text, I have listed the sources for the fragments, which in their cataloguing indicate the order in which they have been arranged in other versions, particularly that of the Washington Papers Project at the University of Virginia.

On Independence Day of the inauguration year, David Humphreys delivered an oration before the State Society of the Cincinnati in

Connecticut. This Fourth of July address was a recasting of the "discarded inaugural." Many of the passages we have in Washington's hand also appear there, edited to Humphreys' third-party use. The oration cannot be employed as an exact template to establish the order of Washington's fragments, but it does serve definitively to demonstrate that the pagination entered on the fragments does not correspond to the order of Washington's address.

I have omitted any probable fragments that the Humphreys version of the address might be said to supply, even though it is clear that some of them must have derived from the original address. Humphreys in all probability obtained license to use the address once Washington had discarded it. The editing to which he subjected it, however, suggests that the original could not have reflected his work alone, thereby bolstering our confidence that the "discarded inaugural" reflects Washington's own thoughts. Humphreys' oration was published in his "Miscellaneous Works" in *1804*, now available in a reprint edition.

Inauguration. The Constitutional Convention had recommended that the Confederation Congress set the place and time to commence proceedings under the new Constitution. They set the first Wednesday in January as the date by which presidential electors had to have been chosen in the states. Electors were to meet and cast their votes on the first Wednesday in February. The sessions of the Senate and the House of Representatives would open the first Wednesday in March. New York was chosen as a provisional capital.

On April *14*, Charles Thomson, Secretary to Congress, handed Washington a letter from John Langdon, president pro tempore of the Senate, stating that Washington had been unanimously elected President of the United States. He left Mount Vernon on April *16*, *1789* and bade farewell to his friends and neighbors in Alexandria. He arrived at New York on April *23*.

The Senate and the House of Representatives completed the plans for the inauguration and ceremony on April *27*. The event followed on April *30*. Shortly after noon, on the balcony of Federal Hall in front of the Senate chamber, the oath of office was administered to Washington by Robert R. Livingston, Chancellor of the State of New York. Washington then addressed his assembled countrymen.

The Annual Addresses. Washington pursued three objects in his eight annual addresses to Congress. The first was to recount the conduct of the executive in relation to legislation that had been previously enacted. The second was to recommend deliberation upon prospective legislation. Third, and most important, Washington encouraged the cooperation of all the representatives in making provision for the general welfare. In all the addresses, of course, Washington was fulfilling the constitutional obligation to report to Congress on the "state of the union."

The first addresses focussed almost exclusively upon the responsibilities of the officers of government. As the years passed, however, and corresponding with the growth of political parties and increasing dissension, Washington devoted greater attention to addressing the general public, including the much-remarked *1794* passage in which he condemned the "self-created democratic societies" which had become implicated in the Whiskey Rebellion.

The Farewell Address. **With a presidential election and the prospect of a third term of office looming before him, Washington decided upon a definitive retirement in *1796*. He devoted considerable thought as to the appropriate manner in which to effectuate his retirement, so as to render it, too, an advantage to his countrymen. On May *10*, *1796*, he asked Alexander Hamilton to help in preparing a valedictory address. Washington sent to Hamilton a draft, parts of which had been written by James Madison, upon whose offices Washington had called four years earlier—prematurely, as it turned out. The draft contained the outline of and the objects to be considered in the address. There followed four months of correspondence until Washington's objective had been achieved. Hamilton enlisted the aid of John Jay in the project. Washington published the address on Monday, September *15*, *1796*, in** Claypoole's American Daily Advertiser.

167

FRAGMENTS OF THE DISCARDED
FIRST INAUGURAL ADDRESS

April 1789

We are this day assembled on a solemn and important occa- 1
sion.

not as a ceremony without meaning, but with a single refer- 2
ence to our dependence

upon the Parent of all good. It becomes a pleasing commence- 3
ment of my office to offer my heart-felt congratulations on the
happy

Justice, and unanimity in those States 4

fairs. It will doubtless be conceded 5

fore we entered upon the performance of our several func- 6
tions, it seemed to be our indispensable part, as rational Be-
ings,

reputation and a decent respect for the sentiments of others, 7
require that something should be said by way of apology for
my

need be bestowed in exculpating myself from any suggestions, 8
which might be made "that the incitement of pleasure or gran-
deur, or power have wrought a change in my resolution."
Small indeed must be the resources for happiness in the mind
of that man, who cannot find a refuge from the tediousness of

445

solitude but in a sound of dissipation, the pomp of state, or the homage of his fellowmen. I am not conscious of being in that predicament. But if there should be a single citizen of the United States, to whom the tenor of my life is so little known, that he could imagine me capable of being so smitten with the allurements of sensual gratification, the frivolities of ceremony or the baubles of ambition, as to be induced from such motives to accept a public appointment: I shall only lament his imperfect acquaintance with my heart, and leave him until another retirement (should Heaven spare my life for a little space) shall work a conviction of his error. In the meantime it may not, perhaps, be improper to mention one or two circumstances which will serve to obviate the jealousies that might be entertained of my having accepted this office, for a desire of enriching myself or aggrandising my posterity.

In the first place, if I have formerly served the community without a wish for pecuniary compensation, it can hardly be suspected that I am at present influenced by avaricious schemes. In the next place, it will be recollected, that the Divine Providence hath not seen fit, that my blood should be transmitted or my name perpetuated by the endearing, though sometimes seducing channel of immediate offspring. I have no child for whom I could wish to make a provision—no family to build in greatness upon my country's ruins. Let then the Adversaries to this Constitution—let my personal enemies if I am so unfortunate as to have deserved such a return from

9   from any one of my countrymen—point to the sinister object, or to the earthly consideration beyond the hope of rendering some little service to our parent country, that could have persuaded me to accept this appointment.

10   myself with the idea it was all that would ever be expected at my hand. But in this I was disappointed. The Legislature of Virginia in opposition to my express desire signified in the clearest terms to the Governor of that State, appointed me a Delegate to the federal Convention. Never was my embarrassment or hesitation more extreme or dis

11   tressing. By letters from some of the wisest and best men in almost every quarter of the Continent, I was advised, that it was my indispensable duty to attend, and that, in the deplorable condition to which our affairs were reduced, my refusal would be considered a desertion of

by my country for repelling force by force; yet it is known, I   *12*
was so far from aspiring to the chief military command, that I
accept[ed] it with unfeigned reluctance.—My fellow soldiers of
the late patriotic army will bear me testimony that when I
accepted that appointment, it was not to revel

in luxury, to grow proud of rank, to eat the bread of idleness,   *13*
to be insensible to the sufferings, or to refuse a share in the
toils and dangers to which they were exposed. I need not say
what were the complicated cares, the cruel reverses or the
unusual perplexities inseparable from my office, to

to prove that I have prematurely grown old in the Service of   *14*
my Country. For in truth, I have now arrived at that sober age,
when, aside of any extraordinary circumstances to deter me
from encountering new fatigues, and then, without having
met with any par

ticular shocks to injure the constitution the love of retirement   *15*
naturally encreases; while the objects of human pursuit, which
are most laudable in themselves and most

as in their consequences, lose much in captivating [   ].—   *16*
It is then high [time] to have learnt the vanity of this foolish
dream of life. It is then high [time] to contract the sphere of
action, to [   ] the remnant of our days peculiarly [   ],
and to compensate for the [inquietude]

tude of turbulent scenes by the tranquility of domestic repose.   *17*
After I had rendered an account of my military trust to Congress and retired to my farm, I flattered myself that this
unenviable lot was reserved for my latter years. I was delighted
with agricultural affairs and excepting a few avocations

set up my own judgment as the standard of perfection? And   *18*
shall I arrogantly pronounce that whosoever differs from me,
must discern the subject through a distorting medium, or be
influenced by some nefarious design? The mind is so formed
in different persons as to contemplate the same object in different points of view. Hence originates the difference on questions of the greatest import, both human and Divine. In all
Institutions of the former kind, great allowances are doubtless
to be made for the fallibility and imperfection of their authors.
Although the agency I had in forming this system, and the
high opinion I entertained of my Colleagues for their ability

and integrity may have tended to warp my judgment in its favour; yet I will not pretend to say that it appears absolutely perfect to me, or that there may not be many faults which have escaped my discernment. I will only say, that, during and since the session of the Convention, I have attentively heard and read every oral and printed information on both sides of the question that could be procured. This long and laborious investigation, in which I endeavoured as far as the frailty of nature would permit to act with candour has resulted in a fixed belief that this Constitution, is really in its formation a government of the people; that is to say, a government in which all power is derived from, and at stated periods reverts to them—and that, in its operation, it is purely, a government of Laws made and executed by the fair substitutes of the people alone. The election of the different branches of Congress by the Freemen, either directly or indirectly is the pivot on which turns the first wheel of the government—a wheel which communicates motion to all the rest. At the same time the exercise of this right of election seems to be so regulated as to afford less opportunity for corruption and influence; and more for stability and system than[t] has usually been incident to popular governments. Nor can the members of Congress exempt themselves from consequences of any unjust and tyrannical acts which they may impose upon others. For in a short time they will mingle with the mass of the people. Their interests must therefore be the same, and their feelings in sympathy with those of their Constituents. Besides, their re-election must always depend upon the good reputation which they shall have maintained in the judgment of their fellow citizens. Hence I have been induced to conclude that this government must be less obnoxious to well-founded objections than most which have existed in the world. And in that opinion I am confirmed on three accounts;—*first*—because every government ought to be possessed of powers adequate to the purposes for which it was instituted:—Secondly, because no other or greater powers appear to me to be delegated to this government than are essential to accomplish the objects for which it was instituted, to wit, the safety and happiness of the governed:—and thirdly because it is clear to my conception that no government before introduced among mankind ever contained so many checks and such efficacious restraints to prevent it from degenerating into any species of oppression. It is unnecessary to be insisted upon, because it is well known, that the impotence of Congress under the former Confederation, and the inexpediency of trusting more ample prerogatives to a simple Body, gave birth to the different branches which constitute the present government. Convinced as I am that the balances arising from the distribution of the Legislative, Executive and Judicial powers, are the best that have been instituted; I presume now[t] to assert, that better may not still be devised. On the article of proposed amendments I shall say a few words in another place. But if it was a point acknowledged on all parts that the late federal government could not have existed much longer; if without some speedy remedy a dissolution of the Union must have ensued, if without adhering to the Union we

But the result, after very many trials, was infinitely distant *19*
from what we had been led to expect. As the process was strictly in conformity to the presented rules, I knew not to what cause the failure of success should be attributed.

to any favoured nation. We have purchased wisdom by experi- *20*
ence. Mankind are believed to be naturally averse to the coercion of government. But when our countrymen had experienced the inconveniences, arising from the feebleness of our

affairs were seen[k] to decline. I will ask your patience for a *21*
moment, while I speak on so unpleasant a subject as the rotten part of our old Constitution. It is not a matter for wonder that the first projected plan of a federal government, formed on the defective models of some foreign confederacies, in the midst of a war, before we had much experience; and while, from the concurrence of external danger and

At the beginning of the late War with Great Britain, when we *22*
thought ourselves justifiable in resisting to blood, it was known to those best acquainted with the different condition of the combatants & the probable cost of the prize in dispute, that the expense in comparison with our circumstances as Colonists must be enormous—the struggle protracted, dubious & severe. It was known that the resources of Britain were, in a manner, inexhaustible, that her fleets covered the Ocean, and that her troops had harvested laurels in every quarter of the globe. Not then organised as a Nation, or known as a people upon the earth—we had no preparation. Money, the nerve of

War, was wanting. The Sword was to be forged on the Anvil of necessity: the treasury to be created from nothing. If we had a secret resource of a nature unknown to our enemy, it was in the unconquerable resolution of our Citizens, the conscious rectitude of our cause, and a confident trust that we should not be forsaken by Heaven. The people willingly offered themselves to the battle; but the means of arming, clothing & subsisting them; as well as of procuring the implements of hostility were only to be found in anticipations of our future wealth. Paper bills of credit were emitted: monies borrowed for the most pressing emergencies: and our brave troops in the field unpaid for their services. In this manner, Peace, attended with every circumstance that could gratify our reasonable desires, or even inflate us with ideas of national importance, was at length obtained. But a load of debt was left upon us. The fluctuations of and speculations in our paper currency, had, but in too many instances, occasioned vague ideas of property, generated licentious appetites & corrupted the morals of men. To these immediate consequences of a fluctuating medium of commerce, may be joined a tide of circumstances that flowed together from sources mostly opened during and after the war. The ravage of farms, the conflagration of towns, the diminution

23   But Congress, constituted in most respects as a diplomatic body, possessed no power of carrying into execution a simple Ordinance, however strongly dictated by prudence, policy or justice. The individual States, knowing there existed no power of coercion, treated with neglect, whenever it suited their convenience or caprice, the most salutary measures of the most indispensable requisitions [acquisitions] of Congress. Experience taught

24   We are now[t] to take upon ourselves the conduct of that government. But be

25   of this government, it may be proper to give assurances of our friendly dispositions to other Powers. We may more at our leisure, meditate on such Treaties of Amity and Commerce, as shall be judged expedient to be propounded to or received from any of them.

In all our appointments of persons to fill domestic and foreign offices, let us be careful to select only such as are distin-

guished for morals and abilities. Some attention should likewise be paid, when

ever the circumstances will conveniently admit, to the distribu-   26
tion of Offices among persons, belonging to the different
parts of the Union. But my knowledge of the characters of
persons, through an extent of fifteen hundred miles, must be
so imperfect as to make me liable to fall into mistakes: which,
in fact, can only be avoided by the disinterested aid of my
coadjutors. I forbear to enlarge on the delicacy there certainly
will be, in discharging this part of our trust with fidelity, and
without giving occasion for uneasiness. It

It appears to me, that it would be a favorable circumstance, if   27
the characters of Candidates could be known, without their
having a pretext for coming forward themselves with personal
applications. We should seek to find the Men who are best
qualified to fill offices: but never give our consent to the creation of Offices to accommodate men.

It belongs to you especially to take measures for promoting   28
the general welfare. It belongs to you to make men honest in
their dealings with each other, by regulating the coinage and
currency of money upon equitable principles as well as by
establishing just weights and measures upon an uniform plan.
Whenever an opportunity shall be furnished to you as public
or as private men, I trust you will not fail to use your best
endeavours to improve the education and manners of a people; to accelerate the progress of arts and Sciences; to patronize works of genius; to confer rewards for inventions of utility;
and to cherish institutions favourable to humanity. Such are
among the best of all human employments. Such exertions of
your talents will render your situations truly dignified and
cannot fail of being acceptable in the sight of the Divinity.

By a series of disinterested services it will be in our power to
show, that we have nothing

Certain propositions for taking measures to obtain explana-   29
tions and amendments on some articles of the Constitution,
with the obvious intention of quieting the minds of the good
people of these United States, will come before you and claim
a dispassionate consideration. Whatever may not be deemed
incompatible with the fundamental principles of a free and

efficient government ought to be done for the accomplishment of so desirable an object.

The reasonings which have been used, to

30 prove that amendments could never take place after this Constitution should be adopted, I must avow, have not appeared conclusive to me. I could not understand, by any mathematical analogy, why the whole number of States in the Union should be more likely to concur in any proposed amendment, than three fourths of that number: before the adoption, the concurrence of the former was necessary for effecting this measure—since the adoption, only the latter. Here I will not presume to dictate as to the time, when it may be most expedient to attempt to remove all the redundancies or supply all the defects, which shall be discovered in this complicated machine. I will barely suggest, whether it would not be the part of prudent men to observe it fully in movement, before they undertook to make such alterations, as might prevent a fair experiment of its effects? And whether, in the meantime, it may not be practicable for this Congress (if their proceedings shall meet with the approbation of three fourths of the Legislatures) in such manner to secure to the people all their justly esteemed privileges as shall produce extensive satisfaction?

The complete organization of the Judicial Department was left by the Constitution to the ulterior arrangement of Congress. You will be pleased therefore to let a supreme regard for equal justice and the inherent rights of the citizens be visible in all your proceedings on that important subject.

I have a confident reliance that your wisdom and patriotism will be exerted to raise the supplies for discharging the interest on the national debt and for supporting the government during the current year, in a manner as little burdensome to the people as possible. The necessary estimates will be laid before you. A general, moderate Impost upon imports; together with a higher tax upon certain enumerated articles, will, undoubtedly, occur to you in the course

31 It might naturally be supposed that I should not silently pass by the subject of our defense. After excepting the unprovoked hostility committed against us by one of the Powers of Barbary, we are now at peace with all the nations of the globe. Separated as we are from them, by intervening Oceans, an exemption from the burden of maintaining numerous fleets and

Armies must ever be considered as a singular felicity in our National lot. It will be in our choice to train our youths to such industrious and hardy professions as that they may grow into an unconquerable force, without our being obliged to draw unprofitable Drones from the hive of Industry. As our people have a natural genius for Naval affairs and as our materials for navigation are ample; if we give due encouragement to the fisheries and the carrying trade, we shall possess such a nursery of Seamen and such skill in maritime operations as to enable us to create a navy almost in a moment. But it will be wise to anticipate events and to lay a foundation in time. Whenever the circumstances will permit, a grand provision of war like stores, arsenals and dock-yards ought to be made.

As to any invasion that might be meditated by foreigners against us on the land, I will only say, that, if the Mighty Nation with which we lately contended could not bring us under the yoke, no nation on the face of the earth can ever effect it; while we shall remain United and faithful to ourselves. A well organised Militia would constitute a strong defence [degree]; of course, your most serious attention will be turned to such an establishment. In your recess, it will give me pleasure, by making such reviews, as opportunities may allow, to attempt to revive the ancient military spirit. During the present impoverished state of our Finances I would not wish to see any expense incurred by augmenting our regular

on the one hand and an unalterable habit of error on the other, are points in policy equally desirable; though, I believe, a power to effect them never before existed. Whether the Constitutional door that is opened for amendments in ours, be not the wisest and apparently the happiest expedient that has ever been suggested by human prudence I leave to every unprejudiced mind to determine.   *32*

Under these circumstances I conclude it has been the part of wisdom to ad[vise] it. I pretend to no unusual foresight into futurity, and therefore cannot undertake to decide, with certainty, what may be its ultimate fate. If a promised good should terminate in an unexpected evil, it would not be a solitary example of disappointment in this mutable state of existence. If the blessings of Heaven showered thick around us should be spilled on the ground or converted to curses, through the fault of those for whom they were intended, it would not be the first instance of folly or perverseness in short-sighted mortals. The blessed Religion revealed in the word of God will remain an eternal and awful monument to prove that the best Institutions may be abused by human depravity; and that they may even, in some instances be made subservient to the vilest purposes. Should, hereafter, those who are entrusted with the management of this government, incited by the lust of power and prompted by the Supineness or venality of their Constituents, overleap the known barriers of this Constitution and violate the unalienable rights of humanity: it will only serve to shew, that no compact among men (however provident in its construction and sacred in its ratification) can be pronounced everlasting and inviolable, and if I may so express myself, that no Wall of words, that no mound of parchm[en]t can be so formed as to stand against the sweeping torrent of boundless ambition on the one side, aided by the sapping current of corrupted morals on the other. But

33   been happily diffused or fostered among them

34   of the soil and the Sea, for the wares and merchandize of other Nations is open to all. Notwithstanding the embarrassments under which our trade has hitherto laboured, since the peace, the enterprising spirit of our citizens has steered our vessels to almost every region of the known world. In some distant and heretofore unfrequented countries, our new Constellation has been received with tokens of uncommon regard. An energetic government will give to our flag still greater respect: While a sense of reciprocal benefits will serve to connect us with the rest of mankind in stricter ties of amity. But an external commerce is more in our power; and may be of more importance. The surplus of produce in one part of the United States, will, in many instances, be wanted in another. An intercourse of this kind is well calculated to multiply Sailors, exterminate prejudices, diffuse blessings, and increase the friendship of the inhabitants of one State for those of another. While the [the] individual States shall be occupied in facilitating the means of transportation, by opening canals and improving roads, you will not forget that the purposes of business and Society may be vastly promoted by giving cheapness, dispatch and security to communications through the regular Posts. I need not say how satisfactory it would be, to gratify the useful curiosity of our citizens by the conveyance of News Papers and periodical Publications in the public vehicles without expense.

Notwithstanding the rapid growth of our population, from the facility of obtaining subsistence, as well as from the accession of strangers, yet we shall not soon become a manufacturing people. Because men are ever better pleased with labouring on their farms, than in their workshops. Even the mechanics who come from Europe, as soon as they can procure a little land of their own, commonly turn Cultivators. Hence it will be found more beneficial, I believe, to continue to exchange our Staple commodities for the finer manufactures we may want, than to undertake to make them ourselves. Many articles however, in wool, flax, cotton, and hemp; and all in leather, iron, fur and wood may be fabricated at home with great advantage. If the quantity of wool, flax, cotton and hemp should be increased to ten-fold its present amount (as it easily could be) I apprehend the whole might in a short time be manufactured. Especially by the introduction of machines for multiplying the effects of labor, in diminishing the number of hands employed upon it. But it will rest with you to investigate what proficiency we are capable of making in manufactures, and what encouragement should be given to particular branches of them. In almost every house, much Spinning might be done by hands which otherwise would be in a manner idle.

It remains for you to make, out of a Country poor in the precious metals and comparatively thin of inhabitants a flourishing State. But here it is particularly incumbent on me to express my idea of a flourishing state with precision; and to distinguish between happiness and splendour. The people of this Country may doubtless enjoy all the great blessings of the social State: and yet United America may not for a long time to come make a brilliant figure as a nation, among the nations of the earth. Should this be the case, and should the people be actuated by principles of true magnanimity, they will not suffer their ambition to be awakened. They should guard against ambition as against their greatest enemy. We should not, in imitation of some nations which have been celebrated for a false kind of patriotism, wish to aggrandize our own Republic at the expense of the freedom and happiness of the rest of mankind. The prospect that the Americans will not act upon so narrow a scale affords the most comfortable reflections to [in] a benevolent mind. As their remoteness from other nations in a manner precludes them from foreign quarrels: so their extent of territory and gradual settlement, will enable them to maintain something like a war of posts, against the invasion of luxury, dissipation, and corruption. For after the larger cities and old establishments on the borders of the Atlantic, shall, in the progress of time, have fallen a prey to those Invaders; the Western States will probably long retain their primaeval simplicity of manners and incorruptible love of liberty. May we not reasonably expect, that, by those manners and this patriotism, uncommon prosperity will be entailed on the civil institutions of the American world? And may you not console yourselves for any irksome circumstances which shall occur in the performance of your task, with the pleasing consideration, that you are now employed in laying the foundation of that durable prosperity?

35   when they shall witness the return of more prosperous times. I feel the consolatory joys of futurity in contemplating the immense deserts, yet untrodden by the foot of man, soon to become fair as the garden of God, soon to be animated by the activity of multitudes & soon to be made vocal with the praises of the *Most High*. Can it be imagined that so many peculiar advantages, of soil & of climate, for agriculture & for navigation were lavished in vain—or that this Continent was not created and reserved so long undiscovered as a Theatre, for those glorious displays of Divine Munificence, the salutary consequences of which shall flow to another Hemisphere & extend through the interminable series of ages? Should not our Souls exult in the prospect? Though I shall not survive to perceive with these bodily senses, but a small portion of the blessed effects which our Revolution will occasion in the rest of the world; yet I enjoy the progress of human society & human happiness in anticipation. I rejoice in a belief that intellectual light will spring up in the dark corners of the earth; that freedom of enquiry will produce liberality of conduct; that mankind will reverse the absurd position that *the many* were, made for *the few*; and that they will not continue slaves in one part of the globe, when they can become freemen in another.

Thus I have explained the general impressions under which I have acted: omitting to mention until the last, a principal reason which induced my acceptance. After a consciousness that all is right within and an humble hope of approbation in Heaven—nothing can, assuredly, be so grateful to a virtuous

456

man as the good opinion of his fellow citizens Tho' the partiality of mine led them to consider my holding the Chief Magistracy as a matter of infinitely more consequence than it really is; yet my acceptance must be ascribed rather to an honest willingness to satisfy that partiality, than to an overweening presumption upon my own capacity. Whenever a government is to be instituted or changed by Consent of the people, confidence in the person placed at the head of it, is, perhaps, more peculiarly necessary

rest, neither life or reputation has been accounted dear in my *36* sight. And, from the bottom of my Soul, I know, that my motives on no [on] former occasion were more innocent than in the present instance. At my time of life and in my situation I will not suppose that many moments need

situation could be so agreeable to me as the condition of a *37* private citizen. I solemnly assert and appeal to the searcher of hearts to witness the truth of it, that my leaving home to take upon myself the execution of this Office was the greatest personal sa

crifice I have ever, in the course of my existence, been called *38* upon to make. Altho' when the last war had become inevitable, I heartily concurred in the measures to

I have now again given way to my feelings, in speaking with- *39* out reserve, according to my best judgment, the words of soberness and affection. If anything in disrespect or foreign to the occasion has been spoken, your candour, I am convinced will not impute it to an unworthy motive. I come now to a conclusion by addressing my humble petition to the

which will conduce to their temporal & eternal peace—I most *40* earnestly supplicate that Almighty God, to whose holy keeping I commend my dearest country, will never suffer so fair an inheritance to become a prey to [Anar-]

to all the protection & emoluments of the general govern- *41* ment—I wish that every unkind distinction may be entirely done away; and that the word, once used to signify opposition to a federal government, may be consigned to eternal oblivion.—But let antirepublican

While others in their political conduct shall demean them- *42* selves as [or] may seem [   ] to them, let us be honest. Let us

457

be firm. Let us advance directly forward in the path of our duty. Should the path at first prove intricate and thorny, it will grow plain and smooth as we go. In public as in private life, let the eternal line that separates right from wrong, be the fence to

SOURCES OF THE FRAGMENTS

The order in which the fragments were presented by the Washington Papers Project at the University of Virginia is designated by the number following "Univ. of Va." in the notes below. In a number of cases, a fragment consists of a numbered page, or several such pages, in the manuscript original, and this information is also here presented when it exists. Sources other than the University of Virginia are cited; note however that copies are in the Virginia collection, as indicated. Note also that two fragments are merely *probable* portions of the discarded address.

For the Nathaniel Stein version of the address, the reader is directed to the publication in *Manuscripts* 10(2), Spring 1958.

1. Univ. of Va. 1
2. Univ. of Va. 13
3. Univ. of Va. 2
4. Univ. of Va. 31
5. Univ. of Va. 30
6. Univ. of Va. 3
7. Univ. of Va. 5
8. Univ. of Va. 6
9. Univ. of Va. 7, from p. 21 of the original
10. Univ. of Va. 19
11. Univ. of Va. 20

12. A probable fragment of the address in the Univ. of Va. collection, numbered 36 but not definitively collated; also No. 86669 in the de Coppert Collection, Princeton Univ.

13. No. 89695, *The Collector* magazine; copy in the Univ. of Va. collection

14. Univ. of Va. 24
15. Univ. of Va. 15

16. A probable fragment in the Univ. of Va. collection, numbered 37 but not definitively collated; also cf. xyz: 84670

17. Ibid.

18. Univ. of Va. 10, from p. 27 of the original; p. 28 beginning at "oral and printed information"; p. 29 beginning at "any unjust and

tyrannical acts"; p. 30 beginning at "before introduced among mankind"

19. Univ. of Va. 12

20. Univ. of Va. 8, from p. 22 of the original

21. Univ. of Va. 32

22. Univ. of Va. 4, from p. 5 of the original; p. 6 beginning at "offered themselves"

23. Univ. of Va. 33

24. Univ. of Va. 14

25. Univ. of Va. 35

26. Univ. of Va. 16, from p. 45 of the original

27. Univ. of Va. 34

28. Univ. of Va. 34, from p. 62 of the original

29. Univ. of Va. 17, from p. 46 of the original

30. Univ. of Va. 18, from p. 47 of the original; p. 48 beginning at "justly esteemed privileges"

31. Univ. of Va. 26

32. Univ. of Va. 11, from p. 33 of the original; p. 34 beginning at "or perverseness"

33. Univ. of Va. 29

34. Univ. of Va. 25, from p. 57 of the original; p. 58 beginning at "While the [the] individual states"; p. 59 beginning at "our Staple commodities"; p. 60 beginning at "It remains for you"; p. 61 beginning at "reflections to [in] a benevolent"

35. Univ. of Va. 9, from p. 23 of the original; p. 24 beginning at "I rejoice in a belief"

36. Univ. of Va. 21

37. Univ. of Va. 22

38. Univ. of Va. 23

39. Univ. of Va. 27

40. Duke Univ. collection; copy in the Univ. of Va. collection

41. No. 77926, Strafford Historical Society collection; copy in the Univ. of Va. collection

42. Univ. of Va. 28

168

THE FIRST INAUGURAL SPEECH

New York, Thursday, April 30, 1789

Fellow-citizens of the Senate
and of the House of Representatives:

Among the vicissitudes incident to life, no event could have filled me with greater anxieties than that of which the notification was transmitted by your order, and received on the fourteenth day of the present month. On the one hand, I was summoned by my country, whose voice I can never hear but with veneration and love, from a retreat which I had chosen with the fondest predilection, and, in my flattering hopes, with an immutable decision, as the asylum of my declining years—a retreat which was rendered every day more necessary as well as more dear to me, by the addition of habit to inclination, and of frequent interruptions in my health to the gradual waste committed on it by time. On the other hand, the magnitude and difficulty of the trust to which the voice of my country called me, being sufficient to awaken in the wisest and most experienced of her citizens a distrustful scrutiny into his qualifications, could not but overwhelm with despondence, one, who, inheriting inferior endowments from nature, and unpractised in the duties of civil administration, ought to be peculiarly conscious of his own deficiencies. In this conflict of emotions, all I dare aver, is, that it has been my faithful study to collect my duty from a just appreciation of every circumstance by which it might be affected. All I dare hope, is, that if, in executing this task, I have been too much swayed by a grateful remembrance of former instances, or by an affectionate sensibility to this transcendent proof of the confidence of my fellow citizens, and have thence too little consulted my incapacity as well as disinclination, for the weighty and untried cares before me; my *error* will be palliated by the motives which misled me, and its consequences be judged by my country with some share of the partiality in which they originated.

Such being the impressions under which I have, in obedience to the public summons, repaired to the present station, it would be peculiarly improper to omit, in this first official act, my fervent supplications to that Almighty Being who rules over the universe; who presides in the councils of nations; and whose providential aid can supply every human defect; that his benediction may consecrate to the liberties and happiness of the People of the United States, a Government instituted by themselves for these essential purposes, and may enable every instrument employed in its administration, to execute with success the functions allotted to his charge. In tendering this homage to the Great Author of every public and private good, I assure myself that it expresses your sentiments not less than my own; nor those of my fellow citizens at large less than either. No people can be bound to acknowledge and adore the invisible hand which conducts the affairs of men, more than the people of the United States. Every step by which they have advanced to the character of an independent nation seems to have been distinguished by some token of providential agency. And in the important revolution just accomplished in the system of their united government, the tranquil deliberations and voluntary consent of so many distinct communities, from which the event has resulted, cannot be compared with the means by which most governments have been established, without some return of pious gratitude, along with an humble anticipation of the future blessings which the past seem to presage. These reflections, arising out of the present crisis, have forced themselves too strongly on my mind to be suppressed. You will join with me, I trust, in thinking that there are none under the influence of which the proceedings of a new and free government can more auspiciously commence.

By the article establishing the Executive Department, it is made the duty of the President "to recommend to your consideration such measures as he shall judge necessary and expedient." The circumstances under which I now meet you will acquit me from entering into that subject, further than to refer to the great constitutional charter under which you are assembled, and which, in defining your powers, designates the objects to which your attention is to be given. It will be more consistent with those circumstances, and far more congenial with the feelings which actuate me, to substitute, in place of a recommendation of particular measures, the tribute that is due to the talents, the rectitude, and the patriotism, which adorn the characters selected to devise and adopt them. In these honorable qualifications, I behold the surest pledges that, as on one side no local prejudices or attachments—no

461

separate views, nor party animosities, will misdirect the comprehensive and equal eye which ought to watch over this great assemblage of communities and interests; so on another, that the foundations of our national policy will be laid in the pure and immutable principles of private morality, and the preeminence of free government be exemplified by all the attributes which can win the affections of its citizens, and command the respect of the world. I dwell on this prospect with every satisfaction which an ardent love for my country can inspire: since there is no truth more thoroughly established, than that there exists in the economy and course of nature, an indissoluble union between virtue and happiness; between duty and advantage; between the genuine maxims of an honest and magnanimous policy, and the solid rewards of public prosperity and felicity: since we ought to be no less persuaded that the propitious smiles of Heaven can never be expected on a nation that disregards the external rules of order and right, which Heaven itself has ordained: and since the preservation of the sacred fire of liberty, and the destiny of the republican model of government, are justly considered as *deeply*, perhaps as *finally*, staked on the experiment entrusted to the hands of the American People.

Besides the ordinary objects submitted to your care, it will remain with your judgment to decide how far an exercise of the occasional power, delegated by the fifth article of the constitution, is rendered expedient at the present juncture, by the nature of objections which have been urged against the system, or by the degree of inquietude which has given birth to them. Instead of undertaking particular recommendations on this subject, in which I could be guided by no lights derived from official opportunities, I shall again give way to my entire confidence in your discernment and pursuit of the public good: for I assure myself, that, whilst you carefully avoid every alteration which might endanger the benefits of an united and effective government, or which ought to await the future lessons of experience, a reverence for the characteristic rights of freemen, and a regard for the public harmony, will sufficiently influence your deliberations on the question, how far the former can be more impregnably fortified, or the latter be safely and advantageously promoted.

To the preceding observations I have one to add, which will be most properly addressed to the House of Representatives.

It concerns myself, and will therefore be as brief as possible. When I was first honored with a call into the service of my country, then on the eve of an arduous struggle for its liberties, the light in which I contemplated my duty, required that I should renounce every pecuniary compensation. From this resolution I have in no instance departed. And being still under the impressions which produced it, I must decline, as inapplicable to myself, any share in the personal emoluments which may be indispensably included in a permanent provision for the Executive Department; and must accordingly pray, that the pecuniary estimates for the station in which I am placed, may, during my continuance in it, be limited to such actual expenditures as the public good may be thought to require.

Having thus imparted to you my sentiments, as they have been awakened by the occasion which brings us together, I shall take my present leave; but not without resorting once more to the benign Parent of the human race, in humble supplication, that, since he has been pleased to favor the American People with opportunities for deliberating in perfect tranquillity, and dispositions for deciding with unparalleled unanimity on a form of government for the security of their union, and the advancement of their happiness, so his divine blessing may be equally *conspicuous* in the enlarged views, the temperate consultations, and the wise measures, on which the success of this Government must depend.

GEO. WASHINGTON.

On Monday, May 18, 1789, the Senate waited on the President of the United States, and the Vice President, in their name, delivered to him the following.

Sir:

We, the Senate of the United States, return you our sincere thanks for your excellent speech delivered to both Houses of Congress; congratulate you on the complete organization of the Federal Government; and felicitate ourselves and our fellow-citizens on your elevation to the office of President—an office highly important by the powers constitutionally annexed to it, and extremely honorable from the manner in which the appointment is made. The unanimous suffrage of the elective body in your favor, is peculiarly expressive of the gratitude, confidence, and affection, of the citizens of

America, and is the highest testimonial, at once of your merit and their esteem. We are sensible, sir, that nothing but the voice of your fellow-citizens could have called you from a retreat, chosen with the fondest predilection, endeared by habit, and consecrated to the repose of declining years. We rejoice, and with us all America, that, in obedience to the call of our common country, you have returned once more to public life. In you all parties confide; in you all interests unite; and we have no doubt that your past services, great as they have been, will be equalled by your future exertions; and that your prudence and sagacity as a statesman will tend to avert the dangers to which we were exposed, to give stability to the present government, and dignity and splendor to that country which your skill and valor, as a soldier, so eminently contributed to raise to independence and empire.

When we contemplate the coincidence of circumstances, and wonderful combination of causes, which gradually prepared the People of this country for independence: when we contemplate the rise, progress, and termination of the late war, which gave them a name among the nations of the earth; we are, with you, unavoidably led to acknowledge and adore the Great Arbiter of the universe, by whom empires rise and fall. A review of the many signal instances of divine interposition in favor of this country, claims our most pious gratitude; and permit us, sir, to observe, that, among the great events which have led to the formation and establishment of a Federal Government, we esteem your acceptance of the office of President as one of the most propitious and important.

In the execution of the trust reposed in us, we shall endeavor to pursue that enlarged and liberal policy to which your speech so happily directs. We are conscious that the prosperity of each State is inseparably connected with the welfare of all; and that, in promoting the latter, we shall effectually advance the former. In full persuasion of this truth, it shall be our invariable aim to divest ourselves of local prejudices and attachments, and to view the great assemblage of communities and interests committed to our charge with an equal eye. We feel, sir, the force, and acknowledge the justness of the observation, that the foundation of our national policy should be laid in private morality. If individuals be not influenced by moral principles, it is in vain to look for public virtue; it is, therefore, the duty of legislators to enforce, both by precept and example, the utility, as well as the necessity, of a strict adherence to the rules of distributive justice. We beg you to be assured that the Senate will, at all times, cheerfully co-operate in every measure which may strengthen the Union, conduce to the happiness, or secure and perpetuate the liberties of this great confederated republic.

We commend you, sir, to the protection of Almighty God, earnestly beseeching him long to preserve a life so valuable and dear to the People of the United States, and that your administration may be prosperous to the nation and glorious to yourself.

To which the President of the United States replied as follows:

Gentlemen:

I thank you for your address, in which the most affectionate sentiments are expressed in the most obliging terms. The coincidence of circumstances which led to this auspicious crisis; the confidence reposed in me by my fellow-citizens; and the assistance I may expect from counsels which will be dictated by an enlarged and liberal policy; seem to presage a more prosperous issue to my administration than a diffidence of my abilities had taught me to anticipate. I now feel myself inexpressibly happy in a belief that Heaven, which has done so much for our infant nation, will not withdraw its providential influence before our political felicity shall have been completed, and in a conviction that the Senate will at all times co-operate in every measure which may tend to promote the welfare of this confederated republic. Thus supported by a firm trust in the Great Arbiter of the universe, aided by the collected wisdom of the Union, and imploring the divine benediction on our joint exertions in the service of our country, I readily engage with you in the arduous but pleasing task of attempting to make a nation happy.

GEO. WASHINGTON.

On Friday, May 8, 1789, the Speaker, attended by the members of the House of Representatives, waited on the President of the United States, and presented to him the following.

Sir:

The Representatives of the People of the United States present their congratulations on the event by which your fellow-citizens have attested the pre-eminence of your merit. You have long held the first place in their esteem. You have often received tokens of their affection. You now possess the only proof that remained of their gratitude for your services, of their reverence for your wisdom, and of their confidence in your virtues. You enjoy the highest, because the truest honor of being the first Magistrate, by the unanimous choice of the freest people on the face of the earth.

We well know the anxieties with which you must have obeyed a summons from the repose reserved for your declining years, into public scenes, of which you had taken your leave for ever. But the obedience was due to the occasion. It is already applauded by the universal joy which welcomes you to your station. And we cannot doubt that it will be rewarded with all the satisfaction with which an ardent love for your fellow-citizens must review successful efforts to promote their happiness.

This anticipation is not justified merely by the past experience of your signal services: it is particularly suggested by the pious impressions under which you commence your administration, and the enlightened maxims by which you mean to conduct it. We feel with you the strongest obligations to adore the invisible hand which has led the American People through so many difficulties, to cherish a conscious responsibility for the destiny of republican liberty; and to seek the only sure means of preserving and recommending the precious deposite in a system of legislation founded on the principles of an honest policy, and directed by the spirit of a diffusive patriotism.

The question arising out of the fifth article of the constitution will receive all the attention demanded by its importance; and will, we trust, be decided under the influence of all the considerations to which you allude.

In forming the pecuniary provisions for the Executive department, we shall not lose sight of a wish resulting from motives which give it a peculiar claim to our regard. Your resolution, in a moment critical to the liberties of your country, to renounce all personal emolument, was among the many presages of your patriotic services, which have been amply fulfilled; and your scrupulous adherence now to the law then imposed on yourself, cannot fail to demonstrate the purity, whilst it increases the lustre, of a character which has so many titles to admiration.

Such are the sentiments which we have thought fit to address to you. They flow from our own hearts, and we verily believe, that, among the millions we represent, there is not a virtuous citizen whose heart will disown them.

All that remains is, that we join in our fervent supplications for the blessings of Heaven on our country, and that we add our own for the choicest of these blessings on the most beloved of her citizens.

To which the President of the United States made the following reply:

Gentlemen:

Your very affectionate address produces emotions which I know not how to express. I feel that my past endeavors in the service of my country are far overpaid by its goodness; and I fear much that my future ones may not fulfil your kind anticipation. All that I can promise, is, that they will be invariably directed by an honest and an ardent zeal; of this resource my heart assures me; for all beyond, I rely on the wisdom and patriotism of those with whom I am to co-operate, and a continuance of the blessings of Heaven on our beloved country.

169

FIRST ANNUAL MESSAGE

Friday, January 8, 1790

*Fellow-citizens of the Senate
and House of Representatives:*

I embrace, with great satisfaction, the opportunity which now presents itself of congratulating you on the present favorable prospects of our public affairs. The recent accession of the important State of North Carolina to the constitution of the United States (of which official information has been received), the rising credit and respectability of our country; the general and increasing good will towards the government of the Union; and the concord, peace, and plenty, with which we are blessed, are circumstances auspicious in an eminent degree to our national prosperity.

In resuming your consultations for the general good, you

cannot but derive encouragement from the reflection, that the measures of the last session have been as satisfactory to your constituents, as the novelty and difficulty of the work allowed you to hope. Still further to realize their expectations, and to secure the blessings which a gracious Providence has placed within our reach, will, in the course of the present important session, call for the cool and deliberate exertion of your patriotism, firmness, and wisdom.

Among the many interesting objects which will engage your attention, that of providing for the common defence will merit particular regard. To be prepared for war, is one of the most effectual means of preserving peace.

A free people ought not only to be armed, but disciplined; to which end, a uniform and well digested plan is requisite: and their safety and interest require that they should promote such manufactories as tend to render them independent on others for essential, particularly for military supplies.

The proper establishment of the troops which may be deemed indispensable, will be entitled to mature consideration. In the arrangements which may be made respecting it, it will be of importance to conciliate the comfortable support of the officers and soldiers, with a due regard to economy.

There was reason to hope that the pacific measures adopted with regard to certain hostile tribes of Indians, would have relieved the inhabitants of our southern and western frontiers from their depredations; but you will perceive, from the information contained in the papers which I shall direct to be laid before you, (comprehending a communication from the Commonwealth of Virginia) that we ought to be prepared to afford protection to those parts of the Union, and, if necessary, to punish aggressors.

The interests of the United States require, that our intercourse with other nations should be facilitated by such provisions as will enable me to fulfil my duty in that respect, in the manner which circumstances may render most conducive to the public good; and to this end, that the compensations to be made to the persons who may be employed, should, according to the nature of their appointments, be defined by law; and a competent fund designated for defraying the expenses incident to the conduct of our foreign affairs.

Various considerations also render it expedient that the terms on which foreigners may be admitted to the rights of citizens, should be speedily ascertained by a uniform rule of naturalization.

Uniformity in the currency, weights, and measures, of the United States, is an object of great importance, and will, I am persuaded, be duly attended to.

The advancement of agriculture, commerce, and manufactures, by all proper means, will not, I trust, need recommendation; but I cannot forbear intimating to you the expediency of giving effectual encouragement, as well to the introduction of new and useful inventions from abroad, as to the exertions of skill and genius in producing them at home; and of facilitating the intercourse between the distant parts of our country by a due attention to the post office and post roads.

Nor am I less persuaded, that you will agree with me in opinion, that there is nothing which can better deserve your patronage, than the promotion of science and literature. Knowledge is, in every country, the surest basis of public happiness. In one in which the measures of government receive their impression so immediately from the sense of the community as in ours, it is proportionably essential. To the security of a free constitution it contributes in various ways: by convincing those who are entrusted with the public administration, that every valuable end of government is best answered by the enlightened confidence of the people; and by teaching the people themselves to know and to value their own rights; to discern and provide against invasions of them; to distinguish between oppression and the necessary exercise of lawful authority; between burthens proceeding from a disregard to their convenience, and those resulting from the inevitable exigences of society; to discriminate the spirit of liberty from that of licentiousness—cherishing the first, avoiding the last; and uniting a speedy but temperate vigilance against encroachments, with an inviolable respect to the laws.

Whether this desirable object will be best promoted by affording aids to seminaries of learning already established; by the institution of a national university; or by any other expedients, will be well worthy of a place in the deliberations of the Legislature.

Gentlemen of the House of Representatives:

I saw, with peculiar pleasure, at the close of the last session, the resolution entered into by you, expressive of your opinion that an adequate provision for the support of the public credit, is a matter of high importance to the national honor and prosperity. In this sentiment I entirely concur. And, to a perfect confidence in your best endeavors to devise such a provision as will be truly consistent with the end, I add an equal reliance on the cheerful co-operation of the other branch of the Legislature. It would be superfluous to specify inducements to a measure in which the character and permanent interests of the United States are so obviously and so deeply concerned, and which has received so explicit a sanction from your declaration.

Gentlemen of the Senate and House of Representatives:

I have directed the proper officers to lay before you, respectively, such papers and estimates as regard the affairs particularly recommended to your consideration, and necessary to convey to you that information of the state of the Union which it is my duty to afford.

The welfare of our country is the great object to which our cares and efforts ought to be directed. And I shall derive great satisfaction from a co-operation with you in the pleasing, though arduous task, of ensuring to our fellow-citizens the blessings which they have a right to expect from a free, efficient, and equal government.

GEO. WASHINGTON.

170

SECOND ANNUAL MESSAGE

Wednesday, December 8, 1790

Fellow-citizens of the Senate
and House of Representatives:

In meeting you again, I feel much satisfaction in being able to repeat my congratulations on the favorable prospects which continue to distinguish our public affairs. The abundant fruits of another year have blessed our country with plenty, and with the means of a flourishing commerce. The progress of public credit is witnessed by a considerable rise of American stock, abroad as well as at home; and the revenues allotted for this and other national purposes, have been productive beyond the calculations by which they were regulated. This latter circumstance is the more pleasing, as it is not only a proof of the fertility of our resources, but as it assures us of a further increase of the national respectability and credit; and, let me add, as it bears an honorable testimony to the patriotism and integrity of the mercantile and marine part of our citizens. The punctuality of the former in discharging their engagements has been exemplary.

In conforming to the powers vested in me by acts of the last session, a loan of three millions of florins, towards which some provisional measures had previously taken place, has been completed in Holland. As well the celerity with which it has been filled, as the nature of the terms, (considering the more than ordinary demand for borrowing, created by the situation of Europe) give a reasonable hope that the further execution of those powers may proceed with advantage and success. The Secretary of the Treasury has my direction to communicate such further particulars as may be requisite for more precise information.

Since your last sessions, I have received communications, by which it appears that the district of Kentucky, at present a part of Virginia, has concurred in certain propositions contained in a law of that State; in consequence of which, the district is to become a distinct member of the Union, in case the requisite sanction of Congress be added. For this sanction application is now made. I shall cause the papers on this very important transaction to be laid before you. The liberality and harmony with which it has been conducted, will be found to do great honor to both the parties; and the sentiments of warm attachment to the Union and its present government, expressed by our fellow citizens of Kentucky, cannot fail to add an affectionate concern for their particular welfare to the great national impressions under which you will decide on the case submitted to you.

It has been heretofore known to Congress, that frequent incursions have been made on our frontier settlements by certain banditti of Indians from the northwest side of the Ohio. These, with some of the tribes dwelling on and near the Wabash, have of late been particularly active in their depredations; and, being emboldened by the impunity of their crimes, and aided by such parts of the neighboring tribes as could be seduced to join in their hostilities, or afford them a retreat for their prisoners and plunder, they have, instead of listening to the humane invitations and overtures made on the part of the United States, renewed their violences with fresh alacrity and greater effect. The lives of a number of valuable citizens have thus been sacrificed, and some of them under circumstances peculiarly shocking; whilst others have been carried into a deplorable captivity.

These aggravated provocations rendered it essential to the safety of the western settlements that the aggressors should be made sensible that the government of the Union is not less capable of punishing their crimes, than it is disposed to respect their rights and reward their attachments. As this object could not be effected by defensive measures, it became necessary to put in force the act which empowers the President to call out the militia for the protection of the frontiers; and I have accordingly authorized an expedition, in which the regular troops in that quarter are combined with such draughts of militia as were deemed sufficient: the event of the measure is yet unknown to me. The Secretary of War is directed to lay before you a statement of the information on which it is founded, as well as an estimate of the expense with which it will be attended.

The disturbed situation of Europe, and particularly the critical posture of the great maritime Powers, whilst it ought to make us the more thankful for the general peace and security enjoyed by the United States, reminds us, at the same time, of the circumspection with which it becomes us to preserve these blessings. It requires, also, that we should not overlook the tendency of a war, and even of preparations for a war, among the nations most concerned in active commerce with this country, to abridge the means, and thereby at least enhance the price of transporting its valuable productions to their proper markets. I recommend it to your serious reflections, how far, and in what mode, it may be expedient to guard against embarrassments from these contingencies, by such encouragements to our own navigation as will render our commerce and agriculture less dependent on foreign bottoms, which may fail us in the very moments most interesting to both of these great objects. Our fisheries, and the transportation of our own produce, offer us abundant means for guarding ourselves against this evil.

Your attention seems to be not less due to that particular

branch of our trade which belongs to the Mediterranean. So many circumstances unite in rendering the present state of it distressful to us, that you will not think any deliberations misemployed which may lead to its relief and protection.

The laws you have already passed for the establishment of a judiciary system, have opened the doors of justice to all descriptions of persons. You will consider, in your wisdom, whether improvements in that system may yet be made; and particularly whether an uniform process of execution, on sentences issuing from the federal courts, be not desirable through all the States.

The patronage of our commerce, of our merchants, and seamen, has called for the appointment of consuls in foreign countries. It seems expedient to regulate by law the exercise of that jurisdiction, and those functions which are permitted them, either by express convention, or by a friendly indulgence in the places of their residence. The consular convention, too, with His Most Christian Majesty, has stipulated, in certain cases, the aid of the national authority to his consuls established here. Some legislative provision is requisite to carry these stipulations into full effect.

The establishment of the militia, of a mint, of standards of weights and measures, of the post office and post roads, are subjects which I presume you will resume of course, and which are abundantly urged by their own importance.

Gentlemen of the House of Representatives:

The sufficiency of the revenues you have established for the objects to which they are appropriated, leaves no doubt that the residuary provisions will be commensurate to the other objects for which the public faith stands now pledged. Allow me, moreover, to hope that it will be a favorite policy with you, not merely to secure a payment of the interest of the debt funded, but, as far and as fast as the growing resources of the country will permit, to exonerate it of the principal itself. The appropriation you have made of the western lands, explains your dispositions on this subject; and I am persuaded the sooner that valuable fund can be made to contribute, along with other means, to the actual reduction of the public debt, the more salutary will the measure be to every public interest, as well as the more satisfactory to our constituents.

Gentlemen of the Senate and House of Representatives:

In pursuing the various and weighty business of the present session, I indulge the fullest persuasion that your consultations will be equally marked with wisdom, and animated by the love of your country. In whatever belongs to my duty, you shall have all the co-operation which an undiminished zeal for its welfare can inspire. It will be happy for us both, and our best reward, if, by a successful administration of our respective trusts, we can make the established government more and more instrumental in promoting the good of our fellow-citizens, and more and more the object of their attachment and confidence.

GEO. WASHINGTON.

171

THIRD ANNUAL MESSAGE

Tuesday, October 25, 1791

Fellow-citizens of the Senate,

and of the House of Representatives:

I meet you upon the present occasion with the feelings which are naturally inspired by a strong impression of the prosperous situation of our common country, and by a persuasion, equally strong, that the labors of the session which has just commenced, will, under the guidance of a spirit no less prudent than patriotic, issue in measures conducive to the stability and increase of national prosperity.

Numerous as are the providential blessings which demand our grateful acknowledgments, the abundance with which another year has again rewarded the industry of the husbandman is too important to escape recollection.

Your own observations in your respective situations will have satisfied you of the progressive state of agriculture, manufactures, commerce, and navigation. In tracing their causes, you will have remarked, with particular pleasure, the happy effects of that revival of confidence, public as well as private, to which the constitution and laws of the United States have so eminently contributed; and you will have observed, with no less interest, new and decisive proofs of the increasing reputation and credit of the nation. But you, nevertheless, cannot fail to derive satisfaction from the confirmation of these circumstances, which will be disclosed in the several official communications that will be made to you in the course of your deliberations.

The rapid subscription to the Bank of the United States, which completed the sum allowed to be subscribed in a single day, is among the striking and pleasing evidences which present themselves, not only of confidence in the Government, but of resource in the community.

In the interval of your recess, due attention has been paid to the execution of the different objects which were specially provided for by the laws and resolutions of the last session.

Among the most important of these, is the defence and security of the western frontiers. To accomplish it on the most humane principles was a primary wish. Accordingly, at the same time that treaties have been provisionally concluded, and other proper means used to attach the wavering, and to confirm in their friendship the well disposed tribes of Indians, effectual measures have been adopted to make those of a hostile description sensible that a pacification was desired upon terms of moderation and justice.

These measures having proved unsuccessful, it became necessary to convince the refractory of the power of the United States to punish their depredations. Offensive operations have therefore been directed, to be conducted, however, as consistently as possible with the dictates of humanity. Some of these have been crowned with full success, and others are yet depending. The expeditions which have been completed were carried on under the authority, and at the expense of the United States, by the militia of Kentucky; whose enterprise, intrepidity, and good conduct, are entitled to peculiar commendation.

Overtures of peace are still continued to the deluded tribes, and considerable numbers of individuals belonging to them have lately renounced all further opposition, removed from their former situations, and placed themselves under the immediate protection of the United States.

It is sincerely to be desired that all need of coercion in future may cease; and that an intimate intercourse may succeed, calculated to advance the happiness of the Indians, and to attach them firmly to the United States.

In order to this, it seems necessary—

That they should experience the benefits of an impartial dispensation of justice;

That the mode of alienating their lands, the main source of discontent and war, should be so defined and regulated as to obviate imposition, and, as far as may be practicable, controversy concerning the reality and extent of the alienations which are made;

That commerce with them should be promoted under regulations tending to secure an equitable deportment towards them, and that such rational experiments should be made, for imparting to them the blessings of civilization, as may, from time to time, suit their condition;

That the Executive of the United States should be enabled to employ the means to which the Indians have been long accustomed for uniting their immediate interests with the preservation of peace;

And that efficacious provision should be made for inflicting adequate penalties upon all those who, by violating their rights, shall infringe the treaties, and endanger the peace of the Union.

A system corresponding with the mild principles of religion and philanthropy, towards an unenlightened race of men, whose happiness materially depends on the conduct of the United States, would be as honorable to the national character as conformable to the dictates of sound policy.

The powers specially vested in me by the act laying certain duties on distilled spirits, which respect the subdivisions of the districts into surveys, the appointment of officers, and the assignment of compensations, have likewise been carried into effect. In a matter in which both materials and experience were wanting to guide the calculation, it will be readily conceived that there must have been difficulty in such an adjustment of the rates of compensation as would conciliate a reasonable competency with a proper regard to the limits prescribed by the law. It is hoped that the circumspection which has been used, will be found, in the result, to have secured the last of the two objects; but it is probable, that, with a view to the first, in some instances a revision of the provision will be found advisable.

The impressions with which this law has been received by the community, have been, upon the whole, such as were to be expected among enlightened and well disposed citizens, from the propriety and necessity of the measure. The novelty, however, of the tax, in a considerable part of the United States, and a misconception of some of its provisions, have given occasion, in particular places, to some degree of discontent. But it is satisfactory to know that this disposition yields to proper explanations and more just apprehensions of the true nature of the law. And I entertain a full confidence that it will, in all, give way to motives which arise out of a just sense of duty, and a virtuous regard to the public welfare.

If there are any circumstances in the law, which, consistently with its main design, may be so varied as to remove any well intentioned objections that may happen to exist, it will consist with a wise moderation to make the proper variations. It is desirable, on all occasions, to unite, with a steady and firm adherence to constitutional and necessary acts of government, the fullest evidence of a disposition, as far as may be practicable, to consult the wishes of every part of the community, and to lay the foundations of the public administration in the affections of the People.

Pursuant to the authority contained in the several acts on that subject, a district of ten miles square, for the permanent seat of the Government of the United States, has been fixed, and announced by proclamation; which district will comprehend lands on both sides of the river Potomac, and the towns of Alexandria and Georgetown. A city has also been laid out, agreeably to a plan which will be placed before Congress; and as there is a prospect, favored by the rate of sales which have already taken place, of ample funds for carrying on the necessary public buildings, there is every expectation of their due progress.

The completion of the census of the inhabitants, for which provision was made by law, has been duly notified, (excepting one instance, in which the return has been informal, and another, in which it has been omitted or miscarried,) and the returns of the officers who were charged with this duty, which will be laid before you, will give you the pleasing assurance that the present population of the United States borders on four millions of persons.

It is proper also to inform you, that a further loan of two millions and a half of florins has been completed in Holland; the terms of which are similar to those of the one last announced, except as to a small reduction of charges. Another, on like terms, for six millions of florins, had been set on foot under circumstances that assured an immediate completion.

Gentlemen of the Senate:

Two treaties, which have been provisionally concluded with the Cherokees and Six Nations of Indians, will be laid before you for your consideration and ratification.

Gentlemen of the House of Representatives:

In entering upon the discharge of your legislative trust, you must anticipate with pleasure, that many of the difficulties necessarily incident to the first arrangements of a new government for an extensive country, have been happily surmounted by the zealous and judicious exertions of your predecessors, in co-operation with the other branch of the Legislature. The important objects which remain to be accomplished, will, I am persuaded, be conducted upon principles equally comprehensive, and equally well calculated for the advancement of the general weal.

The time limited for receiving subscriptions to the loans proposed by the act making provision for the debt of the United States having expired, statements from the proper department will, as soon as possible, apprise you of the exact result. Enough, however, is already known, to afford an assurance that the views of that act have been substantially fulfilled. The subscription, in the domestic debt of the United States, has embraced by far the greatest proportion of that debt; affording, at the same time, proof of the general satisfaction of the public creditors with the system which has been proposed to their acceptance, and of the spirit of accommodation to the convenience of the Government with which they are actuated. The subscriptions in the debts of the respective States, as far as the provisions of the law have permitted, may be said to be yet more general. The part of the debt of the United States which remains unsubscribed, will naturally engage your further deliberations.

It is particularly pleasing to me to be able to announce to you, that the revenues which have been established promise to be adequate to their objects, and may be permitted, if no unforeseen exigency occurs, to supersede, for the present, the necessity of any new burthens upon our constituents.

An object which will claim your early attention, is a provision for the current service of the ensuing year, together with such ascertained demands upon the Treasury as require to be immediately discharged, and such casualties as may have arisen in the execution of the public business, for which no specific appropriation may have yet been made; of all which a proper estimate will be laid before you.

Gentlemen of the Senate
and of the House of Representatives:

I shall content myself with a general reference to former communications for several objects, upon which the urgency of other affairs has hitherto postponed any definitive resolution. Their importance will recall them to your attention, and I trust that the progress already made in the most arduous arrangements of the Government, will afford you leisure to resume them with advantage.

There are, however, some of them, of which I cannot forbear a more particular mention. These are: the militia; the post office and post roads; the mint; weights and measures; a provision for the sale of the vacant lands of the United States.

The first is certainly an object of primary importance, whether viewed in reference to the national security, to the satisfaction of the community, or to the preservation of order. In connexion with this, the establishment of competent magazines and arsenals, and the fortification of such places as are peculiarly important and vulnerable, naturally present themselves to consideration. The safety of the United States, under divine protection, ought to rest on the basis of systematic and solid arrangements; exposed as little as possible to the hazards of fortuitous circumstances.

The importance of the post office and post roads, on a plan sufficiently liberal and comprehensive, as they respect the expedition, safety, and facility of communication, is increased by the instrumentality in diffusing a knowledge of the laws and proceedings of the Government; which, while it contributes to the security of the people, serves also to guard them against the effects of misrepresentation and misconception. The establishment of additional cross posts, especially to some of the important points in the western and northern parts of the Union, cannot fail to be of material utility.

The disorders in the existing currency, and especially the scarcity of small change—a scarcity so peculiarly distressing to the poorer classes—strongly recommend the carrying into immediate effect the resolution already entered into concerning the establishment of a mint. Measures have been taken, pursuant to that resolution, for procuring some of the most necessary artists, together with the requisite apparatus.

An uniformity in the weights and measures of the country is among the important objects submitted to you by the constitution; and if it can be derived from a standard at once invariable and universal, must be no less honorable to the public councils than conducive to the public convenience.

A provision for the sale of the vacant lands of the United States is particularly urged, among other reasons, by the important considerations, that they are pledged as a fund for reimbursing the public debt; that, if timely and judiciously applied, they may save the necessity of burthening our citizens with new taxes for the extinguishment of the principal; and that, being free to discharge the principal but in a limited proportion, no opportunity ought to be lost for availing the public of its right.

GEO. WASHINGTON.

172

FOURTH ANNUAL MESSAGE

Tuesday, November 6, 1792

Fellow-citizens of the Senate
and of the House of Representatives:

It is some abatement of the satisfaction with which I meet you on the present occasion, that, in felicitating you on a continuance of the national prosperity, generally, I am not able to add to it information that the Indian hostilities, which have, for some time past, distressed our northwestern frontier, have terminated.

You will, I am persuaded, learn, with no less concern than I communicate it, that reiterated endeavors towards effecting a pacification, have hitherto issued only in new and outrageous proofs of persevering hostility on the part of the tribes with whom we are in contest. An earnest desire to procure tranquillity to the frontier; to stop the further effusion of blood; to arrest the progress of expense; to forward the prevalent wish of the nation for peace; has led to strenuous efforts, through various channels, to accomplish these desirable purposes: in making which efforts, I consulted less my own anticipations of the event, or the scruples which some considerations were calculated to inspire, than the wish to find the object attainable; or, if not attainable, to ascertain unequivocally that such is the case.

A detail of the measures which have been pursued, and of their consequences, which will be laid before you while it will confirm to you the want of success, thus far, will, I trust, evince that means as proper and as efficacious as could have been devised have been employed. The issue of some of them, indeed, is still depending; but a favorable one, though not to be despaired of, is not promised by any thing that has yet happened.

In the course of the attempts which have been made, some valuable citizens have fallen victims to their zeal for the public service. A sanction, commonly respected even among savages, has been found, in this instance, insufficient to protect from massacre the emissaries of peace. It will, I presume, be duly considered whether the occasion does not call for an exercise of liberality towards the families of the deceased.

It must add to your concern to be informed, that, besides the continuation of hostile appearances among the tribes north of the Ohio, some threatening symptoms have of late been revived among some of those south of it.

A part of the Cherokees, known by the name of Chickamagas, inhabiting five villages on the Tennessee river, have long been in the practice of committing depredations on the neighboring settlements.

It was hoped that the treaty of Holston, made with the Cherokee nation in July, 1791, would have prevented a repetition of such depredations. But the event has not answered this hope. The Chickamagas, aided by some banditti of another tribe in their vicinity, have recently perpetrated wanton and unprovoked hostilities upon the citizens of the United States in that quarter. The information which has been received on this subject will be laid before you. Hitherto, defensive precautions only have been strictly enjoined and observed.

It is not understood that any breach of treaty, or aggression whatsoever, on the part of the United States, or their citizens, is even alleged as a pretext for the spirit of hostility in this quarter.

I have reason to believe that every practicable exertion has been made (pursuant to the provision by law for that purpose) to be prepared for the alternative of a prosecution of the war, in the event of a failure of pacific overtures. A large proportion of the troops authorized to be raised have been recruited, though the number is still incomplete; and pains have been taken to discipline and put them in condition for the particular kind of service to be performed. A delay of operations (besides being dictated by the measures which were pursuing towards a pacific termination of the war) has been in itself deemed preferable to immature efforts. A statement from the proper department, with regard to the number of troops raised, and some other points which have been suggested, will afford more precise information as a guide to the legislative consultations; and, among other things, will enable Congress to judge whether some additional stimulus to the recruiting service may not be advisable.

In looking forward to the future expense of the operations which may be found inevitable, I derive consolation from the information I receive, that the product of the revenues for the present year is likely to supersede the necessity of additional burthens on the community for the service of the ensuing year. This, however, will be better ascertained in the course of the session; and it is proper to add, that the information alluded to proceeds upon the supposition of no material extension of the spirit of hostility.

I cannot dismiss the subject of Indian affairs, without again recommending to your consideration the expediency of more adequate provision for giving energy to the laws throughout our interior frontier; and for restraining the commission of outrages upon the Indians; without which, all pacific plans must prove nugatory. To enable, by competent rewards, the employment of qualified and trusty persons to reside among them, as agents, would also contribute to the preservation of peace and good neighborhood. If, in addition to these expedients, an eligible plan could be devised for promoting civilization among the friendly tribes, and for carrying on trade with them, upon a scale equal to their wants, and under regulations calculated to protect them from imposition and extortion, its influence in cementing their interests with ours could not but be considerable.

The prosperous state of our revenue has been intimated. This would be still more the case, were it not for the impediments which, in some places, continue to embarrass the collection of the duties on spirits distilled within the United States. These impediments have lessened, and are lessening, in local extent; and, as applied to the community at large, the contentment with the law appears to be progressive.

But symptoms of increased opposition having lately manifested themselves in certain quarters, I judged a special interposition on my part proper and advisable; and, under this impression, have issued a proclamation, warning against all unlawful combinations and proceedings, having for their object or tending to obstruct the operation of the law in question, and announcing that all lawful ways and means would be strictly put in execution for bringing to justice the infractors thereof, and securing obedience thereto.

Measures have also been taken for the prosecution of offenders; and Congress may be assured, that nothing within constitutional and legal limits, which may depend on me, shall be wanting to assert and maintain the just authority of the laws. In fulfilling this trust, I shall count entirely upon the full co-operation of the other departments of the Government, and upon the zealous support of all good citizens.

I cannot forbear to bring again into the view of the Legislature the subject of a revision of the judiciary system. A representation from the judges of the supreme court, which will be laid before you, points out some of the inconveniences that are experienced. In the course of the execution of the laws, considerations arise out of the structure of that system, which, in some cases, tend to relax their efficacy. As connected with this subject, provisions to facilitate the taking of bail upon processes out of the courts of the United States, and a supplementary definition of offences against the constitution and laws of the Union, and of the punishment for such offences, will, it is presumed, be found worthy of particular attention.

Observations on the value of peace with other nations are unnecessary. It would be wise, however, by timely provisions, to guard against those acts of our own citizens which might tend to disturb it, and to put ourselves in a condition to give that satisfaction to foreign nations which we may sometimes have occasion to require from them. I particularly recommend to your consideration the means of preventing those aggressions by our citizens on the territory of other nations, and other infractions of the law of nations, which, furnishing just subject of complaint, might endanger our peace with them; and, in general, the maintenance of a friendly intercourse with foreign Powers will be presented to your attention by the expiration of the law for that purpose, which takes place, if not renewed, at the close of the present session.

In execution of the authority given by the Legislature, measures have been taken for engaging some artists from abroad to aid in the establishment of our mint; others have been employed at home. Provision has been made for the requisite buildings, and these are now putting into proper condition for the purposes of the establishment. There has also been a small beginning in the coinage of half dimes, the want of small coins in circulation calling the first attention to them.

The regulation of foreign coins, in correspondency with the principles of our national coinage, as being essential to their due operation, and to order in our money concerns, will, I doubt not, be resumed and completed.

It is represented that some provisions in the law which establishes the post office, operate, in experiment, against the transmission of newspapers to distant parts of the country. Should this, upon due inquiry, be found to be the fact, a full conviction of the importance of facilitating the circulation of political intelligence and information, will, I doubt not, lead to the application of a remedy.

The adoption of a constitution for the State of Kentucky has been notified to me. The Legislature will share with me in the satisfaction which arises from an event interesting to the happiness of the part of the nation to which it relates, and conducive to the general order.

It is proper likewise to inform you, that, since my last communication on the subject, and in further execution of the acts severally making provision for the public debt and for the reduction thereof, three new loans have been effected, each for three millions of florins; one at Antwerp, at the annual interest of four and one half per cent with an allowance of four per cent in lieu of all charges; and the other two at Amsterdam, at the annual interest of four per cent with an allowance of five and one half per cent in one case, and of five per cent, in the other, in lieu of all charges. The rates of these loans, and the circumstances under which they have been made, are confirmations of the high state of our credit abroad.

Among the objects to which these funds have been directed to be applied, the payments of the debts due to certain foreign officers, according to the provision made during the last session, has been embraced.

Gentlemen of the House of Representatives:

I entertain a strong hope that the state of the national finances is now sufficiently matured to enable you to enter upon a systematic and effectual arrangement for the regular redemption and discharge of the public debt, according to the right which has been reserved to the Government; no measure can be more desirable, whether viewed with an eye to its intrinsic importance, or to the general sentiment and wish of the nation.

Provision is likewise requisite for the reimbursement of the loan which has been made of the Bank of the United States, pursuant to the eleventh section of the act by which it is incorporated. In fulfilling the public stipulations in this particular, it is expected a valuable saving will be made.

Appropriations for the current service of the ensuing year, and for such extraordinaries as may require provision, will demand, and I doubt not will engage, your early attention.

Gentlemen of the Senate
and of the House of Representatives:

I content myself with recalling your attention, generally, to such objects, not particularized in my present, as have been suggested in my former communications to you.

Various temporary laws will expire during the present session. Among these, that which regulates trade and intercourse with the Indian tribes will merit particular notice.

The results of your common deliberations hitherto, will, I trust, be productive of solid and durable advantages to our constituents; such as, by conciliating more and more their ultimate suffrage, will tend to strengthen and confirm their attachment to that constitution of government, upon which, under divine Providence, materially depend their union, their safety, and their happiness.

Still further to promote and secure these inestimable ends, there is nothing which can have a more powerful tendency than the careful cultivation of harmony, combined with a due regard to stability in the public councils.

GEO. WASHINGTON.

173

THE SECOND INAUGURAL SPEECH

Monday, March 4, 1793

Fellow-citizens:

I am again called upon, by the voice of my country, to execute the functions of its Chief Magistrate. When the occasion proper for it shall arrive, I shall endeavor to express the high sense I entertain of this distinguished honor, and of the confidence which has been reposed in me by the People of United America.

Previous to the execution of any official act of the President, the constitution requires an oath of office. This oath I am now about to take, and in your presence; that, if it should be found, during my administration of the Government, I have, in any instance, violated willingly or knowingly, the injunction thereof, I may, (besides incurring constitutional punishment) be subject to the upbraidings of all who are now witnesses of the present solemn ceremony.

174

FIFTH ANNUAL MESSAGE

Philadelphia, Tuesday, December 3, 1793

Fellow-citizens of the Senate
and of the House of Representatives:

Since the commencement of the term for which I have been again called into office, no fit occasion has arisen for expressing to my fellow-citizens at large the deep and respectful sense which I feel of the renewed testimony of public approbation. While, on the one hand, it awakened my gratitude for all those instances of affectionate partiality with which I have been honored by my country; on the other, it could not prevent an earnest wish for that retirement from which no private consideration should ever have torn me. But, influenced by the belief that my conduct would be estimated according to its real motives, and that the People, and the authorities derived from them, would support exertions having nothing personal for their object, I have obeyed the suffrage which commanded me to resume the Executive power; and I humbly implore that Being, on whose will the fate of nations depends, to crown with success our mutual endeavors for the general happiness.

As soon as the war in Europe had embraced those Powers with whom the United States have the most extensive relations, there was reason to apprehend that our intercourse with them might be interrupted, and our disposition for peace drawn into question by the suspicions too often entertained by belligerent nations. It seemed, therefore, to be my duty to admonish our citizens of the consequences of a contraband trade, and of hostile acts to any of the parties; and to obtain, by a declaration of the existing legal state of things, an easier admission of our right to the immunities belonging to our situation. Under these impressions, the proclamation which will be laid before you was issued.

In this posture of affairs, both new and delicate, I resolved to adopt general rules, which should conform to the treaties, and assert the privileges, of the United States. These were reduced into a system, which will be communicated to you. Although I have not thought myself at liberty to forbid the sale of the prizes, permitted by our treaty of commerce with France to be brought into our ports, I have not refused to cause them to be restored when they were taken within the protection of our territory, or by vessels commissioned or equipped in a warlike form within the limits of the United States.

It rests with the wisdom of Congress to correct, improve, or enforce, this plan of procedure; and it will probably be found expedient to extend the legal code and the jurisdiction of the courts of the United States to many cases which, though dependent on principles already recognized, demand some further provisions.

Where individuals shall, within the United States, array themselves in hostility against any of the Powers at war; or enter upon military expeditions or enterprises within the jurisdiction of the United States; or usurp and exercise judicial authority within the United States; or where the penalties on violations of the law of nations may have been indistinctly marked, or are inadequate: these offences cannot receive too early and close an attention, and require prompt and decisive remedies.

Whatsoever those remedies may be, they will be well administered by the judiciary, who possess a long established course of investigation, effectual process, and officers in the habit of executing it.

In like manner, as several of the courts have doubted, under particular circumstances, their power to liberate the vessels of a nation at peace, and even of a citizen of the United States, although seized under a false color of being hostile property, and have denied their power to liberate certain captures within the protection of our territory, it would seem proper to regulate their jurisdiction in these points; but if the Executive is to be the resort in either of the two last mentioned cases, it is hoped that he will be authorized by law to have facts ascertained by the courts, when, for his own information, he shall request it.

I cannot recommend to your notice measures for the fulfilment of our duties to the rest of the world, without again pressing upon you the necessity of placing ourselves in a condition of complete defence, and of exacting from them the fulfilment of their duties towards us. The United States ought not to indulge a persuasion, that, contrary to the order of human events, they will forever keep at a distance those painful appeals to arms with which the history of every other nation abounds. There is a rank due to the United States, among nations, which will be withheld, if not absolutely lost, by the reputation of weakness. If we desire to avoid insult, we must be able to repel it; if we desire to secure peace, one of the most powerful instruments of our rising prosperity, it must be known that we are at all times ready for war. The documents which will be presented to you will shew the amount and kinds of arms and military stores now in our magazines and arsenals; and yet an addition even to these supplies cannot, with prudence, be neglected, as it would leave nothing to the uncertainty of procuring a warlike apparatus in the moment of public danger.

Nor can such arrangements, with such objects, be exposed to the censure or jealousy of the warmest friends of republican government. They are incapable of abuse in the hands of the militia, who ought to possess a pride in being the depositary of the force of the republic, and may be trained to a degree of energy equal to every military exigency of the United States. But, it is an inquiry which cannot be too solemnly pursued, whether the act "more effectually to provide for the national defence, by establishing an uniform militia throughout the United States," has organized them so as to produce their full effect; whether your own experience in the several States has not detected some imperfections in the scheme; and whether a material feature, in an improvement of it, ought not to be, to afford an opportunity for the study of those branches of the military art which can scarcely ever be attained by practice alone.

The connexion of the United States with Europe has become extremely interesting. The occurrences which relate to it and have passed under the knowledge of the Executive, will be exhibited to Congress in a subsequent communication.

When we contemplate the war on our frontiers, it may be truly affirmed that every reasonable effort has been made to adjust the causes of dissension with the Indians north of the Ohio. The instructions given to the commissioners evince a moderation and equity proceeding from a sincere love of peace and a liberality having no restriction but the essential interests and dignity of the United States. The attempt, however, of an amicable negotiation, having been frustrated, the troops have marched to act offensively. Although the proposed treaty did not arrest the progress of military preparation, it is doubtful how far the advance of the season, before good faith justified active movements may retard them, during the remainder of the year. From the papers and intelligence which relate to this important subject, you will determine, whether the deficiency in the number of troops, granted by law, shall be compensated by succors of militia, or additional encouragement shall be proposed to recruits.

An anxiety has been also demonstrated by the Executive for peace with the Creeks and the Cherokees. The former have been relieved with corn and with clothing, and offensive measures against them prohibited during the recess of Congress. To satisfy the complaints of the latter, prosecutions have been instituted for the violences committed upon them. But the papers which will be delivered to you disclose the critical footing on which we stand in regard to both those tribes; and it is with Congress to pronounce what shall be done.

After they shall have provided for the present emergency, it will merit their most serious labors to render tranquillity with the savages permanent, by creating ties of interest. Next to a rigorous execution of justice on the violaters of peace, the establishment of commerce with the Indian nations, in behalf of the United States, is most likely to conciliate their attachment. But it ought to be conducted without fraud, without extortion, with constant and plentiful supplies; with a ready market for the commodities of the Indians, and a stated price for what they give in payment and receive in exchange. Individuals will not pursue such traffic, unless they be allured by the hope of profit; but it will be enough for the United States to be reimbursed only. Should this recommendation accord with the opinion of Congress, they will recollect that it cannot be accomplished by any means yet in the hands of the Executive.

Gentlemen of the House of Representatives:

The commissioners, charged with the settlement of accounts between the United States and individual States concluded their important functions within the time limited by law; and the balances struck in their report, which will be laid before Congress, have been placed on the books of the Treasury.

On the first day of June last, an instalment of one million of florins became payable on the loans of the United States in Holland. This was adjusted by a prolongation of the period of reimbursement, in nature of a new loan at an interest of five per cent for the term of ten years; and the expenses of this operation were a commission of three per cent.

The first instalment of the loan of two millions of dollars, from the Bank of the United States, has been paid, as was directed by law. For the second it is necessary that provision should be made.

No pecuniary consideration is more urgent than the regular redemption and discharge of the public debt; of none can delay be more injurious, or an economy of time more valuable.

The productiveness of the public revenues hitherto, has continued to equal the anticipations which were formed of it;

but it is not expected to prove commensurate with all the objects which have been suggested. Some auxiliary provisions will, therefore, it is presumed, be requisite; and it is hoped that these may be made, consistently with a due regard to the convenience of our citizens, who cannot but be sensible of the true wisdom of encountering a small present addition to their contributions, to obviate a future accumulation of burthens.

But here I cannot forbear to recommend a repeal of the tax on the transportation of public prints. There is no resource so firm for the Government of the United States as the affections of the people, guided by an enlightened policy; and to this primary good nothing can conduce more than a faithful representation of public proceedings, diffused without restraint, throughout the United States.

An estimate of the appropriations necessary for the current service of the ensuing year, and a statement of a purchase of arms and military stores, made during the recess, will be presented to Congress.

Gentlemen of the Senate
and of the House of Representatives:

The several subjects to which I have now referred, open a wide range to your deliberations, and involve some of the choicest interests of our common country. Permit me to bring to your remembrance the magnitude of your task. Without an unprejudiced coolness, the welfare of the Government may be hazarded; without harmony, as far as consists with freedom of sentiment, its dignity may be lost. But, as the legislative proceedings of the United States will never, I trust, be reproached for the want of temper or of candor, so shall not the public happiness languish from the want of my strenuous and warmest co-operation.

GEO. WASHINGTON.

175

SIXTH ANNUAL MESSAGE

Wednesday, November 19, 1794

Fellow-citizens of the Senate

and of the House of Representatives:

When we call to mind the gracious indulgence of Heaven, by which the American People became a nation, when we survey the general prosperity of our country, and look forward to the riches, power, and happiness, to which it seems destined; with the deepest regret do I announce to you that, during your recess, some of the citizens of the United States have been found capable of an insurrection. It is due, however, to the character of our Government, and to its stability, which cannot be shaken by the enemies of order, freely to unfold the course of this event.

During the session of the year one thousand seven hundred and ninety, it was expedient to exercise the legislative power, granted by the constitution of the United States, "to lay and collect excises." In a majority of the States scarcely an objection was heard to this mode of taxation. In some, indeed, alarms were at first conceived, until they were banished by reason and patriotism. In the four western counties of Pennsylvania, a prejudice, fostered and embittered by the artifice of men, who labored for an ascendency over the will of others, by the guidance of their passions, produced symptoms of riot and violence. It is well known, that Congress did not hesitate to examine the complaints which were presented; and to relieve them, as far as justice dictated, or general convenience would permit. But, the impression which this moderation made on the discontented, did not correspond with what it deserved. The arts of delusion were no longer confined to the efforts of designing individuals. The very forbearance to press prosecutions was misinterpreted into a fear of urging the execution of the laws, and associations of men began to denounce threats against the officers employed. From a belief, that, by a more formal concert, their operation might be defeated, certain self-created societies assumed the tone of condemnation. Hence, while the greater part of Pennsylvania itself were conforming themselves to the acts of excise, a few counties were resolved to frustrate them. It was now perceived, that every expectation from the tenderness which had been hitherto pursued was unavailing, and that further delay could only create an opinion of impotency or irresolution in the Government. Legal process was therefore delivered to the marshal against the rioters and delinquent distillers.

No sooner was he understood to be engaged in this duty, than the vengeance of armed men was aimed at *his* person, and the person and property of the inspector of the revenue. They fired upon the marshal, arrested him and detained him, for some time, as a prisoner. He was obliged, by the jeopardy of his life, to renounce the service of other process, on the west side of the Allegheny mountain; and a deputation was afterwards sent to him to demand a surrender of that which he *had* served. A numerous body repeatedly attacked the house of the inspector, seized his papers of office, and finally destroyed by fire his buildings and whatsoever they contained. Both of these officers, from a just regard to their safety, fled to the seat of government—it being avowed, that the motives to such outrages were to compel the resignation of the inspector; to withstand by force of arms the authority of the United States; and thereby to extort a repeal of the laws of excise, and an alteration in the conduct of Government.

Upon the testimony of these facts, an associate justice of the supreme court of the United States notified to me that, "in the counties of Washington and Allegheny, in Pennsylvania, laws of the United States were opposed, and the execution thereof obstructed, by combinations too powerful to be suppressed by the ordinary course of judicial proceedings, or by the powers vested in the marshal of that district." On this call, momentous in the extreme, I sought and weighed what might best subdue the crisis. On the one hand, the judiciary was pronounced to be stripped of its capacity to enforce the laws; crimes, which reached the very existence of social order, were perpetrated without control; the friends of government were insulted, abused, and overawed into silence, or an apparent acquiescence; and, to yield to the treasonable fury of so small a portion of the United States, would be to violate the fundamental principle of our constitution, which enjoins that the will of the majority shall prevail. On the other, to array citizen against citizen, to publish the dishonor of such excesses, to encounter the expense, and other embarrasments, of so distant an expedition, were steps too delicate, too closely interwoven with many affecting considerations, to be lightly adopted. I postponed, therefore, the summoning of the militia immediately into the field but I required them to be held in readiness, that, if my anxious endeavors to reclaim the deluded, and to convince the malignant of their danger, should be fruitless, military force might be prepared to act, before the season should be too far advanced.

My proclamation of the 7th of August last was accordingly issued, and accompanied by the appointment of commissioners, who were charged to repair to the scene of insurrection. They were authorized to confer with any bodies of men or individuals. They were instructed to be candid and explicit in stating the sensations which had been excited in the Executive, and his earnest wish to avoid a resort to coercion; to represent, however, that, without submission, coercion *must* be the resort; but to invite them, at the same time, to return to the demeanor of faithful citizens, by such accommodations as lay within the sphere of Executive power. Pardon, too, was tendered to them by the Government of the United States, and that of Pennsylvania, upon no other condition than a satisfactory assurance of obedience to the laws.

Although the report of the commissioners marks their firmness and abilities, and must unite all virtuous men, shewing that the means of conciliation have been exhausted, all of those who had committed or abetted the tumult did not subscribe the mild form which was proposed as the atonement; and the indications of a peaceable temper were neither sufficiently general nor conclusive to recommend or warrant the farther suspension of the march of the militia.

Thus, the painful alternative could not be discarded. I ordered the militia to march, after once more admonishing the insurgents, in my proclamation of the 25th of September last.

It was a task too difficult to ascertain with precision the lowest degree of force competent to the quelling of the insurrection. From a respect, indeed, to economy, and the ease of my fellow-citizens belonging to the militia, it would have gratified me to accomplish such an estimate. My very reluctance to ascribe too much importance to the opposition, had its extent been accurately seen, would have been a decided inducement to the smallest efficient number. In this uncertainty, therefore,

I put into motion fifteen thousand men, as being an army which, according to all human calculation, would be prompt and adequate in every view, and might, perhaps, by rendering resistance desperate, prevent the effusion of blood. Quotas had been assigned to the States of New Jersey, Pennsylvania, Maryland, and Virginia; the Governor of Pennsylvania having declared, on this occasion, an opinion which justified a requisition to the other States.

As commander in chief of the militia, when called into the actual service of the United States, I have visited the places of general rendezvous, to obtain more exact information, and to direct a plan for ulterior movements. Had there been room for a persuasion, that the laws were secure from obstruction; that the civil magistrate was able to bring to justice such of the most culpable as have not embraced the proffered terms of amnesty, and may be deemed fit objects of example; that the friends to peace and good government were not in need of that aid and countenance which they ought always to receive, and, I trust, ever will receive, against the vicious and turbulent; I should have caught with avidity the opportunity of restoring the militia to their families and home. But, succeeding intelligence has tended to manifest the necessity of what has been done; it being now confessed by those, who were not inclined to exaggerate the ill conduct of the insurgents, that their malevolence was not pointed merely to a particular law, but that a spirit, inimical to all order, has actuated many of the offenders. If the state of things had afforded reason for the continuance of my presence with the army, it would not have been withholden. But every appearance assuring such an issue as will redound to the reputation and strength of the United States, I have judged it most proper to resume my duties at the seat of government, leaving the chief command with the Governor of Virginia.

Still, however, as it is probable that, in a commotion like the present, whatsoever may be the pretence, the purposes of mischief and revenge may not be laid aside, the stationing of a small force, for a certain period, in the four western counties of Pennsylvania will be indispensable, whether we contemplate the situation of those who are connected with the execution of the laws, or of others, who may have exposed themselves by an honorable attachment to them. Thirty days from the commencement of this session being the legal limitation of the employment of the militia, Congress cannot be too early occupied with this subject.

Among the discussions which may arise from this aspect of our affairs, and from the documents which will be submitted to Congress, it will not escape their observation, that not only the inspector of the revenue, but other officers of the United States, in Pennsylvania, have, from their fidelity in the discharge of their functions, sustained material injuries to their property. The obligation and policy of indemnifying them are strong and obvious. It may also merit attention, whether policy will not enlarge this provision to the retribution of other citizens, who, though not under the ties of office, may have suffered damage by their generous exertions for upholding the constitution and the laws. The amount, even if all the injured were included, would not be great; and on future emergencies, the Government would be amply repaid by the influence of an example, that he, who incurs a loss in its defence, shall find a recompence in its liberality.

While there is cause to lament that occurrences of this nature should have disgraced the name, or interrupted the tranquillity, of any part of our community, or should have diverted, to a new application, any portion of the public resources, there are not wanting real and substantial consolations for the misfortune. It has demonstrated, that our prosperity rests on solid foundations, by furnishing an additional proof, that my fellow-citizens understand the true principles of government and liberty; that they feel their inseparable union; that, notwithstanding all the devices which have been used to sway them from their interest and duty, they are now as ready to maintain the authority of the laws against licentious invasions, as they were to defend their rights against usurpation. It has been a spectacle, displaying to the highest advantage the value of republican government, to behold the most and the least wealthy of our citizens standing in the same ranks, as private soldiers, pre-eminently distinguished by being the army of the constitution; undeterred by a march of three hundred miles over rugged mountains, by the approach of an inclement season, or by any other discouragement. Nor ought I to omit to acknowledge the efficacious and patriotic co-operation which I have experienced from the Chief Magistrates of the States to which my requisitions have been addressed.

To every description, indeed, of citizens, let praise be given. But let them persevere in their affectionate vigilance over that precious depository of American happiness, the constitution of the United States. Let them cherish it, too, for the sake of those who, from every clime, are daily seeking a dwelling in our land. And when, in the calm moments of reflection, they shall have retraced the origin and progress of the insurrection, let them determine whether it has not been fomented by combinations of men, who, careless of consequences, and disregarding the unerring truth, that those who rouse cannot always appease a civil convulsion, have disseminated, from an ignorance or perversion of facts, suspicions, jealousies, and accusations, of the whole Government.

Having thus fulfilled the engagement which I took, when I entered into office, "to the best of my ability to preserve, protect, and defend, the constitution of the United States," on you, gentlemen, and the people by whom you are deputed, I rely for support.

In the arrangements to which the possibility of a similar contingency will naturally draw your attention, it ought not to be forgotten that the militia laws have exhibited such striking defects as could not have been supplied but by the zeal of our citizens. Besides the extraordinary expense and waste, which are not the least of the defects, every appeal to those laws is attended with a doubt on its success.

The devising and establishing of a well regulated militia would be a genuine source of legislative honor, and a perfect title to public gratitude. I, therefore, entertain a hope, that the present session will not pass, without carrying, to its full energy, the power of organizing, arming, and disciplining, the militia; and thus providing, in the language of the constitution, for calling them forth to execute the laws of the Union, suppress insurrections, and repel invasions.

As auxiliary to the state of our defence, to which Congress can never too frequently recur, they will not omit to inquire, whether the fortifications, which have been already licensed by law, be commensurate with our exigencies.

The intelligence from the army under the command of General Wayne is a happy presage to our military operations against the hostile Indians north of the Ohio. From the advices which have been forwarded, the advance which he has made must have damped the ardor of the savages, and weakened their obstinacy in waging war against the United States. And yet, even at this late hour, when our power to punish them cannot be questioned, we shall not be unwilling to cement a lasting peace, upon terms of candor, equity, and good neighborhood.

Towards none of the Indian tribes have overtures of friendship been spared. The Creeks, in particular, are covered from encroachment by the interposition of the General Government and that of Georgia. From a desire, also, to remove the discontents of the Six Nations, a settlement meditated at Presqu' isle, on Lake Erie, has been suspended; and an agent is now endeavoring to rectify any misconception into which they may have fallen. But, I cannot refrain from again pressing upon your deliberations the plan which I recommended at the last session, for the improvement of harmony with all the Indians within our limits, by the fixing and conducting of trading houses upon the principles then expressed.

Gentlemen of the House of Representatives:

The time which has elapsed since the commencement of our fiscal measures has developed our pecuniary resources, so as to open the way for a definitive plan for the redemption of the public debt. It is believed that the result is such as to encourage Congress to consummate this work without delay. Nothing can more promote the permanent welfare of the nation, and nothing would be more grateful to our constituents. Indeed, whatsoever is unfinished of our system of public credit, cannot be benefited by procrastination; and, as far as may be practicable, we ought to place that credit on grounds which cannot be disturbed, and to prevent that progressive accumulation of debt, which must ultimately endanger all governments.

An estimate of the necessary appropriations, including the expenditures into which we have been driven by the insurrection, will be submitted to Congress.

Gentlemen of the Senate
and of the House of Representatives:

The mint of the United States has entered upon the coinage of the precious metals; and considerable sums of defective coins and bullion have been lodged with the director, by individuals. There is a pleasing prospect that the institution will, at no remote day, realize the expectation which was originally formed of its utility.

In subsequent communications, certain circumstances of our intercourse with foreign nations will be transmitted to Congress. However, it may not be unseasonable to announce that my policy, in our foreign transactions, has been to cultivate peace with all the world; to observe treaties with pure and absolute faith; to check every deviation from the line of impartiality; to explain what may have been misapprehended, and correct what may have been injurious to any nation; and, having thus acquired the right, to lose no time in acquiring the ability, to insist upon justice being done to ourselves.

Let us unite, therefore, in imploring the Supreme Ruler of nations to spread his holy protection over these United States; to turn the machinations of the wicked to the confirming of our constitution; to enable us, at all times, to root out internal sedition, and put invasion to flight; to perpetuate to our country that prosperity, which his goodness has already conferred; and to verify the anticipations of this government being a safeguard to human rights.

GEO. WASHINGTON.

176

SEVENTH ANNUAL MESSAGE

Tuesday, December 8, 1795

Fellow-citizens of the Senate
and of the House of Representatives:

I trust I do not deceive myself, while I indulge the persuasion that I have never met you at any period, when, more than at the present, the situation of our public affairs has afforded just cause for mutual congratulation, and for inviting you to join with me in profound gratitude to the author of all good for the numerous and extraordinary blessings we enjoy.

The termination of the long, expensive, and distressing war in which we have been engaged with certain Indians northwest of the Ohio, is placed in the option of the United States, by a treaty which the commander of our army has concluded provisionally with the hostile tribes in that region. In the adjustment of the terms, the satisfaction of the Indians was deemed an object worthy no less of the policy than of the liberality of the United States, as the necessary basis of durable tranquillity. This object, it is believed, has been fully attained. The articles agreed upon will immediately be laid before the Senate, for their consideration.

The Creek and Cherokee Indians, who, alone, of the southern tribes, had annoyed our frontier, have lately confirmed their pre-existing treaties with us, and were giving evidence of a sincere disposition to carry them into effect, by the surrender of the prisoners and property they had taken. But we have to lament, that the fair prospect in this quarter has been once more clouded by wanton murders, which some citizens of Georgia are represented to have recently perpetrated on hunting parties of the Creeks, which have again subjected that frontier to disquietude and danger; which will be productive of further expense, and may occasion more effusion of blood. Measures are pursuing to prevent or mitigate the usual consequences of such outrages, and with the hope of their succeeding, at least to avert general hostility.

A letter from the Emperor of Morocco announces to me his recognition of our treaty made with his father, the late Emperor, and, consequently, the continuance of peace with that Power. With peculiar satisfaction I add, that information has been received from an agent deputed on our part to Algiers, importing that the terms of a treaty with the Dey and Regency of that country had been adjusted in such a manner as to authorize the expectation of a speedy peace, and the restoration of our unfortunate fellow-citizens from a grievous captivity.

The latest advices from our envoy at the court of Madrid, give, moreover, the pleasing information that he had received assurances of a speedy and satisfactory conclusion of his negotiation. While the event, depending upon unadjusted particulars, cannot be regarded as ascertained, it is agreeable to cherish the expectation of an issue, which, securing amicably very essential interests of the United States, will, at the same time, lay the foundation of lasting harmony with a Power whose friendship we have uniformly and sincerely desired to cultivate.

Though not before officially disclosed to the House of Representatives, you, gentlemen, are all apprised that a treaty of amity, commerce, and navigation, has been negotiated with

Great Britain, and that the Senate have advised and consented to its ratification, upon a condition which excepts part of one article. Agreeably thereto, and to the best judgment I was able to form of the public interest, after full and mature deliberation, I have added my sanction. The result on the part of His Britannic Majesty is unknown. When received, the subject will, without delay, be placed before Congress.

This interesting summary of our affairs, with regard to the foreign Powers between whom and the United States controversies have subsisted; and with regard, also, to those of our Indian neighbors with whom we have been in a state of enmity or misunderstanding; opens a wide field for consoling and gratifying reflections. If, by prudence and moderation on every side, the extinguishment of all the causes of external discord, which have heretofore menaced our tranquillity, on terms compatible with our national rights and honor, shall be the happy result, how firm and how precious a foundation will have been laid for accelerating, maturing, and establishing, the prosperity of our country.

Contemplating the internal situation, as well as the external relations, of the United States, we discover equal cause for contentment and satisfaction. While many of the nations of Europe, with their American dependencies, have been involved in a contest unusually bloody, exhausting, and calamitous, in which the evils of foreign war have been aggravated by domestic convulsion and insurrection; in which many of the arts most useful to society have been exposed to discouragement and decay; in which scarcity of subsistence has embittered other sufferings, while even the anticipations of a return of the blessings of peace and repose are alloyed by the sense of heavy and accumulating burthens, which press upon all the departments of industry, and threaten to clog the future springs of Government; our favored country, happy in a striking contrast, has enjoyed general tranquillity—a tranquillity the more satisfactory, because maintained at the expense of no duty. Faithful to ourselves, we have violated no obligation to others. Our agriculture, commerce, and manufactures, prosper beyond former example; the molestations of our trade (to prevent a continuance of which, however, very pointed remonstrances have been made,) being over-balanced by the aggregate benefits which it derives from a neutral position. Our population advances with a celerity which, exceeding the most sanguine calculations, proportionally augments our strength and resources, and guarantees our future security. Every part of the Union displays indications of rapid and various improvement; and, with burthens so light as scarcely to be perceived; with resources fully adequate to our present exigencies; with governments founded on the genuine principles of rational liberty; and with mild and wholesome laws; is it too much to say, that our country exhibits a spectacle of national happiness, never surpassed, if ever before equalled?

Placed in a situation every way so auspicious, motives of commanding force impel us, with sincere acknowledgment to Heaven, and pure love to our country, to unite our efforts to preserve, prolong, and improve, our immense advantages. To co-operate with you in this desirable work, is a fervent and favorite wish of my heart.

It is a valuable ingredient in the general estimate of our welfare, that the part of our country which was lately the scene of disorder and insurrection, now enjoys the blessings of quiet and order. The misled have abandoned their errors, and pay the respect to our constitution and laws which is due from good citizens to the public authorities of the society. These circumstances have induced me to pardon, generally, the offenders here referred to, and to extend forgiveness to those who had been adjudged to capital punishment: for, though I shall always think it a sacred duty to exercise with firmness and energy the constitutional powers with which I am vested, yet it appears to me no less consistent with the public good, than it is with my personal feelings, to mingle in the operations of government every degree of moderation and tenderness which the national justice, dignity, and safety, may permit.

Gentlemen:

Among the objects which will claim your attention in the course of the session, a review of our military establishment is not the least important. It is called for by the events which have changed, and may be expected still further to change, the relative situation of our frontiers. In this review you will doubtless allow due weight to the considerations, that the questions between us and certain foreign Powers are not yet finally adjusted; that the war in Europe is not yet terminated; and that our western posts, when recovered, will demand provision for garrisoning and securing them. A statement of our present military force will be laid before you by the Department of War.

With the review of our army establishment is naturally connected that of the militia. It will merit inquiry, what imperfections in the existing plan further experience may have unfolded. The subject is of so much moment, in my estimation, as to excite a constant solicitude that the consideration of it may be renewed, till the greatest attainable perfection shall be accomplished. Time is wearing away some advantages for forwarding the object, while none better deserves the persevering attention of the public councils.

While we indulge the satisfaction which the actual condition of our western borders so well authorizes, it is necessary that we should not lose sight of an important truth, which continually receives new confirmations, namely, that the provisions heretofore made with a view to the protection of the Indians from the violences of the lawless part of our frontier inhabitants, are insufficient. It is demonstrated that these violences can now be perpetrated with impunity. And it can need no argument to prove that, unless the murdering of Indians can be restrained, by bringing the murderers to condign punishment, all the exertions of the Government to prevent destructive retaliations by the Indians, will prove fruitless, and all our present agreeable prospects illusory. The frequent destruction of innocent women and children, who are chiefly the victims of retaliation, must continue to shock humanity, and an enormous expense to drain the Treasury of the Union.

To enforce upon the Indians the observance of justice, it is indispensable that there shall be competent means of rendering justice to them. If these means can be devised by the wisdom of Congress, and especially if there can be added an adequate provision for supplying the necessities of the Indians, on reasonable terms, (a measure, the mention of which I the more readily repeat, as, in all the conferences with them, they urge it with solicitude,) I should not hesitate to entertain a strong hope of rendering our tranquillity permanent. I add, with pleasure, that the probability even of their civilization is not diminished by the experiments which have been thus far made under the auspices of Government. The accomplishment of this work, if practicable, will reflect undecaying lustre on our national character, and administer the most grateful consolations that virtuous minds can know.

Gentlemen of the House of Representatives:

The state of our revenue, with the sums which have been borrowed and reimbursed, pursuant to different acts of Congress, will be submitted from the proper department, together with an estimate of the appropriations necessary to be made for the service of the ensuing year.

Whether measures may not be advisable to reinforce the provision for the redemption of the public debt will naturally engage your examination. Congress have demonstrated their sense to be, and it were superfluous to repeat mine, that whatsoever will tend to accelerate the honorable extinction of our public debt, accords as much with the true interest of our country as with the general sense of our constituents.

Gentlemen of the Senate
and House of Representatives:

The statements which will be laid before you relative to the mint, will show the situation of that institution, and the necessity of some further legislative provisions for carrying the business of it more completely into effect, and for checking abuses which appear to be arising in particular quarters.

The progress in providing materials for the frigates, and in building them; the state of the fortifications of our harbors; the measures which have been pursued for obtaining proper sites for arsenals, and for replenishing our magazines with military stores; and the steps which have been taken towards the execution of the law for opening a trade with the Indians, will likewise be presented for the information of Congress.

Temperate discussion of the important subjects which may arise in the course of the session, and mutual forbearance where there is a difference of opinion, are too obvious and necessary for the peace, happiness, and welfare, of our country, to need any recommendation of mine.

GEO. WASHINGTON.

177

EIGHTH ANNUAL MESSAGE

Wednesday, December 7, 1796

Fellow-citizens of the Senate
and of the House of Representatives:

In recurring to the internal situation of our country, since I had last the pleasure to address you, I find ample reason for a renewed expression of that gratitude to the Ruler of the Universe, which a continued series of prosperity has so often and so justly called forth.

The acts of the last session, which required special arrangements, have been, as far as circumstances would admit, carried into operation.

Measures calculated to ensure a continuance of the friendship of the Indians, and to preserve peace along the extent of our interior frontier, have been digested and adopted. In the framing of these, care has been taken to guard, on the one hand, our advanced settlements from the predatory incursions of those unruly individuals who cannot be restrained by their tribes; and on the other hand to protect the rights secured to the Indians by treaties to draw them nearer to the civilized state; and inspire them with correct conceptions of the power as well as justice of the Government.

The meeting of the deputies from the Creek nation at Colerain, in the State of Georgia, which had for a principal object the purchase of a parcel of their land by that State, broke up without its being accomplished—the nation having, previous to their departure, instructed them against making any sale; the occasion however, has been improved, to confirm, by a new treaty with the Creeks, their pre-existing engagements with the United States, and to obtain their consent to the establishment of trading houses and military posts within their boundary; by means of which, their friendship, and the general peace, may be more effectually secured.

The period during the late session at which the appropriation was passed for carrying into effect the treaty of amity, commerce, and navigation, between the United States and his Britannic Majesty, necessarily procrastinated the reception of the posts stipulated to be delivered, beyond the date assigned for that event. As soon however, as the Governor General of

Canada could be addressed with propriety on the subject, arrangements were cordially and promptly concluded for their evacuation, and the United States took possession of the principal of them, comprehending Oswego, Niagara, Detroit, Michilimakinac, and Fort Miami, where such repairs and additions have been ordered to be made, as appeared indispensable.

The Commissioners appointed on the part of the United States and of Great Britain, to determine which is the river St. Croix, mentioned in the treaty of peace of 1783, agreed in the choice of Egbert Benson, Esq. of New York for the third commissioner. The whole met at St. Andrew's, in Passamaquoddy, Bay, in the beginning of October and directed surveys to be made of the rivers in dispute; but, deeming it impracticable to have these surveys completed before the next year, they adjourned, to meet at Boston, in August, 1797, for the final decision of the question.

Other commissioners, appointed on the part of the United States, agreeably to the seventh article of the treaty with Great Britain, relative to captures and condemnation of vessels and other property, met the commissioners of his Britannic Majesty, in London, in August last, when John Trumbull, Esq. was chosen by lot, for the fifth commissioner. In October following, the Board were to proceed to business. As yet, there has been no communication of commissioners on the part of Great Britain, to unite with those who have been appointed on the part of the United States, for carrying into effect the sixth article of the treaty.

The treaty with Spain required that the commissioners for running the boundary line between the territory the United States and his Catholic Majesty's provinces of East and West Florida should meet at the Natchez before the expiration of six months after the exchange of the ratifications, which was effected at Aranjuez on the twenty-fifth day of April; and the troops of his Catholic Majesty occupying any posts within the limits of the United States, were, within the same period, to be withdrawn. The commissioner of the United States, therefore, commenced his journey for the Natchez in September; and troops were ordered to occupy the posts from which the Spanish garrisons should be withdrawn. Information has been recently received of the appointment of a commissioner on the part of his Catholic Majesty, for running the boundary line;

but none of any appointment for the adjustment of the claims of our citizens whose vessels were captured by the armed vessels of Spain.

In pursuance of the act of Congress passed in the last session, for the protection and relief of American seamen, agents were appointed, one to reside in Great Britain, and the other in the West Indies. The effects of the agents in the West Indies are not yet fully ascertained; but those which have been communicated afford grounds to believe the measure will be beneficial. The agent destined to reside in Great Britain declining to accept the appointment, the business has consequently devolved on the Minister of the United States in London, and will command his attention until a new agent shall be appointed.

After many delays and disappointments, arising out of the European war, the final arrangements for fulfilling the engagements made to the Dey and Regency of Algiers, will, in all present appearance, be crowned with success but under great, though inevitable disadvantages, in the pecuniary transactions, occasioned by that war, which will render a further provision necessary. The actual liberation of all our citizens who were prisoners in Algiers, while it gratifies every feeling heart, is itself an earnest of a satisfactory termination of the whole negotiation. Measures are in operation for effecting treaties with the Regencies of Tunis and Tripoli.

To an active external commerce, the protection of a naval force is indispensable. This is manifest with regard to wars in which a State is itself a party. But besides this, it is in our own experience, that the most sincere neutrality is not a sufficient guard against the depredations of nations at war. To secure respect to a neutral flag, requires a naval force, organized and ready to vindicate it from insult or aggression. This may even prevent the necessity of going to war, by discouraging belligerent Powers from committing such violations of the rights of the neutral party, as may, first or last, leave no other option. From the best information I have been able to obtain, it would seem as if our trade to the Mediterranean, without a protecting force, will always be insecure, and our citizens exposed to the calamities from which numbers of them have but just been relieved.

These considerations invite the United States to look to the means, and to set about the gradual creation of a navy. The increasing progress of their navigation promises them, at no distant period, the requisite supply of seamen; and their means, in other respects, favor the undertaking. It is an encouragement, likewise, that their particular situation will give weight and influence to a moderate naval force in their hands. Will it not then be advisable to begin, without delay, to provide and lay up the materials for the building and equipping of ships of war, and to proceed in the work, by degrees, in proportion as our resources shall render it practicable without inconvenience; so that a future war of Europe may not find our commerce in the same unprotected state in which it was found by the present?

Congress have repeatedly, and not without success, directed their attention to the encouragement of manufactures. The object is of too much consequence not to ensure a continuance of their efforts in every way which shall appear eligible. As a general rule, manufactures on public account are inexpedient; but where the state of things in a country leaves little hope that certain branches of manufactures will, for a great length of time, obtain; when these are of a nature essential to the furnishing and equipping of the public force, in time of war; are not establishments for procuring them on public account, to the extent of the ordinary demand for the public service, recommended by strong considerations of national policy, as an exception to the general rule? Ought our country to remain in such cases dependent on foreign supply, precarious, because liable to be interrupted? If the necessary article should, in this mode, cost more in time of peace, will not the security and independence thence arising, form an ample compensation? Establishments of this sort, commensurate only with the calls of the public service in time of peace, will, in time of war, easily be extended in proportion to the exigencies of the Government, and may even perhaps be made to yield a surplus for the supply of our citizens at large, so as to mitigate the privations from the interruption of their trade. If adopted, the plan ought to exclude all those branches which are already or likely soon to be established in the country; in order that there may be no danger of interference with pursuits of individual industry.

It will not be doubted that, with reference either to individual or national welfare, agriculture is of primary importance. In proportion as nations advance in population and other circumstances of maturity, this truth becomes more apparent, and renders the cultivation of the soil more and more an object of public patronage. Institutions for promoting it, grow up, supported by the public purse: and to what object can it be dedicated with greater propriety? Among the means which have been employed to this end, none have been attended with greater success than the establishment of Boards, composed of proper characters, charged with collecting and diffusing information, and enabled, by premiums and small pecuniary aids, to encourage and assist a spirit of discovery and improvement. This species of establishment contributes doubly to the increase of improvement, by stimulating to enterprise and experiment, and by drawing to a common centre the results every where of individual skill and observation, and spreading them thence over the whole nation. Experience accordingly has shown, that they are very cheap instruments of immense national benefits.

I have heretofore proposed to the consideration of Congress, the expediency of establishing a national university, and also a military academy. The desirableness of both these institutions has so constantly increased with every new view I have taken of the subject, that I cannot omit the opportunity of once for all recalling your attention to them.

The assembly to which I address myself, is too enlightened not to be fully sensible how much a flourishing state of the arts and sciences contributes to national prosperity and reputation. True it is, that our country, much to its honor, contains many seminaries of learning, highly respectable and useful; but the funds upon which they rest are too narrow to command the ablest professors in the different departments of liberal knowledge, for the institution contemplated, though they would be excellent auxiliaries.

Amongst the motives to such an institution, the assimilation of the principles, opinions, and manners, of our countrymen, by the common education of a portion of our youth from every quarter, well deserves attention. The more homogeneous our citizens can be made in these particulars, the greater will be our prospect of permanent union; and a primary object of such a national institution should be, the education of our youth in the science of *government*. In a republic, what species of knowledge can be equally important? and what duty more pressing on its legislature, than to patronize a plan for communicating it to those who are to be the future guardians of the liberties of the country?

The institution of a military academy is also recommended by cogent reasons. However pacific the general policy of a nation may be, it ought never to be without an adequate stock of military knowledge for emergencies. The first would impair the energy of its character, and both would hazard its safety, or expose it to greater evils when war could not be avoided. Besides, that war might often not depend upon its own choice. In proportion as the observance of pacific maxims might exempt a nation from the necessity of practising the rules of the military art, ought to be its care in preserving and transmitting, by proper establishments, the knowledge of that art. Whatever argument may be drawn from particular examples, superficially viewed, a thorough examination of the subject will evince, that the art of war is at once comprehensive and complicated; that it demands much previous study; and that the possession of it, in its most improved and perfect state, is always of great moment to the security of a nation. This, therefore, ought to be a serious care of every government; and for this purpose an academy, where a regular course of instruction is given, is an obvious expedient, which different nations have successfully employed.

The compensations to the officers of the United States, in various instances, and in none more than in respect to the most important stations, appear to call for legislative revision. The consequences of a defective provision are of serious import to the Government. If private wealth is to supply the defect of public retribution, it will greatly contract the sphere within which the selection of character for office is to be made, and will proportionally diminish the probability of a choice of men able as well as upright. Besides, that it would be repugnant to the vital principles of our Government, virtually to exclude from public trusts, talents and virtue, unless accompanied by wealth.

While, in our external relations, some serious inconveniences and embarrassments have been overcome, and others lessened, it is with much pain and deep regret I mention, that circumstances of a very unwelcome nature have lately occurred. Our trade has suffered, and is suffering, extensive injuries in the West Indies, from the cruisers and agents of the French republic; and communications have been received from its minister here, which indicate the danger of a further disturbance of our commerce by its authority; and which are, in other respects, far from agreeable.

It has been my constant, sincere, and earnest wish, in conformity with that of our nation, to maintain cordial harmony and a perfectly friendly understanding with that republic. This wish remains unabated; and I shall persevere in the endeavor to fulfil it, to the utmost extent of what shall be consistent with a just and indispensable regard to the rights and honor of our country; nor will I easily cease to cherish the expectation, that a spirit of justice, candor, and friendship, on the part of the republic, will eventually ensure success.

In pursuing this course, however, I cannot forget what is due to the character of our government and nation; or to a full and entire confidence in the good sense, patriotism, self-respect, and fortitude, of my countrymen.

I reserve for a special message a more particular communication on this interesting subject.

Gentlemen of the House of Representatives:

I have directed an estimate of the appropriations, necessary for the service of the ensuing year, to be submitted from the proper department; with a view of the public receipts and expenditures to the latest period to which an account can be prepared.

It is with satisfaction I am able to inform you, that the revenues of the United States continue in a state of progressive improvement.

A reinforcement of the existing provisions for discharging our public debt was mentioned in my address at the opening of the last session. Some preliminary steps were taken towards it, the maturing of which will, no doubt, engage your zealous attention during the present. I will only add, that it will afford me a heartfelt satisfaction to concur in such further measures as will ascertain to our country the prospect of a speedy extinguishment of the debt. Posterity may have cause to regret, if, from any motive, intervals of tranquillity are left unimproved for accelerating this valuable end.

Gentlemen of the Senate
and of the House of Representatives:

My solicitude to see the militia of the United States placed on an efficient establishment, has been so often and so ardently expressed, that I shall but barely recall the subject to your view on the present occasion; at the same time that I shall submit to your inquiry, whether our harbors are yet sufficiently secured?

The situation in which I now stand, for the last time, in the midst of the Representatives of the People of the United States, naturally recalls the period when the administration of the present form of government commenced; and I cannot omit the occasion to congratulate you, and my country, on the success of the experiment; nor to repeat my fervent supplications to the Supreme Ruler of the universe and Sovereign Arbiter of nations, that his providential care may still be extended to the United States; that the virtue and happiness of the People may be preserved; and that the government which they have instituted for the protection of their liberties may be perpetual.

GEO. WASHINGTON.

178

FAREWELL ADDRESS

United States, September 19, 1796

Friends, and Fellow-Citizens:

The period for a new election of a Citizen, to Administer the Executive government of the United States, being not far distant, and the time actually arrived, when your thoughts must be employed in designating the person, who is to be cloathed with that important trust, it appears to me proper, especially as it may conduce to a more distinct expression of the public voice, that I should now apprise you of the resolution I have formed, to decline being considered among the number of those, out of whom a choice is to be made.

Declining to run again for presidency

I beg you, at the same time, to do me the justice to be assured, that this resolution has not been taken, without a strict regard to all the considerations appertaining to the relation, which binds a dutiful citizen to his country, and that, in withdrawing the tender of service which silence in my situation might imply, I am influenced by no diminution of zeal for your future interest, no deficiency of grateful respect for your past kindness; but am supported by a full conviction that the step is compatible with both.

The acceptance of, and continuance hitherto in, the office to which your Suffrages have twice called me, have been a uniform sacrifice of inclination to the opinion of duty, and to a deference for what appeared to be your desire. I constantly hoped, that it would have been much earlier in my power, consistently with motives, which I was not at liberty to disregard, to return to that retirement, from which I had been reluctantly drawn. The strength of my inclination to do this, previous to the last Election, had even led to the preparation of an address to declare it to you; but mature reflection on the then perplexed and critical posture of our Affairs with foreign Nations, and the unanimous advice of persons entitled to my confidence, impelled me to abandon the idea. *Previous wish to retire after first term*

I rejoice, that the state of your concerns, external as well as internal, no longer renders the pursuit of inclination incompatible with the sentiment of duty, or propriety; and am persuaded whatever partiality may be retained for my services, that in the present circumstances of our country, you will not disapprove my determination to retire.

The impressions, with which I first undertook the arduous trust, were explained on the proper occasion. In the discharge of this trust, I will only say, that I have, with good intentions, contributed towards the Organization and Administration of the government, the best exertions of which a very fallible judgment was capable. Not unconscious, in the outset, of the inferiority of my qualifications, experience in my own eyes, perhaps still more in the eyes of others, has strengthned the motives to diffidence of myself; and every day the encreasing weight of years admonishes me more and more, that the shade of retirement is as necessary to me as it will be welcome. Satisfied that if any circumstances have given peculiar value to my services, they were temporary, I have the consolation to believe, that while choice and prudence invite me to quit the political scene, patriotism does not forbid it.

In looking forward to the moment, which is intended to terminate the career of my public life, my feelings do not permit me to suspend the deep acknowledgment of that debt of gratitude wch. I owe to my beloved country, for the many honors it has conferred upon me; still more for the stedfast *Debt of gratitude to country* confidence with which it has supported me; and for the opportunities I have thence enjoyed of manifesting my inviolable attachment, by services faithful and persevering, though in usefulness unequal to my zeal. If benefits have resulted to our country from these services, let it always be remembered to your praise, and as an instructive example in our annals, that, under circumstances in which the Passions agitated in every direction were liable to mislead, amidst appearances sometimes dubious, viscissitudes of fortune often discouraging, in situations in which not unfrequently want of Success has countenanced the spirit of criticism, the constancy of your support was the essential prop of the efforts, and a guarantee of the plans by which they were effected. Profoundly penetrated with this idea, I shall carry it with me to my grave, as a strong incitement to unceasing vows that Heaven may continue to you the choicest tokens of its beneficence; that your Union and brotherly affection may be perpetual; that the free constitution, which is the work of your hands, may be sacredly maintained; that its Administration in every department may be stamped with wisdom and Virtue; that, in fine, the happiness of the people of these States, under the auspices of liberty, may be made complete, by so careful a preservation and so prudent a use of this blessing as will acquire to them the glory of recommending it to the applause, the affection, and adoption of every nation which is yet a stranger to it.

Solicitude for future welfare of nation

Here, perhaps, I ought to stop. But a solicitude for your welfare, which cannot end but with my life, and the apprehension of danger, natural to that solicitude, urge me on an occasion like the present, to offer to your solemn contemplation, and to recommend to your frequent review, some sentiments; which are the result of much reflection, of no inconsiderable observation, and which appear to me all important to the permanency of your felicity as a People. These will be offered to you with the more freedom, as you can only see in them the disinterested warnings of a parting friend, who can possibly have no personal motive to biass his counsel. Nor can I forget, as an encouragement to it, your endulgent reception of my sentiments on a former and not dissimilar occasion.

Interwoven as is the love of liberty with every ligament of your hearts, no recommendation of mine is necessary to fortify or confirm the attachment.

The Unity of Government which constitutes you one people is also now dear to you. It is justly so; for it is a main Pillar in the Edifice of your real independence, the support of your tranquility at home; your peace abroad; of your safety; of your prosperity; of that very Liberty which you so highly prize. But as it is easy to foresee, that from different causes and from different quarters, much pains will be taken, many artifices employed, to weaken in your minds the conviction of this truth; as this is the point in your political fortress against which the batteries of internal and external enemies will be most constantly and actively (though often covertly and insidiously) directed, it is of infinite moment, that you should properly estimate the immense value of your national Union to your collective and individual happiness; that you should cherish a cordial, habitual and immoveable attachment to it; accustoming yourselves to think and speak of it as of the Palladium of your political safety and prosperity; watching for its preservation with jealous anxiety; discountenancing whatever may suggest even a suspicion that it can in any event be abandoned, and indignantly frowning upon the first dawning of every attempt to alienate any portion of our Country from the rest, or to enfeeble the sacred ties which now link together the various parts.

Unity of government, liberty, independence

National union and collective and individual happiness

For this you have every inducement of sympathy and interest. Citizens by birth or choice, of a common country, that country has a right to concentrate your affections. The name of AMERICAN, which belongs to you, in your national capacity, must always exalt the just pride of Patriotism, more than any appellation derived from local discriminations. With slight shades of difference, you have the same Religion, Manners, Habits and political Principles. You have in a common cause fought and triumphed together. The independence and liberty you possess are the work of joint councils, and joint efforts; of common dangers, sufferings and successes.

A common cause

But these considerations, however powerfully they address themselves to your sensibility are greatly outweighed by those which apply more immediately to your Interest. Here every portion of our country finds the most commanding motives for carefully guarding and preserving the Union of the whole.

The *North*, in an unrestrained intercourse with the *South*, protected by the equal Laws of a common government, finds

North and South

in the productions of the latter, great additional resources of Maritime and commercial enterprise and precious materials of manufacturing industry. The *South* in the same Intercourse, benefitting by the Agency of the *North*, sees its agriculture grow and its commerce expand. Turning partly into its own channels the seamen of the *North*, it finds its particular navigation envigorated; and while it contributes, in different ways, to nourish and increase the general mass of the National navigation, it looks forward to the protection of a Maritime strength, to which itself is unequally adapted. The *East*, in a like intercourse with the *West*, already finds, and in the progressive improvement of interior communications, by land and water, will more and more find a valuable vent for the commodities which it brings from abroad, or manufactures at home. The *West* derives from the *East* supplies requisite to its growth and comfort, and what is perhaps of still greater consequence, it must of necessity owe the *secure* enjoyment of indispensable *outlets* for its own productions to the weight, influence, and the future Maritime strength of the Atlantic side of the Union, directed by an indissoluble community of Interest as *one Nation.* Any other tenure by which the *West* can hold this essential advantage, whether derived from its own seperate strength, or from an apostate and unnatural connection with any foreign Power, must be intrinsically precarious.

East and West

While then every part of our country thus feels an immediate and particular Interest in Union, all the parts combined cannot fail to find in the united mass of means and efforts greater strength, greater resource, proportionably greater security from external danger, a less frequent interruption of their Peace by foreign Nations; and, what is of inestimable value! they must derive from Union an exemption from those broils and Wars between themselves, which so frequently afflict neighbouring countries, not tied together by the same government; which their own rivalships alone would be sufficient to produce, but which opposite foreign alliances, attachments and intriegues would stimulate and imbitter. Hence likewise they will avoid the necessity of those overgrown Military establishments, which under any form of Government are inauspicious to liberty, and which are to be regarded as particularly hostile to Republican Liberty: In this sense it is, that your Union ought to be considered as a main prop of your

Union's security and lessened rivalry

Military establishments

liberty, and that the love of the one ought to endear to you the preservation of the other.

These considerations speak a persuasive language to every reflecting and virtuous mind, and exhibit the continuance of the UNION as a primary object of Patriotic desire. Is there a doubt, whether a common government can embrace so large a sphere? Let experience solve it. To listen to mere speculation in such a case were criminal. We are authorized to hope that a proper organization of the whole, with the auxiliary agency of governments for the respective Subdivisions, will afford a happy issue to the experiment. 'Tis well worth a fair and full experiment. With such powerful and obvious motives to Union, affecting all parts of our country, while experience shall not have demonstrated its impracticability, there will always be reason, to distrust the patriotism of those, who in any quarter may endeavor to weaken its bands.

Union over extensive territory

In contemplating the causes wch. may disturb our Union, it occurs as matter of serious concern, that any ground should have been furnished for characterizing parties by *Geographical* discriminations: *Northern* and *Southern*; *Atlantic* and *Western*; whence designing men may endeavour to excite a belief that there is a real difference of local interests and views. One of the expedients of Party to acquire influence, within particular districts, is to misrepresent the opinions and aims of other Districts. You cannot shield yourselves too much against the jealousies and heart burnings which spring from these misrepresentations. They tend to render Alien to each other those who ought to be bound together by fraternal affection. The Inhabitants of our Western country have lately had a useful lesson on this head. They have seen, in the Negociation by the Executive, and in the unanimous ratification by the Senate, of the Treaty with Spain, and in the universal satisfaction at that event, throughout the United States, a decisive proof how unfounded were the suspicions propagated among them of a policy in the General Government and in the Atlantic States unfriendly to their Interests in regard to the Mississippi. They have been witnesses to the formation of two Treaties, that with G: Britain and that with Spain, which secure to them every thing they could desire, in respect to our Foreign relations, towards confirming their prosperity. Will it not be their wisdom to rely for the preservation of these advantages on the

Geographical discriminations which may disturb union

Union by wch. they were procured? Will they not henceforth be deaf to those advisers, if such there are, who would sever them from their Brethren and connect them with Aliens?

To the efficacy and permanency of Your Union, a Government for the whole is indispensable. No Alliances however strict between the parts can be an adequate substitute. They must inevitably experience the infractions and interruptions which all Alliances in all times have experienced. Sensible of this momentous truth, you have improved upon your first essay, by the adoption of a Constitution of Government, better calculated than your former for an intimate Union, and for the efficacious management of your common concerns. This government, the offspring of our own choice uninfluenced and unawed, adopted upon full investigation and mature deliberation, completely free in its principles, in the distribution of its powers, uniting security with energy, and containing within itself a provision for its own amendment, has a just claim to your confidence and your support. Respect for its authority, compliance with its Laws, acquiescence in its measures, are duties enjoined by the fundamental maxims of true Liberty. The basis of our political systems is the right of the people to make and to alter their Constitutions of Government. But the Constitution which at any time exists, 'till changed by an explicit and authentic act of the whole People, is sacredly obligatory upon all. The very idea of the power and the right of the People to establish Government presupposes the duty of every Individual to obey the established Government.

All obstructions to the execution of the Laws, all combinations and Associations, under whatever plausible character, with the real design to direct, controul counteract, or awe the regular deliberation and action of the Constituted authorities are distructive of this fundamental principle and of fatal tendency. They serve to organize faction, to give it an artificial and extraordinary force; to put in the place of the delegated will of the Nation, the will of a party; often a small but artful and enterprizing minority of the Community; and, according to the alternate triumphs of different parties, to make the public administration the Mirror of the ill concerted and incongruous projects of faction, rather than the organ of consistent and wholesome plans digested by common councils and modefied by mutual interests. However combinations or Associa-

The new Constitution

Faction

tions of the above description may now and then answer popular ends, they are likely, in the course of time and things, to become potent engines, by which cunning, ambitious and unprincipled men will be enabled to subvert the Power of the People, and to usurp for themselves the reins of Government; destroying afterwards the very engines which have lifted them to unjust dominion.

Towards the preservation of your Government and the permanency of your present happy state, it is requisite, not only that you steadily discountenance irregular oppositions to its acknowledged authority, but also that you resist with care the spirit of innovation upon its principles however specious the pretexts. one method of assault may be to effect, in the forms of the Constitution, alterations which will impair the energy of the system, and thus to undermine what cannot be directly overthrown. In all the changes to which you may be invited, remember that time and habit are at least as necessary to fix the true character of Governments, as of other human institutions; that experience is the surest standard, by which to test the real tendency of the existing Constitution of a country; that facility in changes upon the credit of mere hypotheses and opinion exposes to perpetual change, from the endless variety of hypotheses and opinion: and remember, especially, that for the efficient management of your common interests, in a country so extensive as ours, a Government of as much vigour as is consistent with the perfect security of Liberty is indispensable. Liberty itself will find in such a Government, with powers properly distributed and adjusted, its surest Guardian. It is indeed little else than a name, where the Government is too feeble to withstand the enterprises of faction, to confine each member of the Society within the limits prescribed by the laws and to maintain all in the secure and tranquil enjoyment of the rights of person and property.

Spirit of innovation and the Constitution

Liberty and the Constitution

I have already intimated to you the danger of Parties in the State, with particular reference to the founding of them on Geographical discriminations. Let me now take a more comprehensive view, and warn you in the most solemn manner against the baneful effects of the Spirit of Party, generally.

Spirit of party, in general

This spirit, unfortunately, is inseperable from our nature, having its root in the strongest passions of the human Mind. It exists under different shapes in all Governments, more or less stifled, controuled, or repressed; but, in those of the popular form it is seen in its greatest rankness and is truly their worst enemy.

The alternate domination of one faction over another, sharpened by the spirit of revenge natural to party dissention, which in different ages and countries has perpetrated the most horrid enormities, is itself a frightful despotism. But this leads at length to a more formal and permanent despotism. The disorders and miseries, which result, gradually incline the minds of men to seek security and repose in the absolute power of an Individual: and sooner or later the chief of some prevailing faction more able or more fortunate than his competitors, turns this disposition to the purposes of his own elevation, on the ruins of Public Liberty.

Without looking forward to an extremity of this kind (which nevertheless ought not to be entirely out of sight) the common and continual mischiefs of the spirit of Party are sufficient to make it the interest and the duty of a wise People to discourage and restrain it.

It serves always to distract the Public Councils and enfeeble the Public administration. It agitates the Community with ill founded jealousies and false alarms, kindles the animosity of one part against another, foments occasionally riot and insurrection. It opens the door to foreign influence and corruption, which find a facilitated access to the government itself through the channels of party passions. Thus the policy and the will of one country, are subjected to the policy and will of another.

Parties in free countries

There is an opinion that parties in free countries are useful checks upon the Administration of the Government and serve to keep alive the spirit of Liberty. This within certain limits is probably true, and in Governments of a Monarchical cast Patriotism may look with endulgence, if not with favour, upon the spirit of party. But in those of the popular character, in Governments purely elective, it is a spirit not to be encouraged. From their natural tendency, it is certain there will always be enough of that spirit for every salutary purpose. And there being constant danger of excess, the effort ought to be, by force of public opinion, to mitigate and assuage it. A fire not to be quenched; it demands a uniform vigilance to prevent its bursting into a flame, lest instead of warming it should consume.

Separation of powers

It is important, likewise, that the habits of thinking in a free Country should inspire caution in those entrusted with its administration, to confine themselves within their respective Constitutional spheres; avoiding in the exercise of the Powers of one department to encroach upon another. The spirit of encroachment tends to consolidate the powers of all the departments in one, and thus to create whatever the form of government, a real despotism. A just estimate of that love of power, and proneness to abuse it, which predominates in the human heart is sufficient to satisfy us of the truth of this position. The necessity of reciprocal checks in the exercise of political power; by dividing and distributing it into different depositories, and constituting each the Guardian of the Public Weal against invasions by the others, has been evinced by experiments ancient and modern; some of them in our country and under our own eyes. To preserve them must be as necessary as to institute them. If in the opinion of the People, the distribution or modification of the Constitutional powers be in any particular wrong, let it be corrected by an amendment in the way which the Constitution designates. But let there be no change by usurpation; for though this, in one instance, may be the instrument of good, it is the customary weapon by which free governments are destroyed. The precedent must always greatly overbalance in permanent evil any partial or transient benefit which the use can at any time yield.

Of all the dispositions and habits which lead to political prosperity, Religion and morality are indispensable supports. *Religion and morality* In vain would that man claim the tribute of Patriotism, who should labour to subvert these great Pillars of human happiness, these firmest props of the duties of Men and citizens. The mere Politician, equally with the pious man ought to respect and to cherish them. A volume could not trace all their connections with private and public felicity. Let it simply be asked where is the security for property, for reputation, for life, if the sense of religious obligation *desert* the oaths, which are the instruments of investigation in Courts of Justice? And let us with caution indulge the supposition, that morality can be maintained without religion. Whatever may be conceded to the influence of refined education on minds of peculiar structure, reason and experience both forbid us to expect that National morality can prevail in exclusion of religious principle.

'Tis substantially true, that virtue or morality is a necessary spring of popular government. The rule indeed extends with more or less force to every species of free Government. Who that is a sincere friend to it, can look with indifference upon attempts to shake the foundation of the fabric

General diffusion of knowledge

Promote then as an object of primary importance, Institutions for the general diffusion of knowledge. In proportion as the structure of a government gives force to public opinion, it is essential that public opinion should be enlightened

Public credit

As a very important source of strength and security, cherish public credit. One method of preserving it is to use it as sparingly as possible: avoiding occasions of expence by cultivating peace, but remembering also that timely disbursements to prepare for danger frequently prevent much greater disbursements to repel it; avoiding likewise the accumulation of debt, not only by shunning occasions of expence, but by vigorous exertions in time of Peace to discharge the Debts which unavoidable wars may have occasioned, not ungenerously throwing upon posterity the burthen which we ourselves ought to bear. The execution of these maxims belongs to your Representatives, but it is necessary that public opinion should cooperate. To facilitate to them the performance of their duty, it is essential that you should practically bear in mind, that towards the payment of debts there must be Revenue; that to have Revenue there must be taxes; that no taxes can be devised which are not more or less inconvenient and unpleasant; that the intrinsic embarrassment inseperable from the selection of the proper objects (which is always a choice of difficulties) ought to be a decisive motive for a candid construction of the Conduct of the Government in making it, and for a spirit of acquiescence in the measures for obtaining Revenue which the public exigencies may at any time dictate.

Taxation

Policy towards foreign nations

Observe good faith and justice towds. all Nations. Cultivate peace and harmony with all. Religion and morality enjoin this conduct; and can it be that good policy does not equally enjoin it? It will be worthy of a free, enlightened, and, at no distant period, a great Nation, to give to mankind the magnanimous and too novel example of a People always guided by an exalted justice and benevolence. Who can doubt that in the course of time and things the fruits of such a plan would richly repay any temporary advantages wch. might be lost by a steady adherence to it? Can it be, that Providence has not connected the permanent felicity of a Nation with its virtue? The experiment, at least, is recommended by every sentiment which ennobles human Nature. Alas! is it rendered impossible by its vices?

In the execution of such a plan nothing is more essential than that permanent, inveterate antipathies against particular Nations and passionate attachments for others should be excluded; and that in place of them just and amicable feelings towards all should be cultivated. The Nation, which indulges towards another an habitual hatred, or an habitual fondness, is in some degree a slave. It is a slave to its animosity or to its affection, either of which is sufficient to lead it astray from its duty and its interest. Antipathy in one Nation against another, disposes each more readily to offer insult and injury, to lay hold of slight causes of umbrage, and to be haughty and intractable, when accidental or trifling occasions of dispute occur. Hence frequent collisions, obstinate envenomed and bloody contests. The Nation, prompted by ill will and resentment sometimes impels to War the Government, contrary to the best calculations of policy. The Government sometimes participates in the national propensity, and adopts through passion what reason would reject; at other times, it makes the animosity of the Nation subservient to projects of hostility instigated by pride, ambition and other sinister and pernicious motives. The peace often, sometimes perhaps the Liberty, of Nations has been the victim.

So likewise, a passionate attachment of one Nation for another produces a variety of evils. Sympathy for the favourite nation, facilitating the illusion of an imaginary common interest, in cases where no real common interest exists, and infusing into one the enmities of the other, betrays the former into a participation in the quarrels and Wars of the latter, without adequate inducement or justification: It leads also to concessions to the favourite Nation of priviledges denied to others, which is apt doubly to injure the Nation making the concessions; by unnecessarily parting with what ought to have been retained; and by exciting jealousy, ill will, and a disposition to retaliate, in the parties from whom eql. priviledges are withheld: And it gives to ambitious, corrupted, or deluded citizens (who devote themselves to the favourite Nation) facility to betray, or sacrifice the interests of their own country, without odium, sometimes even with popularity; gilding with the appearances of a virtuous sense of obligation a commendable deference for public opinion, or a laudable zeal for public good, the base or foolish compliances of ambition corruption or infatuation.

As avenues to foreign influence in innumerable ways, such attachments are particularly alarming to the truly enlightened and independent Patriot. How many opportunities do they afford to tamper with domestic factions, to practice the arts of seduction, to mislead public opinion, to influence or awe the public Councils! Such an attachment of a small or weak, towards a great and powerful Nation, dooms the former to be the satellite of the latter.

Wiles of foreign influence

Against the insidious wiles of foreign influence, (I conjure you to believe me fellow citizens) the jealousy of a free people ought to be *constantly* awake; since history and experience prove that foreign influence is one of the most baneful foes of Republican Government. But that jealousy to be useful must be impartial; else it becomes the instrument of the very influence to be avoided, instead of a defence against it. Excessive partiality for one foreign nation and excessive dislike of another, cause those whom they actuate to see danger only on one side, and serve to veil and even second the arts of influence on the other. Real Patriots, who may resist the intriegues of the favourite, are liable to become suspected and odious; while its tools and dupes usurp the applause and confidence of the people, to surrender their interests.

The Great rule of conduct for us, in regard to foreign Nations is in extending our commercial relations to have with them as little *political* connection as possible. So far as we have already formed engagements let them be fulfilled, with perfect good faith. Here let us stop.

Europe and America

Europe has a set of primary interests, which to us have none, or a very remote relation. Hence she must be engaged in frequent controversies, the causes of which are essentially foreign to our concerns. Hence therefore it must be unwise in us to implicate ourselves, by artificial ties, in the ordinary vicissitudes of her politics, or the ordinary combinations and collisions of her friendships, or enmities:

Our detached and distant situation invites and enables us to pursue a different course. If we remain one People, under an efficient government, the period is not far off, when we may defy material injury from external annoyance; when we may take such an attitude as will cause the neutrality we may at any time resolve upon to be scrupulously respected; when belligerent nations, under the impossibility of making acquisitions upon us, will not lightly hazard the giving us provocation; when we may choose peace or war, as our interest guided by our justice shall Counsel.

Why forego the advantages of so peculiar a situation? Why quit our own to stand upon foreign ground? Why, by interweaving our destiny with that of any part of Europe, entangle our peace and prosperity in the toils of European Ambition, Rivalship, Interest, Humour or Caprice?

'Tis our true policy to steer clear of permanent Alliances, with any portion of the foreign world. So far, I mean, as we are now at liberty to do it, for let me not be understood as capable of patronising infidility to existing engagements (I hold the maxim no less applicable to public than to private affairs, that honesty is always the best policy). I repeat it therefore, let those engagements be observed in their genuine sense. But in my opinion, it is unnecessary and would be unwise to extend them. *Alliances*

Taking care always to keep ourselves, by suitable establishments, on a respectably defensive posture, we may safely trust to temporary alliances for extraordinary emergencies.

Harmony, liberal intercourse with all Nations, are recommended by policy, humanity and interest. But even our Commercial policy should hold an equal and impartial hand: neither seeking nor granting exclusive favours or preferences; consulting the natural course of things; diffusing and deversifying by gentle means the streams of Commerce, but forcing nothing; establishing with Powers so disposed; in order to give to trade a stable course, to define the rights of our Merchants, and to enable the Government to support them; conventional rules of intercourse, the best that present circumstances and mutual opinion will permit, but temporary, and liable to be from time to time abandoned or varied, as experience and circumstances shall dictate; constantly keeping in view, that 'tis folly in one Nation to look for disinterested favors from another; that it must pay with a portion of its Independence for whatever it may accept under that character; that by such acceptance, it may place itself in the condition of having given equivalents for nominal favours and yet of being reproached with ingratitude for not giving more. There can be no greater error than to expect, or calculate upon real favours from Na- *Commercial policy* tion to Nation. 'Tis an illusion which experience must cure, which a just pride ought to discard.

In offering to you, my Countrymen these counsels of an old and affectionate friend, I dare not hope they will make the strong and lasting impression, I could wish; that they will controul the usual current of the passions, or prevent our Nation from running the course which has hitherto marked the Destiny of Nations: But if I may even flatter myself, that they may be productive of some partial benefit, some occasional good; that they may now and then recur to moderate the fury of party spirit, to warn against the mischiefs of foreign Intriegue, to guard against the Impostures of pretended patriotism; this hope will be a full recompence for the solicitude for your welfare, by which they have been dictated.

How far in the discharge of my Official duties, I have been guided by the principles which have been delineated, the public Records and other evidences of my conduct must Witness to You and to the world. To myself, the assurance of my own conscience is, that I have at least believed myself to be guided by them.

Neutral conduct In relation to the still subsisting War in Europe, my Proclamation of the 22d. of April 1793 is the index to my Plan. Sanctioned by your approving voice and by that of Your Representatives in both Houses of Congress, the spirit of that measure has continually governed me; uninfluenced by any attempts to deter or divert me from it.

After deliberate examination with the aid of the best lights I could obtain I was well satisfied that our Country, under all the circumstances of the case, had a right to take, and was bound in duty and interest, to take a Neutral position. Having taken it, I determined, as far as should depend upon me, to maintain it, with moderation, perseverence and firmness.

The considerations, which respect the right to hold this conduct, it is not necessary on this occasion to detail. I will only observe, that according to my understanding of the matter, that right, so far from being denied by any of the Belligerent Powers has been virtually admitted by all.

The duty of holding a Neutral conduct may be inferred, without any thing more, from the obligation which justice and humanity impose on every Nation, in cases in which it is free to act, to maintain inviolate the relations of Peace and amity towards other Nations.

The inducements of interest for observing that conduct will best be referred to your own reflections and experience. With me, a predominant motive has been to endeavour to gain time to our country to settle and mature its yet recent institutions, and to progress without interruption, to that degree of strength and consistency, which is necessary to give it, humanly speaking, the command of its own fortunes.

Though in reviewing the incidents of my Administration, I am unconscious of intentional error, I am nevertheless too sensible of my defects not to think it probable that I may have committed many errors. Whatever they may be I fervently beseech the Almighty to avert or mitigate the evils to which they may tend. I shall also carry with me the hope that my Country will never cease to view them with indulgence; and that after forty five years of my life dedicated to its Service, with an upright zeal, the faults of incompetent abilities will be consigned to oblivion, as myself must soon be to the Mansions of rest. *Conclusion*

Relying on its kindness in this as in other things, and actuated by that fervent love towards it, which is so natural to a Man, who views in it the native soil of himself and his progenitors for several Generations; I anticipate with pleasing expectation that retreat, in which I promise myself to realize, without alloy, the sweet enjoyment of partaking, in the midst of my fellow Citizens, the benign influence of good Laws under a free Government, the ever favourite object of my heart, and the happy reward, as I trust, of our mutual cares, labours and dangers.

CHAPTER TWELVE

WASHINGTON

Washington the President

1789 – 1791

*W*E *principally behold Washington, in the follow-ing pages, describing the character of his country and administration in general correspondence, rath-er than in official acts. Thus it is that, in the course of* pro forma *responses to congratulatory letters, Washing-ton candidly declared what he conceived as the breadth and limits of religious freedom. There also emerges here a sugges-tive portrait of Washington's use of indirection, as opposed to direct command, to accomplish the aims of policy. The clearest indication of a settled policy conviction are his notes on a "Plan of American Finance" sketched in his own hand. Several of the items printed here are not found in the Fitzpatrick* Writings.

As Washington undertook the task of organizing the new govern-ment under the Constitution, he was alert to the significance of every word and deed for subsequent practice. His efforts to establish healthy precedents speak for themselves, but this emphatic concern produced at least one humorous irony. Washington enlisted the aid of James Madison in drafting his first inaugural address. After he delivered it, each house of Congress responded with a written ad-dress (adopting the custom of the colonial legislatures, which always responded to Royal Governors' official addresses that opened their legislative sessions). Madison wrote the address for the House of Representatives (but not, of course, that of the Senate). Then Wash-ington summoned Madison's aid in drafting his response to each of the responses from Congress. Thus, Madison was involved in lengthy conversation with himself as Washington sought to establish satisfac-tory principles under the conviction that "everything in our situation will serve to establish a precedent."

179

TO JAMES MADISON

New York, May 5, 1789

My dear Sir:

Notwithstanding the conviction I am under of the labour which is imposed upon you by *Public* Individuals as well as public bodies; yet, as you have begun, so I could wish you to finish, the good work in a short reply to the Address of the House of Representatives (which I now enclose) that there may be an accordance in this business.

Thursday 12 Oclock, I have appointed to receive the Address. The proper plan is with the House to determine. As the first of everything, *in our situation* will serve to establish a Precedent, it is devoutly wished on my part, that these precedents may be fixed on true principles. With Affectionate regard etc.

180

TO THE UNITED BAPTIST CHURCHES IN VIRGINIA

[May 10, 1789]

Gentlemen:

I request that you will accept my best acknowledgements for your congratulation on my appointment to the first office in the nation. The kind manner in which you mention my past conduct equally claims the expression of my gratitude.

After we had, by the smiles of Heaven on our exertions, obtained the object for which we contended, I retired at the conclusion of the war, with an idea that my country would have no farther occasion for my services, and with the intention of never entering again into public life. But when the exigence of my country seemed to require me once more to engage in public affairs, an honest conviction of duty superseded my former resolution, and became my apology for deviating from the happy plan which I had adopted.

Religious freedom   If I could have entertained the slightest apprehension that the Constitution framed in the Convention, where I had the honor to preside, might possibly endanger the religious rights of any ecclesiastical society, certainly I would never have placed my signature to it; and if I could now conceive that the general government might ever be so administered as to render the liberty of conscience insecure, I beg you will be persuaded that no one would be more zealous than myself to establish effectual barriers against the horrors of spiritual tyranny, and every species of religious persecution. For you, doubtless, remember that I have often expressed my sentiment, that every man, conducting himself as a good citizen, and being accountable to God alone for his religious opinions, ought to be protected in worshipping the Deity according to the dictates of his own conscience.

While I recollect with satisfaction that the religious society of which you are members, have been, throughout America, uniformly, and almost unanimously, the firm friends to civil liberty, and the persevering promoters of our glorious revolution; I cannot hesitate to believe that they will be the faithful supporters of a free, yet efficient general government. Under this pleasing reflection I rejoice to assure them that they may rely on my best wishes and endeavors to advance their prosperity.

In the meantime be assured, Gentlemen, that I entertain a proper sense of your fervent supplications to God for my temporal and eternal happiness.

G. Washington

181

TO THE GENERAL ASSEMBLY OF PRESBYTERIAN CHURCHES

May 1789

While I reiterate the professions of my dependence upon Heaven as the source of all public and private blessings; I will observe that the general prevalence of piety, philanthropy, honesty, industry, and oeconomy seems, in the ordinary course of human affairs, particularly necessary for advancing and conforming the happiness of our country. While all men within our territories are protected in worshipping the Deity according to the dictates of their consciences; it is rationally to be expected from them in return, that they will be emulous of evincing the sanctity of their professions by the innocence of their lives and the beneficence of their actions; for no man, who is profligate in his morals, or a bad member of the civil community, can possibly be a true Christian, or a credit to his own religious society.

I desire you to accept my acknowledgments for your laudable endeavors to render men sober, honest, and good Citizens, and the obedient subjects of a lawful government.

182

TO THE ANNUAL MEETING OF QUAKERS

September 1789

Government being, among other purposes, instituted to protect the persons and consciences of men from oppression, it certainly is the duty of rulers, not only to abstain from it themselves, but, according to their stations, to prevent it in others.

The liberty enjoyed by the people of these states of worshipping Almighty God agreeably to their consciences, is not only among the choicest of their *blessings*, but also of their *rights*. While men perform their social duties faithfully, they do all that society or the state can with propriety demand or expect; and remain responsible only to their Maker for their religion, or modes of faith, which they may prefer or profess.

Your principles and conduct are well known to me;* and it is doing the people called Quakers no more than justice to say, that (except their declining to share with others the burden of the common defense) there is no denomination among us, who are more exemplary and useful citizens.

I assure you very explicitly, that in my opinion the conscientious scruples of all men should be treated with great delicacy and tenderness; and it is my wish and desire, that the laws may always be as extensively accommodated to them, as a due regard to the protection and essential interests of the nation may justify and permit.

183

THANKSGIVING PROCLAMATION

City of New York, October 3, 1789

Whereas it is the duty of all Nations to acknowledge the providence of Almighty God, to obey his will, to be grateful for his benefits, and humbly to implore his protection and favor, and Whereas both Houses of Congress have by their joint Committee requested me "to recommend to the People of the United States a day of public thanks-giving and prayer to be observed by acknowledging with grateful hearts the many signal favors of Almighty God, especially by affording them an opportunity peaceably to establish a form of government for their safety and happiness."

Purpose of Thanksgiving

Now therefore I do recommend and assign Thursday the 26th. day of November next to be devoted by the People of these States to the service of that great and glorious Being, who is the beneficent Author of all the good that was, that is, or that will be. That we may then all unite in rendering unto him our sincere and humble thanks, for his kind care and protection of the People of this country previous to their becoming a Nation, for the signal and manifold mercies, and the favorable interpositions of his providence, which we experienced in the course and conclusion of the late war, for the great degree of tranquillity, union, and plenty, which we have

---

*Washington is addressing a regional meeting assembling Quakers from Pennsylvania, New Jersey, Delaware, Maryland, and Virginia.

since enjoyed, for the peaceable and rational manner in which we have been enabled to establish constitutions of government for our safety and happiness, and particularly the national One now lately instituted, for the civil and religious liberty with which we are blessed, and the means we have of acquiring and diffusing useful knowledge and in general for all the great and various favors which he hath been pleased to confer upon us.

And also that we may then unite in most humbly offering our prayers and supplications to the great Lord and Ruler of Nations and beseech him to pardon our national and other transgressions, to enable us all, whether in public or private stations, to perform our several and relative duties properly and punctually, to render our national government a blessing to all the People, by constantly being a government of wise, just and constitutional laws, discreetly and faithfully executed and obeyed, to protect and guide all Sovereigns and Nations (especially such as have shown kindness unto us) and to bless them with good government, peace, and concord. To promote the knowledge and practice of true religion and virtue, and the encrease of science among them and Us, and generally to grant unto all Mankind such a degree of temporal prosperity as he alone knows to be best.

184

SKETCH OF A PLAN
OF AMERICAN FINANCE

[October ? 1789]

Preliminary. Consider all requisitions heretofore made by Congress on the states, as if they had never been made. This gets rid of the adjustment of quotas for the past. The contributions in money, provisions &ca. made by each State to the Union, become a debt from the Union to the respective State, deduct from this all monies advanced to that State by the Union; the balance will constitute the debt of the Union to the State. Let that debt bear an interest of 6 pr Ct. With that interest each state may pay annually the interest of the debts they owe, and the annual expences of their Government. They will then have no occasion for Taxes and consequently may abandon all the subjects of taxation to the Union.

Impost on imports   I. Let the Union lay an Impost of 5 pr Cent on Importations. Suppose it worth from 1½ to 2 millions of Dollars. Open a loan in Europe sufficient to pay the foreign debts, and to support the government a year or two. Suppose this to be 12 millions of dollars at 5 pr Cent interest. 600,000 Dollars a year.

Appropriate this Impost

1. to pay the interest of the New loan, suppose about 600,000 Dolrs a year

2. the surplus to form an aggregate fund.

Produce tax   II. Lay a direct tax of ½₀ of all produce, payable in kind, but commutable for *half* its worth in money. Should this produce more than the State's quota, let the Surplus belong to the State. The State Legislature may then be entrusted with fixing the objects on which it is to fall, their value, the places of delivery, Sale of the produce, conduct of the receivers &ca:

Appropriate it

1. to the Military and Naval establishments

2. to pay the interest of the debts of the Union to the respective States.

3. the surplus to form an Aggregate fund

Postages and tax on civil process   III. Postages and a Tax on Civil Process may form a third fund.

Appropriate it

1. to the Civil list.

2. the Surplus to the aggregate fund.

The aggregate fund thus formed of the residuary parts of all Taxes.

Appropriate it

1. to pay the interest of the Domestic Debt

2. to contingencies.

3. to be applied as a sinking fund to pay off the capitol of the general debts of the Union. Fix such an order of payment as will retire the sinking the whole Capitol in time. But leave a portion

of the sinking fund free, to be employed by the Executive at their discretion in buying up the general debts at their market price.

185

TO CATHERINE MACAULAY GRAHAM

New York, January 9, 1790

Madam:

Your obliging letter, dated in October last, has been received; and, as I do not know when I shall have more leisure than at present to throw together a few observations in return for yours, I take up my Pen to do it by this early occasion.

In the first place I thank you for your congratulatory sentiments on the event which has placed me at the head of the American Government; as well as for the indulgent partiality, which it is to be feared, however, may have warped your judgment too much in my favor. But you do me no more than justice in supposing that, if I had been permitted to indulge my first and fondest wish, I should have remained in a private Station. Although neither the present age or Posterity may possibly give me full credit for the feelings which I have experienced on the subject; yet I have a consciousness, that nothing short of an absolute conviction of duty could ever have brought me upon the scenes of public life again. The establishment of our new Government seemed to be the last great experiment for promoting human happiness by reasonable compact in civil Society. It was to be, in the first instance, in a considerable degree a government of accommodation as well as a government of Laws. Much was to be done by *prudence*, much by *conciliation*, much by *firmness*. Few who are not philosophical spectators can realize the difficult and delicate part which a man in my situation had to act. All see, and most admire, the glare which hovers round the external trappings of elevated office. To me there is nothing in it, beyond the lustre which may be reflected from its connection with a power of promoting human felicity. In our progress towards political happiness my station is new; and, if I may use the expression, I walk on untrodden ground. There is scarcely any part of my conduct wch. may not hereafter be drawn into precedent.

Return to public life

Thoughts on the new American government

On the conduct of the first President

Under such a view of the duties inherent to my arduous office, I could not but feel a diffidence in myself on the one hand; and an anxiety for the Community that every new arrangement should be made in the best possible manner on the other. If after all my humble but faithful endeavours to advance the felicity of my Country and mankind, I may indulge a hope that my labours have not been altogether without success, it will be the only real compensation I can receive in the closing of life.

On the actual situation of this Country under its new Government I will, in the next place, make a few remarks. That the Government, though not absolutely perfect, is one of the best in the world, I have little doubt. I always believed that an unequivocally free and equal Representation of the People in the Legislature, together with an efficient and responsable Executive, were the great Pillars on which the preservation of American Freedom must depend. It was indeed next to a Miracle that there should have been so much unanimity, in points of such importance, among such a number of Citizens, so widely scattered, and so different in their habits in many respects as the Americans were. Nor are the growing unanimity and encreasing goodwill of the Citizens to the Government less remarkable than favorable circumstances. So far as we have gone with the new Government (and it is completely organized and in operation) we have had greater reason than the most sanguine could expect to be satisfied with its success.

Recovery and progress of the nation

Perhaps a number of accidental circumstances have concurred with the real effects of the Government to make the People uncommonly well pleased with their situation and prospects. The harvests of wheat have been remarkably good, the demand for that article from abroad is great, the encrease of Commerce is visible in every Port, and the number of new manufactures introduced in one year is astonishing. I have lately made a tour through the Eastern States. I found the country, in a great degree, recovered from the ravages of War, the Towns flourishing, and the People delighted with a government instituted by themselves and for their own good. The same facts I have also reason to believe, from good authority, exist in the Southern States. By what I have just observed, I think you will be persuaded that the ill-boding Politicians who prognosticated that America would never enjoy any fruits from her Independence, and that she would be obliged to have recourse to a foreign Power for protection, have at least been mistaken.

I shall sincerely rejoice to see that the American Revolution has been productive of happy consequences on both sides of the Atlantic. The renovation of the French Constitution is indeed one of the most wonderful events in the history of mankind; and the agency of the Marquis de la Fayette in a high degree honorable to his character. My greatest fear has been, that the nation would not be sufficiently cool and moderate in making arrangements for the security of that liberty, of which it seems to be fully possessed.

Mr. Warville, the French Gentleman you mention, has been in America and at Mount Vernon; but has returned sometime since to France.

Mrs. Washington is well and desires her compliments may be presented to you. We wish the happiness of your fireside, as we also long to enjoy that of our own at Mount Vernon. Our wishes, you know, were limited; and I think that our plans of living will now be deemed reasonable by the considerate part of our species. Her wishes coincide with my own as to simplicity of dress, and everything which can tend to support propriety of character without partaking of the follies of luxury and ostentation. I am, etc.

186

TO DAVID STUART

New York, March 28, 1790

Dear Sir:

Your letter of the 15. enclosing the act of Assembly authorising an agreement with Mr. Alexander came to my hand in the moment my last to you was dispatched.

I am sorry such jealousies as you speak of should be gaining *Discontent in the* ground, and are poisoning the minds of the southern people; *southern states* but admit the fact which is alledged as the cause of them, and give it full scope, does it amount to more than what was known to every man of information before, at, and since the adoption of the Constitution? Was it not always believed that there are some points which peculiarly interest the eastern States? and did any One, who reads human nature, and more especially the character of the eastern people conceive that they would not pursue them steadily by a combination of their force. Are there not other points which equally concern the southern States? If these States are less tenacious of their interest, or, if whilst the eastern move in a solid phalanx to effect their views, the southern are always divided, which of the two is most to be blamed? That there is a diversity of interests in the Union none has denied. That this is the case also in every State is equally certain. And that it even extends to the Counties of individual States can be as readily proved. Instance the southern and northern parts of Virginia, the upper and lower parts of south Carolina, &ca. have not the interests of these always been at variance? Witness the County of Fairfax, have not the interests of the people of that County varied, or the Inhabitants been taught to believe so? These are well known truths, and yet it did not follow that separation was to result from the disagreement.

Diversity of interests in the union

To constitute a dispute there must be two parties. To understand it well both parties and all the circumstances must be fully heard, and to accommodate differences, temper and mutual forbearance are requisite. Common danger brought the States into confederacy, and on their union our safety and importance depend. A spirit of accommodation was the basis of the present constitution, can it be expected then that the Southern or the Eastern part of the Empire will succeed in all their measures? certainly not; but I will readily grant that more points will be carried by the latter than the former, and for the reason which has been mentioned, namely, that in all great national questions they move in unison whilst the others are divided; but I ask again which is most blame-worthy, those who see, and will steadily pursue their interest, or those who cannot see, or seeing will not act wisely? And I will ask another question, of the highest magnitude in my mind, to wit, if the eastern and northern States are dangerous *in Union*, will they be less so in separation? If self interest is their governing principle will it forsake them or be less restrained by such an event? I hardly think it would. Then, independent, of other considerations what would Virginia (and such other States as might be inclined to join her) gain by a separation? Would they not, most unquestionably, be the weaker party?

Dangers of separation

Men who go from hence without feeling themselves of so much consequence as they wished to be considered, and disappointed expectants, added to malignant, designing characters, who miss no opportunity of aiming a blow at the Constitution, paint highly on one side without bringing into view the arguments which are offered on the other.

It is to be lamented that the Editors of the different Gazettes in the Union, do not more generally, and more correctly (instead of stuffing their papers with scurrility, and nonsensical declamation, which few would read if they were apprised of the contents) publish the debates in Congress on all great national questions, and this with no uncommon pains, everyone of them might do. The principles upon which the difference of opinion arises, as well as the decisions would then come fully before the public, and afford the best data for its judgment. Mr. Madison, on the question of discrimination, was actuated, I am convinced, by the purest motives, and most heartfelt conviction; but the subject was delicate, and perhaps had better never been stirred.

Publication of Congressional debates

The assumption of the State debts by the United States is another subject that has given rise to long and labored debates, without having yet taken a final form.

The memorial of the Quakers (and a very mal-apropos one it was) has at length been put to sleep, and will scarcely awake before the year 1808. I am etc.

187

TO DAVID STUART

New York, June 15, 1790

Dear Sir:

Your letter of the 2nd Instant came duly to hand. If there are any Gazettes among my files at Mount Vernon which can be of use to you they are at your Service.

Your description of the public Mind, in Virginia, gives me pain. It seems to be more irritable, sour and discontented than (from the information received) it is in any other State in the Union, except Massachusetts; which, from the same causes, but on quite different principles, is tempered like it.

Discontentment of Virginia

That Congress does not proceed with all that dispatch which people at a distance expect; and which, were they to hurry business, they possibly might; is not to be denied. That meas-

Defense of Congress

ures have been agitated wch. are not pleasing to Virginia; and others, pleasing perhaps to her, but not so to some other States; is equally unquestionable. Can it well be otherwise in a Country so extensive, so diversified in its interests? And will not these different interests naturally produce in an Assembly of Representatives who are to Legislate for, and to assimilate and reconcile them to the general welfare, long, warm and animated debates? Most undoubtedly; and if there was the same propensity in Mankind to investigate the motives, as there is for censuring the conduct of public characters, it would be found that the censure so freely bestowed is oftentimes unmerited and uncharitable; for instance, the condemnation of Congress for sitting only four hours in the day. The fact is, by the established rules of the House of Representatives, no Committee can sit whilst the House is sitting; and this is, and has been for a considerable time, from ten o'clock in the forenoon until three, often later, in the afternoon; before and after which the business is going on in Committees. If this application is not as much as most Constitutions are equal to, I am mistaken. Many other things which undergo malignant constructions wd. be found, upon a candid examination to wear other faces than are given to them. The misfortune is the enemies to the Government, always more active than its friends and always upon the watch to give it a stroke, neglect no opportunity to aim one. If they tell truth, it is not the whole truth; by which means one side only of the picture appears; whereas if both sides were exhibited it might, and probably would assume a different form in the opinion of just and candid men who are disposed to measure matters on a Continental Scale. I do not mean however, from what I have here said, to justify the conduct of Congress in all its movements; for some of these movements, in my opinion, have been injudicious and others unseasonable, whilst the questions of Assumption; Residence and other matters have been agitated with a warmth and intemperence; with prolixity and threats; which it is to be feared has lessened the dignity of that body and decreased that respect which was once entertained for it. And this misfortune is increased by many members, even among those who wish well to the Government, ascribing in letters to their respective States when they are unable to carry a favourite measure, the worst motives for the conduct of their opponents; who, viewing matters through a different medium may, and do retort in their turn; by which means jealousies and distrusts are spread most impolitickly, far and wide; and will, it is to be feared, have a most unhappy tendency to injure our public affairs, which, if wisely conducted might make us (as we are now by Europeans thought to be) the happiest people upon Earth. As an evidence of it, our reputation has risen in every part of the Globe; and our credit, especially in Holland, has got higher than that of *any* Nation in Europe (and where our funds are above par) as appears by *Official* advices just received. But the conduct we seem to be pursuing will soon bring us back to our late disreputable condition. The introductions of the (Quaker) Memorial respecting Slavery, was to be sure, not only an illjudged piece of business, but occasioned a great waste of time. The final decision thereon, however, was as favourable as the proprietors of that species of property could have expected considering the great dereliction to Slavery in a large part of this Union.

America's reputation abroad

The question of Assumption has occupied a great deal of time, and no wonder; for it is certainly a very important one; and, under *proper* restrictions, and scrutiny into Accounts will be found, I conceive to be just. The Cause in which the expenses of the War was incurred, was a Common Cause. The States (in Congress) declared it so at the beginning and pledged themselves to stand by each other. If then, some States were harder pressed than others, or from particular or local circumstances contracted heavier debts, it is but reasonable when this fact is ascertained (though it is a sentiment I have not made known here) that an allowance ought to be made them when due credit is given to others. Had the invaded, and hard pressed States believed the case would have been otherwise; opposition in them would very soon, I believe, have changed to submission; and given a different termination to the War.

Assumption of states' debts

In a letter of last year to the best of my recollection, I informed you of the motives, which *compelled* me to allot a day for the reception of idle and ceremonious visits (for it never has prevented those of sociability and friendship in the afternoon, or at any other time) but if I am mistaken in this, the history of this business is simply and shortly as follows. Before the custom was established, which now accommodates foreign characters, Strangers, and others who from motives of curiosity, respect to the Chief Magistrate, or any other cause, are

Management of public visits and ceremonies

induced to call upon me, I was unable to attend to any business *whatsoever;* for Gentlemen, consulting their own convenience rather than mine, were calling from the time I rose from breakfast, often before, until I sat down to dinner. This, as I resolved not to neglect my public duties, reduced me to the choice of one of these alternatives, either to refuse them *altogether,* or to appropriate a time for the reception of them. The first would, I well knew, be disgusting to many. The latter, I *expected,* would undergo animadversion, and blazoning from those who would find fault, *with,* or *without* cause. To please everybody was impossible; I therefore adopted that line of conduct which combined public advantage with private convenience, and which in my judgment was unexceptionable in itself. That I have not been able to make bows to the taste of poor Colonel Bland, (who, by the by, I believe never saw one of them) is to be regretted especially too as (upon those occasions) they were indiscriminately bestowed, and the best I was master of; would it not have been better to throw the veil of charity over them, ascribing their stiffness to the effects of age, or to the unskillfulness of my teacher, than to pride and dignity of office, which God knows has no charms for me? for I can truly say I had rather be at Mount Vernon with a friend or two about me, than to be attended at the Seat of Government by the Officers of State and the Representatives of every Power in Europe.

Description of meetings with the public

These visits are optional. They are made without invitation. Between the hours of three and four every Tuesday I am prepared to receive them. Gentlemen, often in great numbers, come and go, chat with each other, and act as they please. A Porter shews them into the room, and they retire from it when they please, and without ceremony. At their *first* entrance they salute me, and I them, and as many as I can talk to I do. What pomp there is in all this, I am unable to discover. Perhaps it consists in not sitting. To this two reasons are opposed, first it is unusual; secondly, (which is a more substantial one) because I have no room large enough to contain a third of the chairs, which would be sufficient to admit it. If it is supposed that ostentation, or the fashions of courts (which by the by I believe originates oftener in convenience, not to say necessity than is generally imagined) gave rise to this custom, I will boldly affirm that *no* supposition was ever more erroneous; for, if I was to give indulgence to my inclinations, every moment that I could withdraw from the fatigues of my station should be spent in retirement. That they are not proceeds from the sense I entertain of the propriety of giving to every one as free access, as consists with that respect which is due to the Chair of government; and that respect I conceive is neither to be acquired or preserved but by observing a just medium between much state and too great familiarity.

Similar to the above, but of a more sociable kind are the visits every Friday afternoon to Mrs. Washington where I always am. These public meetings and a dinner once a week to as many as my table will hold, with the references *to* and *from* the different Departments of State, and *other* Communications with *all* parts of the Union is as much, if not more, than I am able to undergo; for I have already had within less than a year, two *severe* attacks; the last worse than the first; a third more than probable, will put me to sleep with my fathers; at what distance this may be I know not. Within the last twelve months I have undergone more, and severer sickness than thirty preceding years afflicted me with, put it all together. I have abundant reason however to be thankful that I am so well recovered; though I still feel the remains of the violent affection of my lungs. The cough, pain in my breast, and shortness in breathing not having entirely left me. I propose in the recess of Congress to visit Mount Vernon; but when this recess will happen is beyond my ken, or the ken I believe of any of its members. I am &c.

Poor health

188

TO THE HEBREW CONGREGATIONS

January, 1790

Gentlemen:*

The liberal sentiment towards each other which marks every political and religious denomination of men in this country stands unrivalled in the history of nations. The affection of such a people is a treasure beyond the reach of calculation; and the repeated proofs which my fellow citizens have given of

---

*Washington replies to Hebrew congregations in Philadelphia, Newport, Charleston, and Richmond.

their attachment to me, and approbation of my doings form the purest source of my temporal felicity. The affectionate expressions of your address again excite my gratitude, and receive my warmest acknowledgements.

The power and goodness of the Almighty were strongly manifested in the events of our late glorious revolution and his kind interposition in our behalf has been no less visible in the establishment of our present equal government. In war he directed the sword and in peace he has ruled in our councils. My agency in both has been guided by the best intentions, and a sense of the duty which I owe my country. And as my exertions hitherto have been amply rewarded by the approbation of my fellow citizens, I shall endeavor to deserve a continuance of it by my future conduct.

May the same temporal and eternal blessings which you implore for me, rest upon your congregations.

G. Washington

189

TO THE ROMAN CATHOLICS IN THE UNITED STATES OF AMERICA

[March 15], 1790

Gentlemen:

While I now receive with much satisfaction your congratulations on my being called, by an unanimous vote, to the first station in my country; I cannot but duly notice your politeness in offering an apology for the unavoidable delay. As that delay has given you an opportunity of realizing, instead of anticipating, the benefits of the general government, you will do me the justice to believe, that your testimony of the increase of the public prosperity, enhances the pleasure which I should otherwise have experienced from your affectionate address.

I feel that my conduct, in war and in peace, has met with more general approbation than could reasonably have been expected and I find myself disposed to consider that fortunate circumstance, in a great degree, resulting from the able support and extraordinary candour of my fellow-citizens of all denominations.

The prospect of national prosperity now before us is truly animating, and ought to excite the exertions of all good men to establish and secure the happiness of their country, in the permanent duration of its freedom and independence. America, under the smiles of a Divine Providence, the protection of a good government, and the cultivation of manners, morals, and piety, cannot fail of attaining an uncommon degree of eminence, in literature, commerce, agriculture, improvements at home and respectability abroad.

As mankind become more liberal they will be more apt to allow that all those who conduct themselves as worthy members of the community are equally entitled to the protection of civil government. I hope ever to see America among the foremost nations in examples of justice and liberality. And I presume that your fellow-citizens will not forget the patriotic part which you took in the accomplishment of their Revolution, and the establishment of their government; or the important assistance which they received from a nation in which the Roman Catholic faith is professed.

I thank you, gentlemen, for your kind concern for me. While my life and my health shall continue, in whatever situation I may be, it shall be my constant endeavour to justify the favourable sentiments which you are pleased to express of my conduct. And may the members of your society in America, animated alone by the pure spirit of Christianity, and still conducting themselves as the faithful subjects of our free government, enjoy every temporal and spiritual felicity.

G. Washington

190

TO THE HEBREW CONGREGATION IN NEWPORT

[August], 1790

Gentlemen:

While I received with much satisfaction your address replete with expressions of esteem, I rejoice in the opportunity of assuring you that I shall always retain grateful remembrance of the cordial welcome I experienced on my visit to Newport from all classes of citizens.

The reflection on the days of difficulty and danger which are past is rendered the more sweet from a consciousness that they are succeeded by days of uncommon prosperity and security.

If we have wisdom to make the best use of the advantages with which we are now favored, we cannot fail, under the just administration of a good government, to become a great and happy people.

The citizens of the United States of America have a right to applaud themselves for having given to mankind examples of an enlarged and liberal policy—a policy worthy of imitation. All possess alike liberty of conscience and immunities of citizenship.

It is now no more that toleration is spoken of as if it were the indulgence of one class of people that another enjoyed the exercise of their inherent natural rights, for, happily, the Government of the United States, which gives to bigotry no factions, to persecution no assistance, requires only that they who live under its protection should demean themselves as good citizens in giving it on all occasions their effectual support.

It would be inconsistent with the frankness of my character not to avow that I am pleased with your favorable opinion of my administration and fervent wishes for my felicity.

May the children of the stock of Abraham who dwell in this land continue to merit and enjoy the good will of the other inhabitants—while every one shall sit in safety under his own vine and fig tree and there shall be none to make him afraid.

May the father of all mercies scatter light, and not darkness, upon our paths, and make us all in our several vocations useful here, and in His own due time and way everlastingly happy.

G. Washington

191

TO THE HEBREW CONGREGATIONS OF THE CITY OF SAVANNAH, GEORGIA

Gentlemen:

I thank you with great sincerity for your congratulations on my appointment to the office which I have the honor to hold by the unanimous choice of my fellow-citizens, and especially the expressions you are pleased to use in testifying the confidence that is reposed in me by your congregations.

As the delay which has naturally intervened between my election and your address has afforded me an opportunity for appreciating the merits of the Federal Government and for communicating your sentiments of its administration, I have rather to express my satisfaction rather than regret at a circumstance which demonstrates (upon experiment) your attachment to the former as well as approbation of the latter.

I rejoice that a spirit of liberality and philanthropy is much more prevalent than it formerly was among the enlightened nations of the earth, and that your brethren will benefit thereby in proportion as it shall become still more extensive; happily the people of the United States have in many instances exhibited examples worthy of imitation, the salutary influence of which will doubtless extend much farther if gratefully enjoying those blessings of peace which (under the favor of heaven) have been attained by fortitude in war, they shall conduct themselves with reverence to the Deity and charity toward their fellow-creatures.

May the same wonder-working Deity, who long since delivered the Hebrews from their Egyptian oppressors, planted them in a promised land, *whose providential agency has lately been conspicuous in establishing these United States as an independent nation*, still continue to water them with the dews of heaven and make the inhabitants of every denomination participate in the temporal and spiritual blessings of that people whose God is Jehovah.

G. Washington

192

TO THE CHIEFS AND COUNSELORS
OF THE SENECA NATION

Philadelphia, December 29, 1790

I the President of the United States, by my own mouth, and by a written Speech signed with my own hand [and sealed with the Seal of the U S] Speak to the Seneka Nation, and desire their attention, and that they would keep this Speech in remembrance of the friendship of the United States.

I have received your Speech with satisfaction, as a proof of your confidence in the justice of the United States, and I have attentively examined the several objects which you have laid before me, whether delivered by your Chiefs at Tioga point in the last month to Colonel Pickering, or laid before me in the present month by the Cornplanter and the other Seneca Chiefs now in Philadelphia.

Friendship with the Six Nations

In the first place I observe to you, and I request it may sink deep in your minds, that it is my desire, and the desire of the United States that all the miseries of the late war should be forgotten and buried forever. That in future the United States and the six Nations should be truly brothers, promoting each other's prosperity by acts of mutual friendship and justice.

Effect of new Constitution on Indian relations

I am not uninformed that the six Nations have been led into some difficulties with respect to the sale of their lands since the peace. But I must inform you that these evils arose before the present government of the United States was established, when the separate States and individuals under their authority, undertook to treat with the Indian tribes respecting the sale of their lands.

But the case is now entirely altered. The general Government only has the power, to treat with the Indian Nations, and any treaty formed and held without its authority will not be binding.

Here then is the security for the remainder of your lands. No State nor person can purchase your lands, unless at some public treaty held under the authority of the United States. The general government will never consent to your being defrauded. But it will protect you in all your just rights.

Hear well, and let it be heard by every person in your Nation, That the President of the United States declares, that the general government considers itself bound to protect you in all the lands secured you by the Treaty of Fort Stanwix, the 22nd of October 1784, excepting such parts as you may since had fairly sold to persons properly authorized to purchase of you.

You complain that John Livingston and Oliver Phelps have obtained your lands, assisted by Mr. Street of Niagara, and they have not complied with their agreement.

It appears upon enquiry of the Governor of New York, that John Livingston was not legally authorized to treat with you, and that every thing he did with you has been declared null and void, so that you may rest easy on that account.

But it does not appear from any proofs yet in the possession of government, that Oliver Phelps has defrauded you.

If however you should have any just cause of complaint against him, and can make satisfactory proof thereof, the federal Courts will be open to you for redress, as to all other persons.

But your great object seems to be the security of your remaining lands, and I have therefore upon this point, meant to be sufficiently strong and clear.

That in future you cannot be defrauded of your lands. That you possess the right to sell, and the right of refusing to sell your lands.

That therefore the sale of your lands in future, will depend entirely upon yourselves. *Future sale of Indian lands*

But that when you may find it for your interest to sell any parts of your lands, the United States must be present by their Agent, and will be your security that you shall not be defrauded in the bargain you may make.

[It will however be important, that before you make any further sales of your land that you should determine among yourselves, who are the persons among you that shall give sure conveyances thereof as shall be binding upon your Nation and forever preclude all disputes related to the validity of the sale.]

That besides the [before mentioned] security for your land, you will perceive by the law of Congress, for regulating trade and intercourse with the Indian tribes, the fatherly care the United States intend to take of the Indians. For the particular meaning of this law, I refer you to the explanations given thereof by Colonel Pickering at Tioga, which with the law, are herewith delivered to you.

You have said in your Speech "That the game is going away from among you, and that you thought it the design of the great Spirit, that you should till the ground, but before you speak upon this subject, you want to know whether the United States meant to leave you any land to till?"

You now know that all the lands secured to you by the Treaty of Fort Stanwix, excepting such parts as you may since have fairly sold are yours, and that only your own acts can convey them away; speak therefore your wishes on the subject of tilling the ground. The United States will be happy to afford you every assistance in the only business which will add to your numbers and happiness.

Murder of Indians

The murders that have been committed upon some of your people, by the bad white men I sincerely lament and reprobate, and I earnestly hope that the real murderers will be secured, and punished as they deserve. This business has been sufficiently explained to you here, by the Governor of Pennsylvania, and by Colonel Pickering on behalf of the United States, at Tioga.

The Senekas may be assured, that the rewards offered for apprehending the murderers, will be continued until they are secured for trial, and that when they shall be apprehended, that they will be tried and punished as if they had killed white men.

Bad Indians

Having answered the most material parts of your Speech, I shall inform you, that some bad Indians, and the outcast of several tribes who reside at the Miamee Village, have long continued their murders and depredations upon the frontiers, lying along the Ohio. That they have not only refused to listen to my voice inviting them to peace, but that upon receiving it, they renewed their incursions and murders with greater violence than ever. I have therefore been obliged to strike those bad people, in order to make them sensible of their madness. I sincerely hope they will hearken to reason, and not require to be further chastised. The United States desire to be the friends of the Indians, upon terms of justice and humanity. But they will not suffer the depredations of the bad Indians to go unpunished.

My desire is that you would caution all the Senekas and six Nations, to prevent their rash young men from joining the Miamee Indians. For the United States cannot distinguish the tribes to which bad Indians belong, and every tribe must take care of their own people.

The merits of the Cornplanter, and his friendship for the United States are well known to me, and shall not be forgotten. And as a mark of the esteem of the United States, I have directed the Secretary of war to make him a present of Two hundred and Fifty Dollars, either in money or goods, as the Cornplanter shall like best. And he may depend upon the future care and kindness of the United States. And I have also directed the Secretary of War to make suitable presents to the other Chiefs present in Philadelphia. And also that some further tokens of friendship to be forwarded to the other Chiefs, now in their Nation.

Remember my words Senekas, continue to be strong in your friendship for the United States, as the only rational ground of your future happiness, and you may rely upon their kindness and protection.

An Agent shall soon be appointed to reside in some place convenient to the Senekas and six Nations. He will represent the United States. Apply to him on all occasions.

If any man brings you evil reports of the intentions of the United States, mark that man as your enemy, for he will mean to deceive you and lead you into trouble. The United States will be true and faithful to their engagements.

193

TO MARQUIS DE LAFAYETTE

Philadelphia, July 28, 1791

I have, my dear Sir, to acknowledge the receipt of your favors *Events in France* of the 7 of March and 3 of May, and to thank you for the communications which they contain relative to your public affairs. I assure you I have often contemplated, with great anxiety, the danger to which you are personally exposed by your peculiar and delicate situation in the tumult of the times, and your letters are far from quieting that friendly concern. But to one, who engages in hazardous enterprises for the good of his country, and who is guided by pure and upright views, (as I am sure is the case with you) life is but a secondary consideration.

To a philanthropic mind the happiness of 24 millions of people cannot be indifferent; and by an American, whose country in the hour of distress received such liberal aid from the French, the disorders and incertitude of that Nation are to be peculiarly lamented. We must, however, place a confidence in that Providence who rules great events, trusting that out of confusion he will produce order, and, notwithstanding the dark clouds, which may threaten at present, that right will ultimately be established.

Paris

The tumultuous populace of large cities are ever to be dreaded. Their indiscriminate violence prostrates for the time all public authority, and its consequences are sometimes extensive and terrible. In Paris we may suppose these tumults are peculiarly disastrous at this time, when the public mind is in a ferment, and when (as is always the case on such occasions) there are not wanting wicked and designing men, whose element is confusion, and who will not hesitate in destroying the public tranquillity to gain a favorite point. But until your Constitution is fixed, your government organized, and your representative Body renovated, much tranquillity cannot be expected; for, until these things are done, those who are unfriendly to the revolution, will not quit the hope of bringing matters back to their former state.

Commercial measures of the National Assembly

The decrees of the National Assembly respecting our tobacco and oil do not appear to be very pleasing to the people of this country; but I do not presume that any hasty measures will be adopted in consequence thereof; for we have never entertained a doubt of the friendly disposition of the French Nation toward us, and are therefore persuaded that if they have done any thing which seems to bear hard upon us, at a time when the Assembly must have been occupied in very important matters, and which perhaps would not allow time for a due consideration of the subject, they will, in the moment of calm deliberation, alter it and do what is right.

I readily perceive, my dear Sir, the critical situation in which you stand, and never can you have greater occasion to show your prudence, judgment, and magnanimity.

Tour of the southern states

On the 6 of this month I returned from a tour through the southern States, which had employed me for more than three months. In the course of this journey I have been highly gratified in observing the flourishing state of the Country, and the good dispositions of the people. Industry and economy have become very fashionable in these parts, which were formerly noted for the opposite qualities, and the labours of man are assisted by the blessings of Providence. The attachment of all Classes of citizens to the general Government seems to be a pleasing presage of their future happiness and respectability.

The complete establishment of our public credit is a strong mark of the confidence of the people in the virtue of their Representatives, and the wisdom of their measures; and, while in Europe, wars or commotions seem to agitate almost every nation, peace and tranquillity prevail among us, except on some parts of our western frontiers, where the Indians have been troublesome, to reclaim or chastise whom proper measures are now pursuing. This contrast between the situation of *Contrasts with* the people of the United States, and those of Europe is too *Europe* striking to be passed over, even by the most superficial observer, and may, I believe, be considered as one great cause of leading the people here to reflect more attentively on their own prosperous state, and to examine more minutely, and consequently approve more fully of the government under which they live, than they otherwise would have done. But we do not wish to be the only people who may taste the sweets of an equal and good government; we look with an anxious eye to the time, when happiness and tranquillity shall prevail in your country, and when all Europe shall be freed from commotions, tumults, and alarms.

Your friends in this country often express their great attachment to you by their anxiety for your safety. Knox, Jay, Hamilton, Jefferson remember you with affection; but none with more sincerity and true attachment than etc.

194

TO GOUVERNEUR MORRIS

Philadelphia, July 28, 1791

Dear Sir:

I have now before me your favors of the 22 of November 1 and 24 of December 1790, and of the 9 of March 1791. The Plateaux which you had the goodness to procure for me arrived safe, and the account of them has been settled, as you desired, with Mr. Robert Morris. For this additional mark of attention to my wishes you must accept my thanks.

The communications in your several letters, relative to the state of affairs in Europe, are very gratefully received; and I should be glad if it was in my power to reply to them more in detail than I am able to do. But my public duties, which are at all times sufficiently numerous, being now much accumulated by an absence of more than three months from the seat of government, make the present a very busy moment for me.

Change of systems in Europe

The change of systems, which have so long prevailed in Europe, will, undoubtedly, affect us in a degree proportioned to our political or commercial connexions with the several nations of it. But I trust we shall never so far lose sight of our own interest and happiness as to become, unnecessarily, a party in their political disputes. Our local situation enables us to keep that state with them, which otherwise could not, perhaps, be preserved by human wisdom. The present moment seems pregnant with great events; But, as you observe, it is beyond the ken of mortal foresight to determine what will be the result of those changes which are either making or contemplated in the general system of Europe. Altho' as fellow-men we sincerely lament the disorders, oppressions, and incertitude which frequently attend national events, and which our European brethren must feel; yet we cannot but hope that it will terminate very much in favor of the Rights of man; and that a change there will be favorable to this Country I have no doubt. For, under the former system we were seen either in the distresses of war, or viewed after the peace in a most unfavorable light through the medium of our distracted state. In neither point could we appear of much consequence among Nations. And should affairs continue in Europe in the same state they were when these impressions respecting us were received, it would not be an easy matter to remove the prejudices imbibed against us. A change of system will open a new view of things, and we shall then burst upon them, as it were with redoubled advantages.

Treaties with Europe

Should we under the present state of affairs form connexions, other than we now have, with any European powers, much must be considered in effecting them, on the score of our increasing importance as a Nation; and, at the same time, should a treaty be formed with a Nation whose circumstances may not at this moment be very bright much delicacy would be necessary in order to shew that no undue advantages were taken on that account. For unless treaties are mutually beneficial to the Parties, it is in vain to hope for a continuance of them beyond the moment when the one which conceives itself to be over-reached is in a situation to break off the connexion. And I believe it is among nations as with individuals, the party taking advantage of the distresses of another will lose infinitely more in the opinion of mankind and in subsequent events than he will gain by the stroke of the moment.

In my late tour through the southern States I experienced great satisfaction in seeing the good effects of the general Government in that part of the Union. The people at large have felt the security which it gives and the equal justice which it administers to them. The Farmer, the Merchant, and the Mechanic have seen their several interests attended to, and from thence they unite in placing a confidence in their representatives, as well as in those in whose hands the execution of the laws is placed. Industry has there taken place of idleness, and economy of dissipation. Two or three years of good crops, and a ready market for the produce of their lands, has put every one in good humour; and, in some instances they even impute to the Government what is due only to the goodness of Providence. *Tour of the southern states*

The establishment of public credit is an immense point gained in our national concerns. This I believe exceeds the expectation of the most sanguine among us; and a late instance, unparalleled in this country, has been given of the confidence reposed in our measures by the rapidity with which the subscriptions to the Bank of the United States were filled. In two hours after the books were opened by the Commissioners the whole number of shares were taken up, and 4000 more applied for than were allowed by the Institution. This circumstance was not only pleasing as it related to the confidence in government; but as it exhibited an unexpected proof of the resources of our Citizens. *Bank of the United States*

In one of my letters to you the account which I gave of the number of inhabitants which would probably be found in the United States on enumeration, was too large. The estimate was then founded on the ideas held out by the Gentlemen in Congress of the population of their several States, each of whom (as was very natural) looking thro' a magnifying glass *First census* would speak of the greatest extent, to which there was any probability of their numbers reaching. Returns of the Census have already been made from several of the States and a tolerably just estimate has been formed now in others, by which it appears that we shall hardly reach four millions; but one thing is certain our *real* numbers will exceed, greatly, the official returns of them; because the religious scruples of some, would not allow them to give in their lists; the fears of others that it was intended as the foundation of a tax induced them to conceal or diminished theirs, and thro' the indolence of the people, and the negligence of many of the Officers numbers are omitted. The authenticated number however is far greater, I believe, than has ever been allowed in Europe, and will have no small influence in enabling them to form a more just opinion of our present and growing importance than has yet been entertained there.

This letter goes with one from Mr. Jefferson, to which I must refer you for what respects your public transactions, and I shall only add to it the repeated assurances of regard and affection etc.

195

TO ARTHUR YOUNG

Philadelphia, December 5, 1791

Sir:

In a letter which I addressed to you on the 15th. of August, acknowledging the receipt of your favor dated the 25th. of January preceeding, I promised to answer the queries contained in it, in detail.

Reply to agricultural survey

Accordingly, I took measures for that purpose, by writing to some of the most intelligent Farmers in the States of New York, New Jersey, Pennsylvania, Maryland and Virginia; as you will perceive by the circular letter herewith enclosed: and have obtained the answers from the three last mentioned States that are thereunto annexed. I did not extend my enquiries to the Northward of New York, nor to the Southward of Virginia; because in neither extremity of the Union, in my opinion, is the climate, Soil, or other circumstances well adapted to the pursuits of a *mere* Farmer, or congenial to the growth of the smaller Grains.

I have delayed the information I am about to give you, in expectation of receiving answers which have been promised me from the States of New York and New Jersey; but as they are not yet arrived, and a Vessel is on the point of Sailing for London, I shall put this Packet under cover to Joshua Johnson Esqr. our Consul at that Port; with a request to him, that it may be forwarded to you, by a safe conveyance. The others shall follow as opportunities may present; it being my wish to give you a comprehensive view of the different parts of this Country: although I have no hesitation in giving it at the sametime as my opinion, if I had a new establishment to make in it, that it would be, under the knowledge I entertain of it at present *A comprehensive* (and I have visited all parts from New Hampshire to Georgia *view of different* inclusively) in one of the three States of which you are fur- *parts of the* nished with particular Accounts. New York and New Jersey do *country* not differ much in Soil, or Climate, from the Northern parts of Pennsylvania. Both are pleasant, and both are well improved, particularly the first. But the Country beyond these, to the Eastward, (and the farther you advance that way it is still more so) is unfriendly to Wheat, which is subject to a blight or mill-dew, and of late years, to a fly, which has almost discouraged the growth of it. The lands, however, in the New England States are strong, and productive of other Crops; are well improved; populously seated; and as pleasant as it can be in a Country fast locked in Snow sevl. months in the year.

To the Southward of Virginia the climate is not well adapted to Wheat; and less and less so as you penetrate the warmer latitudes; nor is the Country so thickly settled, or well cultivated. In a word, as I have already intimated, was I to commence my career of life anew, I shd. not seek a residence north of Pennsylvania, or South of Virginia: nor, but this I desire may be received with great caution, for I may, without knowing I am so, be biassed in favor of the River on which I live, should I go more than 25 miles from the margin of the Potomac, in less than half the distance, in some places I might seat myself either in Pennsylvania, Maryland or Virginia, as local circumstances might prompt me.

Having said thus much, some of the reasons which lead to *Advantages of* this opinion, may be expected in support of it. Potomac River *Potomac region* then, is the centre of the Union. It is between the extremes of heat and cold. It is not so far to the south as to be unfriendly to grass, nor so far north as to have the produce of the Summer consumed in the length, and severity of the winter. It waters that soil, and runs in that climate, which is most congenial to English grains, and most agreeable to the Cultivators of them.

It is the River, more than any other, in my opinion, which must, in the natural progress of things, connect by its inland navigation (now nearly compleated 190 measured miles up to Fort Cumberland, at the expence of £50,000 Sterlg. raised by private subscription) the Atlantic States with the vast region which is populating (beyond all conception) to the Westward of it. It is designed by law for the seat of the Empire; and must, from its extensive course through a rich and populous country become, in time, the grand Emporium of North America. To these reasons may be added, that, the lands within, and surrounding the district of Columbia are as high, as dry, and as healthy as any in the United States; and that those above them, in the Counties of Berkeley in Virginia, Washington in Maryland, and Franklin in Pennsylvania (adjoining each other) at the distance of from Sixty to 100 miles from Columbia, are inferior in their natural state to none in America.

The general Map of North America, which is herewith enclosed, will shew the situation of this district of the United States. And on Evan's Map of the Middle Colonies, which is on a larger scale, I have marked the district of Columbia with double red lines; and the Counties adjacent to, and above it, of which particular mention has been made, with single red lines.

The last mentioned Map shews the proximity of the Potowmac (which is laid down from actual Survey) to the Western Waters, and it is worthy of observation, that the Shenandore, in an extent of 150 miles from its confluence, through the richest tract of land in the State of Virginia, may (as is supposed) be made navigable for less than £2,000. The South branch of Potowmac (100 miles higher up, and) for a hundred miles of its extent, may be made navigable for a much less sum. And the intermediate waters on the Virginia side, in that proportion, according to their magnitude. On the Maryland side (the river Potowmac to the head of the North branch being the boundary between the two States) the Monocasy and Conogocheag are capable of improvement to a degree which will be convenient and benificial to the Inhabitants of the State, and to parts of Pennsylvania.

The local, or State taxes, are enumerated in the answers to the circular letter; and these from the nature of the Government, will probably decrease. The taxes of the General Government will be found in the Revenue laws, which are contained in the volume that accompanies this letter.

"The Pennsylvania Mercury, and Philadelphia Price current" is sent that you may see what is, and has been, the prices of the several enumerated Articles which have been bought, and sold in this market at different periods, within the last twelve months.

An English farmer must entertain a contemptible opinion of our husbandry, or a horrid idea of our lands, when he shall be informed that not more than 8 or 10 bushels of Wheat is the yield of an Acre; but this low produce may be ascribed, and principally too, to a cause which I do not find touched by either of the Gentlemen whose letters are sent to you, namely, that the aim of the farmers in this Country (if they can be called farmers) is not to make the most they can from the land, which is, or has been cheap, but the most of the labour, which is dear, the consequence of which has been, much ground has been *scratched* over and none cultivated or improved as it ought to have been; Whereas a farmer in England, where land is dear and labour cheap, finds it his interest to improve and cultivate highly, that he may reap large crops from a small quantity of ground. That this last is the true, and the first an erroneous policy, I will readily grant, but it requires time to conquer bad habits, and hardly anything short of necessity is able to accomplish it. That necessity is approaching by pretty rapid strides.

Low productivity of American farmers

If from these communications you shall derive information or amusement, it will be but a small return for the favors I have received from you; and I shall feel happy in having had it in my power to render them. As they result from your letter of the 25th. of January, and are intended for your private satisfaction it is not my wish that they should be promulgated as coming from me. With very great esteem I am etc.

CHAPTER THIRTEEN

PRESIDENT WASHINGTON

Trials of Division

1792 – 1796

*W*ASHINGTON'S *administration of the government under the Constitution was not untroubled.
During those eight years the founding itself was consummated, yet during that same period Americans witnessed the birth of what ultimately became the system of
political parties. Washington's unanimous election to the
presidency was never to be repeated, for statesmen of the
founding era discovered room to contest the "administration" of the
government within the protective confines of the established Constitution. Washington himself became the tacit head of the Federalist
Party, direct heir to the Federalists who prevailed in the struggle
over adoption of the Constitution. The opposition party, the Democratic-Republican Party, was headed by James Madison and
Thomas Jefferson. In the last six years of Washington's administration, the growing party discord figured as the most pressing political
development. These years witnessed the emergence of party presses
and party organizations. Most significantly, the discord divided
Washington's administration itself; for the chief party spokesmen,
apart from Madison, were members of Washington's cabinet. Alexander Hamilton, Secretary of the Treasury, headed the Federalists,
and Thomas Jefferson spearheaded the organization of the Demo-
cratic-Republicans, even while he was Secretary of State. Madison,
whose 1791–92 essays in the* National Gazette *laid out the Republican platform, had been the principal Federalist spokesman in Congress. To all appearances, therefore, the cemented union for which
Washington had so long labored was being fractured in a contest
over the spoils of victory. While maintaining the principle of energetic government, Washington sought to contain the damage of division, praying that "the cup which has been presented may not be
snatched from our lips by a discordance of action."*

The Whiskey Rebellion. Congress first imposed an excise tax on distilled liquor in 1791. A group of western Pennsylvania farmers thought the tax burdensome and refused to pay it. In 1792 Congress decreased the tax, but the farmers still refused to pay. On September 15, 1792, Washington issued a proclamation imploring obedience to the law. Possibly encouraged by the formation of Democratic Societies inspired by the French Revolution, the farmers ignored the presidential urgings, attacked federal officers, and burned buildings. Washington insisted on August 7, 1794, that the farmers desist from unlawful actions. Determined that the nation's law must be observed and enforced, he called out the militia on September 25. Fifteen thousand militiamen responded, and the insurrection was subdued with virtually no casualties. Most of the captured insurgents were pardoned by the President on July 10, 1795.

The Proclamation of Neutrality. President Washington was at Mount Vernon early in April 1793 when news reached America of a declaration of war against Great Britain by the Republic of France. He cut short his Virginia vacation and returned to Philadelphia to confer with his cabinet as to the best means to protect the United States in the crisis. Washington circulated inquiries among the Secretaries and the Attorney General, asking them to consider what measures would be proper for the United States to observe, especially in light of the defensive treaty of alliance consummated with the French monarchy during the American Revolution. He ultimately determined that the United States would follow a neutral course, desiring to give neither belligerent cause for complaint. Accordingly, he issued the Proclamation of Neutrality on April 22, 1793.

196

TO JAMES MADISON

Mount Vernon, May 20, 1792

My dear Sir:

As there is a possiblity if not a probability, that I shall not see you on your return home; or, if I should see you, that it may be on the road and under circumstances which will prevent my speaking to you on the subject we last conversed upon; I take the liberty of committing to paper the following thoughts, and requests.

I have not been unmindful of the sentiments expressed by you in the conversations just alluded to: on the contrary I have again, and again revolved them, with thoughtful anxiety; but without being able to dispose my mind to a longer continua- tion in the Office I have now the honor to hold. I therefore still look forward to the fulfilment of my fondest and most ardent wishes to spend the remainder of my days (which I can not expect will be many) in ease and tranquility.

Continuation in office

Nothing short of conviction that my deriliction of the Chair of Government (if it should be the desire of the people to continue me in it) would involve the Country in serious dis- putes respecting the chief Magestrate, and the disagreeable consequences which might result therefrom in the floating, and divided opinions which seem to prevail at present, could, in any wise, induce me to relinquish the determination I have formed: and of this I do not see how any evidence can be obtained previous to the Election. My vanity, I am sure, is not of that cast as to allow me to view the subject in this light.

Under these impressions then, permit me to reiterate the request I made to you at our last meeting, namely, to think of the proper time, and the best mode of anouncing the intention; and that you would prepare the latter. In revolving this subject myself, my judgment has always been embarrassed. On the one hand, a previous declaration to retire, not only carries with it the appearance of vanity and self importance, but it may be construed into a manoeuvre to be invited to remain. And on the other hand, to say nothing, implys consent; or, at any rate, would leave the matter in doubt, and to decline afterwards might be deemed as bad, and uncandid.

I would fain carry my request to you farther than is asked above, although I am sensible that your compliance with it must add to your trouble; but as the recess may afford you leizure, and I flatter myself you have dispositions to oblige me, I will, without apology desire (if the measure in itself should strike you as proper, and likely to produce public good, or private honor) that you would turn your thoughts to a *Planned farewell* Valadictory address from me to the public; expressing in plain *address* and modest terms: that having been honored with the Presidential Chair, and to the best of my abilities contributed to the Organization and Administration of the government, that having arrived at a period of life when the private Walks of it, in the shade of retirement, becomes necessary, and will be most pleasing to me; and the spirit of the government may render a rotation in the Elective Officers of it more congenial with their ideas of liberty and safety, that I take my leave of them as a public man; and in bidding them adieu (retaining no other concern than such as will arise from fervent wishes for the prosperity of my Country) I take the liberty at my departure from civil, as I formerly did at my military exit, to invoke a continuation of the blessings of Providence upon it; and upon all those who are supporters of its interests, and the promoters of harmony, order and good government.

That to impress these things it might, among other things be observed, that we are *all* the Children of the same country; a Country great and rich in itself; capable, and promising to be, as prosperous and as happy as any the Annals of history have ever brought to our view. That our interest, however, deversified in local and smaller matters, is the same in all the great and essential concerns of the Nation. That the extent of our Country, the diversity of our climate and soil, and the various productions of the States consequent to both, are such as to make one part not only convenient, but perhaps indispensably necessary to the other part; and may render the whole (at no distant period) one of the most independant in the world. That the established government being the work of our own hands, with the seeds of amendment engrafted in the Constitution, may by wisdom, good dispositions, and mutual allowances; aided by experience, bring it as near to perfection as any human institution ever aproximated; and therefore, the only strife among us ought to be, who should be foremost in facilitating and finally accomplishing such great and desirable objects; by giving every possible support, and cement to the Union. That however necessary it may be to keep a watchful eye over public servants, and public measures, yet there ought to be limits to it; for suspicions unfounded, and jealousies too lively, are irritating to honest feelings; and oftentimes are productive of more evil than good.

To enumerate the various subjects which might be introduced into such an Address would require thought; and to mention them to you would be unnecessary, as your own judgment will comprehend *all* that will be proper; whether to touch, specifically, any of the exceptionable parts of the Constitution may be doubted. All I shall add therefore at present, is, to beg the favor of you to consider: 1st. the propriety of such an Address. 2d. if approved, the several matters which ought to be contained in it; and 3d. the time it should appear: that is, whether at the declaration of my intention to withdraw from the service of the public; or to let it be the closing Act of my Administration; which, will end with the next Session of Congress (the probability being that that body will continue sitting until March,) when the House of Representatives will also dissolve.

'Though I do not wish to hurry you (the cases not pressing) in the execution of either of the publications beforementioned, yet I should be glad to hear from you generally on both; and to receive them in time, if you should not come to Philadelphia until the Session commences, in the form they are finally to take. I beg leave to draw your attention also to such things as you shall conceive fit subjects for Communication on that occasion; and, noting them as they occur, that you would be so good as to furnish me with them in time to be prepared, and engrafted with others for the opening of the Session. With very sincere and Affectionate regard etc.

197

TO MARQUIS DE LAFAYETTE

Philadelphia, June, 10, 1792

My dear Sir:

In the revolution of a great Nation we must not be surprized at the vicissitudes to which individuals are liable; and the changes they experience will always be in proportion to the weight of their public character; I was therefore not surprised, my dear Sir, at receiving your letter dated at Metz which you had the goodness to write me on the 22d of January. That personal ease and private enjoyment is not your primary object I well know, and until peace and tranquillity are restored to your Country upon permanent and honorable grounds I was fully persuaded, in my own mind, that you could not be permitted long to enjoy that domestic retirement, into which you had fondly entered.

Events in Europe

Since the commencement of your revolution our attention has been drawn, with no small anxiety, almost to France alone; but at this moment Europe in general seems pregnant with great events, and to whatever nation we turn our eyes there appears to be more or less cause to believe, that an important change will take place at no very distant period. Those philanthropic spirits who regard the happiness of mankind are now watching the progress of things with the greatest solicitude, and consider the event of the present crisis as fixing the fate of man. How great! How important, therefore, is the part, which the actors in this momentous scene have to perform! Not only the fate of millions of the present day depends upon them, but the happiness of posterity is involved in their decisions.

You who are on the spot cannot, I presume, determine when or where these great beginnings will terminate, and for us, at this distance to pretend to give an opinion to that effect would at least be deemed presumptuous. We are however, anxious that the horrors of war may be avoided, if possible, and the rights of man so well understood and so permanently fixed, as while despotic oppression is avoided on the one hand, licentiousness may not be substituted for liberty nor confusion take place of order on the other. The just medium cannot be expected to be found in a moment, the first vibrations always go to the extremes, and cool reason, which can alone establish a permanent and equal government, is as little to be expected in the tumults of popular commotion, as an attention to the liberties of the people is to be found in the dark Divan of a despotic tyrant.

I assure you, my dear Sir, I have not been a little anxious for your personal safety, and I have yet no grounds for removing that anxiety; but I have the consolation of believing that, if you should fall it will be in defence of that cause which your heart tells you is just. And to the care of that Providence, whose interposition and protection we have so often experienced, do I chearfully commit you and your nation, trusting that he will bring order out of confusion, and finally place things upon the ground on which they ought to stand.

Concern for Lafayette's safety

The affairs of the United States still go on in a prosperous train. We encrease daily in numbers and riches, and the people are blessed with the enjoyment of those rights which can alone give security and happiness to a Nation. The War with the Indians on our western frontier will, I hope, be terminated in the course of the present season without further effusion of blood; but, in case the measures taken to promote a pacification should fail, such steps are pursued as must, I think, render the issue by the sword very unfavorable to them.

Indian War

Soon after the rising of Congress I made a journey to Mount Vernon, from whence I returned but a few days ago, and expect, (if nothing of a public nature should occur to detain me here) to go there again some time next month with Mrs. Washington and her two little grand children, where we shall continue 'till near the next meeting of Congress.

Your friends in this Country are interested in your welfare, and frequently enquire about you with an anxiety that bespeaks a warm affection. I am afraid my Nephew George, your old Aid, will never have his health perfectly re-established, he has lately been attacked with the alarming symptom of spitting large quantities of blood, and the Physicians give no hopes of a restoration unless it can be effected by a change of air, and a total dereliction of business, to which he is too anxiously attentive. [He will, if he should be taken from his family and friends leave three fine childn. viz. two Sons and a daughter, the eldest of the boys he has given the name of Fayette to and a fine looking child he is.]

Hamilton Knox Jay and Jefferson are well and remember you with affection. Mrs. Washington desires to be presented to you in terms of friendship and warm regard, to which I add my most affectionate wishes and sincere prayers for your health and happiness, and request you to make the same acceptable to Madm. le Fayette and your children. [I am &c.]

198

TO THE SECRETARY OF THE TREASURY

Private and Confidential

Mount Vernon, July 29, 1792

My dear Sir:*

I have not yet received the new regulation of allowances to the Surveyors, or Collectors of the duties on Spirituous liquors; but this by the bye. My present purpose is to write you a letter on a more interesting and important subject. I do it in strict confidence, and with frankness and freedom.

Concern with sentiments towards public measures

On my way home, and since my arrival here, I have endeavoured to learn from sensible and moderate men, known friends to the Government, the sentiments which are entertained of public measures. These all agree that the Country is prosperous and happy; but they seem to be alarmed at that system of policy, and those interpretations of the Constitution which have taken place in Congress. Others, less friendly perhaps to the Government, and more disposed to arraign the conduct of its Officers (among whom may be classed my neigbour, and quandom friend Colo. M) go further, and enumerate a variety of matters, wch. as well as I can recollect, may be adduced under the following heads. Viz.

Public debt

First. That the public debt is greater than we can possibly pay before other causes of adding new debt to it will occur;

---

*Alexander Hamilton

and that this has been artificially created by adding together the whole amount of the debtor and creditor sides of the accounts, instead of taking only their balances; which could have been paid off in a short time.

2d. That this accumlation of debt has taken forever out of our power those easy sources of revenue, which, applied to the ordinary necessities and exigencies of Government, would have answered them habitually, and covered us from habitual murmerings against taxes and tax gatherers; reserving extraordinary calls, for extraordinary occasions, would animate the People to meet them.

3d. That the calls for money have been no greater than we must generally expect, for the same or equivalent exigencies; yet we are already obliged to strain the *impost* till it produces clamour, and will produce evasion, and war on our Citizens to collect it, and even to resort to an *Excise* law, of odious character with the people; partial in its operation; unproductive unless enforced by arbitrary and vexatious means; and committing the authority of the Government in parts where resistance is most probable, and coercion least practicable.

4th. They cite propositions in Congress, and suspect other projects on foot, still to encrease the mass of the debt.

5th. They say that by borrowing at ⅔ of the interest, we might have paid off the principal in ⅔ of the time; but that from this we are precluded by its being made irredeemable but in small portions, and long terms.

6th. That this irredeemable quality was given it for the avowed purpose of inviting its transfer to foreign Countries.

7th. They predict that this transfer of the principal, when compleated, will occasion an exportation of 3 millions of dollars annually for the interest; a drain of Coin, of which as there has been no example, no calculation can be made of its consequences.

8th. That the banishment of our Coin will be compleated by the creation of 10 millions of paper money, in the form of Bank-bills, now issuing into circulation. *Paper money*

9th. They think the 10 or 12 pr. Ct. annual profit, paid to the lenders of this paper medium, are taken out of the pockets of the people, who would have had without interest the coin it is banishing.

10th. That all the Capitol employed in paper speculation is

barren and useless, producing, like that on a gaming table, no accession to itself, and is withdrawn from Commerce and Agriculture where it would have produced addition to the common mass.

Nourishment of vice

11th. That it nourishes in our citizens vice and idleness instead of industry and morality.

12th. That it has furnished effectual means of corrupting such a portion of the legislature, as turns the balance between the honest Voters whichever way it is directed.

13th. That this corrupt squadron, deciding the voice of the legislature, have manifested their dispositions to get rid of the limitations imposed by the Constitution on the general legislature; limitations, on the faith of which, the States acceded to that instrument.

Overthrow of Republican government

14th. That the ultimate object of all this is to prepare the way for a change, from the present republican form of Government, to that of a monarchy; of which the British Constitution is to be the model.

15th. That this was contemplated in the Convention, they say is no secret, because its partisans have made none of it; to effect it then was impracticable; but they are still eager after their object, and are predisposing every thing for its ultimate attainment.

16th. So many of them have got into the legislature, that, aided by the corrupt squadron of paper dealers, who are at their devotion, they make a majority in both houses.

17th. The republican party who wish to preserve the Government in its present form, are fewer even when joined by the two, three, or half a dozen antifederalists, who, tho' they dare not avow it, are still opposed to any general Government: but being less so to a republican than a Monarchical one, they naturally join those whom they think pursuing the lesser evil.

Elections as hope for the future

18th. Of all the mischiefs objected to the system of measures before mentioned, none they add is so afflicting, and fatal to every honest hope, as the corruption of the legislature. As it was the earliest of these measures it became the instrument for producing the rest, and will be the instrument for producing in future a King, Lords and Commons; or whatever else those who direct it may chuse. Withdrawn such a distance from the eye of their Constituents, and these so dispersed as to be inaccessible to the public information, and particularly to that of the conduct of their own Representatives, they will form the worst Government upon earth, if the means of their corruption be not prevented.

19th. The only hope of safety they say, hangs now on the numerous representation which is to come forward the ensuing year; but should the majority of the new members be still in the same principles with the present; shew so much dereliction to republican government, and such a disposition to encroach upon, or explain away the limited powers of the Constitution in order to change it, it is not easy to conjecture what would be the result, nor what means would be resorted to for the correction of the evil. True wisdom they acknowledge should direct temperate and peaceable measures; but add, the division of sentiment and interest happens unfortunately, to be so geographical, that no mortal can say that what is most wise and temperate, would prevail against what is more easy and obvious; they declare, they can contemplate no evil more incalculable than the breaking of the Union into two, or more parts; yet, when they view the mass which opposed the original coalescence, when they consider that it lay chiefly in the Southern Quarter, that the legislature have availed themselves of no occasion of allaying it, but on the contrary whenever Northern and Southern prejudices have come into conflict, the latter have been sacrificed and the former soothed.

Corruption of legislature

Northern and Southern prejudices

20th. That the owers of the debt are in the Southern and the holders of it in the Northern division.

21st. That the antifederal champions are now strengthened in argument by the fulfilment of their predictions, which has been brought about by the Monarchical federalists themselves; who, having been for the New government merely as a stepping stone to Monarchy, have themselves adopted the very construction, of which, when advocating its acceptance before the tribunal of the people, they declared it insusceptable; whilst the republican federalists, who espoused the same government for its intrinsic merits, are disarmed of their weapons, that which they denied as prophecy being now become true history. Who, therefore, can be sure they ask, that these things may not proselyte the small number which was wanting to place the majority on the other side; and this they add is the event at which they tremble.

Monarchical federalists and republican federalists

These, as well as my memory serves me, are the sentiments which, directly and indirectly, have been disclosed to me. To obtain light, and to pursue truth, being my sole aim; and wishing to have before me *explanations* of as well as the *complaints* on measures in which the public interest, harmony and peace is so deeply concerned, and my public conduct so much involved; it is my request, and you would oblige me by furnishing me, with your ideas upon the discontents here enumerated; and for this purpose I have thrown them into heads or sections, and numbered them that those ideas may apply to the corrispondent numbers. Although I do not mean to hurry you in giving your thoughts on the occasion of this letter, yet, as soon as you can make it convenient to yourself it would, for more reasons than one, be agreeable, and very satisfactory to me.

The enclosure in your letter of the 16th was sent back the Post after I received it, with my approving signature; and in a few days I will write to the purpose mentioned in your letter of the 22d. both to the Secretary of War and yourself. At present all my business, public and private, is on my own shoulders; the two young Gentlemen who came home with me, being on visits to their friends, and my Nephew, the Major, too much indisposed to afford me any aid, in copying or in other matters. With affectionate regard &c.

199
——————

TO THE SECRETARY OF STATE

Private

Mount Vernon, August 23, 1792

My dear Sir:*

Your letters of the 12th. and 13th came duly to hand, as did that enclosing Mr. Blodgets plan of a Capitol. The latter I forwarded to the Commissioners, and the enclosures of the two first are now returned to you.

I believe we are never to hear *from* Mr. Carmichael; nor *of him* but through the medium of a third person. His ——— I really do not know with what epithet to fill the blank, is, to me, amongst the most unaccountable of all the unaccountable

——————————
*Thomas Jefferson

things! I wish much to hear of the arrival of Mr. Short at
Madrid, and the result of their joint negotiations at that Court,
as we have fresh, and much stronger Representations from
Mr. Seagrove of the extraordinary interference of the
Spaniards in West Florida, to prevent running the boundary
line which had been established by treaty between the United
States and the Creeks, of their promising them support in case
of their refusal; and of their endeavouring to disaffect the four
Southern tribes of Indians towards this Country. In the execution of these projects Seagrove is convinced McGillivray and
his partner Panton are embarked, and have become principal
agents; and there are suspicions entertained, he adds, that the
Capture of Bowles was a preconcerted measure between the
said Bowles and the Spaniards. That the former is gone to
Spain (and to Madrid I think) is certain. That McGillivray has
removed from little Tellassee to a place he has within, or bor-
dering on the Spanish line. That a Captn. Oliver, a French-
man, but an Officer in a Spanish Regiment at New Orleans,
has taken his place at Tellassee and is holding talks with the
Chiefs of the several Towns in the Nation. And that every
exertion is making by the Governor of West Florida to obtain a
full and general meeting of the Southern Tribes at Pensicola,
are facts that admit of *no doubt*. It is also affirmed that five
Regiments of about 600 men each, and a large quantity of
Ordnance and Stores arrived lately at New Orleans, and that
the like number of Regiments (but this can only be from report) was expected at the same place from the Havanna. Recent accts. from Arthur Campbell (I hope without *much* foundation) speak of very hostile dispositions in the lower
Cherokees, and of great apprehension for the safety of Govr.
Blount and Genl. Pickens who had set out for the proposed
meeting with the Chicasaws and Choctaws at Nashville, and
for the Goods which were going down the Tenessee by Water,
for that Meeting.

Our accounts from the Western Indns. are not more favourable than those just mentioned. No doubt remains of their
having put to death Majr. Trueman and Colo. Hardin; and
the Harbingers of their mission. The report from their grand
Council is, that War was, or soon would be, decided on; and
that they will admit no Flags. The meeting was numerous and
not yet dissolved that we have been informed of. What influ-

ence our Indn. Agents may have at it, remains to be known. Hendricks left Buffaloe Creek between the 18th. and 20th. of June, accompanied by two or three of the Six Nations; some of the Chiefs of those Nations were to follow in a few days, only waiting, it was said, for the Caughnawaga Indians from Canada. And Captn. Brandt would not be long after them. If these attempts to disclose the just and pacific disposition of the United States to these people, should also fail, there remains no alternative but the Sword, to decide the difference; and recruiting goes on heavily. If Spain is really intrieguing with the Southern Indians as represented by Mr. Seagrove, I shall entertain strong suspicions that there is a very clear understanding in all this business between the Courts of London and Madrid; and that it is calculated to check, as far as they can, the rapid encrease, extension and consequence of this Country; for there cannot be a doubt of the wishes of the former (if we may judge from the conduct of its Officers) to impede any eclaircissment of ours with the Western Indians, and to embarrass our negotiations with them, any more than there is of their Traders and some others who are subject to their Government, aiding and abetting them in acts of hostilities.

Internal dissensions   How unfortunate, and how much is it to be regretted then, that whilst we are encompassed on all sides with avowed enemies and insidious friends, that internal dissensions should be harrowing and tearing our vitals. The last, to me, is the most serious, the most alarming, and the most afflicting of the two. And without more charity for the opinions and acts of one another in Governmental matters, or some more infalible criterion by which the truth of speculative opinions, before they have undergone the test of experience, are to be forejudged than has yet fallen to the lot of fallibility, I believe it will be difficult, if not impracticable, to manage the Reins of Government or to keep the parts of it together: for if, instead of laying our shoulders to the machine after measures are decided on, one pulls this way and another that, before the utility of the thing is fairly tried, it must, inevitably, be torn asunder. And, in my opinion the fairest prospect of happiness and prosperity that ever was presented to man, will be lost, perhaps for ever!

My earnest wish, and my fondest hope therefore is, that instead of wounding suspicions, and irritable charges, there may be liberal allowances, mutual forebearances, and temporising yieldings on *all sides*. Under the exercise of these, matters will go on smoothly, and, if possible, more prosperously. Without them every thing must rub; the Wheels of Government will clog; our enemies will triumph, and by throwing their weight into the disaffected Scale, may accomplish the ruin of the goodly fabric we have been erecting.

I do not mean to apply these observations, or this advice to any particular person, or character. I have given them in the same general terms to other Officers of the Government; because the disagreements which have arisen from difference of opinions, and the Attacks wch. have been made upon almost all the measures of government, and most of its Executive Officers, have, for a long time past, filled me with painful sensations; and cannot fail I think, of producing unhappy consequences at home and abroad.

The nature of Mr. Seagroves communications was such, and the evidence in support of them so strongly corroborative, that I gave it as my sentiment to Genl. Knox that the Commissioners of Spain ought to have the matter brought before them again in the manner it was before, but in stronger (though not in committing) language; as the Government was embarrassed, and its Citizens in the Southern States made uneasy by such proceedings, however unauthorized they might be by their Court.

200

TO THE SECRETARY
OF THE TREASURY

Private

Mount Vernon, August 26, 1792

My dear Sir:*

Your letter of the 18th. enclosing answers to certain objections communicated to you in my letter of the 29th. Ulto. came duly to hand; and although I have not, at yet, from a variety of causes, been able to give them the attentive reading I mean to

---

*Alexander Hamilton

bestow, I feel myself much obliged by the trouble you have taken to answer them; as I persuade myself, from the full manner in which you appear to have taken up the Subject, that I shall receive both satisfaction and profit from the perusal.

Differences in political opinions

Differences in political opinions are as unavoidable as, to a certain point, they may, perhaps, be necessary; but it is exceedingly to be regretted that subjects cannot be discussed with temper on the one hand, or decisions submitted to without having the motives which led to them improperly implicated on the other: and this regret borders on chagrin when we find that men of abilities, zealous patriots, having the same *general* objects in view, and the same upright intentions to prosecute them, will not excercise more charity in deciding on the opinions and actions of one another. When matters get to such lengths, the natural inference is, that both sides have strained the Cords beyond their bearing, and, that a middle course would be found the best, until experience shall have decided on the right way, or, which is not to be expected, because it is denied to mortals, there shall be some *infallible* rule by which we could *fore-judge* events.

Having premised these things, I would fain hope that liberal allowances will be made for the political opinions of each other; and instead of those wounding suspicions, and irritating charges, with which some of our Gazettes are so strongly impregnated, and cannot fail if persevered in, of pushing matters to extremity, and thereby to tare the Machine asunder, that there might be mutual forbearances and temporizing yieldings *on all sides*. Without these I do not see how the Reins of government are to be managed, or how the Union of the States can be much longer preserved.

How unfortunate would it be if a fabric so goodly, erected under so many Providential circumstances, and in its first stages, having acquired such respectability, should from diversity of sentiments or internal obstructions to some of the acts of Government (for I cannot prevail on myself to believe that these measures are as yet the deliberate acts of a determined party) should be harrowing our vitals in such a manner as to have brought us to the verge of dissolution. Melancholy thought! But one at the same time that it shows the consequences of diversified opinions, when pushed with too much tenacity, it exhibits evidence also of the necessity of accommodation, and of the propriety of adopting such healing measures as may restore harmony to the discordant members of the Union, and the Governing powers of it.

I do not mean to apply this advice to any measures which are passed or to any particular character; I have given it in the same *general* terms to other Officers of the Government. My earnest wish is, that balsam may be poured into *all* the wounds which have been given, to prevent them from gangrening and from those fatal consequences which the community may sustain if it is with held. The friends of the Union must wish this; those who are not, but wish to see it rended, will be disappointed, and all things I hope will go well.

We have learnt through the medium of Mr. Harrison to Doctr. Craik, that you have some thoughts of taking a trip this way. I felt pleasure at hearing it, and hope it is unnecessary to add that it would be considerably encreased by seeing you under this roof; for you may be assured of the sincere and Affecte. regard of yours, &c.

PS: I pray you to Note down whatever may occur to you, not only in your own department but other matters also of general import that may be fit subjects for the Speech at the opening of the ensuing Session.

201

TO THE ATTORNEY GENERAL

Private

Mount Vernon, August 26, 1792

My dear Sir:*

The purpose of this letter is merely to acknowledge the receipt of your favors of the 5th. and 13th. instt., and to thank you for the information contained in both without entering into the details of either.

With respect, however, to the interesting subject treated on in that of the 5th., I can express but one sentiment at this time,

---

*Edmund Randolph

and that is a wish, a devout one, that whatever my ultimate determination shall be, it may be for the best. The subject never recurs to my mind but with additional poignancy; and from the declining State in the health of my Nephew, to whom my concerns of a domestic and private nature are entrusted it comes with aggrivated force. But as the allwise disposer of events has hitherto watched over my steps, I trust that in the important one I may soon be called upon to take, he will mark the course so plainly, as that cannot mistake the way. In full hope of this, I will take no measure, yet a while, that will not leave me at liberty to decide from circumstances, and the best lights, I can obtain on the Subject.

Newspaper abuse   I shall be happy in the mean time to see a cessation of the abuses of public Officers, and of those attacks upon almost every measure of government with which some of the Gazettes are so strongly impregnated; and which cannot fail, if persevered in with the malignancy they now teem, of rending the Union asunder. The Seeds of discontent, distrust, and irritations which are so plentifully sown, can scarcely fail to produce this effect and to Mar that prospect of happiness which perhaps never beamed with more effulgence upon any people under the Sun; and this too at a time when all Europe are gazing with admiration at the brightness of our prospects. And for what is all this? Among other things, to afford Nuts for our transatlantic, what shall I call them? Foes!

In a word if the Government and the Officers of it are to be the constant theme for News-paper abuse, and this too without condescending to investigate the motives or the facts, it will be impossible, I conceive, for any man living to manage the helm, or to keep the machine together. But I am running from my text, and therefore will only add assurances of the Affecte. esteem and regard with which I am &c.

202

PROCLAMATION

Private

September *15, 1792*

Whereas certain violent and unwarrantable proceedings have lately taken place tending to obstruct the operation of the laws of the United States for raising a revenue upon spirits distilled within the same, enacted pursuant to express authority delegated in the constitution of the United States; which proceedings are subversive of good order, contrary to the duty that every citizen owes to his country, and to the laws, and of a nature dangerous to the very being of a government:

Concerning the whiskey excise tax

And whereas such proceedings are the more unwarrantable, by reason of the moderation which has been heretofore shewn on the part of the government, and of the disposition which has been manifested by the Legislature (who alone have authority to suspend the operation of laws) to obviate causes of objection, and to render the laws as acceptable as possible: And whereas it is the particular duty of the Executive "to take care that the laws be faithfully executed"; and not only that the duty, but the permanent interests and happiness of the people require, that every legal and necessary step should be pursued, as well to prevent such violent and unwarrantable proceedings, as to bring to justice the infractors of the laws and secure obedience thereto.

Now therefore I George Washington, President of the United States, do by these presents most earnestly admonish and exhort all persons whom it may concern, to refrain and desist from all unlawful combinations and proceedings whatsoever having for object or tending to obstruct the operation of the laws aforesaid; inasmuch as all lawful ways and means will be strictly put in execution for bringing to justice the infractors thereof and securing obedience thereto.

And I do moreover charge and require all Courts, Magistrates and Officers whom it may concern, according to the duties of their several offices, to exert the powers in them respectively vested by law for the purposes aforesaid, hereby also enjoining and requiring all persons whomsoever, as they tender the welfare of their country, the just and due authority of government and the preservation of the public peace, to be aiding and assisting therein according to law.

203

TO THE SECRETARY OF STATE

Philadelphia, October 18, 1792

My dear Sir:*

Urges reconciliation of Hamilton and Jefferson

I did not require the evidence of the extracts which you enclosed me, to convince me of your attachment to the Constitution of the United States, or of your disposition to promote the general Welfare of this Country. But I regret, deeply regret, the difference in opinions which have arisen, and divided you and another principal Officer of the Government; and wish, devoutly, there could be an accommodation of them by mutual yieldings.

A Measure of this sort would produce harmony, and consequent good in our public Councils; the contrary will, inevitably, introduce confusion, and serious mischiefs; and for what? because mankind cannot think alike, but would adopt different means to attain the same end. For I will frankly, and solemnly declare that, I believe the views of both of you are pure, and well meant; and that experience alone will decide with respect to the salubrity of the measures wch. are the subjects of dispute. Why then, when some of the best Citizens in the United States, Men of discernment, Uniform and tried Patriots, who have no sinister views to promote, but are chaste in their ways of thinking and acting are to be found, some on one side, and some on the other of the questions which have caused these agitations, shd. either of you be so tenacious of your opinions as to make no allowances for those of the other? I could, and indeed was about to add more to this interesting subject; but will forbear, at least for the present; after expressing a wish that the cup wch. has been presented, may not be snatched from our lips by a discordance of *action* when I am persuaded there is no discordance in your *views*. I have a great,

*Thomas Jefferson

Trials of Division

a sincere esteem and regard for you both, and ardently wish that some line could be marked out by which both of you could walk. I am &c.

204

PROCLAMATION

Philadelphia, December 12, 1792

Whereas I have received authentic information, that certain lawless and wicked persons, of the western frontier in the State of Georgia, did lately invade, burn, and destroy a town belonging to the Cherokee nation, although in amity with the United States, and put to death several Indians of that nation; and whereas such outrageous conduct not only violates the rights of humanity, but also endangers the public peace, and it highly becomes the honor and good faith of the United States to pursue all legal means for the punishment of those atrocious offenders; I have, therefore, thought fit to issue this my proclamation, hereby exhorting all the citizens of the United States, and requiring all the officers thereof, according to their respective stations, to use their utmost endeavours to bring those offenders to justice. And I do moreover offer a reward of five hundred dollars for each and every of the above-named persons, who shall be so apprehended and brought to justice, and shall be proved to have assumed or exercised any command or authority among the perpetrators of the crimes aforesaid, at the time of committing the same.

Crimes against the Cherokee nation

205

PROCLAMATION OF NEUTRALITY

Philadelphia, April 22, 1793

Whereas it appears that a state of war exists between Austria, Prussia, Sardinia, Great Britain, and the United Netherlands, on the one part, and France on the other; and the duty and interest of the United States require, that they should with sincerity and good faith adopt and pursue a conduct friendly and impartial towards the belligerent powers:

Policy toward the war in Europe

I have therefore thought fit by these presents, to declare the disposition of the United States to observe the conduct aforesaid towards those powers respectively; and to exhort and warn the citizens of the United States carefully to avoid all acts and proceedings whatsoever, which may in any manner tend to contravene such disposition.

And I do hereby also make known, that whosoever of the citizens of the United States shall render himself liable to punishment or forfeiture under the law of nations, by committing, aiding or abetting hostilities against any of the said powers, or by carrying to any of them, those articles which are deemed contraband by the modern usage of nations, will not receive the protection of the United States against such punishment or forfeiture; and further that I have given instructions to those officers to whom it belongs, to cause prosecutions to be instituted against all persons, who shall, within the cognizance of the Courts of the United States, violate the law of nations, with respect to the powers at war, or any of them.

206

TO GOVERNOR HENRY LEE

Private

Philadelphia, July 21, 1793

Dear Sir:

I should have thanked you at an earlier period for your obliging letter of the 14th. ulto. had it not come to my hands a day or two only before I set out for Mount Vernon; and at a time when I was much hurried, and indeed very much perplexed with the disputes, memorials and what not, with which the Government were pestered by one or other of the petulant representatives of the powers at War: and because, since my return to this City (nine days ago) I have been more than ever overwhelmed with their complaints. In a word, the trouble they give is hardly to be described.

My journey to and from Mount Vernon was sudden and rapid, and as short as I could make it. It was occasioned by the unexpected death of Mr. Whitting (my manager) at a critical season for the business with wch. he was entrusted. Where to supply his place, I know not; of course my concerns at Mount Vernon are left as a body without a head; but this by the bye.

The communications in your letter were pleasing and grateful; for, although I have done no public act with which my mind upbraids me, yet it is highly satisfactory to learn that the things which I do (of an interesting tendency to the peace and happiness of this Country) are generally approved by my fellow Citizens. But, were the case otherwise, I should not be less inclined to know the sense of the people upon every matter of great public concern; for, as I have no wish superior to that of promoting the happiness and welfare of this Country, so, consequently, it is only for me to know the means to accomplish the end, if it be within the compass of my powers.

That there are in this, as well as in all other Countries, discontented characters, I well know; as also that these characters are actuated by very different views: Some good, from an opinion that the measures of the General Government are impure: some bad, and (if I might be allowed to use so harsh an expression) diabolical; inasmuch as they are not only meant to impede the measures of that Government generally, but more especially (as a great mean towards the accomplishment of it) to destroy the confidence, which it is necessary for the people to place (until they have unequivocal proof of demerit) in their public servants; for in this light I consider myself, whilst I am an occupant of office; and, if they were to go further and call me their slave, (during this period) I would not dispute the point. *Opposition to the government*

But in what will this abuse terminate? The result, as it respects myself, I care not; for I have a consolation within, that no earthly efforts can deprive me of, and that is, that neither ambitious nor interested motives have influenced my conduct. The arrows of malevolence, therefore, however barbed and well pointed, never can reach the most vulnerable part of me; though, whilst I am *up* as a *mark*, they will be continually aimed. The publications in Freneau's and Bache's papers are outrages on common decency; and they progress in that style, in proportion as their pieces are treated with contempt, and are passed by in silence, by those at whom they are aimed. The tendency of them, however, is too obvious to be mistaken by men of cool and dispassionate minds, and, in my opinion, *Philip Freneau and Benjamin Bache* ought to alarm them; because it is difficult to prescribe bounds to the effect.

The light in which you endeavored to place the views and conduct of this Country to Mr. G[enet]; and the sound policy thereof, as it respected his own, was, unquestionably the true one, and such as a man of penetration, left to himself, would most certainly have viewed them in; but mum on this head. Time may unfold more, than prudence ought to disclose at present. As we are told, that you have exchanged the rugged and dangerous field of Mars, for the soft and pleasurable bed of Venus, I do in this, as I shall in every thing you may pursue like unto it good and laudable, wish you all imaginable success and happiness being, with esteem &c.

207

PROCLAMATION

City of Philadelphia, March 24, 1794

Warning on enlisting troops in the United States

Whereas I have received information that certain persons, in violation of the laws, have presumed, under color of a foreign authority, to enlist citizens of the United States and others within the State of Kentucky, and have there assembled an armed force for the purpose of invading and plundering the territories of a nation at peace with the said United States;* and

Whereas such unwarrantable measures, being contrary to the laws of nations and to the duties incumbent on every citi-

---

*Having put a formal end to the troublesome career of Citizen-Genet (French Ambassador to the United States, 1793) with his January 20, 1794, message to Congress announcing Genet's recall, Washington hoped to be free of concerns about foreigners raising armies within the United States to fight in international crusades. Nevertheless, not all of Genet's machinations faded so quickly into the background as he did. A "commission" which Genet had granted the aging General George Rogers Clark had produced efforts to raise an army in Kentucky in the winter and spring of 1793–94. The purpose of the army was to invade the dominions of Spain (Britain's ally) at the base of the Mississippi. A sympathetic Kentucky governor, Isaac Shelby, along with two Frenchmen, Auguste Lachaise and Charles Delpeau, designed to orchestrate the expedition, lending credibility to Administration fears of unwanted foreign entanglements at a time when war fever against Britain was already running high. This proclamation was the first in a series of moves through 1794 intended to reduce the likelihood of general war.

zen of the United States, tend to disturb the tranquillity of the same, and to involve them in the calamities of war; and

Whereas it is the duty of the Executive to take care that such criminal proceedings should be suppressed, the offenders brought to justice, and all good citizens cautioned against measures likely to prove so pernicious to their country and themselves, should they be seduced into similar infractions of the laws:

I have therefore thought proper to issue this proclamation, hereby solemnly warning every person, not authorized by the laws, against enlisting any citizen or citizens of the United States, or levying troops, or assembling any persons within the United States for the purposes aforesaid, or proceeding in any manner to the execution thereof, as they will answer for the same at their peril; and I do also admonish and require all citizens to refrain from enlisting, enrolling, or assembling themselves for such unlawful purposes and from being in anywise concerned, aiding, or abetting therein, as they tender their own welfare, inasmuch as all lawful means will be strictly put in execution for securing obedience to the laws and for punishing such dangerous and daring violations thereof.

And I do moreover charge and require all courts, magistrates, and other officers whom it may concern, according to their respective duties, to exert the powers in them severally vested to prevent and suppress all such unlawful assemblages and proceedings, and to bring to condign punishment those who may have been guilty thereof, as they regard the due authority of Government and the peace and welfare of the United States.

208

PROCLAMATION

Philadelphia, August 7, 1794

Whereas combinations to defeat the execution of the laws laying duties upon spirits distilled within the United States, and upon stills, have from the time of the commencement of those laws existed in some of the Western parts of Pennsylvania:

Opposition to duties on spirits and stills

And whereas the said combinations, proceeding in a manner subversive equally of the just authority of Government and of the rights of individuals, have hitherto effected their dangerous and criminal purpose; by the influence of certain irregular meetings, whose proceedings have tended to encourage and uphold the spirit of opposition; by misrepresentations of the laws calculated to render them odious; by endeavors to deter those, who might be so disposed from accepting offices under them, through fear of public resentment and of injury to person and property, and to compel those who had accepted such offices, by actual violence to surrender or forbear the execution of them; by circulating vindictive menaces against all those who should otherwise directly or indirectly aid in the execution of the said laws, or who, yielding to the dictates of conscience, and to a sense of obligation, should themselves comply therewith; by actually injuring and destroying the property of persons who were understood to have so complied; by inciting cruel and humiliating punishments upon private citizens for no other cause, than that of appearing to be friends of the laws; by intercepting the public officers on the highways, abusing, assaulting, and otherwise ill-treating them; by going to their houses in the night, gaining admittance by force, taking away their papers, and committing other outrages, employing for these unwarrantable purposes the agency of armed banditti disguised in such manner as for the most part to escape discovery:

And whereas the endeavors of the Legislature to obviate objections to the said laws, by lowering the duties and by other alterations conducive to the convenience of those whom they immediately affect (though they have given satisfaction in other quarters,) and the endeavors of the executive officers to conciliate a compliance with the laws, by explanations, by forbearance, and even by particular accommodations, founded on the suggestions of local considerations, have been disappointed of their effect by the machinations of persons whose industry to excite resistance has increased with every appearance of a disposition among the people to relax in their opposition and to acquiesce in the laws, insomuch that many persons in the said Western parts of Pennsylvania have at length been hardy enough to perpetrate acts which I am advised amount to treason, being overt acts of levying war against the United States; the said persons having on the sixteenth and *Attacks on public* seventeenth of July last past proceeded in arms (on the second *servants* day, amounting to several hundreds) to the house of John

Neville, inspector of the revenue for the fourth survey of the district of Pennsylvania, having repeatedly attacked the said house with the persons therein, wounding some of them; having seized David Lenox, marshal of the district of Pennsylvania, who, previous thereto, had been fired upon while in the execution of his duty, by a party of armed men, detaining him for some time prisoner, till, for the preservation of his life and the obtaining of his liberty, he found it necessary to enter into stipulations to forbear the execution of certain official duties touching processes issuing out of a Court of the United States; and having finally obliged the said inspector of the revenue, and the said marshal, from considerations of personal safety, to fly from that part of the country, in order, by a circuitous route, to proceed to the seat of Government; avowing as the motives of these outrageous proceedings an intention to prevent by force of arms the execution of the said laws, to oblige the said inspector of the revenue to renounce his said office, to withstand by open violence the lawful authority of the Government of the United States, and to compel thereby an alteration in the measures of the Legislature and a repeal of the laws aforesaid.

And whereas, by a law of the United States, entitled "An act to provide for calling forth the militia to execute the laws of the Union, suppress insurrections, and repel invasions," it is enacted,

that whenever the laws of the United States shall be opposed or the execution of them obstructed in any State by combinations too powerful to be suppressed by the ordinary course of judicial proceedings, or by the powers vested in the marshals by that act, the same being notified by an Associate Justice or the District Judge, it shall be lawful for the President of the United States to call forth the militia of such State to suppress such combinations, and to cause the laws to be duly executed. And if the militia of a State where such combinations may happen shall refuse, or be insufficient to suppress the same, it shall be lawful for the President, if the Legislature of the United States shall not be in session, to call forth and employ such numbers of the militia of any other State or States, most convenient thereto, as may be necessary; and the use of the militia so to be called forth may be continued, if necessary, until the expiration of thirty days after the commencement of the ensuing session: *Provided, always,* That whenever it may be necessary, in the judgment of the President, to use the military force hereby directed to be called forth, the President shall forthwith, and previous thereto, by proclamation, command such insurgents to disperse and retire peaceably to their respective abodes within a limited time.

And whereas James Wilson, an Associate Justice, on the fourth instant, by writing under his hand, did, from evidence which had been laid before him, notify to me that

in the counties of Washington and Alleghany, in Pennsylvania, laws of the United States are opposed, and the execution thereof obstructed by combinations too powerful to be suppressed by the ordinary course of judicial proceedings, or by the powers vested in the marshal of the district.

Calling forth the militia

And whereas it is, in my judgment, necessary, under the circumstances of the case, to take measures for calling forth the militia, in order to suppress the combinations aforesaid, and to cause the laws to be duly executed, and I have accordingly determined so to do, feeling the deepest regret for the occasion, but withal the most solemn conviction that the essential interests of the Union demand it; that the very existence of Government, and the fundamental principles of social order, are materially involved in the issue, and that the patriotism and firmness of all good citizens are seriously called upon, as occasion may require, to aid in the effectual suppression of so fatal a spirit.

Wherefore, and in pursuance of the proviso above recited, I, George Washington, President of the United States, do hereby command all persons, being insurgents as aforesaid, and all others whom it may concern, on or before the first day of September next, to disperse and retire peaceably to their respective abodes. And I do moreover warn all persons whomsoever against aiding, abetting, or comforting the perpetrators of the aforesaid treasonable acts; and do require all officers and other citizens, according to their respective duties and the laws of the land, to exert their utmost endeavors to prevent and suppress such dangerous proceedings.

209

TO GOVERNOR HENRY LEE

Private

German Town, August 26, 1794

Dear Sir:

Your favor of the 17th. came duly to hand, and I thank you for its communications. As the Insurgents in the western counties of this State are resolved (as far as we have yet been able to learn from the Commissioners, who have been sent among them) to persevere in their rebellious conduct untill what they call the excise Law is repealed, and acts of oblivion and amnesty are passed; it gives me sincere consolation amidst the regret with which I am filled, by such lawless and outrageous conduct, to find by your letter above mentioned, that it is held in general detestation by the good people of Virginia; and that you are disposed to lend your *personal* aid to subdue this spirit, and to bring those people to a proper sense of their duty.

Insurgency against the excise law

On this latter point I shall refer you to letters from the War office; and to a private one from Colo. Hamilton (who in the absence of the Secretary of War, superintends the *military* duties of that department) for my sentiments on this occasion.

It is with equal pride and satisfaction I add, that as far as my information extends, this insurrection is viewed with universal indignation and abhorrence; except by those who have never missed an opportunity by side blows, or otherwise, to aim their shafts at the general government; and even among these there is not a Spirit hardy enough, yet, *openly* to justify the daring infractions of Law and order; but by palliatives are attempting to suspend all proceedings against the insurgents until Congress shall have decided on the case, thereby intending to gain time, and if possible to make the evil more extensive, more formidable, and of course more difficult to counteract and subdue.

I consider this insurrection as the first *formidable* fruit of the Democratic Societies; brought forth I believe too prematurely for their own views, which may contribute to the annihilation of them.

Democratic Societies

That these societies were instituted by the *artful* and *designing* members (many of their body I have no doubt mean well, but know little of the real plan,) primarily to sow the seeds of jealousy and distrust among the people, of the government, by destroying all confidence in the administration of it; and that these doctrines have been budding and blowing ever since, is not new to any one, who is acquainted with the characters of their leaders, and has been attentive to their manoeuvres. I early gave it as my opinion to the confidential characters around me, that, if these Societies were not counteracted (not by prosecutions, the ready way to make them grow stronger) or did not fall into disesteem from the knowledge of their origin, and the views with which they had been instituted by their father, Genet, for purposes well known to the Government; that they would shake the government to its foundation. Time and circumstances have confirmed me in this opinion, and I deeply regret the probable consequences, not as they will affect me personally, (for I have not long to act on this theatre, and sure I am that not a man amongst them can be more anxious to put me aside, than I am to sink into the profoundest retirement) but because I see, under a display of popular and fascinating guises, the most diabolical attempts to destroy the best fabric of human government and happiness, that has ever been presented for the acceptance of mankind.

A plan to create discord

A part of the plan for creating discord, is, I perceive, to make me say things of others, and others of me, wch. have no foundation in truth. The first, in many instances I *know* to be the case; and the second I believe to be so; but truth or falsehood is immaterial to them, provided their objects are promoted.

False accusations of attack on Patrick Henry

Under this head may be classed, I conceive, what it is reported I have said of Mr. Henry, and what Mr. Jefferson is reported to have said of me; on both of which, particularly the first, I mean to dilate a little. With solemn truth then I can declare, that I never expressed such sentiments of that Gentleman, as from your letter, he has been led to believe. I had heard, it is true, that he retained his enmity to the Constitution; but with very peculiar pleasure I learnt from Colo. Coles (who I am sure will recollect it) that Mr. Henry was acquiescent in his conduct, and that though he could not give up his opinions respecting the Constitution, yet, unless he should be called upon by official duty, he wd. express no sentiment unfriendly to the exercise of the powers of a government, which had been chosen by a majority of the people; or words to this effect.

Except intimating in this conversation (which to the best of my recollection was introduced by Colo. Coles) that report had made Mr. Henry speak a different language; and afterwards at Prince Edward Court house, where I saw Mr. Venable, and finding I was within eight or ten miles of Mr. Henry's seat, and expressing my regret at not seeing him, the conversation might be similar to that held with Colo. Coles; I say, except in these two instances, I do not recollect, nor do I believe, that in the course of the journey to and from the Southward I ever mentioned Mr. Henrys name in conjunction with the Constitution, or the government. It is evident therefore, that these reports are propagated with evil intentions, to create personal differences. On the question of the Constitution Mr. Henry and myself, it is well known, have been of different opinions; but personally, I have always respected and esteemed him; nay more, I have conceived myself under obligations to him for the friendly manner in which he transmitted to me some insidious anonymous writings that were sent to him in the close of the year 1777, with a view to embark him in the opposition that was forming against me at that time.

I well recollect the conversations you allude to in the winter preceeding the last; and I recollect also, that difficulties occurred which you, any more than myself, were not able to remove. 1st., though you believed, yet you would not undertake to *assert*, that Mr. Henry would be induced to accept *any appointment* under the General Government; in which case, and supposing him to be inemical to it, the wound the government would receive by his refusal, and the charge of attempting to silence his opposition by a place, would be great; 2d., because you were of opinion that *no* office which would make a residence at the Seat of government essential would comport with his disposition, or views; and 3dly., because if there was a vacancy in the supreme Judiciary at that time (of which I am not at this time certain) it could not be filled from Virginia without giving two Judges to that State, which would have excited unpleasant sensations in other States. Any thing short of one of the great Offices, it could not be presumed he would have accepted; nor would there (under any opinion he might entertain) have been propriety in offering it. What is it then, you have in contemplation, that you conceive would be relished? and ought there not to be a moral certainty of its acceptance? This being the case, there wd. not be wanting a disposition on my part; but strong inducements on public and private grounds, to invite Mr. Henry into any employment under the General Government to which his inclination might lead, and not opposed by those maxims which has been the invariable rule of my conduct.

Jefferson's views　　With respect to the words said to have been uttered by Mr. Jefferson, they would be enigmatical to those who are acquainted with the characters about me, unless supposed to be spoken ironically; and in that case they are too injurious to me, and have too little foundation in truth, to be ascribed to him. There could not be the trace of doubt on his mind of predilection in mine, towards G. Britain or her politics, unless (which I do not believe) he has set me down as one of the most deceitful, and uncandid men living; because, not only in private conversations between ourselves, on this subject; but in my meetings with the confidential servants of the public, he has heard me often, when occasions presented themselves, express very different sentiments with an energy that could not be mistaken by *anyone* present.

Having determined, as far as lay within the power of the Executive, to keep this country in a state of neutrality, I have made my public conduct accord with the system; and whilst so acting as a public character, consistency, and propriety as a private man, forbid those intemperate expressions in favor of one Nation, or to the prejudice of another, wch. many have indulged themselves in, and I will venture to add, to the embarrassment of government, without producing any good to the Country. With very great esteem &c.

210

TO BURGESS BALL

Philadelphia, September 25, 1794

Dear Sir:

Your letter of the 10th. instt. from the Sulpher Springs has been recd.

When General Knox (who for several days has been expected) returns, I will deliver your letter to him, and from him (in whose department the business lyes) you will receive an answer to your proposition.

I hear with the greatest pleasure of the spirit which so generally pervades the Militia of every State that has been called upon, on the present occasion; and of the decided discountenance the Incendiaries of public peace and order have met with in their attempt to spread their nefarious doctrines, with a view to poison and discontent the minds of the people against the government; particularly by endeavouring to have it believed that their liberties were assailed, and that all the wicked and abominable measures that cod. be devised (under specious guises) are practiced to sap the Constitution, and lay the foundation of future Slavery.

The Insurrection in the Western counties of this State is a striking evidence of this; and may be considered as the first *ripe fruit* of the Democratic Societies. I did not, I must confess; expect their labours would come to maturity so soon; though I never had a doubt, that such conduct would produce some such issue; if it did not meet the frown of those who were well disposed to order and good government, in time; for can any thing be more absurd, more arrogant, or more pernicious to the peace of Society, than for self created bodies, forming themselves into *permanent* Censors, and under the shade of Night in a conclave, resolving that acts of Congress which have undergone the most deliberate, and solemn discussion by the Representatives of the people, chosen for the express purpose, and bringing with them from the different parts of the Union the sense of their Constituents, endeavouring as far as the nature of the thing will admit, to form *that will* into Laws for the government of the whole; I say, under these circumstances, for a self created, *permanent* body, (for no one denies the right of the people to meet occasionally, to petition for, or to remonstrate against, any Act of the Legislature &ca) to declare that *this act* is unconstitutional, and *that* act is pregnant of mischief; and that all who vote contrary to their dogmas are actuated by selfish motives, or under foreign influence; nay in plain terms are traiters to their Country, is such a stretch of arrogant presumption as is not to be reconciled with laudable motives: especially when we see the same set of men endeavouring to destroy all confidence in the Administration, by arraigning all its acts, without knowing on what ground, or

Intent of Democratic societies

with what information it proceeds and this without regard to decency or truth. These things were evidently intended, and could not fail without counteraction, to disquiet the public mind; but I hope, and trust, they will work their own cure; especially when it is known, more generally than it is, that the Democratic Society of this place (from which the others have emanated) was instituted by Mr. Genet for the express purpose of dissention, and to draw a line between the people and the government, after he found the Officers of the latter would not yield to the hostile measures in which he wanted to embroil this Country.

I hope this letter will find you, Mrs. Ball and the family in better health than when you wrote last. remember me to them, and be assured that I remain Your Affectionate.

211

PROCLAMATION

Philadelphia, September 25, 1794

Whereas, from a hope that the combinations against the Constitution and laws of the United States, in certain of the Western counties of Pennsylvania, would yield to time and reflection, I thought it sufficient, in the first instance, rather to take measures for calling forth the militia than immediately to embody them; but the moment is now come, when the overtures of forgiveness, with no other condition than a submission to law, have been only partially accepted; when every form of conciliation not inconsistent with the being of Government has been adopted, without effect; when the well-disposed in those counties are unable by their influence and example to reclaim the wicked from their fury, and are compelled to associate in their own defence; when the proffered lenity has been perversely misinterpreted into an apprehension that the citizens will march with reluctance; when the opportunity of examining the serious consequences of a treasonable opposition has been employed in propagating principles of anarchy, endeavoring through emissaries to alienate the friends of order from its support, and inviting enemies to perpetrate similar acts of insurrection; when it is manifest, that violence would continue to be exercised upon every attempt to enforce the laws; when, therefore, Government is set at defiance, the contest being whether a small proportion of the United States shall dictate to the whole Union, and, at the expense of those who desire peace, indulge a desperate ambition;

Now, therefore, I, George Washington, President of the United States, in obedience to that high and irresistible duty, consigned to me by the Constitution, "to take care that the laws be faithfully executed"; deploring that the American name should be sullied by the outrages of citizens on their own Government; commiserating such as remain obstinate from delusion; but resolved, in perfect reliance on that gracious Providence which so signally displays its goodness towards this country, to reduce the refractory to a due subordination to the laws; do hereby declare and make known, that, with a satisfaction which can be equalled only by the merits of the militia summoned into service from the States of New Jersey, Pennsylvania, Maryland, and Virginia, I have received intelligence of their patriotic alacrity, in obeying the call of the present, though painful, yet commanding necessity; that a force, which, according to every reasonable expectation, is adequate to the exigency, is already in motion to the scene of disaffection; that those who have confided or shall confide in the protection of Government, shall meet full succor under the standard and from the arms of the United States; that those who having offended against the laws have since entitled themselves to indemnity, will be treated with the most liberal good faith, if they shall not have forfeited their claim by any subsequent conduct, and that instructions are given accordingly.

Militia summoned into national service

And I do, moreover, exhort all individuals, officers, and bodies of men, to contemplate with abhorrence the measures leading directly or indirectly to those crimes, which produce this resort to military coercion; to check, in their respective spheres, the efforts of misguided or designing men to substitute their misrepresentation in the place of truth, and their discontents in the place of stable government; and to call to mind, that as the people of the United States have been permitted, under the Divine favor, in perfect freedom, after solemn deliberation, in an enlightened age, to elect their own Government, so will their gratitude for his inestimable blessing be best distinguished by firm exertions to maintain the Constitution and the laws.

And, lastly, I again warn all persons, whomsoever and

wheresoever, not to abet, aid, or comfort the insurgents afore-said, as they will answer the contrary at their peril; and I do also require all officers and other citizens, according to their several duties, as far as may be in their power, to bring under the cognizance of the law all offenders in the premises.

212

TO THE SECRETARY OF STATE

Private

Fort Cumberland, October 16, 1794

Dear Sir:*

Assembly of troops

Your letters of the 11th. instt. were received this morning at my stage 15 miles short of this place. We arrived here in the afternoon of this day; and found a respectable force assembled from the States of Virginia and Maryland; and I am informed that about 1500 more (from the former state) either is or will be at Frankfort (ten miles on our left) this evening or tomor-row at farthest. Nothing more precise, than you were in-formed of in my last, from Carlisle, has been heard from the Insurgent counties. All accts. agree however, that they are much alarmed at the serious appearance of things: The truth of which I expect to be better informed of to morrow, or next day, by persons whom I have sent amongst them and whose return may be looked for about that time.

I do not expect to be here more than two days; thence to Bedford, where, as soon as matters are arranged, and a plan settled, I shall shape my course for Philadelphia; but not be-cause the impertinence of Mr. Bache, or his corrispondents has undertaken to pronounce, that I cannot, constitutionally, command the Army whilst Congress are in Session.

Threat of self-created societies

I believe the eyes of all the *well* disposed people of this Country will soon be opened, and that they will clearly see, the tendency if not the design of the leaders of these self created societies. As far as I have heard them spoken of, it is with strong reprobation. I should be extremely sorry therefore if

---

*Edmund Randolph

Mr. M——n *from any cause whatsoever* should get entangled with them, or their politics.

As the Speech will be composed of several distinct subjects, my wish was that each of these shd. receive its final dress; subject however to revision; that part especially which relates to the insurrection and the proceedings thereupon. The subjects themselves, will naturally point to the order, in which they ought to follow each other; and the throwing them into it cannot, at any time, be more than the work of a few minutes after the materials are all provided. It will appear evident, on a moments reflection, that the continual interruptions in a militia camp, where every thing is to be provided, and arranged, will allow no time to clothe the speech in a correct or handsome garb; nor will there be time to do it after my return.

My mind is so perfectly convinced, that if these self created societies cannot be discountenanced, that they will destroy the government of this Country that I have asked myself whilst I have been revolving on the expence and inconvenience of drawing so many men from their families and occupations as I have seen on their march where wd. be the impropriety of glancing at them in my Speech by some such idea as the following;

That however distressing this Expedition will have proved to individuals, and expensive to the Country, the pleasing spirit which it has drawn forth in support of Law and Govt. will immortalize the American character and is a happy presage, that future attempts of a certain description of people will not, tho' accompanied by the same industry, sow the seed of distrust and disturb the public tranquillity will prove equally abortive.

I have formed no precise ideas of what is best to be done or said on this subject, nor have I time to express properly what has occurred to me, as I am now writing at an hour when I ought to be in bed; because all the day, from business or ceremonious introductions I have been unable to do it sooner. I am, &c.

213

TO JOHN JAY

Private

Philadelphia, November 1[–5], 1794

My dear Sir:

On tuesday last I returned from my tour to the Westward; on monday, Congress, by adjournment, are to meet; and on the day following, Mr. Bayard, according to his present expectation, is to leave this city for London.

Thus circumstanced (having so little time between my return, and the opening of the Session, to examine papers and to prepare my communications for the Legislature) you will readily perceive that my present address to you must be hurried; at the same time my friendship and regard for you, would not let an opportunity, so good as the one afforded by Mr. Bayard, pass without some testimony of my remembrance of you; and an acknowledgment, of the receipt of your private letters to me, dated the 23d of June, 21st of July, and 5th and 11th of August. These comprehend *all* the letters I have recd. from you since your arrival in England, to the present date.

Jay's negotiations with England

That of the 5th. of August, dawns more favorably upon the success of your mission than any that had preceeded it; and for the honor, dignity and interest of this country; for your own reputation and glory; and for the peculiar pleasure and satisfaction I shd. derive from it, as well on private, as on public considerations, no man more ardently wishes you *compleat* success than I do. But, as you have observed in some of your letters, that it is hardly possible in the early stages of a negociation to foresee all the results, so much depending upon fortuitous circumstances, and incidents which are not within our controul; so, to deserve success, by employing the means with which we are possessed, to the best advantage, and trusting the rest to the all wise disposer, is all that an enlightened public, and the virtuous, and well disposed part of the community, can reasonably expect; nor in which will they I am sure be disappointed. Against the malignancy of the discontented, the turbulant, and the vicious, no abilities; no exertions; nor the most unshaken integrity, are any safeguard.

As far as depends upon the Executive, measures preparatory for the worst, while it hopes for the best, will be pursued; and I shall endeavor to keep things in statu quo until your negotiation assumes a more decisive form; which I hope will soon be the case, as there are many hot heads and impetuous spirits among us who with difficulty can be kept within bounds. This, however, ought not to precipitate your conduct; for, as it has been observed, there is a "tide in human affairs" that ought always to be watched; and because I believe all who are acquainted with you, will readily concede, that considerations both public and private combine to urge you to bring your mission to a close with as much celerity as the nature of it will admit.

As you have been, and will continue to be, fully informed by the Secretary of State of all transactions of a public nature, which relate to, or may have an influence on the points of your mission, it would be unnecessary for me to touch upon any of them in this letter; was it not for the presumption, that, the insurrection in the western counties of this State has excited much speculation, and a variety of opinions abroad; and will be represented differently according to the wishes of some, and the prejudices of others, who may exhibit it as an evidence of what has been predicted "that we are unable to govern ourselves." Under this view of the subject, I am happy in giving it to you as the general opinion that this event having happened at the time it did, was fortunate, altho' it will be attended with considerable expence.

That the self-created Societies, wch. have spread themselves over this country, have been labouring incessantly to sow the seeds of distrust, jealousy, and of course discontent; thereby hoping to effect some revolution in the government, is not unknown to you. That they have been the fomenters of the Western disturbances, admits of no doubt in the mind of any one who will examine their conduct. But fortunately, they have precipitated a crisis for which they were not prepared; and thereby have unfolded views which will, I trust, effectuate their annihilation sooner than it might otherwise have happened; at the sametime that it has afforded an occasion for the people of this country to shew their abhorrence of the result, and their attachment to the Constitution and the laws; for I

Attack on self-created societies

believe that five times the number of militia that was required, would have come forward, if it had been necessary, in support of them.

The Spirit which blazed out on this occasion, as soon as the object was fully understood, and the lenient measures of the government were made known to the people, deserved to be communicated: for there are instances of General Officers going at the head of a single Troop, and of light companies; of field Officers, when they came to the places of rendezvous and found no command for them in that grade, turning into the ranks and proceeding as private Soldiers, under their own Captains, and of numbers, possessing the first fortunes in the Country, standing in the ranks as private men and marching day by day with their knapsacks and haversacks at their backs; sleeping on straw, with a single blanket, in a Soldiers tent, during the frosty nights which we have had; by way of example to others. Nay more, many young Quakers (not discouraged by the Elders) of the first families, charactrs. and property having turned into the Ranks and are marchg. with the Troops.

These things have terrified the Insurgents, who had no conception that such a spirit prevailed; but, while the thunder only rumbled at a distance, were boasting of their strength, and wishing for, and threatening the militia by turns; intimating, that the arms they should take from them, would soon become a magazine in their hands. Their language is much changed indeed but their principles want correction.

I shall be more prolix in my speech to Congress, on the commencement and progress of this insurrection, than is usual in such an instrument, or, than I should have been, on any other occasion: but, as numbers (at home and abroad) will hear of the insurrection, and will read the speech, that may know nothing of the documents to which it might refer, I conceived, it would be better to encounter the charge of prolixity, by giving a cursory detail of facts (that would show the prominent features of the thing) than to let it go naked into the world, to be dressed up according to the fancy or the inclination of the readers, or the policy of our enemies.

I write nothing in answer to the letter of Mr. Wangenheim (enclosed by you to me). Were I to enter into corrispondencies of that sort (admitting there was no impropriety in the measure) I should be unable to attend to my ordinary duties. I have established it as a maxim, neither to envite, nor to discourage emigrants. My opinion, is that they will come hither as fast as the true interest and policy of the United States will be benefited by foreign population. I believe many of these, as Mr. Wangenheim relates, have been, and I fear will continue to be, imposed upon by Speculators in land, and other things. But I know of no prevention but caution, nor any remedy except the Laws. Nor is military, or other employment so easily obtained as foreigners conceive, in a country where offices bear no proportion to the seekers of them. with sincere esteem &c.

PS. Novr. 5th. Your corrisponde. with New York is, I have no doubt, too frequent and regulr. to render any acct. of Mrs. Jay from me necessary; yet as I was told yesterday by Mr. King that she and all yr. family were well, I chose to mention it. For want of a Senate, Congress cannot proceed to business.

214

TO THE COMMISSIONERS OF THE DISTRICT OF COLUMBIA

Philadelphia, January 28, 1795

Gentlemen:

A plan for the establishment of an University in the federal City, has frequently been the subject of conversation; but in what manner it is proposed to commence this important institution; on how extensive a scale, the means by which it is to be effected; how it is to be supported; or what progress is made in it; are matters altogether unknown to me.

On education and the establishment of a university

It has always been a source of serious reflection and sincere regret with me, that the youth of the United States should be sent to foreign countries for the purpose of education. Altho' there are doubtless many under these circumstances who escape the danger of contracting principles, unfriendly to republican government; yet we ought to deprecate the hazard attending ardent and susceptible minds, from being too strongly, and too early prepossessed in favor of other political systems, before they are capable of appreciating their own.

For this reason, I have greatly wished to see a plan adopted by which the arts, Sciences and Belles lettres, could be taught in their *fullest* extent; thereby embracing *all* the advantages of European tuition with the means of acquiring the liberal knowledge which is necessary to qualify our citizens for the exigencies of public, as well as private life; and (which with me, is a consideration of great magnitude) by assembling the youth from the different parts of this rising republic, contributing from their intercourse, and interchange of information, to the removal of prejudices which might perhaps, sometimes arise, from local circumstances.

The federal City, from its centrality, and the advantages which, in other respects it must have over any other place in the U: States, ought to be preferred, as a proper site for such a University. And if a plan can be adopted upon a scale as *extensive* as I have described; and the execution of it shall commence under favorable auspices, in a reasonable time, with a fair prospect of success; I will grant, in perpetuity, fifty shares in the navigation of Potomac River towards the endowment of it.

Endowment of proposed university

What annuity will arise from these fifty shares, when the navigation is in full operation, can, at this time, be only conjectured; and those who are acquainted with the nature of it, can form as good a judgment as myself.

As the design of this University has assumed no form with which I am acquainted; and as I am equally ignorant who the persons are that have taken, or are disposed to take, the maturation of the plan upon themselves, I have been at a loss to whom I should make this communication of my intentions. If the Commrs. of the federal city have any particular agency in bringing the matter forward, then the information I now give to them, is in its proper course. If, on the other hand, they have no more to do in it than others, who may be desirous of seeing so important a measure carried into effect, they will be so good as to excuse my using them as the medium for disclosing these intentions; for as much, as it appears necessary, that the funds for the establishment and support of the Institution, should be known to the promoters of it; and because I saw no mode more eligable of making known mine. For these reasons I give you the trouble of this Address, and the assurance of being Gentlemen, &c.

TO THOMAS JEFFERSON

Philadelphia, March 15, 1795

Dear Sir:

I received your letter of the 23d. Ulto.; but not at so early a period as might have been expected from the date of it. My mind has always been more disposed to apply the shares in the inland navigations of Potomac and James Rivers (which were left to my disposal by the legislature of Virginia) towards the endowment of a *University* in the U States, than to any other object it had contemplated. In pursuance of this idea, and understanding that other means are in embryo, for establishing so useful a seminary in the federal city; I did, on the 28th. of Jany. last, announce to the Commrs. thereof, my intention of vesting, in perpetuity, the fifty shares I hold under that act in the navigation of Potomac; as an additional mean of carrying the plan into effect; provided, it should be adopted upon a scale so liberal, and so extensive, as to embrace a *compleat* system of education.

I had but little hesitation in giving the federal dist. a preferrence of all other places for this Institution, and for the following reasons. 1st. on account of its being the permanent Seat of the government of this Union, and where the laws and policy of it must be better understood than in any local part thereof. 2d, because of its centrality. 3d, because one half (or near it) of the district of Columbia, is within the Commonwealth of Virginia; and the whole of the State not inconvenient thereto. 4th, because as *part* of the endowment, it would be useful; but *alone*, would be inadequate to the end. 5th, because many advantages, I conceive, would result from the Jurisdiction which the general government will have over it, wch. no other spot would possess. And, lastly, as this Seminary is contemplated for the *completion* of education, and study of the sciences (not for boys in their rudiments) it will afford the Students an opportunity of attending the debates in Congress, and thereby becoming more liberally, and better acquainted with the principles of law, and government.

My judgment and my wishes point equally strong to the application of the James River shares to the same object, at the same place; but considering the source from whence they were

Establishment of a university

derived, I have, in a letter I am writing to the Executive of Virginia on this subject, left the application of them to a Seminary, *within the State*, to be located by the Legislature.

Hence you will perceive that I have, in a degree, anticipated your proposition. I was restrained from going the whole length of the suggestion, by the following considerations: 1st, I did not know to what extent, or when any plan would be so matured for the establishment of an University, as would enable any assurance to be given to the application of Mr. D'Ivernois. 2d, the propriety of transplanting the Professors in a *body*, might be questioned for several reasons; among others, because they might not be all good characters; nor all sufficiently acquainted with our language; and again, having been at variance with the levelling party of their own country, the measure might be considered as an aristocratical movement by more than those who, without any just cause that I have been able to discover, are continually sounding the alarm bell of aristocracy. and 3d, because it might preclude some of the first Professors in other countries from a participation; among whom some of the most celebrated characters in Scotland, in this line, I am told might be obtained.

Something, but of what nature I am unable to inform you, has been written by Mr. Adams to Mr. D'Ivernois. Never having viewed my intended donation as more than a part of the means, that was to set this establishment afloat; I did not incline to go too far in the encouragement of Professors before the plan should assume a more formal shape; much less to induce an entire College to migrate. The enclosed is the answer I have received from the Commissioners: from which, and the ideas I have here expressed, you will be enabled to decide on the best communication to be made to Mr. D'Ivernois.

My letter to the Commissioners has bound me to the fulfilment of what is therein engaged; and if the legislature of Virginia, in considering the subject, should view it in the same light I do, the James River shares will be added thereto; for I think one good Institution of this sort, is to be preferred to two imperfect ones; which, without other aids than the shares in *both* navigations, is more likely to fall through, than to succeed upon the plan I contemplate. Which, in a few words, is to supercede the necessity of sending the youth of this country abroad, for the purpose of education (where too often principles and habits not friendly to republican government are imbibed, which are not easily discarded) by instituting such an one of our own, as will answer the end; and by associating them in the same seminary, will contribute to wear off those prejudices, and unreasonable jealouses, which prevent or weaken friendships and, impair the harmony of the Union. With very great esteem &c.

PS: Mr. Adams laid before me the communications of Mr. D'Ivernois; but I said nothing to him of my intended donation towards the establishment of a University in the Federal District. My wishes would be to fix this on the Virga. side of the Potomac, therein; but this would not embrace, or accord with those other means which are proposed for this establishment.

216

TO ALEXANDER HAMILTON

Private and perfectly confidential

Philadelphia, July 3, 1795

My dear Sir:

The treaty of Amity, Commerce and Navigation, which has lately been before the Senate, has, as you will perceive, made its public entry into the Gazettes of this city. Of course the merits, and demerits of it will (especially in its unfinished state) be freely discussed. *Treaty with Great Britain*

It is not the opinion of *those* who were determined (before it was promulgated) to *support*, or *oppose* it, that I am sollicitous to obtain; for *these* I well know rarely do more than examine the side to which they lean; without giving the reverse the consideration it deserves; possibly without a wish to be apprised of the reasons, on which the objections are founded. My desire is to learn from dispassionate men, who have knowledge of the subject, and abilities to judge of it, the genuine opinion they entertain of *each* article of the instrument; and the *result* of it in the aggregate. In a word, placed on the footing the matter now stands, it is, more than ever, an incumbent duty on me, to do what propriety, and the true interest of this country shall appear to require at my hands on so important a subject, under such delicate circumstances.

You will be at no loss to perceive, from what I have already said, that my wishes are, to have the favorable, and unfavorable side of *each* article stated, and compared together; that I may see the bearing and tendency of them: and, ultimately, on which side the balance is to be found.

This treaty has, I am sensible, many relations, which, in deciding thereon, ought to be attended to; some of them too are of an important nature. I know also, that to judge with precision of its commercial arrangements, there ought likewise to be an intimate acquaintance with the various branches of commerce between this Country and Great Britain as it *now* stands; as it will be placed by the treaty; and as it may affect our present, or restrain our future treaties with other nations. All these things I am persuaded you have given as much attention to as most men; and I believe that your late employment under the General government afforded you more opportunities of deriving knowledge therein, than most of them who had not studied and practiced it scientifically, upon a large and comprehensive scale.

I do not know how you may be occupied at present; or how incompatible this request of mine may be to the business you have in hand. All I can say is, that however desirous I may be of availing myself of your sentiments on the points I have enumerated, and such others as are involved in the treaty, and the resolution of the Senate; (both of which I send you, lest they should not be at hand) it is not my intention to interrupt you in that business; or, if you are disinclined to go into the investigation I have requested, to press the matter upon you: for of this you may be assured, that with the most unfeigned regard, and with every good wish for your health and prosperity I am etc.

PS: Admitting that his B: Majesty will consent to the suspension of the 12th. article of the treaty, is it necessary that the treaty should again go to the Senate? or is the President authorized by the resolution of that body to ratify it without?

217

TO ALEXANDER HAMILTON

Private

Mount Vernon, July 29, 1795

My dear Sir:

Your letters of the 20th and 21st. Instt. found me at this place, after a hot and disagreeable ride.

As the measures of the government, respecting the treaty, were taken before I left Philadelphia, something more imperious than has yet appeared, must turn up to occasion a change. Still, it is very desirable to ascertain, if possible, after the paroxysm of the fever is a little abated, what the real temper of the people is, concerning it; for at present the cry against the Treaty is like that against a mad-dog; and every one, in a manner, seems engaged in running it down.

That it has received the most tortured interpretation, and that the writings agt. it (which are very industriously circulated) are pregnant of the most abominable mis-representations, admits of no doubt; yet, there are to be found, so far as my information extends, many well disposed men who conceive, that in the settlement of *old* disputes, a proper regard to reciprocal justice does not appear in the Treaty; whilst others, also well enough affected to the government, are of opinion that to have had *no* commercial treaty would have been better, for this country, than the restricted one, agreed to; inasmuch, say they, the nature of our Exports, and imports (without any extra: or violent measures) would have forced, or led to a more adequate intercourse between the two nations; without any of those shackles which the treaty has imposed. In a word, that as our *exports* consist chiefly of *provisions* and *raw materials*, which to the manufacturers in G. Britain, and to their Islands in the West Indies, affords employment and food; they must have had them on *our* terms, if they were not to be obtained on their *own*; whilst the *imports* of this country, offers the best mart for their fabricks; and, of course, is the principal support of their manufacturers: But the string which is most played on, because it strikes with most force the popular ear, is the violation, as they term it, of our engagements with France; or in other

Doubts concerning treaty with Great Britain

words, the prediliction shown by that instrument to G. Britain at the expence of the French nation.

Interests of the French

The consequences of which are more to be apprehended than any, which are likely to flow from other causes, as ground of opposition; because, whether the fact is, in *any* degree true, or not, it is the interest of the French (whilst the animosity, or jealousies betwn. the two nations exist) to avail themselves of such a spirit, to keep *us* and *G. Britain* at variance; and they will, in my opinion, accordingly do it. To what *length* their policy may induce them to carry matters, is too much in embryo at this moment to decide: but I predict much embarrassment to the government therefrom, and in my opinion, too much pains cannot be taken by those who speak, or write, in favor of the treaty, to place this matter in its true light.

Camillus letters

I have seen with pleasure, that a writer in one of the New York papers under the Signature of Camillus, has promised to answer, or rather to defend the treaty, which has been made with G. Britain. To judge of this work from the first number, which I have seen, I auger well of the performance; and shall expect to see the subject handled in a clear, distinct and satisfactory manner: but if measures are not adopted for its dissimination a few only will derive lights from the knowledge, or labour of the author; whilst the opposition pieces will spread their poison in all directions; and Congress, more than probable, will assemble with the unfavorable impressions of their constituents. The difference of conduct between the friends, and foes of order, and good government, is in nothg. more striking than that, the latter are always working, like bees, to distil their poison; whilst the former, depending, often times *too much*, and *too long* upon the sense, and good dispositions of the people to work conviction, neglect the means of effecting it. With sincere esteem and regard I am your Affecte.

218

TO ALEXANDER HAMILTON

Private and confidential

Philadelphia, October 29, 1795

My dear Sir:

A voluminous publication is daily expected from Mr. R_____. The paper alluded to in the extract of his letter to me, of the 8th. instt., and inserted in all the Gazettes, is a letter of my own, to him; from which he intends (as far as I can collect from a combination of circumstances) to prove an inconsistency in my conduct, in ratifying the Treaty with G. Britain, without making a rescinding (by the British government) of what is commonly called the Provision order, equally with the exception of the 12th. article, by the Senate, a condition of that ratification. Intending thereby to shew, that my *final* decision thereon, was the result of party-advice; and that that party was under British influence. It being a letter of my own which he has asked for, I did not hesitate a moment to furnish him therewith; and to authorise him to publish every private letter I ever wrote, and every word I ever uttered to him, if *he* thought they wd. contribute to his vindication: But the paper he asked for, is but a mite of the volume that is to appear; for without any previous knowledge of mine, he had compiled every official paper (before this was asked) for publication; the knowledge of which can subserve the purposes he has in view; and why they have not made their appearance before this, I know not, as it was intimated in the published extract of his letter to me, that nothing retarded it but the want of the paper then applied for, which was furnished the day after my arrival in this city; where (on the 20th. instt) I found his letter, after it had gone to Alexandria, and had returned.

I shall now touch upon another subject, as unpleasant as the one I have just quitted. What am I to do for a Secretary of State? I ask frankly, and with solicitude; and shall receive kindly, any sentiments you may express on the occasion. That there may be no concealment; and that the non-occupancy of the Office until this time may be accounted for (I tell you in confidence that) Mr. Paterson of New Jersey; Mr. Thos. Johnson of Maryland; Genl. Pinckney of So. Carolina; and Mr. Patrick Henry of Virginia; in the order they are mentioned, have all been applied to and refused. Would Mr. King accept it? You know the objections I have had to the nomination, to office, any person from either branch of the Legislature; and you will be at no loss to perceive, that at the present crisis, another reason might be adduced against this appointment. But maugre all objections, if Mr. King wd. accept, I would look no further. Can you sound, and let me know soon, his sentiments on this occasion. If he should feel disposed to listen to the proposition, tell him *candidly*, all that I have done in this matter; that neither he, nor I, may be made uneasy thereafter from the discovery of it; he will, I am confident, perceive the ground upon which I have acted in making these essays; and will, I am persuaded, appreciate my motives. If he should decline also, pray learn with precision from him, what the qualifications of Mr. Potts the Senator are, and be as diffusive as you can with respect to others, and I will decide on nothing until I hear from you, pressing as the case is.

To enable you to judge of this matter with more lights still; I add, that Mr. Marshall of Virginia has declined the Office of Attorney General, and I am pretty certain would accept of no other: And I know that Colo. Carrington would not come into the War department (if a vacancy should happen therein). Mr. Dexter, it is said, would accept the Office of Attorney General. No person is yet absolutely fixed on for that Office. Mr. Smith of So. Carolina would, sometime ago, have had no objection to filling a respectable office under the Genl. government; but what his views might lead to, or his abilities particularly fit him for, I am an incompetent judge: and besides, on the ground of popularity, his pretensions would, I fear, be small. Mr. Chase of Maryland is, unquestionably, a man of abilities; and it is supposed by some, that he wd. accept the appointment of Attorney General. Though opposed to the adoption of the Constitution, it is said he has been a steady friend to the general government since it has been in operation. But he is violently opposed in his own State by a party, and is besides, or to speak more correctly has been, accused of some impurity in his conduct. I might add to this catalogue, that Colo. Innis is among the number of those who have passed in review; but his extreme indolence renders his abilities (great as they are said to be) of little use. In short, what with the non-acceptance of some; the known dereliction of those who are most fit; the exceptionable drawbacks from others; and a wish (if it were practicable) to make a geographical distribution of the *great* officers of the Administration, I find the selection of proper characters an arduous duty.

The period is approaching, indeed is already come, for selecting the proper subjects for my communications to Congress at the opening of next Session, and the manner of treating them merits more than the consideration of a moment. The crisis, and the incomplete state in which most of the important affairs of this country are, at present, make the first more difficult, and the latter more delicate than usual.

Preparation for annual message

The Treaty with G. Britain is not yet concluded. After every consideration, however, I could bestow on it (and after entertaining very serious doubts of the propriety of doing it, on account of the Provision order) it has been ratified by me: what has been, or will be done by the governmt. of G. Britain relative to it, is not now and probably will not be known by the meeting of Congress: Yet, such perhaps is the state of that business, as to make a communication thereof to the Legislature necessary: whether in the concisest form, or to accompany it with some expression of my sense of the thing itself, and the manner in which it has been treated, merits deep reflection. If good would flow from the latter, by a just and temperate communication of my ideas to the community at large, through this medium; guarded so as not to add fuel to passions prepared to blaze, and at the sametime so expressed as not to excite the criticisms, or animadversions of European Powers, I would readily embrace it. But I would, decidedly, avoid every expression which could be construed a deriliction of the powers of the President with the advice and consent of the Senate to make Treaties; or into a shrinking from any act of mine relative to it. In a word, if a conciliatory plan can be assimilated with a firm, manly and dignified conduct in this business, it would be desirable; but the latter I will never yield. On this head it may not be amiss to add, that no official (nor indeed other) accounts have been received from France of the reception of the Treaty with G. Britain, by the National Convention. Perhaps it is too soon to expect any.

Supports treaty with Great Britain

Our negociations with Spain, as far as accts. have been recd. from Mr. Pinckney (soon after his arrival there, but after a

Negotiations with Spain

conference with the Duke de la Alcudia on the subject, before, however, the Peace between France and that Country was publicly known) stands upon the same procrastinating, trifling, undignified (as it respects that government), and insulting as it relates to this country, ground as they did at the commencement of them. Under circumstances like these, I shall be at a loss (if nothing more decisive shall arrive between this and the Assembling of Congress) what to say on this subject, especially as this procrastination and trifling, has been accompanied by encroachments on our territorial rights. There is no doubt of this fact, but persons have, nevertheless, been sent both by Govr. Blount and Genl. Wayne, to know by what authority it is done. The conduct of Spain (after having herself, invited this negociation, and throughout the whole of its progress) has been such, that I have, at times, thought it best to express this sentiment at once in the Speech, and refer to the proceedings. At other times, to say only, that matters are in the same inconclusive state they have been; and that if no alteration for the better, or a conclusion of it should take place before the Session is drawing to a close, that the proceedings will be laid fully before Congress.

From Algiers no late accts. have been received; and little favorable, it is to be feared, is to be expected from that quarter.

From Morocco, the first communications, after our Agent arrived there, were pleasing, but the final result, if any has taken place is yet unknown, and are more clouded.

Western Indians   Our concerns with the Indians will tell well. I hope, and believe, the Peace with the Western Indians will be permanent; unless renewed difficulties with G. Britain shd. produce (as it very likely would do) a change in their conduct. But whether this matter can be mentioned in the Speech with propriety before it is advised and consented to by the Senate, is questionable. And nothing, I am sure, that is so, and is susceptible of caval or criticism, will escape the anonymous writers (if it should go unnoticed elsewhere). It will be denominated by these gentry, a bolster. All the hostile Indians to the Southward have renewed the treaties of Amity and friendship with the United States; and have given the best proof in their power of their sincerity, to wit, a return of Prisoners and property; and peace prevails from one end of our frontier to the other. Peace also has been produced between the Creeks and Chickasaws by the intervention of this government, but something untoward and unknown here, has occasioned a renewal of hostilities on the part of the Creeks.

The Military establishment is of sufficient importance to claim a place in the general communication, at the opening of the Session; and my opinion is, that circumstanced as things are at present, and the uncertainty of what they may be next year, it would be impolitic to reduce it; but whether to express any opinion thereupon, or leave it entirely to their own decision may be considered.

Military establishment

Whether a report from the Secretary of the Treasury relative to Fiscal matters, particularly on the loans of money, and another from the Secretary of War respecting the Frigates, Arsenals, Military Stores directed to be provided; and the train, in wch. the Trade with the Indians is, agreeably to the several Acts of Legislature may not be proper, and to be referred to in the Speech.

Having desired the late Secretary of State to note down every matter as it occurred, proper either for the speech at the opening of the Session, or for messages afterwards, the enclosed paper contains everything I could extract from that Office. Aid me I pray you with your sentiments on these points and such others as may have occurred to you relative to my communications to Congress. With affectionate regard etc.

219

TO GOUVERNEUR MORRIS

Private

Philadelphia, December 22, 1795

My dear Sir:

I am become so unprofitable a corrispondent, and so remiss in my corrispondencies, that nothing but the kindness of my friends in overlooking these deficiencies, could induce them to favor me with a continuance of their letters; which, to me, are at once pleasing, interesting, and useful. To a man immersed in debt, and seeing no prospect of extrication but by an act of insolvency (perhaps absolvency would be a better word) I compare myself: and like him too, affraid to examine the items of the account, I will, at once, make a lumping acknowledgment of the receipt of many interesting private letters from you, previous to your last arrival in England; and will begin with those of the 3d. of July and 22d. of Augt. subsequent thereto.

As the British government has repealed the order for seizing our Provision Vessels, little more need be said on that head than that it was the *principle* which constituted the most obnoxious and exceptionable part thereof; and the predicament in which this country was thereby placed in her relations with France. Admitting therefore that the compensation to *some* individuals was adequate to what it might have been in another quarter, yet the exceptions to it on these grounds, remained the same.

Continued grievances with Great Britain

I do not think Colo. Innes's report to the Govr. of Kentucky was entirely free from exceptions; but let the report be accompanied with the following remarks. 1. That the one which Lord Grenville might have seen published, was disclaimed by Colo. Innes as soon as it appeared in the public Gazettes, on account of its incorrectness. 2. An irritable spirit at that time pervaded all our people at the Westward, arising from a combination of causes (but from none more powerful than the analogous proceedings of Great Britain in the North, with those of Spain in the South, towards the United States and their Indian borderers) which spirit required some management and soothing. But 3. and principally, Lord Grenville if he had adverted to the many remonstrances which have gone from this country against the conduct of his own; which I will take the liberty to say has been as impolitic for their Nation (if Peace and a good understanding with this, was its object) as it has been irritating to us. And that it may not be conceived that I am speaking at random, let his Lordship be asked if we have not complained, that some of their naval Officers have insulted and menaced us in our *own Ports?* That they have violated our national rights, by searching Vessels, and impressing Seamen within our acknowledged Jurisdiction? and in an outrageous manner have seized the latter by *entire crews* in the West Indies, and done the like, but not so extensively, in all parts of the World? That the Bermudian Privateers, or to speak more correctly, Pirates; and the Admiralty Court of that Island, have committed the most atrocious depredations and violences on our Commerce in capturing, and in their adjudications afterwards, as were never tolerated in any well organized or efficient government? That their Governor of Upper Canada has ordered, in an official, and formal manner, Settlers within our own territory (and far removed from the Posts they have withheld from us) to withdraw, and forbid others to settle on the same? That the persons to whom their Indian Affairs are entrusted, have taken unwearied pains, and practiced every deception to keep those people in a state of irritation and disquietude with us; and, to the *last* moment, exerted every nerve to prevent the Treaty which has lately been concluded between the United States and them, from taking effect?

These complaints were not founded in vague and idle reports, but on indubitable facts. Facts not only known to the government, but so notorious as to be known to the people also; who charge to the last item of the above enumeration, the expenditure of a million, or more dollars annually, for the purpose of self defence against Indian tribes thus stimulated, and for chastising them for the ravages and cruel murders which they had committed on our frontier Inhabits. Our Minister at the Court of London has been directed to remonstrate against these things, with force and energy. The answer, it is true, has been (particularly with respect to the interferences with the Indians) a disavowal. Why then are not the Agents of such unauthorised, offensive, and injurious measures, made examples of? For wherein, let me ask, consists the difference *to us* between their being the acts of government, or the acts of unauthorised Officers, or Agents of the government; if we are to sustain all the evils which flow from such measures?

To this catalogue may be added, the indifference, nay more than indifference, with which the government of Great Britain received the advances of this country towards a friendly intercourse with it; even after the adoption of the present Constitution, and since the operation of the government; and also, the ungracious and obnoxious characters (rancorous refugees, as if done with design to insult the country) which they have sent among us as their Agents; who retaining all their former enmity, could see nothing through a proper medium, and becoming the earwigs of their Ministers (who bye the by does not possess a mind capacious enough, or a temper sufficiently conciliatory, to view things and act upon a great and liberal scale) were always labouring under some unfavorable information

Attitude of British government

619

and impression; And, probably not communicating them in a less exceptionable manner than they received, or conceived them themselves.

I give you these details (and if you should again converse with Lord Grenville on the subject, you are at liberty, unofficially, to mention them, or any of them, according to circumstances) as evidences of the impolitic conduct, for so it strikes me, of the British government towards these United States; that it may be seen how difficult it has been for the Executive, under such an accumulation of irritating circumstances, to maintain the ground of neutrality which had been taken; at a time when the remembrance of the aid we had received from France in the Revolution, was fresh in every mind, and when the partizans of that country were continually contrasting the affections of that people with the unfriendly disposition of the *British government* and that too, as I have observed before, while the recollection of their *own* sufferings during the War with the latter, had not been forgotten.

Peace with England and Europe

It is well known that Peace has been (to borrow a modern phraze) the order of the day with me, since the disturbances in Europe first commenced. My policy has been, and will continue to be, while I have the honor to remain in the administration of the government, to be upon friendly terms with, but independant of, all the nations of the earth. To share in the broils of none. To fulfil our own engagements. To supply the wants, and be carriers for them all: being thoroughly convinced that it is our policy and interest to do so; and that nothing short of self respect, and that justice which is essential to a national character, ought to involve us in War; for sure I am, if this country is preserved in tranquillity twenty years longer, it may bid defiance, in a just cause, to any power whatever, such, in that time, will be its population, wealth, and resource.

If Lord Grenville conceives that the United States are not well disposed towards Great Britain, his candour, I am persuaded, will seek for the causes; and his researches will fix them as I have done. If this should be the case, his policy will, I am persuaded, be opposed to the continuance, or renewal of the irritating measures which I have enumerated; for he may be assured, tho' the assurance will not, it is probable, carry conviction with it from me to a member of the British administration, that a liberal policy will be one of the most effectual means of deriving advantages to their trade and manufactures from the people of the United States; and will contribute more than any thing else, to obliterate the impressions which have been made by their late conduct towards it.

In a government as free as ours where the people are at liberty, and will express their sentiments, oftentimes imprudently, and for want of information sometimes unjustly, allowances must be made for occasional effervescences; but after the declaration which I have here made of my political creed, you can run no hazard in asserting, that the Executive branch of this government never has, nor will suffer, while I preside, any improper conduct of its officers to escape with impunity; or will give its sanctions to any disorderly proceedings of its citizens.

Defense of executive branch

By a firm adherence to these principles, and to the neutral policy which has been adopted, I have brought on myself a torrent of abuse in the factious papers in this country, and from the enmity of the discontented of all descriptions therein: But having no sinister objects in view, I shall not be diverted from my course by these, nor any attempts which are, or shall be made to withdraw the confidence of my constituents from me. I have nothing to ask, and discharging my duty, I have nothing to fear from invective. The acts of my Administration will appear when I am no more, and the intelligent and candid part of mankind will not condemn my conduct without recurring to them.

The Treaty entered into with G. Britain has (as you have been informed) undergone much, and severe animadversion; and tho' a more favorable one were to have been wished, which the policy perhaps of Great Britain might have granted, yet the demerits thereof are not to be estimated by the opposition it has received; nor is the opposition sanctioned by the great body of the yeomanry in these States: for they (whatever their opinion of it may be) are disposed to leave the decision where the Constitution has placed it. But an occasion was wanting, and the instrument by those who required it, was deemed well calculated for the purpose of working upon the affections of the people of this country, towards those of France; whose interests and rights under our treaty with them, they represented as being violated: and with the aid of the Provision order, and other irritating conduct of the British Ships of War, and agents, as mentioned before, the means

Opposition to treaty with Great Britain

were furnished, and more pains taken, than upon any former occasion, to raise a general ferment with a view to defeat the Treaty.

But knowing that you have other corrispondents who have more leizure, and equally capable of detailing these matters, I will leave you to them, and the Gazettes, for fuller information thereon; and for a more minute account of the prevailing politics. And thanking you for the interesting information, and opinions contained in your letter of the 22d. of August, I shall only add that with sincere esteem etc.

PS: We have not heard through any other channel than your letter, of the intended resignation of Mr. Skipwith, and of the proposed recommendation of Mr. Montflorence.

220

TO THE HOUSE OF
REPRESENTATIVES

United States, March 30, 1796

Gentlemen of the House of Representatives:

Power to make treaties residing with the President

With the utmost attention I have considered your resolution of the 24th. instant, requesting me to lay before your House, a copy of the instructions to the Minister of the United States who negotiated the Treaty with the King of Great Britain, together with the correspondence and other documents relative to that Treaty, excepting such of the said papers as any existing negotiation may render improper to be disclosed.

In deliberating upon this subject, it was impossible for me to lose sight of the principle which some have avowed in its discussion; or to avoid extending my views to the consequences which must flow from the admission of that principle.

I trust that no part of my conduct has ever indicated a disposition to withhold any information which the Constitution has enjoined upon the President as a duty to give, or which could be required of him by either House of Congress as a right; And with truth I affirm, that it has been, as it will continue to be, while I have the honor to preside in the Government, my constant endeavour to harmonize with the other branches thereof; so far as the trust delegated to me by the People of the

United States, and my sense of the obligation it imposes to "preserve, protect and defend the Constitution" will permit.

The nature of foreign negotiations requires caution; and their success must often depend on secrecy: and even when brought to a conclusion, a full disclosure of all the measures, demands, or eventual concessions, which may have been proposed or contemplated, would be extremely impolitic: for this might have a pernicious influence on future negotiations; or produce immediate inconveniences, perhaps danger and mischief, in relation to other powers. The necessity of such caution and secrecy was one cogent reason for vesting the power of making Treaties in the President, with the advice and consent of the Senate, the principle on which that body was formed confining it to a small number of Members.

To admit then a right in the House of Representatives to demand, and to have as a matter of course, all the Papers respecting a negotiation with a foreign power, would be to establish a dangerous precedent.

It does not occur that the inspection of the papers asked for, can be relative to any purpose under the cognizance of the House of Representatives, except that of an impeachment, which the resolution has not expressed. I repeat, that I have no disposition to withhold any information which the duty of my station will permit, or the public good shall require to be disclosed: and in fact, all the Papers affecting the negotiation with Great Britain were laid before the Senate, when the Treaty itself was communicated for their consideration and advice.

The course which the debate has taken, on the resolution of the House, leads to some observations on the mode of making treaties under the Constitution of the United States.

Having been a member of the General Convention, and knowing the principles on which the Constitution was formed, I have ever entertained but one opinion on this subject; and from the first establishment of the Government to this moment, my conduct has exemplified that opinion, that the power of making treaties is exclusively vested in the President, by and with the advice and consent of the Senate, provided two thirds of the Senators present concur, and that every treaty so made, and promulgated, thenceforward became the Law of the land. It is thus that the treaty making power has been understood by foreign Nations: and in all the treaties made with them, *we* have declared, and *they* have believed, that when ratified by the President with the advice and consent of the Senate, they became obligatory. In this construction of the Constitution every House of Representatives has heretofore acquiesced; and until the present time, not a doubt or suspicion has appeared to my knowledge that this construction was not the true one. Nay, they have more than acquiesced: for till now, without controverting the obligation of such treaties, they have made all the requisite provisions for carrying them into effect.

There is also reason to believe that this construction agrees with the opinions entertained by the State Conventions, when they were deliberating on the Constitution; especially by those who objected to it, because there was not required, in *commercial treaties*, the consent of two thirds of the whole number of the members of the Senate, instead of two thirds of the Senators present; and because in treaties respecting territorial and certain other rights and claims, the concurrence of three fourths of the whole number of the members of both houses respectively, was not made necessary.

It is a fact declared by the General Convention, and universally understood, that the Constitution of the United States was the result of a spirit of amity and mutual concession. And it is well known that under this influence the smaller States were admitted to an equal representation in the Senate with the larger States; and that this branch of the government was invested with great powers: for on the equal participation of those powers, the sovereignty and political safety of the smaller States were deemed essentially to depend.

If other proofs than these, and the plain letter of the Constitution itself, be necessary to ascertain the point under consideration, they may be found in the journals of the General Convention, which I have deposited in the office of the department of State. In these journals it will appear that a proposition was made, "that no Treaty should be binding on the United States which was not ratified by a Law"; and that the proposition was explicitly rejected.

As therefore it is perfectly clear to my understanding, that the assent of the House of Representatives is not necessary to the validity of a treaty: as the treaty with Great Britain exhibits in itself all the objects requiring legislative provision; And on these the papers called for can throw no light: And as it is essential to the due administration of the government, that the boundaries fixed by the constitution between the different departments should be preserved: A just regard to the Constitution and to the duty of my Office, under all the circumstances of this case, forbids a complyance with your request.

CHAPTER FOURTEEN

LIFE MASK OF WASHINGTON

A Work Completed

1796 – 1799

*W*ASHINGTON *confidently speaks of "the happy reward of our mutual cares, labors, and dangers" in his "Farewell Address." He left the presidency with no less pleasure than he had had in resigning his military commission thirteen years earlier, when he declared that he resigned "with satisfaction the appointment he accepted with diffidence." The spontaneous and universal acclaim which welcomed him home from the war in 1783 was duplicated in 1796. This time, however, he had completed a much more trying task, the increasingly bitter party strife having made even him a target.*

In preparing for his first inauguration, Washington opted for expressions of diffidence instead of confidence in addressing the people. By the time of the "Farewell Address," he could speak with some confidence. He could consistently lay claim to satisfaction upon this last retirement. Not only had the country been solidified and its finances put in order, but the ominous threats of war which had loomed over his last five years in office had been greatly lessened even as the country had been strengthened to meet any eventuality. At the same time, his resignation removed him from that unfamiliar position of being held up to public scorn and ridicule by infamous scribblers.

221

TO ALEXANDER HAMILTON

Private and Confidential

Philadelphia, May 8, 1796

My dear Sir:

Your note of the 5th instant accompanying the information given to you by G —— M—— on the 4th. of March, came safe on friday. The letter he refers to, as having been written to me, is not yet received; but others from Mr. Monroe of similar complexion, and almost of as imperious a tone from that government, have got to hand.

That justice and policy should dictate the measures with which we are threatned, is not to be conceived; and one would think that even folly and madness on their part, would hardly go such lengths, without supposing a stimulus of a more serious nature than the Town meetings, and the partial resolutions which appeared in the course of last Summer and Autumn on ours. Yet, as it seems to be the Aera of strange vicissitudes, and unaccountable transactions; attended with a sort of irrisistable fatality in many of them, I shall not be surprized at any event that may happen, however extraordinary it may be; and therefore, it may not be amiss to ruminate upon the information which has been received in its fullest latitude; and be prepared to answer the demands on the extensive scale wch. has been mentioned.

Opposition to Jay's Treaty

What then do you think ought to be said in case G——M——s information should prove true, *in all its parts*? And what, if the proceedings, and Instructions of the French Directory should not exceed my conjecture, which is, that encouraged by the proceedings of last Summer on the Treaty (as already mentioned) and aided perhaps by communications of influential men in *this* country, thro' a medium which ought to have been the last to engage in it, that that government *may*, and I believe *will* send out an Envoy extraordinary, with Instructions to make strong remonstrances against the unfriendliness (as they will term it), and the tendency of our Treaty with Great Britain; accompanied probably, and expectedly, with discretionary powers to go farther, according to circumstances, and the existing state of matters when he shall have arrived here. Perhaps these Instructions may extend to a releasement from that part of our Treaty with *them*, which claims exemption from the Seisure of Enemies goods in *our* Vessels. Perhaps, to demand the fulfilment of our guarantee of their West India Islds. as the most likely means of affording them relief, under the circumstances they labor at present. Perhaps too, to endeavor to render null and void our Treaty with G: Britain. Possibly *all of them*, or the dissolution of the Alliance. But I cannot bring my mind to believe that they seriously mean, or that they could accompany this Envoy with a Fleet, to *demand* the annihilation of the Treaty with G. Britain in fifteen days; or that War, in case of refusal, must follow as a consequence.

Were it not for the unhappy differences among ourselves, *my* answer wd. be short and decisive, to this effect. We are an Independent Nation, and act for ourselves. Having fulfilled, and being willing to fulfil, (as far as we are able) our engagements with other Nations, and having decided on, and strictly observed a Neutral conduct towards the Belligerent Powers, from an unwillingness to involve ourselves in War. We will not be dictated to by the Politics of any Nation under Heaven, farther than Treaties require of us.

Whether the *present*, or any circumstances should do more than *soften* this language, may merit consideration. But if we are to be told by a foreign Power (if our engagements with it are not infracted) what we *shall do*, and what we shall *not do*, we have Independence yet to seek, and have contended hitherto for very little.

If you have communicated this purport of G —— M——s letter to Mr. Jay, I wish you would lay this also before him, *in confidence*, and that you and he would be so good as to favor me with your sentiments, and opinions on both; and on the measures which you think would be most advisable to be taken, in case we should have to encounter the difficulties with which we are threatened: which, assuredly, will have been brought on us by the misconduct of some of our own intemperate people; who seem to have preferred throwing themselves into the Arms of France (even under the present circumstances of that Country) to that manly, and Neutral conduct which is so essential, and would so well become us, as an Independent Nation.

Before I close this letter, I will mention another subject; which, tho' in a smaller degree, is nevertheless embarrassing. This also is communicated in confidence. It respects the wishes of young Fayette, relative to his father. As is very natural, and what might have been expected, he is extremely solicitous that something should be attempted to obtain the liberation of him; and has brought forward several plans (suggested by Doctr. Ballman; who, it is to be feared will be found a troublesome guest among us) to effect it.

Lafayette in prison

These will be better understood by the enclosures now sent, than by any details I could give, when I add to them, the supposition of Fayette and Frestal, that the Doctor is without funds, and will be more embarrassing *to them* the longer he remains here. No mention, however, that has come to my knowledge of his going away.

The result of my reflection on this subject, and which I have communicated to the two young Men, is, that altho' I am convinced in my own mind that Mr. La Fayette will be held in confinement by the combined Powers until Peace is established; yet to satisfy them, and their friends of my disposition to facilitate their wishes, as far as it can be done with any propriety on my part; I would, *as a private person*, express in a letter to the Emperor, my wish, and what I believe to be the wishes of this Country towards that Gentleman; viz, that the liberation of him, conditioned on his repairing hither, would be a grateful measure. That this letter I would put under cover to Mr. Pinckney, to be forwarded or not, according to the view he might have of its success; after conversing indirectly with the Diplomatic characters of the combined Powers in London.

But that I could not, while in Public Office, have any Agency in, or even knowledge of, any projects that should require concealment, or that I should be unwilling to appear openly and avowedly in. That as Doctr. Ballman had committed an Act (however meritorious and pleasing it might be to the friends of Mr. de la Fayette) which was viewed in a very obnoxious light by the Power in whose possession the prisoner was. Had narrowly escaped condign punishment for it himself. And was released upon the express condition that he should never again appear in those Dominions; that I could neither shew him countenance, nor could I furnish him with money to extricate himself from difficulties (if he was in any). Seeing but little difference between giving before, or after, to a man who stands in the light he does between that Power and the Executive of the U States; but that, if he was disposed to quit the latter, I had no doubt, and he might be so assured, that the friends of Mr. de la Fayette would raise a sufficient sum to enable him to do this, and to defray his expences since he has been in this Country. What they will say to him, or he do in this matter, I know not.

If you and Mr. Jay see no impropriety in such a letter as I have mentioned, to be used at the discretion of Mr. Pinckney, I would thank either of you, for drafting it. Mr. Jay in particular having been in the habit, and better acquainted with the stile and manner of addressing these sort of characters than I am, would be able to give it a better shape. To return the papers now sent, with the draught required, as soon as convenient, would be acceptable to Dear Sir Your etc.

222

TO THE EMPEROR OF GERMANY

Philadelphia, May 15, 1796

It will readily occur to your Majesty, that occasions may sometimes exist, on which official considerations would constrain the Chief of a Nation to be silent and passive, in relation even to objects which affect his sensibility, and claim his interposition as a man. Finding myself precisely in this situation at present, I take the liberty of writing this *private* Letter to your

Majesty; being persuaded, that my motives will also be my appology for it.

In common with the people of this Country, I retain a strong and cordial sense of the services rendered to them by the Marquis De la Fayette; and my friendship for him has been constant and sincere. It is natural, therefore, that I should sympathize with him and his family in their misfortunes, and endeavour to mitigate the calamities which they experience; among which his present confinement is not the least distressing.

On behalf of Lafayette

I forbear to enlarge on this delicate subject. Permit me only to submit to your Majesty's consideration, whether his long imprisonment, and the confiscation of his Estate, and the Indigence and dispersion of his family, and the painful anxieties incident to all these circumstances, do not form an assemblage of sufferings, which recommend him to the mediation of *Humanity?* Allow me, Sir! on this occasion to be its organ; and to entreat that he may be permitted to come to this Country on such conditions and under such restrictions, as your Majesty may think it expedient to prescribe.

As it is a maxim with me not to ask what under similar circumstances, I would not grant, your Majesty will do me the justice to believe, that this request appears to me to correspond with those great principles of magnanimity and wisdom, which form the Basis of sound Policy and durable Glory.

May the almighty and merciful Sovereign of the universe keep your Majesty under his protection and guidance.

223

TO ALEXANDER HAMILTON

Philadelphia, May 15, 1796

My dear Sir:

On this day week, I wrote you a letter on the subject of the information received from G —— M—— and put it with some other Papers respecting the case of Mr. De la Fayette, under cover to Mr. Jay: to whom also I had occasion to write. But in my hurry (making up the dispatches for the Post Office next morning) I forgot to give it a Superscription; of course it had

Discussion of the
farewell address

to return from N. York for one, and to encounter all the delay occasioned thereby, before it could reach your hands.

Since then, I have been favored with your letter of the 10th. instt. and enclose (in its rough State) the paper mentioned therein, with some alteration in the first page (since you saw it) relative to the reference at foot. Having no copy by me (except of the quoted part), nor the notes from wch. it was drawn, I beg leave to recommend the draught now sent, to your particular attention.

Even if you should think it best to throw the *whole* into a different form, let me request, notwithstanding, that my draught may be returned to me (along with yours) with such amendments and corrections, as to render it as perfect as the formation is susceptible of; curtailed, if too verbose; and relieved of all tautology, not necessary to enforce the ideas in the original or quoted part. My wish is, that the whole may appear in a plain stile; and be handed to the public in an honest; unaffected; simple garb.

It will be perceived from hence, that I am attached to the quotation. My reasons for it are, that as it is not only a fact that such an Address *was written*, and on the point of being published, but *known also to one or two* of those characters who are now strongest, and foremost in the opposition to the Government; and consequently to the person Administering of it contrary to their views; the promulgation thereof, as an evidence that it was much against my inclination that I continued in Office, will cause it more readily to be believed, that I could have *no* view in extending the Powers of the Executive beyond the limits prescribed by the Constitution; and will serve to lessen, in the public estimation the pretensions of that Party to the patriotic zeal and watchfulness, on which they endeavor to build their own consequence at the expence of others, who have differed from them in sentiment. And besides, it may contribute to blunt, if it does not turn aside, some of the shafts which it may be presumed will be aimed at my annunciation of this event; among which, conviction of fallen popularity, and despair of being re-elected, will be levelled at me with dexterity and keenness.

Having struck out the reference to a *particular character* in the first page of the Address, I have less (if any) objection to expunging those words which are contained within parenthesis's in pages 5, 7 and 8 in the quoted part, and those in the

18th page of what follows. Nor to discarding the egotisms (however just they may be) if you think them liable to fair criticism, and that they had better be omitted; notwithstanding some of them relate facts which are but little known to the Community.

My object has been, and must continue to be, to avoid personalities; allusions to particular measures, which may appear pointed; and to expressions which could not fail to draw upon me attacks which I should wish to avoid, and might not find agreeable to repel.

Avoid attacks on personalities

As there will be another Session of Congress before the Political existence of the *present* House of Representatives, or my own, will constitutionally expire, it was not my design to say a word to the Legislature on this subject; but to withhold the promulgation of my intention until the period, when it shall become indispensably necessary for the information of the Electors, previous to the Election (which, this year, will be delayed until the 7th of December). This makes it a little difficult, and uncertain what to say, so long beforehand, on the part marked with a pencil in the last paragraph of the 2d page.

All these ideas, and observations are confined, as you will readily perceive, to *my draft* of the valedictory Address. If you form one anew, it will, of course, assume such a shape as you may be disposed to give it, predicated upon the Sentiments contained in the enclosed Paper.

With respect to the Gentleman you have mentioned as Successor to Mr P—— there can be no doubt of his abilities, nor in *my mind* is there any of his fitness. But you know as well as I, what has been said of his political sentiments, with respect to another form of Government; and from thence, can be at no loss to guess at the Interpretation which would be given to the nomination of him. However, the subject shall have due consideration; but a previous resignation would, in my opinion, carry with it too much the appearance of Concert; and would have a bad, rather than a good effect. Always, and sincerely I am yours.

Rufus King and Timothy Pickering

224

TO THOMAS PINCKNEY

Private

Philadelphia, May 22, 1796

Dear Sir:

Jay's Treaty in the House of Representatives

To my letters of the 20th. of February and 5th. of March, I beg leave to refer you for the disclosure of my sentiments on the subjects there mentioned to you. Very soon afterwards, a long and animated discussion in the House of Representatives relative the Treaty of Amity, Commerce, and Navigation with Great Britain, took place; and continued, in one shape or another, until the last of April; suspending, in a manner, all other business; and agitating the public mind in a higher degree than it has been at any period since the Revolution. And nothing, I believe, but the torrent of Petitions, and remonstrances which were pouring in from all the Eastern and middle States, and were beginning to come pretty strongly from that of Virginia, requiring the necessary provisions for carrying the Treaty into effect, would have produced a division (51 to 48) in favor of the appropriation.

But as the debates, which I presume will be sent to you from the Department of State, will give you a view of this business, more in detail than I am able to do, I shall refer you to them.

Fisher Ames

The enclosed Speech, however, made by Mr. Aimes at the close of the discussion, I send to you; because, in the opinion of most that heard it delivered, or have read it since, his reasoning is unanswerable.

The doubtful issue of the dispute, added to the *real* difficulty in finding a character to supply your place, at the Court of London, has occasioned a longer delay than may have been convenient or agreeable to you. But as Mr. King of the Senate (who it seems had resolved to quit his Seat at that board) has accepted the appointment, and will embark as soon as matters can be arranged, you will soon be relieved.

In my letter of the 20th of Feby, I expressed in pretty strong terms, my sensibility on acct. of the situation of the Marquis De la Fayette. This is increased by the visible distress of his Son, who is now with me, and grieving for the unhappy fate of his parents. This circumstance, giving a poignancy to my own feelings on this occasion, has induced me to go a step further than I did in the letter above mentioned; as you will perceive by the enclosed Address (a copy of which is also transmitted for your information) to the Emperor of Germany: to be forwarded by you in such a manner, and under such auspices as, in your judgment, shall be deemed best: or to arrest it, if from the evidence before you (derived from former attempts) it shall appear *clear,* that it would be of no avail to send it.

Before I close this letter, permit me to request the favor of you to embrace some favorable occasion to thank Lord Grenville, in my behalf, for his politeness in causing a special permit to be sent to Liverpool for the shipment of two sacks of the field Peas, and the like quantity of Winter Vetches, which I had requested our Consul at that place to send me, for Seed; but which it seems could not be done without an Order from government. A circumstance which did not occur to me, or I certainly should not have given it the trouble of issuing one, for such a trifle. With very great esteem &c.

225

TO ALEXANDER HAMILTON

Mount Vernon, June 26, 1796

My dear Sir:

Your letter without date, came to my hands by wednesdays Post; and by the first Post afterwards I communicated the purport of it (withholding the names) to the Secretary of State; with directions to bestow the closest attention to the subject, and if the application which had been made to the Minister of France, consequent on the Capture of the Ship Mount Vernon, had not produced such an answer as to supercede the necessity, then to endeavor to obtain such explanation of the views of the French government relatively to our Commerce with Great Britain, as the nature of the case appeared to require.

French reaction to Jay's Treaty

That the fact is, as has been presented to you, I have very little, if any doubt. Many, very many circumstances are continually happening in confirmation of it: among which, it is evident Bache's Paper, which *receives* and *gives* the tone, is endeavouring to prepare the Public mind for this event, by representing it as the *predicted*, and *natural* consequence of the Ratification of the Treaty with Great Britn.

Let me ask therefore. Do you suppose that the Executive, in the recess of the Senate, has power in such a case as the one before us, especially if the measure should not be *avowed* by authority, to send a special character to Paris, as Envoy Extraordinary, to give, and receive explanations? And if there be a doubt, whether it is not probable, nay, more than probable, that the French Directory would, in the present state of things, avail themselves of the unconstitutionallity of the measure, to decline receiving him? The policy of delay, to avoid explanations, would induce them to adopt any pretext to accomplish it. Their reliance upon a party in this country for support, would stimulate them to this conduct; And we may be assured they will not be deficient in the most minute details of every occurrence, and every opinion, worthy of communication. If then an Envoy cannot be sent to Paris without the Agency of the Senate, will the information you have received, admitting it should be realized, be sufficient ground for convening that body?

These are serious things; they may be productive of serious consequences; and therefore require very serious and cool deliberation. Admitting, however, that the Powers of the President during the recess, were adequate to such an appointment, where is the character who would go, that unites the proper qualifications for such a Mission; and would not be obnoxious to one party or the other? And what should be done with Mr. M—— in that case?

As the affairs of this country in their administration, receive great embarrassment from the conduct of characters among ourselves; and as every act of the Executive is mis-represented, and tortured with a view to make it appear odious, the aid of the friends to government is peculiarly necessary under such circumstances; and at such a crises as the present: It is unnecessary therefore to add, that I should be glad upon the present, and all other important occasions, to receive yours: and as I have great confidence in the abilities, and purity of Mr. Jays views, as well as in his experience, I should wish that his sentiments on the purport of this letter; and other interesting matters as they occur, may accompany yours; for having no other wish than to promote the true and permanent interests of this country, I am anxious, always, to compare the opinions of those in whom I confide with one another; and those again (without being bound by them) with my own, that I may extract all the good I can.

Having from a variety of reasons (among which a disinclination to be longer buffited in the public prints by a set of infamous scribblers) taken my ultimate determination "To seek the Post of honor in a private Station" I regret exceedingly that I did not publish my valedictory address the day after the Adjournment of Congress. This would have preceeded the canvassing for Electors (wch is commencing with warmth, in this State). It would have been announcing *publicly*, what seems to be very well understood, and is industriously propagated, *privately.* It would have removed doubts from the mind of *all*, and left the field clear for *all*: It would, by having preceeded any unfavorable change in our foreign relations (if any should happen) render my retreat less difficult and embarrassing. And it might have prevented the remarks which, more than probable will follow a late annunication, namely, that I delayed it long enough to see, that the current was turned against me, before I declared my intention to decline. This is one of the reasons which makes me a little tenacious of the draught I furnished you with, to be modified and corrected.

Decision to retire from public life

Having passed, however, what *I now* conceive would have been the *precise* moment to have Addressed my Constituents, let me ask your opinion (under a full conviction that nothing will shake my determination to withdraw) of the *next* best time, considering the present, and what may, probably, be the existing state of things at different periods previous to the Election; or rather, the middle of Octr; beyond which the promulgation of my intentions cannot be delayed. Let me hear from you as soon as it is convenient; and be assured always of the sincere esteem, and affecte. regard of.

226

TO THOMAS JEFFERSON

Mount Vernon, July 6, 1796

Dear Sir:

When I inform you, that your letter of the 19th. Ulto. went to Philadelphia and returned to this place before it was received by me; it will be admitted, I am persuaded, as an apology for my not having acknowledged the receipt of it sooner.

If I had entertained any suspicions before, that the queries, which have been published in Bache's Paper, proceeded from you, the assurances you have given of the contrary, would have removed them; but the truth is, I harboured none. I am at no loss to *conjecture* from what source they flowed; through what channel they were conveyed; and for what purpose they and similar publications, appear. They were known to be in the hands of Mr. Parker, in the early part of the last Session of Congress; They were shown about by Mr. Giles during the Cession, and they made their public exhibition about the close of it.

Perceiving, and probably, hearing, that no abuse in the Gazettes would induce me to take notice of anonymous publications, against me; those who were disposed to do me *such friendly Offices*, have embraced without restraint every opportunity to weaken the confidence of the People; and, by having the *whole* game in their hands, they have scrupled not to publish things that do not, as well as those which do exist; and to mutilate the latter, so as to make them subserve the purposes which they have in view.

Jefferson and his friends

As you have mentioned the subject yourself, it would not be frank, candid, or friendly to conceal, that your conduct has been represented as derogatory from that opinion *I* had conceived you entertained of me. That to your particular friends and connexions you have described, and they have denounced me, as a person under a dangerous influence; and that, if I would listen *more* to some *other* opinions, all would be well. My answer invariably has been, that I had never discovered any thing in the conduct of Mr. Jefferson to raise suspicions, in my mind, of his insincerity; that if he would retrace my public conduct while he was in the Administration, abundant proofs would occur to him, that truth and right decisions, were the *sole* objects of my pursuit; that there were as many instances within his *own* knowledge of my having decided *against*, as in *favor of* the opinions of the person evidently alluded to; and moreover, that I was no believer in the infallibility of the politics, or measures of *any man living.* In short, that I was no party man myself, and the first wish of my heart was, if parties did exist, to reconcile them.

To this I may add, and very truly, that, until within the last year or two ago, I had no conception that Parties would, or even could go, the length I have been witness to; nor did I believe until lately, that it was within the bonds of probability; hardly within those of possibility, that, while I was using my utmost exertions to establish a national character of our own, independent, as far as our obligations, and justice would permit, of every nation of the earth; and wished, by steering a steady course, to preserve this Country from the horrors of a desolating war, that I should be accused of being the enemy of one Nation, and subject to the influence of another; and to prove it, that every act of my administration would be tortured, and the grossest, and most insidious mis-representations of them be made (by giving one side *only* of a subject, and that too in such exaggerated and indecent terms as could scarcely be applied to a Nero; a notorious defaulter; or even to a common pickpocket). But enough of this; I have already gone farther in the expression of my feelings, than I intended.

Political parties and foreign connections

The particulars of the case you mention (relative to the Little Sarah) is a good deal out of my recollection at present, and I have no public papers here to resort to. When I get back to Philadelphia (which, unless I am called there by something new, will not be 'till towards the last of August) I will examine my files.

It must be pleasing to a Cultivator, to possess Land which will yield Clover kindly; for it is certainly a great Desiderata in Husbandry. My Soil, without very good dressings, does not produce it well: owing, I believe, to its stiffness; hardness at bottom; and retention of Water. A farmer, in my opinion, need never despair of raising Wheat to advantage, upon a Clover lay; with a single ploughing, agreeably to the Norfolk and Suffolk practice. By a misconception of my Manager last year, a field at one of my Farms which I intended shd. have been fallowed for Wheat, went untouched. Unwilling to have my crop of Wheat at that place so much reduced, as would

Virginia agriculture

have been occasioned by this omission, I directed, as soon as I returned from Philadelphia (about the middle of September) another field, not in the usual rotation, which had lain out two years, and well covered with mixed grasses, principally white clover, to be turned over with a good Bar-share; and the Wheat to be sown, and harrowed in at the tail of the Plough. It was done so accordingly, and was, by odds, the best Wheat I made this year. It exhibits an unequivocal proof to my mind, of the great advantage of Clover lay, for Wheat. Our Crops of this article, hereabouts, are more or less injured by what some call the Rot; others the Scab; occasioned, I believe, by high winds and beating rain when the grain is in blossom, and before the Farina has performed its duties.

Desirous of trying the field Peas of England, and the Winter Vetch, I sent last fall to Mr. Marray of Liverpool for 8 bushels of each sort. Of the Peas he sent me two kinds (a white and dark, but not having the letter by me, I am unable to give the names). They did not arrive until the latter end of April; when they ought to have been in the ground the beginning of March. They were sown however, but will yield no Seed; of course the experiment I intended to make, is lost. The Vetch is yet on hand for Autumn Seeding. That the Albany Peas will grow well with us, I know from my own experience: but they are subject to the same bug which perforates, and injures the Garden Peas, and will do the same, I fear, to the imported Peas, of any sort from England, in this climate, from the heat of it.

I do not know what is meant by, or to what uses the Caroline drill is applied. How does your Chicorium prosper? Four years since I exterminated all the Plants raised from Seed sent me by Mr. Young, and to get into it again, the seed I purchased in Philadelphia last Winter, and what has been sent me by Mr. Murray this Spring, has cost me upwards of twelve pounds Sterling. This, it may be observed, is a left handed way to make money; but the first was occasioned by the manager I then had, who pretended to know it well in England and pronounced it a noxious weed; the restoration of it, is indebted to Mr. Strickland and others (besides Mr. Young) who speak of it in exalted terms. I sowed mine broad-cast; some with and some without grain. It has come up well; but there seems to be a serious struggle between *it* and the grass and weeds; the issue of which (as I can afford no relief to the former) is doubtful at present, and may be useful to know.

If you can bring a moveable threshing Machine, constructed upon simple principles to perfection, it will be among the most valuable institutions in this Country; for nothing is more wanting, and to be wished for on our farms. Mrs. Washington begs you to accept her best wishes, and with very great esteem etc.

227

TO ALEXANDER HAMILTON

Private

Philadelphia, August 25, 1796

My dear Sir:

I have given the Paper herewith enclosed, several serious and attentive readings; and prefer it greatly to the other draughts, being more copious on material points; more dignified on the whole; and with less egotism. Of course less exposed to criticism, and better calculated to meet the eye of discerning readers (foreigners particularly, whose curiosity I have little doubt will lead them to inspect it attentively and to pronounce their opinions on the performance).

When the first draught was made, besides having an eye to the consideration above mentioned, I thought the occasion was fair (as I had latterly been the subject of considerable invective) to say what is there contained of myself; and as the Address was designed in a more especial manner for the Yeomanry of this Country I conceived it was proper they should be informed of the object of that abuse; the silence with which it had been treated; and the consequences which would naturally flow from such unceasing and virulent attempts to destroy all confidence in the Executive part of the Government; and that it was best to do it in language that was plain and intelligible to their understandings.

Considerations on farewell address

The draught now sent comprehends the most, if not all these matters; is better expressed; and I am persuaded goes as far as it ought with respect to any personal mention of myself.

I should have seen no occasion myself, for its undergoing a revision. But as your letter of the 30th. Ulto. which accompanied it, intimates a wish to do this, and knowing that it can be more correctly done after a writing has been out of sight for sometime than while it is in hand, I send it in conformity thereto; with a request, however, that you wd. return it as soon as you have carefully reexamined it; for it is my intention to hand it to the Public before I leave this City, to which I came for the purpose of meeting General Pinckney; receiving the Ministers from Spain and Holland; and for the dispatch of other business which could not be so well executed by written communications between the heads of Departments and myself as by oral conferences. So soon as these are accomplished I shall return; at any rate I expect to do so by, or before the tenth of next month for the purpose of bringing up my family for the Winter.

I shall expunge all that is marked in the paper as unimportant &ca. &ca. and as you perceive some marginal notes, written with a pencil, I pray you to give the sentiments so noticed mature consideration. After which, and in every other part, if change or alteration takes place in the draught, let them be so clearly interlined, erazed, or referred to in the Margin as that no mistake may happen in copying it for the Press.

To what Editor in *this* City do you think it had best be sent for Publication? Will it be proper to accompany it with a note to him, expressing (as the principal design of it is to remove doubts at the next Election) that it is hoped, or expected, that the State Printers will give it a place in their Gazettes; or preferable to let it be carried by my private Secretary to that Press which is destined to usher it to the World and suffer it to work its way afterwards? If you think the first most eligable, let me ask you to sketch such a note as you may judge applicable to the occasion. With affectionate regard I am always yours.

228

TALK TO THE CHEROKEE NATION

City of Philadelphia, August 29, 1796

Beloved Cherokees:

Many years have passed since the White people first came to America. In that long space of time many good men have considered how the condition of the Indian natives of the country might be improved; and many attempts have been made to effect it. But, as we see at this day, all these attempts have been nearly fruitless. I also have thought much on this subject, and anxiously wished that the various Indian tribes, as well as their neighbours, the White people, might enjoy in abundance all the good things which make life comfortable and happy. I have considered how this could be done; and have discovered but one path that could lead them to that desirable situation. In this path I wish all the Indian nations to walk. From the information received concerning you, my beloved Cherokees, I am inclined to hope that you are prepared to take this path and disposed to pursue it. It may seem a little difficult to enter; but if you make the attempt, you will find every obstacle easy to be removed. Mr. Dinsmoor, my beloved agent to your nation, being here, I send you this talk by him. He will have it interpreted to you, and particularly explain my meaning.

Improvement of the condition of the Indians

Beloved Cherokees, You now find that the game with which your woods once abounded, are growing scarce; and you know when you cannot meet a deer or other game to kill, that you must remain hungry; you know also when you can get no skins by hunting, that the traders will give you neither powder nor cloathing; and you know that without other implements for tilling the ground than the hoe, you will continue to raise only scanty crops of corn. Hence you are sometimes exposed to suffer much from hunger and cold; and as the game are lessening in numbers more and more, these sufferings will increase. And how are you to provide against them? Listen to my words and you will know.

My beloved Cherokees, Some among you already experience the advantage of keeping cattle and hogs: let all keep them and increase their numbers, and you will ever have a plenty of meet. To these add sheep, and they will give you

Indian husbandry

cloathing as well as food. Your lands are good and of great extent. By proper management you can raise live stock not only for your own wants, but to sell to the White people. By using the plow you can vastly increase your crops of corn. You can also grow wheat, (which makes the best bread) as well as other useful grain. To these you will easily add flax and cotton, which you may dispose of to the White people, or have it made up by your own women into cloathing for yourselves. Your wives and daughters can soon learn to spin and weave; and to make this certain, I have directed Mr. Dinsmoor, to procure all the necessary apparatus for spinning and weaving, and to hire a woman to teach the use of them. He will also procure some plows and other implements of husbandry, with which to begin the improved cultivation of the ground which I recommend, and employ a fit person to shew you how they are to be used. I have further directed him to procure some cattle and sheep for the most prudent and industrious men, who shall be willing to exert themselves in tilling the ground and raising those useful animals. He is often to talk with you on these subjects, and give you all necessary information to promote your success. I must therefore desire you to listen to him; and to follow his advice. I appointed him to dwell among you as the Agent of the United States, because I judged him to be a faithful man, ready to obey my instructions and to do you good.

Indian agents

But the cares of the United States are not confined to your single nation. They extend to all the Indians dwelling on their borders. For which reason other agents are appointed; and for the four southern nations there will be a general or principal agent who will visit all of them, for the purpose of maintaining peace and friendship among them and with the United States; to superintend all their affairs; and to assist the particular agents with each nation in doing the business assigned them. To such general or principal agent I must desire your careful attention. He will be one of our greatly beloved men. His whole time will be employed in contriving how to do you good, and you will therefore act wisely to follow his advice. The first general or principal agent will be Colonel Benjamin Hawkins, a man already known and respected by you. I have chosen him for this office because he is esteemed for a good man; has a knowledge of Indian customs, and a particular love and friendship for all the Southern tribes.

A Work Completed

Beloved Cherokees, What I have recommended to you I am myself going to do. After a few moons are passed I shall leave the great town and retire to my farm. There I shall attend to the means of increasing my cattle, sheep and other useful animals; to the growing of corn, wheat, and other grain, and to the employing of women in spinning and weaving; all which I have recommended to you, that you may be as comfortable and happy as plenty of food, clothing and other good things can make you.

Beloved Cherokees, When I have retired to my farm I shall hear of you; and it will give me great pleasure to know that you have taken my advice, and are walking in the path which I have described. But before I retire, I shall speak to my beloved man, the Secretary of War, to get prepared some medals, to be given to such Cherokees as by following my advice shall best deserve them. For this purpose Mr. Dinsmoor is from time to time to visit every town in your nation. He will give instructions to those who desire to learn what I have recommended. He will see what improvements are made; who are most industrious in raising cattle; in growing corn, wheat, cotton and flax; and in spinning and weaving; and on those who excel these rewards are to be bestowed.

Beloved Cherokees, The advice I here give you is important as it regards your nation; but still more important as the event *Cherokees to set* of the experiment made with you may determine the lot of *example* many nations. If it succeeds, the beloved men of the United States will be encouraged to give the same assistance to all the Indian tribes within their boundaries. But if it should fail, they may think it vain to make any further attempts to better the condition of any Indian tribe; for the richness of the soil and mildness of the air render your country highly favorable for the practice of what I have recommended.

Beloved Cherokees, The wise men of the United States meet together once a year, to consider what will be for the good of all their people. The wise men of each separate state also meet together once or twice every year, to consult and do what is good for the people of their respective states. I have thought that a meeting of your wise men once or twice a year would be alike useful to you. Every town might send one or two of its wisest counsellors to talk together on the affairs of your nation, and to recommend to your people whatever they should think would be serviceable. The beloved agent of the United

States would meet with them. He would give them information of those things which are found good by the white people, and which your situation will enable you to adopt. He would explain to them the laws made by the great council of the United States, for the preservation of peace; for the protection of your lands; for the security of your persons; for your improvement in the arts of living, and for promoting your general welfare. If it should be agreeable to you that your wise men should hold such meetings, you will speak your mind to my beloved man, Mr. Dinsmoor, to be communicated to the President of the United States, who will give such directions as shall be proper.

Beloved Cherokees, That this talk may be known to all your nation, and not forgotten, I have caused it to be printed, and directed one, signed by my own hand, to be lodged in each of your towns. The Interpreters will, on proper occasions, read and interpret the same to all your people.

Beloved Cherokees, Having been informed that some of your chiefs wished to see me in Philadelphia, I have sent them word that I would receive a few of the most esteemed. I now repeat that I shall be glad to see a small number of your wisest chiefs; but I shall not expect them 'till November. I shall take occasion to agree with them on the running of the boundary line between your lands and ours, agreeably to the treaty of Holston. I shall expect them to inform me what chiefs are to attend the running of this line, and I shall tell them whom I appoint to run it; and the time and place of beginning may then be fixed.

I now send my best wishes to the Cherokees, and pray the Great spirit to preserve them.

229

TO ALEXANDER HAMILTON

Private

Philadelphia, September 1, 1796

My dear Sir:

About the middle of last Week I wrote to you; and that it might escape the eye of the Inquisitive (for some of my letters have lately been pried into) I took the liberty of putting it under a cover to Mr. Jay.

Since then, revolving on the Paper that was enclosed therein; on the various matters it contained; and on the first expression of the advice or recommendation which was given in it, I have regretted that another subject (which in my estimation is of interesting concern to the well-being of this country) was not touched upon also: I mean Education *generally* as one of the surest means of enlightening and givg. just ways of thinkg to our Citizens, but particulary the establishment of a university; where the Youth from *all parts* of the United States might receive the polish of Erudition in the Arts, Sciences and Belle Letters; and where those who were disposed to run a political course, might not only be instructed in the theory and principles, but (this Seminary being at the Seat of the General Government) where the Legislature wd. be in Session half the year, and the Interests and politics of the Nation of course would be discussed, they would lay the surest foundation for the practical part also.

Public education

National university

But that which would render it of the highest importance, in my opinion, is, that the Juvenal period of life, when friendships are formed, and habits established that will stick by one; the youth, or young men from different parts of the United States would be assembled together, and would by degrees discover that there was not that cause for those jealousies and prejudices which one part of the Union had imbibed against another part: of course, sentiments of more liberality in the general policy of the Country would result from it. What, but the mixing of people from different parts of the United States during the War rubbed off these impressions? A century in the ordinary intercourse, would not have accomplished what the Seven years association in Arms did: but that ceasing, prejudices are beginning to revive again, and never will be eradicated so effectually by any other means as the intimate intercourse of characters in early life, who, in all probability, will be at the head of the councils of this country in a more advanced stage of it.

To shew that this is no *new* idea of mine, I may appeal to my early communications to Congress; and to prove how seriously I have reflected on it since, and how well disposed I have been, and still am, to contribute my aid towards carrying the measure into effect, I enclose you the extract of a letter from me to the Governor of Virginia on this Subject, and a copy of the resolves of the Legislature of that State in consequence thereof.

I have not the smallest doubt that this donation (when the Navigation is in complete operation, which it certainly will be in less than two years), will amount to twelve or £1500 Sterlg a year, and become a rapidly increasing fund. The Proprietors of the Federal City have talked of doing something handsome towards it likewise; and if Congress would appropriate some of the Western lands to the same uses, funds sufficient, and of the most permanent and increasing sort might be so established as to envite the ablest Professors in Europe, to conduct it.

Let me pray you, therefore, to introduce a Section in the Address expressive of these sentiments, and recommendatory of the measure; without any mention, however, of my proposed personal contribution to the plan.

Such a Section would come in very properly after the one which relates to our religious obligations, or in a preceeding part, as one of the recommendatory measures to counteract the evils arising from Geographical discriminations. With Affecte. regard etc.

230

TO ALEXANDER HAMILTON

Private

Philadelphia, November 2, 1796

My dear Sir:

On monday afternoon I arrived in this City, and among the first things which presented themselves to my view, was Mr. Adets letter to the Secretary of State, published by his order, in the moment it was presented.*

Reception of Minister Adet

The object in doing this is not difficult of solution; but whether the *publication* in the manner it appears, is by order of the Directory, or an act of his own, is yet to be learnt. If the first, he has executed a duty only; if the latter, he has exceeded it, and is himself responsible for the indignity offered to this Government by such publication, without allowing it time to reply, or to take its own mode of announcing the intentions of his country towards the Commerce of these United States.

In either case, should there be in your opinion, any difference in my reception and treatment of that Minister, in his visits at the public Rooms (I have not seen him yet, nor do not expect to do it before tuesday next), and what difference should be made if any?

He complains in his letter, that he had received no answers to the remonstrances in former communications (the dates of which are given). The fact is, that one at least of those remonstrances, were accompanied by as indecent charges, and as offensive expressions as the letters of Genet were ever marked with; and besides, the same things on former occasions, had been replied to (as the Secretary of State informs me) over and over again.

That the letter which he has now given to the public will be

---

*P.-A. Adet, yet another troublesome Jacobin French Ambassador to the United States, had opened a diplomatic communication to public view, publishing it in the party press. In this letter the French government effectively threatened to treat the United States as a hostile force in reprisal for the Jay Treaty, ratified shortly before. Adet went on to exceed this excess by publishing an endorsement of Thomas Jefferson for the presidency in the election of 1796.

answered, and (to a candid mind) I hope satisfactorily, is certain; but ought it to be published *immediately,* or *not*? This question has two sides to it; both of which are important. If the answer does not accompany the letter, the antidote will not keep pace with the poison, and it may, and undoubtedly would be said, it is because the charges are just, and the consequences had been predicted. On the other hand, may not the dignity of the Government be committed by a Newspaper dispute with the Minister of a foreign Nation, and an apparent appeal to the People? and would it not be said also that we can bear *every thing* from one of the Belligerent Powers, but *nothing* from another of them? I could enlarge on this subject, but add nothing, I am certain, that your own reflections thereon will not furnish. Whether the answer is published now, or not, would it be proper do you conceive, at the ensuing Session, which will close the political Scene with me, to bring the French Affairs, since the controversy with Genet fully before Congress? In doing this it is to be noticed, that there is such a connexion between them and our transactions with Great Britain as to render either imperfect without the other; and so much of the latter as relates to the Treaty with that country has already been refused to that body: not because there was any thing contained therein that all the world might not have seen, but because it was claimed as a matter of right, and the compliance therewith would have established a dangerous precedent.

A national agricultural institution

Since I wrote to you from Mount Vernon, on the eve of my departure from that place, and on my way hither, I received a letter from Sir John Sinclair, an extract of which I enclose you, on the subject of an Agricultural establishment. Though not such an enthusiast as he is, I am nevertheless deeply impressed with the benefits which would result from such an institution, and if you see no impropriety in the measure, I would leave it as a recommendatory one in the Speech at the opening of the session; which, probably, will be the last I shall ever address to that, or any other public body.

It must be obvious to every man, who considers the Agriculture of this country, (even in the best improved parts of it) and compares the produce of our lands with those of other countries, no ways superior to them in *natural fertility,* how miserably defective we are in the management of them; and that if we do not fall on a better mode of treating them, how ruinous it will prove to the landed interest. Ages will not produce a systematic change without public attention and encouragement; but a few years more of increased sterility will drive the Inhabitants of the Atlantic States Westwardly for support; whereas if they were taught how to improve the old, instead of going in pursuit of new and productive Soils, they would make those acres which now scarcely yield them any thing, turn out beneficial to themselves, to the Mechanics, by supplying them with the staff of life on much cheaper terms, to the Merchants, by encreasing their Commerce and exportation, and to the Community generally, by the influx of Wealth resulting therefrom.

In a word, it is in my estimation, a great national object, and if stated as fully as the occasion and circumstances will admit, I think it must appear so. But whatever may be the reception, or fate of the recommendation, I shall have discharged my duty in submitting it to the consideration of the Legislature.

As I have a very high opinion of Mr. Jay's judgment, candour, honor and discretion (tho' I am not in the habit of writing so freely to him as to you) it would be very pleasing to me if you would shew him this letter (although it is a hurried one, my time having been much occupied since my arrival by the heads of the Departments, and with the Papers which have been laid before me) and let me have, for consideration, your joint opinion on the several matters therein stated.

You will recollect that the conduct to be observed towards Mr. Adet must be decided on before tuesday next; that is, if he comes to the public room, whether he is to be received with the same cordiality as usual, or with coolness; and you will do me the justice to believe that in this instance, and every other, I wish it to be such as will promote the true policy and interest of the country, at the sametime that a proper respect for its dignity is preserved. My own feelings I put out of the question. *French duplicity*

There is in the conduct of the French government relative to this business, an inconsistency, a duplicity, a delay, or a something else, which is unaccountable upon honorable ground. It appears that the order under which Mr. Adet has acted is dated in July (early) and yet Mr. Monroe has been led to believe (though much dissatisfaction he says has appeared) that no such order had, or would be, issued unless Great Britain set the example; and in a letter of August the 28th he writes Mr. King to that effect; as the latter officially informs the Secretary of State: But I am fatigued with this and other

matters which croud upon me, and shall only add that I am
Very Affectionately Yours.

PS: I find I have not time before the hour for closing the
mail arrives, to take the promised extract from Sir John Sin-
clairs letter, I therefore send the original, with a request that it
may soon be returned as I have given it no acknowledgment
yet. the articles which he requests my acceptance of are not yet
come to hand.

231
_____

TO JONATHAN TRUMBULL

Philadelphia, March 3, 1797

My dear Sir:

*Reflections on
last day in office*

Before the curtain drops on my political life, which it will do
this evening, I expect for ever; I shall acknowledge, although
it be in a few hasty lines only, the receipt of your kind and
affectionate letter of the 23d. of January last.

When I add, that according to custom, all the Acts of the
Session; except two or three very unimportant Bills, have been
presented to me within the last four days, *you* will not be surprised at the pressure under which I write at present; but it
must astonish *others* who know that the Constitution allows the
President ten days to deliberate on *each Bill* that is brought
before him that he should be allowed by the Legislature less
than half that time to consider *all* the business of the Session;
and in some instances, scarcely an hour to revolve the most
important. But as the scene is closing, with me, it is of little
avail *now* to let it be with murmers.

I should be very unhappy if I thought my relinquishing the
Reins of government wd. produce any of the consequences
which your fears forebode. In all free governments, contention in elections will take place; and, whilst it is confined to our
own citizens it is not to be regretted; but severely indeed ought
it to be reprobated when occasioned by foreign machinations.
I trust however, that the good sense of our Countrymen will
guard the public weal against this, and every other innovation;
and that, altho' we may be a little wrong, now and then, we
shall return to the right path, with more avidity. I can never
believe that Providence, which has guided us so long, and

through such a labirinth, will withdraw its protection at this Crisis.

Although I shall resign the chair of government without a single regret, or any desire to intermeddle in politics again, yet there are many of my compatriots (among whom be assured I place you) from whom I shall part sorrowing; because, unless I meet with them at Mount Vernon it is not likely that I shall ever see them more, as I do not expect that I shall ever be twenty miles from it after I am tranquilly settled there. To tell you how glad I should be to see you at that place is unnecessary; but this I will add, that it would not only give me pleasure, but pleasure also to Mrs. Washington, and others of the family with whom you are acquainted; and who all unite in every good wish for you, and yours, with Dear Sir, Your sincere friend and Affectionate Servant.

232

TO MARQUIS DE LAFAYETTE

Mount Vernon, December 25, 1798

My dear Sir:

I am indebted to you for the following letters, dated the 6th of Octr. and 20th of Decr. of the last year. And 26th. of April, 20th. of May, 20th. of August and 5th. of Septr. in the present. If more have been written they have fallen into other hands, or miscarried on their passage.

Convinced as you must be of the fact, it wd. be a mere waste of time to assure you of the sincere and heartfelt pleasure I derived from finding by the above letters, that you had not only regained your liberty; but were in the enjoyment of better health than could have been expected from your long and rigorous confinement; and that madame La Fayette and the young ladies were able to Survive it attall. On these desirable events I can add with truth, that amongst your numerous friends none can offer his congratulations with more warmth, or who prays more sincerely for the perfect restoration of your ladies health, than I do.

It is equally unnecessary for me to apologize to you for my long silence; when by a recurrence to your own Letters you will find my excuse; for by these it will appear that if you had embarked for this country at the epochs mentioned therein no letters of mine cou'd have arrived in Europe before your departure from thence; untill by your favor of the 20th. of Augt. I was informed, that your voyage to America was postponed for the reasons then given, and which conveyed the first Idea to my mind that a letter from me might find you in Europe.

The letter last mentioned together with that of the 5th. of September, found me in Phila. whither I had gone for the purpose of making some military arrangements with the Secretary of War, and where every moment of my time was so much occupied in that business, as to allow no leisure to attend to any thing else.

Declaration of friendship

I have been thus circumstantial in order to impress you with the true cause of my silence and to remove from your mind if a doubt had arisen there that my friendship for you, had undergone no diminution or change. And that no one in the United States would receive you with open arms, or with more ardent affection than I should, after the differences between this Country and France are adjusted and harmony between the nations is again restored. But it would be uncandid and incompatible with that friendship I have always professed for you, to say (and on your own account) that I wish it before. For you may be assured my dear Sir that the Scenes you wou'd meet with, and the part you wou'd be stimulated to act, in case of an open rupture or even if matters should remain in Statu quo, would be such as to place you in a Situation in which no address or human prudence, could free you from embarrassment. In a word you would lose the Confidence of one party or the other (perhaps) both were you here under these circumstances.

Politics of opposition

To give you a Complete View of the politics and Situation of things in this Country would far exceed the limits of a letter; and to trace effects to their Causes would be a work of time. But the sum of them may be given in a few words, and amounts to this. That a party exists in the United States, formed by a Combination of Causes, which oppose the Government in all its measures, and are determined (as all their Conduct evinces) by Clogging its Wheels indirectly to change the nature of it, and to subvert the Constitution. To effect this no means which have a tendency to accomplish their purposes are left unessayed. The friends of Government who are anxious to maintain its neutrality, and to preserve the Country in peace, and adopt measures to produce these, are charged by them as being Monarchists, Aristocrats, and infractors of the Constitution; which according to their interpretation of it would be a mere Cypher; while they arrogated to themselves, (until the eyes of the people began to discover how outrageously they had been treated in their Commercial concerns by the Directory of France, and that, that was a ground on which they could no longer tread). The sole merit of being the friends of France, when in fact they had no more regard for that Nation than for the Grand Turk, further than their own views were promoted by it; denouncing those who differed in Opinion; whose principles are purely American; and whose sole view was to observe a strict neutrality, with acting under British influence, and being directed by her counsels, now with being her Pensioners.

This is but a short sketch, of what requires much time to illustrate; and is given with no other view, than to shew you what would be your situation here at this crisis under such circumstances as it unfold.

You have expressed a wish, worthy [of] that benevolence of your heart, that I would exert all my endeavors to avert the Calamitous effects of a rupture between our Countries. Believe me my dear friend that no man can deprecate an event of this sort with more horror than I should and that no one, during the whole of my Administration laboured more incessantly and with more sincerity and zeal than I did to avoid this, and to render every justice, nay favor to France, consistently with the neutrality which had been proclaimed to these sanctioned by Congress and approved by the State legislatures, and the people at large in their Town and County meetings. But neutrality was not the point at which France was aiming, for whilst it was crying peace, Peace, and pretending that they did not wish us to be embroiled in their quarrel with great Britain they were pursuing measures in *this Country* so repugnant to its Sovereignty, and so incompatible with every principle of neutrality, as *must* inevitably, have produced a war with the latter. And when they found that the Government *here* was resolved to adhere steadily to its plan of neutrality, their next step was to destroy the confidence of the people in, and to seperate them from it; for which purpose their diplomatic agents were specially instructed; and in the attempt were aided by inimical characters among ourselves not as I observed

French reaction to American neutrality

before because they loved France more than any other nation, but because it was an instrument to Facilitate the destruction of their own Government.

Hence proceeded those charges which I have already enumerated, against the friends to peace and order. No doubt remains on this side of the water, that to the representations of and encouragement given by these people, is to be ascribed in a great measure, the intentions of our Treaty with France; their violation of the Laws of nations, disregard of Justice and even of sound policy. But herein they have not only deceived France, but were deceived themselves, as the event has proved, for no sooner did the yeomanry of this Country come to a right understanding of the nature of the dispute, than they rose as one man with a tender of their Services; their lives and their fortunes, to support the Government of their choice, and to defend their country. This has produced a declaration from them (how sincere let others judge), that, if the French should attempt to invade this Country that they themselves would be amongst the foremost to repel the attack.

Response of the United States government

You add in another place that the Executive Directory are disposed to accommodation of all differences. If they are Sincere in this declaration, let them evidence it by actions, for words unaccompanied therewith will not be much regarded now. I would pledge myself, that the Government and people of the United States will meet them heart and hand at *fair* negotiation; having no wish more ardent, than to live in peace with all the world, provided they are suffered to remain undisturbed in their just rights. Of this their patience, forbearance, and repeated solicitations under accumulated injuries and insults are incontestable proofs; but it is not to be infered from hence that they will suffer any nation under the sun (while they retain a proper sense of Virtue and Independence) to trample upon their rights with impunity, or to direct, or influence the internal concerns of their Country.

It has been the policy of France and that of the opposition party among ourselves, to inculcate a belief that all those who have exerted themselves to keep this Country in peace, did it from an overweening attachment to Great Britain. But it is a solemn truth and you may count upon it, that it is void of foundation; and propagated for no other purpose, than to excite popular clamour against those whose aim was peace, and whom they wished out of their way.

That there are many among us, who wish to see this Country embroiled on the side of Great Britain, and others who are anxious that we should take part with France against her, admits of no doubt. But it is a fact on which you may entirely and absolutely rely, that the Governing powers of the Country, and a large part of the people are truly Americans in principle, attached to the interest of it; And unwilling under any circumstances whatsoever to participate in the Politics or Contests of Europe: Much less since they have found that France, having forsaken the ground she first took, is interfering in the internal concerns of all nations, Neutral as well as Belligerent, and setting the world in an uproar. *Unwillingness to participate in European politics*

After my valedictory address to the people of the United States you would no doubt be somewhat surprised to hear, that I had again consented to Gird on the Sword. But, having Struggled Eight or nine Years against the invasion of our rights by one power, and to establish an Independence of it, I could not remain an unconcerned spectator of the attempt of another Power to accomplish the same object, though in a different way, with less pretensions indeed without any at all. *Consent to return to national service*

On the Politics of Europe I shall express no Opinion, nor make any inquiry who is Right or who is Wrong. I wish well to all nations and to all men. My politics are plain and simple. I think every nation has a Right to establish that form of Government under which It conceives It shall live most happy; provided it infracts no Right or is not dangerous to others. And that no Governments ought to interfere with the internal concerns of Another, except for the security of what is due to themselves.

I sincerely hope that Madame la Fayette will accomplish all her wishes in France and return safe to you with renovated health. I congratulate you on the marriage of your eldest daughter, and beg to be presented to them both and to Virginia in the most Respectful and affectionate terms; to George I have written. In all these things Mrs. Washington (as the rest of the family would do if they were at home) most cordially joins me: as she does in wishing you and them every felicity which this life can afford, as some consolation for your long cruel, and painful Confinement and Sufferings.

I shall now only add what you knew well before that with the most Sincere friendship and affectionate regard, I am always &c.

PS: Your old aid de camp, and my worthy nephew George A. Washington; died about 5 years ago of a palmanory Complaint, he left 3 fine Children a daughter and two Sons, the eldest of the boys was called after you.

The letters herewith enclosed and directed one to yourself, another to George, and the third to Mr. Frestel, have been some time in my possession and detained to be delivered to you *here* upon the same principle that prevented me from writing to you at an earlier period.

233

TO PATRICK HENRY

Confidential

Mount Vernon, January 15, 1799

Dear Sir:

At the threshold of this letter, I ought to make an apology for its contents; but if you will give me credit for my motives, I will contend for no more, however erroneous my sentiments may appear to you.

It would be a waste of time, to attempt to bring to the view of a person of your observation and discernment, the endeavors of a certain party among us, to disquiet the Public mind among us with unfounded alarms; to arraign every act of the Administration; to set the People at variance with their Government; and to embarrass all its measures. Equally useless would it be to predict what must be the inevitable consequences, of such policy, if it cannot be arrested.

Virginia and Kentucky resolutions

Unfortunately, and extremely do I regret it, the State of Virginia has taken the lead in this opposition. I have said the *State*, Because the conduct of its Legislature in the Eyes of the world, will authorise the expression; because it is an incontrovertable fact, that the principle leaders of the opposition dwell in it; and because no doubt is entertained, I believe, that with the help of the Chiefs in other States, all the plans are arranged; and systematically pursued by their followers in other parts of the Union; though in no State except Kentucky (that I have heard of) has Legislative countenance been obtained, beyond Virginia.

It has been said, that the great mass of the Citizens of this State are well affected, notwithstanding, to the General Government, and the Union; and I am willing to believe it, nay do believe it: but how is this to be reconciled with their suffrages at the Elections of Representatives; both to Congress and their State Legislature; who are men opposed to the first, and by the tendency of their measures would destroy the latter? Some among us have endeavoured to account for this inconsistency, and though convinced themselves, of its truth, they are unable to convince others; who are unacquainted with the internal policy of the State.

One of the reasons assigned is, that the most respectable, and best qualified characters amongst us, will not come forward. Easy and happy in their circumstances at home, and believing themselves secure in their liberties and property, will not forsake them, or their occupations, and engage in the turmoil of public business, or expose themselves to the calumnies of their opponents, whose weapons are detraction.

Need for leadership at times of crisis

But at such a crisis as this, when every thing dear and valuable to us is assailed; when this Party hangs upon the Wheels of Government as a dead weight, opposing every measure that is calculated for defence and self preservation; abetting the nefarious views of another Nation, upon our Rights; prefering, as long as they durst contend openly against the spirit and resentment of the People, the interest of France to the Welfare of their own Country; justifying the first at the expence of the latter: When every Act of their own Government is tortured by constructions they will not bear, into attempts to infringe and trample upon the Constitution with a view to introduce monarchy; When the most unceasing, and the purest exertion; were making, to maintain a Neutrality which had been proclaimed by the Executive, approved unequivocally by Congress, by the State Legislatures, nay, by the People themselves, in various meetings; and to preserve the Country in Peace, are charged as a measure calculated to favor Great Britain at the expence of France, and all those who had any agency in it, are accused of being under the influence of the former; and her Pensioners; When measures are systematically, and pertinaciously pursued, which must eventually dissolve the Union or produce coercion. I say, when these things are become so obvious, ought characters who are best able to rescue their Country from the pending evil to remain at home? rather, ought they not to come forward, and by their talents and influence, stand in the breach wch. such conduct has made on the Peace and happiness of this Country, and oppose the widening of it?

*Threats to peace
and happiness
from civil discord*

Vain will it be to look for Peace and happiness, or for the security of liberty or property, if Civil discord should ensue; and what else can result from the policy of those among us, who, by all the means in their power, are driving matters to extremity, if they cannot be counteracted effectually? The views of Men can only be known, or guessed at, by their words or actions. Can those of the *Leaders* of Opposition be mistaken then, if judged by this Rule? That they are *followed* by numbers who are unacquainted with their designs, and suspect as little, the tendency of their principles, I am fully persuaded. But, if their conduct is viewed with indifference; if there is activity and misrepresentation on one side, and supineness on the other, their numbers, accumulated by Intriguing, and discontented foreigners under proscription, who were at war with their own governments; and the greater part of them with *all* Government, their numbers will encrease, and nothing, short of Omniscience, can foretel the consequences.

*Urges Henry to
run for office*

I come now, my good Sir, to the object of my letter, which is, to express a hope, and an earnest wish, that you wd. come forward at the ensuing Elections (if not for Congress, which you may think would take you too long from home) as a candidate for representation, in the General Assembly of this Commonwealth.

There are, I have no doubt, very many sensible men who oppose themselves to the torrent that carries away others, who had rather swim with, than stem it, without an able Pilot to conduct them; but these are neither old in Legislation, nor well known in the Community. Your weight of character and influence in the Ho. of Representatives would be a bulwark against such dangerous sentiments as are delivered there at present. It would be a rallying point for the timid, and an attraction of the wavering. In a word, I conceive it of immense importance at this Crisis, that you should be there; and I would fain hope that all minor considerations will be made to yield to the measure.

If I have erroneously supposed that your sentiments on these subjects are in unison with mine; or if I have assumed a liberty which the occasion does not warrant, I must conclude as I began, with praying that my motives may be received as an apology; and that my fear, that the tranquillity of the Union, and of this State in particular, is hastening to an awful crisis, has extorted them from me.

With great, and very sincere regard, and respect, I am &c.

Epilogue

WASHINGTON *lived only three years beyond his resignation from the presidency. He returned once again to a Mount Vernon fallen to a point beyond which his labors could hope to restore it. Nevertheless, he plunged back into his favorite pursuits of agricultural development and experimentation and the design and organization of Mount Vernon. He was again to find himself under a constant press of correspondence and visitation. He was even summoned back as commander of American military forces when war with France seemed imminent. That crisis passed, however, and with it Washington's countrymen's claims upon him. His claims upon his countrymen would reach beyond his death, as made evident in the two items reproduced here.*

Throughout his life, Washington had created the most pervasive of the myths about his own person and character, above all the idea that he somehow lacked full intellectual power. This habitual self-effacement rivaled his famous self-possession. Washington had never accepted a public charge without forswearing any opinion that he was worthy of it. Concluding his affairs in 1799, he insisted for the last time that his merit in no way exceeded that of any of his countrymen, and he requested that he be laid away "in a private manner, without parade, or funeral oration."

234

TO GOVERNOR JONATHAN TRUMBULL

Mount Vernon, August 30, 1799

My Dear Sir:

Your favor of the 10th instant came duly to hand. It gave me pleasure to find by the contents of it, that your sentiments respecting the comprehensive project of Colo. Trumbull, co-incided with those I had expressed to him.

A very different state of Politics must obtain in this Country, and more unanimity prevail in our Public councils than is the case at present, 'ere such a measure could be undertaken with the least prospect of success. By unanimity *alone* the plan could be accomplished: while then a party, and a strong one too, is hanging upon the Wheels of Government, opposing measures calculated solely for Internal defence, and is endeavouring to defeat all the Laws which have been passed for this purpose, by rendering them obnoxious, to attempt anything beyond this, would be to encounter *certain* disappointment. And yet, if the Policy of this Country, or the necessity occasioned by the existing opposition to its measures, should suffer the French to Possess themselves of Louisiana and the Floridas, either by exchange or otherwise, I will venture to predict, without the gift of *"second sight"* that there will be "no peace in Israel." Or, in other words, that the restless, ambitious, and Intriguing spirit of that People, will keep the United States in a continual state of Warfare with the numerous tribes of Indians that inhabit our Frontiers. For doing which their "Diplomatic skill" is well adapted.

Lack of unity in public councils

Epilogue

Declines to run again for the Presidency

With respect to the other subject of your letter, I must again express a strong, and ardent wish and desire that, no eye, no tongue, no thought, may be turned towards me for the purpose alluded to therein. For, besides the reasons which I urged against the measures in my last, and which, in my judgment, and by my feelings, are insurmountable, you, yourself, have furnished a cogent one.

You have conceded, what before was self-evident in my mind, namely, that not a single vote would, thereby, be drawn from the anti-federal Candidate. You add, however, that it might be a means of uniting the federal Votes. Here then, my dear Sir, let me ask, what satisfaction, what consolation, what safety, should I find in support, which depends upon caprice?

If *Men*, not *Principles*, can influence the choice on the part of the Federalists, what but fluctuations are to be expected? The favorite today, may have the Curtain dropped on him tomorrow, while steadiness marks the conduct of the Anti's; and whoever is not on *their* side must expect to be loaded with all the calumny that malice can invent; in addition to which, I should be charged with inconsistency, concealed ambition, dotage, and a thousand more et ceteras.

The Federalist cause

It is too interesting not to be again repeated, that if principles, instead of men, are not the steady pursuit of the Federalists, their cause will soon be at an end. If *these* are pursued, they *will not divide* at the next Election of a President; If they do divide on so *important* a point, it would be dangerous to trust them on any other; and none except those who might be solicitous to fill the Chair of Government would do it. In a word, my dear Sir, I am too far advanced into the vale of life to bear such buffiting as I should meet with, in such an event. A mind that has been constantly on the stretch since the year 1753, with but short intervals, and little relaxation, requires rest, and composure; and I believe that nothing short of a serious Invasion of our Country (in which case I conceive it to be the duty of every citizen to step forward in its defence) will ever draw me from my present retirement. But let me be in that, or in any other situation, I shall always remain your sincere friend and Affectionate &c.

235

LAST WILL AND TESTAMENT

July 9, 1799

In the name of God amen

I George Washington of Mount Vernon, a citizen of the United States, and lately President of the same, do make, orda[in] and declare this Instrument; w[hic]h is written with my own hand [an]d every page thereof subscribed [wit]h my name, to be my last Will and [Tes]tament, revoking all others.

Imprimus. All my [deb]ts, of which there are but few, and none of magnitude, are to be punctu[al]ly and speedily paid; and the Legaci[es her]einafter bequeathed, are to be disc[ha]rged as soon as circumstances will [pe]rmit, and in the manner directe[d].

Item. To my dearly [be]loved wife Martha Washington [I] give and bequeath the use, profit [an]d benefit of my whole Estate, real and p[e]rsonal, for the term of her natural li[fe;] except such parts thereof as are s[pec]ifically disposed of hereafter: [My improved] lot in the Town of Alex[andria, situated on] Pitt and Cameron [Streets, I give to her and] her heirs fore[ver, as I also do my household] and Kitc[hen] furniture of every sort and kind, w[it]h the liquors and groceries which may be on hand at the time of my decease; to be used and disposed of as she may think proper.

Item Upon the decease [of] my wife, it is my Will and desire th[at] all the Slaves which I hold in [*my*] *own right*, shall receive their free[dom.] To emancipate them during [her] life, would, tho' earnestly wish[ed by] me, be attended with such insu[perab]le difficulties on account of thei[r interm]ixture by Marriages with the [Dow]er Negroes, as to excite the most pa[i]nful sensations, if not disagreeabl[e c]onsequences from the latter, while [both] descriptions are in the occupancy [of] the same Proprietor; it not being [in] my power, under the tenure by which[h t]he Dower Negroes are held, to man[umi]t them. And whereas among [thos]e who will receive freedom ac[cor]ding to this devise, there may b[e so]me, who from old age or bodily infi[rm]ities, and others who on account of [thei]r infancy, that will be unable to [su]pport themselves; it is [my] Will a[nd de]sire that all who [come under the first] and second descrip[tion shall be comfor]tably cloathed and [fed by my heirs while] they live; and that such of the latter descrip-

667

tion as have no parents living, or if living are unable, or unwilling to provide for them, shall be bound by the Court until they shall arrive at the age of twenty five years; and in cases where no record can be produced, whereby their ages can be ascertained, the judgment of the Court upon its own view of the subject, shall be adequate and final. The Negros thus bound, are (by their Masters or Mistresses) to be taught to read and write; and to be brought up to some useful occupation, agreeably to the Laws of the Commonwealth of Virginia, providing for the support of Orphan and other poor Children. And I do hereby expressly forbid the Sale, or transportation out of said Commonwealth, of any Slave I may die possessed of, under any pretence whatsoever. And I do moreover most pointedly, and most solemnly enjoin it upon my Executors hereafter named, or the Survivors of them, to see that *this* [cl]ause respecting Slaves, and every part thereof be religiously fulfilled at the Epoch at which it is directed to take place; without evasion, neglect or delay, after the Crops which may then be on the ground are harvested, particularly as it respects the aged and infirm; Seeing that a regular and permanent fund be established for their Support so long as there are subjects requiring it; not trusting to the uncertain provision to be made by individuals. And to my Mulatto man William (calling himself William Lee) I give immediate freedom; or if he should prefer it (on account of the accidents which have befallen him, and which have rendered him incapable of walking or of any active employment) to remain in the situation he now is, it shall be optional in him to do so: In either case however, I allow him an annuity of thirty dollars during his natural life, which shall be independent of the victuals and cloaths he has been accustomed to receive, if he chuses the last alternative; but in full, with his freedom, if he prefers the first; and this I give him as a testimony of my sense of his attachment to me, and for his faithful services during the Revolutionary War.

Item To the Trustees (Governors, or by whatsoever other name they may be designated) of the Academy in the Town of Alexandria, I give and bequeath, in Trust, four thousand dollars, or in other words twenty of the shares which I hold in the Bank of Alexandria, towards the support of a Free school established at, and annexed to, the said Academy; for the purpose of Educating such Orphan children, or the children of such other poor and indigent persons as are unable to accomplish it with their own means; and who, in the judgment of the Trustees of the said Seminary, are best entitled to the benefit of this donation. The aforesaid twenty shares I give and bequeath in perpetuity; the dividends only of which are to be drawn for, and applied by the said Trustees for the time being, for the uses above mentioned; the stock to remain entire and untouched; unless indications of a failure of the said Bank should be so apparent, or a discontinuance thereof should render a removal of this fund necessary; in either of these cases, the amount of the Stock here devised, is to be vested in some other Bank or public Institution, whereby the interest may with regularity and certainly be drawn, and applied as above. And to prevent misconception, my meaning is, and is hereby declared to be, that these twenty shares are in lieu of, and not in addition to, the thousand pounds given by a missive letter some years ago; in consequence whereof an annuity of fifty pounds has since been paid towards the support of this Institution.

Item Whereas by a Law of the Commonwealth of Virginia, enacted in the year 1785, the Legislature thereof was pleased (as a an evidence of Its approbation of the services I had rendered the Public during the Revolution; and partly, I believe, in consideration of my having suggested the vast advantages which the Community would derive from the extension of its Inland Navigation, under Legislative patronage) to present me with one hundred shares of one hundred dollars each, in the incorporated company established for the purpose of extending the navigation of James River from tide water to the Mountains: and also with fifty shares of one hundred pounds sterling each, in the Corporation of another company, likewise established for the similar purpose of opening the Navigation of the River Potomac from tide water to Fort Cumberland; the acceptance of which, although the offer was highly honorable, and grateful to my feelings, was refused, as inconsistent with a principle which I had adopted, and had never departed from, namely, not to receive pecuniary compensation for any services I could render my country in its arduous struggle with great Britain, for its Rights; and because I had evaded similar propositions from other States in the Union; adding to this refusal, however, an intimation that, if it should be the pleasure of the Legislature to permit me to appropriate the said shares to *public uses*, I would receive them on those terms with due sensibility; and this it having consented to, in flattering terms, as will appear by a subsequent Law, and sundry resolutions, in the most ample and honourable manner, I proceed after this recital, for the more correct understanding of the case, to declare:

That as it has always been a source of serious regret with me, to see the youth of these United States sent to foreign Countries for the purpose of Education, often before their minds were formed, or they had imbibed any adequate ideas of the happiness of their own; contracting, too frequently, not only habits of dissipation and extravagence, but principles unfriendly to Republican Governmt. and to the true and genuine liberties of mankind; which, thereafter are rarely overcome. For these reasons, it has been my ardent wish to see a plan devised on a liberal scale which would have a tendency to sprd. systematic ideas through all parts of this rising Empire, thereby to do away local attachments and State prejudices, as far as the nature of things would, or indeed ought to admit, from our National Councils. Looking anxiously forward to the accomplishment of so desirable an object as this is (in my estimation) my mind has not been able to contemplate any plan more likely to effect the measure than the establishment of a university in a central part of the United States, to which the youth of fortune and talents from all parts thereof might be sent for the completion of their Education in all the branches of polite literature; in arts and Sciences, in acquiring knowledge in the principles of Politics and good Government; and (as a matter of infinite Importance in my judgment) by associating with each other, and forming friendships in Juvenile years, be enabled to free themselves in a proper degree from those local prejudices and habitual jealousies which have just been mentioned; and which, when carried to excess, are never failing sources of disquietude to the Public mind, and pregnant of mischievous consequences to this Country: Under these impressions, so fully dilated,

Item I give and bequeath in perpetuity the fifty shares which I hold in the Potomac Company (under the aforesaid Acts of the Legislature of Virginia) towards the endowment of a university to be established within the limits of the District of Columbia, under the auspices of the General Government, if that government should incline to extend a fostering hand towards it; and until such Seminary is established, and the funds arising on these shares shall be required for its support, my further Will and desire is that the profit accruing therefrom shall, whenever the dividends are made, be laid out in purchasing Stock in the Bank of Columbia, or some other Bank, at the discretion of my Executors; or by the Treasurer of the United States for the time being under the direction of Congress; provided that Honourable body should Patronize the measure, and the Dividends proceeding from the purchase of such Stock is to be vested in more stock, and so on, until a sum adequate to the accomplishment of the object is obtained, of which I have not the smallest doubt, before many years passes away; even if no aid or encouraged is given by Legislative authority, or from any other source.

Item The hundred shares which I held in the James River Company, I have given, and now confirm in perpetuity to, and for the use and benefit of Liberty-Hall Academy, in the County of Rockbridge, in the Commonwealth of Virga.

Item I release exonerate and discharge, the estate of my deceased brother Samuel Washington, from the payment of the money which is due to me for the land I sold to Philip Pendleton (lying in the County of Berkeley) who assigned the same to him the said Samuel; who, by agreement was to pay me therefor. And whereas by some contract (the purport of which was never communicated to me) between the said Samuel and his son Thornton Washington, the latter became possessed of the aforesaid Land, without any conveyance having passed from me, either to the said Pendleton, the said Samuel, or the said Thornton, and without any consideration having been made, by which neglect neither the legal nor equitable title has been alienated; it rests therefore with me to declare my intentions concerning the Premises; and these are, to give and bequeath the said land to whomsoever the said Thornton Washington (who is also dead) devised the same; or to his heirs forever if he died Intestate: Exonerating the estate of the said Thornton, equally with that of the said Samuel from payment of the purchase money; which, with Interest; agreeably to the original contract with the said Pendleton, would amount to more than a thousand pounds. And whereas two other Sons of my said deceased brother Samuel, namely, George Steptoe Washington and Lawrence Augustine Washington, were, by the decease of those to whose care they were committed, brought under my protection, and in conseqe. have occasioned advances on my part for their Education at College, and other Schools, for their board, clothing, and other incidental expences, to the amount of near five thousand dollars over and above the Sums furnished by their Estate whc. Sum may be inconvenient for them, or their fathers Estate to refund. I do for these reasons acquit them, and the said estate, from the payment thereof. My intention being, that all accounts between them and me, and their fathers estate and me shall stand balanced.

Item The balance due to me from the Estate of Bartholomew Dandridge deceased (my wife's brother) and which amounted on the first day of October 1795 to four hundred and twenty five pounds (as will appear by an account rendered by his deceased son John Dandridge, who was the acting Exr. of his fathers Will) I release and acquit from the payment thereof. And the Negros, (then thirty three in number) formerly belonging to the said estate, who were taken in execution, sold, and purchased in on my account in the year _____ and ever since have remained in the possession, and to the use of Mary, Widow of the said Bartholomew Dandridge, with their increase, it is my Will and desire shall continue, and be in her possession, without paying hire, or making compensation for the same for the time past or to come, during her natural life; at the expiration of which, I direct that all of them who are forty years old and upwards, shall receive their freedom; all under that age and above sixteen, shall serve seven years and no longer; and all under sixteen years, shall serve until they are twenty five years of age, and then be free. And to avoid disputes respecting the ages of any of these Negros, they are to be taken to the Court of the County in which they reside, and the judgment thereof, in this relation, shall be final; and a record thereof made; which may be adduced as evidence at any time thereafter, if disputes should arise concerning the same. And I further direct, that the heirs of the said Bartholomew Dandridge shall, equally, share the benefits arising from the Services of the said negros according to the tenor of this devise, upon the decease of their Mother.

Item If Charles Carter who intermarried with my niece Betty Lewis is not sufficiently secured in the title to the lots he had of me in the Town of Fredericksburgh, it is my Will and desire that my Executors shall make such conveyances of them as the Law requires, to render it perfect.

Item To my Nephew William Augustine Washington and his heirs (if he should conceive them to be objects worth prosecuting) and to his heirs, a lot in the Town of Manchester (opposite to Richmond) No 265 drawn on my sole account, and also the tenth of one or two, hundred acre lots, and two or three half acre lots in the City, and vicinity of Richmond, drawn in partnership with nine others, all in the lottery of the deceased William Byrd are given; as is also a lot which I purchased of John Hood, conveyed by William Willie and Samuel Gordon Trustees of the said John Hood, numbered 139 in the Town of Edinburgh, in the County of Prince George, State of Virginia.

Item To my Nephew Bushrod Washington, I give and bequeath all the Papers in my possession, which relate to my Civel and Military Administration of the affairs of this Country; I leave to him also, such of my private Papers as are worth preserving; and at the decease of [my] wife, and before, if she is not inclined to retain them, I give and bequeath my library of Books, and Pamphlets of every kind.

Item Having sold Lands which I possessed in the State of Pennsylvania, and part of a tract held in equal right with George Clinton, late Governor of New York, in the State of New York; my share of land, and interest, in the Great Dismal Swamp, and a tract of land which I owned in the County of Gloucester; withholding the legal titles thereto, until the consideration money should be paid. And having moreover leased, and conditionally sold (as will appear by the tenor of the said leases) all my lands upon the Great Kanhawa, and a tract upon Difficult Run, in the county of Loudoun, it is my Will and direction, that whensoever the Contracts are fully, and respectively complied with, according to the spirit, true intent and meaning thereof, on the part of the purchasers, their heirs or Assigns, that then, and in that case, Conveyances are to be made, agreeably to the terms of the said Contracts; and the money arising therefrom, when paid, to be vested in Bank stock; the dividends whereof, as of that also wch. is already vested therein, is to inure to my said Wife during her life; but the Stock itself is to remain, and be subject to the general distribution hereafter directed.

Item To the Earl of Buchan I recommit "the Box made of the Oak that sheltered the Great Sir William Wallace after the battle of Falkirk" presented to me by his Lordship, in terms too flattering for me to repeat, with a request "to pass it, on the event of my decease, to the man in my country, who should appear to merit it best, upon the same conditions that have induced him to send it to me." Whether easy, or not, to select *the man* who might comport with his Lordships opinion in this respect, is not for me to say; but conceiving that no disposition of this valuable curiosity can be more eligable than the recommitment of it to his own Cabinet, agreeably to the original design of the Goldsmith Company of Edenburgh, who presented it to him, and at his request, consented that it should be transfered to me; I do give and bequeath the same to his Lordship, and in case of his decease, to his heir with my grateful thanks for the distinguished honour of presenting it to me; and more especially for the favourable sentiments with which he accompanied it.

Item To my brother Charles Washington I give and bequeath the gold headed Cane left me by Doctr. Franklin in his Will. I add nothing to it, because of the ample provision I have made for his Issue. To the acquaintances and friends of my Juvenile years, Lawrence Washington and Robert Washington of Chotanck, I give my other two gold headed Canes, having my Arms engraved on them; and to each (as they will be useful where they live) I leave one of the Spy-glasses which constituted part of my equipage during the late War. To my compatriot in arms, and old and intimate friend Doctr. Craik, I give my Bureau (or as the Cabinet makers call it, Tambour Secretary) and the circular chair, an appendage of my Study. To Doctor David Stuart I give my large shaving and dressing Table, and my Telescope. To the Reverend, now Bryan, Lord Fairfax, I give a Bible in three large folio volumes, with notes, presented to me by the Right reverend Thomas Wilson, Bishop of Sodor and Man. To General de la Fayette I give a pair of finely wrought steel Pistols, taken from the enemy in the Revolutionary War. To my Sisters in law Hannah Washington and Mildred Washington; to my friends Eleanor Stuart, Hannah Washington of Fairfield, and Elizabeth Washington of Hayfield, I give, each, a mourning Ring of the value of one hundred dollars. These bequests are not made for the intrinsic value of them, but as mementos of my esteem and regard. To Tobias Lear, I give the use of the Farm which he now holds, in virtue of a Lease from me to him and his deceased wife (for and during their natural lives) free from Rent, during his life;

at the expiration of which, it is to be disposed as is hereinafter directed. To Sally B. Haynie (a distant relation of mine) I give and bequeath three hundred dollars. To Sarah Green daughter of the deceased Thomas Bishop, and to Ann Walker daughter of Jno. Alton, also deceased, I give, each one hundred dollars, in consideration of the attachment of their fathers to me, each of whom having lived nearly forty years in my family. To each of my Nephews, William Augustine Washington, George Lewis, George Steptoe Washington, Bushrod Washington and Samuel Washington, I give one of the Swords or Cutteaux of which I may die possessed; and they are to chuse in the order they are named. These Swords are accompanied with an injunction not to unsheath them for the purpose of shedding blood, except it be for self defence, or in defence of their Country and its rights; and in the latter case, to keep them unsheathed, and prefer falling with them in their hands, to the relinquishment thereof.

And now Having gone through these specific devises, with explanations for the more correct understanding of the meaning and design of them; I proceed to the distribution of the more important parts of my Estate, in manner following:

First To my Nephew Bushrod Washington and his heirs (partly in consideration of an intimation to his deceased father while we were Bachelors, and he had kindly undertaken to superintend my Estate during my Military Services in the former War between Great Britain and France, that if I should fall therein, Mount Vernon (then less extensive in domain than at present) should become his property) I give and bequeath all that part thereof which is comprehended within the following limits, viz: Beginning at the ford of Dogue run, near my Mill, and extending along the road, and bounded thereby as it now goes, and ever has gone since my recollection of it, to the ford of little hunting Creek at the Gum spring until it comes to a knowl, opposite to an old road which formerly passed through the lower field of Muddy hole Farm: at which, on the north side of the said road are three red, or Spanish Oaks marked as a corner, and a stone placed. Thence by a line of trees to be marked, rectangular to the back line, or outer boundary of the tract between Thomson Mason and myself. Thence with that line Easterly (now double ditching with a Post and Rail fence thereon) to the run of little hunting Creek. Thence with that run which is the boundary between the

675

Lands of the late Humphrey Peake and me, to the tide water of the said Creek; thence by that water to Potomac River. Thence with the River to the mouth of Dogue Creek. And thence with the said Dogue Creek to the place of beginning at the aforesaid ford; containing upwards of four thousand Acres, be the same more or less; together with the Mansion house and all other buildings and improvemts. thereon.

Second In consideration of the consanguinity between them and my wife, being as nearly related to her as to myself, as on account of the affection I had for, and the obligation I was under to, their father when living, who from his youth had attached himself to my person, and followed my fortunes through the viscissitudes of the late Revolution; afterwards devoting his time to the Superintendence of my private concerns for many years, whilst my public employments rendered it impracticable for me to do it myself, thereby affording me essential Services, and always performing them in a manner the most felial and respectful: for these reasons I say, I give and bequeath to George Fayette Washington, and Lawrence Augustine Washington and their heirs, my Estate East of little hunting Creek, lying on the River Potomac; including the Farm of 360 Acres, Leased to Tobias Lear as noticed before, and containing in the whole, by Deeds, Two thousand and Seventy seven acres, be it more or less. Which said Estate it is my Will and desire should be equitably, and advantageously divided between them, according to quantity, quality and other circumstances when the youngest shall have arrived at the age of twenty one years, by three judicious and disinterested men; one to be chosen by each of the brothers, and the third by these two. In the meantime, if the termination of my wife's interest therein should have ceased, the profits arising therefrom are to be applied for thir joint uses and benefit.

Third And whereas it has always been my intention, since my expectation of having Issue has ceased, to consider the Grand children of my wife in the same light as I do my own relations, and to act a friendly part by them; more especially by the two whom we have reared from their earliest infancy, namely: Eleanor Parke Custis, and George Washington Parke Custis. And whereas the former of these hath lately intermarried with Lawrence Lewis, a son of my deceased Sister Betty Lewis, by which union the inducement to provide for them both has been increased; Wherefore, I give and bequeath to the said Lawrence Lewis and Eleanor Parke Lewis, his wife, and their heirs, the residue of my Mount Vernon Estate, not already devised to my Nephew Bushrod Washington, comprehended within the following description. viz: All the land North of the Road leading from the ford of Dogue run to the Gum spring as described in the devise of the other part of the tract, to Bushrod Washington, until it comes to the Stone and three red or Spanish Oaks on the knowl. Thence with the rectangular line to the back line (between Mr. Mason and me) thence with that line westerly, along the new double ditch to Dogue run, by the tumbling Dam of my Mill; thence with the said run to the ford aforementioned; to which I add all the Land I possess West of the said Dogue run, and Dogue Crk. bounded Easterly and Southerly thereby; together with the Mill, Distillery, and all other houses and improvements on the premises, making together about two thousand Acres, be it more or less.

Fourth Actuated by the principal already mentioned, I give and bequeath to George Washington Parke Custis, the Grandson of my wife, and my Ward, and to his heirs, the tract I hold on four mile run in the vicinity of Alexandria, containing one thousd. two hundred acres, more or less, and my entire Square, number twenty one, in the City of Washington.

Fifth All the rest and residue of my Estate, real and personal, not disposed of in manner aforesaid. In whatsoever consisting, wheresoever lying, and whensoever found, a schedule of which, as far as is recollected, with a reasonable estimate of its value, is hereunto annexed: I desire may be sold by my Executors at such times, in such manner, and in such credits (if an equal, valid, and satisfactory distribution of the specific property cannot be made without), as, in their judgment shall be most condusive to the interest of the parties concerned; and the monies arising therefrom to be divided into twenty three equal parts, and applied as follows, viz:

To William Augustine Washington, Elizabeth Spotswood, Jane Thornton, and the heirs of Ann Ashton; son, and daughters of my deceased brother Augustine Washington, I give and bequeath four parts; that is, one part to each of them.

To Fielding Lewis, George Lewis, Robert Lewis, Howell Lewis and Betty Carter, sons and daughter of my deceased Sister Betty Lewis, I give and bequeath five other parts, one to each of them.

To George Steptoe Washington, Lawrence Augustine Washington, Harriot Parks, and the heirs of Thornton Washington, sons and daughter of my deceased brother Samuel Washington, I give and bequeath other four parts, one part to each of them.

To Corbin Washington, and the heirs of Jane Washington, Son and daughter of my deceased Brother John Augustine Washington, I give and bequeath two parts; one part to each of them.

To Samuel Washington, Frances Ball and Mildred Hammond, son and daughters of my Brother Charles Washington, I give and bequeath three parts; one part to each of them. And to George Fayette Washington, Charles Augustine Washington and Maria Washington, sons and daughter of my deceased Nephew Geo: Augustine Washington, I give one other part; that is, to each a third of that part.

To Elizabeth Parke Law, Martha Parke Peter, and Eleanor Parke Lewis, I give and bequeath three other parts, that is a part to each of them.

And to my Nephews Bushrod Washington and Lawrence Lewis, and to my ward, the grandson of My wife, I give and bequeath one other part; that is, a third thereof to each of them. And if it should so happen, that any of these persons whose names are here ennumerated (unknown to me) should now be deceased, or should die before me, that in either of these cases, the heirs of such deceased persons shall, notwithstanding, derive all the benefits of the bequest; in the same manner as if he, or she, was actually living at the time.

And by way of advice, I recommend it to my Executors not to be precipitate in disposing of the landed property (herein directed to be sold) if from temporary causes the Sale thereof should be dull; experience having fully evinced, that the price of land (especially above the Falls of the Rivers, and on the Western Waters) have been progressively rising, and cannot be long checked in its increasing value. And I particularly recommend it to such of the Legatees (under this clause of my Will) as can make it convenient, to take each share of my Stock in the Potomac Company in preference to the amount of what it might sell for; being thoroughly convinced myself, that no uses to which the money can be applied will be so productive as the Tolls arising from this navigation when in full operation (and this from the nature of things it must be 'ere long) and more especially if that of the Shanondoah is added thereto.

The family Vault at Mount Vernon requiring repairs, and being improperly situated besides, I desire that a new one of Brick, and upon a larger Scale, may be built at the foot of what is commonly called the Vineyard Inclosure, on the ground which is marked out. In which my remains, with those of my deceased relatives (now in the old Vault) and such others of my family as may chuse to be entombed there, may be deposited. And it is my express desire that my Corpse may be Interred in a private manner, without parade, or funeral Oration.

Lastly I constitute and appoint my dearly beloved wife Martha Washington, My Nephews William Augustine Washington, Bushrod Washington, George Steptoe Washington, Samuel Washington, and Lawrence Lewis, and my ward George Washington Parke Custis (when he shall have arrived at the age of twenty years) Executrix and Executors of this Will and testament, In the construction of which it will readily be perceived that no professional character has been consulted, or has had any Agency in the draught; and that, although it has occupied many of my leisure hours to digest, and to through it into its present form, it may, notwithstanding, appear crude and incorrect. But having endeavoured to be plain, and explicit in all the Devises, even at the expence of prolixity, perhaps of tautology, I hope, and trust, that no disputes will arise concerning them; but if, contrary to expectation, the case should be otherwise from the want of legal expression, or the usual technical terms, or because too much or too little has been said on any of the Devises to be consonant with law, My Will and direction expressly is, that all disputes (if unhappily any should arise) shall be decided by three impartial and intelligent men, known for their probity and good understanding; two to be chosen by the disputants, each having the choice of one, and the third by those two. Which three men thus chosen, shall, unfettered by Law, or legal constructions, declare their Sense of the Testators intention; and such decision is, to all intents and purposes to be as binding on the Parties as if it had been given in the Supreme Court of the United States.

In witness of all, and of each of the things herein contained, I have set my hand and Seal, this ninth day of July, in the year One thousand seven hundred and ninety and of the Independence of the United States the twenty fourth.

Index of Recipients

Alexandria, mayor, corporation, and citizens of, 436–37
Armstrong, John, 386–89
Army, Continental
  farewell orders to, 266–70
  general orders to, 42–44, 55–57, 70–73, 95–97, 186–88, 195–97, 209–10, 235–38
  "Newburgh Address" to officers (1783), 217–21

Ball, Burgess, 596–98
Banister, John, 98–104
Bermuda, inhabitants of the island of, 45–46
Bland, Theodorick, 231–33

Canada, inhabitants of, 46–48
Chastellux, Marquis de, 393–95
Cherokees, 645–48
Continental Congress, Second, 272–73
  President of, 40, 62–64, 75–81, 120–23, 156–64, 194–95, 214–15, 221–23, 297–300
Craik, James, 282–83
Custis, John Parke, 190–92

Dandridge, Francis, 21–23
Delaware Chiefs, 131–33
District of Columbia, commissioners of the, 605–6
Duane, James, 177–80, 260–66

Estaing, Comte d', 106–11

Fairfax, Bryan, 33–39

Fairfax, George William, 29–32
Fitzhugh, William, 176–77
Frederick William II, King of Prussia, 632–33

Gage, Lt. Gen. Thomas, 44–45
Gordon, Rev. William, 257–60
Graham, Catherine Macaulay, 537–39
Grayson, William, 300–1
Greene, Maj. Gen. Nathanael, 207–8, 229

Hamilton, Alexander, 211–13, 229–30, 369, 370–71, 416–17, 421–23, 572–76, 579–81, 609–17, 629–32, 633–35, 637–39, 643–44, 649–54
Harrison, Benjamin, 116–19, 210–11, 278–79, 287–94, 295–97
Hebrew congregations, 545–46
  in Newport, 547–48
  in Savannah, Ga., 549
Henry, Patrick, 370, 660–63
Hopkinson, Francis, 430–31
House of Representatives, 622–25
Humphreys, David, 301–3, 350–53

Jay, John, 135–37, 323–24, 333–35, 357–59, 409–11, 602–5
Jefferson, Thomas, 283–86, 418–21, 576–79, 584–85, 607–9, 640–43
Johnson, Joshua, 559
Johnson, Thomas, 26–28, 294–95
Jones, Joseph, 144–45, 152–54, 206–7, 215–17, 227–28

Knox, Henry, 348–50, 354–57, 363–65, 398–400

Lafayette, Marquis de, 233–35, 280–82, 304–7, 319–23, 324–27, 382–85, 389–93, 396–98, 400–3, 427–29, 553–55, 570–72, 655–60
Laurens, Henry, 113–15
Laurens, Lt. Col. John, 182–86
Lee, Henry, 316–18, 337–38, 586–88, 593–96
Lee, Richard Henry, 5
Lincoln, Gen. Benjamin, 403–4, 415–16, 423–26, 429–30

McHenry, James, 309–11
Madison, James, 286–87, 314–16, 339–40, 343–47, 360–63, 376–78, 379–82, 385–86, 434–35, 531, 567–70
Mason, George, 23–26, 124–26, 175–76, 311–12
Morris, Gouverneur, 111–13, 129–31, 555–58, 617–22
Morris, Robert Hunter, 20–21, 318–19

Nelson, Thomas, 123
New England States, circular to, 180–81
Nicola, Lewis, 203–4

Pendleton, Edmund, 142–44
Pennsylvania Associators, officers and soldiers of, 74–75
Philadelphia, merchants of, 271–72
Pinckney, Thomas, 636–37
Presbyterian Churches, general assembly of, 533

Quakers, annual meeting of, 533–34

Randolph, Edmund, 308–9, 347,

359–60, 378–79, 581–82, 600–1
Reed, Joseph, 53–55, 57–62, 65–68, 146–52
Reformed German Congregation of New York, ministers, elders, deacons, and members of the, 270–71
Roman Catholics in the United States of America, 546–47

Schuyler, Gen. Philip, 88–90
Seneca Nation, chiefs and counselors of, 550–53
States of the Union, circular to, 133–35, 154–56, 164–70, 239–49
Stuart, David, 374–75, 539–45
Sullivan, John, 188–90

Tilghman, Lt. Col. Tench, 238–39
Trumbull, Jonathan, Jr., 277–78, 411–12, 654–55, 665–66

Unidentified correspondent, 85–86
United Baptist Churches in Virginia, 531–32

Vanderkemp, Rev. Francis Adrian, 395–96
Virginia militia, 19

Warren, James, 86–88, 126–28, 312–14
Washington, Bushrod, 335–36, 341–42, 371–74
Washington, George Steptoe (nephew), 431–34
Washington, John Augustine, 69–70, 104–6, 255–57
Washington, Lund, 82–84, 192–93
Washington, Martha, 40–42
Webster, Noah, 413–14

Young, Arthur, 558–61

Subject Index

Adam, 30
Adams, 608, 609
Adams, John, 430
Adet, P. A., 651–53
Agriculture, 342, 421, 558–61
  best regions for, 559–60
  calling out the militia as
    injurious to, 122
  deficiencies in management of,
    652–53
  in eighth annual message
    (1796), 508–9
  in Great Britain, 561
  Indian, 646
  low productivity of American
    farmers, 561
  peas from England, 637, 642
  proposal for an agricultural
    institution, 652
  seeds for France, 307
  survey on (1791), 558–59
  technical discussion of, 641–43
Alarm posts, 72
Alcoholic beverages, taxes on. *See*
  Distilled spirits, duties on
Alexander, William (Lord
  Stirling), 235
Alexander the Great, 397
Alexandria, 292
  academy in, will provision on,
    668–69
Algiers, 318, 401, 500, 507, 616
Allegheny Mountains, Indians of,
  31
Allegheny River, 288
Ambition, as greatest enemy of
  United States, 455

Amendments to the Constitution,
  373–75, 378, 384, 420, 521
adoption of Constitution
  should not depend on, 387–
  88
in first draft on first inaugural
  address ("discarded
  inaugural"), 451–52
Pennsylvania antifederalists
  and, 415
premature, apprehension
  about, 415–16, 424
ratification of the Constitution
  should precede, 391
American empire, foundation of,
  240–41
American Revolution, 449–50. *See
  also* Army, Continental
accommodation with Great
  Britain rejected, 66–67
Bermudans urged to take
  American side in, 45–46
blessed effects of, in the rest of
  the world, 456
contributions of different
  states, 149
critical time for. *See also* state of
  affairs of *below*
  1776, 71
  1778, 118–19
  1783, 241–42
end of war. *See also* Peace
  treaty (1783)
  not in sight, 124–25
  order for cessation of
    hostilities, 236
  prospects for (1779), 121–22

American
Revolution

rejoicing in, 229–30, 236–37, 238
European balance of power and, 135–36
European negotiations and (1778), 100–1
explained to Canadians, 46–47
federal government's defects in prosecution of war, 248
financial aspects of, 111–12, 144, 176, 182–85, 212, 449–50. *See also* Army, Continental, supplies for; Trade
as determining factor, 147–48
errors in administration of finances, 182
foreign aid, 182, 185
French finances, 148
loans needed, 183, 184
public dissatisfaction with, 183
France and, 144, 146, 406
alliance with France, 92, 100, 107*n*, 184–86
finances, 148
French troops needed, 184–85
gratitude for French cooperation at Yorktown (1781), 194–97
naval operations, 107–11, 138–39, 142, 143
in historical perspective, 208, 282
Indians and, 131–33, 261
indifference and lethargy of the public, 146
naval warfare during, 114
British superiority, 109
captured ships, 67–68
d'Estaing's role in, 107–11
need for superiority in, 184
new plan to conduct war needed, 176
persistence of the enemy, 116–17
political dissolution, danger of, 212

public discontent with conduct of war, 169, 185–86
records and papers of W. and writing history of, 260
recovery of nation from war, 538
review of war, 267–68
state of affairs of. *See also* critical time for *above*
in 1780, 175–76
in 1781, 182–86
in 1783, 212
vigorous offensive needed (1781), 184
weariness of war, American people's, 99–100
Ames, Fisher, 636
Amusements, advice to nephew on, 432
Annapolis Convention (1786), 349, 352, 353
Annual addresses of W. as President, 442–43
first (1790), 467–70
second (1790), 470–74
third (1791), 474–80
census, 477
currency, 479–80
duties on distilled spirits, 476–77
Indians, 475–76, 478
loan from Holland, 477–78
militia, 479
permanent seat of the government of the United States, 477
Post Office and post roads, 479
public debt, 477–78
weights and measures, uniformity in, 480
fourth (1792), 480–86
duties on spirits, 483
Indians, 480–83, 485
the mint, establishment of, 484
peace with other nations, 483–84

Post Office, 484
public debt, 484–85
fifth (1793), 486–91
defense policy, 488–89
Indians, 489–90
public debt, 490–91
tax on the transportation of
public prints, 491
war in Europe, 487–88
sixth (1794), 492–99
democratic societies, 492,
497
foreign affairs, 499
Indians, 497–98
Mint of the United States,
the, 498–99
public debt, 498
tax revolt in Pennsylvania,
492–95
seventh (1795), 499–504, 615
general welfare and
prosperity, 501–2
Great Britain, relations with,
500–1
Indians, 499–501, 503, 504
military establishment, 502–3,
504
public debt, 504
Spain, relations with (1795),
500
eighth (1796), 505–12
agriculture, 508–9
Barbary states, 507
compensations to officers of
the U.S., 510
financial affairs, 511
France, relations with, 510–11
Indians, 505
manufacturing, 508
militia, 511–12
navy, 507–8
protection and relief of
American seamen, 507
treaty with Great Britain,
505–6
treaty with Spain, 506–7
Anspach, Regiment of, 106
Antifederalists, 399, 574, 575

elections of 1788 and, 415
false reports circulated by, 429–
30
Appointive powers of the
President, 638
Appointments of officials, 451–52
Aristocracy, 211
Armand, Col., 161, 188
Armed forces. *See also* Army,
Continental; Army, U.S.;
Defense policy; Military
establishment; Militia
proclamation against enlistment
of, under color of a foreign
country (1794), 588–89
Army, British, pay of officers in,
76, 99
Army, Continental. *See also*
Military strategy; *specific
battles*
appointment of officers (1775),
42
artillery, 161–62
bounties for soldiers, 76–77, 246
of states, abolition of, 120–21
cavalry, 161
chaplains, 236
appointment of, 73
instructions to, 209–10
civilians, relations with, 89, 90
civil occupations, recom-
mencing of, 268
commissioned officers in, 57
condition of
described to Congress, 62–64,
75–81
in 1779, 130, 133–34
Congress and, 42
appointment of W. as
commander-in-chief, 40, 41
committee of Congress to
reside near headquarters,
proposal for, 144–45
completion of battalions, 120
condition of army described,
62–64, 75–81
jealousy of the army, 102–3
pay for troops and officers,

*Army,
Continental*

Army,
Continental
54, 219–23, 245–46
recruiting, 120–21
standing army urged, 79, 82
conscription into, 152
courts-martial, 72–73, 80, 96–97
of civilians, 97
of John White, 44
desertion from, 63, 72–73
discipline in, 42–43, 55–57, 63–
64, 71–72. *See also* Courts-
martial
punishments, 80-81
discontent in, 204–7
general meeting of officers,
anonymous papers
requesting (1783), 214–18
end of war and, 236–38
congratulations upon, 236–37
disbanding of army, 253,
266–67
discharges after, 238
liquor issued at, 238
tasks after, 237
thanks to troops, in farewell
orders (1783), 269–70
enlistments in, 54, 58–59, 62,
64, 82, 106, 118
system of temporary
enlistments criticized, 165,
169
European armies compared,
158
farewell orders to, 266–70
financing of, 64, 111–12. *See
also* American Revolution,
financial aspects of; supplies
for *below*
furlough rules, 43
general movement eastward
(1778), 109
general orders to, 42–44, 55–57,
70–73, 209–10
health concerns, 43
smallpox in Boston, 55
horses for, 123
intervals between the dismissal
of one army and the
collection of another, 166

James Warren and, 87–88
militia and, 78–79
mutiny and sedition in, 146
in New Jersey line, 186–87
in Pennsylvania line, 180
"Newburgh Address" to officers
(1783), 217–21
number of men in, 59
number of officers to a
regiment, 160
number of regiments in, 156–60
officers of, 81. *See also* pay for
soldiers and officers *below*
resignation of commissions,
98, 99
organization of, 156–64
regiments, 160
overview of problems of, 166–
67
partisan corps, proposal of, 161
patience and perseverance in
the face of adversity, 95–96,
103
as patriot army, 187, 237
pay for soldiers and officers, 54,
75–77, 112, 153, 268. *See also*
Bounties for soldiers
after end of war, 213
circular to the states on (June
14, 1783), 245–46
complaints of officers, 204–5
Congress urged to act on
issue of (1783), 221–23, 227
desperate need for (1780),
181
dissimilarities in the
payments of men in civil
and military life, 232
general meeting of officers,
anonymous papers
requesting (1783), 214–18
half pay for life for officers,
proposal for, 157–58
half pay or commutation of,
245, 246, 256
Joseph Jones urged to press
issue, 227–28
lack of congressional action,

234–35
patriotism and, 99
pleas for justice to army, 217,
    221–23, 231–32
possible consequences of not
    settling accounts, 228
refusal to disband until paid,
    rumors about, 215–16
Pennsylvania, Associated
    Troops of, 74–75
pensions
    for disabled veterans, 247
    for officers, 157, 158
predicament in January–
    February 1776, 59–60, 62–63,
    65–66
prisoners
    exchange of, 124
    treatment of, 43–45, 57
promotion system in, 179
recruiting for, 58. *See also*
    enlistments in *above*
    abolition of state bounties,
        120–21
religious services, 43
resignation of officers from,
    157
rights of civilians respected by,
    155
sacrifices made by officers of,
    153
sentries of, 71, 73
shortage of soldiers, 62–63, 68
size of, 82, 158–59
spirit of, 55, 95–96
standing (permanent) army
    need for, 79, 82, 98–99, 102,
        165, 168, 176, 177, 190–91
    not a threat to government,
        102
state armies versus continental
    armies, 87–88
sufferings of, 186–87
supplies for, 42, 43, 54, 66, 71,
    95, 96, 150
    arms, shortage of, 59–60
    beef, 178–79
    Bermudans asked to take

over supply depot, 46
in Canada, 47–48
clothing, 122, 134–35, 166,
    170, 178
contribution of different
    states, 149
extremity of distress and
    want, 154–56, 170
flour, 149
for Gen. Schuyler, 89
Hudson River, military
    importance of, 108
inefficient method of
    obtaining, 178, 183
patience of the army as
    nearly exhausted, 183
Pennsylvania and, 149, 151
plundering may be necessary
    to obtain, 155, 156
provisions, lack of, 154–55
surgeons in, 79–80
terms of service in, 162
training of recruits, 63, 169
W. as commander-in-chief of
    appointment (1775), 40, 41
    as destiny, 41
    Martha Washington, letter to,
        40–42
    papers and documents
        related to, 282
    pay, 40
    resignation of commission,
        253, 272–73
    role of, 211–12
    unhappiness with situation,
        83
Army, U.S.. *See* Defense policy;
    Military establishment
Arnold, Benedict, 47, 55
Articles of Confederation, 69–70,
    172, 243, 258, 336, 338
    defects of, 213, 230
    need to reform, 230, 323
Artillery, 161–62
Assessment Bill (Virginia, 1785),
    311–12
Attorney General, selection of
    (1795), 614–15

Augusta County

Augusta County, 31
Austria, 319

Bache, Benjamin, 587, 600, 638, 640
Ball, Frances, 678
Ballman, 631
Baltimore, inland navigation of Potomac River and, 284
Bank of the United States, 475, 485, 557
Barbary states, 326, 401, 507
Barlow, Joel, 396–97, 402
Bassett, Fanny, 297
Bayard, 602
Beef for army, 178–79
Belvoir (Fairfax mansion), renting of, 29–30
Benson, Egbert, 506
Bermuda urged to take American side in Revolutionary War, 45–46
Bermudan privateers (pirates), 618–19
Berrien, John, 73
Big Beaver Creek, 292
Bill of Rights, 392
Biographies of W., 282–83
Black people. *See* Slaves
Bland, Col., 544
Bloomery Tract and Works, 32
Blount, William, 577, 616
Boston, 34
    attack on, consideration of (1776), 60, 67
    cause of, as cause of America (1774), 31
    Council of, 107
    defense of, 110
    Intolerable Acts and, 36
    rumors in (1775), 53–54
    siege of (1776), 50–51
    smallpox in, 55
    W. in, 40
Boston Port Bill, 30–31
Boston Tea Party, 31
Bounties for soldiers, 246
    need for, 76–77

of states, abolition of, 120–21
Boycott of British goods, discussion of (1769), 24–26
Brandywine, Battle of (1777), 52
Bravery, 63
    exhortation on, 71
Bribery of military surgeons, 79
Buchan, Earl of, 673–74
Bunker Hill
    attack on, consideration of, 67
    raid on (1776), 60, 66
Burgoyne, Gen. John, defeat forecast for, 89
Burr, Aaron, 96
Byron, Adm. John, 108, 111

California, country of, 303
Camden, Battle of (1780), 169
Camillus, 612
Campbell, Arthur, 577
Canada (Canadians), 39, 55, 66, 70, 167, 264, 288, 299, 619
    American invasion of, 47–48
    American Revolution explained to, 46–47
    British view of, 47
    French expedition to, possibility of, 141
    French interest in, 114–15
    French troops in, 113–14
    Vermont and, 363
Canals, 316, 317, 418
Capital of the United States. *See also* District of Columbia
    establishment of, 300
    selection of, in third annual message (1791), 477
Carleton, Gen. Sir Guy, 210, 280
Carter, Betty, 677
Carter, Charles, 672
    publication of letter to, 381
Caughnawaga Indians, 578
Cavalry, 161
Cayahoga River, 291–92
Census, first, 557–58
    in third annual message (1791), 477
Chapel at Newburgh, 209

688

Chaplains, 236
  appointment of, 73
  instructions to, 209–10
Charles III, King of Spain, 306
Charlestown, 129
Chase, Samuel, 614
Chastellux, Chevalier, 196
Chastellux, Madame de, 393–94
Cheat River, 292, 297
Checks and balances, 383, 448,
  449
  in Farewell Address (1796), 521
Cherokees, 489–90, 500, 577
  agriculture of, 646
  as example to other tribes, 647
  livestock kept by, 645–46
  proclamation on crimes against
    (1792), 585
  treaty with (1791), 478, 481
Chickamauguas, 481
Chickasaws, 577, 616–17
Children, lack of, 446
Choctaws, 577
Choissy, Brig. Gen. de, 196
Christianity
  Indians and, 298–99
  taxes for the support of
    teachers of (Virginia), 311–12
Civility. *See also* Conduct
  rules of, 6–13
  of W. in Massachusetts (1775),
    53–54
Clark, Gen. George Rogers, 588*n*
Clinton, Gen. Henry, 66, 70, 93,
  107*n*, 108, 129, 173, 406
  reinforcements to, 134
Clinton, George, 673
Clock, political system as a, 117,
  125–26
Clothes
  advice to nephew on, 433
  for army, 122, 134–35, 166, 170,
    178
Coercion, government's need for,
  362
  Madison on, 368–69
Coins, scarcity of, 479–80, 484
Colonies, line should be drawn

between Great Britain and,
  39
Commerce, 285. *See also* Trade
  inland waterways and, 289, 291
  regulation of, 309–11, 314–15
Common Sense (Paine), 286–87
Commonweal, 117
Commutable taxes, 346–47
  Patriotic Society and, 342
Conduct. *See also* Civility
  advice to nephew on, 431–34
  W.'s, 53–54, 57–58
Confederation, the, 449. *See also*
  Articles of Confederation;
  Continental Congress,
  Second; Federal government
  inadequacy of, 355
  as shadow without substance,
    312
Congress. *See also* Continental
  Congress, Second; Federal
  government; Legislative
  branch
  defense of, 541–42
  elections of 1788–1789, 427–30
  interests of members of, held
    to be the same as their
    constituents, 448
  place for convening, 415, 420
  publication of debates, 541
Connecticut, 61, 68, 412
  manufacturing in, 429
  ratification of the Constitution
    and, 384, 430
Connecticut River, 109
Conscription into army, 152
Constitution(s). *See also* Articles of
  Confederation
  of Massachusetts, 349
  state, 351–53
Constitution, French, 539
Constitution, U.S., 320. *See also*
  Constitutional Convention
  amendments to, 373–75, 378,
    384, 420, 521
  adoption of Constitution
    should not depend on,
    387–88

Constitution,
U.S.

Constitution,
U.S.

in first draft of first
inaugural address
("discarded inaugural"),
451–52
Pennsylvania antifederalists
and, 415
premature, apprehension
about, 415–16, 424
ratification of the
Constitution should
precede, 391
as basis for union of states, 518
as best that could be obtained,
370, 379
checks and balances under, 383
critical period for, 423–24
in Farewell Address (1796), 518
The Federalist on, 375, 376
praise for, 416–17
Henry sent copy of, 370
imperfections of, 373
Jay and, 376–77
need for a new, 69–70, 234
opponents of, 370–75, 409
more good than evil as
product of, 388
in Virginia, 377–78
the people as ultimate holders
of power under, 373
the Presidency and, 392
President's power to make
treaties under, 623–24
ratification of, 370, 372–73,
376–81, 384, 385, 391, 394–95,
397–400, 402, 404, 411–12,
415, 417. *See also under specific*
states
amendments should not be
condition of, 387–88
Madison on, 369
state legislatures and, 376,
377
in Virginia, 376, 377, 379–80
separation of powers under,
383
support growing for, 415
vigilance over, 497
Constitutional Convention, 258,

321, 375, 407, 574
appointment of delegates to,
343
W., appointment of, 347, 352,
446
attendance of delegates at
Society of the Cincinnati and
W.'s attendance at
convention, 352, 354, 357,
360, 364
W.'s decision whether or not
to attend, 352–55, 357–59,
364
Continental Congress and, 361
resolution recommending the
convention, 358, 359
doubt concerning, 323
expectations for, 363
Jay on, 365–66
legality of, 355, 358
Madison and, 352
prospects for, 349, 369
representation of all states at,
364
second convention opposed,
384
states and, 352–53
W.'s role in, 331
Constitutional rights and liberties,
38
Bill of Rights, 392
Intolerable Acts and, 35
need to ascertain and assert, 39
Continental Army. *See* Army,
Continental
Continental Congress, First
(1774), 30n
Continental Congress, Second
(1775–1776), 69, 101
ablest men should be in, 117,
118, 125, 192
adjournment of, advisability of,
213
appointment of ministers of
war, finance, and foreign
affairs by (1781), 188
army and, 42
appointment of W. as

commander-in-chief, 40, 41
committee of Congress to
 reside near headquarters,
 proposal for, 144–45
completion of battalions, 120
condition of army described,
 62–64, 75–81
half pay and commutation
 for officers, 245–46
jealousy of the army, 102–3
pay for troops and officers,
 54, 219–23
recruiting, 120–21
resignations of officers, 169
standing army urged, 79, 82
attendance of members of,
 285–86
constant versus annual sessions
 of, 286
Constitutional Convention and,
 361
resolution recommending the
 convention, 358, 359
financing of war and, 144
indecision of, 102
Indians and, 132–33
as nugatory body, 312–13
parties in. *See* Parties
political creed regarding, 279
powers of, 257, 362
disinclination of states to
 yield, 278–79
fear of, 259
fear of increasing, 333–34
inadequacy of, 450
increase in, need for, 169,
 170, 176–78, 191, 192, 211,
 239, 242–43, 320–21, 333–34
nomination of commissioners
 to revise, 321
not a danger, 259
prolongation of the war due
 to inadequacy of, 230
regulation of commerce, 309–
 11, 314–15
requisitions to the states by, 334
Contracts, inviolability of, 374,
 375

Conway, Gen. Henry, 61
Cornplanter (Seneca chief), 550,
 553
Cornwallis, Charles (1st Marquis
 Cornwallis), 51–52
surrender at Yorktown (1781),
 194
Corruption of Congress, public
 fears concerning, 574–75
Courage, 73
exhortation on, 71
Courts, 32. *See also* Judiciary
 branch; Judiciary system
Stamp Act and, 22–23
Courts-martial, 72–73, 80, 96–97
of civilians, 97
of John White, 44
Courts of admiralty, 67
Cowardice, 63
Craik, Dr. James, 434, 674
Credit, public, 182–84
establishment of, 555, 557
in Farewell Address (1796), 522
increase in (1790), 470–71
provision for the support of,
 470
Creditors, 231, 478. *See also* Public
 debt
army and, 215
Creeks, 489, 498, 500, 505, 616–17
in West Florida, 577
Criminal defendants,
 transportation to other
 colonies or to Great Britain
 for trial, 34
Currency. *See also* Mint of the
 United States, the; Money;
 Paper money
circulation of, 389
depreciation of, 119, 127, 134,
 143, 182
in fourth annual message
 (1792), 484
scarcity of small change, 479–
 80, 484
shortage of (1774), 32
in third annual message (1791),
 479–80

Currency

Currency uniformity in, 469
Custis, Eleanor Parke, 23, 28,
  676–78
Custis, George Washington
  Parke, 23, 307, 336, 676, 677,
  679
Custis, Jack, 276

Dagworthy, Capt. John, 20*n*
Dandridge, Bartholomew, 307,
  672
Dandridge, John, 672
Dandridge, Mary, 672
David d'Angers, xxii
Debts (debtors). *See also* Foreign
  debt; Public debt
  boycott of British goods and
    (1769), 24–25
  to Great Britain
    non-payment of, 37
    refusal to pay, 34
  of states, assumption of, 543
Declaration of Independence, 73
Defense policy
  in fifth annual message (1793),
    488–89
  in first annual message (1790),
    468
  in first draft of first inaugural
    address ("discarded
    inaugural"), 452–53
  in seventh annual message
    (1795), 502–4
Delaware, 149
  ratification of the Constitution
    and, 376, 384
Delaware Nation, 131
Delaware River, capital site on
  banks of, 300
Democratic governments. *See also*
  Representative government
  tardiness of people's action in,
    306, 320, 356–57
Democratic-Republican Party, 564
Democratic societies, 565, 593–94,
  597–98. *See also* Self-created
  societies
Denmark, 136

Depreciation of currency, 119,
  127, 134, 143, 182
Desertion, 63, 72–73
  from Militia, 78
Despotism. *See also* Tyranny
  parties and, 520
Detroit, 288, 291, 292
  settlers in, 264, 265
Deuxponts, 197
Discipline
  in Continental Army, 42–43,
    55–57, 63–64, 71–72. *See also*
    Courts-martial
  punishments, 80–81
  in Militia, 78
Distilled spirits, duties on, 476–77,
  483
  proclamation against
    combinations to defeat
    execution of (1794), 589–92
  proclamation on (1792), 583–84
District of Columbia, 560. *See also*
  Capital of the United States
Dogs from France, 306
Domestic felicity, 393–94
Donkeys, as gifts from King of
  Spain, 306, 322
Dorchester Heights, 51
Douville, 20*n*
Draft, military (conscription), 152
Dunmore, 4th Earl of (John
  Murray), 30, 54–55

East, the, in Farewell Address
  (1796), 516
East India Company, 34
East Indies, 411
  trade with, 421
Economy, the. *See also* Currency;
  Financial affairs of the U.S.;
  Financial aspects of
  American Revolution;
  Money; Prosperity; Public
  debt; Taxation; Trade
  Spanish, 148
Education, 649. *See also*
  Knowledge
  money for, 389

national university proposed,
509, 605–9, 649–50, 670–71
Ejectments, trial for, in
Pennsylvania, 309
Elections
as pivot on which turns the
first wheel of the
government, 448
of 1788, 415
for delegates to Virginia
Convention, 385, 386
of 1788–1789, 427–30
Elizabeth River, 297
Emancipation of slaves, 235, 322
in will, 667
Emigration
from Europe, 301
from Great Britain, 298–99
from Holland, 395–96
to western lands, 301, 384
Empire, American, foundation of,
240–41
England. *See* Great Britain
Estaing, Count d', 138, 139, 142
Europe (European nations), 121,
125, 230, 231, 279
balance of power in, 135–36
change of systems in, 556
changes in (1791–1792), 570
contrast between United States
and (1791), 555
in Farewell Address (1796),
524–25
Lafayette's tour through, 319–
20
peace in, 301
treaties with, 243, 556–57
United States forearmed as well
as forewarned against evil
contingencies of European
politics, 411
unwillingness to participate in
politics of, 659
war in (1788), 390, 400–1, 418–
19
war in (1793), 487–89
proclamation of neutrality
toward, 585–86

European negotiations (1778),
100–1
Evans, John, 72, 287
Executive branch. *See also*
Presidency, the
principles of Washington's
administration, 621
Executive power, 178

Factions. *See* Parties
Fairfax, Bryan
Intolerable Acts, disagreement
with W. in mode of obtaining
repeal of, 35–36
letter read to Fairfax County
meeting (1774), 35
urged to stand for election to
House of Burgesses, 33
Fairfax, George William, 29–32
Bloomery Tract and Works
and, 32
book of accounts of, 30
fishery at the Raccoon Branch,
29–30
intention of not returning to
Virginia, 30
renting of Belvoir and, 29–30
sale of furniture of, 29, 32
Fairfax, Mrs. George William, 32
Fairfax, Lord, 674
Fairfax County, 34, 35
Farewell Address (1796), 639
on federal government, 518–21
on foreign relations, 517–18,
522–26
Hamilton asked for advice on,
634–35, 643–44
on institutions for the general
diffusion of knowledge, 522
Madison asked to write (1792),
568–70
on military establishment, 516–
17
on neutrality, 524–26
publication of, 644
on public credit, 522
on regional divisions that may
threaten union, 517

Farewell Address
on regions of the country,
common interests of, 515–16
on religion and morality, 521–
22
on separation of powers, 521
third term as President
declined, 512–13
thoughts on contents of, 568–69
on trade, 525
on treaty with Spain, 517
on unity of government, 515
Federal government (federal
system; also called general
government), 341. *See also*
Confederation, the;
Congress; Executive branch;
Judiciary branch; Legislative
branch
alliances among states not a
substitute for, 518
capital for, 300, 477
compensations to officers of
the U.S., 510
concern for fate of (1786), 339
conduct of individuals called to
administer, 387
Constitutional Convention and,
352
defects of, 323, 383
in prosecuting Revolutionary
War, 248
as experiment for promoting
human happiness, 537
in Farewell Address (1796),
518–21
good will of citizens toward,
538
as government of the people,
448
inadequacy of, 356–58
Jay's proposals for, 366
Knox's proposals for revising,
355
Knox's views on, 366–67
Madison's views on, 367–68
opponents of a strong, 369
Patriotic Society and, 342
perfection not claimed for,

447–48
powers of, 256, 383, 448
revision of, 356–58
need for, 355, 361–62
resistance of spirit of
innovation, 519
sovereignty of, 258–59
states' opposition to, 355, 358
states' relationship to, 258–59
weakness of, 312–13
Federalist, The, 375, 376, 382, 388
praise for, 416–17
Federalist Party, 564
Federalists, 564. *See also*
Antifederalists
monarchical versus republican,
575
representatives to Congress
from Virginia, 430
Fee Bill, 32
Financial affairs of the U.S., 617.
See also Currency; Financial
aspects of American
Revolution; Money;
Prosperity; Public debt;
Trade
in eighth annual message,
(1796), 511
in Farewell Address (1796), 522
public concerns regarding, 572–
73
sketch of a plan of American
finance (1789), 535–37
Financial affairs of W.
compensation, 463
shares in navigation companies
given to charitable causes,
295–97, 308
Financial aspects of American
Revolution, 111–12, 144, 176,
182–85, 212, 449–50. *See also*
Army, Continental, supplies
for; Trade
as determining factor, 147–48
errors in administration of
finances, 182
foreign aid, 185
as indispensable, 182

French finances, 148
    loans needed, 183, 184
    public dissatisfaction with, 183
Florida, 128, 140
    West, 577
Flour for army, 149, 155
Food for army, 154–55, 178–79
Foreign affairs (foreign policy),
    243. *See also* Treaties; *and
    specific nations*
    in annual messages as
        President
        first annual message (1790),
            468
        fifth annual message (1793),
            487–89
        sixth annual message (1794),
            499
        seventh annual message
            (1795), 501
        eighth annual message
            (1796), 510–11
    in Farewell Address (1796),
        517–18, 522–s26
    in first draft of first inaugural
        address ("discarded
        inaugural"), 455–56
    friendly terms with all nations
        as goal, 620
    neutrality, 630, 631, 656–59, 661
        in Farewell Address (1796),
            524–26
        French reaction to, 657–58
        not a sufficient protection,
            507
        proclamation of (1793), 565,
            585–86
        trade and, 501
    peace with other nations, 483–
        84
    war in Europe (1793), 487–89
        proclamation of neutrality
            toward, 585–86
Foreign aid, 185
    as indispensable, 182
Foreign debt, 419–20, 536
Fort George, N.Y., necessity of
    evacuating, 89–90

Fort Pitt, 292
Fort Stanwix, Treaty of, 552
France, 66, 112, 132, 135, 136,
    160, 380, 413, 616. *See also*
    French and Indian War;
    French Revolution
    accommodation of differences
        with, 658
    Adet affair and, 651–53
    American Revolution and, 144–
        45, 146, 406
    alliance with France, 92, 100,
        107*n*, 184–86
    finances, 148
    French troops needed, 184–
        85
    gratitude for French
        cooperation at Yorktown
        (1781), 194–97
    naval operations, 107–11,
        138–39, 142, 143
    Canada
        French interest in, 114–15
        French troops in, 113–14
    constitution of, 539
    as first power in the world,
        325–26
    friendship between United
        States and, 324–25
    gratitude to, 382
    Jay's Treaty (1795) and, 611–12,
        621–22, 630, 637, 651*n*
    La Luzerne's conference with
        W., 138–42
    little prospect of trip to, 281
    as more powerful than her
        rivals believe, 390
    neutrality of United States and,
        657–58
    new Minister Plenipotentiary
        of, 382
    political affairs in (1788), 384–
        85
    relations with, in eighth annual
        message (1796), 510–11
    situation in (1788), 401, 419
    trade with, 324–25, 390, 421,
        487, 554

Franklin,
Benjamin

Franklin, Benjamin, 124, 141, 674
Frederick William II, King of
  Prussia, 401
Freedom. *See* Liberty
French and Indian War, 19–21
French Revolution, 553–54, 570–
  71, 620, 631
Freneau, Philip, 587
Frugality, 433
  Stamp Act and, 22
Future of America, 240, 278, 403–
  4, 406, 456
  ultimate fate, inability to
    foresee, 453–54

Gage, Gen. Thomas, 21
  treatment of prisoners held by,
    44–45
  tyranny of, 36, 39
Gates, Maj. Gen. Horatio, 109,
  175
Gattinois, 197
Genet, Edmond Charles Edouard,
  588, 588n
George III, King of Great
  Britain, 210
  loyalty to, 19
  petitions to, as ineffective, 33–
    34, 36, 37
Georgetown, inland navigation of
  Potomac River and, 284
Georgia, 129, 140, 166, 559
  Creeks in, 498, 500, 505
  ratification of the Constitution
    and, 376
Germantown, Battle of (1777), 52
Germany, 319. *See also* Prussia
Gibraltar, 403
Gloucester, N.J., British
  surrender of (1781), 194
Government. *See also* Continental
  Congress, Second; Federal
  government
  British claim that people are
    unfit for their own, 337, 340
  education of youth in the
    science of, 509–10
  forming a new, 69–70

religion and morality as
  indispensable to, 521–22
Governor general
  Jay's proposal for, 366
  Knox's proposal for, 367
Grafton, 3rd Duke of (Augustus
  Henry), 61
Grasse, Count François-Joseph-
  Paul de, 194–95, 413
Great Britain, 320, 380, 401, 419.
  See also American Revolution
  accommodation with, 100
    rejection of, 66–67
  agriculture in, 561
  designs of (1779), 128
  Detroit, Niagara, and Oswego
    retained by, 291
  disunity of the United States
    and, 279
  emigration from, 298–99
  European balance of power
    and, 135–36
  financing of war effort by, 112
  grievances against (1795), 618–
    20
  Indians and, 321, 350, 616
    Indians should not trust
      Great Britain, 131–32
  insurrections and divisions
    fomented by, 350, 351
  Jay's negotiations with, 602
  maritime resources of, 147
  middle states and, 290
  news from (January 1776), 61
  oaths of allegiance to, 84–85
  reconciliation with, 67, 69, 82
  trade with, 291
    British policy, 324, 325
    British trade policy, 305–6
    interference with, declared
      treason by Gage, 36
    1795 treaty and, 611
  treaty with (1783; Peace treaty),
    229–30, 231, 233, 234, 321
    violations of, 333, 334, 350,
      361
  treaty with (1795–1796), 500–1,
    505–6, 517, 609–13, 615, 619,

620–24
western lands and, 321
Great Kanawha River, 292–93,
297, 303
Great Lakes, navigation of, 285
Greed, 119, 125
Green, Sarah, 675
Greene, Gen. Nathanael, 71, 327
appointed to command Army
of the South, 175–77
death of, 349
resignation as Quartermaster
General, 152–53
suspension of, 152–54
Grenville, Lord, 618, 620, 637

Hamilton, Alexander, 188, 200,
211–13, 564, 593
Farewell Address (1796) and,
443
reconciliation with Jefferson
urged, 584–85
Hammond, Mildred, 678
Hampshire County, 31
Happiness
of domestic life in America,
393–94
public (social and political), 240,
241, 462
distinguished from splendor,
455
government as experiment
for promoting, 537
knowledge as basis of, 469
pillars of, 428
Harlem, 187
Harrison, Benjamin, 306
Hawkins, Col. Benjamin, 646
Haynie, Sally B., 675
Health, of W., 343, 365, 545
Henry Huntington Library and
Art Gallery, xvii, xix, xxii
Henry, Patrick, 391, 404, 424, 614
false reports of W.'s criticism
of, 594–96
urged to run for office, 662
Hessians, 51, 69
Holland, 136, 380–81, 386, 395

loans from, 212, 471, 477–78,
484–85, 490
Holston, treaty of (1791), 481
Honesty, 315
Hood, John, 673
Horses, 123
Hounds from France, 306
Hounds from France, 306
Howe, Gen. Richard (Earl Howe),
51, 52
Howe, Gen. William, 62, 66, 107n,
110, 111, 186
proclamation issued by
(November 30, 1776), 84–85
puzzling conduct of, 90
Hudson River, military
importance of, 108
Human nature, 333, 334
Humphreys, Col. David, 400, 412,
435, 440
praised, 302
Huntington, Countess of, 298

Ignorance, 323–324. *See also*
Knowledge
Imports from Great Britain. *See
also* Boycott of British goods;
Trade, with Great Britain
Stamp Act and, 22, 23
Impost Law (1783), 210, 260
Inaugural addresses. *See*
Presidential addresses
Independence, 99
accomplishment of, 237
nothing short of, 101
pillars of, 242
union of the states and, 243
Indian affairs agents, 263–64, 646
Indians, 114, 122, 128, 289, 326,
550–53, 555. *See also* French
and Indian War; *specific tribes*
in annual messages as
President
third annual message (1791),
475–76, 478
fourth annual message
(1792), 480–83, 485
fifth annual message (1793),

Indians

Indians

489–90

sixth annual message (1794),
497–98

seventh annual message
(1795), 499–501, 503, 504

boundary between United
States and, 261–63

confederacy of, 31

Congress and, 132–33

dangers presented by, 31–32

Great Britain and, 321, 350, 616
Indians should not trust
Great Britain, 131–32

improvement of the condition
of, 645

lands of
alienation of, 476
purchase of, 266
sale of, 550–51

murder of, 552

of Ohio Valley, 497–98
Miami Indians, 552–53
raids by, 471–72
in seventh annual message
(1795), 499–501

peace with, 263, 265, 498, 616–
17

prisoners held by, 261

proclamation on crimes against
the Cherokee Nation, 585

protection against attacks by,
468

protection of, from settlers, 503

Revolutionary War and, 131–
33, 261

Spain and, 577–79

spreading Christianity among,
298–99

trade with, 264, 476, 485, 504,
617

treaties with, 476, 478, 552

treatment of, 260–64

in western lands, 302, 616–17
protection of Indians from
settlers, 503
reports concerning (1792),
577–78
war with Indians, 571

Indian vocabularies, 363, 400

Industry, Stamp Act and, 22

Inflation, 112

Inland navigation of Potomac
River, 276, 291–92, 313–14,
418, 560. *See also* Potomac
Company
connection between Potomac
and Ohio rivers needed, 283–
84
engineering aspects of, 28
financing of, 26–28, 284, 292,
305
gift of shares in Potomac
Company given to W. by
Virginia Assembly, 295–97,
308
local jealousies and, 284
Maryland and, 283–85
New York and, 284–85
pre-Revolutionary War plan,
26–28, 284
roads and, 297
survey of Potomac called for,
291

Inland waterways. *See also* Canals;
Inland navigation of Potomac
River; *specific rivers*
benefits of, 315–16
need for, 287–91
Pennsylvania and, 293–94
political and commercial
consequences of, 303
routes for, 288, 291–92
shares in navigation companies
given to charitable causes,
308

Insurgency in Massachusetts,
348–51, 356, 362

Insurrections, British
encouragement of, 350, 351

Intolerable Acts, mode of
obtaining repeal of, 35–37, 39

Invasion by foreign nation, as
certain to fail, 453

James River, 284, 303
navigation of, 292, 293, 295,

297, 305, 308–9, 313–14
survey of, call for, 291
James River Company, shares in,
    will provision on, 669, 671
Jay, John, 119, 318, 322, 361, 631,
    632, 638, 653
    on Constitutional Convention,
    365–66
    Constitution and, 376–77
    Farewell Address (1796) and,
    443
    negotiations with England, 602.
    See also Jay's Treaty (1795).
    summary of letter from, 365–66
Jay's Treaty (1795), 602, 609–13,
    619–24
    Camillus letters and, 612
    doubts concerning, 611–12
    France and, 611–12, 621–22,
    630, 637, 651n
    House of Representatives
    debate on, 636
    opposition to, 621–22, 629
    ratification of, 636–38
    seizure of ships and, 618, 630
    support for, 615
    treaty-making power of the
    President and, 622–24
Jealousies, local. *See* Local
    interests
Jefferson, Thomas, 126, 306, 385,
    391, 392, 558, 564, 594, 596,
    651n
    reconciliation with Hamilton
    urged, 584–85
    relationship with, 640–41
    W's high opinion of, 322
Jersey. *See* New Jersey
Jews, thanked for their support,
    547–49
Johnson, Thomas, 284, 285, 305,
    614
Jones, Comm. Paul, 419
Judiciary branch, 452
    Madison on, 368
Judiciary system
    Indians, courts open to actions
    by, 551

revision of, 483
    in second annual message
    (1790), 473
Jury trial, 392
Justice, 38, 256
    as pillar of independence, 242–
    44

Kentucky, 399
    constitution of, 484
    militia of, 475
    raising army in, for use against
    Spanish colonies, 588
    statehood for, 471
King, Rufus, 614, 635, 653
Knowledge
    as basis of public happiness,
    469
    importance of acquiring, 432
    institutions for the general
    diffusion of, 522
Knox, Gen. Henry, 50–51, 181,
    253, 339, 429, 579, 596–97
    national government proposed
    by, 355
    promotion of, 179
    summary of letter from, 366–67

Lachaise, Auguste, 588n
Lafayette, Marquis de, 107n, 115,
    124, 195–97, 229, 287, 300,
    301, 309, 427–29, 539, 674
    arrival of (1780), 144
    concern for personal safety of,
    571
    Constitution explained to, 382–
    84
    emancipation of slaves by, 322
    European tour of, 319–20
    friendship with, 656
    German emperor asked to
    allow Lafayette to come to
    United States (1796), 633
    gratitude toward, for serving
    American cause, 234
    hounds obtained for W. by, 306
    imprisonment of, 636–37
    invited to Mount Vernon

Lafayette, Marquis de
(1784), 281
political advice to, 401
in prison, 631–33
reasons for not replying more
promptly to letters of, 304
Land jobbing and monopolizing,
in Indian lands, 263
Landownership by W., 116
Lands, Indian
alienation of, 476
purchase of, 266
sale of, 550–51
Land sales
Indian lands, 550–51
in third annual message (1791),
480
in the west, 384
western lands, 300, 306, 384. *See
also* Northwest Ordinance
(1785)
Langdon, John, 442
Languedoc, canal of, 418
Laurens, Col. Henry, 195, 371
Law, Elizabeth Parke, 678
Laws
coercion needed to enforce, 362
military, 315
of Virginia, 314
Lear, Tobias, 353, 435
Lechmere Point, Mass., 68
Lee, Col. R. H., 377–79, 424
Lee, Francis L., 378
Lee, Gen. Charles, 42, 44, 60–61,
70, 93
in Battle of Monmouth (1778),
105
Legionary Corps, 161
Legislative branch. *See also*
Congress; Continental
Congress
checks on, 386
Letchmore's Point, 54
Lewis, Col. Fielding, 32
Lewis, Eleanor Parke (née Custis),
23, 28, 676–78
Lewis, Fielding, 677
Lewis, George, 675, 677
Lewis, Howell, 677

Lewis, Lawrence, 676–79
Lewis, Robert, 677
Liberal arts, 397
Liberality, 230, 239, 241, 547–49
differences in political opinions
and, 580
internal dissensions and (1792),
578–79
among religious
denominations, 545
Liberty (liberties), 256. *See also*
Constitutional rights and
liberties; Religious freedom
as basis of United States, 242
of Canadians, 47
exhortation on, 71
in Farewell Address (1796),
515–19
maintenance and defense of,
different tactics considered in
(1769), 23–24
military establishment as
unfavorable to, 516–17
Stamp Act as attack on, 22
Lincoln, Gen. Benjamin, 140, 196,
197, 412
publication of letter to, 381
Literature, promotion of, 469
Littlepage, 318, 322, 323
Livestock, Indian, 645–46
Livingston, John, 551
Livingston, Robert R., 442
Loans from Holland, 212, 471,
477–78, 484–85, 490
Local interests (jealousies or
prejudices), 231, 256, 258,
277–78, 312, 339, 341, 461–62,
540
broader interests threatened by,
233–34
inland navigation of Potomac
River and, 284, 285
inland waterways and, 289, 291
in Massachusetts (1775), 53–54
need to forget, 242
state jealousies of Congress and
of one another, 278–79
unreasonable versus proper, 310

Longchamp, 309
Long Island, Battle of (1776),
    51
Louis XVI, King of France, 233,
    401, 419
Loyalists (Tories)
    pardon of, 104
    proclamation of (January 25,
        1777) and, 84–86
Loyalty to George III, 19
Luzerne, Chevalier Anne-César
    de la, 210
    conference between W. and,
        138–42

McGillivray, Alexander, 577
Madison, James, 360–63, 424, 541,
    564
    asked to write Farewell Address
        (1792), 568–70
    Constitutional Convention and,
        352
    Farewell Address (1796) and,
        443
    help in drafting reply to the
        Address of the House of
        Representatives requested by
        W., 531
    summary of letter from, 367–69
Manners, 6–13. *See also* Conduct
Manufactured goods
    Stamp Act and, 22, 23
    trade of raw materials for, 325
Manufacturing, 421
    agriculture deemed preferable
        to, 455
    encouragement of, 428–29
    in eighth annual message
        (1796), 508
    in first annual message (1790),
        468, 469
    possibility of British attempt to
        restrict American, 24
Martial law, in Pennsylvania, 150–
    52
Maryland, 149, 189, 424
    agriculture in, 558
    elections in (1789), 430

inland navigation of Potomac
    River and, 27, 283–85, 292
inland waterways and, 288, 297,
    316
paper emission question in, 349
ratification of the Constitution
    and, 391, 393, 394, 397, 402
Mason, Col. George, 33, 84, 98,
    338, 381, 391
Massachusetts, 138, 336, 412
    American Revolution and, 155
    civility of W. towards
        gentlemen of (1775), 53–54
    constitution of, 349
    exports from, 421
    insurgency in (1786), 337–40,
        348–51, 356, 362
    manufacturing in, 429
    ratification of the Constitution
        and, 380, 381, 384, 385, 391
Massachusetts Bay Colony,
    charter withdrawn from, 34,
    36
Mercer, Gen. Hugh, 52, 71
Merchants (mercantile interests),
    32. *See also* Trade
    British, Stamp Act and, 23
    regulation of trade and, 305
Miami Indians, 552–53
Mifflin, Gen. Thomas, 42, 70–71
Military academy, call for
    establishment of (1796), 509,
    510
Military certificates, 353
Military establishment, 617
    in Farewell Address (1796),
        516–17
    in seventh annual message
        (1795), 502–3
Military laws, 315
Military strategy. *See also*
    American Revolution
    lines as a kind of trap, 90
Militia, 64, 68, 71, 453, 503
    called to suppress opposition to
        tax on distilled spirits (1794),
        591–92, 597, 599
    disadvantages of, 77–79, 82,

Militia

Militia
122, 130, 165–66, 168–69, 191
discipline in, 78
in eighth annual message
(1796), 511–12
establishment of regular and
uniform, 247
Indian raids and, 472
of Kentucky, 475
legislation concerning, 497
tax revolt in Pennsylvania put
down by (1794), 494–96
in third annual message (1791),
479
unhappiness with, 82–83
Minot, George Richards, 415
Mint, the, 479, 484
Mint of the United States, the,
498–99
Mississippi River, 293
navigation of, 303, 338, 349, 399
Monarchy, 200–1, 334
Nicola's offer to make W. King,
203–4
opposition to, 361
parties and, 520
prosperity and happiness of his
people in a, 401–2
public suspicion of plot to
establish a, 574, 575
Money, 125. *See also* Currency;
Financial affairs of the U.S.;
Greed; Mint, the; Paper
money; Pay; Speculation
circulation of, 389
Monmouth, Battle of (1778), 93,
104–6
Monongahela River, 292, 297
Monroe, James, 629, 653
Montgomery, Gen. Richard, 62,
167
Morality, 462
as indispensable support of
government, 521–22
Morgan, Gen. Daniel, 416
Morocco, 318, 500, 616
Morris, Gouverneur, 421, 427,
630, 631, 633, 638
Morris, Robert, 556

Morristown, New Jersey, 52
Morse, 350
Mount Vernon, 571, 586–87, 664
additions to, 33
British in, 192–93
repairs in, 83–84
after war's end, 276
in will, 675–77, 679
Moustiers, Count de, 421
Music, Hopkinson's, 430–31
Muskingum River, 291
Mutiny, 146
in New Jersey line, 186–87
in Pennsylvania line, 180

National character, 294, 339
establishment of, 231, 233, 241,
256
pillars of, 242
National Gazette, 564
National supremacy, Madison's
views on, 367, 368
National university, call for
establishment of, 509, 605–9,
649–50, 670–71
Naturalization, 469
Natural rights, 38
Naval warfare, 114. *See also* Ships,
captured
British superiority in, 109
d'Estaing's role in, 107–11
need for superiority in, 184
Navigation. *See* Inland navigation
of Potomac River; Inland
waterways
Navigation Act, 310, 311
Navy, British
compared to French and
Spanish navies, 147
treatment of ships captured
from, 67–68
Navy, French, 147
in American Revolution, 138,
142, 143
Navy, Spanish, 147
Navy, U.S., 452–53. *See also* Naval
warfare
need for, in eighth annual

message (1796), 507–8
Negroes, 55. *See also* Slaves
Nelson, Thomas, 123, 197
Netherlands, the. *See* Holland
Neutrality, 630, 631, 656–59, 661
  in Farewell Address (1796),
    524–26
  French reaction to, 657–58
  not a sufficient protection, 507
  proclamation of (1793), 565,
    585–86
  trade and, 501
Newburgh Addresses, 201, 214*n*,
  217–21
New England states, agriculture
  in, 559
Newfoundland, 114, 141
New Hampshire, 68, 559
  ratification of the Constitution
    and, 399, 400, 404
New Jersey, 61, 149, 559
  mutiny in New Jersey line,
    186–87
  ratification of the Constitution
    and, 384
New-Levies, 71
New Orleans, 114
Newport, R.I., 107*n*
Newspapers, 320
  abuse of public officers in, 582
  attacks on W. in, 640
  Freneau's and Bache's attacks
    on W., 587–88
  insurgency in Massachusetts as
    reported by, 351
  mailing of, 409–10, 454–55
  tax on transportation of, 491
New York, 70, 109, 139, 149, 321,
  362, 559
  American Revolution and, 413,
    414
  Indians in, 262
  inland navigation of Potomac
    River and, 284–85
  inland waterways and, 288
  ratification of the Constitution
    and, 381, 399, 402, 404, 412,
    417

New York Circular Letter, 415–17
New York City, 60, 110, 143
  British evacuation of (1783),
    280
  lodgings in, 435
  as provisional capital, 442
Niagara, 291
Nicola, Col. Lewis, 200–1
Nisbet, Dr., 389
Noailles, Louis Marie, Viscount
  de, 195
Non-importation scheme, 24–26,
  37
Norfolk County, Va., 70
North, Lord Frederick
  speech and bills offered to
    Parliament (1778), 102, 104
North Carolina, 70, 298, 315
  ratification of the Constitution
    and, 376, 380, 404, 412, 424,
    467
Northern colonies, boycott of
  British goods and (1769), 24
Northern states, in Farewell
  Address (1796), 515–16
North River (N.Y.–N.J.), 90, 105,
  106, 109, 110, 137
Northwest Ordinance (1785), 300,
  302–3, 306
Nova Scotia, 141

Oaths of allegiance
  to Great Britain, 84–85
  to the United States of
    America, 85, 86
Ohio
  inland navigation of Potomac
    River and, 28
  opened to immigrants, 304–5
Ohio River, 292, 303
  connection between Potomac
    River and, 283–84
  inland waterways and, 291–92
Oneidas, 266
Onondagas, 132
Oswego, 291
Ottoman Empire ("the Porte"),
  385, 390, 401, 419

Paine, Thomas

Paine, Thomas, 286–87
Paper money, 118
  emission of, 339
    Maryland Assembly and, 349
    Virginia Assembly and, 353
  public concern regarding, 573–74
Papers, public and private, will provision on, 673
Parks, Harriot, 678
Parliament, British
  not governed by the principles of justice, 38
  petitions to, as ineffective, 36–38
  remonstrances to, as ineffective, 23, 34
  taxation power of, 34–37, 39
Parsons, Maj. Gen. Samuel Holden, 187, 188, 384
Parties (factions; partisanship), 118, 131, 190, 564
  attacks on W. by, 641
  baneful effects of the spirit of, generally, 519–20
  Congress as rent by, 126
  in Farewell Address (1796), 517–20
  in monarchical versus free governments, 520
  opposition, 656–58, 660–62
  in Pennsylvania, 151
  regional jealousies fomented by, 517
  as subverting government, 518–19
Partisan corps, proposal for, 161
Paterson, William, 614
Patriotic Society, 330, 341–42
Patriotism, 96, 187, 515
  as insufficient for conducting a war, 99
  merchants and other citizens of Philadelphia, 271
  union of states as object of, 517
Pay. *See also* Bounties
  of soldiers and officers, 54, 75–77, 112, 153, 268

circular to the states on (June 14, 1783), 245–46
complaints of officers, 204–5
Congress urged to act on issue of (1783), 221–23, 227
desperate need for (1780), 181
dissimilarities in the payments of men in civil and military life, 232
after end of war, 213
general meeting of officers, anonymous papers requesting (1783), 214–18
half pay for life for officers, proposal for, 157–58
half pay or commutation of, 245, 246, 256
Joseph Jones urged to press issue, 227–28
lack of congressional action, 234–35
patriotism and, 99
pleas for justice to army, 217, 221–23, 231–32
possible consequences of not settling accounts, 228
refusal to disband until paid, rumors about, 215–16
of W. as commander-in-chief, 40
Peace, 304
  British attempt to use specious allurements of, 99–100
  in Europe, 301
  as first priority (1795), 620
  independence as only terms for, 101
  with other nations, 483–84
  prospects for (1779), 121–22, 134, 210
Peace treaty (1783), 229–30, 231, 233, 234, 321
  violations of, 333, 334, 361
  as pretext for British interference, 350
Peas, 637, 642
Pendleton, Col. Edmund, 41

Pendleton, Philip, 671
Pennsylvania, 272, 424
  agriculture in, 558
  American Revolution and, 155
    Associated Troops, 74–75
    importance of Pennsylvania,
      149–50
    martial law, 150–52
    mutiny in Pennsylvania line;
      180
  Constitution increasingly
    supported in, 415
  ejectments trial for W.'s land
    in, 309
  inland waterways and, 293–94,
    316
  manufacturing in, 429
  ratification of the Constitution
    and, 376, 384
  road from Fort Cumberland to
    the Yohoganey, 297
  tax revolt in (1794), 492–96,
    593, 600–1, 603–4
    Democratic Societies and,
      593–94, 597–98
    militia called to suppress
      insurrections, 591–92, 597,
      599
    proclamations on, 589–92,
      598–600
Pensions for officers of army,
  157, 158
Peter, Martha Parke, 678
Peterborough, Bishop of, 61
Philadelphia Agricultural Society,
  313
Philadelphia Convention. *See*
  Constitutional Convention
Pickering, Col. Timothy, 550–52,
  635
Pinckney, Charles, 614–15, 631,
  632, 644
Poetry, 396–97
Politics, *See also* Parties
  differences in political opinions
    and, 580
  discontent with government,
    587, 602–3

dissensions, internal (1792),
  578–79
fate of America, 398
lack of unity in public councils,
  665
opposition, 656–58, 660–62
W.'s political creed, 279
Population growth, 455, 501–2
Portugal, 136
Postage, 536
Post Office
  in fourth annual message
    (1792), 484
  mailing of newspapers and,
    409–10
  newspapers, mailing of, 454
  roads, 479
  stagecoaches used by, 410–11
  in third annual message (1791),
    479
Potomac Company, 294, 322, 335,
  375, 418
  canals and, 316, 317
  directors of, 305
  general meeting of (1785), 301
  shares held by W.
    will provisions on, 669–71,
      678
    given to charitable causes,
      308, 607–8, 650, 670–71
  survey to be undertaken by,
    309
Potomac River
  advantages of region near, 559–
    60
  canal works and, 316, 317
  inland navigation of. *See* Inland
    navigation of Potomac River;
    Potomac Company
  survey of, 309
  call for, 291
Potts, 614
Prayer. *See also* Religious services
  in circular to the states (June
    14, 1783), 249
Presidency, the
  appointive powers during
    recess of the Senate, 638

Presidency, the   Constitution and, 392
declines to run again for, 666
election of W. to, feeling about
    possibility of, 392–93
inauguration of the President,
    441–42
treaty-making power, 623–24
W. as President, 407. *See also*
    Presidential addresses
annual addresses. *See* Annual
    addresses of W. as
    President
conduct of the first
    President, 537–38
Farewell Address (1796), 443
farewell to Alexandria
    citizens, 436–37
feelings about possibility of
    becoming President, 417,
    422–25, 428, 460
gratitude for public support,
    545–46, 549
inauguration, 442
last day in office, 654–55
motivations for accepting
    Presidency, 445–47, 456–57,
    460
plans to go to New York to
    assume office, 434–35
principles of W.'s
    administration, 621
public opinion's role in
    decision to accept
    Presidency, 457
reception of idle and
    ceremonious visits, 543–45
reluctance to become
    President, 428
third term declined (1796),
    512–13
Presidential addresses. *See also*
    Annual addresses of W. as
    President
Farewell Address (1796), 639
on federal government, 518–
    21
on foreign relations, 517–18,
    522–26

Hamilton asked for advice
    on, 634–35, 643–44
on institutions for the
    general diffusion of
    knowledge, 522
Madison asked to write, 568–
    70
on military establishment,
    516–17
on neutrality, 524–26
publication of, 644
on public credit, 522
on regional divisions that
    may threaten union, 517
on regions of the country,
    common interests of, 515–
    16
on religion and morality,
    521–22
on separation of powers, 521
third term as President
    declined, 512–13
thoughts on contents of, 568–
    69
on trade, 525
on treaty with Spain, 517
on unity of government, 515
first draft of first inaugural
    address ("discarded
    inaugural"), 440–41, 445–58
agriculture, 455
amendments to the
    Constitution, 451–52
appointments of officials,
    451–52
defense policy, 452–53
election as pivot on which
    turns the first wheel of the
    government, 448
foreign affairs, 455–56
general welfare, measures for
    promoting, 451
manufacturing, 455
motivations for accepting
    Presidency, 445–47, 456–57
perfection not claimed for
    federal system, 447–48
powers of government, 448–49

Index

retirement, love of, 447
Revolutionary War, 449–50
separation of powers, 449
first inaugural speech, 460–67
feelings about accepting
Presidency, 460
House of Representatives'
reply, 465–67
W.'s response to, 467
pecuniary compensation
rejected, 463
prayers and thanks to God,
460–61
Senate's reply, 463–65
W.'s response to, 465
second inaugural speech, 486
Prices of everyday objects, 112
Princess Anne County, Va., 70
Princeton, Battle of (1777), 51–52
Prisoners
exchange of, 124, 177
of Indians, 261
treatment of, 43–45, 57
Private life, W.'s, 302. *See also*
Retirement, W.'s
desire for, 255–56
relative isolation, 355
return to, 276, 278
enjoyment of, 280
sacrifice of, 386–87
secretary or clerk sought by W.,
299
Proclamation of 1763, 116
Promotions, 204
army's system of, 179
Prosperity, 501–2, 546, 547
Providence, 258, 412
United States favored by, 403–4
Prussia, 319, 401, 419
treaty with, 326
Public credit(ors), 182–84, 478. *See
also* Public debt
establishment of, 555, 557
in Farewell Address (1796), 522
increase in (1790), 470–71
provision for support of, 470
Public debt, 339. *See also* Public
credit

in annual messages as
President
second annual message,
(1790), 473
third annual message (1791),
477–78
fourth annual message
(1792), 484–85
fifth annual message (1793),
490–91
sixth annual message (1794),
498
seventh annual message
(1795), 504
eighth annual message
(1796), 511
Impost Law and (1783), 210
justice to creditors, 244, 272,
420
payment of, 185, 231, 244
public concerns regarding, 572–
73, 575
to states, 535–36
Public opinion. *See also*
Reputation of W.
attendance by W. at
Constitutional Convention
and, 357, 364
of Congress, 117–18
decision to accept Presidency
and, 457
discontent with conduct of war,
185–86
enlightened, 522
and financing of war effort,
183
government supported by, 538–
39
gratitude for support shown to
his Presidency, 545–46
interest in, 587
issues of concern to (1792),
572–76
W. as out of touch with, 355–56
Public papers, 282, 673
Publius. *See Federalist, The*
Punishments, in Continental
Army, 80–81

*Punishments, in
Continental Army*

707

Putnam, Maj. Gen. Israel, 42, 384

Quakers, 318–19, 541, 604
   praise for, 534
   slavery and, 543
Quebec, 62, 114

Raccoon Branch, Fairfax's fishery
   at, 29–30
Raleigh Tavern, meeting at
   (1774), 30*n*, 31
Randolph, Edmund, 391
Ray, John, Jr., 73
Reed, Joseph, 42
   fleet under command of, 58
   full discretionary power of,
   150–51
Regiments
   number of, 156–60
   number of officers in, 160
   organization of, 160
Regions of the United States, 575
   divisions may threaten union,
   517
   shared interests of, 515–16
Religion. *See also* Christianity
   as indispensable support of
   government, 521
Religious denominations, liberal
   sentiments among, 545
Religious freedom (liberty), 271,
   532, 533
   Assessment Bill (Virginia, 1785)
   and, 311–12
Religious services, 209
   attendance of officers and
   soldiers at, 43
Religious toleration, 548
Representative government, 335–
   36. *See also* Democratic
   governments
   national matters and, 341
Republican form of government,
   public suspicion of plot to
   overthrow, 574
Reputation of W., 65, 116
Retirement, W.'s, 238–40, 386,

387, 443. *See also* Private life,
   W.'s
   gratitude to country, 513–14
   love of, 447
   return to public life, 537
   after second term as President,
   443, 628, 629. *See also*
   Farewell Address (1796)
   announcing the intention to
   retire, 568
   declines to run again for
   Presidency (1796), 666
   last day in office, 654–55
   looking forward to, 567
   wish to retire after first term,
   513
Revolutionary War. *See* American
   Revolution
Rhode Island, 108, 139, 143
   Impost Law and (1783), 211
   ratification of the Constitution
   and, 404, 412
Rights
   constitutional. *See*
   Constitutional rights and
   liberties
   of mankind, 240–41
   natural, 38
   of prisoners, 44–45
Rinds Gazette, 30
Rivers. *See* Inland waterways
Roads, inland waterways and, 297
Roanoke, Va., 297
Rochambeau, Count Jean de, 173,
   185, 194, 197, 406
Roman Catholics, thanked for
   their support, 546–47
"Rules of Civility and Decent
   Behavior in Company and
   Conversation," 6–13
Rumsey, James, 294
Russia, 126, 135, 401

St. Clair, Gen. Arthur
   suspension of, 153–54
St. Croix River, 506
St. Simon, Marquis de, 196, 322
Schuyler, Gen. Philip, 42, 47, 145,

260, 262, 266
evacuation of Fort George
   recommended by, 89–90
supplies for, 89
suspension of, 153–54
Schuylkill River, 288, 292
Science, promotion of, 469
Seagrove, James, 577–79
Secrecy, as characteristic of good
   government, 362
Secretary, W.'s search for a, 299
Secretary of State, selection of
   (1795), 613–14
Sedition, 146
Seeds for the Kings Garden at
   Versailles or elsewhere, 307
Self-created societies. *See also*
   Democratic societies
   attack on, 603–4
   threat posed by, 600–1
Senecas, 550–53
Sentries, 71, 73
Separation of powers, 383
   in Farewell Address (1796), 521
   in first draft of first inaugural
      address ("discarded
      inaugural"), 449
Settlers in western lands, 262–65
   inland waterways and, 290, 291
Ships, captured
   British repeal of order for
      seizing provision vessels
      (1795), 618
   treatment of, 67–68
   treaty with Great Britain (1796)
      and, 506
Six Nations, 262, 498, 553, 578
   friendship with, 550
   treaty with (1791), 478
Slaves (slavery), 30, 39
   emancipation of, 235, 322
      in will, 667
   opposition to slavery, 319
   Quakers and, 318, 543
   W.'s, 193
      in will, 667–69
Smallpox, 55, 70
Societies, Bushrod W.'s views on,

response to, 335–36
Society of the Cincinnati, 343–46,
   351–52
changes in, 345
nonattendance by W. at
   meeting of, 343–45
purpose of, 344–45
W.'s attendance at
   Constitutional Convention
   and, 352, 354, 357, 360, 364
Southa, 308
South Carolina, 129, 140, 166
   ratification of the Constitution
      and, 376, 391, 394–95, 398,
      402
Southern colonies, 70
Southern states, 538
   discontent in, 539–40
   end of hostilities in, 207
   in Farewell Address (1796),
      515–16
   Gen. Greene appointed to
      command army in, 175–77
   monarchical ideas in, 361
   peace prospects and (1779),
      121–22
   ratification of the Constitution
      and, 376
   relief of, 129
   Spain and, 140–41
   tour of (1791), 554–55, 557
   unity of the states and, 310
Sovereignty, federal, 361, 362
   Jay on, 366
Spain, 126, 128, 135, 338, 401
   American Revolution and, 148
      wish that Spain enter war,
         112, 114
   donkeys from, 306, 322
   economy of, 148
   Florida and, 140
   Indians and, 577–79
   inland waterways and, 290
   negotiations with (1795), 615–16
   raising of army in Kentucky to
      invade the dominions of
      (1793–1794), 588n
   relations with (1795), 500

Spain

Spain

southern states and, 140–41
treaty with (1796), 506–7, 517
West Florida and, 577
Sparks, Jared, 440
Specie, 189. *See also* Money
Speculation, 119, 125, 127, 128
Spies, need for, 110
Spotswood, Elizabeth, 677
Stamp Act, 22–23
Standing army (permanent force)
need for, 79, 82, 98–99, 165,
168, 176, 177, 190–91
not a threat to government, 102
State constitutions, 351–53
State legislatures
appeal to (1780), 177
congressional powers and, 321
States of the Union. *See also*
Southern states
as badly represented in
Congress, 117–18, 125
coercion of, to enforce
obedience to laws, 362
Constitutional Convention and,
352–53
general interest of the United
States and, 258–59
jealousy of Congress and of
one another, 278–79
Knox's proposals for revising,
355
pay for army and, 213
state armies versus continental
armies, 87–88
as too much engaged in their
local concerns, 117
trade and, 390
wickedness in the conduct of,
317–18, 323
Stein, Nathaniel, 440
Steuben, Baron Friedrich von,
197, 231, 371
Stewart, Col. Walter, 196
Stirling, Lord (William
Alexander), 235
Stony Point, N.Y., 143
Street, Mr., 551
Stuart, David, 674

Sullivan, Gen. John, 106
Surgeons, military, 79–80
Susquehanna River, 27, 288, 292

Tariffs (imposts), 305, 321
British-American trade and,
305, 310–11
proposal for (1789), 536
Taxation (taxes; duties), 260, 420,
561. *See also* Stamp Act
circular to the states on (June
14, 1783), 244–45
on civil process, 536
commutable taxes, 342, 346–47,
374, 375
on distilled spirits and stills,
476–77, 483. *See also* Whiskey
Rebellion
proclamation against
combinations to defeat
execution of (1794), 589–92
proclamation on (1792), 583–
84
excise, 573
in Farewell Address (1796), 522
for inland navigation of
Potomac River, 284
insurgency against the excise
law in Pennsylvania, 593
non-payment of taxes, 212
Parliament's power (or right)
of, 34–37, 39
Patriotic Society and, 342
Pennsylvania, tax revolt in
(1794), 492–96, 593, 600–1,
603–4
Democratic Societies and,
593–94, 597–98
militia called to suppress
insurrections, 591–92, 597,
599
proclamations on, 589–92,
598–600
on produce, 536
in sixth annual message (1794),
492–93
to support teachers of
Christianity (Virginia), 311–12

on transportation of public
prints, 491
without consent, 31, 36–37
Tellassee, 577
Ternay, Chevalier de (Charles
Louis d'Arsac), 185
Thanksgiving proclamation, 534–
35
Thornton, Jane, 677
Threshing machine, 642
Tidewater, extension of
navigation to Wills's Creek,
284
Tilghman, Lt. Col. Tench, 195,
235, 327
Tobacco, as commutable, 342, 346
Tobacco colonies, boycott of
British goods and (1769), 24
Toby's Creek, 288, 292
Tories. *See* Loyalists
Trade. *See also* Tariffs
of agricultural commodities for
manufactured goods, 455
boycott of British goods,
discussion of (1769), 24–26
curtailed for want of credit, 428
with East Indies, 421
in eighth annual message
(1796), 510–11
with enemy during
Revolutionary War, 189
with Europe, threats to (1790),
472–73
in Farewell Address (1796), 525
in first draft of first inaugural
address ("discarded
inaugural"), 454
with France, 324–25, 390, 421,
487, 554
fur and peltry, 289
with Great Britain, 291
1795 treaty and, 611
British policy, 324, 325
British trade policy, 305–6
interference with, declared
treason by Gage, 36
with Indians, 264, 476, 485, 504,
617

influence on humanity and
society in general, 326
inland navigation of Potomac
River and, 27, 28
inland waterways and, 289
with Mediterranean nations,
473
neutrality and, 501
non-importation scheme, 24–26,
37
paying for exports in money or
raw materials, 325
regulation of, 305–6, 309–11,
313–15, 390
in second annual message
(1790), 472–73
Stamp Act and, 22, 23
usefulness of, 313
Virginia Assembly and, 362
with West Indies, French
interference with (1796), 510–
11
Treaties. *See also* Peace treaty
(1783)
with European nations, 556–57
with Great Britain (1795–1796),
500–1, 505–6, 517, 609–13,
615, 619–24
with Indians, 476, 478, 552
President's power to make,
623–24
with Spain (1796), 506–7, 517
Trenton, Battle of (1776), 51
Tripoli, 507
Trumbull, John, 506
Trumbull, Jonathan, 277
Tunis, 507
Turks. *See* Ottoman Empire ("the
Porte")
Tyranny, 256
checks and barriers against the
introduction of, 383
of European monarchs, 320
of Gage, 36, 39

Union (unity) of colonies
Canadians asked to join (1775),
47

*Union (unity) of
colonies*

Union (unity) of colonies
during French and Indian War, 21
Intolerable Acts and, 39
Union (unity) of states, 315. *See also* Articles of Confederation
alliances among states not a substitute for, 518
commercial regulation and, 310–11
Constitution needed for, 234
dangers of separation, 540
desirability of, 372
in Farewell Address (1796), 515–17
inland navigation and, 313–14
liberty and, 515–17
local interests as threatening, 233–34
as pillar of independence and national character, 242
principles of, 242–43
regional divisions may threaten, 517
taxes and, 245
ties with middle states (western lands), 290
United Netherlands. *See* Holland
United States. *See also* Confederation, the
diversity of interests in, 540
God's design for, 456
industry and frugality of the people, 402–3
internal dissensions (1792), 578–79
pillars of, 242
place among the nations of the world, 455
political fate of, 398
prayer for, 249
prospects for, 240, 278, 403–4, 406, 456
ultimate fate of, inability to foresee, 453–54
University, national, call for establishment of a, 509, 605–9, 649–50, 670–71

Valley Forge, Pa., 92, 166
Vanity, wish to forestall any imputation of, 282–83
Vermont, admittance into the Union, 363
Vice, 433
Vice President, appointment of a, 425–26
Virginia, 54, 149, 339. *See also* Virginia Assembly
agriculture in, 558
American Revolution and, 413
Assessment Bill in (1785), 311–12
boycott of British goods and (1769), 25–26
discontent in, 541
elections of 1788 for delegates to Convention, 385, 386
Impost Law and (1783), 210
inland navigation of Potomac River and, 27, 285
inland waterways and, 288, 290–91
money for reenlisting troops in, 103
ratification of the Constitution and, 391, 398, 399, 404, 411–12
representatives to Congress from, 430
resignation of officers in, 98
volunteer plan, 103–4
western lands and, 285
claims relinquished, 189
Virginia and Kentucky resolutions, 660–61
Virginia Assembly (House of Burgesses), 343, 349
appropriation for militia by, 21
army and, 118
Bryan Fairfax urged to stand for election to, 33
Custis in, 190
dissolution of (1774), 30–31
inland navigation of Potomac River and, 294, 295
gift of shares in Potomac

Company given to W. by,
    295–97
inland waterways and, 297
law code being considered by,
    314
Potomac Company and, 375
praise for, 343
ratification of the Constitution
    and, 376, 377, 379–80
trade and, 362, 390
Virginia Convention (1774), 30n,
    69, 70
Virginia militia
    address to (1756), 19
    appropriation by Assembly for,
    21
Virtue, 533
Volunteer plan (Virginia), 103–4

Walker, Ann, 675
War. *See also* American
    Revolution
    as plague to mankind, 301
    waste of, 394
Ward, Artemus, 42
Washington, Bushrod (nephew),
    330, 673, 675, 678, 679
Washington, Charles (brother),
    674
Washington, Charles Augustine,
    678
Washington, Corbin (nephew),
    678
Washington, Elizabeth (friend),
    674
Washington, Ferdinand, 255
Washington, George (nephew),
    660
    health of, 571–72
Washington, George Fayette (son
    of nephew), 676, 678
Washington, George Steptoe
    (nephew), 671–72, 675, 678,
    679
    advice on conduct to, 431–34
Washington, Hannah (friend),
    674
Washington, Hannah (sister-in-

law), 674
Washington, Lawrence (friend),
    674
Washington, Lawrence (nephew),
    433, 434
Washington, Lawrence Augustine
    (nephew), 671–72, 676, 678
Washington, Lund, refreshment
    given to British by, 192–93
Washington, Maria (daughter of
    nephew), 678
Washington, Martha (wife), 28,
    53, 276, 545, 571
    concern for happiness of, 41
    health of, 307
    Francis Dandridge's
    disapproval of W.'s marriage
    to, 22
    relatives of, 23
    smallpox inoculation, 70
    in will, 667, 679
Washington, Mildred (sister-in-
    law), 674
Washington, Robert (friend), 674
Washington, Samuel (brother),
    671
Washington, Samuel (nephew),
    675, 678, 679
Washington, Thornton (nephew),
    671, 678
Washington, William Augustine
    (nephew), 673, 675, 677, 679
Watertown, stores at, 44
Waterways. *See* Inland waterways
Wayne, Gen. Anthony, 497, 616
Wealthy, the (monied gentry)
    boycott of British goods and
    (1769), 25
    inland navigation of Potomac
    River and, 27, 28
Webster, Noah, xxiii, 406
Weights and measures,
    uniformity in, 469, 480
Westchester, N.Y., 187
Western lands, 128, 268, 473. *See
    also* Inland waterways
    conduct towards Indians and
    citizens in, 261–63

Western lands

defense of frontiers, 475
emigration to, 384
in Farewell Address (1796), 516
Great Britain and, 321
Indians of, 302, 616–17
  protection of Indians from
    settlers, 503
  reports concerning (1792),
    577–78
  spreading Christianity
    among, 298–99
  war with Indians, 571
inland waterways to, 287–90
Northwest Ordinance (1785)
  and, 300, 302–3, 306
sale of, 300, 306, 384. *See also*
  Northwest Ordinance (1785)
as second land of promise, 301,
  304–5
settlement of, 262–65
  inland waterways and, 290,
    291
Virginia and, 285
West Florida, 577

West Indies
  coordination of French Navy
    and American Army in, 138–
    39, 143
  trade with, French interference
    with (1796), 510–11
West Point, N.Y., garrison at, 159
Wheat, 559, 561, 641–42
Wheatley, Phillis, 68
Whiskey Rebellion, 565
Wilkinson, Gen. James, 377
Will, W.'s, 41, 667–79
Wills's Creek, extension of
  navigation from tidewater to,
  284
Wilson, James, 592
Wilson, Thomas, 674
Winchester, French and Indian
  War and, 20*n*

Yohoghaney River, 292
Yorktown, Battle of (1781), 173,
  194–97, 406

This book was set in New Baskerville, a typeface
derived from designs cut by the British printer
John Baskerville (1706–1775) for use on his own press.
In creating his design, Baskerville broke with tradition
to reflect the rounder, yet more sharply cut lettering
of eighteenth-century stone inscriptions and copy-books.
The type foreshadows modern design in such characteristics
as the increase in contrast between thick and thin strokes
and the shifting of stress from the diagonal to the
vertical strokes. Realizing that his new style of letter
would be most effective if cleanly printed on smooth paper
with genuinely black ink, he built his own presses,
developed a method of hot-pressing the printed sheet
to a smooth, glossy finish, and experimented
with special inks.

One of Baskerville's customers was another well-known
printer, Benjamin Franklin.

BOOK DESIGN BY
BETTY BINNS GRAPHICS,
NEW YORK, NEW YORK

EDITORIAL SERVICE AND INDEX BY
HARKAVY PUBLISHING SERVICE,
NEW YORK, NEW YORK

TYPOGRAPHY BY
ALEXANDER TYPESETTING COMPANY,
INDIANAPOLIS, INDIANA,
ON A MERGENTHALER LINOTRON 202.

PRINTING AND BINDING BY
WORZALLA PUBLISHING COMPANY,
STEVENS POINT, WISCONSIN